A COMPILATION VOLUME OF *The Penguin Book of Australian Jokes, The Penguin Book of More Australian Jokes, The Penguin Book of Jokes from Cyberspace* AND *The Penguin Book of Schoolyard Jokes*, COLLECTED BY

Phillip Adams and Patrice Newell

THE **GIANT** PENGUIN BOOK OF AUSTRALIAN JOKES

PHILLIP ADAMS is an odd assortment of people who write things, film things, say things on wireless and appear on television. All of whom share an anthropological fascination for jokes. The Adams' hobbies are levity and levitation.

PATRICE NEWELL has been a model, a television researcher, a newsreader and a presenter of public affairs programs on both SBS and the Nine Network. She now raises politicall
cattle property.

THE PENGUIN BOOK OF AUSTRALIAN JOKES

collected by Phillip Adams and Patrice Newell

Penguin Books

Penguin Books Australia Ltd
487 Maroondah Highway, PO Box 257
Ringwood, Victoria 3134, Australia
Penguin Books Ltd
Harmondsworth, Middlesex, England
Penguin Putnam Inc.
375 Hudson Street, New York, New York 10014, USA
Penguin Books Canada Limited
10 Alcorn Avenue, Toronto, Ontario, Canada M4V 3B2
Penguin Books (NZ) Ltd
Cnr Rosedale and Airborne Roads, Albany, Auckland, New Zealand
Penguin Books (South Africa) (Pty) Ltd
5 Watkins Street, Denver Ext 4, 2094, South Africa
Penguin Books India (P) Ltd
11, Community Centre, Panchsheel Park, New Delhi 110 017, India

The Penguin Book of Australian Jokes first published by Penguin Books Australia Ltd 1994
The Penguin Book of More Australian Jokes first published by Penguin Books Australia Ltd 1996
The Penguin Book of Jokes from Cyberspace first published by Penguin Books Australia Ltd 1995
The Penguin Book of Schoolyard Jokes first published by Penguin Books Australia Ltd 1997
This combined volume first published by Penguin Books Australia Ltd 1999

10 9 8 7 6 5 4 3 2 1

Cover illustration by Ned Culic
Typeset by Midland Typesetters, Maryborough, Victoria
Made and printed in Australia by Australian Print Group, Maryborough, Victoria

National Library of Australia
Cataloguing-in-Publication data:

The Giant Penguin Book of Australian Jokes

Includes index.
ISBN 0 14 029911 4.

1. Australian wit and humor. 2. Internet (Computer network) - Humor. 3. Schools - Australia - Humor. I. Title: The Penguin book of more Australian jokes. II.Title: The Penguin book of Australian jokes. III. Title: The Penguin book of schoolyard jokes. IV. Title: The Giant Penguin Book of Australian Jokes

A828.02

www.penguin.com.au

Acknowledgements

The Editors wish to thank the countless citizens who submitted jokes for this collection. Whilst many were not included because they were too slanderous or obscene, the main reason for rejection was an utter lack of funniness, even when read aloud in a character voice. Other jokes were rejected because they were minor variations on a familiar theme.

CONTENTS

The stupidest book in the world is a book of jokes.
J.C. Holland, Everyday Topics, 1876

Have You Heard the One About . . .

Why do fish shoal? That's neither riddle nor joke but a serious question that, recently, a number of piscatorially correct academics sought to answer. While the overwhelming majority of fish shoal on a full or part-time basis, the reason remained mysterious. What is shoaling's social and/or evolutionary purpose? Are we witnessing a form of fishy fascism, wherein members of submarine communities are forced into conformity, or is the impulse more democratic?

When you think about it, the shoaling of little fish seems to offer larger fish or the professional fisherman an easier target. If fish were more solitary, you'd hardly be able to spot one in the immensities of the ocean. Thus their sticking together smacks of a suicidal form of self-advertisement.

So the academics went to work with a will, as is their wont, and discovered all sorts of interesting things. First of all, we're not dealing with demagoguery in the deep as there's no leader of the pack in a fish shoal. Any fish can take on the task, a bit like the 'king for the day' notion encouraged by Kleisthenes in the Athens of 508 BC. The only thing that's rigidly enforced is the *mathematics* of the shoal – the lattice-like format that defines it. It seems that fish have little sensors on their gills that facilitate their flying in formation, and that they're required to maintain an average distance apart over the course of a day. Thus sometimes they'll shoal a little closer, sometimes further apart. When you do the calculations, however, you'll find that there's been a mathematical maintenance of the status quo.

But why bother with formation flight, particularly when it produces a larger blip on the enemy's radar? Well, it turns out to be wonderfully simple. Yes, a shoal is more visible than a fish flying solo, but when attacked by something higher on the food chain – a shark or a seal – the lattice explodes outwards, as if responding to a central detonation. The effect on the predator is highly confusing. It's rather like having dinner at a posh restaurant and being presented with an over-large menu. Cobwebs form and moss grows on the waiter whilst he waits for you, the perplexed diner, to order.

The academics were triumphant when they observed that, again and again, a fish attacking an exploding shoal could be observed flailing around trying to grab this fish or that fish only to finish up missing out entirely.

The point of this aquatic detour is to emphasise that traits and foibles, as well as a creature's design, should make evolutionary sense, which, according to a wide variety of scientists, jokes don't. Our reading of the literature on humour reveals that for decades academics have been scratching their heads. What is the evolutionary purpose of smiling, of laughter? How do jokes help the survival of the species? To what extent is the selection of a joke a part of the process of natural selection?

The fact that scientists seem flummoxed is deeply encouraging. It's painfully obvious that scholars should be kept at arm's length from any manifestation of humour. God forbid that what semiotics has done to the cinema, what deconstruction has wreaked on the novel, should find a parallel in the realm of the joke, that most democratic form of creativity.

For a glimpse of the danger posed by academic inquiry, consider the following description of the physiological process of laughter by one Norbert Dearborn:

There occur in laughter and more or less in smiling, clonic spasm of the diaphragm, in number ordinarily about eighteen perhaps, and contraction of most of the muscles of the face. The upper eyelid is elevated, as are also, to some extent, the brows, the skin over the glabella, and the upper lip, while the skin at the outer canthi of the eyes is characteristically puckered. The nostrils are moderately dilated and drawn upwards, the tongue slightly extended, and the cheeks distended and drawn somewhat upward; in persons with the pinnal muscles largely developed, the pinnae tend to incline forwards. The lower jaw vibrates or is somewhat withdrawn (doubtless to afford all possible air to the distending lungs), and the head, in extreme laughter, is thrown backward; the trunk is straightened even to the beginning of bending backward, until (and this usually happens soon), fatigue-pain in the diaphragm and accessory abdominal muscles causes a marked proper flexion of the trunk for its relief. The whole arterial vascular system is dilated, with consequent blushing from the effect on the dermal capillaries of the face and neck, and at times the scalp and hands. From the same cause, in the main, the eyes often slightly bulge forwards and the lachrymal gland becomes active, ordinarily to a degree only to cause a 'brightening' of the eyes, but often to such an extent that the tears overflow entirely their proper channels.

Or take Charles Darwin's description of a smile, quilled more than a century ago:

By drawing backwards and upwards of the corners of the mouth, through the contraction of the great zygomatic muscles, and by the raising of the upper lip, the cheeks are drawn upwards. Wrinkles are thus formed under the eyes, and, with old people, at the outer ends. As in laughing and broadly smiling the cheeks and upper lip are much raised, the nose appears to be shortened, and the skin on the bridge becomes finely wrinkled in transverse lines, with other oblique longitudinal lines on the sides. The upper front teeth are commonly exposed. A well marked naso-labial ford is formed, which runs from the wing of each nostril to the corner of the mouth.

And here's another scientific observation, worthy of inclusion in a Python sketch:

Spontaneous laughter is a motor reflex produced by the co-ordinated contraction of 15 facial muscles in a stereotyped pattern and accompanied by altered breathing. Electrical stimulation of the main lifting muscle of the upper lip, the zygomatic major, with currents of varying intensity produces facial expressions ranging from the faint smile through the broad grin to the contractions typical of explosive laughter.

Ambrose Bierce is less wanton with his words in *The Devil's Dictionary:* Laughter, n. An interior convulsion producing a distortion of the features and accompanied by inarticulate noises.

Some of the most solemn explorations of the joke came from Sigmund Freud who didn't hesitate to explore it as he had the dream, seeking its relation to the unconscious:

Anyone who has at any time had occasion to enquire from the literature of aesthetics and psychology what light can be thrown on the nature of jokes and on the position they occupy will probably have to admit that jokes have not received nearly as much philosophical consideration as they deserve in view of the part they play in our mental life, he complained. He agreed with Kuno Fischer that *if what is ugly is concealed, it must be uncovered in the light of the comic way of looking at things: if it is noticed only a little or scarcely at all, it must be brought forward and made obvious, so that it lies clear and open to the light of day... in this way caricature comes about.*

Freud then proceeds to render a number of jokes as unfunny as possible by rigorous analysis. Even a simple two-liner like: A horse dealer was recommending a saddle-horse to a customer. 'If you take this horse and get on it at four in the morning you'll be at Pressburg by half past six.' 'What should I be doing in Pressburg at half past six in the morning?'

On re-reading the sainted Sigmund's deconstruction of that snippet of text, you can't help feeling that it's the analysis that's funny rather than the joke. Because as soon as you start thinking about the construction and purpose of a joke the humour evaporates. It's like confusing sexual intercourse with gynaecology or art with criticism. Because it must be remembered that among the many things that jokes mock is reason itself. Jokes are anathema to logic and, consequently, hostile to analysis.

Nonetheless let us persist in examining the matter scientifically. It's said that tranquillising endorphins are found in tears of grief. Could tears of laughter be similarly spiked to produce a natural high? There's much speculation that something of the sort is going on in Near Death Experiences, that the brain produces a narcotic to numb the terrors. Isn't it likely, therefore, that a few million years of evolution have provided something similar for the thousands of little NDEs that flesh is heir to, the profusion and confusion of alarms, anxieties and humiliations that are our lot?

The one aspect of humour on which there seems to be scholarly agreement involves how our children learn to smile and laugh. The consensus is that both originate as expressions of fear or fright. Thus laughter begins when a baby is shocked by something – such as being lifted aloft by a playful parent. Within a nano-second it discovers that it is not, after all, being threatened, that all is well, that it's going to survive. The lungful of air that was to provide a drawn-out scream is, instead, employed in an explosive release of tension. The scream becomes the laugh, just as the gasp becomes the chuckle. And the smile, which began as a grimace of terror, softens as panic passes.

(It's said that the scientist's purpose is to achieve synthesis, whereas the artist aims at a juxtaposition of the familiar and the eternal. The humorist's game is different – to contrive a collision. This has led to another observation on the actual sound of laughter that runs along these lines. The discoverer's 'Eureka!' cry is identified as the ah ha! reaction. The delight of the aesthetic experience becomes the aaah . . . reaction. Whereas laughter is described as the ha-ha reaction.)

There was a time when anthropologists felt that humans could be identified as human by their use of tools. Their observation of other creatures showed that chimps used rocks for hammers, sticks for spoons and boughs for levers. We've long favoured the notion that humans alone contemplate their own mortality. Our dread of death undergoes a wondrous alchemy and becomes humour, so that Rabelais can say: 'Laughter is what characterises man.' Humour, sharing its place in the dictionary with humiliation, humility and human, is essentially about horror. The gift of humour is the evolutionary mechanism that allows us to cope with the great practical joke of life, with all its essential tragedy.

Faced by the horrors that assail us on all sides, faced with the abyss of death, we have the choice of screaming or laughing. Sometimes we do both at once – hence terms like 'a scream of laughter'. Nonetheless humour remains our best defence mechanism against horror.

In early western physiology humour was one of the four fluids of the body that were thought to determine a person's temperament and features. In ancient physiology still current in the Middle Ages and later, the four cardinal humours were blood, phlegm, choler (yellow bile) and melancholy (black bile). The variant mixtures of these humours in different persons determined their 'complexions' or 'temperaments', their physical and mental qualities and their dispositions. By further extension humour in the sixteenth century came to denote usually an unbalanced mental condition, a mood of unreasonable caprice, or a fixed folly or vice.

Which is why the greatest humour is born in various forms of adversity. Thus the bleakest, most self-deprecating humour has been provided by the people described by Arthur Koestler as 'the exposed nerve ends of mankind'. Over the millennia, and certainly within the century of Holocaust, a completely disproportionate number of jokes, and of comedians to tell them, have come from the Jews.

In a sense, terms like Jewish humour, gallows humour and black humour should be contradictions in terms. But as laughter begins as an abbreviation of fear, humour grows as an attempt to deal with the dread of despair.

Having fought its losing battle with death, humour mounts many a quixotic campaign against oppression, dispossession and fear. Humour gives the powerless a tiny bit of power over those who tyrannise them. Though the best jokes thumb their noses at the cosmos, many of the better ones are aimed at the authority figures, the pompous, the bigots. But first and foremost jokes are used to ward off the Grim Reaper like the crucifix does Dracula. Case in point, Woody Allen, who, not content with being Jewish, nurtures a deep fear of his own mortality, and everyone else's. Allen returns to the theme over and over again, as in: 'More than any other time in history, mankind faces a crossroad. One path leads to despair and hopelessness. The other, to total extinction. Let us pray we have the wisdom to choose correctly.' And less amusingly: 'Life is a concentration camp. You're stuck here and there's no way out and you can only rage impotently against your persecutors.'

Everything dies but only humans seem painfully aware of it. Death follows us around like Captain Hook's crocodile, the alarm clock ticking in its tummy. Death casts its dark shadow over every aspect of human life and in an attempt to cope with it, to deny it, even to defeat it, we've invented religions, philosophy, science and medicine. Nonetheless we still die and it remains a lonely and terrifying business. Our sense of humour allows us to blow a raspberry at the fates, to defy the nemesis we cannot escape.

Many people who've been revived after clinical death describe the Near Death Experience or NDE, involving coming into contact with a 'light of transcendental love'. Whilst Tony Staley remembers dying as a highly pleasurable, almost orgasmic experience, other friends who've died and returned – Robyn Williams and Kerry Packer – describe no loving luminosity. Both glumly report that they 'just died'. Game, set and match. Subsequently they've preferred to deal with their terminal dramas with irony and humour, the antidote that evolution has made available to all of us, irrespective of religious belief.

Perhaps that's why religions are, by and large, so humourless. 'The secret source of humour is not joy but sorrow,' wrote Mark Twain. 'There is no humour in heaven.'

Jules Renard agreed. 'We are in the world to laugh. In Purgatory or in Hell we shall no longer be able to do so. And in Heaven it would not be proper.'

Then there's that ingenious Italian novel, *The Name of the Rose*, wherein Umberto Eco faithfully explored the fundamental threat that humour poses to religious hierarchies. Interestingly the Old Testament contains twenty-five references to laughter, out of which thirteen are linked with scorn, derision, mocking and contempt. Only two usages relate laughter to joy.

Not only does humour subvert dogma and religious certainty but, of course, religion is in direct competition with humour as a method of ameliorating mortality's bleak implications. There is an implicit acknowledgement in humour that, finally, we're all stuffed, whereas religion tries to persuade us that life isn't meaningless and, against all the evidence, that we're cherished and protected by a deity who will allow us to survive death to rise from our graves like so many missiles from their silos. To allow people the pleasure of laughter would be to offer them another method of dealing with the darkness. And humour's method is devoid of much in the way of prohibition or dogma or ritual, and tries its best to defeat guilt.

Moreover one suspects that religion is incultured whereas humour is innate, that it is as primitive a response to the essential tragedy of life as a child's first chuckle of relief to a more immediate threat.

If it is true, as it seems to be, that we are the only creatures who apprehend our own extinction, then humour is the first line of defence. While it might fight a losing battle with the immensity of mortal dread, it never stops trying. The whole notion of absurdity, so fashionable in this century, and dazzlingly refined by the likes of Ionesco and Spike Milligan, involves using humour to protect us from cosmic gloom and general ghastliness. Humour, much more than religion, is the opium of the people.

Of course, increasingly, opium is the opium of the people. People take a wide range of recreational narcotics to dull the pain. Humour, nonetheless, remains as useful as Valium and Dettol for dealing with life's little problems, as well as the big ones. For on every level, from the macro to the micro, the joke begins with the things we do not find funny at all. It begins with the things that trouble us, disgust us, appal us.

At their best, jokes wound and heal in the same instant, just as they indict and pardon, diminish and enlarge. Whatever its origin, it is with the absurdity of the joke that we get through the larger absurdity of life.

Which is why jokes, in any quantity, are such depressing things. Please extend your sympathies to the humble editors of this compilation for we have been exposed to the most unimaginable misery and unpleasantness. A joke in isolation may be 'a thing of beauty and a joy forever'. Jokes in bulk, however, jokes in bulging mailbags, are appalling. Almost without exception they deal in bigotry, sexism, racism, ageism and all the other politically incorrect isms. They clearly help people deal with their deep distaste for their own sexuality, their excremental functions, their foreign neighbours, their political masters and an infinite variety of things that go bump in the night. Jokes are to self-hatred what hypocrisy is to salacity, what guilt is to desire. Indeed, apart from jokes involving innocent plays on words, almost every genre is fundamentally an act of verbal aggression against a fear or an enemy, be it defiantly targeted or dimly perceived.

A couple of years ago, this book would have been full of dingo jokes as people dealt with the Lindy Chamberlain case as worst they could. One typical example: They've reopened the Harold Holt case and are looking for a dingo with flippers. Here was a story blending many elemental and mythic ingredients: our suspicion of other people's religions, our fear of Australia's brooding hinterland, ancient notions of 'sacrifice in the desert' and the vengeance of animals on the humans who butcher them. Here were misogyny, allegations of murder, hints of Aboriginal mythology, blurred notions of guilt and innocence. So the slanderous jokes proliferated, as ugly and numerous as cane toads. Here we saw an entire nation trying to deal with its demons. The dingo genre of jokes has now disappeared, although the prejudices that gave it birth seem not only to endure but to intensify.

You can see some of it in the jokes [sic] about Aborigines. Almost without exception they're quintessential expressions of the hostility that accrues to blacks in our cities and country towns. They're included because it is important to understand what mainstream Australia regards as funny in the 1990s. To censor them would be to entirely distort the collection. We'd hoped to offset them with jokes told by Aborigines about white people, but found these elusive. Energetic attempts to track down examples utterly failed. But then, there's a distinction between jokes and humour and while Aboriginal communities have a sense of humour reminiscent of Jewish communities – and for much the same reason – these are not encoded in the form of the joke.

We discussed this at length with Kooris and Nugget Coombs who talked happily about the playfulness and humour he'd observed in Aboriginal life. However, structured jokes, with beginnings, middles and ends, seem to belong to our cultural convention, not to theirs.

In a final, desperate attempt to find Aboriginal jokes aimed at the white community, to balance the fairly repulsive Aboriginal jokes that are essentially anti-Aboriginal, we made an appeal on national television. The result was some hundreds of letters containing the same piece of verbal kitsch.

From black fellah to white fellah.
Dear white fellah,
Coupla tings you orta no.
Firstly
Wen I am born, I'm black.
Wen I grow up, I'm black.
Wen I get sick, I'm black.
Wen I go out in a sun, I'm black.
Wen I'm cold, I'm black.
And wen I get scared, yes, I'm black.
And wen I die, I'm still black.

But you white fellah.
Wen you born, you pink.
Wen you grow up, you white.
Wen you get sick, you green.
Wen you go out in a sun, you go red.
Wen you get cold, you go blue.
Wen you get scared, you yellow.
And wen you die, you purple.

And you got the cheek to call *me* coloured.

Hundreds of correspondents insisted that this was an authentic, 'ethnic' Aboriginal joke, some even providing spurious anthropological evidence for its authenticity, as if it were a verbal counterpart to an ancient cave painting.

Incidentally, many of the first anti-Aboriginal jokes in Australia were told by blacks. By African Americans. At the end of the Civil War, freed slaves tried to set up companies to compete with the white man's Black and White Minstrel Shows. Why shouldn't they sing their own Negro spirituals or perform the Stephen Foster medleys? Ironically it became necessary for them to copy the white man's make-up – so the blacks appeared on stage wearing the cosmetic masks of 'black face' whites. However, their intrusion on a highly successful business wasn't welcomed, and white entrepreneurs ran them out of town – and some of them ran straight to Australia where they began entertaining the citizens of Melbourne, Sydney and the goldfields. The productions were enormous and energetic, so much so that they soon drove the

English music hall entertainment to the wall. It seems that the Negro entertainers were not subjected to much in the way of prejudice, that they were both welcomed and admired. But to separate themselves from the Aborigines, they didn't hesitate to tell anti-Aboriginal jokes about 'the loobras at La Perouse'. It's a story explained in fascinating detail by Richard Waterhouse in *From Minstrel Show to Vaudeville: the Australian Popular Stage 1788 to 1914* (published by the New South Wales University Press in 1990) and marks the beginning of American influence, and finally domination of Australian popular culture.

Anti-Aboriginal jokes have been included to demonstrate a sorry truth to the reader. Namely, that we laugh at these jokes, albeit guiltily. We may strive for proper attitudes, to shun prejudice, to atone for sins of the past yet, despite our best intentions, we continue to laugh at jokes that embody old hostilities. If anything, our laughter may be intensified by our sense of shock and shame that we're laughing at all.

Increasingly, racial vilification legislation will prevent the publication of broadcasting of this sort of material, but that will not stop their informal circulation as long as people find them funny or therapeutic, even if they're simultaneously apologising for their laughter. 'I know we shouldn't laugh but . . .'

As such, jokes about racial or sexual relationships are the most honest of indicators about what we are really feeling. The opinions we express to pollsters may be muted, modified or cautious. Jokes are far more self-revelatory.

Of course the jokes of bigots can be turned against them. Or the powerless can seek protection from rampaging infections of bigotry by inoculating themselves with self-deprecating jokes. Thus Jewish jokes are not a lot different from anti-Jewish jokes. Indeed a good Jewish joke can become an anti-Semitic joke simply by being told by the wrong person. Finally it's not what the joke says but what it means that makes the difference. There are comics in Australia – like those associated with 'Wogs Out of Work' and 'Acropolis Now' – who'd argue that jokes of racial vilification are redeemed simply by the victims becoming the performers. You tell the joke against us, it's an insult. We tell the joke about us, it's okay. Similarly there are stand-up (or, more correctly, wobble-up) comics who, being disabled themselves, can get away with jokes about disability.

It's an interesting argument, but not entirely convincing. The unreconstructed bigot is unlikely to be won over. Impervious to the subtlety of the shift, the bigots laugh on, which leads to growing pressure, and well-meaning regulations, to censor jokes about/against a growing list of minority groups. Apart from the impracticality of the undertaking, many of us regard the censorship of jokes as entirely counter-productive. It may well prove to be a cure that is worse than the disease. As if 'political correctness' wasn't a sufficient downer, humour becomes a target of regulation in an era when deregulation is the driving force in public policy. Moreover the queue of pressure groups demanding protection now stretches round the block.

Recently, in America, a well-dressed man pulled a machine-gun from his attaché case and massacred a large group of lawyers. Within hours the head of the California Bar Association was trying to have anti-lawyer jokes outlawed, arguing that they'd led to widespread anti-lawyer feelings throughout the United States and, by implication, to the massacre. Fortunately other lawyers laughed him out of court.

This is not to say that there isn't a link between the unpleasant joke and the unpleasant social outcome. Good intentions may or may not pave the way to hell but anti-Semitic jokes certainly provided the mortar for the bricks of the crematoria.

Yes, there's a problem here. Many of the jokes in this book are entirely repulsive. But to deny their existence would be, in the long run, as hopeless an exercise as, for example, Tito's attempts to 'deep freeze' hatreds in the Balkans. Bottled up, resentments intensify rather than dissipate. Finally, down the track, they erupt.

Perhaps it's better to do what Richard Glover, a journalist with the *Sydney Morning Herald*, does – to invent a genre of anti-bigot jokes (some of the jokes he has created are printed on pages 141–4 and 273–5). Censorship solves nothing. The underlying human fear of difference, in all its manifestations, is unlikely to disappear. Certainly the way we use jokes makes a mockery of the famous utterance of G.K. Chesterton that Malcolm Muggeridge once told us. 'When you've got hold of a vulgar joke, you may be certain you've got hold of a subtle and spiritual idea.' It sounds marvellous, but we've never been able to imagine what it was G.K. was on about. Was it, perhaps, a joke?

This experience makes you suspect that, finally, the joke is a cultural artifact. There isn't much evidence of 'jokes' as such in previous centuries. Oh, there's word play galore and all sorts of funny stories. Yet the essential character of the joke, as distinct from the anecdote or exaggerated yarn or verbal stream from a stand-up comic, lies in its distinctive structure of set-up and punchline. And this seems very much of our time and space. We have a collection of antiquities containing ancient Islamic tiles in which talk balloons, almost identical to those employed in modern comics, are depicted emerging from the ceramic mouths of human beings. Nonetheless the joke seems as contemporary in form as the three-panel newspaper comic.

An anthropologist made an exhaustive study of the Kalahari bushmen of South West Africa.

On the way home we saw and shot a springbok, as there was no meat left in the camp. The bullet hit the springbok in the stomach and partly eviscerated him, causing him to jump and kick before he finally died. The bushmen thought this was terribly funny, and they laughed, slapping their thighs and kicking their heels to imitate the springbok, showing no pity at all, but then they regard animals with great detachment. (Elizabeth Marshall Thomas, *The Harmless People*, Knopf, New York, 1959.)

This was seen as evidence of 'pre-historic' humour, disapprovingly so. Yet the same detachment, the same enjoyment of cruelty, can be seen in white jokes about Aborigines, or about any of the other racial victims you'll find in this book. Everything is funny as long as it happens to somebody or something else.

Whilst professional comedians used to tell jokes – with beginnings, middles and ends – the stand-up comics of today tend to bombard the audience with various forms of verbal aggression. The humour derives from the same sources as the structured joke, exploiting the same ingredients of sexuality, bigotry and absurdity. The form, however, is essentially different, more flowing, less formal. Just as 'Monty Python' and 'Fast Forward' both decided to dump the punchline in their sketches (apart from any other consideration, they're so hard to write) the stand-up comic tends to leave joke-telling to the amateurs. In a sense, the joke is impersonal and authorless, something that is passed from person to person in a social ritual, whereas the stand-up comic likes to pretend that his or her material comes directly from his or her experience, and the delivery involves momentum and escalation rather than the old style 'Did you hear the one about . . . '

(Incidentally, we must remember that stand-up comics are so intensely aware of mortality that their jargon invariably reflects it. 'I killed them,' they say in triumph, after a good gig. Or, alternatively, 'I died.')

There was a time when the joke seemed to be the main mode of humorous transmission. Not any more. Television sitcoms, comedy shows like 'Full Frontal' and the D-Gen's 'Late Show' and the aggressive soliloquys of the likes of Wendy Harmer make little use of jokes as such. Just as other forms of narrative are less and less reliant on traditional plot, humour seems less reliant on the mini plots of jokes which have an increasingly traditional, even anachronistic look in a post-modernist era. Perhaps the use and distribution of jokes, previously told in groups or printed in magazines, will be replaced by these new modes in these comparatively new media.

We've certainly found much evidence of computers being used as modes of transport for the joke while one of the few known cases where the authorship of a joke was unequivocally demonstrated involves computer networking. Within a few hours of the Challenger tragedy, people around America were saying that NASA stood for 'Need Another Seven Astronauts'. (A journalist, determined to trace the new meaning of NASA, that acrimonious acronym, worked his way back through the umpteen computer contacts. Finally he found a bloke who happily confessed. And he was exhilarated to discover that his little joke had gone around the United States and the world within a few hours.)

This brings us to the question of a joke's Australianness. Sadly it must be reported that there seem to be very few genuinely Australian jokes. Even the aforementioned anti-Aboriginal jokes derive from jokes told against African Americans or Native Americans which are reworked for local conditions and consumption. This is emphatically true in the case of political jokes. Again and again what seemed to be an authentic local joke concerning, for example, former New South Wales Premier Nick Greiner, would be revealed as having originated as a Margaret Thatcher joke. But perhaps it wasn't 'originally' a Margaret Thatcher joke at all but one of more ancient origin, repeatedly recycled.

For example, the most common political jokes these days are aimed at Paul Keating. Some of the most vehement turn out to be recycled anti-Hitler jokes told in Munich clubs in the 1930s, specifically by two courageous comedians who ended up in Dachau. Over the years people have replaced Hitler's name with the name of whichever politician they sought to demonise.

One of Australia's most famous jokes in recent years – told by Andrew Denton – concerns a woman's desire to perform oral sex on David Hill in an ABC lift. The story earned Denton a considerable amount of notoriety at the time but turned out to have been recycled from a New York joke concerning Donald Trump. What is interesting about the joke is that Trump and Hill are seen as similar in personality, in vanity. If the joke fits, wear it. As Finley Peter Dunne observed in 1901: 'Th' las' man that makes a joke owns it.'

You can observe similar recycling in jokes that seek to decry the intellectual limitations of this or that race or group. Thus jokes told about the allegedly dim-witted Irish are all but identical to jokes told about Poles, many of which, with modification, are then targeted at blondes. Writers of novels, plays and feature films tell us that there are only about a dozen basic plots which are endlessly rejigged and reused – American writers of top television dramas have told us how script editors have asked them to 'Lear-up' an episode, or have required yet another variation on the Romeo and Juliet theme. If that is true of drama it seems trebly, painfully true of jokes.

Classic Irish jokes are frequently retold as indigenous Dad 'n Dave jokes. Moreover, no two people tell the same joke exactly the same way, so that you get a spectrum of stories based on the same core joke, with variations on names, places and punchline.

Our book contains a great many jokes that were collected at considerable personal risk by editors whose senses of humour may never recover. We have not attempted to censor the stories. To soften the words, to mute the essential nastiness would have been to mislead the reader, and to confuse the archaeologists who will try to make sense of this text in a thousand years' time. Virtually the only jokes that have been eliminated are those entirely dependent on quality of performance, involving vocal devices for which there are no typographic equivalents. Moreover, most of the jokes have been reprinted in much the form we heard them or received them, in the hope of preserving something of their spirit. So spare us pedantic letters complaining about syntax and the splitting of infinitives.

Virginia Woolf observed that humour is the first of the gifts to perish in a foreign tongue. Jokes, verbal devices in their essence, a part of oral culture, don't necessarily survive translation to the page. Believe it or not, some of the jokes you'll read in this book were once very funny indeed. But it was in the telling. In the facial expression, the gesture, the quality of performance. We can only hope that some of the better jokes that lie flat on the Penguin's pages are destined to be recycled and revived by talented joke tellers.

Nonetheless we confess, we emphasise that, at the end of the day, this collection of jokes is not particularly Australian. This is not the collection that would have been gathered twenty or thirty years ago when the idiom had been less subjected to the bombardment of global media. There may still be jokes of local origin but they would be all but impossible to identify. We must accept that, overwhelmingly, jokes are a global, floating currency subject to instant conversion. Finally the definition of 'jokes currently circulating in Australia'. What follows are the most often told jokes of recent vintage. Thus the joke of 'Pierre, the bridge builder' was recently transmogrified into 'Spiro, the boat builder', an inevitable outcome given the comparative populations of French and Greek migrants.

Yet if the hypothesis about humour holds – that it's strengthened by adversity – then Australians should have at least a great sense of irony. And jokes aside, examples abound of a highly advanced sense of the absurd. When life plays such immense practical jokes as afflicting you with drought, followed by fire which is immediately drenched by flood, you have to be laconic to survive.

So there's Ned Kelly, standing on the gallows, the noose around his neck, the knot being tightened at his ear by a bureaucratic butcher. And what does he say? What are his last words as the trapdoor opens? 'Such is life.'

Those words should be the motto on our coat of arms, emblazoned on the shield between those big-bummed, small-brained creatures that so eloquently signify Australia: the kangaroo and the emu.

Perhaps we should replace the animals with the heraldic device of that famous *Bulletin* cartoon showing a couple of builders' labourers dangling over an abyss. One clings to a girder, the other to his mate's trousers which are slowly slipping from his hips. 'Stop laughing,' says one to the other, 'this is serious.'

It's a toss up which of those two contributions would be the most apt. But both of them celebrate something about our national character that we'd like to believe in. We escape the gravitational pull of disaster – whether tumbling from a girder or falling through the gallows' trapdoor – by being flippant, courageous. Our humour, at its best, meets the definition of death defiance.

If this was a collection of Australian cartoons, it would be easy to present hundreds of marvellous examples of the laconic, the tough, the ironic, the magnificently bleak. Ever since the *Bulletin* days, the era of Bruce Petty and Mike Leunig, Australia's black and white artists have been as tough in their commentary as Samuel Beckett in Godot. But in the spoken or written joke, we are less original, less distinctive.

Yet there's one that has some of the ingredients. It is politically incorrect and distinctly chauvinist. Yet in its austerity, brevity and basic decency it speaks of an ethos that links us to the time of Lawson.

A couple of farmers with neighbouring properties were working together repairing a buggered fence. One says to the other: 'I reckon I might have a bit of a problem now the shearin's done. Head down to Synny.'

'Yeah? I hear Synny's pretty interesting. What route will you take?'

'Oh, I reckon I'll take the missus. After all she stuck by me through the drought.'

Few and far between, like gum trees on the Hay plain. But memorable in their ruggedness, a handful of such jokes survive. For the rest, they are the world's jokes, dressed up in Akubras and Drizabones.

The only serious, academic attempt to analyse Australian humour that we can identify is a contribution to *National Styles of Humour*, edited by someone with the jokey name of Avner Ziv and published by Greenwood in New York in 1988 as a part of a series on the study of popular culture. Heading essays on humour in Belgium, France, Great Britain, Israel, Italy, the United States and what used to be Yugoslavia, Hyram Davies and Peter Crofts (the former an actor and writer, the latter a stand-up comedian) tell the world about everything from *Coles Funny Picture Book* to Steele

Rudd. They cover humour in Australian film, radio, television, theatre and the visual arts and provide a comprehensive bibliography from Afferback Lauder to A.J. Wilkes' *Dictionary of Australian Colloquialisms*. But though their wide net captures everyone from Roy Rene to Barry Humphries, from Wally and the Major to Norman Gunston, their essay is more an inventory than an explanation.

It's a Who's Who and What's What of Australian humour, embracing Lawson, Banjo Paterson, Norman Lindsay, George Wallace, Ed Dyson, C.J. Dennis, John O'Grady, Stan Cross, Pat Oliphant, Bill Wannan and Ross Campbell. 'Mavis Bramston' and 'The Aunty Jack Show' are explained to scholars of humour around the world. But a definition, a differentiation of Australian humour remains elusive.

But that's not to say they don't try very hard, restating our mythology of mirth. There's talk about our 'tortured beginnings' and they argue that

the whole tradition of humour was spawned in those first fledgling years. Apart from a small birth of ethnic influence, it is the same sardonic irreverence and lack of respect for authority which characterises the mainstream of indigenous humour to this day . . . The underdog battling to survive in a hostile environment, and the realisation that things are so lousy that you can only laugh, that you can't win, is a constant text in Australian humour. The harsh and mysterious land, with its inhabitants of convicts and free settlers and law and judiciary, soon imprinted its character on the people. The

Cockney twang and soft lilt of Ireland and gentle vowels of English counties and Scottish inflections, all flattened together and became the laconic Australian accent ... The ribald aggressiveness of the humour finds expression in the mateship of segregation and does not include women in its aura.

They describe the Australian pub as

the home of the country's true-blue, dinky-di humourous expression ... without the tradition of many touring professional shows, no repertory or provisional theatre, the pub became the stage for many amateur comedians, practical jokers, and raconteurs, locally known as wits, wags, and whackers. They would spin one another yarns, tell traditional stories and tall tales about tricksters, heroes, and hoaxsters, all the time holding their small territory around a hotel bar in an ambience of mateship, eulogised in Australia as perhaps the single most important virtue that the Australian male can possess.

The Australian joke is very much like those told by Australians in pubs: always masculine, at times cruel, uncouth, disrespectful, and often racist. Australians rarely came into contact with the butt of their jokes, so there was little of the strident venom of the true racist; and more often than not, the jokes were dirty and quite often directed at themselves.

Fair enough. But the sad truth remains that very, very few jokes are pristine in their ocker ethnicity. Show us an Australian joke and we'll show you an

English, an American or a German joke that has been on a long journey. Thus the 'what route are you taking?' yarn may well have had its origins elsewhere, where the culture allows route and root to be confused.

This collection also excludes the exaggerated yarns beloved of the late Frank Hardy. All but endless anecdotes whose Australianness teeters between the triumphant and the tedious are still being told around the country – indeed some communities organise competitions and Yarn Fests. But a few examples would all but have filled this volume. Also judged to be outside our terms of reference were political anecdotes which arrived in their hundreds from MPs in every State and Territory. There were enough Whitlam stories alone – both true and apocryphal – to justify a separate volume. But anecdotes are no more 'jokes' than yarns.

There may have been a time when the Australian joke, evolving in isolation, produced something of distinct comicality, analogous to the oddity of the kangaroo or platypus. But it's a long time since cultural influences arrived by sail, blown by the trade winds. Now jokes blow in on electronic winds, at the speed of light, though their internal circulation is achieved by more traditional means. The pub, however, is losing its cultural dominance and flesh and blood friendships are replaced by cathode substitutes. The dynamics of suburbia have been extensively modified, with neighbours replaced by 'Neighbours'. Our researches indicate that, these days, jokes are as likely to be communicated by fax (we received any number of Faxyarns from a service of that name) or by computer, just as the traditional 'rubbing' of rice paper and charcoal has been replaced by people putting their bums on photocopiers.

Similarly, the rich world of Australian colloquialism lives on in the works of Bill Wannan, is parodied in the glossaries of Barry Humphries and is preserved in the Macquarie Dictionary. But unless you have a copy of Lenny Lower or C.J. Dennis or Steele Rudd you'll find the words are being replaced by international jargon. Thus drongo is rarely heard. Dickhead prevails. The words like battler and wowser that gave the language such potency are now anachronisms, while phrases like 'not much chop' and 'she'll be right' seem doomed to die. Whilst there was a neo-classic period following the film version of Barry Humphries, '*The Adventures of Barry McKenzie*', it's important to recognise that many of McKenzie's colloquial efforts were pastiche. Yet people around Australia and the world started 'pointing Percy at the porcelain' or equating dryness with 'a dead dingo's donger'.

As the global culture intensifies, as the all-at-onceness of electronic communication triumphs over separate cultures, perhaps there'll be a last stand. Perhaps a few Australians, like Ned at Glenrowan, will plate themselves in thick idiom and blaze away at the cultural imperialists. Even so, such heroic figures are doomed to fall in the dust, as cultures hybridise.

DAD 'N DAVE 'N THE BUSH

31

The Australian hayseeds, Dad 'n Dave, first appeared as characters in *On Our Selection* by Steele Rudd. The Rudd stories were turned into films by the veteran Australian director, Ken Hall, with a very young Peter Finch playing Dave. The sexual escapades of Dave and Mabel have been a staple of Australian humour ever since, with most jokes focusing on the two innocents dealing with the wickedness of the big city. A familiar theme in Australian popular culture, it was recently recycled for the *Crocodile Dundee* films.

Dad and Dave were standing watching a dingo licking its privates. Dave said to Dad, 'Just between you and me, I wanted to do that all my life.'

Dad said, 'Go ahead, but I'd pat him a bit first. He looks pretty vicious to me.'

Dave was going to marry Mabel, so he went down to Melbourne to book a room for the wedding night. He found a pub he liked, in he went, in high spirits, very jaunty. 'Gidday. I'd like to book a room for me honeymoon night, luv.'

'Yes,' said the female receptionist, 'bridal suite?'

'Ahh, no thanks dear, I'll just hang onto her ears.'

Dave returned to Snake Gully after a brief trip to Europe. Dad said, 'Reckon you saw a lot of mighty fine things in that Europe.'

'Sure did, Dad. Cathedrals, palaces, mansions. But what impressed me most were the dunnies. They sure have got terrific dunnies. And they all flush.'

'Well, son,' said Dad, 'reckon you ought to build yourself one of those posh dunnies. But you'll have to get rid of the old shithouse first.'

'Nothing to it, Dad.' Dave took out a hand grenade that he happened to have on him, pulled out the pin and threw it at the shithouse.

Dad's a slow thinker and a slow mover. After a while he said, 'I don't reckon you should have done that, son.'

Out of the debris staggered Mum. She lurched up to Dad and said, 'Reckon it must have been something I ate.'

Mum sends Dave off to the market to buy a few things and Mabel tags along, as usual. After investing in a new bucket, a straw broom, a couple of live chickens and a poddy calf, Dave is struggling home, with the calf baulking and the chickens flapping and the bucket clanking – all in different directions. As they pass through a bit of bush Mabel says, 'Aw gee, Dave, I'm scared!'

Dave yanks the calf and recovers a chicken and says, 'Yeah! What of, Mabel?'

'Aw gee, you might take advantage of me in this lonely bush!' says Mabel.

'Come off it, Mabel,' says Dave, grabbing the bucket. 'Look how busy I am with this lot!'

Quick as a flash, Mabel says, 'But couldn't you put the chickens down on the ground with the bucket on top of them, and push the broom into the ground and tie the calf to it?'

Dave rode back from the Melbourne Show with a jar of liquid. Dad was curious to know what the sideshow shysters had sold Dave this time, and followed him to the old cow shed, whereupon Dave pulled a worm out of the cowyard's mud and dipped it into the little jar. Immediately the worm became rigid. Dave then used it as a nail to fix a wobbly weatherboard on the shed.

That arvo, Dad said to Dave, 'How much was that concoction?'

Dave replied, '$10 for 100 mls.'

Dad said, 'If you get me a litre of it, I'll buy you a new Porsche.'

So Dave raced off to Melbourne on his horse and returned two days later with the litre pack. He spent the next day fixing fences in the bottom paddock. When he got back to the homestead, Dad was taking it easy on the verandah, alongside of which was a nice new sporty Mazda. 'D'ya like the car, Dave?' Dad asked.

Dave exploded with rage. 'You old coot! You promised me a Porsche!'

'I did, I did,' said Dad. 'It's in the garage. The Mazda's a present from Mum!'

Dad and Dave go to town but, because of their divergent interests, decide to take separate cars. So Dad takes the Holden ute and Dave takes the Falcon. They arrange to meet in a fortnight's time at a pub near Centennial Park that they remember from the Royal Show.

When Dad turns up, he's really pissed off. 'I'm glad we're going back home. I couldn't park anywhere without some bastard giving me a ticket.'

To which Dave replies, 'You think you had troubles! I parked the Falcon outside a Catholic church and the bastards raffled it!'

When Dave goes to Ashton's Circus, he sees an elephant for the first time. A spieler exploits his innocence and sells him a pair of coconuts as elephants' eggs. 'Think of all the work elephants could do around your farm,' he's told. 'But you'll have to hatch them by taking them to bed for a week.'

Mabel wonders why Dave is spending so much time in bed. He explains that he's incubating the elephant eggs. She puts her hand under the blankets and feels Dave's genitalia. 'Ugghh . . .' she says, pulling her hand out quickly. 'It's gruesome.'

Dave says, 'Mabel, you'd better put yer 'and back . . . it's grew some more.'

Mum is working in the kitchen when Dad enters with his first erection in years. 'Mum . . . get into bed,' he says. She takes off her apron, puts all the ingredients and utensils away, washes her hands, gets into bed . . . but too late. Dad has withered away.

'Ya know . . . we can't 'ave this 'appen agin,' says Dad. 'Next time I git one of these, I'll ring the firebell so you start gittin' ready when youse hears it. When I git to the house, we'll be right.'

A year goes by. Mum's in the kitchen. She hears the firebell. She goes through all the preparations. Dad comes pounding into the house, through the kitchen, into the bedroom where Mum lies waiting for him. He looks at her and says, 'Get up, yer oversexed fool . . . the barn's on fire!'

Dad and Dave are in Paris, walking down the Champs Élysées. They are intrigued by the most beautiful marble building. There's absolutely nothing like it back in Snake Gully. What could it be? They decide to go inside and ask. They discover an extremely courteous Frenchwoman sitting at a Louis XV desk.

'*Messieurs*, is there anything I can do for you?' she enquires.

Dave leers at her and says, 'How about a blonde?'

'*Mais oui*,' says the Mademoiselle. 'Go up to the *cinquième* floor, room *vingt-six*.'

Dave goes up and finds a beautiful blonde lying sprawled over an elegant divan. There is an energetic cultural exchange. He retreats to the marble foyer and asks the Mademoiselle if there's a bill.

'*Mais* no, *monsieur*. This is *pour vous*,' and she hands him 500 francs. Dad is astonished. He decides to try his luck. As he's in the process of lighting his pipe with a box of Australian matches, he asks for a redhead.

'*Mais oui, monsieur*. Go to room *trois* on the *huitième* floor.'

He does so and, lo and behold, there's a redhead straight from a Degas painting. They have truck.

Dad returns to the foyer, slightly wobbly on his legs. Like Dave, he asks for the bill but once again, the Mademoiselle insists on giving him some francs. This time it's an even thicker wad – 5000. Dad puts the money in his pocket and says to the Mademoiselle, 'Look, I don't like to grizzle, but my son didn't get as much of this Frog money as me.'

To which the Mademoiselle replies, 'But he was only on the local Parisienne news, whereas you, *mon cher monsieur*, were seen over the entire network.'

'Dad, there's a new pub in Snake Gully. And for a dollar you get one of those new light beers, then they take you out the back and you get a root.'

'Really,' says Dad, 'are you sure about this, Dave?'

'Yep.'

'Have you been in there?'

'No, Dad, but Mabel has.'

Dad and Dave, having made some money with booming wool prices, decided to spend a bit of the proceeds down in the Big Smoke. They booked into their hotel, a commodious Edwardian pile not far from the CBD. They repaired to the saloon bar for a couple of jugs but continued their wassail well into the evening. Finally they retired to their room with its huge four-poster. Soon snores filled the room. Suddenly Dad woke up, shook his recumbent son and shouted, 'Dave, I'm as thirsty as buggery. Nip down to the bathroom and bring me back a glass of water.'

Dave did as he was bidden and came back with a brimming tumbler. Dad gulped it in one swallow and said, 'That's better – now for a bit more shut-eye.'

After half an hour he woke again and made the same request of Dave. And the procedure was repeated over and over again. But on the last occasion Dave returned without the water.

'Where's me drink, son?'

'Gee Dad, I'm sorry,' Dave replied, 'but when I went down to the bathroom, I couldn't get any. Some silly bastard was sitting on the well.'

During the rural recession, Dave got a job working a signal post on the Cairns to Townsville line. After a couple of weeks, there was a spot inspection by the local boss. 'What would you do if you had two trains coming at each other on the same line?'

Dave replied, 'I'd put all the lights on red and stop them.'

'Your lights are out of action,' says the inspector, 'what now?'

'I'd fire the flares,' said Dave.

'They're damp and won't work,' snarls the inspector, 'and by this time the trains are really close.'

'Well,' says Dave, 'as a last resort I'd go and get Mabel.'

'What could she do?' growls the inspector.

'Nothing,' replies Dave, 'but she's never seen a train crash before.'

Dad and Dave were watching a documentary on television, showing a rabbit plague in Victoria. The narrator explained that rabbits had been introduced to Australia by an Englishman. He'd imported four or five pairs for his favourite sport of shooting.

Looking at all the millions of bunnies hopping around, Dave said, 'He must have been a crook shot.'

Because he and Mabel were going to live with Dad and Mum when they got married, Dave wanted Dad to build a new dunny to replace the existing dilapidated one. Dad resisted the idea strongly.

'It's been good enough for Mum and me for all these years, so it's good enough for you and Mabel.'

Dave was determined, so he fitted a fuse and a cap to a plug of gelignite, dropped it into the dunny and retreated behind a stump to watch. He had just made it to the stump, when Dad came out of the kitchen and headed for the dunny. He rushed from behind the stump and yelled at Dad to save him from a disaster. But Dad thought he was trying to beat him to the dunny and put his head down and ran faster.

'You young blokes ain't as good as yer think you are,' he yelled. Dad got there first and had barely entered the building, when up it went. Ka-boom. Dave rushed to Dad's aid and extricated him from the wreckage.

'Are you all right, Dad?' he asked.

'I'm all right son, but stone the crows yer mother would have been annoyed if I'd let that one go in the kitchen.'

Dave and Mabel were out walking along the river bank one Sunday afternoon when they came across Herb Wilson sitting by a large tree with a fishing line in the river.

'Are yer catchin' any?' asked Dave.

'Just a few,' said Herb.

'How big?'

'Just tiddlers,' said Herb, 'about the size of your diddle.'

Dave and Mabel retreated to the other side of the tree and started to have a cuddle. Shortly after, Mabel called out to Herb. 'Eh! Herb,' she called.

'Yes, Mabel.'

'I'll bet yer catchin' some woppers, now.'

Dad and Dave went to the Royal Easter Show and were very interested in the new tractors that were on display. One salesman demonstrated his machine and then offered them a deal.

'You can have this model for $10 000 and I'll take off 10 per cent for cash.' They went away to discuss the deal.

'What's he mean by take off 10 per cent cash?' asked Dad. 'How much would he take orf?'

'I dunno,' replied Dave.

'Listen Dave, you're in pretty good with that barmaid at the pub and she looks like a pretty intelligent sort of girl, how about you ask her?' So Dave approached the barmaid.

'Tell me, Mary, if I gave you $10 000 less 10 per cent, how much would you take orf?'

'Dave,' she said, 'if you gave me $10 000 less 10 per cent, I'd take off everything bar me garters and you could use them for stirrups.'

Dave and Mabel became parents and Dave met Herb Wilson in town.

'Gee! Mabel and me 'ave got a baby. I bet yer can't guess what it is.'

'A boy?' says Herb.

'No,' says Dave, 'have another guess.'

The taxi driver took Dave to the railway station to catch a train to Sydney.

'You want to watch them wild wimmen down there,' warned the taxi driver.

'Don't worry about me,' says Dave, 'I'm as smart as them, any day.'

A fortnight later Dave gets off the train and hails the taxi.

'I want yer to take me an' the wife out to the farm,' says Dave.

The taxi driver looks at the woman standing on the station and couldn't help but notice that she was about six months pregnant. 'Is this yer wife?' he asks.

'Yeah,' says Dave, with a big grin on his face.

'But she's gonna have a baby.'

'That's right,' grins Dave.

'But it won't be your baby?'

'Course it's my baby,' protested Dave.

'How do yer make out it's your baby?'

'Well,' says Dave, 'if you buy a cow and it has a calf, the calf's yours, ain't it?'

In the days before TV and quiz shows, spelling bees were all the rage on the radio. Dave was the champion speller of Snake Gully and the whole team was involved when Dave went down to Sydney for a spelling contest. But just as Dave's turn came, a violent electrical storm cut off Snake Gully from the outside world. The whole town turned up the next morning to meet the train bringing Dave back from the Big Smoke.

'How did you go, Dave, how did you go?' boomed the Mayor as soon as Dave set foot to ground.

'No bloody good,' drawled Dave. 'Do you know what them silly buggers reckon in Sydney. They reckon you spell horse piss a-u-s-p-i-c-e.'

Dave decided to take Mabel to the Snake Gully café for lunch. Dave looked at the menu and said, 'They've got sheep tongues on the menu, Mabel. I think I'll have that. What about you?'

Mabel said, 'No, Dave, I couldn't eat anything that came out of an animal's mouth.'

'What would you like then, Mabel?' said Dave.

Mabel said, 'I think I'll have an egg.'

Dave and Mabel decided to raise pigs, but not knowing much about the facts of life, thought all they needed was a sow which could be served by a boar, and piglets would be there next morning. They approached farmer Brown down the road who informed them he charged $5, $10 or $20 per serve, depending on which boar was chosen.

'I think as we are just starting we should try the $5 boar,' said Mabel.

'Okay,' said Dave.

So they put the old sow in the wheelbarrow and wheeled it down to farmer Brown's boar. Dave got up early next morning expecting a litter of piglets.

'Gee, Mabel, I think we should have gone for the $10 boar.'

Mabel agreed so they put the old sow in the wheelbarrow and wheeled it down to farmer Brown's $10 boar. The next morning they were disappointed to find no piglets again. So Mabel said to Dave, 'Gee, Dave, we should have gone for the $20 boar in the first place.' Dave agrees, so back into the barrow goes the old sow, down to farmer Brown's for the $20 serve.

The next morning Mabel got up early because she was sure there would be piglets this time.

'Any piglets there this morning?' called Dave.

'No, Dave, but the old sow is sitting in the wheelbarrow!'

'What's the meaning of indecent?' the shearer asked his mate.

'Well,' replied his companion, 'I'd say if it was long enough, thick enough, hard enough and in far enough, it'd be in decent.'

Thirty years ago, one of the most famous and fast shearers in Australia was a bloke called Charlie Gibbs. Charlie shore all the 'long runs' between Queensland and NSW, shearing 200 a day, day after day, week after week, month after month. It was said of him that he was one of the very few shearers to have shorn 50 000 in a year. Well, this story relates to an incident that occurred after Charlie arrived back in Bourke after a very long run. As he walked into the hotel, the publican caught his eye and said, 'Charlie, there's a cocky just out of town who wants to know if you'll shear his sheep. Can you give him a ring?' Charlie sauntered off to the telephone and rang the cocky.

'Oh, Mr Gibbs,' (cockies always call shearers 'Mister' before they shear the sheep), 'I heard your shed had cut out and was wondering if it would be possible for you to come and shear my sheep.'

'Oh, I suppose so,' said Charlie. 'How many have you got?'

'Three hundred and twelve,' replied the cocky.

There was a silence and Charlie said, 'What are their names?'

The gun shearer had been invited to the very aristocratic squatter's for an end-of-season evening meal. The squatter's wife, a very distinguished matron, enquired, 'Would you care to wash your hands before dinner?'

He replied, 'No thanks, Mam. I already washed them over against that fence.'

An old swaggie turned up at the shearing shed and it was painfully obvious that he hadn't washed in years. So the shearers manhandled him into a bath and, after stripping off several layers of never-before-removed clothing, they noticed a peculiar bulge on his upper back. After a few more old flannels and singlets were peeled off, they found . . . a schoolbag.

A swagman who had tramped many kilometres along a rough outback track came to a small pub named 'George and the Dragon' and made his way around to the back in search of a handout. Before he had time to ask, the publican's wife came on the scene and gave the tramp the greatest verbal thrashing of his life. She called him a lazy good-for-nothing loafer and added if he was hoping to get even a crust of bread he could forget it. The tramp heard her out in silence, then just stood there.

'Well,' she snapped, 'now what is it you want?'

'I was wonderin',' said the man, 'if I could have a word with George?'

In 1919 a stockman was taking a mob of cattle to the Gulf country when he camped out one night with the rabbit-proof fence man. This lonely bloke hadn't seen anyone for years, so they sat around the campfire catching up with the news. After a lull in the conversation, the stockman said, 'By the way, we won the war.'

'That's good,' said the rabbit-proof fence man. 'I never could stand them Boers.'

These two rabbit trappers had been around the traps and were busy gutting the rabbits, of which there were hundreds. One of the trappers announced that he had to go into the bush to excrete. His mate said, 'All right,' and continued to gut, flinging the rabbits' entrails well out of the way so as to keep the work area comparatively clean.

One set of entrails landed directly under the rabbiter as he answered the call of nature. He was gone a bit longer than usual and when he came out of the bush his face was deathly pale and he was barely able to walk. His mate said, 'Strike me pink, sport, what's wrong?'

'You wouldn't believe it,' said the sick and sorry rabbiter, 'but I strained so hard that I passed some of my guts on the ground.'

'Strewth,' said his mate, 'we'll have to get you to a doctor.'

'No, I'll be all right soon,' said the reeling

rabbiter. 'With the help of God and a little stick I got 'em all back in again.'

Two men in a small country town shared a sizeable lottery prize. A reporter from the local newspaper interviewed them and asked each what they would do with their money. The first, a businessman, said that he would buy a new motor car, take an overseas trip and invest the remainder. The other, a farmer, said, 'I dunno, I think I will just keep farming until it's all gone.'

An old farmer was worried about his favourite bull. It was ignoring the cows. So he went to the vet and got some medicine. Next day he was telling a neighbour about it. 'I gave that Brahmin of mine one dose and within half an hour he'd serviced eight cows.'

'Blimey,' said the neighbour, 'what's the stuff called?'

'Well, the label's come off the bottle,' said the farmer, 'but it tastes like peppermint.'

A city boy was sent to the country to spend a holiday on his bushwhacker uncle's farm. When he returned home he was bubbling over with news of everything he'd seen. His mum asked him to name all his uncle's animals. 'Well, I saw horses and pigs and some bulls and cows and some fuckers.'

'Some fuckers?'

'Well, Uncle Harry called them 'eifers but I knew what he meant.'

A couple of farmers with neighbouring properties were working together repairing a buggered fence. One says to the other, 'I reckon I might have a bit of a problem now the shearin's done. Head down to Synny.'

'Yeah? I hear Synny's pretty interesting. What route will you take?'

'Oh, I reckon I'll take the missus. After all she stuck by me through the drought.'

Two old bushies were sitting on the verandah of the pub, chatting over a couple of beers. They were discussing 'the new metric system' which meant they had to talk metres instead of yards, kilos instead of pounds and hectares instead of acres. They shook their heads sorrowfully. 'What next? I suppose we'll have to drive on the right-hand side of the road.'

'Well, that'd be all right provided they brought it in gradual.'

A farmer returned from a holiday in Bali. 'Christ, those coconuts are beaut. You can get milk out of them without having to get up at 3 o'clock in the morning and risk being kicked in the balls.'

A young city bloke inherited a cattle station. On taking up residence he soon discovered that cattle were being stolen in considerable numbers. Moreover, it was obvious that the cattle duffer was his neighbour. He discussed the matter with another local who said, 'Be careful. He's a tough bastard and he's just as likely to shoot you if you accuse him of pinching your steers.'

So the young bloke had a good think and sent off a letter ending with ' . . . and I would appreciate it if you would refrain from leaving your hot branding iron lying around where my foolish cattle can sit down on it.'

A newly graduated geologist got a job with a mining company and was posted to a very remote region of far west Queensland. After he'd been there a month, and being young and fit, he started to need a woman, so he asked the resident engineer where he could find a bit of female company.

'Nothing round here, son,' said the engineer. 'The nearest town is two hours' drive away and it's been empty for years, except for a fettlers' camp and the sergeant of the Stock Squad who stops there once a month.'

'Well,' said the young bloke, 'where do all the rest of our blokes go, all clean and dressed up on a Friday night?'

'Didn't you know?' asked the engineer. 'They've got your problem, so they go out after the sheep.'

'The sheep? Dirty bastards. I won't be in that!' exclaimed the young man.

'Well, suit yourself,' said the older man easily, 'I'm only telling you what's available.'

But after another month, the young geologist was desperate and, Friday night, he spruced himself up, had a couple of stubbies at the canteen and dashed off with the rest of the men. The next morning, he woke up with a splitting headache and realised he was in a cell. Standing next to him was the engineer.

'You're awake, then. Come on, I've bailed you out.'

'What happened, why am I in a cell? I didn't have much to drink, but I've got an awful headache. What's going on?'

'You've got a headache because the sergeant

sconed you with his rifle and, if you don't go quietly, he'll charge you with bestiality.'

'Why me, for Christ's sake? What about the others – they've been doing it for bloody months!'

'Maybe, but you had to pick the Sergeant's girlfriend, didn't you!'

Two boundary riders were camped for the night by a windmill. Having finished their meal they were sitting around the fire enjoying a 'makins'. One got up and walked into the darkness to answer a call of nature. After a minute or so he called out to his cobber, 'Say, Bert, have you ever smoked a cigarette that's been pissed on?'

Bert pondered this hypothesis for a while and answered, 'No, Alf, I can't say 'as I 'ave.'

There was a studied silence till the reply came. 'Well, you 'aven't bloody missed much.'

A motorist was driving quietly along the road when, suddenly, his eyes goggled as, believe it or not, he espied a three-legged chook running beside him. It suddenly made a right hand turn, heading up a side track towards a nearby farm house. Intrigued, the motorist decided to follow the chook. At the end of the track, he met a farmer leaning on a gate.

The motorist said, 'You probably won't believe this, but I reckon I saw a three-legged chook running this way.'

The farmer was nonchalant in response. 'Yep, we breed them here.'

'But why?' asked the motorist.

'Well, you see, I like a leg, my wife likes a leg, and me son likes a leg.'

'And what do they taste like?'

'Dunno,' replied the farmer, 'no one can catch the little bastards.'

Out for a Sunday drive, a bloke passed a gate to a property where a three-legged pig was standing near the fence. He stopped, backed up for a better look, became aware of the cocky standing nearby. 'Strange pig that . . . three legs . . . how did it happen?'

'Wonderful pig, that. Dived into the dam last Christmas and saved me youngest from drowning. Pulled him out like a lifesaver. Marvellous animal.'

'Is that how it lost the leg?'

'No. Then there was the bushfire. We'd all have been burned in our beds if that pig hadn't battered down the door and woken us up.'

'Leg injured in the fire, was it?'

'Oh, no. Then I remember the time that pig fought off those three dingos in the lambing paddock. Covered with blood 'e was. Killed two of the sods.'

'So the dingos got his leg?'

'No . . .'

'Then, how?'

'Well, mate, a pig like that, such a bloody marvellous animal, almost a member of the family, you might say. A pig like that – you couldn't eat him all at once now, could you?'

Bert was the station master on a rather large property out west. One day he needed some fencing work done on one of the farm boundaries, so he called in Bill, one of his stockmen. 'Bill, I want you to go out to Bennett's boundary and fix the fence there. You can take the four-wheel drive and if you have any trouble give me a call on the two-way radio.' So Bill set off. About ten hours later Bert got a call on the two-way. 'Boss, this is Bill. I've got a bit of a problem.'

'Yes, mate, what is it?'

'Well, I was driving along in the four-wheel drive and I ran into a pig.'

'So, what's the problem?'

'Well, he got stuck in the bullbars and he's still alive and kicking and squealing so much that I can't get him free.'

'Okay mate. In the back of the four-wheel drive you'll find a .303. Take it out. Put the muzzle close to the pig's head and shoot it. It'll go all limp, and you'll be able to get it off the bullbar. Then drag it into the bush and leave it there.'

'Okay boss, I'll do that. Thanks for your help.'

About a quarter of an hour later, there was another call. 'Yes, Bill what is it?'

'Well, I took out the .303, shot the pig in the head and he went limp just like you said. And I got him off the bullbar and dumped him in the bush but I still can't go on.'

'Why not, mate?'

'Well, it's his motorbike. It's still stuck under the four-wheel drive.'

Once upon a time there was a farmer who had a very randy rooster. The rooster wasn't so bad when he was sober but in the cold evenings the farmer often had a brandy before he went to bed and would also give the rooster a cup. The only trouble was that the rooster would then charge off to the henhouse, full of brandied libido and screw the hens half to death. The farmer was getting a bit worried about this because in the morning he'd go to the henhouse and find feathers all over the place and all his hens looking totally plucked. So he told the rooster that he's going to have to lay off the booze for a while because otherwise the hens are going to be plucked to death. For a few weeks he doesn't give the rooster any brandy and all is okay.

Eventually the farmer has to go away for a week so he tells the rooster that while he's away there's to be no brandy because if he gets back and finds any of his hens plucked to death he's going to cut the rooster's crest off. This is the worst fate to befall a rooster, to be crestless, so the rooster is appropriately chastised. So the farmer goes away and, after a couple of nights, the rooster is sitting on the windowsill of the farmhouse when he notices a bottle of brandy sitting on the table inside and that the window is slightly ajar. Well the rooster is sorely tempted and even though he takes himself all the way to the other side of the farmyard he can't get the sight of this brandy out of his mind. Eventually he thinks to himself 'just a sip will be okay', so he goes back to the farmhouse, gets in through the window and has a sip of brandy. This goes down really well and he gets the taste for it. So he thinks 'well, just one glass will be all right,' and pours himself a glass. After drinking this he's well on the way, so he has another and then another and eventually staggers out of the farmhouse with the bottle under his arm off to the henhouse.

When the farmer gets back he goes to the henhouse and finds a total disaster area. There are feathers all over the place, and nearly all the hens are lying on their backs, feet in the air, dead as doornails. 'That's it,' he decides, 'I've had enough of this horny drunken rooster.' So he grabs the rooster and cuts his crest off. For the next couple of weeks the rooster mopes around the farmyard totally dejected, holding his head, looking about as crestfallen as a crestless rooster can look.

The farmer starts to feel sorry for him and decides he'll try to do something to cheer him up. He's going to his sister's wedding at the weekend so he takes the rooster with him thinking they'll have a good time at the reception and this will cheer him up. When they get to the reception, the ladies and gents have to enter through different doors, ladies to the left, gents to the right. There is a piano in between the doors so the farmer sits the rooster on the piano and asks him to tell the guests which door to go through. The rooster is doing this just fine until a waiter comes past with a tray of drinks. The rooster asks for and gets a brandy and is sitting happily on the piano drinking his brandy telling the guests 'ladies to the left, gents to the right,' when the farmer's bald uncle walks in with his wife. Whereupon the rooster says 'ladies to the left, gents to the right. And you, you baldheaded chicken fucker, up on the piano with me!'

Two kangaroo shooters, way out the back of Bourke. Their ute breaks down. They do the right thing – stay with it. But no one comes along. So they decide to walk out. The temperature is 40 plus. After two days, they're on their last drop of radiator water when they climb a rise and find, nailed to a tree, a sign saying MERCY, POPULATION 12. In the distance, a collection of ramshackle tin huts. They arrive. One hut is identified as a café. They enter. A lady appears, very proper. 'Yis,' she says.

'Bring us a drink, luv. Make it long and quick.'

'We only serve one thing here.'

'What's that?'

'Koala tea.'

'Well, bring it love, only make it quick!'

She brings it, and she is not kidding. Pathetic little paws grip the edge of the billy and little furry ears poke through the murky surface. Well, kangaroo shooters are pretty tough but they're not this tough. They look at each other and beg the woman to 'take it away please, and strain it'.

'What?' she says, 'The Koala Tea of Mercy is not strained!'

Once upon a time, way out past the back of Bourke, two grizzled old drovers were leaning on the bar of the local pub, discussing the relative merits of various dogs. 'Now, I reckon my Blue Heeler's the smartest dog in the country,' said one, ' . . . do anything that it's told.'

'Nah,' said the other, 'me Kelpie's master. 'e thinks for 'imself.' They argued back and forth across the mounting pile of empty glasses, the yarns about what each dog could do getting wilder and more far-fetched. But neither could agree with the other. 'Tell you what,' one said, 'let's put it to the test. Meet you out by the chicken run termorrer mornin'.'

Morning rose bright and early. The two old codgers rose bluff and bleary, and went out to the chicken run with their dogs.

'Right, Bluey,' said the bloke with the Heeler.

'Now you listen here and you listen good, coz I'm only gonna tell yer once.' The dog sat and watched him, eyes bright and ears erect. 'Now Blue, I want yer to go down that road for about a kilometre and yer'll come ter a gate. Go through the gate, up over the hill, ter yer left and yer'll come ter a brick wall with another gate. Open the gate, go through and yer'll find three poddy calves. Round up the calves, bring 'em through the gate, close it, bring 'em back over the hill, through the second gate and back here. Yer got that?' The dog barked, wheeled, scampered off down the road, through the gate, over the hill, got the calves, closed the gate, over the hill, through the gate, closed it, and brought the calves back to his master.

'Geez, that's pretty smart,' said the bloke with the kelpie, 'but that's nothing. You watch this . . . Oi, Kelly! Breakfast!' The dog looked around, dashed off down the road, came back, with a billy of water, collected some sticks, begged a match off his master, lit the fire, put the billy on to boil, scrabbled his way under the wire of the chicken coop, collected an egg, put it in the water, sat and watched it for three and a half minutes, took the billy off the fire, gently tipped the egg out at the bloke's feet, then stood on its head.

'Geez, that's bloody clever,' said the bloke with the Heeler, 'but what's the silly bugger doing standing on 'is 'ead?'

'Ah!' said the other bloke, ''e's not so silly. 'e knows I haven't got an eggcup.'

It appeared that a bullocky with his team hooked up and hitched to a large log, was snigging it to the loading ramp for cartage to the mill. The team had been mooching along fairly well, when suddenly they stopped. The bullocky, in a few well-chosen words, told the team what was expected of them – but they wouldn't budge. So he went up the front to check on the track. And there, right across the road in front of the leaders, was a dirty great goanna. So the bullocky got a strong piece of rope and tied it round the goanna's tail. He then unhooked two of the bullocks, and tied the rope to them, but these two bullocks couldn't move the goanna. So then he unhooked the whole team from the jinker and hooked them onto the goanna. He gave the bullocks explicit instructions as to what to do, but they couldn't move the goanna. To his horror, the next thing that happened was that the goanna took off! The last thing the bullocky saw was the goanna pulling the bullocks down the hill, through the bush to the gully below.

A SENSE OF IDENTITY

An Australian tour guide was showing a group of American tourists the Top End. On their way to Kakadu he was describing the abilities of the Australian Aborigine to track man or beast over land, through the air, under the sea. The Americans were incredulous.

Then, later in the day, the tour rounded a bend on the highway and discovered, lying in the middle of the road, an Aborigine. He had one ear pressed to the white line whilst his left leg was held high in the air. The tour stopped and the guide and the tourists gathered around the prostrate Aborigine.

'Jacky,' said the tour guide, 'what are you tracking and what are you listening for?'

The Aborigine replied, 'Down the road about 25 miles is a 1971 Valiant ute. It's red. The left front tyre is bald. The front end is out of whack and it has dents in every panel. There are nine black fellows in the back, all drinking warm sherry. There are three kangaroos on the roof rack and six dogs on the front seat.'

The American tourists moved forward,

astounded by this precise and detailed knowledge.

'Goddammit man, how do you know all that?' asked one.

The Aborigine replied, 'I fell out of the bloody thing about half an hour ago.'

Botha to Evans: Do your blacks have the vote?

Evans to Botha: Only if they live to be 18.

Two Aboriginal men were talking. 'How's your brother?'

'He passed away,' his friend replied.

'I'm sorry,' said the first man, 'I didn't know he'd been arrested.'

A young Aboriginal lad observed that there seemed to be some advantages in being white, so he went off and painted himself white all over. He went and showed his mother who roused on him, and told him to go and show his father. This he did, and his father not only roared at him for being so silly, but cuffed him over the ears and sent him on his way. The boy went on and sat on his favourite log pondering his position and feeling very glum. His mate came along and asked him what was wrong.

'I've only been a white kid for half an hour,' he replied, 'and I hate those black bastards already.'

A university researcher goes up to a blackfella and says, 'I'm researching people's religious beliefs. Tell me, do you believe in reincarnation?'

'Dunno, mate. What's it mean?'

'It means that, after death, you return to the earth in another form – a snake, or a brolga, whatever. Anyway, suppose there was reincarnation, what would you like to come back as?'

'I reckon I'd come back as a dog's turd.'

'A dog's turd? What on earth for?'

'Look at it this way, mate. Nobody'd stand on you, nobody'd drive over you and, after three days in the sun, you'd be white.'

An Aborigine walked into an enormous pig farm looking for work. He met the foreman who told him with a smirk that he had the perfect job for him. All he had to do was arrive at 5 a.m. and load a truckload of pigs by 9 a.m. The foreman knew that it usually took a couple of experienced blokes all day to get the buggers on board. The following day the Aborigine turned up at 5 and the foreman left him to it. By 6 a.m. he bowled up to his boss and said that the job was done.

'Who are you kidding?' said the astonished foreman.

But it was true. The truck was loaded with all the pigs.

'How the hell did you do that?' the foreman asked. 'It must have been beginner's luck.'

The Aborigine smiled and the foreman fumed.

The next two mornings the same thing happened. The Aborigine got the job done in a fraction of the usual time. On the fourth day the foreman decided to spy on him and hid in the bushes.

The Aborigine let the pigs out of the yard, stood on the back of the truck and starting singing, 'Come on, Aussie, come on!'

Whitey was walking along the road and saw an Aborigine. 'Hey Jacky, how far is Ayers Rock?'

The Aborigine asked, 'How do you know my name's Jacky?'

Whitey replied, 'I guessed it.'

To which the Aborigine said, 'Well, bloody well guess how far is Ayers Rock.'

An Aborigine walks into a bar with one thong on. The barman asks, 'Did ya lose a thong, mate?'

'Nah, I found one.'

Feeling generous, the publican in an outback pub invited the Aboriginal yardman to have a glass of beer. The yardman drank it appreciatively and the publican then asked him, 'How was the beer, Jacky?' The yardman answered, 'Just right boss, just right.'

The publican said, 'What do you mean, just right?'

The yardman answered, 'Any worse and I couldn't have drunk it; any better and you'd have sold it.'

Two white men and an Aborigine were in prison together. One of the whites said he was in for ten years for attempted rape, but thought himself lucky he hadn't actually done the rape or he would be in for twenty years.

The other white said he was in for fifteen years for attempted murder, but was lucky his victim had lived, or he would be doing life.

The Aborigine then said he was in for twenty-five years for riding his bike without a light, but reckoned he was lucky it wasn't night time.

A man in Canberra decides the way to make a fortune is to open a ten-pin bowling alley. He builds the ultimate bowling alley with twenty lanes, two restaurants and various bars. On the afternoon before the official opening he is standing around admiring his creation when he realises he's forgotten to order bowling balls. He rings the manufacturer in Sydney and orders 1000 balls. The supplier advises that he has them in stock and all he has to do is drill and polish them and then he can air-freight them to Canberra. The bowling alley proprietor says this will cost too much in freight and asks that they be sent by road in a 22-wheeler semitrailer.

The supplier works into the night and the balls are loaded and despatched. Travelling at great speed and in the middle of nowhere the truck driver sees two blokes standing on the side of the road. He stops to offer assistance and the two guys, who he sees are Aborigines, say that their bike has broken down on the way to Canberra and they are stranded. He offers them a lift, but says they must travel in the back because company policy prevents passengers in the cabin. They climb in with their bike and he speeds off.

Shortly after he's pulled up by the police. One policeman says to his mate, 'You book him while I check his load.' He opens the back but quickly slams and locks the door. And he runs to his mate and says, 'Forget booking him. Let's just get him across the border and out of New South Wales.' Despite his mate's protests, they head off at great speed to the Canberra border, escorting the truck.

At the border they stop and the truck hurtles on.

The policeman then says to his mate, 'Will you tell me why I couldn't book him and we had to escort him here?'

He replies, 'When I opened the back I could see it was full of Abo eggs. We had to get them out of the state because two had already hatched and one of them had stolen a bike!'

Jacky was sitting on the stoop in an inner-suburban street. It was garbage day, and the council garbage truck stopped right by him.

'Where's ya bin?' demanded the garbo.

'I bin away,' answered Jacky.

'No—where's ya wheely bin?' asked the garbo impatiently.

'Oh,' said Jacky, 'I *weely* bin in prison, but I tell me friends I've bin on holidays in Mullumbimby!'.

What does an Aborigine call a boomerang that doesn't come back?

A stick.

A lot of new Australians live in Fortitude Valley, Brisbane. A Chinaman had a fruit and vegie shop. Every Friday his neighbour, a Greek bloke with a snack bar, used to pass his shop on the way to bank his takings and he always called out, 'What day is it, Chinaman?'

The Chinaman always replied, 'Flyday, you Gleek plick.'

'Not "Flyday", you dozey bastard, "F-r-r-ri-day". Why don't you learn to talk English proper?'

So, the Chinaman practised all week. The next Friday, the Greek called out, as usual, 'What day is it, Chinaman?'

'F-r-r-ri-day, you Gleek plick.'

A young Chinese student was travelling in a train compartment with a ferocious Red Guard, an old lady and a pretty young girl. The train went through a tunnel. In the darkness they heard a kiss followed by a resounding smack. When they came out of the tunnel the Red Guard was rubbing a very swollen face, and they each contemplated what must have happened.

The old lady thought, 'What a proper young lady that is to chastise the Red Guard for his unwelcome advances.'

The young lady thought, 'Why should the Red Guard want to kiss the old lady instead of an attractive person like me?'

The Red Guard thought, 'That student is a lucky

chap. He kisses the young lady and I get the smack.'

But the student knew, 'I'm a cunning fellow. I kiss the back of my hand, smack the Red Guard, and get away with it!'

Two upper class Pommy brothers, one very hard of hearing, were having a quiet drink in a Chelsea pub where a drunken loud-mouthed Aussie was regaling the bar with his opinions. 'What a place England is. Free and open and as friendly as buggery,' spruiked the Australian.

'What did he say?' asked the hard-of-hearing brother.

'He said he likes England,' said the other.

'And Pommy women are fantastic movers,' said the Aussie very loudly. 'They're terrific sports, do anything in bed, fucking great.'

'What was that?' asked brother number 1.

'He says he likes English women.'

The Aussie continued. 'And last night I picked up a brassy old broad who took me home and fucked me stupid all night. Gee, she knew some tricks. The silly old bitch. What a fuck!'

'What did he say?' asked the deafish bastard.

'He said he'd met Mother.'

The Great Australian Dream – an Italian swimming out through Sydney Heads with a Pom under each arm.

Did you hear about the Pom who came out here, married an Australian prostitute and dragged her down to his level?

Did you hear about the Pommy taxidermist who went home because Australians kept telling him to get stuffed?

Dear Dorothy Dix,

I am shortly to become engaged to a wonderful man. My psychiatrist tells me that an open, honest relationship is the foundation of a happy marriage. But there are a few things about my family that are difficult to raise in conversation. For instance, my father is a heroin dealer and touches up little boys. My mother has always been a hooker and now runs a small brothel in the Cross. My brother ran out on bail for murder and went to England where he got married and is hiding out under a false name. My eldest sister is a lesbian.

My main question is this: should I tell my fiancé that my brother has married a Pom?'

A Pommy businessman was visiting Germany. He was alone and lonely in the lounge after work when a stunning Fräulein approached him, offering company. They dined together and his melancholy mood began to lift. He offered, she accepted, coffee and liqueur in the anteroom. He invited her to his suite for port and she came willingly. He proposed an even better remedy for loneliness and she complied. The next morning he was profusely thankful. 'You've been so kind to me,' he said, 'can I offer you some money? Perhaps 50 or 60 pounds?'

She said, 'That would be nice, but I'd prefer Marks.'

'How spiffing of you,' said the Pommy, 'I'd say about seven out of ten.'

A Pommy got a job at a cattle station. He mucked up everything he was given to do. Finally the farmer gave him a last chance. He told the Pommy to take a heifer into a paddock with a Hereford bull. Later the farmer asked the Pommy how things had gone. 'Top hole, old chap,' said the Pom. 'Christ, you stuffed it up again,' said the farmer.

Outside Bullen's Lion Park there's a notice stating the fees for driving cars and buses through. It also states that Poms on bicycles would be admitted free.

A bloke's car broke down on a country road. He walked to the nearest farm and knocked on the door. The most beautiful blonde with a perfect figure opened it, with a charming smile. He explained that he needed mechanical help and she said, 'See my husband. He's around the back.'

The bloke went to the back of the house and discovered an old Aborigine trying to make a fire with two sticks. He returned to the front of the house and said, 'How come a beautiful girl like you married an old bloke like that?'

She said, 'Oh, I haven't done so bad. My sister married a Pommy.'

An American journalist was sent to England to search for a typical English joke. After several fruitless weeks, he found himself in a country pub. He approached a group of locals and explained his problem. One of them told him this story which they all agreed was typical English humour.

'Approaching a road intersection was a man walking. On another road was a man riding a bicycle; on another a man driving a car; on another a man riding a horse. They all arrived at the corner at the same time. On the corner was a pretty girl who was greeted by one of these men. Which one?'

Naturally, the American hadn't the faintest idea, so the storyteller told him, 'The horseman knew her.'

When the journalist returned to New York, he told his boss this typical English joke. 'There's a dolly bird standing on the crossroad. Along one of these roads is a guy strolling towards the corner. On another street is a bicyclist; on another a guy in an automobile, and on the other is a guy on a horse. Which one of these guys knew the gal on the corner?'

The editor said, 'Hell, I don't know.'

'Neither do I,' said the journo, 'but the answer's "horse shit"!'

This is the story of an aviator – handsome, dashing, with big dark eyes, thick, black swept-back hair, and a bushy handlebar moustache. A Frenchman from the days when men were men, women were pleased, and the planes were built of wood, fabric, and flown on sinew.

Pierre is back from a successful mission, has wined and dined a pretty young lady and taken her back to his room. He kisses her forehead, eyelids and the tip of her nose. 'Oooo,' she thinks. Suddenly Pierre goes off, gets a bottle of red wine, sprinkles it on her lips and passionately kisses her. 'Oooo,' she says as they come up for breath. 'That's very nice – but why the red wine?'

'Aha,' he says, 'I am Pierre, the famous fighter pilot. When I 'ave red meat, I 'ave red wine!'

They continue. Clothing is gradually discarded. He kisses her chin, her neck, her cleavage. 'Oooo,' she thinks. Pierre goes and gets a bottle of white wine, sprinkles it onto her breasts and kisses them passionately. 'Oooo,' she says, 'that's very nice, but why the white wine?' 'Aha,' he says, 'I am Pierre, the famous fighter pilot. When I 'ave white meat, I 'ave white wine!'

Matters progress further. More clothing is discarded. He kisses her navel, her stomach, her mons. 'Oooo,' she thinks, 'OOOO!' Pierre then goes and gets a bottle of cognac, sprinkles it liberally over the fluffy bits and sets it alight. 'AAAAHH!' she screeches, leaping off the bed and beating out the burning bush. 'You silly fool! What did you do that for?'

'Aha,' he said, 'I am Pierre, the famous fighter pilot. When I go down . . . I go down in flames!'

Quasimodo was run down and his doctor ordered him to take a complete break from his job. But he felt that Notre Dame required its bells to be rung as usual, so that he shouldn't take leave until he found a suitable replacement bellringer. He advertised the temporary vacancy in *Le Monde* but there was only one applicant. It was a funny looking bloke who had no arms.

'This is crazy,' said Quasi. 'You've got no arms. How do you expect to ring the bells?'

'I'll use my head,' said the little man and took a running leap at the nearest bell, scoring a direct hit and making quite an acceptable sound.

'Not too bad at all,' said Quasi. 'Try the one on the left!'

The little man took another running leap, but his timing was out and he went over the parapet, falling 100 metres to the pavement below. Quasi limped his way down to the street. A gendarme was standing next to the shapeless remains.

'Do you know this man?' interrogated the policeman.

'Not really, but his face rings a bell.'

The next day another applicant appeared. Obviously he was the identical twin brother, also minus arms. Same deal. A demo of ringing the bells. Same outcome. Squished. Same gendarme standing over gruesome remains down on the footpath.

'Did you know this man?' asks the gendarme.

'No,' said Quasimodo,' but he's a dead ringer for his brother.'

Bruce arrives in Paris and is gazing around at the sights in wonderment. As he walks beneath the Eiffel Tower, gazing up, he bumps into a little

Frenchman and sends him sprawling. 'Sorry, mate,' says Bruce, dusting him down and picking him up. 'Look, let me buy you a beer.' The Frenchman introduces himself as Pierre, and, rather mournfully, agrees.

'What's the trouble, cobber?' asks Bruce, observing that Pierre is still looking very sorry for himself, even after a few beers.

'*Mon ami*,' says Pierre, 'do you see that cathedral over there by the river Seine? I, Pierre, I built that cathedral. But do they call me Pierre the Cathedral Builder? And do you see the bridge by the cathedral? I, Pierre, I built that bridge. But do they call me Pierre the Bridge Builder? And do you see that magnificent sculpture standing in the middle of that park? I, Pierre, I created that sculpture. But do they call me Pierre the Great Sculptor? But suck just *one* cock . . .!'

How do French women hold their liquor?

By the ears.

An aristocratic family in Delhi sent their favourite son to Harvard, whence he returned with that most desirable of degrees, an MBA. Determined to demonstrate his managerial brilliance, he approached the government with a brilliant idea. To raise money for the Indian Treasury he will conduct, on their behalf, the biggest lottery in the history of the world. The entire population of India will be encouraged to buy tickets. Although each will pay only a few rupees, the amount of money raised will be immense.

The ticket sales go very well. Finally comes the day of the draw. The young man with the MBA has arranged for all the ticket stubs to be deposited in a vast wooden barrel which is positioned high above the swelling crowds, on an elaborately carved platform. And on the platform, many of India's most famous political and cultural celebrities. A magnificently painted elephant has been trained to turn the barrel, so that the stubs are properly mixed, and India's most beauteous film star is on hand to call out the winning numbers. The entire event is compered by the young MBA, whilst the actual prize will be read out by India's Treasurer.

At the appointed time, the crowd has grown to immense proportions, stretching from one end of India to the other. The elephant churns the barrel and the movie star is asked to pull out the number of the third prize winner. The MBA proclaims the number through his microphone, his voice echoing through thousands and thousands of loudspeakers strung up lamp posts, trees and minarets. Finally there is a response from far, far away in the crowd and a thin figure in a *dhoti* is seen weaving his way through the multitude crying, 'It's me, it's me!' At last he arrives breathless on the platform. The Treasurer announces the third prize. You have won two first-class airline tickets from Air India to take you anywhere you wish around the world, along with 1000 English pounds spending money. The crowd goes wild.

Now the elephant churns the mighty barrel and the sequence is repeated for the second prize. This time the winner has to run even further, almost all the way from Jaipur.

'Congratulations,' says the Treasurer, 'you have won second prize. Here it is, this beautiful fruit cake.' The little Indian chap is very upset. 'A fruit cake? But the third prize was airline tickets and lots of money.'

Attempting to soothe the indignant prizewinner the MBA explains, 'But this is no ordinary fruit cake . . . this fruit cake was baked . . .' and he takes a deep breath as he makes the proud announcement ' . . . by Madam Gandhi!'

To which the prizewinner responds, 'Fuck Madam Gandhi!'

'Ah no no no,' says the MBA, with a characteristically Indian shake of the head, 'that is first prize!'

One of Madam Gandhi's nephews wanted to become a fully-fledged Brahmin. He was told there was an initiation ceremony. He had to do three things within an hour. Firstly, drink a full bottle of scotch. Then make love to a woman, and thirdly, shoot a man-eating tiger. After forty-seven minutes he'd downed the whisky. He returned from the jungle torn to pieces with three minutes to go, pulled out his gun and said, 'Now where's this bloody sheila I'm suppose to shoot?'

Two blokes are walking down Lygon Street in Carlton. One of them is notorious for his prejudice against Italians. Yet when he sees an Italian organ grinder with a monkey, he throws $5 into the monkey's hat. The friend is surprised. 'But people have been telling me for years how much you hated Italians, and here you do that.' To which the bloke replies, 'Well, they're so cute when they're little.'

Maria went to Luigi's fruit and vegetable shop every week. She walked in on this particular day and said, 'Hello, Luigi. I woulda lika two kilos of tomatoes pleasa.'

'Ah, Maria, so sorry, I have no tomatoes today.'

'Luigi, don'ta you joka with me. You know that I always buy my tomatoes from you. Just give me my tomatoes, Luigi.'

'Maria, I told you, I have no tomatoes today.'

'Luigi, I'm in a hurry, please give me two kilos of tomatoes.'

'Maria, it's lika this. How you say "carrots", without the "c"?'

'Arrots.'

'How you say "potatoes" without the "p"?'

'Otatoes.'

'How you say "tomatoes" without the "f"?'

'There's no "f" in tomatoes.'

'That's whata I been trying to tell you, Maria. There's no effing tomatoes!'

Luigi, the fisherman, is out on Port Phillip Bay when his boat springs a leak and starts sinking. He frantically starts radioing for help.

'This is-a Luigi. Send-a me *plane*, and-a quick!'

Search and Rescue radios back. 'We hear you Luigi, and we're sending you a Fokker Friendship.'

To which Luigi replies, 'I don't want-a you fokker friendship! I want a fokker *plane*!'

It's necessary to register the birth of the twins (a boy and a girl) at the Almoner's office section of Births, Deaths and Marriages. As Dad speaks poor English, he asks his proud brother to do the registration. The woman on the counter asks, 'And what is the little girl called?'

'Denise.'

'A lovely name. And the boy?'

'Denephew.'

An American oil-drilling company was erecting new offshore platforms in total isolation. Their industrial psychologist was concerned about the effect this might have on the crew. It was therefore decided to test the reactions of three men. An Englishman, an American and the inevitable Irishman were selected and told to pick out their favourite leisure gear to help them cope with the next three months completely on their own in the middle of the ocean.

The American turned up with a suitcase, the Englishman with five huge plastic bags and the Irishman with only his hands in his pockets.

The industrial psychologist was, naturally, very curious. The American explained that he was taking his Linguaphone records and books to learn languages. The Englishman said he had 5000 golf balls to improve his game. Then they quizzed the Irishman who produced a packet of tampons from his pocket, reading aloud from the label. 'With this you can go swimming, scuba diving, aerogliding, dancing and do aerobics.'

Mary, a strictly brought up Catholic girl, wanted to marry Richard Todd, a Protestant. Their families were horrified, but when they could see she was determined, asked if she would first have a talk with Father O'Toole. Father O'Toole pointed out the pitfalls of mixed marriages, but he was a wise priest and could see Mary was not convinced. He therefore suggested she kneel before the statue of the Blessed Virgin, ask permission and abide by her words.

Mary thought about this, eventually agreed and, kneeling reverently before the statue said, 'Holy Mary, Mother of God, may I marry Dickie Todd?'

The priest, who'd nipped around behind the statue, replied in a rather deep voice, 'No!'

'Shut up, God,' said Mary, 'I'm talking to yer mother.'

An Irishman collected a large insurance settlement after an auto accident by pretending that his injuries had put him in a wheelchair for life. When the inspector from the insurance company warned him that he would be pursued by them for the rest of his life until they established the fraudulence of his claim, he responded by telling him that they would be following him to the Catholic religious shrine at Lourdes and 'there you're going to see the greatest miracle in your life'.

Needing to conduct a pathology test, a doctor asked a simple Irish washerwoman for a specimen. Not wishing to confess her ignorance, she returned home and went next door to ask her neighbour the meaning of the doctor's request. She came back bruised and dishevelled. When her husband asked her what had happened, she said, 'I asked her what a specimen was and she told me to go and pee in a bottle. So I said, "Go shit in your hat," and the fight was on.'

Two Irishmen rented a boat at Williamstown, rowed out into Port Phillip Bay and caught a couple of snapper. 'We should mark the spot,' one said, so they painted a big black 'X' on the bottom of the boat. 'That's no good,' said one of them, on careful re-evaluation. 'Next time we mightn't get the same boat.'

An Irishman visited Australia. When he got back to Dublin they asked him about the place. He said it was a wonderful country, that the Australians were marvellous. But he couldn't stand the white bastards.

A gridiron football match in Boston. A vociferous lady with a strong Irish accent on the fence, giving her views. As the opposing scrums inclined together for battle, she shouted, 'Give the ball to Muldoon!'

A wild scuffle, the ball emerged and was slung to a player. He was borne down by a pride of opponents and carried off on a stretcher. His replacement ran on. Still the lady shouted, 'Give the ball to Muldoon!' Another scrum. Again the ball passed to a player who was promptly flung heavily to the ground and was assisted, limping, from the arena. As his substitute ran on, the lady still shouted, 'This time, give the ball to Muldoon!'

A figure stood up in the scrum, cupped his hands and shouted back, 'Muldoon say he don't want the ball!'

When I was flying to Singapore I asked the man sitting next to me where he was going. His reply was, 'DDDDDDDDUUUUUUBBBBBBBBLLLLLLIIIINNNN.' I then asked what he was going to do in Dublin. His reply was that he was going to Dublin 'TTTTTOOOOO BBBBBEEEE AAAAAAA RRRRRAAAACCCCIIIINNNNGGGGG BBBRRRRROOOAAADDDDCCCAAAASSSTTEEERRRR.'

I asked him if he really expected to get the job. 'NNNNNNOOOOO. They'll probably give it to a bloody Catholic.'

Two IRA men planted some explosives and were sheltering behind another building. After the detonation, a human head rolled along and stopped at their feet. After a minute, one of the IRA men said, 'You know, that looked like Father McGillicuddy.' The other said, 'It couldn't be. We gave him plenty of warning!'

So they decided to see the priest's housekeeper, Mrs O'Flaherty. Holding the head by the hair, they knocked on the door. She opened it and asked, 'Well, boys, what's the trouble?' When they explained, she said, 'Hold it up!' The fellow with the head lifted it up above his own, so she could have a good look.

'No, that's not him,' said Mrs O'Flaherty, 'he's too tall.'

Paddy was an Irishman with some experience in the building trade. But when he arrived in Melbourne he found that the recession and the troubles of the BLF made it very, very hard to get a job. He kept trying and trying. 'Oid loik a job, sir,' Paddy would say. 'Well, now,' said a foreman who wasn't too enthusiastic about the Irish. 'Before we employ anyone on this site, we always have a quick intelligence test.'

'That's or'right, sir,' said Paddy, 'you just foir away.'

'Well,' said the foreman, 'can you tell me what's the difference between a girder and a joist?'

'Well now sir, just off the top of me head, oid say Goethe wrote *Faust* and Joyce wrote *Ulysses*.'

An Irishman goes on 'Sale of the Century' and chooses Irish history as his category.

'In what year was the Easter rising?'

'Pass,' he replies.

'Who was Parnell?'

'Pass,' he replies.

'What's the difference between the Orange and the Green?'

'Pass,' he replies.

'Good man, Seamus!' comes a voice from the audience, 'tell them nothing!'

Kerry Packer had a set of dominoes with huge diamonds instead of spots. An Irishman broke into his house and stole the double blank.

'What have you got in your pocket?' one Irishman asks another.

'I'll give you a clue. It begins with "N".'

'A napple,' said the first Irishman.

'No, I told you it begins with "N".'

'A norange!'

'No, I'm telling you for the last time that it begins with an "N".'

'Would it be a nonion?'

'You've got it at last.'

There's a riot in an Irish prison and the Governor tells the guards to evict the troublemakers.

'What's that on your leg, Seamus?'

'A birthmark.'

'How long have you had it?'

A boss decides to sack his lazy Irish cleaning lady.

'Look, Bridget, I can write my name in the dust on this desk.'

'Can you now, sir?' she replied. 'Isn't education a wonderful thing!'

Have you heard about the Irishmen who waited outside a brothel for hours because the red light wouldn't turn green?

Judge: Do you want to challenge any member of the jury?

Paddy: I reckon I could fight that little bloke on the end.

There's a court case in Dublin. A German sailor's been charged with being drunk and disorderly. 'I can't understand a word he's saying,' complains the judge. 'Is there anyone in court who can translate German?'

'I'll do it,' said an Irishman.

'Good,' said the Judge, 'ask him what his name is?' 'Vot iss your name?' said the Irishman.

Seamus had BO so his girlfriend told him to go home and have a bath. 'And afterwards, use some deodorant and toilet water.'

Next day he reappeared swathed in bandages. 'Holy Virgin!' she asked, 'what happened?'

'The toilet seat hit me on the head.'

An Irishman is taking an IQ test. 'What's black and is worn on the left foot in wet weather?' The Irishman didn't know.

'It's a Wellington boot! Now, think carefully before you answer the next question. What's black and worn on the right foot in wet weather?' The Irishman shook his head in bewilderment.

'A pair of Wellington boots. Now, here's the final question. Who lives in the White House and rules over millions of Americans?'

'I know that one,' shouted the Irishman. 'Three Wellington boots!'

When an Irishman couldn't get a dance his friend decided to tell him the truth. 'Look, it's the smell from your socks. Go home and change them and you'll have no trouble.' Later in the evening the Irishman complained that he still couldn't get a dance.

'Did you change your socks?'

'Of course I did,' said the Irishman, pulling them from his pocket.

An Irishman joined the Army and was being assessed by an officer to see what regiment he should join.

'Can you shoot a gun?'

'No.'

'Well, what can you do?'

'I can take messages, sir.'

'Good. We'll assign you to the pigeon corps in charge of vital messages being carried from the front by pigeons.'

After a week's intensive training the Irishman was given his first job – to intercept a pigeon from the front bearing a message. He returned after an hour, covered in feathers and pigeon poop.

'Well,' said the officer, 'what's the message?'

'Coo, coo,' said the Irishman.

A bloke went into a pub. Seated at the bar beside an Irishman was a huge dog. 'Does your dog bite?' he asked the Irishman.

'No,' said the Irishman, 'he's as gentle as a lamb.'

So the bloke patted him and the dog just about tore his arm off.

'You told me your dog didn't bite,' he screamed.

'Yes,' said the Irishman, 'but that's not my dog.'

An Irishman, a very good Catholic, was hanging off a cliff by one arm praying for God to save him. A fishing boat passed by, and the fisherman shouted for the Irishman to let go and be rescued.

'No,' said the Irishman, 'God will save me.'

Then a helicopter came and dangled a rope over the cliff.

'Grab the rope,' shouted the pilot.

'No,' said the Irishman, 'God will save me.'

Then a submarine surfaced and the captain called out to the Irishman to jump.

'No,' said the Irishman, 'God will save me.'

A few hours later he fell off the cliff and drowned. When he arrived in Heaven he said, 'God, why didn't you save me?'

'Look,' said God, 'I sent a boat, a helicopter and a submarine. What else could I bloody well do?'

An Irishman had been missing for weeks. His wife told the police. Next day the police arrived to say that her husband's body had been found floating in the Yarra. 'Sure, that couldn't be him,' she said, 'because he couldn't swim.'

Two Irishmen escaped from Pentridge and hid up separate gum trees. Some cops arrived with tracker dogs and surrounded the first tree. 'Who's up there?'

'Miaow,' said the first Irishman.

'Let's try the other tree,' said the policeman, 'there's only a cat up that one.' So they went to the second tree and a policeman yelled, 'Who's up there?'

'Another cat,' said the second Irishman.

Did you hear about the Irishman who tried to kill himself by taking a hundred painkillers.

After two he began to feel better.

Seamus and Brendan had been on the piss. When they woke up in the morning the blinds were drawn. 'Is it day or night?' asked Seamus.

'I'll go and have a look,' said Brendan. So he lifted the blind and looked out.

'Well,' said Seamus, 'is it day or night?'

'I can't remember,' said Brendan.

What events did the Irish win at Barcelona?

Heading the shot and catching the javelin.

A wealthy Dublin woman comes into the undertakers and identifies a corpse as her father. She orders a very expensive funeral. But just as she's leaving, the corpse's jaw opens and exposes a set of false teeth.

'My father didn't have false teeth! Cancel the funeral!'

When she left, Seamus hauled the body out of the coffin and said, 'You fool, you'd have gone first class if only you'd kept your damn mouth shut.'

Seamus and Paddy were out driving together.

'Are we getting near a town?' asked Seamus.

'We must be,' said Paddy, 'we seem to be knocking more people down.'

'Well, drive slower then,' said Seamus.

'What do you mean drive slower?' said Paddy. 'I thought you were driving!'

Dear Patrick,

I have not written to you for a long time. I know that you are not a very fast reader, so I am writing this letter very slowly. You might be interested to know that your Uncle Seamus has got a new and important job. He has 500 people under him. He's in charge of a cemetery . . .

Paddy had been working for an Australian company for awhile when the management called in some efficiency experts. They required all the employees to have an IQ test. Thoroughly alarmed, Paddy asked his mate, Bob, about it.

'Hey Bob, what's this IQ test?'

'Don't worry, Paddy. They just go around and ask a lot of questions and, depending on how you answer them, they give you a certain score.'

'What's the score for?' asked Paddy.

'Well, the higher you get,' explained Bob, 'the better job you'll get.'

Even more alarmed, Paddy asked, 'What's a good score?'

'Well, suppose you get 100,' said Bob, 'they'd give you a job up in the office somewhere, in the main building.'

'But suppose I only got 80?' asked Paddy.

'Well, you'd probably keep the job you've got now, out here in the yard stacking timber.'

'But suppose I only got 60 or 40 or 30?' wailed Paddy.

'Look, if you only got 30 or 40, you wouldn't have enough intelligence to do up your shoelaces.'

Whereupon Paddy burst out laughing. 'Now I know why all Australians wear thongs.'

Paddy charged into the newspaper office to insert a funeral notice following the death of his father.

'How much is it ye charge?' he asked the man at the counter.

'Two dollars per inch,' he replied.

'Holy Nellie,' said Paddy, 'and my old Dad was six foot foive!'

Two young Irish lads apply to their nearest police station for jobs as police constables. Mick Murphy is given an interview first while his mate Paddy waits in the anteroom.

Inspector to Murphy, 'I'll ask you three questions. Question one, where's the River Liffey?'

Murphy (a Dublin resident) looks stunned and says, 'Pass.'

Inspector, 'I'll ask you an easier one this time. What's the capital of Ireland?'

Murphy, 'Pass.'

Inspector (becoming exasperated), 'Well, can you at least answer this question ... who killed Jesus Christ our Lord?'

Murphy, 'Pass.'

Inspector, 'I suggest you go away and don't come back until you find out who did.'

Murphy rejoins his mate Paddy who asks, 'Did you get the job?'

Murphy, 'To be sure, and they've put me on a murder case already.'

Two Irish travellers returning home became lost. One said, 'We must be in a cemetery. Look, here's a headstone.'

The other lit a match and peered at the stone. 'Well, he was a grand old age – ninety-five!'

'What was his name?' asked his friend.

'Oh, some fellow called Miles from Dublin.'

Old Pat Muldoon was dying of a terrible contagious disease. As he lay gasping in his bed, he felt he was truly at his end.

'Maggie,' he wheezed to his beloved wife, 'go quick and send for the rabbi. I'm dying.'

'What!' exclaimed his wife, 'all your life you've been such a good Catholic and now you want a rabbi!'

Pat opened one eye, 'What, you want a priest to catch this?' he asked.

The police pulled Paddy in for suspected rape. They put him in line with ten other fellows and the accusing woman was brought in. Paddy jumped forward, 'That's her,' he screamed, 'that's her! I'd recognise her anywhere.'

The old Cork couple had not had a holiday for fifty years and they decided to take a fortnight off. They went to the Glens of Antrim and had a splendid time. But unluckily, no sooner had they arrived home than the husband sickened and died. At the wake a friend went to pay her respects to the dead man. 'How tanned he is looking,' she said to the widow. 'Yes,' she said, 'the two weeks in the Glen did him the world of good!'

An Irishman had a very bad start to the duck season. Everyone else was getting ducks and he wasn't. He finally realised his mistake. He wasn't throwing the dog high enough.

Did you hear about the Irishman who built a bridge over the Nullarbor? They had to tear it down because too many Australians were fishing from it.

Did you hear about the Irishman who immigrated from Ireland to Australia and raised the IQ level in both countries?

An Englishman asked an Irishman, 'Has the Irish language got any equivalent to "*Mañana*" in Spanish? The Irishman thought for a moment, then replied, 'Yes, but it hasn't got quite the same sense of urgency about it.'

The scene is a court room. Patrick is being charged with causing an affray. He looks very much the worse for wear with cuts and bruises. The other contender in the brawl is in court. He is Michael O'Toole. The judge questions Patrick.

'Tell me, Patrick, what happened, in your own words?'

'Well, your honour, I was in the bar minding my own business when Michael there entered it. He had a long bit of four-by-two in his hand and he came at me and began beating me. Oi didn't stand a chance. He's entirely the injuring party.'

'But Patrick,' said the judge, 'will you tell me what you had in your hand?'

'Ah, your honour – all I had in my hand was Mrs Molly O'Toole's right breast. 'Twas a lovely thing in itself, your honour, but no earthly use in a fight.'

An Irishman was walking down town when he felt hungry. Up ahead he saw Joe's Pizza Parlor. He went in and ordered a pizza. When it came out of the oven, Joe asked the Irishman whether he wanted it cut into six or eight pieces. The Irishman said, 'You'd better cut it into six pieces. I couldn't eat eight!'

Pat and Mick were camping in the bush, but the mosquitoes were so bad they decided to pack up and move a few hundred yards. But they'd do so in total darkness, so that the mosquitoes wouldn't know where they'd gone.

They stumbled around in the dark, striking the tent by feel and groping their way through the thick scrub. Somehow they managed to repitch their tent in total darkness and, finally, fell inside exhausted. Whereupon a firefly came through the flap of their tent.

'It's no use,' moaned Pat, 'they're looking for us with hurricane lamps!'

A Pommy bloke had a prang on one of those fancy motorways and was taken to hospital. When he was off the critical list, a surgeon visited him and said, 'This news is good and bad. The good news is that you're out of danger, the bad news is that there is some damage to the brain which is not immediately life-threatening but could cause trouble later on. I strongly recommend that you authorise us to operate and remove the damaged cells.'

'I say, old boy, doesn't sound very nice. How much would have to be removed?'

'About 18 per cent, we estimate,' replied the surgeon.

'And what would be the significance of that, in layman's terms?'

'Well, it would have the effect of lowering your IQ to the level of the average Irish peasant.'

'I say, that doesn't sound at all nice. Still, I suppose you'd better do what has to be done.'

The operation was performed, and the surgeon came in to see the patient. 'The news is good and bad,' he said. 'The good news is that the operation was a complete success. The bad news is that the damage was more extensive than we thought and we had to remove 80 per cent of your brain cells.'

'Fair dinkum?'

An Irishman arrived in Australia and went into a pub in the Outback where he asked for a glass and, having pissed in it, drank it. He then walked out the door, into the chook house and proceeded to knock the hens off their perches prior to going to the paddock, where he lifted the tail of a cow and put his ear to its anus. When he returned to the bar a few minutes later, the publican asked him to explain his strange conduct.

'Before I left Dublin,' he said, 'I met an Aussie who said there are three things I had to do to be a real Australian. Drink the piss. Knock off the birds. And listen to the bullshit.'

Paddy and the priest were walking down the lane. Paddy was putting his hand in his coat pocket, looking for his cigarettes, when a packet of condoms fell on the cobbles. The priest picked up the packet and said, 'What do you use these for?'

Paddy said, 'Well, you can use them for lots of things. Like when it rains. You can put one over your cigarette to keep it dry.' As it was raining lightly at the time, the priest said, 'Then I'll get some.'

Next day he went to the chemist and asked the girl behind the counter for some condoms. She said, 'What size, Father?'

And the priest said, 'To fit a Camel.'

Paddy and Mick emigrate to Australia. Before they leave home, Paddy's dad, an old salt, gives them a bit of advice, 'You watch them Aussie cab drivers, they'll rob you blind. Don't you go paying them what they ask. You haggle.'

At Sydney airport they catch a cab to their hotel. When they reach their destination the cabbie says, 'That'll be twenty dollars, lads.'

'Oh no you don't! My dad warned me about you.

You'll only be getting fifteen dollars from me,' says Paddy.

'And you'll only get fifteen from me too,' adds Mick.

Paddy and Mick walk into the CES looking for work.

'Oh look, it's a pity Seamus wasn't with us.'

'And why would that be?' asks Mick.

'Well, there's a vacancy here for tree fellers and we could have gone for it.'

Paddy finally got the job and went along on his first day. He was given his chainsaw and told he must cut down twenty trees to earn his wages. He returned in the evening tired out.

'How many did you cut today, Paddy?'

'Five.'

'Sorry, no wages today.'

Next day, 'How many today, Paddy?'

'Ten.'

'Sorry Paddy, not enough.'

On the third day, Paddy crawls into the office.

'How many today, Paddy?'

'Fifteen, sir, and it's the best I can do.'

The foreman shook his head. 'I don't understand it. The others all reach their quota. Perhaps there's something wrong with your saw.' He took the chainsaw, started it up.

Paddy leapt back in horror. 'What's that noise?'

A doctor was doing his hospital rounds with an Irish nurse. When he came to one bed he pronounced, 'Nurse, this patient has died.'

The old fellow in the bed said, 'I'm all right. I'm not dead!'

The nurse responded, 'Will you be quiet. The doctor knows best.'

An Irish lady was given a parrot, but when she took it home it started to yell, 'My name's Sally. I'm a hooker and a goodtime girl.' So the lady went to the priest for advice.

'I have the solution,' said the priest. 'My two parrots are god-fearing, say the rosary daily and study the Bible. Put together they will make Sally forget her wicked past.'

When Sally was put in the cage with the other two, one was heard to remark, 'Put away your beads and Bible, Charlie. Our prayers have been answered!'

The ventriloquist was in sparkling form. The audience was in stitches. He'd told how the Jews got the Commandments. ('Free, already? *oi vey*! We'll take ten!'). The English-tourist-in-Wales-gag brought the house down. He'd explained why Scotsmen have thin penises. (They're such tight-fisted wankers.) 'Now,' he announced, 'I have a great Irish joke for you.' Whereupon, to his consternation, a huge man wearing a MacAlpine's jacket, jumped up. 'Listen, boyo,' he said in ominous tones, 'oim not goin' to stand for any o' them stories makin' out that us Oirish is t'ick.' The ventriloquist was somewhat alarmed. 'Now, now my good man,' he stammered, 'it's only a bit of harmless fun. No offence intended.'

'Oim not talkin' to you, mate,' replied the Irishman. 'Oim talkin' to that cheeky little bastard sittin' on yer knee.'

It was wake time in the Rafferty household. When Mulligan called to pay his last respects he found Mrs Rafferty more than usually upset. 'Sure it's his wig, Mick. You know how self-conscious he was about his baldness and how he always liked to look his best. We just can't get the wig to stay on properly.' 'Give me a minute or two wit' the carpse,' volunteered Mick, 'and oil see what oi kin do.' When Mick called Mrs Rafferty back into the room the wig was sitting perfectly on the corpse's head. 'Ah, Mick,' she cried, 'shure'n he's lovely. If only he could see himself. You must let me reward you.'

'Faith, 'twas nuthin',' the modest Mick protested.

'At least let me square up for your expenses,' Mrs Rafferty insisted.

'Well, all roight then,' Mick conceded, 'just give me a couple o' bob for the nails.'

At the height of the trouble in Northern Ireland, one of the most profitable businesses was the glazier trade. Most glaziers were so busy that stopgap measures had to be employed while waiting for new glass. Thus suppliers of plywood also prospered. But imagine the surprise of the person who broke his spectacles one Friday and was informed by the optometrist, 'We can't fit new lenses until next Monday, but we can board them up for you over the weekend.'

The young Irish lass was distraught. No one had ever explained to her the possible consquences of doing 'that'. 'Oh Mammy, Mammy,' she lamented, 'Oim pregnant. Oim goin' to have a baby.' Her mother liked to be clear on these things. 'Holy Mother,' she exclaimed, 'are ye sure it's yours?'

The Irish paratroop sergeant was explaining the technique.

'These 'chutes are army surplus,' he pointed out. 'To avoid strain, don't pull the rip cord until you're about 10 feet off the ground.'

'What if it doesn't open?' asked a worried recruit.

'Jeezus,' the sergeant bellowed, 'ye can jump 10 feet can't ye!'

Two young, teenage, Irish Catholic girls were walking home from a lecture given by the local priest on premarital sex. One said, 'Bridget, did you understand everything that Father said?'

'Oh yes,' replied Bridget, 'I know all about that stuff he was talkin' about.'

'Well, if you do,' said the first lass, 'are you one of them virgins Father was talkin' about?'

'No,' said Bridget, 'not yet!'

Did you hear about the Irishman who had a greyhound?

He had a bus painted on the side of it.

Pat and Mick decided it's time to confess. Mick goes into see the priest and says, 'I've been having a relationship with a young woman.' The priest is aghast. 'Was it Mary Houlihan?'

'No,' says Mick.

'Was it Brenda O'Shaughnessy?'

'No,' says Mick.

'Was it Maureen O'Hara?'

'No,' says Mick.

'Well, say fifty Hail Marys and don't do it again,' says the priest.

Pat is waiting for Mick outside the church. 'How did you go?'

'Marvellous. I got three new names.'

Why do the Irish call their currency a punt?

Because it rhymes with bank manager.

An Australian and an Irishman opened a Beer House in London, which failed badly. 'I know what we'll do,' said the Australian. 'Let's open a brothel on the first floor.'

'What a silly idea,' replied the Irishman. 'If you can't sell beer, how are you going to sell broth?'

A 10 p.m. curfew was imposed in Belfast. Everybody had to be off the streets by 8 p.m. However one citizen was shot at 7.45 p.m.

'Why did you do that?' the soldier was asked.

'I know where he lives,' he replied, 'and he wouldn't have made it.'

The judge in a criminal case in Dublin was shocked when the accused pleaded guilty to the charge but was acquitted by the jury.

'How did you arrive at that verdict?' he asked the foreman of the jury.

'Well, Your Honour,' was the reply, 'everybody except you knows him to be the biggest liar in Ireland.'

A Japanese businessman arrives at the Melbourne airport from Tokyo and goes straight to the airport bank. In return for a 1000 yen, the teller gives him 1260 Australian dollars. A few days later he's flying to Sydney and goes to the same counter for some extra cash. This time the teller hands him 1185 dollars for his 1000 yen. The Japanese complains, saying, 'One thousand yen, one thousand two hundred and sixty dollars, not right, not right.'

The teller calmly explains that the rates change

daily. But the Japanese, by now holding up a number of other customers, continues to demand his 'one thousand two hundred and sixty dollars.'

The teller tries patiently to explain, 'Please understand, it's the world money rate, the differences in currency.' Failing to communicate, he then said loudly, 'It's the fluctuations, the fluctuations!'

To which the angry Japanese replied, 'Well fluck you Aussies too.'

During a goodwill mission to Japan, a high-ranking Australian senator was shown over a factory manufacturing televisions. Pleasantly surprised at the number of employees who spoke English he stopped behind a young girl who was soldering.

'And what do you use for flux?' he asked.

The girl looked at him in surprise. 'Plicks, of course,' she said.

A sadistic captain in the First Fleet discovered that there were two Jews among the convicts. He had them brought before him. 'Jacob Levy and Isaac Cohen, I'm going to make an example of you. You will receive thirty lashes and be put on bread and water until we reach Sydney in three months. If you are still alive when we arrive you will be put in prison until you rot, if we don't hang you first. What do you say to that, you miserable convict Jews?'

The pathetic pair in manacles and tatters looked at each other. Jacob hobbled towards the captain and kicked him in the shin. Isaac looked at Jacob and out of the corner of his mouth said, 'For God's sake, Jacob, don't make trouble.'

A Jewish grandmother was looking after her son's children in a coffee shop in Acland Street. A friend came along and said, 'How old are the children?'

'Well,' replied the grandmother, 'the doctor is 4 and the lawyer will be 2 next week.'

The Australian Opera was halfway through the first act of *Aida* when Mrs Cohen rushed onto the stage calling out, 'Is there a doctor in the house?'

The singing stopped, the orchestra was silent, the curtains plunged and the theatre lights went on. A man in the front row stood up.

'I am a doctor,' he said.

'Would you like to meet a nice Jewish girl?' asked Mrs Cohen.

The Cohens had just married off their fourth daughter. 'That's the last one then,' said the rabbi.

'Good thing,' said Mr Cohen. 'The confetti's getting really grubby.'

Two Jewish businessmen were discussing insurance. 'You need fire insurance, burglary insurance and flood insurance.'

'The fire and theft and burglary I can understand,' said the other, 'but the flood insurance? How do you start a flood?'

A rabbi entered a delicatessen, studying the offerings in the display case very carefully. After a while he pointed to some sliced meat and said, 'Half a kilo of that corned beef please.'

The salesgirl said politely, 'I'm very sorry, sir, but that's ham.'

'And who the hell asked you?' retorted the rabbi.

Mrs Cohen sat next to a well-dressed man on the bus. She immediately peered closely at him and said, 'Pardon me, but are you Jewish?'

'No,' said the man, 'I'm not Jewish.'

'Are you sure?' asked Mrs Cohen.

'I'm absolutely sure,' replied the man.

'Could you be mistaken?' Mrs Cohen persisted.

'No way,' responded the man.

'I've got a feeling that you're Jewish,' said Mrs Cohen yet again.

'Listen, lady, get this, I am not Jewish.'

'Look, Mister, it's just between you and me, all right? You're Jewish, aren't you?'

Worn down, the man said, 'Okay, you got me, I'm Jewish.'

'That's funny,' said Mrs Cohen, 'you don't look Jewish.'

The wife of a Jewish immigrant who'd only recently arrived in Australia dies suddenly. One of the neighbours offers his condolences, mentioning to Isaac that it's an Australian custom to put an ad. in the Classified Columns. So Isaac phones the *Age* and, determined to save money, asks for a two-word message. 'Ruth died.'

When the operator explains that the minimum charge covers five words, he thinks for a moment and adds, 'Toyota for sale.'

The business executive jumps out of a four-storey building and splatters on the footpath. Within a few moments the ambulance arrives and the officers try everything – mouth-to-mouth, heart massage. An old Jewish lady comes up. 'Give him chicken soup. It won't help, it won't hoit.'

Mr Weinstein couldn't attend the final court case of a major commercial litigation, but instructed his lawyer to advise him immediately of the outcome. When he returned to his office, the following fax message was waiting for him. 'Justice prevailed.'

To which he immediately replied, 'Appeal.'

Mr Cohen and Mr Cohen are both hospitalised for severe attacks of sciatica. They share the same room and get the same daily massages, which are extremely painful. While Mr Cohen is crying out loud during the massage, the other Mr Cohen endures his with serenity and calm. After it's been going on for a few days, Cohen asks Cohen, 'How do you manage to take this treatment without yelling?'

'How do I do it? You think I'm such a fool to let them massage my sciatic leg?'

Sol Greenblat was hit by the recession. He was practically broke. He prayed on the Sabbath in the synagogue. 'God, I need your help. I've never asked you before and I promise not to bother you again. All I need is to win the lottery. Just once God, that's all I ask.'

On Monday he looked in the papers – nothing. So next Saturday he went to the synagogue again and his prayers were even more fervent. On Monday – nothing.

So on Wednesday he prayed, 'God, do you really want me to pray again? It's only just a small thing I ask. Please help me.'

And he heard a voice, 'Look mate, you'll have to co-operate a little. You have to buy a ticket.'

Abe Finkelstein had finished his hawking rounds for a week and had done very well. So he thought he would give himself a justly deserved reward and went to a well-known King's Cross brothel. The Madam said, 'Well, you can have this nice Chinese girl over there for $5, then I have a redhead for $10 and this terrific blonde for $15.' Abe decided to spend $10 and had a marvellous time.

More than twenty years later his wife had died and he felt lonely so once again he went to the brothel. He recognised the redhead who was now the Madam, and there was a friendly reunion. Whereupon a huge youngster of about 20 appeared and called out, 'Mum, does this guy bother you?'

'No, no,' said the Madam, 'in fact, John, I'd like you to meet your father.'

'What?' said John, 'this little Jewish bloke's my Dad?'

To which Abe responded, 'Watch your manners! If I hadn't been so generous, you'd have been a Chinaman.'

A big Texan steps off the plane at Ben Gurion airport and hails a taxidriver. He drawls, 'Ah want yew to take me to where yew people are weeping and wailing and rocking and beating your heads against the wall.'

And the taxidriver takes him to the Taxation Department.

Poor Isaac lay dying and his family were at his bedside.

'Are you there, Abe?'

'Yes, father, I'm here.'

'Are you there, Ben?'

'Yes, father, I'm here.'

'Are you there, Rachel?'

'Yes, father, I'm here.'

'Are you there, Anna?'

'Yes, father, I'm here.'

Isaac forces his way up onto his elbows. His eyes

open a little and he yells, 'Who the hell is looking after the business?'

A Jewish shopkeeper rented some space in one of the new shopping malls. Each new tenant was allowed one banner above their space. The retailer on the right asked for 'Best Quality'. The one on his left 'Lowest Prices'. After a moment's reflection, the Jewish shopkeeper demanded 'Enter Here'.

A group of Israelis were discussing recent wars. 'What a shame that we have no Tomb of the Unknown Warrior,' said one, 'representing the fallen who were never found.'

'Of course we have such a tomb,' said another. 'It's on the outskirts of the city. I'll take you to it.' And they came upon a well-kept cemetery, as green as an oasis.

'There,' he said, 'is the Tomb of the Unknown Warrior.'

The first man looked and immediately protested, 'What are you talking about? This is the tomb of Isaac Goldberg, the prominent banker.'

'That's right. As a banker he was remarkable, as a soldier – unknown.'

An old Jewish bloke is crossing the street in Berlin in 1936 when he accidentally bumps into a burly stormtrooper.

'*Schweinhund*,' snarls the Nazi.

'Goldberg,' the old chap replies offering his hand.

Mr Block approaches a Catholic priest regarding the funeral of his deceased sister.

'This must be an error, Mr Block,' says the priest, 'I am a Catholic priest and your sister, God bless her soul, was Jewish.'

'My sister was not only baptised but she entered a convent and died as a nun.'

'That makes, of course, things quite different. Particularly as she has been a bride of Christ, I will be happy to see her to her grave. My fee for the service will be $100.'

Mr Block gives the priest $50, saying, 'My brother-in-law will pay the other half.'

Young Moishe was never good at mathematics and at the end of Term 10 his grades were completely unsatisfactory. When his father took him to task, his explanation was that his teacher was anti-semitic.

'Fine,' said his father, 'if that is the case, I will have you baptised.'

But baptised or not baptised, Moishe again brought a completely unsatisfactory report at the end of the following term.

'Now I have had you baptised and things haven't improved,' reproached his father.

'Come on, father, you know we Christians are no good at maths.'

The President of Israel is visiting the Pope at the Vatican. On the Pope's desk he notices a green telephone. 'What is the purpose of that phone, Your Holiness?'

'Well,' answers the Pope, pointing skywards, 'that's a direct line to you-know-who.'

'Marvellous,' replies the President of Israel. 'May I make a call?'

'Certainly, my son,' replies the Pope, 'but it will cost you about $200.'

A few months later the Pope is paying a return visit to Israel and is in the President's apartments. He espies a green phone on the desk. 'My son, what is the purpose of that phone?'

'Well, Your Holiness,' replies the President, 'that is a direct line to you-know-who.'

'*Benissimo*,' replies the Pope, 'may I make a call? I will be happy to reimburse you.'

'Go right ahead,' replies the President, 'but don't worry about the cost. It's a local call.'

On a long flight, one of the passengers stood up and addressed the others. He said, 'My name is Brown B-R-O-W-N and I'm true blue. I'm an American through and through. I'm white as snow from the top of my head to the tip of my toes, and I hate blacks.' After a while he stood up and again made a speech, 'My name is Brown B-R-O-W-N Brown and I'm true blue, as white as snow from the top of my head to the tip of my toes and I hate Jews.'

After a while a little man stood up and also addressed the passengers saying, 'My name's Schmidt S-C-H-M-I-D-T Schmidt and I'm a Jew. I'm as white as snow from the top of my head to the top of my toes, except for my arse which is brown B-R-O-W-N brown.'

An Irish priest offered 10 cents to the boy who could tell him who was 'the greatest man in history'.

'Columbus,' said one.

'George Washington,' said another.

'St Patrick,' shouted a third.

'The 10 cents is yours. But as the only Jewish boy in class, why did you choose St Patrick?'

'Right down in my heart I knew it was Moses,' he replied, 'but business is business.'

An El Al jumbo jet takes off from London airport bound for Tel Aviv. After climbing a few thousand feet the captain gets on the blower. 'Good afternoon, ladies and gentlemen. Welcome aboard El Al. We'll be cruising at 35 000 feet for most of your journey. Heavy cloud below in some parts, but flying conditions should be very good. A little turbulence on descent maybe . . . but that's all. Estimated time of arrival at Tel Aviv . . . ah . . . 1800 hours . . . to you . . . 1750.'

There are two Jewish business men who, although close friends, have been rivals all through their business lives. Each tries to outdo the other in every field of endeavour. When Max buys a home for one million dollars, Harry responds by buying one for a million, one hundred thousand.

It came to pass that Max went to Europe on his vacation and, on returning, couldn't wait to boast to his friend. 'I didn't want to disappoint the queen, so when she came to meet me at the airport, I agreed to let her put me up at the palace. She really couldn't do enough for me.'

Harry, at this point, is eaten with jealousy. Determined to outdo Max, he embarks on a European journey within days. When he returns after a few weeks he is met at the airport by his friend. 'Well,' asks Max, 'how was it? Was it as good as my trip?'

'I really don't know,' responds Harry. 'I didn't go

to London. I decided to go to Rome. And when I got there, the Pope came to the airport and insisted that I stay at the Vatican.'

This greatly impresses Max. 'The Pope?' he asks breathlessly, 'tell me, what is the Pope really like?'

'Well, I'll tell you,' says the storyteller, 'him I liked, but her I couldn't stand.'

For their fortieth wedding anniversary, Sadie gives Hymie a gift voucher to a high class brothel. Hymie is shocked. 'Sadie, what does this mean?' 'Well, Hymie,' says Sadie, 'our sex life has become so boring that I want you to take this, with my blessing, and go with one of these goils and learn something to put a little sparkle back in our schtupping.' Hymie is dismayed, but Sadie persists and eventually he goes.

The next morning he staggers through the door exhausted and, waving away Sadie's questions, stumbles to bed. By dinner, he's recovered enough to join Sadie and she asks, 'So? How was it?'

'Ahh, it was nothing,' he says.

'Nothing! All that money I spent and you say it was nothing. Surely you learnt something!'

'I didn't, Sadie,' says Hymie, 'I tried everything but everything I tried, we do already.'

'But surely,' says Sadie, 'surely there was one thing.'

'Well,' says Hymie, 'maybe there was one little thing.'

'Yes,' says Sadie, 'yes, what is it?'

'Well,' says Hymie, a little embarrassed, 'she moaned.' Sadie is speechless a moment. 'She moaned?' Hymie guiltily nods. 'And you like this moaning?' says Sadie, and Hymie shrugs and nods. 'Whoo boy,' says Sadie, 'for this I pay all that money. But, okay, if moaning is what you like then who am I to argue.'

That night Sadie and Hymie slide between the sheets and Sadie says, 'You want me to start moaning now?' And Hymie says, 'Not now, Sadie, not now.' Foreplay proceeds and Sadie says, 'Now, Hymie? You want I moan now?' 'Not yet, Sadie,' says Hymie, 'not yet.' And then Hymie climbs aboard Sadie and things, for him anyway, are building to a big crescendo as Sadie waits with wide-eyed anticipation. And then Hymie orgiastically calls out, 'Now, Sadie, moan now!' And Sadie shrugs and says, 'Okay, if that's what you want . . . So, you're not going to believe it, but I went to the butcher's this morning and he had no veal and my corns were hurting and, *oi vey*! Mrs Silverstein wouldn't stop telling me about her son the doctor . . . '

A Jewish socialite, Mrs Beckki Goldstein, had just learnt that she had six months to live. On hearing this she contacted her rabbi and asked him to find her a teacher so she could learn to speak Hebrew. The rabbi asked why she wanted to learn to speak Hebrew.

'Never mind,' she said, 'just find me a teacher.'

The rabbi organised a teacher for her and after six weeks she managed to master the Hebrew language, much to her tutor's amazement. Some time later, the rabbi paid her a visit and enquired how the lessons were proceeding.

'Excellent,' she said. 'I have mastered the Hebrew language in six weeks.'

'This is wonderful and amazing,' said the rabbi, 'after six weeks you have managed to learn Hebrew, a language that has taken scholars many years to perfect. Tell me, Mrs Goldstein, was there a reason for learning Hebrew at your age in life?'

'You bet,' Mrs Goldstein said. 'When I die and go to heaven I want to be able to speak to God in his native tongue.'

'Well, that's all very well, Mrs Goldstein, but what happens if you go to hell after you die?'

'It doesn't matter,' she said. 'I also speak Hungarian.'

As Hyram turned into his driveway, he was surprised to find a brand new Ford Laser parked there. He entered the house and called to his wife, 'Rachel! What's with the new car?'

Rachel ran to her husband, gave him a big kiss, and said excitedly, 'Oh, Hyram! It's all thanks to you. Since we got married, every time we made love I put $50 away. Yesterday I'd saved enough to buy the Laser!'

Hyram looked dejectedly at his wife. 'Oh, Rachel,' he exclaimed, 'if only I'd known. I would have given you all my business and you could have bought a Rolls Royce!'

After twenty years delivering mail to the same area, Abe the postman was retiring. As he went from house to house on his final round, the neighbours gave him little gifts in appreciation of his service. When he arrived at Mrs Goldberg's house she said, 'Postie, for your last day I've made you a lovely lunch. Please come in.' Which he did.

After lunch, Mrs Goldberg then said, 'Now that you've eaten, would you like to come upstairs with me and make love?' Although somewhat surprised, he agreed to her request. As he was leaving, she picked up an envelope from the hall table and gave it to him. He opened it and found that it contained $5.

'Mrs Goldberg,' he said, 'you made me a beautiful lunch; you took me up stairs and we made love. And now you want to give me $5. You are too generous.'

'Oh,' she said, 'you really should thank my husband. This morning I said to him "Abe the postman is retiring. What do you think I should give him?" And my husband said, "Fuck him! Give him $5" but the lunch was my idea!'

Mr Cohen is on a skiing holiday in the alps and gets hopelessly lost. After a few days a search party is sent out to find him. They arrive in the first valley and call out, 'Mr Cohen! Mr Cohen! It's the Red Cross!' Silence.

They struggle on, through deeper and deeper snow, to a second valley. 'Mr Cohen! Mr Cohen! It's the Red Cross!' Nothing.

With immense difficulty they make it to a third valley where, once again, they call out, MR COHEN! MR COHEN! IT'S THE RED CROSS!!'

And they hear a little voice, from far in the distance, 'I gave at the office, already!'

Moses went back up the mountain. 'Excuse me, God, I just want to get this straight. The Arabs get all the oil, and we get to cut the ends off our what????'

Three retired ragtraders, who made a bit of money out of schmutter, meet every week in an Acland Street café for a chat. One tells his friends that he has terrible, terrible news. 'My son has become a Christian.'

'*Oi vey*,' says another, 'so has mine!'

Then the third confesses that his son, too, has traded in the yarmulke for a crucifix. Whereupon the rabbi wanders in and they tell him of their troubles. The rabbi looks shamefaced and says that his son, has also become a Christian. So they troop off to the Synagogue where the rabbi prays to God, reminding Him of the way He had helped the Israelites flee Egypt, taking them safely through the Red Sea and showing them the Promised Land. 'And now, just a few thousand years later, our sons have become Christians.'

'A funny thing,' says God, 'my son too . . .'

The priest in the confessional hears an old man's voice on the other side of the screen. 'I'm 79 years old, married to the same woman for 50 years, and always faithful – never looked at another woman. Yesterday, I made passionate love to a pair of 18-year-old twins.'

Priest: 'When was the last time you went to confession?'

Man: 'What confession? I'm Jewish.'

Priest: 'So why are you telling me?'

Man: 'I'm telling *everybody*!'

The recession hit hard and a Jewish couple getting on in years falls on very hard times. Rachel offers to help by going out on the streets. Abe protests feebly, but Rachel goes. The next morning he's counting the takings. There's $34.50. 'Which lousy schmuck gives you the 50 cents,' he asks.

'All of them.'

What do you get if you cross a Jewish American Princess with a computer?

A system that won't go down on you.

Why do Jewish American Princesses prefer to have sex doggy style?

Because they can't bear to see anyone else enjoying themselves.

Did you hear about the Jewish banker who bought his wife a solid gold diaphragm?

He wanted to come into his own money.

A New Zealander, trying to escape the shame of applying for the dole in an increasingly hostile Australia, approaches a local farmer for a job. He claims to be a great horseman, terrific with cattle and even better with sheep. 'I worked for sux farmers when I was in New Zulland,' he said. 'There's nothing around the farm that I can't do.'

The farmer decides to give him a go. 'I want you to go up to the top of the hill, herd all those cattle down into the yards and then round up the sheep and shear them.'

The New Zealander goes to it. Half an hour later the farmer sees that all the cattle are in the yards, but there's no sign of the sheep. So he goes up to the shearing shed and finds the New Zealander having intercourse with one of his ewes.

'You rotten swine,' yells the farmer, 'I told you to shear them.'

'Not on your life,' said the New Zealander, 'I'm not sharing them with anybody.'

What's long and hard and fucks New Zealanders?

High School.

How do you make a New Zealander successful in small business?

Give him a large business.

An American, an Australian and a New Zealander were walking down a country lane when they chanced upon a ewe caught in a wire fence with its bum facing out to the road. Commenting upon the sheep's gyrations and exertions to escape, the American said, 'Goddam, I wish that was Madonna. I'd give her a reason to wriggle!'

The Australian said, 'I wish that was Kylie Minogue – I'd be up that like a rat up a drain pipe!'

Said the Kiwi, 'I wish it was dark!'

Things were going badly in Te Maika, as in the rest of New Zealand. Brian decided to try his luck in Melbourne, and two months later, his brother Bruce got a letter from him, 'You must come over here. The streets are paved with gold.'

Bruce packed his few belongings, and travelled steerage from Auckland. As he stepped onto the quay at Port Melbourne, he saw a 50-dollar note on the ground. 'Good as gold!' he exclaimed as he bent to pick it up. Then he stopped, straightened up, wiped his brow, and said, 'Hang about. It's Sunday today. I'll start work tomorrow.'

There's a sign outside a Queensland garage, 'Fill up and get a free fuck.' A man fills up and says, 'Well?'

The attendant says, 'Law says there's got to be a little competition. Think of a number.'

'Eight.'

'Bad luck, it's nine.'

The man drives off, stops at the next pub, orders a drink and says to a bloke standing at the bar, 'That garage down the road – it's a bloody take. Signs says "Fill up and get a free fuck" and it's all bullshit.'

The bloke says, 'No, mate, you're wrong. It's fair dinkum. Ridgy-didge. No worries. My wife won twice last month.'

A chap walks into a bar, bubbling over with good humour and says to the barman, 'Look, I've got this incredible joke about banana benders. You set me up with my drink and I'll tell you my incredible joke.' So away goes the barman, prepares the drink and returns with it.

'Just one point, sir, before you start this joke, I think perhaps I ought to mention. I happen to be a Queenslander. And if you notice that gentleman at the end of the bar who is bigger than I am – I happen to know that he also is a Queenslander. And if you glance over to the far corner there and notice the gentleman in the blue shirt who is bigger than both of us put together – he also is a

Queenslander. I just thought you might like to know all that.'

'Oh, well, in that case,' says the chap glancing around, 'perhaps I'll just have the drink. Perhaps I'll not bother you with the joke.'

'Why not? It might be a very interesting joke.'

'Well, hell, I mean,' he says glancing around again, 'I don't want to have to explain it three times over.'

Stalin's corpse was having a very unsettling effect on Soviet citizenry, so Nikita rang President Kennedy and asked him if he'd help with his dilemma by taking Stalin's body. Kennedy said no, and suggested Krushchev ring Macmillan. But Prime Minister Macmillan also refused, as did President de Gaulle. Krushchev then called Ben-Gurion of Israel and explained his problem.

Ben-Gurion said, 'Send it to us, we'll take care of it. But remember, my country has the highest rate of resurrection in the world.'

A Russian official woke Mr Brezhnev one morning saying, 'Comrade Brezhnev, I'm sorry to wake you, but there are two very important items of news which you'll have to know about. One of them is good and one is bad. Which you do want to hear first?'

Brezhnev said, 'I'd better hear the bad news first.' The official said, 'Comrade Brezhnev, the Chinese have landed on the moon.'

Brezhnev said, 'God, that's awful, what's the good news?'

'All of them,' said the official.

Ivan was leaning on his front verandah chewing solemnly. His friend Yuri approached. 'You should be more careful, my friend. It is illegal to have imperialist, capitalist chewing gum in Mother Russia. You might get arrested for being in contact with the enemy.' Ivan looked at Yuri and said, 'It is not chewing gum. I am washing my underpants.'

A Russian decides to buy a motor car. He rings the car factory and asks for a delivery date if an order is placed now. The man at the car factory says five years, which would be a Monday in September. The car buyer asks, 'Would that be in the morning or the afternoon?'

The car salesman says, 'After five years, what does it matter morning or afternoon?'

The car buyer says, 'Because the plumber is calling in the morning.'

Two Russians, a man and a woman, met on the train taking them to work. Said the man, 'Vot are you working at?'

The woman replied, 'I work in a tractor factory. I paint tractors red. And last week my extra production earned me a medal and I was made one of the elite, a Hero Worker. However we are very proud of our achievements and if we keep our production tallies up we have been promised a tour of the salt mines.'

The man listened to all this, then exclaimed, 'Enough of this romance, down with your pants.'

President Gorbachev, at a news conference in London, was asked by a reporter, 'President Gorbachev, what effect on history do you think it would have had if, in 1963, President Krushchev had been assassinated instead of President Kennedy?'

Gorbachev thought for a moment and replied, 'I don't think Mr Onassis would have married Mrs Krushchev.'

Andy McTavish migrated to Australia and took up residence in a boarding house in Melbourne.

'Would y' like me to cut yer some lunch?' asked the landlady as he set out to work.

'Och aye, that would be verra guid.'

So the landlady made him a sandwich from a slice of cheese and put it in a neat paper bag. When he arrived home that evening he said nothing about the lunch. Eventually the landlady, consumed with curiosity, asked him if he had enjoyed the lunch.

'Och aye, it were verra guid, what there was of it.' Taking the hint, the landlady next day gave him two sandwiches. That evening the same question brought forth the same reply. And so this went on – three and then four sandwiches – and always the reply, 'Och aye, verra guid, what there was of it.' So the landlady decided on a desperate measure. She got a large loaf, cut it lengthwise, filled it with everything in the fridge – ham, cheese, salami, peanut butter, tomato, lettuce, hard-boiled eggs, olives – the lot, and wrapped it in several pages of the *Age*. That evening she asked, 'And how did y' like yer lunch today, Mr McTavish?'

'Och aye, it were verra guid, but I see you are back to one sandwich again!'

There were two Scotsmen in a pub in Glasgow comparing scars and old wounds on their respective bodies, legacies of the innumerable fights and brawls they'd been in, and for which much of working-class Glasgow is famous. Each was trying to outdo the other for former acts of bravado and daring.

'See this scar here,' said one in an accent that made Billy Connolly sound like an educated Pommie, 'I got that fra' a big bastard wi' a razor i' Gorbals one night!' He pointed to a white line that ran from below one ear to the middle of his chin.

'Och, tha's nothin',' said the other, 'take a look at this!' He turned his head to display a missing ear lobe. 'Bit off by a sailor in yon boozer doon at they docks!'

'See you and ya wee love bites,' said the former, 'I nearly lost ma nose fra' a chibbin' i' Brig-ton – see they stitches!'

And so it continued, the two so engrossed in their comparisons that they failed to notice they were being observed. Across the other side of the bar, but within earshot, was a monster of a man. Fully 2 metres tall, he had a face that looked like raw meat, hands like hams, and a chest as big as a barrel. He sat alone, his huge bulk dwarfing the table on which he leaned. He listened intently while the erstwhile warriors displayed more and more sections of their battered anatomy. Then he rose, finished his pint, and lumbered over to where they sat.

'See youse two!' he bellowed. Silence fell upon the bar.

'D'youse want ta see a *real* scar, instead o' they scratches on ya scrawny wee bodies?' The two nodded silently, almost paralysed with fear.

Slowly, the huge man unbuttoned his shirt, and then the belt of his trousers, eventually revealing an enormous purple scar that began from under his chin, ran the entire length of his torso, and terminated only centimetres above his pubes. The entire bar was transfixed, gazing unbelievingly at this ultimate trophy, this extraordinary badge of pugilistic pride. The giant completed a full 360 degrees display, ensuring that everyone got a good look.

Finally, one of our two warriors managed to break the silence. 'Jesus Christ!' he spluttered, 'where d'you get that?'

A broad smile split the face of the giant as he uttered but two words. 'Post mortem!'

Two 90-year-old Scotsmen meet in the street and Jock says to Sandy, 'What's this I hear about you being committed on a rape charge? You know that's ridiculous.'

'Och aye,' says Sandy, 'but I was too proud to plead Not Guilty!'

What is a Tasmanian man's idea of foreplay?

You awake, mum?

There was great excitement in Wynyard, Tasmania, as the local football team had won the preliminary final and, for the first time in twenty-nine years, would play in the Grand Final the following week. Discussion of the game had reached a fever pitch in the small coastal town and most of it centred on the injuries of the team's champion players, Ian and Trevor Dick, who were brothers. Ian had strained ligaments and Trevor a corked thigh. Would they be fit for the big day?

The burning question was answered on Friday morning before the game by the *Advocate*, which had the following banner headline on its sports page: WYNYARD TO PLAY WITHOUT DICKS. Not to be outdone, the other newspaper in the region, the *Examiner*, led with a similar headline on Saturday, the morning of the game. It read: WYNYARD TO PLAY WITH DICKS OUT. Needless to say the ground was jam-packed for the big game as people travelled from all over the state to see this historic clash.

How do you get a racist to laugh on a Sunday?

Tell him a racist joke on Friday.

What's the difference between a racist and a bucket of sludge?

The bucket.

Why is a racist like a drunk?

Because whatever he says ends in a slur.

Why is a racist like a dog?

They both mark out territory by spraying walls – and always with something offensive.

What's red and white and peels itself?

A white supremist trying to get a suntan.

What's the definition of 'confused'?

A white supremist watching the Olympic 100-metres men's sprint.

What do you get when you cross a white supremist with a donkey?

Someone who thinks the sun shines out of his own ass.

What do you call a bigot who does well in an IQ test?

A cheat.

Why is a bigot like the announcer at Rosehill?

Because they both start shouting the instant they see a new race.

What's the difference between a schoolyard racist and Adolf Hitler?

Opportunity.

What are the best four years of a racist's life?

Year 6.

Why is racist abuse like pooing your own pants?
Because you only do it when you're really scared.

Why do racists always hang round in gangs?
So they can form a dope ring.

Why *didn't* the racist cross the road?
Because she was afraid of seeing the other side.

Why couldn't the racist get work as a doctor?
Because every time he felt bad about himself, he'd try to put someone down.

How many racists does it take to change a light bulb?
None – because racists hate being enlightened.

Have you heard about the racist who choked on his yoghurt?
Someone told him it grew out of a foreign culture.

Why is a racist like a 'Neighbours' writer?
Because they're both involved in character assassination.

Why do racists compete with others on the basis of colour?
Because if they competed on brains, they'd lose.

Why did the racist punch-out the sophisticated immigrants?

Because if you can't join them, beat them.

Have you heard about the racist who was terrified of getting a culture shock?

That's why she only attacked people without power.

Why is a racist like a drug runner?

Because they're both terrified of foreign customs.

Did you hear about the racist who was invited to address the recycling conference?

He had a lot of experience in talking rubbish.

Two black doctors were walking along a hospital corridor in Johannesburg. One said to the other, 'You know that white fellow in Ward 5 who has cancer?'

'The one in the corner bed?'

'Yes. Have you broken the news to him he has a terminal illness?'

'Well, yes, as a matter of fact I have.'

'You bastard. I wanted to tell him.'

SOCIAL NICETIES

Scene: Collins Street, Melbourne, peak hour. A limo waits at a red light. A tramp knocks on the driver's window. Driver presses button, lowers window.

Tramp: 'Lend us a couple of dollars for a feed, mate.'

Driver removes cigar from mouth: ' "Neither a borrower nor a lender be" – William Shakespeare.'

Replaces cigar, presses button, raises window. Lights change to green, limo proceeds to next intersection, stops again at red light. Tramp runs after limo, again knocks on driver's window.

Driver presses button, lowers window.

Tramp: ' "Cunt" – D.H. Lawrence.'

A rich American family commissioned a well-known author to write a family history, but insisted he should soft-pedal on the case of one particular family skeleton. This was the late Uncle William whose life of crime ended with his death in the electric chair in the 1920s. 'Don't come straight out and say this,' the author was told, 'just skirt around it.'

So this is what he wrote, 'Uncle William occupied a chair of applied electronics in one of our leading government institutions. He was held to the post by the closest of ties and his death came as a real shock.'

Long before the Australian Government decided to let gays into the army, a couple of colonels were travelling in a first class compartment, each reading his newspaper. After a while, one put his paper down and called across to the other, 'Army?' The second put his paper down and replied, 'Yes, as a matter of fact.' They both returned to their papers.

After a while the first one put down his paper again and asked, 'Duntroon?'

'Yes, as a matter of fact,' replied the second. Back to their papers.

Some while later, the first put down his paper again and called across, 'Homo?'

'No.'

'Pity.'

During World War II the train from Liverpool to London was absolutely full and many soldiers had been standing in the corridors for hours. All this time a wealthy dowager in a first class compartment had been occupying two seats, one for herself and one for her tiny dog. A weary English officer asked her politely whether she would mind putting her dog on the floor. She replied, 'I have paid for Fifi's seat and she is going to stay there as long as she wants.'

Eventually the officer could stand it no longer. He picked up Fifi, threw her out the window and sat down. For a moment there was stunned silence. Then an American officer sitting opposite leant towards the English officer. 'You know,' he said, 'you English are a strange lot. You eat with your fork in the wrong hand; you drive on the wrong side of the road, and now you've thrown the wrong bitch out of the window!'

A wizard was strolling about the Botanic Gardens one day and noted two statues, a man statue and a woman statue, perched on each side of the path, staring at each other. 'Look at that,' he murmured to himself. 'There they have been since Federation, in sun and rain, heat and cold, droughts, floods and bushfires and never a move. I will reward them.' So he clicked his fingers and humanised the statues. 'As a reward for your patience,' he told them, 'you can have half an hour as humans.'

The man statue looked at the woman statue and said, 'Will we?'

'Yes, let's,' giggled the woman statue. So they retired behind some bushes, whence for some fifteen minutes came muffled sounds of gasps, giggles and grunts. Then they came out from behind the bushes, pink in the face, and dusting off turf and grass and ferns and lolly papers and beer can labels.

The wizard looked at his watch and said, 'You still have fifteen minutes before you're back to being statues.'

The woman statue said to the man statue, 'Again?'

'Too right,' said the man statue, 'only this time you hold the pigeon and I'll crap on it.'

The Dowager rings for her butler and asks him to:

'Please take off my dress.'

'Please take off my petticoat.'

'Please take off my bra.'

'Please take off my panties.'

All of her requests are answered by a respectful, 'Yes, Ma'am.'

Finally she says, 'And Jeeves, if I catch you wearing my clothes again, you'll be sacked.'

Lady Penelope of Sloane Street, London, is throwing a party. It is to be fancy dress and everyone is to come as an emotion. Lady Penelope has a big black butler called Jeeves whose advances to her are continually knocked back. Comes the night of the big party and a little group of close friends gather behind her at the door to welcome her guests. The doors are opened and first in the queue is dressed entirely in green. 'Let me see,' Lady Penelope says, 'you're green with envy!' The group at the door applauds elegantly.

The second guest steps up to the door dressed entirely in blue. 'Hmmm . . .' considers Lady Penelope, 'you've got the blues.' The group behind her titters and claps genteelly. Her jaw drops as the next to step up is Jeeves, stark naked. Around his waist is strapped a bowl of custard. He's got a cock on him like a sock full of sand and the end of it disappears into the bowl. She gasps, turns pale and puts her gloved hand to her mouth. There is a hush from behind.

Jeeves growls, 'I's fucken d'iscusted.'

Two Englishmen, two Scotsmen, two Welshmen and two Irishmen were stranded on a desert island. The Scotsmen started the Caledonian Club to celebrate all things Scottish – tossing the caber, bagpipes etc. The two Welshmen started an Eisteddford, the two Irishmen formed the IRA and agreed to blow up anything built by the English.

The two Englishmen went to the opposite ends of the island and would not talk to each other as they'd not been introduced.

Two old codgers took their wives along to the ladies' night at their very exclusive club. They chose the club's specialty from the menu – thick blue boiler pea soup made with lashings of ham from the bone. An hour later the inevitable happened. One of the gentlemen emitted a sound from his nether regions which would have been described in less-refined circles as a massive 'Doris Hart'.

'I say, old boy,' said his startled club mate, 'not in front of my wife.'

'Terribly sorry, old chap,' said the contrite offender. 'I wasn't aware it was her turn!'

The speaker was known for the brevity of his speech-making. It was claimed he once made the shortest speech on record. Introduced to a large and expectant audience as 'The World-wide Authority on Sexual Behaviour', he rose and said, 'Ladies and gentlemen, it gives me great pleasure.' And sat down.

An Australian, an Englishman and a Frenchman were arguing as to the meaning of *savoir faire*. The Australian said, 'I'll give you an example. A bloke comes home to find his best cobber screwing his wife in bed. He says, "G'day, Shirl! G'day, George! Never mind me, just carry on. I'll go and get a beer!" That's *savoir faire*!'

The Englishman said, 'Well, I'd almost go along with that, but I'd express it a little differently. A chap comes home, "Good evening, Shirley. Good evening, George. Never mind me, I'll just go and have a gin and tonic." That's *savoir faire*.'

The Frenchman says, 'No, no. A man comes home to find his best friend in bed making passionate love to his wife. He says, "*Ah, bonjour*. Never mind me. You just carry on while I go and get a drink." And if they *can* carry on, that's *savoir faire*!'

The Australian, the Frenchman and the Canadian were bragging about their sexual escapades with their respective wives.

'After I have zee sex wiz my wife,' said the Frenchman, 'I cover her wiz crepes suzette and eat it sensually off her silky bare skin. She becomes so excited she rises centimetres off ze bed.'

'When I screw my wife,' drawled the Canadian, 'I pour maple syrup on her and lick it off slowly. She's in so much goddam ecstasy she rises *feet* off the bed.'

'Me?' says the Aussie. 'When I've finished with my old lady I wipe my dick on the curtains and she hits the roof!'

John saw Bob in the pub. Bob had a black eye.

'What happened?' asked John.

'Well,' said Bob, 'I was in church last Sunday, and we stood up to sing a hymn. I noticed that the dress on the woman in front of me had caught up into the crack of her bum. I thought to myself, that will be uncomfortable when she sits down, and it wouldn't look good for her to be squirming on the seat in church. So I reached forward and pulled the folds of her dress out from where it was caught. She turned around and slugged me, whammo. Black eye.'

'Some people have no gratitude,' opined John.

The following week they meet again. Bob's other eye is blackened.

'Not that woman in church again?' asked John.

'Sure was,' replied Bob. 'Same deal. We stand up to sing a hymn, her dress is caught in the crack of her bum. Only this time it's the guy next to me who pulls it out.'

John asks, 'And did she think it was you and slug you for it?'

'Oh, no. You see, I knew that she didn't like her dress being pulled out of her bum, so I tried to poke it back in again. Whammo. Black eye.'

The Governor-General was visiting the State House for the Confused. In the main assembly hall the inmates were sitting about quietly but periodically one would stand up and shout out a number after which they would all fall about in paroxysms of mirth. When the G-G asked what was going on, the superintendent revealed that because they had all been there so long and had heard all their respective stories many times, they had numbered them. So all an individual had to do was shout out the number of his story and they all knew what it was about. Fascinated, the G-G said he would like to tell a story and see the reaction. The superintendent said, 'Okay, think of a number and when I introduce you, shout it out.'

Having got the attention of the audience, the superintendent introduced the G-G and announced he was going to tell a story. The G-G then shouted '69', which was greeted with a deathly silence. Embarrassed, the official party left the hall and when outside, the G-G asked why they hadn't laughed.

'They knew the story,' the superintendent consoled him, 'they just didn't like the way you told it!'

Two old blokes, obviously mates, were standing on the corner of Spring and Bourke Streets. It was a balmy day. The first bloke sniffed the air and remarked to his friend, 'You didn't fart just then, did you?'

To which his mate took considerable offence. 'Of course I did. You don't think I smell like that all the time do you?'

Two old ladies were sitting on a Sydney bus, circa 1960. 'What do you think of these new fangled tights, Glad?'

'Oh, I suppose they're all right, but the trouble is every time I fart I blow my shoes off.'

A very rich and respected Toorak lady held a tea party for her rich and influential friends, and ate more cucumber sandwiches than was good for her. During one of those deadly silences that happen in even the best of parties, a colossal breaking of wind came from the hostess's direction. Never one to be easily embarrassed, she quickly said to her butler, 'James, stop that immediately!' The butler turned slowly and replied in his most superior voice, 'Certainly madam, which way did it go?'

The Keatings go to London to see the Queen. Because of Paul's 'coming the grope' on her last tour, and because of all the fuss about the republic, relationships are pretty strained and Paul is trying to make the very best impression. Halfway down the Mall the lead horse farted so ferociously that people thought they'd heard a 21-gun salute. 'I do apologise, Mr Keating,' said HM as the smell filled the carriage. 'That's all right, Your Majesty,' replied the Australian Prime Minister, 'I thought it was the horse.'

A young man won $200,000 in the lottery. When he collected his cash he went home and sat down to count each note. On reaching $200,000, he peeled off just one note and gave it to his father. Dad looked at it and said, 'Thanks, son. I'm glad you're keeping thrifty ways like me. I've never taken drink, gambled or played about with loose women. In fact, when you were born, your mother and I were not married.'

Surprised, the son said, 'That's lovely! You know what that makes me?'

'That's right, son,' said his father, 'and what's more, you're a greedy one.'

An Arab gentleman in the doctor's surgery is having his severed left hand re-sewn to his wrist. Another doctor walks into the room and says to the patient, 'I see you won your appeal, Ahmed.'

A soldier in Queensland, training for the Vietnam war, jumped out of the grass and called out, 'Who goes there?'

An officer told him, 'You won't last five minutes in Vietnam. The idea is to stay lying down in the grass and call out "Ho Chi Minh is a bastard". Then, when the VC jumps up, you shoot him.' Some time later, in Vietnam, the officer came across the same bloke in hospital. He was in a very bad way. The officer asked him what happened.

'I did as you told me,' he said. 'Only the VC called out "and Arthur Calwell is a bastard". I jumped up to shake hands with him and we were knocked over by a tank.'

An Englishman, an Irishman and an Australian are at the beach together and see a mermaid sunning herself alluringly on the sand. They are all overcome by her charms. The Englishman marches up to her with great dignity and says, 'My dear, you are an exquisite creature and you must tell me if any man has ever kissed you.' The mermaid demurely answers, 'No, I've never been kissed.' So the Englishman bends down and plants a reverential kiss on her cheek then goes back to his colleagues, blushing with happiness.

The Irishman sidles over to the mermaid and says, 'Sure and you're the most beautiful little morrmaid I ever saw. Tell me, my beauty, has any man ever touched you gently on your perfectly formed, firm young breasts?' The mermaid lowered her gaze and admitted that she'd never been touched there. The Irishman bent down, gave her a feel and went back to the others beaming with satisfaction.

Then the Australian strode over to the mermaid. 'You ever been rooted?' he demanded.

'Actually, no,' said the mermaid.

'Well, you're rooted now, because the tide's gone out.'

A young couple rented a nice little suburban flat. They longed for a place in the bush but could not afford a mortgage. One day the husband came home very excited and called to his wife, 'Great news, I've been promoted and the rise is backdated. I also got a big bonus, so we can afford a mortgage and the deposit.'

After weeks of searching they found what they were looking for: Restored 19th century worker's cottage, on one hectare, easy reach of city by rail or road. So they arranged to inspect the property.

The cottage was beautiful, with stone walls and a newly painted tin roof. A crazy-paving path led across an immaculate lawn to the front verandah. An elderly man opened the door and invited them in. The hallway was hung with genuine horse brasses and Victorian prints. Each room was freshly painted and tastefully furnished. 'I really must compliment you on the condition of the property,' said the young man to the owner but, even as he spoke, his wife tugged his sleeve and reached up to whisper in his ear.

'My wife,' he said to the owner, 'observes that there appear to be no toilet facilities.'

'That's right,' said the owner, 'we haven't got the mains and the dirt's no good for septic. We've got a dunny down the back. Come and see.'

He led them into the back garden, past herbs in pots and neat rows of vegetables, down a brick path at the end of which stood the dunny, resplendent in a new coat of white paint and red roof, flanked by frangipanis in full bloom. The dunny was superbly made of cedar chamfer-board. Its receptacle gleamed inside and out and the seat was more cedar, smoothed and polished through years of use.

'Again,' said the young man, 'I must compliment you on the condition of this, er, facility.' Again his wife tugged and whispered.

'What's the matter this time?' asked the owner.

'My wife observes that there is no lock on the door,' the young man replied diffidently.

The owner considered this question carefully; the demonstrable lack of security appeared to imply considerations that had never previously exercised his mind. 'She's right, you know, there is no lock on the door. But I'll tell you something, mate, I don't know what people are like where you come from, but I've lived here man and boy for seventy years and I've never had a bucket of shit stolen yet.'

Bruce had been to a party held by the friend of a friend of a friend. He had had a wonderful time, and much of the evening had vanished in an amiable alcoholic haze. The next morning he discovered that he had left his wallet at the house, and although he could remember the street the house was in, he couldn't remember the house number or the name of the owner. However, he did remember one unusual feature – the house had a gold-plated toilet seat.

So he started at one end of the street, knocking at doors and asking whether this was the house with the gold-plated toilet seat. He was met with reactions ranging from hostile incredulity to helpful indifference. After he had repeated his litany for the seventy-sixth time, he was met by a stony gaze lasting a full ten seconds.

Then the man in the doorway turned and called over his shoulder, 'Hey, Harry, here's the bloke that pissed in ya tuba!'

OUT OF THE MOUTHS OF BABES

Little Johnny hadn't spoken a word in all his six years of life. Finally, one morning at breakfast he cried out, 'Mum, the toast's burnt!' His amazed and delighted mother hugged him joyfully and asked, 'Johnny, why haven't you spoken before?'

'Well,' he replied, 'everything's been all right up till now.'

Two little boys are sitting on the beach examining each other's navels. 'What are they?'

'Well, when you're born there's a piece of rope hanging out there. And they cut it off and twist the end around and tape it inside.'

'What for?'

'So you won't go psssshhhhh and go down.'

A little girl was sitting at the table drawing. Her mother said, 'What are you drawing, darling?'

The little girl said, 'I'm drawing a picture of God.'

Mother said, 'But how can you do that, dear? Nobody knows what God looks like.'

'They will when I've finished.'

'Where did I come from, Mum?' asked a six-year-old.

Mum had been dreading the question but decided against euphemism. She gave the little boy a very frank, candid description beginning with the sex act and concluding with the dramas of the delivery room. She then awaited his reaction.

'I just wondered,' said the child. 'The boy who sits in front of me came from New Zealand.'

Little Johnny was sitting in the dirt tormenting ants and spiders and things, pouring liquid on them and watching them sizzle. The parish priest, Father Murphy, walked past and enquired, 'What's in the bottle, Johnny?'

'Sulphuric acid, Father,' said the boy with savage glee.

The priest, wishing to deter the lad from these savage entertainments, said, 'You shouldn't use that. You should use this wonderful Holy Water I have here in this bottle.'

'What bloody good's that?' the lad asked querulously.

'Well,' said the priest, 'yesterday I poured some of this on a woman's stomach, and she passed a baby!'

'That's nuthin,' said Johnny. 'I poured some of this on the cat's arse and it passed a fuckin' motorbike!'

A four-year-old was in church on Sunday when the wine and wafers were passed out. His mother leaned over and told him that he was not old enough to understand and was not allowed to take part in the Communion.

Later, the collection plate came by and stopped in front of him. His mother leaned over and tried to coax the coin out of his clenched fist. He shouted, 'If I can't eat, I won't pay!'

Two little kids meet on the corner. She is a very pretty little girl, he is your average boy walking his dog. They are both quite shy of each other, but eventually start talking.

'Hello.'

'Hello.'

'What's your name?' asked the boy.

'My name's Petal,' replied the girl, betraying a very cute young girl lisp. 'What's your name?'

'My name's Troy.'

'What's your doggie called?'

'He's called Porky.'

They both stand there awkwardly for a minute, turning on their heels, hands behind their backs, looking at the ground. Then, 'Petal's a really pretty name. How come you're called Petal?'

'Well,' the little girl said, her lisp getting cuter and cuter as she talked. 'A long, long, long, time ago, before I was ever born, my Mummy and Daddy went on a picnic in the woods. It was a beautiful day – the birds were singing, the sun was shining, the butterflies were fluttering around. So Mummy and Daddy lay down in the long cool grass to talk. After a while the fairies came along and picked a petal off one of the trees and floated it down to where Mummy and Daddy were resting in the grass. "Gee that's pretty," they said, "if we ever have a pretty little girl, we'll call her Petal." And that's how come I'm called Petal.'

The little boy was all teary-eyed as he said, 'That's *beautiful*.'

'Mmmm,' Petal agreed. 'Hey, how come your dog's called Porky?'

Very matter-of-factly Troy answered, 'Because he fucks pigs.'

Bobby and Billy have progressive parents who don't believe in discipline and, as a result, the language of the children leaves a great deal to be desired. One holiday they go to stay with their grandmother, a conservative old lady who scarcely knows the meaning of some of the words she hears. After a week she's on the edge of a nervous breakdown, and seeks advice from a friend.

'If it's that bad,' he says, 'there's only one answer. Next time one of them says something you don't like, wallop him! You'll feel better, and they'll get the message.'

She's hesitant, but nothing else has worked, so she decides to try the new approach. Next morning they're all in the kitchen as usual.

'Bobby,' she asks, 'what would you like for breakfast?'

'Oh,' says Bobby, 'give me some of them fuckin' cornflakes.'

Bang! Next moment he's sitting on the floor looking at Grandma with astonishment.

'And Billy,' she says sweetly, 'what would you like for breakfast?'

Billy looks down at Bobby and up at Grandma. 'Well, I'm not exactly sure,' he says, 'but you can bet your sweet arse it won't be them fuckin' cornflakes . . .'

A small girl went out to where her father was working in the garden and said, 'Daddy, what does sex mean?' Dad scratched the side of his jaw and wondered if he'd heard right.

'What does what mean?' he asked.

'Sex,' she repeated.

'Why . . . er . . . why do you want to know what sex means?'

'Because Mummy told me to tell you lunch will be ready in a couple of them.'

Little Gregory wakes up in the middle of the night feeling alone and scared. He goes into his mother's room for comfort. He sees his mum standing naked in front of the mirror. She's rubbing her chest and groaning sensuously, 'I want a man, I want a man.' Shaking his head in bewilderment, Gregory takes off back to bed. Next night the same thing happens. Little Gregory wakes up feeling scared again and goes to mum's room for company. There she is again, standing naked in front of the mirror, rubbing her chest and groaning, 'I want a man, I want a man!' Little Gregory gives up and goes back to bed. The third night it happens again. Little Gregory wakes up, goes into his mum's room but this time there's a man in bed with his mum.

Gregory's eyes widen. He hoofs it back to his room, whips off his pyjamas, rubs his naked chest and groans, 'I want a bike, I want a bike!'

The lady running a preschool kindergarten was staging a nativity play. The scene was the Inn, and George, aged 5, was the reluctant innkeeper. He was angry because he hadn't been given the part of Joseph. There was a knock at the door.

'Who's there?' growled George.

'It's me, Joseph and Mary, and she's going to have a baby. Can we stay here tonight?'

'No,' snapped George. 'Piss off.'

A young boy came home from school and asked his mother, 'What is vice?' She stammered that his father knew more about that sort of thing.

When Dad got home she said, 'Now's the time to tell our son about the facts of life.' So he took his son into the garden and decided to go the whole hog. He told the lad about sexual intercourse and masturbation and oral sex and prostitution and ejaculation and multiple orgasms and the G-spot. The boy stood there with his mouth open. 'Gee, thanks, Dad.'

'That's all right, son, but why did you ask about vice?'

'Cos they made me Vice Captain at school!'

Mum was having the dickens of a time getting her son ready for school. 'I'm not going,' he screamed. 'The teachers all make fun of me and the kids all hate me. I'm just not going anymore.'

'I'll give you two reasons that you will go, son,' said the mother. 'First you are 49 and second you're the headmaster.'

Little Johnny came home from school to find the family's pet rooster dead in the front yard. Rigor mortis had set in and the rooster was flat on its back, with its legs in the air. When his Dad came home, Johnny said, 'Dad, our rooster's dead. And its legs are sticking up in the air. Why's that?'

His father, thinking quickly, said, 'Johnny, that's so God in his infinite wisdom can reach down from the clouds and lift the rooster straight up to heaven.'

'Gee, Dad, that's great,' said Johnny.

A few days later, when Dad came home from work, Johnny rushed out yelling, 'Dad, Dad, we almost lost Mum today!'

'What do you mean, Johnny?'

'Well, Dad, I happened to come home from school early and walked into your bedroom and there was Mum, flat on her back, legs in the air yelling "Jesus, I'm coming, I'm coming." And if it hadn't been for Uncle George holding her down, we'd have lost her for sure.'

The little boy was to start school and his mother, anxious to give him confidence, said she would take him to meet the teacher. 'Then you'll stay at school until you're 15 and might, in later life, become Prime Minister.'

The little boy started to quiver, his eyes moistened and a tear rolled down his cheek. His mother asked him, 'What's wrong?'

And he stammered, 'Mum, you won't forget to come and get me when I'm 15, will you?'

A boy applied for a job as a men's convenience attendant after his mother had seen an ad in the paper. He was interviewed by an old bloke sitting by a kerosene fire who said, 'Right oh, you can start. Fill out this form.' The boy said, 'I can't write.'

'Well,' said the old bloke, 'you don't qualify for the job.' So the boy went away. On the way home he bought some apples for 20¢ and thought he'd try to sell them for 40¢. Years passed, and he finished up with twenty fruit shops and finally became a millionaire. One day at the bank the manager asked him to sign some papers. 'Sorry,' he said, 'I can't write.' The manager said, 'You can't write? Good heavens, what would you have become if you'd been able to write?'

'A bloody toilet assistant,' replied the man.

The kindergarten teacher with a new class thought the kids should tell each other something about their families.

Said little Johnny, 'Well, Miss, my Dad has two penises!'

'Don't be silly, Johnny, that's just not possible.'

'It's true, Miss,' he persisted. 'He's got a little one he does wees out of, and he's got a really big one that he cleans Mummy's teeth with!'

A young school teacher asked her infant class to nominate some beautiful things. The answers came thick and fast.

'Kittens.'

'Moonlight.'

'A rose in the morning.'

'Young chickens.' etc.

The only other response was little Kevin who proposed, 'A 17-year-old girl who's pregnant.'

'Yes,' said the young school mam, 'a pregnant woman is beautiful at any age, but why did you suggest that?'

'Well,' said Kevin, 'my big sister is 17 and the other night when she told Dad she was pregnant he said, "that's just bloody beautiful, that is!"'

A teacher asked a Grade 4 class to spell whatever they had for breakfast. In response, one spelt B-A-C-O-N. Another spelt E-G-G-S. But Jimmy spelt B-U-G-G-E-R A-L-L. 'Miss' was mortified and ordered him to come in front of the class.

'Now, Jimmy, as your punishment you can be the first in the geography test. Where is the South Australian border?'

'At home in bed with Mum,' replied Jimmy. 'And that's why I had bugger-all for breakfast.'

A young boy asked his father if he could explain the difference between potential and reality. So his father said, 'Go and ask your mother if she would sleep with the milkman for $1 million.' The boy protested, saying he couldn't ask his mother that sort of question. But his father insisted. When the boy returned he said his mother had said yes.

His father then said, 'Now go and ask your sister if she'd sleep with the milkman for $1 million.' Again the boy protested that he couldn't ask that of his sister. And again his father insisted. Once again he told his father the answer was yes.

Then his father said, 'Now go and ask your brother if he'd sleep with the milkman for $1 million.' The boy said, 'But Dad, they're both males.' Father insisted.

So the boy went off and asked his brother the same question. He returned to say that his brother had said he, too, would sleep with the milkman for $1 million.

Father then explained to the young boy, 'Well that's potential and reality. We have the potential to make $3 million. But the reality is we live with two sluts and a poofter.'

'Tomorrow morning, *mes enfants*,' says the teacher at a Paris primary school, 'we will be having our weekly English lesson. And tomorrow the word we'll be studying is "probably".' (This she pronounces as pwobably.)

'Tonight, I want you to think of a sentence that shows you understand the meaning of this interesting English word, pwobably.'

The children copy the word she's written on the blackboard and head for home. Next day she asks Jacques to use 'pwobably' in a sentence.

'Last night my father came into my bedroom just before I was going to sleep. He was *pwobably* going to tell me a story.'

'*Très bien*, Jacques! And now *petite* Bridget?'

'Last night, my mother came into the bathroom when I was having my bath. She was *pwobably* going to dry me with the towel.'

'*Très bien*, Bridget! And now, let us hear from Henri.'

'Yesterday my sister was having a music lesson *avec le* music teacher, Monsieur Chirac. Suddenly the music stopped and I went into *la chambre*.

Monsieur Chirac had his trousers around his ankles and my sister had pulled her skirts up very high. They were *pwobably* going to shit in the piano.'

Several boys from Maribyrnong State School spend their lunchtime playing by the Maribyrnong Creek. When they arrive back late the headmaster hauls them up to his office for an explanation. The first boy explains, 'Sir, we were just throwing peanuts into the creek.'

The headmaster lectures him severely, first for being late and, more especially, for wasting good food in a world where so many are starving. He orders him to write a hundred lines: 'Waste not, want not.' The second boy offers the same excuse and receives the same censure and penalty.

Now it's the third boy's turn to be questioned. Looking a bit bedraggled, he looks up at the headmaster and says, 'Sir, I'm Peanuts.'

It's the new teacher's first morning in class and she's keen to make a good impression on the kids. So she asks a pretty little blonde girl her name. She replies, 'Apple Blossom, teacher.' Noting the teacher's surprise, she explains, 'When I was a baby an apple blossom fell on my head and so Daddy named me his Apple Blossom.'

The teacher then asks a little brunette girl her name. Not to be outdone, she says it's 'Cherry Blossom', explaining it in much the same way. As a baby, she'd been sitting beneath the cherry tree.

The teacher then turns to a poor, miserable-looking little bloke with a twisted nose, lop ears, snaggle teeth. 'And what's your name?' And the poor little bugger says, 'Wardrobe.'

After a series of sex eduction lectures, tapes and videos, the primary school teacher asked the kids to prepare a short burst on the subject and present it to the class next morning. She nominated children to speak. The first was adorable little Jenny who told the class that her cat had had kittens. 'Very good, Jenny,' said the teacher, 'and very appropriate.' And thus it went as the teacher pointed to children around the classroom. A pet budgie had just laid an egg. A cow had given birth to a calf. And all through the simple little stories, the class terror, Freddy, had been waving his hand to be picked. 'Ask me,' he'd chanted over and over. Finally the teacher acquiesced.

'It's an hour before sunset. My dad was in Vietnam when the VC attacked his position. Hundreds and hundreds of them. Dad shot about fifty with his rifle, killed another twenty with hand grenades, stabbed ten to death with his pocket knife and finally strangled the rest.'

'Freddy,' interjected the teacher, 'that's a very

interesting story. But it was supposed to be about the birds and the bees. How does your story relate?'

'It goes to show, Miss,' said Freddy, 'that you shouldn't fuck around with my dad.'

Don Chipp was driving through the Victorian countryside a couple of years ago. With the honesty of a Democrat he conceived [sic] his speedometer needle was perilously close to 120 kph. On the left hand side of the road he noticed two typical 11-year-old boys. At 11 years of age, boys seem to achieve their most unspeakable and insufferable and yet most lovable selves. They also seem to master the cheekiest of toothy grins. These two chaps were no exception. They were wearing red peaked caps and holding up a large homemade sign roughly printed in texta colour SLOW DOWN POLICE CHECK AHEAD. Instinctively Don's foot came off the accelerator and he negotiated the next bend within the speed limit. As he passed the police trap, complete with radar and other paraphernalia, Don gave a royal wave and the smuggest of smiles.

He was having some thoughts of these altruistic lads when he passed the next bend. Here on the left hand side of the road were two other 11-year-olds with a roughly printed sign NOW WASN'T THAT WORTH A BUCK.

ANIMAL CRACKERS

A bear and a rabbit were walking together down a jungle track. The bear suddenly stopped and said, 'Excuse me, old man, call of nature y'know,' and left the track. He came back a few minutes later and they both continued their walk. 'Tell me,' the bear said, 'are you rabbits bothered by shit sticking to your fur?'

'Not at all,' the rabbit replied. 'It doesn't affect us – dry pellets, you know.'

'Good,' said the bear, 'that's all right then,' and picked up the rabbit and wiped his bum with him.

A merchant banker has his apartment redecorated, following a jungle theme. As a finishing touch he buys a brilliantly coloured parrot and sets up its elaborate cage in the loungeroom. The bird is quite chatty, and screeches comments about all manner of things. One evening, when his owner brings a woman home, the parrot screams, 'Hey, you look like a good fuck!'

The banker apologises and cautions the parrot, 'Any more of that and you go into the freezer to cool off.'

The following week the banker brings home another date. 'Hey!' screeches the parrot. 'Great tits!'

The banker grabs the parrot and stuffs him into the freezer, saying, 'A few minutes in there should give you something to think about.'

When he opens the freezer door five minutes later the parrot looks suitably subdued, and with beak chattering, squawks, 'What the hell did that chook in there say?'

What do you do if a bird shits on your windscreen?

You don't take her out again.

A magician is hired to entertain passengers on a long ship voyage. The first night out, he starts his show in the lounge in front of an enthusiastic (if captive) audience. He has just produced a pack of cards out of nowhere, and is about to take his bow, when the ship's parrot, in a cage but also in the lounge, squawks, 'I saw what you did! You pulled those from up your sleeve!' Laughter and derision from the audience.

The next night, the magician was opening with another trick, hiding a coin and making it reappear. As he prepared to take his bow, the parrot squawked again, 'I saw that! You hid that in your shoe!' More laughter and derision from the audience. The magician had had enough. He went to the captain and said something had to be done. 'Very well,' was the reply, 'we'll cover the bird up with a blanket.'

Well satisfied, the magician appeared again on the third night. Just as he was about to launch into one of his disappearing tricks, the ship hit a reef and sank. The magician managed to survive by clinging to a piece of wood, and after a couple of days of floating on his improvised raft, what should float by but the cage, enveloped in the blanket. The magician pulled the cage onto the raft, and whipped off the blanket. The parrot sat in the cage, blinked several times in the light and turned his head slowly from one side to the other, looking round in a puzzled manner. 'All right,' said the parrot, 'I give up – where'd you hide the ship?'

While on a visit to a shopping centre, an elderly bush spinster bought a pair of talking parrots from a pet shop. On her return home she rang back and asked how she could distinguish the male bird from the female.

'Simple,' replied the dealer, 'wait until they're mating and fasten something around the male's neck so he'll be easy to spot.'

The lady bided her time, and in due course tied a strip of white ribbon around the male bird's neck.

A few days later the parson came to visit. The cock bird took one look at him and croaked, 'Ha ha! So the old girl caught you at it too, eh?'

A bloke goes into a pet shop, looking for something suitable for his wife. He spots a very attractive rosella. 'I'll take the parrot.'

'A present?' asks the pet shop owner.

'Yes, for the missus.'

'Well, this is a very intelligent parrot, it's a very talented parrot. You'll be able to teach it to say all sorts of things, but there is a problem.'

'What's that?'

'It's got no feet.'

'Well, how does it sit on the perch?' asks the bloke.

'If you look closely, sir, you'll see that it's grasping the perch with its pecker.'

'I didn't know parrots had peckers.'

'Well, this parrot has a pecker. Look, see how it uses it to balance itself,' says the pet shop owner.

The bloke takes the parrot home and his wife is thrilled to bits. And not only does it learn to talk, it learns to keep an eye on things. So one night when the bloke gets home the parrot tells him that his wife has had a visitor.

'What happened?'

'Well, this chap came in and started kissing your wife.'

'Then what happened?'

'Then he started to undress her.'

'And then what happened?' asked the bloke.

'I don't know,' says the parrot, 'that's when I fell off my perch.'

Squatter Fraser was exhibiting his prize bull at the annual Western District Agricultural Show as he did every year. Two hours before the judging, he noticed the bull's eyes were crossed and knew that this would rule out any chance of a prize. He hurriedly called in the vet, who took one look at the beast and fished a plastic tube out of his black bag. The vet shoved one end of the tube into the bull's bum and blew vigorously through the other end. Instantly, the animal's eyes uncrossed and Squatter Fraser walked off with the blue ribbon.

At the following year's show, the same thing happened. Hoping to save a few bob, Fraser hunted around and found a piece of plastic tubing, knelt down and repeated the vet's routine. But the bull's eyes stayed firmly crossed. In desperation he called in the vet who quickly appraised himself of the situation, pulled the tube out of the bull's rectum, reversed it, pushed it in again and blew.

Hey-presto, the bull looked at the vet straight in the eye, but Squatter Fraser was puzzled. 'Tell me,' he asked the vet, 'why did you turn the tube around?'

The vet regarded him with astonishment. 'You surely didn't think I'd be crazy enough to blow into the same end of the tube as an arsehole like you!'

Four young bulls were boasting of their plans for the future.

'I'm going to Rome to become a Papal bull,' said one.

'I'm going to become a stock market bull,' said another.

'I want to be a bull in a china shop,' said the third.

'Well, I'm not going anywhere,' said the fourth. 'I shall stay here for heifer and heifer and heifer.'

Bruce and Simon were checking out the junk shops in the hope of finding something of value for their antique stall at the Paddo Market. In the doorway of a particularly grotty shop, Bruce noticed a cat lapping milk out of a really great Royal Doulton saucer. He nudged Simon and gave him a knowing wink. Then, acting very casual, Bruce said to the old codger running the shop, 'That's a very nice cat. Like to sell him?'

'Well,' said the old codger, 'I might be willing to let you have him for, say, ten bucks.'

Simon picked up the cat and said, 'We might as well take the saucer as well, seeing that he's used to drinking from it.'

'No way,' said the codger.

'Well, could we buy it from you?'

'No way.'

'But why?'

'Because thanks to that saucer I've already flogged eighty-seven cats.'

How do you make a cat go 'woof'?

Soak it in petrol and throw a match on it.

A young man lived in a garden flat in Paddington with a dog and three cats. He named the dog and two of the cats George. The third cat had no name.

'Why such an odd arrangement?' asked his next-door-neighbour.

'Well,' replied the young man, 'when I return home from work in the evening, I go to the back door and call "George, George, George", and they all come in.'

'But what about the third cat?' queried the neighbour.

'Oh,' said the young man, 'he never goes out.'

In response to sounds of unusual activity in next door's backyard, a neighbour looked over the fence. A great deal of shovelling was taking place. A very large hole was being excavated.

'What are you doing?'

'I'm burying my dead cat.'

'Oh, what a pity. But Tiddles was only a little cat. Why the big hole?'

'Because,' solemnly explained the neighbour, 'he's inside your bloody great Alsatian!'

What is the difference between a coyote and a flea?

The coyote howls about the prairie.

The boys were on a trip to Kakadu and decided to go fishing. On the way to the moorings, they saw a great pair of shoes in a tourist shop window. 'Look at the price,' said Davo, 'five hundred bucks.'

'They're crocodile shoes,' said Wocka, 'I know where we can get plenty of those.'

They headed upriver and Wocka dropped the boys off by a deep pool where they could catch some fish. He headed upstream in the boat. When he hadn't returned in a couple of hours, they went looking for him. And they kept finding crocodiles floating belly up in the water, but no sign of Wocka. Finally, round the next bend, they spotted him, wrestling a huge crocodile in a rock pool.

'What the bloody hell are you up to?' they yelled.

'Well,' said Wocka, 'if this bastard isn't wearing shoes, I'll give up.'

A meeting was arranged by the Western Australian Department of Agriculture aimed at trying to come up with a solution to the dingo problem in WA. The meeting was also attended by representatives from CSIRO, pastoralists and environmentalists with the intention of coming up with a mutually acceptable solution. The pastoralists wanted to kill the dingos while the greenies wanted a 'biological' solution, such as castration of the dingos, as a strategy of population control. At this point one of the pastoralists lost his temper and blurted out, 'Listen, lady, the dingos are eating the sheep, not fucking them!'

How do you make a dog 'meow'?

Pass it quickly over a circular saw.

A man went to the movies to see a re-run of *Gone With the Wind* and was very surprised to see a large dog sitting next to a woman in the row in front of him. What was even more surprising was that the dog seemed to be following the story, sitting with ears pricked, wagging its tail at the happy parts, and sitting downcast with bowed head during the distressing or emotionally intense parts of the story.

At the conclusion of the movie the man could contain his curiosity no longer and, as the audience was filing out of the cinema, walked over to the lady.

'Excuse me, madam. I couldn't help noticing your dog in the movie. He seemed to understand the story and really enjoyed it. It was amazing!'

'Yes,' replied the woman enthusiastically, if a trifled puzzled. 'I was amazed, too. He hated the book!'

I saw a dog sitting with three of my friends playing poker.

'Isn't it amazing,' I said, 'a dog playing poker.'

One of my mates looked up and said, 'Aw, I dunno, every time he gets a good hand he wags his tail.'

A duck walks into a chemist. 'Give us a jar of Vaseline,' it quacks.

'That'll be five dollars,' says the chemist, without batting an eye.

'Put it on my bill, please.'

'Certainly sir. Anything else?'

'Yeah, give me a packet of condoms, too.'

'Yes sir. Shall I put them on your bill?'

'No thanks. I'm not that kind of duck.'

What's grey and comes in pints?

An elephant.

An elephant and a mouse were walking through the jungle when all of a sudden the elephant fell into a hole. It was very deep and steep-sided and the elephant couldn't pull himself out. So the mouse said he'd hail the first car that came along. After a while a shining new Porsche came roaring through the jungle. The mouse hailed it, they got a rope, dropped it down the hole and the Porsche towed the elephant out. The elephant thanked the Porsche driver who went on his way.

Shortly thereafter the mouse fell into a hole and he couldn't climb out. So the elephant dropped his dick down the hole and the mouse climbed up it, and they continued on down the road.

The moral of the story is: if you've got a big enough dick, you don't need a Porsche.

A bloke blundered into a pub in tow with an emu and a cat. He ordered a beer, a vodka and a rum and the three sat at a table. Shortly after, the emu went to the bar and re-ordered, then returned to the table. This happened several times. The barman scratched his head, wondering why the cat didn't buy a shout. So, the next time the bloke fronts up the barman asks, 'Hey, why isn't the cat buying?'

The man sort of smirks, saying, 'It's a long yarn. Y'see, I found this vase, rubbed it and a genie pops out. The genie says "Okay, you got me out. So what do you want?" Well, like any normal bloke, I asked for a bird with long legs and a tight pussy.'

A man driving in the outback sees a farmer staggering from tree to tree carrying a huge emu. The emu is eating acorns from the trees. He stops the car and says, 'Why don't you put the emu down and shake the tree? Then the acorns will fall down and that would save a lot of time.'

The man says, 'What's time to an emu?'

What is the difference between a mountain goat and a goldfish?

The goldfish mucks about the fountain.

A fish goes into the bar. The barman says, 'What do you want?'

The fish croaks, 'Water!'

Two beautiful girls were walking down St George's Terrace when they heard a cry for help. They had some trouble working out where it was coming from, but eventually found a green frog sitting on a window ledge. The frog was in a pretty emotional state and explained that it had been a Perth entrepreneur. He had fallen under the spell of the NSCS and been turned into a green frog. Only one thing could save him. To be kissed by a beautiful girl. They seemed rather doubtful about his approach but he assured them that he was, truly, a Perth entrepreneur, and he promised them anything and indeed everything if one of them would only kiss him and restore him to his previous condition. The girls looked at him for a while. Suddenly one of them opened her handbag, picked up the frog, dropped him inside and snapped it shut. 'Good heavens,' said her friend, 'what are you doing?'

'Well,' said the girl with the handbag, 'I'm no fool. I know that a talking frog is worth a lot more than a Perth entrepreneur.'

The wide-mouthed frog sets out on his travels around Australia. First he meets a kangaroo.

'Hullo,' says the wide-mouthed frog (mouth stretched wide by hooking a forefinger in each corner). 'Who are you?'

'I'm a kangaroo.'

'What do you do?'

'I sleep under a bush all day and hop around the countryside at night, having a wonderful time.'

'That's very nice,' says the wide-mouthed frog and goes on his way. Next he meets a wombat.

'Hullo, who are you?'

'I'm a wombat.'

'What do you do?'

'I sleep in my burrow all day and come out at night to forage around for a good feed.'

'Pleased to meet you,' says the wide-mouthed

frog as he continues his journey. Then he meets a snake.

'Hullo, who are you?'

'I'm a snake.'

'And what do you do?'

'I eat wide-mouthed frogs.'

Wide-mouthed frog, hastily becoming a narrow-mouthed frog (by pushing lips together vertically with forefingers), 'Bet you don't see many of them around.'

Why do you wrap guinea pigs in masking tape?

So they don't burst when you fuck them.

The Director of Taronga Park Zoo called in his deputy.

'Look,' he said, 'we've got a major problem. The gorilla's on heat and we've only got a couple of weeks to mate her. Contact all the leading zoos and see if they can lend us an active male. Tell them we'll cover all the expenses.'

After a couple of days spent telephoning and faxing zoos all over the world, the deputy director reported. 'No luck,' he said. 'All the males are too young to breed or past it.'

'Bugger it,' exclaimed the Director, 'I thought we

were going to be the first zoo successfully to breed a gorilla in captivity.'

'I've got an idea,' said the deputy director. 'You know old Charlie the Pom, the cleaner?'

'What, that dirty, hairy old bastard who cleans out the cages?' 'That's him. He's a simian, if ever I saw one. How about we offer him a couple of thousand dollars?'

'Well,' said the Director, 'it's worth a try.'

So they called in Charlie and explained the problem.

'I dunno,' said Charlie, 'I reckon it would cost a lot more than that to bring a gorilla over here.'

'Oh, all right,' said the Director, 'how about five thousand?'

'Okay,' said Charlie, 'but there are three conditions.'

The Director sighed. 'Righto, what conditions?'

'Number 1, she's got to be chained down, otherwise she might get stroppy and attack me. Number 2, she's got to have a bag over her head, 'cos she's an ugly cow.' Charlie paused.

'All right,' said the Director, getting exasperated, 'what's the third condition?'

'Any children of the union must be brought up Protestant.'

An Australian diplomat living in West Africa was disturbed by a hell of a racket on his roof. He went outside and looked up to see a gorilla ripping off tiles and hurling them down into the garden. He rang the local police station. 'Sorry, sir,' said the sergeant, 'I'm afraid we can't help you. I suggest you look in the yellow pages and under "G" you'll see Gorilla Catchers. Just ring one of those.' The chap did as suggested and the gorilla catcher said, 'Sir, I'll be there in fifteen minutes.'

Sure enough, fifteen minutes later around the corner came a small van. When it pulled up a fellow stepped out built like Tarzan, wearing only a small piece of leopard skin around his hips. In one hand he carried a revolver. Then out of the van jumped a small corgi.

'Good lord,' said the diplomat. 'I would have expected a German shepherd or a bull terrier, but not a corgi.'

The gorilla catcher said, 'Just hold this gun will you?' Then he opened the back of the van and the fellow saw that it was made into a cage with heavy bars. The gorilla catcher opened the barred door and turned to the diplomat. 'Now look here, I'll tell you how it goes. I will climb up onto the roof and wrestle with the gorilla. When I see the opportunity I'll throw him off the roof. As soon as he hits the ground the corgi will race in and bite him in the groin. The gorilla will give a scream and leap up and jump into the cage. Then he'll slam the door shut between himself and the dog. All we have to do is walk up and slip the lock.'

The diplomat was most impressed. 'That's incredible,' he said. 'It's so cleverly worked out. Does it always go like that?'

'Always,' said the gorilla catcher.

'Well, what have I got this gun for?' asked the diplomat.

'Well,' said the gorilla catcher, 'it's always worked out like this in the past. However, just in case, if instead of me throwing down the gorilla, he should throw me down, YOU IMMEDIATELY SHOOT THE CORGI.'

A bloke goes to the CES to get a job. The only one that's available is at Taronga Zoo. On arrival he's told the gorilla has just died but, luckily, they've managed to preserve its skin. His job is to wear it, to pretend to be a gorilla until another can be shipped from Africa.

The days went by and he settled into the new job, coming to thoroughly enjoy his carefree existence, munching bananas and swinging from branch to branch, watched by enthralled spectators. However, he became too enthusiastic and, swinging too far, landed in the lions' cage. As he pulled himself to his feet one of the lions growled fiercely and he ran to the bars screaming for help. Whereupon he heard one of the lions snarling, 'If that dopey bastard doesn't shut up, we'll all lose our jobs.'

An American with a very sick horse went to his Australian neighbour's place and ask him what he gave his horse when it got sick. The neighbour said turpentine. So off went the American. He came back several days later and said, 'My horse died.'

'That's funny,' said the Aussie neighbour, 'so did mine.'

An old horse was employed by the Maitland Cricket Club. Every day a match was scheduled, the horse had to pull a dirty great roller so as to prepare the wicket. Naturally the horse got very bored and so began demanding that he be selected for the Maitland team. Needless to say the captain and the selectors refused. So the horse said, 'No game, no roll. ' Finally the selectors had no choice but to relent.

The local team won the toss and went in to bat. After losing three quick wickets the captain sent in the horse. He struck form at once, began hitting fours and sixes to all points of the compass, taking the Maitland team to a very good score. The visitors didn't fare well, owing to the fact that the horse ran around and caught out most of their best batsmen and even managed to run out a couple of them. In fact, their score was so low that they were obliged to follow on.

Well, Maitland's captain was so delighted with the horse that he asked it to open the bowling in the second innings. The horse only laughed and said, 'Wake up to yourself, horses can't bowl.'

What is the difference between a cavalry horse and a draught horse?

The cavalry horse darts into the fray.

A weary penguin, bleary-eyed after a hard day's fishing in the Ross Sea, hauls his exhausted little body up onto the penguin rookery where he sits looking around him in a somewhat bewildered fashion. After a while he says to the nearest penguin, 'G'day mate, I'm a bit snookered and not sure exactly where I am. Have you seen my wife?'

After a pause the other penguin replies, 'Dunno – what does she look like?'

A stranger walks into the Phillip Island pub and orders a scotch. 'You look a bit upset,' says the barman. 'What's wrong?'

The stranger says, 'I reckon I just ran over a couple of penguins.'

'No way,' says the barman. 'Not at this time of the year.'

'Then you better make that a double scotch,' says the stranger, 'it must have been a couple of nuns.'

An English tourist finds a bedraggled penguin on the beach at Bondi and asks a nearby cop what to do with it. 'I'd take it to the Taronga Park Zoo, mate.' Off goes the tourist.

Next day, to the policeman's astonishment, there's the Pom and the penguin waddling along Bondi Beach together. 'Hey, you,' says the cop, 'I thought I told you to take the penguin to the zoo.'

'I did,' said the tourist, 'and he enjoyed it so much that I'm taking him to the pictures today.'

A young man gets a job assisting the keepers at Taronga Park Zoo.

He is put in charge of the porpoises and given special instructions about their diet; the porpoises are very partial to seagull chicks, which must be collected surreptitiously from the harbour foreshores and fed to the porpoises very early in the morning, before the zoo is open, to avoid trouble with the RSPCA and animal rights activists.

One morning, as the young man is returning to the zoo with his bag of chicks he sees that one of the lions has got out of the lion pit and is sprawled across the entrance to the zoo, snoozing in the sun.

The young man prods the lion, trying to wake him, but when the animal doesn't budge, he decides to feed the porpoises first, and steps over the lion. Just then a siren sounds, a police car screeches to a halt and an officer leaps out to arrest the young man. On what charge? Transporting underage gulls over a prostrate lion for immoral porpoises.

Two lions escaped from Taronga Park Zoo. They went in different directions. One was caught a few hours later and returned to its cage, but it was six months before the other one was captured.

'How come you were able to remain free for so long?' asked the first lion.

'It was no problem. I simply made my way over the Harbour Bridge after dark, then I holed up in an empty room I found on the top floor of some government offices. The place was packed with advisors and advisors to the advisors. Every time I got hungry I just nipped out and ate one and slipped back to my room again. I could have stayed there for years.'

'How come they finally realised that something was going on?' asked the first lion.

'Oh, I made a terrible mistake. One day I ate the tea lady!'

Bullen's lion tamer was performing his new act, one that had never been seen before by the public. The crowd were wildly appreciative, clapping noisily at almost every move he made. Well satisfied and egged on by the crowd response, he approached his finale for the evening. He made the largest of his lions sit in front of him. When he hit it on the head with the handle of his whip, the powerful animal opened its huge jaws. The lion tamer immediately opened his fly and extruded his genitalia, which he promptly put into the lion's mouth. He then hit the lion on the head again with his whip handle and the animal very gently locked its jaws on its master's genitals. The lion tamer flourished his whip and the crowd burst into rapturous applause. He then hit the lion on the head again, the lion opened its jaws and he packed away his genitalia.

Again with a flourish, he quietened the crowd and asked, 'Is there anyone in the crowd who is game enough to try this?' There was a short silence as most of the men in the audience looked embarrassed, but eventually a little old lady put up her hand and nervously said, 'Can I try?'

The lion tamer was rather taken aback and stumbled over his reply, 'Well, um, that's very brave, but you, um, haven't got the required, um . . .' The little old lady defended herself, 'Don't tell me that I can't do it, young man! I am sure I can! But don't you dare hit *me* on the head!'

The circus advertised for a new lion tamer and had two applicants – a young woman, and an old man. The circus manager decided to test their skills with the lion so he first asked the young woman to show him what she could do. She entered the cage, removed all her clothes and the lion walked up and nuzzled her bare legs. The astonished circus owner then said to the old man, 'Can you do that?'

'You're damned right I can,' said the old man, 'just get that lion out of there first.'

What's the difference between the Prince of Wales, a bald man and a monkey's mother?

The Prince of Wales is heir apparent, a bald man has no hair apparent and a monkey's mother is a hairy parent.

A woman wanted to purchase a woollen jumper. As she walked through the mall she saw an attractive jumper in the window of a boutique. She asked the price of the garment and decided it was far too expensive. So she walked on and saw exactly the same garment in another shop for half the price. Having purchased it, she returned to the boutique to complain. The sales woman's response was haughty. 'But Madam, our garment is made from virgin wool.'

'I don't give a damn what the sheep do at night,' said the woman, 'I just want a reasonably priced jumper.'

What does a dingo call a baby in a pram?
Meals on wheels.

Did you hear about the Irish dingo?
It ate the azaleas.

Did you hear about the Italian dingo?
It ate the pastor.

A SPORTING CHANCE

A husband and wife are doing the dishes. She's washing, he's wiping. She hands him a saucer which slips from his fingers and smashes on the floor. Her reaction seems out of all proportion to the incident. 'Tell me, you bastard, where you've been going every Tuesday and Wednesday night? And where do you go on Saturdays when you head out of the door without a word and aren't home for hours?'

The husband looks somewhat embarrassed but brushes off his mysterious absences by saying, 'They're not important. It doesn't matter.'

'I demand an explanation,' she says.

After a few moments' embarrassment, the husband says, 'It's really nothing. I just go to brothels and have sex with prostitutes for money. That's all. Then I come home.'

'You're a liar!' screams the wife. 'You're secretly playing with the Sydney Swans. You go off to practise during the week and you play with the Swans on Saturdays.'

'No! No!' the husband protests his innocence.

'I'm not doing that, I promise you. I'm just going off to fuck hookers.'

'You promise? Cross your heart that's all your doing? That you're not really going off and training and playing with the Swans?'

'Darling, I promise you. Faithfully. All I'm doing is spending hundreds and hundreds of dollars on professional sex.'

She throws herself into his arms, sobbing with relief against his chest. 'Darling, darling, forgive me for being suspicious. I'm sorry that I didn't trust you.' He makes soothing noises and they resume doing the dishes. She hands him another saucer which, once again, he fumbles. It sails up in the air, he grabs at it without success and, once again there's a breakage.

'YOU BASTARD,' she screams. 'YOU ARE PLAYING WITH THE SYDNEY SWANS!'

(The Swans were the first VFL team to move interstate. After initial successes, their downward slide has been spectacular. This joke hints at the magnitude of their humiliation.)

What has thirty-six legs and can't climb a ladder?

The Swans.

During the Queen's first visit to Australia, she was taken to a game of Aussie Rules. At half-time, when introduced to the players, she asked a country boy how he developed his skills.

'Started kickin' mallee roots around. Could hoove the bastards 50 metres across the back paddock.'

The President of the VFL said to the player, 'Now, that's a bit strong.'

To which the player replied, 'Ah, well, 40 bloody metres then.'

Two old mates were barramundi fishing up in the Gulf in the summer. Unfortunately one dropped dead so his mate loaded him in the four-wheel drive and drove to Brisbane, which took him two and a half days. He called at a police station to notify the death and the Sergeant said, 'He must be very smelly by now.'

The mate said, 'He's not too bad – I gutted him.'

Four mates were playing golf. One of them was bending over a putt, concentrating like mad, when a funeral procession passed by on a nearby road. He straightened up, removed his hat, held it over his breast and remained at silent attention until the cortège had passed. His three mates were amazed. They'd never known him to be a man of particular sensitivity and praised him for his respect for the dead. 'It's the least I could do,' he said modestly, 'we would have been married twenty-eight years tomorrow.'

As the golfer trudged towards the 19th hole at the Royal Melbourne, he muttered, 'That was my worst game ever.' To which the caddy replied, 'You mean you've played before?'

A distinguished Australian barrister had always dreamed of playing the St Andrew's course in Scotland. Finally, he received an invitation from a British barrister who was a member and headed immediately for Mascot. Sadly, on arriving in Scotland, he found his friend had died. He was admitted to the clubhouse and told to see a gentleman in the corner, who was reading *The Times*.

'I beg your pardon, your lordship, but my name is Fleetwood-Jones. I'm from a leading law firm in Sydney, Australia, and have always yearned to play a round here, but unfortunately my friend, who was a member here, has just died, and so . . .'

His Lordship lowered *The Times* and asked 'Church?'

'Anglican, sir.'

'Education?' his Lordship continued.

'Cranbrook, sir, and then Oxford.'

'Athletics?'

'Rugby, sir, played for the Wallabies in 62. And rowed number 4 in the crew that beat Cambridge.'

'Military?'

As a matter of fact, got the VC.'

His Lordship considered briefly, then nodded to the Club Secretary and said, 'Nine holes.'

A husband and wife were playing golf together when, unfortunately, the husband smashed a ball straight into her face. Panic-stricken he ran to the club house for a doctor.

'Doctor, come quickly . . . my wife's been hit by a golf ball.'

'Where was she hit?' asked the Doc.

'Between the first and second holes,' gasped the man.

'Oh dear,' replied the doctor, 'that won't leave much room for bandages.'

A big bloke strides up to the bar of a golf clubhouse and orders a beer. As the barman starts pouring the beer the bloke notices a friend, drinking alone at the other end of the bar. He takes his beer up to that end of the bar, taps his friend on the shoulder and asks how he has been. The friend replies in a very hoarse croak, 'Up until today I've been fine.'

The big fellow, surprised at his friend's difficulty in speaking, asks, 'What happened to your voice? It sounds terrible.'

The friend replied, barely audible, 'I'll tell you. I teed off on the sixteenth and sliced the ball badly over the boundary fence and into the trees. So I swore, picked up the tee, grabbed the buggy and went to look for my ball. Just as I was about to walk into the trees, and not knowing how long it would take me to find the ball, I turned around and waved the following group through. I looked for the bloody ball but couldn't see it anywhere. In fact, I was so intent on looking for the ball that a passing cow made me jump with fright. Unbelievable as it may seem, as the cow turned away, I noticed what looked like a ball stuck under its tail. I walked slowly up to the cow, lifted its tail and, sure enough, there was a golf ball. But it wasn't mine! Mine was a white one and this was orange.

'While I still had hold of the cow's tail, I noticed a woman from the following group come into the trees, obviously looking for her ball. I called over to her and she came my way. As she got closer, I lifted up the cow's tail and said, "Does that look like yours" and she wrapped a nine iron around my neck.'

An Irish golfer wasn't very good at the game, which he found pretty frustrating. Then, one day, a leprechaun appeared and said, 'I'll help you become a greater golfer, but every time you do, you'll have to give up part of your sex life.' The golfer agreed.

'Firstly, it's time you sank a ball in par,' said the leprechaun, 'and the cost is one week of celibacy.' So off the golfer drove and with four shots he had his ball in the hole.

They met again in a month's time and the wee feller said he'd decided it was time for the golfer to achieve a birdie. 'But the penalty would be eight weeks of celibacy.' He teed up with considerable enthusiasm and, three shots later, the ball was in the hole.

It was some months later until they met again. The leprechaun said, 'Today, a hole in one. But you'll have to give up screwing for a year.'

'A hole in one is every golfer's dream,' said the golfer. He drove off and straight into the hole went the ball.

'I'll have to leave you now,' said the leprechaun, 'but for the record, what's your name?'

'Father O'Flaherty,' was the reply.

There were two men golfers being held up by two women who wouldn't wave them through. Finally one of the blokes said he'd go up and ask to be let through. But he came back looking very worried. 'What's the matter?' asked his friend.

'Well, it's very awkward. You see, one is my wife and the other is my mistress.'

'I've never met your wife – I'll go up,' said the other.

Shortly thereafter he came back and said, 'It's a small world.'

An elderly member breezed into his golf club late one afternoon when there were still a number of golfers in the lounge. He slapped a $50 note down on the bar and said, 'Drinks all round, barman, if you please.'

The golfers accepted readily, so the old gent pushed the change across the bar and said, 'Let's have another round, barman.' Whilst the party was consuming the second round, the barman came back and said, 'Tell me, sir. You don't often come into the club these days, yet here you are, shouting for the bar. What's the celebration?'

'Well,' replied the old member, 'as you know, I'm a retired army major of 69, and tomorrow I'm being married to a delightful young lass of 19 – daughter of an old army colleague of mine. So I have reason to celebrate. Let's have another round.' So they did, and eventually the major staggered off home.

Some time later, the major reappeared at the club, produced a $100 note and repeated the performance. After the second round, the same barman said to him, 'Major, I remember last time you came in and shouted because you were being married the next day. So what's the celebration for this time?'

'Well, my boy, this morning my wife gave birth to a fine bouncing baby boy. So again I'm celebrating. Another round, please.'

Whilst this round was being served, an experienced golfer, with a good memory for scores, came over and said, 'Major, I overheard your conversation, and I was here last time you were celebrating your impending marriage. Wasn't that only seven months ago?'

'Yes,' said the major, 'and that's what I'm so bloody delighted about – two under par, on a strange course, with concealed holes, using two old balls and an old club with a whippy shaft.'

A young woman decided to take up golf, but had never had a golf club in her hand. So she joined a club and was advised to have some lessons. The pro took her to the practice nets to show her how to stand in relation to the ball and how to swing the club. Unfortunately she had no idea of an acceptable swing, so the pro stood behind her, reaching around to place his hands over hers on the shaft of the club. He then showed her how to commence the backswing, then released his grip and went to step back so she could try again on her own. But he found he was unable to move because the zipper on his fly had caught in the zipper of the young woman's skirt. The more he struggled to separate the zippers the more tightly they became meshed. So with great embarrassment he decided the only thing to do was to return to the pro shop where he would be able to disengage the zippers with the aid of a pair of plyers.

Off they frogmarched back towards the pro shop in view of a number of onlookers who viewed their progress with mixed feelings – wonder, surprise, embarrassment, mirth. As they rounded the corner of the clubhouse, a big Alsatian dog rushed out and threw a bucket of water over them!

An Australian, keen to have a holiday abroad and wishing to improve his golf handicap, takes a holiday in Japan where the excellence of the golf courses is well known, if expensive. He is soon on the first tee of the superbly groomed fairways of the Osaka Resort. This resort specialises in tuition for the average golfer and has introduced a system where the golfer is assigned a little silver robot which accompanies the player around all eighteen holes of the course. The robot is programmed to do everything from dragging the golf buggy around the course to advising on club selection; how to play the shot, correcting errors in the player's swing, scoring and, of course, looking after the player's comfort needs.

After a few basic instructions from the pro, and a substantial hiring fee, the Australian tees off at the first, after taking on board the robot's concern at the bunkers some 192 yards from the yellow tee markers on the left side of the fairway. He smacks his second onto the green (it's a par four and he's on the green for two – rarely happened before) after the robot draws his attention to a basic and easily corrected fault in his grip.

After some further constructive advice as to his stance, a few tasteful but nevertheless funny jokes from the robot and a can of his favourite Aussie beer, our player was feeling pretty good. His score card was steadily improving and halfway through the round he was actually sinking some of the birdie putts which had been bogie putts in previous rounds. He was also beginning to enjoy the ooohs and aaahs and the applause which seemed to him to come from an invisible gallery which was following his every shot, but which in reality was supplied by courtesy of the little silver robot. It was his own British Open, and he had triumphed. By the time he had finished he was three under the card! This from an 18 handicapper.

As he returned to the pro shop he was actually toying with the idea that perhaps a life in golf was not just a dream. A bit more practice on the tips from the robot and who knows? He tipped the pro and (although he still felt a bit silly doing it) bade a fond farewell and thanks to the little silver robot. The robot passed a typically courteous remark and looked forward to 'tearing the course apart' next time with the Aussie.

Well, it was so overwhelming and he played so well, the Aussie booked immediately for holidays next year and even advanced the deposit right there and then. He only asked that he be assigned to the same little silver robot next trip. Not a problem, said the pro, happy to be of service.

It was a difficult year at work, which made the time go slowly, however he was out on his home course at every opportunity and, although playing better than in previous years, he never quite captured his Japanese form of a year ago. It was time to once again take his leave, so off to the Osaka Resort he went. After check-in he was on the doorstep of the pro shop, somewhat alarmed that there were no little silver robots to be seen. So he asked the pro about his robot and was appalled at what he heard.

The pro recounted the whole tragic story thus. Although the little silver robots had proved to be a great success in everything they were supposed to do, on sunny days the glare from their silver panels was off-putting to other golfers and sometimes caused players to hit poor shots. So something had to be done. The Committee met and decided to come up with the ingenious idea of painting the robots black, matt black in fact. 'That must have solved the problem,' said the incredulous Aussie. Matt black paint, no reflection from the sun. What was the problem?

'Problem was,' replied the pro, 'one night the bloody black little robots broke into the clubhouse, got drunk, stole the poker machine takings and did not come back to work next day!'

What do you call a lady who can suck a golf ball up a garden hose?

Darling.

The Englishman, the Scotsman and the Australian were trying to get into the Barcelona Olympic Games without paying. The Englishman got a long stick and sharpened the end to a point. He went to the gate and said, 'David Mitchell, England, javelin.' And was allowed to enter.

The Scot got a tennis ball, rubbed off the fluff and went up to the gate. 'Sandy McGregor, Scotland,' he said, 'shot putt!' He too was allowed to enter.

The Australian found a scrap of barbwire left behind by the building contractors and said, 'Bluey Morgan, Australia, fencing.'

Chap with an impediment in his speech rushed up to a bookmaker after the fifth race and said, 'I bbbbacked a fffive-ttt . . .' 'Look,' said the bookie, 'there was no 5 to 1 winner, so buzz off.'

Not to be deterred the punter said, 'Bbbut I bbbacked a fffive . . .' The bookie got somewhat heated, but the punter persisted. When the bookie could take no more, he pulled a $20 note out of his bag, gave it to the punter and said, 'Now piss off and stop annoying me!'

The punter accepted the note rather reluctantly, and as he left the ring, a mate asked him how he was making out. 'I just met a bloody gggood bbbookie,' he said. 'I tried to tttell him I bbbacked a fffive ton tttruck into his cccar and he gave me twwwenty bucks.'

A Queensland grazier employed a boundary rider with whom he could not resist gambling. Every week when he paid the boundary rider he found himself drawn into some ridiculous bet which involved him in paying his employee two or three times his wages. And the fame of the 'unbeatable' gambler spread throughout the land.

Finally, one day the grazier took the boundary rider aside and said, 'Look, I like you, but I can't go on losing all the money. So I've had a chat with my old mate, Brown, over on the next property. He's agreed to give you a job – same wages and conditions – and he's rather looking forward to the challenge of employing the Great Queensland Gambler. Is that okay?'

'Sure, Mr Smith, that's fine,' said the boundary rider. He shook hands, collected his final wages and rode over to the Browns' property. Mr Brown met his new employee at the boundary fence and they rode together to the homestead. As they were dismounting the Great Queensland Gambler said,

'By cripes, you've got piles badly, haven't you Mr Brown?'

'No,' said Mr Brown. 'Never a suggestion of a pile in my life.'

'I'll bet you you have,' said the gambler. 'I can see by the way you ride. I bet you twenty bucks you've got piles.'

And before he could think of the consequences, Brown said, 'Done!' And shook the hand of the Great Queensland Gambler. Then Brown recovered his presence of mind.

'How are we going to prove that I haven't got piles?' he asked.

'Well, Mr Brown, a bet's a bet. I guess you'll have to let me examine you.'

'Come on,' said Brown. 'I've only just met you. You can't expect me to let you . . .'

'Well, a bet's a bet. We can call if off if you like . . .'

But Brown's desire to beat the unbeatable gambler overcame his inhibitions and, there being nobody else about at the time, he submitted to the indignity of the examination. The boundary rider paid up like a lamb and with good grace.

'No, not a suggestion of a pile, Mr Brown. Here's the twenty bucks,' he said.

Brown was ecstatic. He raced into the homestead and rang Smith. 'You know the great gambler you sent over to work for me,' Brown exalted. 'He wasn't here twenty minutes and I won twenty bucks from him.'

'Cripes!' said Smith, 'How did you do that?'

'Well, he was silly enough to tell me I had piles,'

said Brown, 'and I've never been bothered with them.' 'Now wait a minute,' said Smith, 'how did you prove that?'

'Well, promise me you'll never tell another living soul. I had to let him examine me. But it was worth it to see his face when he lost.'

Smith snarled, 'He didn't lose. He won. And you've just won it for him. You see the last thing he did before he left here was to bet me a hundred bucks that he'd have his finger up your arse within an hour of setting foot on your property.'

The little man walked onto the building site in response to the sign 'Bricklayers Wanted', presented his union ticket and was signed on by the large and unsmiling foreman. About an hour later he called his new brickie over.

'Okay, bloke, your work's all right, but you talk too much for mine. Where do you come from anyway – I haven't seen you around?'

'I don't do much bricklaying these days,' was the reply.

'Oh yeah, what do you do then?'

'Gambling mostly – I'm a professional gambler.'

'Come again – you do what?' The veins on the foreman's temples were swelling.

'Professional gambling – I bet on anything. For instance, I'll bet you ten bucks that by lunchtime you'll have a serious hernia.'

'You're mad – I'm the fittest man on a building

site anywhere in Victoria – Australia for that matter,' said the foreman.

'Do you want the bet or don't you?' replied his new brickie.

'Just to teach you a lesson, I'll take it – a tenner it is – by 12 o'clock, and in the meantime get back to work and keep your trap shut.'

All went well from then on and, as the gangs knocked off for lunch, the foreman couldn't wait to call the little bloke over.

'Okay smart stuff, I want your tenner and I hope you've learnt your lesson.'

'No hernia eh?' said the little bloke, 'I could have sworn. But a tenner's a lot of money – I reckon you ought to allow me to check.'

The foreman looked murderous but the little bloke persisted and so, reluctantly, the big fellow lowered his tweeds for the inspection. 'Seems okay,' said the little bloke as with the tip of his trowel he tested the weight of each testicle. 'I guess I lose this one – here's your tenner.'

'Yeah – and you're fired anyway – so get lost,' said the big man.

'Suits me,' the little bloke said, stepping a pace or two out of the foreman's range, 'I'll just collect my winnings off the fellas and I'll be going.'

'What bloody winnings?'

The little bloke was suddenly cheerful, 'Don't you get it? There's eight blokes over there each owing me a tenner for betting that I wouldn't have your balls on the end of my trowel by lunchtime. Eighty, er seventy bucks is not a bad morning's work!'

Fred and his mate were having a drink in a pub at the Gold Coast when a very wealthy American walked in. They invited him over and got yarning. During the course of the conversation Fred's mate told the American that Fred knew everyone that was important in the whole world.

The American said, 'I just can't swallow that.'

'It's fair dinkum, mate,' said Fred's mate, 'and what's more I can prove it.'

'Well, then, how about you prove to me that Fred knows the President of the United States of America,' said the wealthy American. 'And if you can I'll give you $200,000.'

'Okay then. We'll have to fly to Washington to do that,' said Fred's mate.

'Hold on there,' said Fred, 'it's not right to take this man's dough like that. Everyone knows that I know Bill Clinton.'

'No, I insist,' said the wealthy American. 'I've got a jet waiting for me at Brisbane airport. We'll catch a cab out to the airport and fly to Washington so that you can prove Fred knows Bill Clinton and the $200,000 will be yours.'

They caught the cab, jumped into the plane and headed off to Washington. The next day they all fronted up at the White House, introduced themselves to the guards and were ushered into the President's waiting room. Bill Clinton came to the door of the waiting room and said with a big welcoming smile, 'How are you, Fred? Golly gosh, it's been a long time! Come in, come in.' Fred and Bill were closeted for close on an hour in the Oval Office. When he finally came back to the waiting room, the wealthy American said, 'Well, Fred, you sure proved that you know Bill. I'll write out your cheque. No, on second thoughts, what I'll do is this, I would like you to prove to me that you know Maggie Thatcher. If you can do that, I'll double the $200,000 to $400,000.

Fred looked doubtful at this and said, 'Yeah, I know Maggie Thatcher. She's a good friend of mine. But I don't like to take your money.'

'I insist,' said the wealthy American, 'my jet is all fuelled up. We'll catch a cab to the airport and fly to Heathrow immediately.'

'It's your money,' said Fred, 'let's go.'

They flew to Heathrow and caught a taxi to Parliament House. On the way they were stopped by a cavalcade of official vehicles. They got out of the taxi and started walking past the Rolls Royces, the Jaguars, the Daimlers. They'd only passed a couple when a darkened window of a Daimler was wound down and it was Maggie. She called out, 'Fred! Hello there! Fancy seeing you in London. Come over here and ride with me and we'll catch up on the news.' Fred jumped into the Daimler and off they drove. Fred's mate and the wealthy American went to their hotel and a couple of hours later Fred turned up. The wealthy American said, 'Well Fred, you certainly know Maggie Thatcher. I'll either pay your $400,000 now or I'll double it if you can prove you know the Pope.'

Fred said, 'Sure I know the Pope and if you're silly enough to bet me $800,000 I'll prove it to you. We'll have to fly to the Vatican City though.'

The wealthy American said, 'Done!'

They headed for Heathrow and took off for Rome. When they got there Fred wanted to know what proof the wealthy American needed. The American said, 'I want you to come out on the balcony of the Vatican with the Pope when he makes his daily appearance before the crowds.'

Fred agreed and disappeared into the Vatican. At 2 o'clock the wealthy American and Fred's mate were waiting with the crowds in the square beneath the balcony to see Fred and the Pope. When Fred emerged from the Vatican a few minutes later, he found his mate standing over the body of the collapsed American.

'What happened?' asked Fred.

'Well, everything was fine until this dago standing behind us said, "I know who Fred is, but who's that fella with him?"'

A midget walks into the pub, reaches up and taps on the bar and asks the publican, 'Can a bloke get a bet on here?'

The barman leans over the bar, peers down at the midget and asks, 'You're not a copper, are you?'

There was a bloke who, although he punted on every race every Saturday, had not backed a solitary winner for many years. Every race he'd front up to a bookmaker, slap a tenner on his selection, and then watch it race as if it had rabbit traps attached to all four legs. Lesser gamblers would have given up, but this fellow persisted.

One day, a kind-hearted bookie decided that he would let the punter win for a change. He called the punter over and said, 'You've been backing horses with me for ten years and never had a collect. I'll tell you what I'm going to do – I'm going to put the names of all the fancied runners in next week's big race on slips of paper and place them in my hat. You can draw one of them out and I'll give you – free of charge – the odds about it to $1000. In other words, if you select a 7 to 1 pop and it wins, I'll pay you $7000.'

The punter was thrilled with this arrangement and readily agreed. The slips of paper with the horses' names on them were placed in the bookmaker's hat and the punter drew one.

'What horse did you draw?' asked the bookie, as the punter sadly surveyed the paper.'

'Akubra!'

The producer of *Phar Lap*, John Sexton, restaged the 1930 Melbourne Cup. On looking at the rushes, he realised that not all the horses in the re-enactment finished in the proper sequence. So he called all the jockeys together. 'Gentlemen, we have a problem. The horses must finish in exactly the same order as they did in the original race.'

There was a long silence broken finally by the leading jockey. 'What's the problem?'

Fred got a job driving a racehorse transport truck. He had to take horses to Flemington and Moonee Valley. He was running a bit late one day and had his foot flat to the floor when he was caught in a radar trap and pulled over. 'You were doin' 150, driver, ' said the police officer. 'What's the story?'

'Sorry, sir, but I was late for the first race at Flemington. And the trainer said I'd lose me job if the horses weren't there in time.' Whereupon the cop walked to the back of the truck and looked in.

'What the bloody hell are you talking about?' he yelled. 'There are no horses in here. It's empty!'

'Bugger it,' said Fred, 'they've given me the scratchings again.'

POLITICS AND POWER

Politicians are like a bunch of bananas. They start off green, quickly turn yellow, and there's not a straight one in the whole bunch.

Two rival politicians met face-to-face on a narrow pavement. Neither was willing to step aside for the other, especially since it had been raining heavily and the street was awash. So they glared at each other for a while until, finally, one said, 'I never step aside for fools!'

'Oh, really,' said the other, 'I always do!' and stepped off into the wet street.

A school class was shown over Parliament House and, when they returned to school, the students were asked to write an essay about what they'd seen. One lad wrote just one line, 'All politicians is bastards.' Rather than scold him, the teacher decided to apply psychology and sent the boy back, where he met the Speaker, was introduced to the Premier, sat in the Speaker's chair, met the Leader of the Opposition and was given an official lunch. After this red carpet treatment he went back to school to write another essay. It also consisted of one line, 'All politicians is cunning bastards.'

The leader of the opposition droned on and on, despite warnings from the speaker, who eventually was banging his gavel repeatedly. Finally the speaker lost his temper and hurled his gavel at the politician. He missed and hit someone in the front bench. As he slumped to the ground, the injured man said, 'Hit me again. I can still hear the bastard.'

There are two squashed corpses on the Hume Highway. One is a dead possum, the other a dead politician. What's the difference?

There are skid marks before the possum.

It happened in the early 1970s. There was this almighty flood. In one of the rescue helicopters – apart from the pilot – there was an odd group of three people. A young hippie, a simple country clergyman and a half-sozzled bloke in a crumpled suit. Suddenly the machine developed a serious fault. Ashen-faced, the pilot turned around and said, 'I'm terribly sorry, but you'll have to bail out because we're going to crash. The problem is that we've only got two parachutes.'

Before he finished speaking, the business-suited bloke spoke up, 'I'm a Rhodes scholar,' he said, 'and I'm in charge of all the workers in Australia. I have the brains, the drive and the connections to become the PM of this great country. I am clearly indispensable.' So saying, he grabbed the pack nearest to hand and jumped out.

'Son,' said the padre, 'I am an old man, I suffer from arthritis and am near the end. You have your life ahead of you – you take the other parachute.'

'What's with you, man?' asked the hippie, 'there's still two chutes. That self-important idiot jumped out with my back-pack.'

Once upon a time, a little nonconforming swallow decided not to fly south for the winter. He was unsure of the rationale behind the annual pilgrimage of his contemporaries and, being suspicious of unproved advice, decided to test the claim that it was necessary to avoid the life-threatening winter. So he wouldn't budge.

Gradually the winter started to close in. The swallow grew colder and colder. Finally he decided to head south after the others. But he'd left it too late. As he flew, the winter became more and more bitter. Ice formed on his wings. Eventually, he fell to earth in a frost-covered field. As he gasped his last breath, a cow wandered through the field and crapped on him. The warmth of the manure thawed his wings, warmed his body and revived him. He was so overjoyed by this turn of events that he raised his little head and whistled a happy little bird song. Just at that moment, a cat walking through the field heard the happy little chirping sound. It found the mound of dung, uncovered the little swallow and ate him.

There are three morals to this story:

1. Everyone who craps on you is not necessarily your enemy.
2. Everyone who extricates you from crap is not necessarily your friend.
3. If you are warm and comfortable in a pile of crap, keep your mouth shut.

A medical doctor, an engineer and a politician were discussing their professions. Which was the oldest? The medical officer reminded the others that the Book of Genesis clearly states that the first woman was created from the rib of a man. This was a medical function, so one must agree that his profession was the oldest. Whereupon the engineer argued that earlier in the Book of Genesis there was reference to the fact that God created order and calm out of chaos and mayhem. 'That would take an engineer.'

'Oh no,' cried the politician. '*We* go back further. Who do you think created the chaos?'

There was a young couple typically in love who had an all-consuming problem. That is, she was a staunch Liberal and he was a dedicated Labor supporter. They decided to marry under the solid rule that politics would not be discussed, but immediately after the reception they had a fierce political argument. Later that night in the nuptial bed the girl relented and tapped the fellow on the shoulder and said, 'There is a split in the Liberal Party ranks and it is likely if a Labor member stood then he would get in unopposed.' To which there was a prompt reply, 'It is too late, he stood independently and has blown his deposit.'

A politican was driving a constituent and her young son through Kings Cross when the son pointed out some women loitering on the footpath and asked her, 'What are those ladies waiting for?'

To which she replied, 'Son, they are waiting for their husbands to come and pick them up after work.' Whereupon the politician, obviously Labor, cut in and said, 'Lady, you can't shield your son from the real world. Admit to him that they're prostitutes.' The boy then asked, 'Mother, do prostitutes have babies?' To which the mother replied, 'Of course, son, where do you think politicians come from!'

A New Zealand Minister had been forced to resign, and while he was packing up he looked out the window of his office, high above the streets of Wellington, and said to his staff, 'See that new school over there? Well, last year I persuaded Cabinet to vote the money for that school. Yes, I built that school. But do you think the voters will remember me for that?

'And see that new hospital down the street? Well, the year before I built the school I had to call in every political debt owed me to get Cabinet to back that hospital. But I did it. And I built that hospital. But will the voters ever remember me for that? Course they bloody won't!

'And see that six-lane freeway out to the airport? Well, the first year I was a Minister, the year after we just managed to win the election, I had to squeeze Cabinet like you wouldn't believe to get the money for that, and I built that freeway, and you can bet the voters won't ever give me a second thought for that either.

'But screw one sheep and they never forget!'

The political candidate knocked hopefully on the door of a prospective supporter in the electorate and introduced himself. Much to his surprise, the lady of the house remarked, 'I'm certainly not going to vote for you!'

'But,' said the candidate, 'you've never seen my opponent.'

'No,' said the lady, 'but I've had a damn good look at you.'

My favourite jokes are one-liners which can be pinned more or less at random on one's political opponents:

'He's always been insufferable. In fact, he was so insufferable as a child that at the age of nine both parents ran away from home.'

'When he was born he was so unprepossessing that his parents hired a team of lawyers to try to find a loophole in his birth certificate.'

A businessman, disappointed in his career, decided to volunteer for the first brain transplant. A brilliant surgeon offered him a choice of three samples from his brain bank: one from a leading brain surgeon at $1000, one from a leading research scientist at $1000 and one from a retired politician at $5000. He enquired why the last one was so much dearer. 'It's never been used,' said the brain surgeon.

Why do so many people take an instant dislike to Senator Bishop?

Because it saves time.

Senator John Button was staying at a hotel in Los Angeles where there was a convention of comic book superheroes – Batman, Spiderman, Wonderwoman, etc. At breakfast Button was interrupted by the arrival of Superman, who said he was feeling the worse for wear after a heavy night. Button enquired what had taken place. Superman said that he'd come back to his room after a party and was preparing for bed when his X-ray vision revealed that Wonderwoman was lying naked in the next room. Superman said he could do nothing else but crash through the wall, landing on the bed. So Button said to Superman, 'Well, that must have surprised Wonderwoman!' To which Superman replied, 'Not nearly as much as it surprised the Invisible Man!'

Hillary Clinton was out jogging one morning. As she passed a small boy she saw that he had a boxful of puppies. She stopped and asked the young man what kind of puppies he had. He looked up proudly and said, 'They're all Democrats.' Hillary was pleased as she jogged away. She returned home and told her husband the story.

About a week later Bill was jogging by a young man with a box of small puppies. He stopped and asked the young boy what kind of puppies they were. The boy looked up confidently and said, 'They're all Republicans.' Somewhat puzzled, Bill asked him if he was the same boy that had told Hillary about his Democrat pups. The boy said that, yes, he was the same boy. Bill then asked him if he had a new box of puppies.

'No,' said the boy, 'they are the same puppies.'

Bill asked, 'How can they be Democrats last week and Republicans this week?'

The small boy said cheerfully, 'Last week, when they had their eyes closed, they were Democrats. Now that their eyes are open they are Republicans.'

Whilst campaigning in 1992, Bill Clinton discovered that his wife, Hillary, had almost married a small town mechanic. On pointing out to Hillary how close she came to not being First Lady, she replied that had she married the mechanic, *he* would have been President.

Nick Greiner was having great difficulty getting any good press coverage. So he called his press secretary and demanded that all the press be assembled under the Harbour Bridge for a major announcement at noon the next day. The due time arrived and all the State's media were assembled. The Premier said, 'I'm sick and tired of all this bad coverage, so I'm going to do something that nobody here can complain about.' He then proceeded to walk on the water across Sydney Harbour. The Premier awoke next morning to find that the *Sydney Morning Herald* proclaimed: GREINER CAN'T SWIM while the *Telegraph* was emblazoned with the banner GOVERNMENT RORTS; GREINER DOESN'T PAY THE TOLL.

A prostitute decides to undertake a new marketing technique by applying tattoos to her inner thighs. On one thigh is tattooed the face of Nick Greiner, on the other that of Wal Murray. Any client identifying one or the other receives a 50 per cent discount. If they can identify both, they get a freebie. A succession of customers identify either Nick or Wal. Then the lady happens to pick up an off-duty policeman who can't recognise either. 'Nup, I give up,' he says, 'but the one in the middle looks like Ted Pickering.'

Bob Hawke visited George Bush during the Gulf War and couldn't help but be impressed by the quality of the White House staff. So he said to Bush, 'George, where do you get all these great staffers?'

Bush replied, 'It is very simple. Every morning I ask a staff member a trick question. Watch this . . .' Bush then called for Dan Quayle. The VP walked in and Bush said, 'Dan, your mother has a child. It's not your brother, it's not your sister, who is it?'

Quayle replied, 'That's very simple, George. It's me.'

'Well done, Dan,' said the President, and Hawke was duly impressed. 'I've got to try that out.'

On his return to Canberra, he took his car straight into the office and put the same question to Paul Keating. 'Paul, your mother has a child. It's not your brother and it's not your sister. Who is it?'

Keating said, 'Gee, Bob, that's a tough one. I don't know the answer but I'll find out.' So he ran down to Johnny Button, well known as the brightest man in the Government, and said, 'John, your mother has a child. It's not your brother, it's not your sister. So who is it?' Button looked at him, half took off his glasses like he always does, and said, 'Paul, you moron, it's me!'

Keating was delighted. 'Right! I've got it!' He ran back to Hawke and said, 'Bob, my mother has a child. It's not my brother and it's not my sister. But I know who it is.'

Hawke said, 'Well, who?'

Keating responded, 'John Button!'

Hawke looked at him and said, 'Don't be bloody silly, Paul. It's Dan Quayle!'

If an intelligent politician, an intelligent woman and the Easter Bunny got into a lift together and discovered a $10 note lying on the floor, who would pick it up?

The intelligent woman. The other two don't exist.

There was a meeting between Bob Hawke, Presidents Bush and Gorbachev. While they were discussing world problems, the Angel of the Lord appeared to announce that God was not pleased and intended destroying the world in three weeks. Each travelled back to their respective countries to make the announcement. George told the Americans that he had good news and bad news.

The good news was that he had proof of God's existence. The bad news was that He was going to pull the plug. President Gorbachev told the Russians that he had bad news and worse news. The bad news was that God existed, despite Communist beliefs to the contrary, and the worse news was that the world was to be destroyed. Bob Hawke, meanwhile, appeared on national television to tell us that he had good news and terrific news. Although he hadn't believed it previously, there really was a God. And the terrific news was that no child would be living in poverty in a month's time.

Bob Hawke was flying home to Canberra after a particularly successful day kicking the shit out of the left wing. And since he was in such a good mood he decided he would do something to make an Australian happy. So he asked the steward if he could toss a $10 note out of the plane, so that whoever found it would share in some of his joy. The steward suggested that he throw ten $1 coins out of the plane since that would make ten Australians happy. Bob said, 'What a great idea. Maybe some poor kids will find them and I'll have less of them to worry about being in poverty by 1990.' A left-winger sitting behind him overheard all this and piped up with, 'Why don't you throw yourself out of the plane? Then you'd make all Australia happy.'

I've had a lot of trouble knowing when Bob Hawke is telling the parliament lies,' said the journo. 'When he raises his eyes he's telling the truth. When he rolls his eyes he's telling the truth. When he scratches his chin he's telling the truth. Now I know when he's lying. It's when he opens his mouth.'

Gary Hart meets Margaret Thatcher. Mrs Thatcher tells him, 'I want your hands off Nicaragua, your hands off Afghanistan and your hands off my knee.'

Why does Dr Hewson's Ferrari go backwards? Because it's negatively geared.

A specially chartered Lufthansa flight arrives at Buenos Aires airport. It taxis away from the main terminal and, under cover of darkness, a number of shadowy figures emerge. They immediately pile into a Mercedes and are driven off into the night. They arrive at an impressive mansion outside of town purchased some years earlier by the local BMW agent. The men knock nervously at the door. After a time, steps approach. The door opens and reveals an old man with a familiar lock of hair dangling over the forehead. Except after all these years the lock is thin and grey.

'Yes?'

'*Mein Führer*,' says the spokesman, 'we have come to beg you to return to Berlin, to lead your people in the Fourth Reich!'

'No,' snarls the old man, 'been there, done that.'

'But, *Mein Führer*, the entire population is ready for you. The neo-Nazi movement has never been stronger.'

'The German people were not worthy of me,' snarls the old man.

'True, *Mein Führer*. But now a United Germany is ready to follow you anywhere, to fulfil your greatest dream.'

The old man ruminates. He talks about having a peaceful, private life with Eva and the great-grandchildren, about how well BMW sales are going. But, finally, he is prevailed upon.

Then he makes one proviso. 'Okay, but this time, no more Mr Nice Guy.'

David Hill is going to work one day and he gets in the David Hill lift and goes up to the David Hill suite. The lift makes an unscheduled stop on the third floor and in walks a very attractive blonde who David had never seen before. The woman obviously doesn't work for the ABC because she is not carrying anything in triplicate.

She and David look at each other and she says, 'David Hill?'

And he says, 'Yes.'

And she says, 'I'd like to give you a blow job.'

And this is the mark of the man. David Hill looks at her and says, 'Yes . . . fine, but what's in it for me?'

David Hill and his wife were in bed today.

'God . . .' she said, to which he responded, 'You may call me David when we're in bed.'

Saddam Hussein disappeared down the bunker where he addressed his magic mirror, 'Magic mirror on the wall who is the biggest bastard of them all?' The magic mirror said, 'Saddam Hussein, you are the biggest bastard of all.' Saddam was so delighted with the response that he raced out and ordered a thousand of his faithful followers to be put to the sword.

The next week he disappeared down the bunker again. 'Magic mirror on the wall, who is the biggest bastard of all?'

'Saddam Hussein, you are still the biggest bastard of all.'

Saddam again was so delighted he declared war on the Kurds. The next week he went into the bunker, but didn't return. His worried aides finally decided to seek him out. When they arrived there was Saddam crying uncontrollably in the corner.

'Sire, sire,' they cried, 'what's wrong?'

'Who's Paul Keating?' sobbed Saddam.

Keating dies and turns up at the pearly gates. He asks for admission, explaining that he was 'the world's greatest Treasurer' and undoubtedly Australia's greatest Prime Minister. Peter sends him down below because he isn't on the list. Up comes an old man with a long white beard who insists that *he* is the real Keating. And Peter lets him in. A man who's been watching goes up to Peter and asks why he let in this imposter whilst denying the genuine article. 'No, he's not Keating. He's God. But he thinks he's Keating.'

Three plastic surgeons meet at a conference. The first, an American, talks about the latest triumph in Californian reconstruction. 'A guy was shot to pieces in a shoot-out. All we had left was his right ear. We took that ear, reconstituted the entire body and now he's back at work. As a matter of fact, he replaced six men.'

The English plastic surgeon promptly tops the story. 'We had a nuclear accident at a power station, and all that was left was a single hair. We took that hair, reconstructed the entire human being and now he's back at work at the power station. Where he's replaced *twenty* men.'

The Australian plastic surgeon is unimpressed. 'I was walking down Collins Street a few weeks ago and smelt a fart. I trapped it in a bottle, got back to the hospital, managed to constitute it into an arsehole and then into an entire human body. That bloke's now the Prime Minister of Australia, and he's put a million people out of work.'

Paul Keating entered a pub with a pig on a leash. He ordered two beers, one for him and one for the pig. After a couple of rounds, the barman's curiosity got the better of him. 'Where did you get him?' he asked. 'I won him in a raffle,' replied the pig.

The former Treasurer of Australia, Paul Keating, rushed into the office of the Prime Minister, Bob Hawke.

'Bob! Bob! I've just seen your new business card and you've got C^3I after your name. I thought that was a high-tech buzz word standing for Command,

Control, Communications and Intelligence. You don't have any of those qualities.'

Bob Hawke pompously replies, 'Paul, you've got it all wrong again. Those letters stand for Charisma, Credibility and Integrity.'

'But, Bob, what does the other C stand for?' blurts out the former greatest treasurer on the planet.

'I couldn't think of another suitable word beginning with C,' says our esteemed leader. 'You suggest one.'

Paul Keating, the Indian High Commissioner and the Israeli Ambassador are forced to seek emergency accommodation when their car breaks down in the middle of the bush. A farmer is happy to help, but has only two spare beds . . . 'So someone will have to sleep in the barn.'

The Israeli Ambassador volunteers. 'We Jewish people are used to sleeping in barns – it is part of our history.' But he returns to the house when he discovers that he'll be cohabiting with a pig, which just isn't kosher. Then the Indian High Commissioner steps forward, only to be knocking at the door a few minutes later, protesting the presence of a cow. 'The cow is sacred to us Indians,' he exclaims. 'I couldn't possibly sleep with one.' 'Okay, scumbags,' says Paul, 'I'll go and sleep in the barn.'

After five minutes there's another knocking on

the door. The farmer opens it only to be confronted with the pig and the cow.

Paul Keating visits the Canberra cemetery to negotiate a plot. He's taken to a grassy knoll, beside a eucalypt, with a splendid view. 'How much is this one?' he asks.

'Five thousand dollars,' says the cemetery official.

'Have you got anything cheaper?'

'Well, yes, there's one down the hill for $2000. But the view isn't very good.'

'Two thousand is still too much. What else have you got?'

'The only other plot we have is behind the tool shed.'

'How much is that?'

'Two hundred dollars. But sir, an ex-Prime Minister of Australia can't be buried in a $200 plot.'

'No worries,' says Keating, 'I'm only going to be there three days.'

Paul Keating took his Cabinet colleagues into the parliamentary dining room for dinner. The waiter approached the Prime Minister and asked for his order.

The PM said, 'The steak.'

'Well done or rare?' asked the waiter.

'Rare,' said Keating.

'And what about the vegetables?' asked the waiter.

'They'll have what I have,' replied Keating.

Senator Graham Richardson has just explained his actions about the Marshall Islands affair to a forgiving Prime Minister.

Richo says, 'Paul, mate, you've got a hole in your pants.'

Keating replies, 'Richo, I told you to take that damn cigar out of your mouth before you kissed me goodbye.'

Paul Keating was tripping along a country road when the car ran over a pig. He told the chauffeur to go to the nearby farmhouse and explain what had happened, apologise and offer to pay for the animal. The driver was gone a long time and when he returned had lipstick all over his face, was smoking a cigar and clutching an empty champagne bottle. 'I had a marvellous time, boss,' he said. 'The farmer gave me a cigar, his sons kept giving me champagne and his daughters made passionate love to me.'

'Good grief,' exclaimed Paul, 'what on earth did you say to them?'

'Just what you told me, boss,' said the chauffeur. 'I knocked on the door and said, "G'day, I'm Paul Keating's chauffeur and I've just killed the pig."'

Henry Kissinger was midway through one of his diplomatic marathons. He was sitting at the airport at Tel Aviv, waiting for a jet to take him to a small but important sultanate. Oddly enough the airport terminal was all but deserted except for a rather serious-looking young Israeli who reminded Henry of Woody Allen. 'And what do you do, son?' enquired Henry, to pass the time. 'Oh, I've just passed my university course and I'm looking for a job,' said the boy. 'And what do you do?' Though stunned by the boy's ignorance, Henry made a joke of it. 'Oh, I'm a sort of marriage broker.'

'Gee, do you think you could get me a good marriage?'

'Certainly. Just watch me.' Whereupon Henry had the airport officials contact the head of the Rothschild family in Paris. After a few pleasantries, Henry told Baron Rothschild that he had a young friend who'd be the perfect husband for his attractive daughter.

'Ah, Henry, everyone says that. Can you imagine how many suitors that girl has?'

'Ah, yes, but how many of her suitors represent David Rockefeller here in the Middle East?'

Whereupon Baron Rothschild agreed that the young man should press his suit.

Next Henry rang David Rockefeller in New York and said, 'David, I've got a young bloke here who wants to be your representative in the Middle East.'

David Rockefeller laughed. 'But Henry, there are hundreds of young men who want to be my representative in the Middle East.'

'Perhaps,' said Henry, 'but how many of them are engaged to Baron Rothschild's daughter?'

Talleyrand once asked Napoleon, 'Why is it that your brothers hate you so much?' After a pause, Napoleon said, 'They believe that I have robbed them of the inheritance of our late father, the King.'

Mr Dan Quayle landed at Sydney airport carrying a personal letter to Paul Keating from the President of the United States. Standing on the tarmac, he handed it to Keating as the photographers captured the moment. What did the letter say?

'Please ignore this man, he is an idiot.'

President Reagan wakes one winter's morn and goes to the window of his bedroom to look at the freshly fallen snow on the White House lawn and is aghast to see, written in what is obviously urine, the legend 'Reagan sucks'. Furious, he calls in his CIA chief and bellows that this incident has ruined his whole day and they'd better find the culprit immediately. The CIA chief scuttles off and later that day fronts Reagan in the Oval Office and says, 'Sir, we have good news and we have bad news. The good news is we can unequivocally tell you who the culprit is. We've run the piss sample through spectrometers, the CIA computers and a urine-inspect-o-nalysis doo-dad and without a shadow of a doubt I can tell you, it was Frank Sinatra!'

President Reagan reels in shock and gasps, 'Frank Sinatra! That's the good news. What on earth could be the bad news?'

'Well, sir,' says the CIA chief, 'the handwriting's Nancy's.'

During the Fraser years, when John Stone still led the Treasury, a small dispute between clerical officers and the government resulted in a one-man picket at the bottom of the Treasury steps. The lone picketer was having limited success convincing his fellow unionists to join the strike, but even Stone's arrival at work did not deter him. 'SCAB!' he called after Stone, who turned around to give the striker a lengthy lecture about the distortion of allocation of labour, the imbalanced power of unions and the benefits of government labour policy. Satisfied he had made his point, Stone continued up the stairs only to hear the cry 'SCAB!' again at his back. Patiently he returned to the picketer and again (with more emotion) gave the man a diatribe on the many benefits of Tory labour policy. This time the striker would surely understand. Stone returned to his climb up the stairs. 'SCAB!' the call came for the third time. Exasperated, Stone returned to the picket, saying with conviction, 'You have heard my views. I just don't know what to say to people like you,' and he turned on his heel to stomp up the stairs. The picketer paused before calling after Stone 'INARTICULATE SCAB!'

A Short Poppy asked a Tall Poppy over to his place to swim in his pool. When the TP got there the pool was one of those squat, low vases. The SP had a lovely time, but the TP barely wet his toes.

The TP asked the SP over to his place to swim in his pool. When the SP got there the pool was one of those long thin vases you use for single red roses. The TP had a lovely time, but the SP was floundering, struggling, sinking.

Finally, as the SP was going down for the third time, he shouted, 'Help me! I can't touch the bottom!' 'Oh you can touch the bottom all right,' said the Tall Poppy, 'it's the top you can't touch!'

A Short Poppy and a Tall Poppy went to the Cenotaph. The TP said, 'Look at those mosaics on the ceiling; those fine, athletic soldiers looking like Greek gods! And look at those stained glass windows; pure artistry in light, it makes you feel close to God!'

The Short Poppy was looking down at their reflections in the polished marble floor.

'I don't know about that,' he said, 'but my balls are twice as big as yours!'

Four things wrong with being a Tall Poppy:

You take twice as long to grow to your full height.

While you're growing the short poppies are down in the dirt having all the fun.

When you do reach your full height everybody sneers at you and says you don't deserve it.

Then, on every 11th November, an old man cuts you off at the knees, sticks you in a hole in his jacket, and when you ask him why, he falls silent.

THE LAW IS AN ASS

The Pope dies. As he mounts the stairs to the Pearly Gates he wonders why he doesn't hear any trumpets. Nor is St Peter waiting for him. However, the gates are ajar so His Holiness pushes his way in. Needless to say, he's in his best outfit, complete with his most impressive papal crook. Well, you only die once, and he wanted to make a grand entrance. So he's very, very disappointed by the reception. Perhaps they'll jump out from behind a cloud and chorus 'Welcome to Heaven'. Perhaps they're going to have a surprise party for him.

But for twenty minutes absolutely nothing happens. Suddenly a bloke runs by with a big tray of sandwiches. And the Pope yells out, 'Hey you, over there!' The fellow stops and says, 'Oh, Your Holiness, we were expecting you. I'm sorry we weren't there to meet you, but we're holding a brunch for you tomorrow around 11 o'clock. You'll enjoy it. Welcome to heaven.'

The Pope says, 'Hang on, I'm the bloody Pope!'

'We've got lots of popes. We've got hundreds of popes here. You'll meet a lot of them at the brunch. Anyway, welcome to heaven, but right now we've got to go and meet Mr Meyers.' And off he goes. And the Pope is left wondering who the hell Mr Meyers is.

So he follows the bloke around the corner where a band's tuning up and there's St Peter with a list in his hand organising things 'The anchovies . . . not many people like anchovies. Put them down at the end of the banquet table. The artichokes are very puny. That won't do for heaven, and certainly not for Mr Meyers. Get bigger artichokes – do a miracle, or something.'

Just then St Peter looks up and says, 'Oh, Your Holiness. Hi, I'm St Peter. Awfully sorry I wasn't there to meet you, but Mr Meyers is coming.'

The Pope says, 'Who is this Mr Meyers? And why is he more important than the Pope?'

'Well, he's our first lawyer.'

And the Pope says, 'A lawyer? What's a lawyer doing in heaven?'

'Oh, here he comes now, Your Holiness. Excuse me I'll be right back.'

St Peter runs off to the gate and the Pope catches a glimpse of a fellow in a pinstripe suit with a briefcase in his hand. He's led into heaven looking a bit puzzled. But St Peter couldn't be nicer. He takes the briefcase from him, shakes his hand, puts an arm around his shoulder and says, 'I'm St Peter. Welcome to heaven.'

Mr Meyers looks really puzzled and says, 'How did I get into heaven?'

'Believe me, Mr Meyers, it's not based on your work or your character or anything you've done during your life. But it's because you're the oldest man ever to come to heaven.'

'What do you mean? I was 46 when I died of a heart attack just this afternoon. What do you mean old?'

'Well, according to our records you're over 500 years old.'

'Nonsense,' protests Mr Meyers, 'I told you I'm 46.'

St Peter said, 'Well, we have your office records right here.'

Mr Meyers says, 'Oh no, you've just added up the hours I charge my clients.'

A lawyer was sitting in his office one afternoon, all by himself, doing some paperwork, when suddenly there's a big puff of smoke in the corner and the smell of brimstone. When the smoke cleared the lawyer saw – the Devil.

He said, 'What can I do for you?'

The Devil said, 'I want to offer you a great deal.'

'I'm a lawyer, I'll tell you whether this deal is great or not. What are the terms?'

The Devil said, 'Well, first of all, I guarantee that you'll live to be at least 150 years of age and that you'll have the body and lust of a teenager and an endless succession of nymphomaniacal secretaries, each one of which will be more beautiful, voluptuous and enthusiastic than the last one. Women will do anything you want – all you'll have to do is think about it. Moreover, you'll have a job with the biggest law firm in Melbourne. You just name it, you'll be the head of that law firm on the most fabulous six-figure salary. You'll have eight weeks holidays every few months if you want.'

The lawyer said, 'Hold on, this sounds too good. What do I have to give in return?'

The Devil said, 'Oh, it's very simple. Your faithful wife of twenty-four years and your two beautiful children will have to die right now. In extreme agony. And go to hell to burn for the rest of eternity.'

The lawyer paused for a minute and said, 'Oh, all right, but what's the catch?'

What happens to a lawyer who jumps out of a plane at 35 000 feet with no parachute?

Who cares?

A couple of blokes set off in a balloon. They're determined they are going to stay up longer than anyone else in ballooning history. But two days later there's a huge storm that wrecks all their radio equipment. And while they're being buffeted around, their food falls overboard. Worse still, they don't know where they are. They might be anywhere. On the other side of the world. So they decide to lose altitude until they come in sight of land. Down they go, very slowly, descending through the clouds. And they sigh with relief because they're over land. Peering down from the basket they see cars and think, 'Well, they're driving on the left side of the road. That means we're probably in the UK or Australia. And they're playing tennis. So it must be a civilised country.'

They come within hailing distance of the tennis court and call out to one of the players, 'Hello, down there!'

The two fellows stop playing tennis and look up. 'Yeah, what do you want?'

'Where are we?'

'You got any money?'

'Yes, what do you want with money?'

'Throw it down,' says the man on the ground.

So they throw a wallet down and one of the blokes on the ground picks it up, takes the money out, splits it with the fellow on the other side of the net and puts the wallet in his pocket. Finally he says, 'Now, what was your question?'

'Where are we?'

'You're in a balloon.'

At that moment they rise above the clouds and the two partners look at one another helplessly. 'That was useless,' said one.

'No, at least we know where we are.'

'What do you mean we know where we are?'

'Well, we're over a civilised country. They drive on the left hand side of the road. And those two fellows are lawyers.'

'How can you tell they're lawyers?'

'Well, first of all, they wouldn't do a thing for us until we paid them. And what they said was absolutely true and totally useless.'

University research psychologists decided not to use white rats in experiments any more. They opted to use lawyers instead.

First, they're much more plentiful – you can get lawyers anywhere. Second, sometimes experimenters get a little too attached to their white rats and if something nasty happens to them you feel bad. And with lawyers you just don't have that problem. Third, they've found out there are some things that white rats just won't do.

But the latest development is they've stopped using lawyers. They're back to using white rats again. The reason's simple. They weren't into it very long before they found out that lawyers aren't that close to human beings.

An engineer, a doctor and a lawyer were on a ship. It began taking water and sinking, and the cowardly crew abandoned the ship and the passengers. The three found themselves trying to stay afloat in a two-man dinghy. It was obvious that it was not going to work, and that sacrifice by one of the three was necessary to enhance the survival prospects of the other two. Without fuss, the lawyer went over the side and struck out confidently for what looked like a smudge of land on the horizon.

Suddenly, several menacing triangular fins broke the surface and the two in the dinghy thought the lawyer was about to pay the ultimate price. To their amazement, however, two of the sharks started leading the way to the island in the distance, while the remainder formed a protective circle around the lone swimmer.

Watching dumbfounded from the dinghy, the doctor stammered, 'That's the most amazing thing I've ever seen!'

'Not amazing,' replied the engineer, 'simply a matter of professional courtesy.'

A lawyer working for the family court forgot that he was due at a divorce settlement. By the time he arrived he saw his Aboriginal client, a woman, leaving the court holding a sheet of rusty galvanised iron.

'I'm terribly sorry I wasn't here in time,' he said.

'It's okay,' said the woman, 'I managed fine without you. Look, I got half the house.'

Two 88-year-old pensioners visit the lawyer. 'We want a divorce,' they chorus in quavering voices.

The lawyer is both amused and curious. 'Why on earth have you waited so long?'

'We were waiting for the kids to die.'

Two Justices of the Peace, having become slightly 'point-o-pissed' together one Friday evening, were promptly arrested by the unsuspecting new plod who had arrived in town to enforce the law. All parties were embarrassed when the facts emerged. However, the question of bail was not in issue, since each of these gentlemen, with a stroke of the legal pen, granted the other co-offender freedom on the condition that he would appear in the magistrates court on the following Monday morning. On Monday morning the question arose, who should sit on the bench first.

'*I* will,' said the first gentleman of the law, hoping that he could set a precedent for his brother justice. 'This is a serious matter, this drunkenness in a public place,' he said. 'However, as this is your first offence, I shall treat the matter with a degree of leniency and place you on a good behaviour bond.'

He then stepped down from the bench and took his turn standing in the dock. His brother justice, with whom he had previously been imbibing, stepped up and sat on the bench. 'There is a prevalence of this type of offence coming before the courts, and something must be done about it. Why, this is the second example of such behaviour that the court has had to listen to this morning. Fined $100!'

A Queensland farmer is seeking damages for injuries sustained when his horse was hit by a car. In court, the defence counsel asks, 'After the accident, didn't someone come over to you and ask how you felt?'

Farmer: 'Yes, I believe that is so.'

Defence counsel: 'And didn't you tell him that you never felt better in your life?

Farmer: 'Yes, I guess I did.' The defence counsel then sits down and the plaintiff's counsel stands up.

Plaintiff's counsel: 'Will you tell His Honour the circumstances in which you made the response?'

Farmer: 'Yes. Not long after the accident, my horse, which had sustained broken legs, was thrashing around. A policeman came up to the horse, put his revolver to its ear and shot it dead. Then he went over to my dog, which had a broken back and was howling miserably. He put his revolver to the dog's ear and shot it. Then he came over to me and asked, "How do you feel?"

I said, "I never felt better in my life."'

Three Sydney men, who were called for jury service but failed to attend, were summoned to appear before a judge and account for themselves. The first of them to front the judge was lectured on the seriousness of the offence and asked for an explanation. 'Your Honour,' he said. 'I realise how serious this matter is. The night before I was due to report for jury service I set my alarm clock to wake me in plenty of time. But the clock broke down – it didn't go off and I slept in. Even so I hurried and got ready to leave without breakfast, but I couldn't start my car. The battery was flat. I immediately phoned for a taxi. When it came I told the driver the situation and asked him to hurry. We were doing fine until we reached Pyrmont Bridge, but then we ran into a milk cart and killed the horse.'

The judge muttered something about that being 'a likely story' and told the man to sit down and wait while the second man was interviewed.

This man's story started off exactly the same way: the alarm clock that didn't ring, the car that wouldn't start, the taxi . . . The judge interrupted, 'And when you got to the Pyrmont Bridge,' he suggested, 'you ran into a milk cart and the horse was killed?'

'That's right,' said the man. 'How did you know?'

'Never mind,' said the judge, 'sit over there and wait.'

The third man appeared before the judge, who eyed him sceptically and said, 'Did you set an alarm clock that failed to go off?'

'Yes, sir.'

'And then your car wouldn't start because the battery was flat?'

'Yes, sir.'

'So you called a cab and told the driver to hurry.'

'Yes, sir.'

The judge smiled sourly. 'I can hardly wait to hear what happened at Pyrmont Bridge,' he sneered.

'Ah,' said the man, 'that's where the hold-up happened – there were two dead horses on the bridge.'

What do you call a bigot in a wig?

Your Honour.

What do you call a few hundred bigots in wigs?

The Australian judicial system.

Why are Australian judges like Mother Teresa?

Because everything they say makes you want to launch an appeal.

Why is an Australian judge like a dyslexic?

Because they both stuff up their sentences.

Why is an Australian judge like a drunk?

Because his judgment suffers from too many years at the bar.

Why is an Australian judge like Old Sydney Town?

Because both offer a variety of 18th-century views.

Why is a woman in the court system like a ship on the ocean?

Because, at the end of it all, it will be her in the dock.

What do you call a judge driving through a working-class suburb?

Lost.

Is it true that Australian judges are all from the same class?

Yes. Mr Tompkin's Latin class at Melbourne Grammar, 1914.

Why are Australian judges so prejudiced against women?

Because they never met any at Melbourne Grammar.

What is right and old and goes round and round in circles?

An Australian judge endeavouring to blame the victim.

What is black and angry and going nowhere?

An Aboriginal Australian expecting a fair trial.

Why do white men get such lenient sentences?

Because the judges have to save prison space for the blacks.

Have you heard about the Australian judge who got confused?

He was prejudiced in favour of a woman.

Why is an Australian judge like a remedial speech teacher?

They both worry that men won't be able to cope with a long sentence.

Why do people address judges as 'the bench'?

Because they're both about as sensitive as a block of wood.

How many Australian judges does it take to change a light bulb?

None – the judiciary hasn't changed anything in years.

Why is an Australian judge like Halley's Comet?

Because they've both spun out of touch with the real world.

Why did the judge stop his wife plugging in the iron?

Because he couldn't cope with a woman being close to power.

What do you call fifty sexist, racist judges stuck at the bottom of the ocean?
A bloody good start.

Why are Australian judges often called wharfies?
They sit on cases.

There are two farmers over in C Division – Farmer Fred and Farmer Pete. Farmer Fred is doing six months for rooting a cow. Farmer Pete is in for aiding and abetting. He held up the cow's tail.

The little accountant had got three years for some heavy embezzlement, and went into prison with horror stories of prisoner assault. He was sure he was going to be reamed out. His worst fears were realised when his cell mate turned out to be a monster bikie – 2 metres tall, tatts, scars, and missing teeth and various other bits. But his fears were allayed slightly when the bikie revealed himself to be a bit simple, and invited the accountant to play with his toys – his jigsaw, his trains, and his comics. Eventually, the bikie said, 'Right, now we'll play Mummies and Daddies. Do you want to be the Mummy or the Daddy?'

A little uneasily, the accountant opted to be Daddy.

'That's fine,' said the bikie, 'now come over here and suck Mummy's cock!'

Two lawyers meet up in the Executive Lounge before a flight. One is looking slightly flustered and his friend enquires about the problem.

Says the first lawyer, 'I've just done something very embarrassing. You know how sometimes your words can get all jumbled and you say something you didn't mean to? I was at the check-in counter – there's a very beautiful young woman on duty – and I said, 'Good morning. Two pickets to Titsburg, please.'

His friend smiled. 'Yeah, similar thing happened to me at breakfast this morning. I poured myself a coffee then said to my wife, "You fucking bitch, you're ruining my life. I want out", when what I *meant* to say was, "Pass me the sugar bowl please, darling."'

A new partner in a law firm was known for bragging and attempting to outdo anyone else's stories at social functions.

At a dinner to entertain a potentially lucrative client, all progressed smoothly while the guest of honour held the floor. He described the new saltwater pool being installed at his beachside retreat – black slate, landscaped surrounds, spa. As he paused for a drink, the lawyer launched in, 'Oh, they're great, of course, but you should be looking at a pool larger than 20 metres. I had one installed last year, 30 metres long' – his boss mouthed the word FIRED at him across the table – 'and ah, 5 centimetres deep.'

A motorist is cruising along the Hume Highway at normal speed when he notices a police car right behind him. So he accelerates to 100 kilometres, and then to 115 kilometres, and so on. No matter what the increment in speed, the police car remains close behind. Finally it overtakes and passes the motorist and signals him to stop. A very angry constable demands an explanation of this erratic and illegal behaviour.

'It's like this, Sarge. Last week one of your officers ran away with my wife and I was afraid he was bringing her back.'

A few years back there was a mug local cop who hadn't made an arrest in a long, long time. His sergeant was crooked on him. The young cop said, 'There's no one around my beat doing anythin' wrong.'

So the Sergeant says, 'Next Saturday night, when the pub's closing, you'll see a bloke go down the back lane. Follow him, flash your torch on him and arrest him for urinating.'

Come Saturday night, the young constable saw a bloke and his girlfriend going down the lane. He followed them, flashed his torch on them and said, 'What are you up to?'

'I'm having sex with this young lady,' the bloke replied.

And the young cop said, 'You're damn lucky you weren't pissing. I'd have to run you in.'

A surgeon from outback Queensland is apprehended by police for driving his Rolls Royce in an erratic manner.

'Now, sir, would you blow into this breathaliser?'

'No, I cannot.'

'Why?'

'Because I have emphysema.'

'Well, sir, you must submit to a blood test.'

'Sorry, that's not possible.'

'Why?'

'Because I'm a haemophiliac.'

'Well, you must get out of your car and walk along a straight line.'

'No.'

'Why?'

'Because I'm pissed!'

CRIMINAL: A person found at home in bed at 3 a.m.

DESPERATE CRIMINAL: An Aboriginal person found at home in bed at 3 a.m.

WHITE VICTIM: A person whose family should be given $50,000 compensation.

BLACK VICTIM: A person whose family should be given no compensation.

POLICE INTELLIGENCE: Something used in order to raid the wrong house.

THE LAW: A system devised by do-gooders to hamper police operations.

INNOCENT PERSON: A person whose background requires further investigation.

INNOCENT VICTIM: An innocent person who's been shot by the Tactical Response Group and whose background thus requires *substantial* further investigation.

A bloke was in court in the backblocks of Queensland charged with cattle duffing – taking somebody else's unbranded cattle and whacking his own brand on them. The jury consisted of local farmers who'd all done a bit of duffing in their time, and the accused was a drinking mate from the Linga-Longa Pub. So when the judge sent them off to consider the verdict, their deliberations took about five minutes flat.

The clerk of the court says, 'Have you reached a verdict?

'Yeah,' said the foreman of the jury.

'Do you find the defendant guilty or not guilty?'

'We reckon he's not guilty, but he's got to give the cattle back.'

The judge was infuriated and started banging away with his gavel. 'You cannot reach a verdict with such conditions attached! The man is either guilty or not guilty. Now go away and reconsider your verdict.'

The jury shuffled grumpily out of the court, only to return seconds later.

'Well!' said the judge. 'How do you find?'

'We find him not guilty, and he can keep the bloody cattle!'

A bloke was driving home after a long lunch. He knew he'd had a few, so he was being particularly careful, doing everything by the book. Inevitably, he was pulled over. Before the cop reached the window, the driver was explaining how he'd really only had a couple and he was ... The cop cut him short. 'If you'd just get out of the vehicle please, sir.'

The man tried to explain how watchful he was being. The cop insisted. The man got out of the car. The cop led him around to the back and pointed.

'Are you aware, sir,' he said, 'that your left-hand brakelight is not working?' The man slumped to his knees and burst into tears.

'It *is* only a brake light, sir,' the cop said.

'Oh, fuck the brake light,' said the man, 'where's my bloody caravan?'

A vintage car buff had broken down and a fellow in a Porsche offered to tow him, 'but', he said, 'I'm in a hurry. If you see a police car, give a hoot.'

A little while later a traffic policeman returned to his base. 'I thought I'd seen everything,' he said, 'but today I give up. I was chasing this vintage car at 120 kilometres, but when I started my siren, the crazy guy starts hooting to overtake a Porsche.'

THE WORK ETHIC

Tarzan comes home pooped and says to Jane, 'It's a jungle out there.'

If a magician's wand is used for cunning stunts what is a policeman's baton used for?

There was a long drought in Central Africa. The witch doctor had tried all his rainmaking dances, imprecations, but to no avail. One of the elders observed that rain was never a problem in England, so why not send the witch doctor to London to learn the secret. Off he went to England, learned the secret, and returned to the tribe. He informed the leaders that these crazy white men had a big paddock of grass enclosed by a white picket fence. In the middle were two lots of sticks driven into the ground. Two men, each with a club, stood next to these sticks and waited for a lot of other men to spread themselves all over the paddock. Then two more men, wearing black trousers, four sweaters and six hats, came out to keep a close watch on the men with the clubs. Then one man got a red rock and threw it at one of the fellers with a club. AND DOWN CAME THE RAIN!

Why is it a good thing that there are female astronauts?

When the crew gets lost in space, at least the woman will ask for directions.

What does NASA stand for?

Need Another Seven Astronauts.

What's the difference between NASA and Margaret Fulton?

Margaret Fulton teaches cooks and NASA cooks teachers.

What's the difference between a rottweiler and a social worker?

The rottweiler eventually gives the child back.

(Joan Kirner, then Premier of Victoria, told this story when a large number of children had been seized from parents who belonged to a religious cult. The joke proved as controversial as the police action.)

What's an astronaut's favourite drink?

Seven-up.

When Australia got its space program going up the Cape, the scientists decided to send up three astronauts with a monkey. Before blast off, each was given an envelope, not to be opened until they'd got into orbit. Everything went pretty well, so they opened their envelopes.

The monkey's letter listed his tasks:

1. Recheck fuel supplies.
2. Review the instrument panel.
3. Adjust the solar power.
4. Recycle all urine for drinking purposes.
5. Check the automatic guiding systems.
6. Conduct the ten scientific experiments outlined on the next page.

The three astronauts opened their letters containing identical instructions. 'Don't forget to feed the monkey.'

It seemed like an appalling affront to the dignity of the upper class bank in an upper class area of Melbourne when a scruffy-looking male, about 25, walked in. Noses sniffed in disdain. He approached the upper class, snooty-looking female teller and said, 'I wanna open a fuckin' cheque account.' Her surprise was barely contained by her practised dignity. She told him she would most certainly not serve a man so rude and would he please leave the establishment. Instead, he repeated his request. 'I wanna open a fuckin' cheque account, ya bitch.' She left her cage with icy decorum and fetched the grey-suited, silvery-looking manager who approached with a supercilious expression. In an accent appropriate to the suburb, he chastened the young guy and impressed upon him the bank's strong belief in manners, decorum, cleanliness and presentation.

In spite of this the scruff repeated, 'I just wanna open a fuckin' cheque account, arsehole.'

The manager raised an eyebrow and asked, very icily, 'And how much would your initial deposit be, perchance?'

The reply came, 'Three-and-a-half million dollars. I just won Tattslotto.'

To which the manager said, 'And what cock-sucking little slut refused to serve you?'

A bloke walked into a bank and joined a very long queue. Finally he made it to a teller and asked for an appointment with the bank's manager. The teller apologised. 'Sadly, the bank manager passed away last week.' Whereupon the man thanked her and rejoined the still lengthy queue, only to be given the same message by the second teller. He then joined the long queue yet again, finally putting the same question to the third teller, who protested, 'But I just overheard my colleague explaining that the bank manager recently passed away!'

The gentleman thanked him but explained he just liked hearing the good news.

What do you call a bank manager with a big dick?

A tight-fisted wanker.

A woman goes into a bank and hands the teller a $100 note.

He looks at it closely. 'This is a forgery,' he says.

'Oh no,' cried the woman, 'I've been raped again.'

A wealthy and unusually idealistic merchant banker was pottering around the backyard of his mansion one day when an itinerant handyman came round and asked him for a bit of casual work. Feeling sorry for the fellow, the banker produced 5 litres of enamel paint and a brush and told the handyman he would like him to go and paint the front porch.

An hour later the handyman was around the back again to collect his earnings. The banker commended him on the speed of his work and handed him ten dollars. As he was leaving the handyman remarked, 'By the way, it's not a Porsche, it's a Mercedes.'

A couple of burly Melbourne brickies, Mick and Tiny, had the reputation of being the fastest in the trade. They could've dammed the Yarra overnight at the drop of a hod. One Friday night they were bragging as usual about their prowess with the trowel. Come closing time, they were about to stagger out into Lygon Street when a swarthy gent sidled up to them. 'You wanna make lotsa money?' he asked.

'Yeah, yer not wrong there, mate,' said Mick.

'Good. I have heard of your reputation. Fantastic. I represent the richest Sheik in the Middle East, and he wants a 10-metre brick wall built round his 200-room harem. The British want tea-breaks, the Americans leave gum all over the place, the Italians would serenade the concubines, the Germans speak German, and the French complain about the food. So we're trying Australians.'

'Good on yer,' said Tiny.

'But you must leave tonight.'

'We weren't doin' anythin' partic'lar.'

'And you must finish the wall within twenty-four hours of starting, otherwise you will be used to plug an oil well.'

'No worries, mate. Lead us to it.'

Mick and Tiny found themselves bundled aboard a private Concorde, and settled back into a beer-induced stupor. Next thing they knew, the cabin door was opened, and in streamed the Sahara sunlight. The first desert they'd ever set eyes on. They stared at it in total disbelief, dune upon dune as far as the horizon.

'Christ!' breathed Mick, 'will you look at all that sand!'

'Yeah,' said Tiny. 'Let's get the hell outta here before they bring the cement!'

The civic councillors of a small country town are reviewing the architectural plans for a new amenities block in the local park. One of the councillors is bemused by the terms being bandied around and finally quietly asks a fellow councillor what the architect means by the word urinal. When this is explained, the first councillor nods wisely, then announces, 'Well, why stop at a urinal? We should probably build an arsenal, too!'

An American, a Frenchman and an Australian were sitting in a bar overlooking Sydney Harbour. 'Do you know why America is the wealthiest country in the world?' asked the American. 'It's because we build big and we build fast. We put up the Empire State Building in six weeks.'

'Six weeks, *mon dieu*, so long!' snapped the Frenchman, 'ze Eiffel Tower we put up in one month *exactement*. And you,' he continued, turning to the Australian, 'what has Australia done to match that?'

'Ah, nuthin' mate. Not that I know of.'

The American pointed to the Harbour Bridge. 'What about that?' he asked.

The Australian looked over his shoulder. 'Dunno, mate. Wasn't there yesterday.'

An economist is a person who marries Elle Macpherson for her money.

An engineer and a scientist met in a pub to discuss a mathematical problem. On a table 4 metres away was a carton of beer. The problem was to reach the table, with a first step of any size, a second step half the first, a third step half the second and so on.

Quickly the scientist said that this was a geometric progression, was asymptotic to zero, and no matter how many steps you took, you'd never actually reach the table, and said it couldn't be done.

The engineer leapt 2 metres, strode 1 metre, minced half a metre, leaned over, picked up the beer and triumphantly declared, 'Fuckin' near enough's good enough.'

A workshop foreman was sent a young man for 'work experience' and, being busy for the moment, handed the young fellow a broom with the polite request to tidy up the floor a bit until someone could show him some proper work.

'But I'm a graduate engineer!' protested the young man.

'I'm so sorry, I didn't think,' apologised the foreman, taking the broom. 'Look, this is how you do it.'

The Italian-Australian retired from his factory job. He went to the nearest chicken hatchery and said, 'I ama retiring to open a chicken farma. Please sella me 10 000 day-olda chicks.' He took delivery and went on his way. Three days later he approached the hatchery sales clerk again. 'I wanna 10 000 day-olda chicks.' He took delivery and went on his way. Three days later he was back at the counter. 'I wanna 10 000 day-olda chicks.' The salesperson enquired, 'You certainly have bought a lot of chicks. Have you got a very large farm?'

The old man replied, 'No, all the others died. I think I might be planting them too deep.'

Propelled by two rows of sweating galley slaves straining at the long oars, a Roman warship glided across the sparkling Mediterranean. Suddenly one of the older chained rowers gave a strangled cry, clutched his chest and collapsed over the oar, stone dead. The guards released him from his chains, carried him on deck and threw the body into the sea.

Meanwhile the slave master strode rapidly up and down the aisle separating the two banks of rowers, giving each slave a lash with his whip. Then he said, 'Right, you know what to do.' Whereupon each slave released his grip on the oar, lay back on his seat and urinated into the air. Everyone was drenched. A recently-sentenced slave whispered into the ear of a neighbour. 'What was all that about?' Speaking from the side of his mouth, the neighbour replied, 'An old Roman tradition, son. Every time there's a death on board, we have a quick whip around and a piss-up.'

On his first day as a member of the galley crew, a slave remarked to the oarsman beside him that it was a beautiful day to be sculling around the Mediterranean. 'Won't be tomorrow,' said his mate, 'we're booked to take Antony and Cleopatra waterskiing.'

Four insurance companies decided to amalgamate. At the first joint board meeting it was agreed that the new company should have its own coat of arms. So the College of Heralds was called in and the requirements stated, which were that it should embody some element identifying each company while also indicating their union. In due course the College of Heralds representative returned and unrolled a vellum scroll to be viewed by the board members. On it was a large shield suitably decorated and divided into four quarters in each of which was depicted a double bed occupied by a couple.

'What on earth is this?' asked the Chairman. 'It's not at all what we asked for. How does it show the identity of the original companies?'

'Quite simple,' was the reply. 'The first quarter shows a man in bed with his wife. That's Legal and General.

'The second quarter shows a man in bed with his fiancée. That's Mutual Trust.

'The third quarter shows a man in bed with his secretary. That's Employers Liability.

'The fourth quarter shows a man in bed with a prostitute. That's Commercial Union.'

A young man can't believe his luck when he is allocated a seat beside a very attractive girl on a flight to Sydney, and decides to strike up a conversation. So he starts by asking her where she's going.

'I'm going to a nymphomaniacs' convention in Sydney,' replies the girl.

He suddenly becomes very interested, and asks her, 'What sort of men do you like?'

'I like policemen,' she replies, 'because they're big and strong and honest.'

'I see,' says the young man, 'well, what's your second choice?'

'Cowboys,' she says, 'because they look so manly with their leather and spurs and horses.'

'What about your third choice?' he asks.

'Well, I like Jewish men because they're artistic, sensitive and caring.'

'What's your name?' she asks the young man.

'I'm Sergeant Hopalong Bernstein.'

A businessman was faced with the dilemma of firing two of his three secretaries. All were good at their jobs, and he didn't know how he was going to choose between them. Finally he decided to put an extra $100 in each of their pay envelopes and judge their reactions. The first secretary surreptitiously pocketed the extra money and didn't say a word. The second came to him and said, 'Look, I've been overpaid $100, so I went out and invested it in bonds at twelve-and-a-half per cent.' And the third secretary came to him and said, 'Look, I was overpaid $100. It's not mine. I haven't earned it. I want to give it back.'

Which one kept her job? The good-looking one with the big tits.

A man was visiting Sydney for the first time in 30-odd years. He wanted to drive down Martin Place in style, but when he got there Martin Place had vanished under acres of amenities. The old Hotel Australia had gone, so had the privy and the clock, too. Sadly he drove to Railway Square, but the tram shelters were no longer there. Marcus Clarke had disappeared and the Empire was now Her Majesty's. He was about to leave forever when, in the corner, he saw the shop of Gus, the cobbler. He went in and, sure enough, there was Gus, mouth full of nails. Nothing had changed.

'Gus,' he said with some emotion, 'remember me?'

Gus shook his head.

'I went bush over thirty years ago and I've never been back. Matter of fact, I left some shoes here.'

'Aw,' said Gus, 'well, I never throw anything out. What was your name again?' And he rummaged in the shadows. 'Brown plain toes?'

'Yes, yes,' cried the bloke.

'About size 9?'

'Yes.'

'And with lace-up fronts?'

'Yes, that's them!'

Gus called out, 'Be ready next Tuesday.'

The locals were drinking prior to closing time when an obviously English gent with a monocle entered through the swinging doors. An awed hush fell upon the assembled throng as the visitor announced in clipped British tones, 'I'd like a whisky and soda, please.'

One local approached the visitor and asked him, 'Whaddaya doin' up 'ere, mate?'

'Well,' he replied, 'I'm a taxidermist and I'm having a wonderful time. Yesterday I stuffed a kangaroo and today I stuffed a koala and they do tell me, if I can stay a few more days, I'll be able to stuff a wombat.'

The inquisitor returned to his group and said, 'The bastard reckons he's a taxi driver. But, if you ask me, the bugger's a bloody drover just like the rest of us.'

They had so many strikes on the Melbourne wharf that they asked the workers not to clock on or off. Instead they suggested they might like to sign the visitors' book.

Two wharfies are unloading a container. One checks a consignment document, scratches his head, and says, 'What's a cubic foot?' His mate frowns then replies, 'Dunno. Reckon we can claim compo for it though.'

Woman: 'Officer, I've been half-raped.'
Policeman: 'What do you mean half-raped?'
Woman: 'It was a wharfie and it started to rain.'

Four union members were discussing how smart their dogs were. The first, a member of the Vehicle Builders' Union, had a dog called T-Square. He said he could do maths calculations. He told him to go to the blackboard and draw a square, a circle and a triangle. This the dog did with consummate ease.

The Amalgamated Metal Workers' Union member had a dog named Slide Rule who he thought was even cleverer. He told him to fetch twelve biscuits and divide them into four piles, which Slide Rule did without problems.

The Liquor Trades' Union member admitted that both were quite good, but he thought his dog could outperform them. His dog was named Measure, and he told him to go and get a stubby of beer and to pour half a litre into a 1-litre bottle. The dog did this without a flaw.

They turned to the Waterside Workers' Union member and said, 'What can your dog do?' The waterside worker called his dog, who was named Tea Break, and said to him, 'Show these bastards what you can do, mate.'

Tea Break went over and ate the biscuits, drank the beer, pissed on the blackboard, screwed the other three dogs, claimed that he'd injured his back, filed a worker's compensation claim form and shot through on sick leave.

After a former leader of the Liberal Party retired from Parliament, he became internationally known for producing some of the world's best daffodils. He was often asked if he could send daffodil bulbs around the world but, in most cases, they'd perish before they'd arrive. As the years rolled on, he became more and more crippled with arthritis and needed to use his crutches to get around. This disability did not deter him from his enthusiasm for producing daffodils and one day he struck upon a perfect way to export the bulbs – he used a condom with a little water in it. The daffodil arrived at its destination hale and hearty. Having proof that the experiment worked, he then collected all his orders, which amounted to 144.

On a Friday evening he walked with some difficulty into the local chemist shop, and asked the chemist for 144 çondoms, not explaining the purpose to which he intended putting them. The chemist was somewhat taken aback but handed over the cache. The old man spent the weekend filling each condom with a daffodil and, as well, received a phone call from a customer ordering a further 144 bulbs. He returned to the chemist on Monday morning and asked him for another 144 condoms, adding, 'And this time give me 144. You short-changed me by 5 on Friday night!'

Two men formerly employed at a sheltered workshop that has been closed front up to Social Security to claim unemployment benefits. The counter clerk addresses the first man: 'What was the nature of your previous work?'

'I sewed the crotches into ladies' underpants,' he replies.

'Right, you're entitled to $100 a week as a compensation for lost wages,' says the clerk.

He turns to the second man: 'Previous work?'

'Diesel fitter,' he replies.

'You're entitled to $200 a week compensation,' says the clerk.

The first man objects, 'Why is he getting more? I had the really skilled job, with the sewing. When I finished a pair of pants, all *he* did was pull them over his head and say, "Dese'll fit 'er."'

FOOD FOR THOUGHT

There is a very famous international restaurant in London, just off Berkeley Square. They claim they can serve any national dish and, if they fail, the customer is given £100 reward. So an Australian bloke called Bruce thinks he'll try them on. He asks for kangaroo balls on toast. The waiter receives the order without blinking an eye, but after a very long time has elapsed, the dish fails to appear. Bruce then does his lolly and demands his £100. The waiter slips it to him hidden in a starched serviette, so that no other restaurant guest can observe the transaction, 'Please take the money,' says the waiter, 'but don't tell anybody. It would be very, very bad for business. You see, it's never happened before, never in our history.'

'Well,' said Bruce, in a conciliatory voice, 'I suppose that kangaroo balls are a bit hard to . . .'

'You don't understand, sir,' interrupted the waiter, 'we ran out of bread.'

A traveller staying at a rough bush pub was annoyed when the girl who brought his customary morning tea failed to materialise. After waiting some time, he dressed and made his way to the kitchen. 'Say, where's the chambermaid?' he asked the swarthy, barefoot cook.

'Blowed if I know, mister,' replied the woman, busily wiping out cups with her greasy apron. 'But the rest of the crockery comes from Japan.'

A city bloke was visiting the outback and he booked into an old hotel with an outside toilet. After he'd put his suitcase on the bed, the first thing he did was go to the toilet. Trouble was, he couldn't get near it for blowflies. So he went and saw the manager to make a complaint.

'I just went to the toilet and couldn't get near it for blowies.'

The manager looked up at the bar room clock and said, 'It's only 11.30, mate. Could you hang on for another half hour? Until 12 o'clock? The blowies will all be in the dining room then.'

Cucumbers are better than men because:

* the average cucumber is 15 centimetres long
* cucumbers stay hard for a week

* a cucumber never suffers from performance anxiety
* you can follow a cucumber in the supermarket – and you know how hard it is when you take it home
* cucumbers can get away any weekend
* a cucumber will always respect you
* you only eat cucumbers when you feel like it
* cucumbers don't need a round of applause
* cucumbers don't ask 'Am I the best?' How was it? Did you come?' and 'How many times?'
* a cucumber won't mind hiding in the fridge when your mother comes over
* a cucumber can stay up all night – and you never have to sleep in a wet patch.

The worst things about being an egg are:

* you only get laid once
* you come in a box with eleven other blokes
* only your mother ever sits on your face.

Tarzan, having swung through the trees all day, was feeling a bit crook, so he went home early. 'What's for tea?' he asked Jane. She pointed at a pot. He lifted the lid and saw that it was full of tiny finches. He pulled a face. 'What else have you got going?'

Jane pointed to a bigger pot. Tarzan lifted the lid and discovered chimpanzees floating around in the thick sauce.

'Oh, bugger,' he said, 'boring old finch and chimps again.'

Two roadworkers sit down for their lunch break. One opens his brown paper bag and exclaims in disgust, 'Aw, look mate! Flamin' raspberry jam sandwiches again!'

His mate says, 'Why don't yer go crook at yer missus and git her to give yer somethin' else?'

To which the first bloke replies, 'That's me trouble, mate. She's away and so I have to cut me own lunch!'

A little old lady with slightly failing eyesight was in the butcher's shop. 'Can I help you?' said the butcher.

'Yes, please. I would like a kilogram of your pissoles.'

'My dear lady,' said the butcher, indicating the appropriate sign. 'That is an "R", not a "P"!'

'Oh, all right then – give me a kilogram of arsoles.'

For the best part of six months, Mrs Martin had religiously visited her local butcher shop on Saturdays and bought four slices of bacon, half a kilo of sausages, three lamb chops and fourteen tins of Dinky-Di dog food. Curiosity eventually got the better of the butcher who asked how many dogs she had at home to eat all the tinned stuff she bought every week. A little embarrassed, Mrs Martin whispered to the butcher that the dog food was actually for her husband who ate two whole tins of it day in, day out.

The butcher was horrified. 'You shouldn't let him eat that,' he cautioned. 'It's not meant for humans, just dogs. At the rate he's putting it away I wouldn't be surprised if it killed him before much longer.'

'Don't you think I've told him that?' replied Mrs Martin. 'But it's all he wants and I'm tired of the arguments, so he can eat all he likes. Anyhow, it's none of your concern. Just fill my order, please.'

And so it continued, until one Saturday some six weeks later, Mrs Martin told the butcher she didn't want the fourteen tins of Dinky-Di any more, just the usual meat order. 'Great,' said a much relieved butcher, 'you've finally talked some sense into your old man and he's given up eating dog food.'

'If only that was true,' said a sad Mrs Martin. 'Actually, my husband is dead.'

'Ha hah,' mocked the butcher, 'I told you. Didn't I tell you the dog stuff would finish him off one day? I knew it'd happen. Why didn't you listen to me?'

'It wasn't the Dinky-Di at all,' sobbed the widow Martin.

'Okay, then,' roared the butcher, 'if it wasn't the blasted dog food, what killed your husband?'

Mrs Martin touched a tissue to her eyes, sighed deeply and said, 'Poor old thing. Last Wednesday he was quietly sitting in the middle of the road licking his dick and a car ran over him.'

A man went into a pub and ordered a dry martini. The olive went into a small glass jar he had brought with him. He drank quickly and ordered another. And another. Always putting the olive into the jar. After about an hour the jar was full and the man staggered out with it.

'What a weirdo!' exclaimed a customer.

'Not really,' said the barman. 'What would *you* do if your wife sent you out to get a jar of olives for tonight's party, and the shops were all shut?'

A woman who had eaten at a country pub visited the Ladies. On the way out as she was leaving the place she said to the waitress, 'You can tell the owner of this dump that I found your graffiti in very bad taste.'

'Okay,' said the waitress, 'but next time you should try our spaghetti.'

A road train heading west to the Channel country struck and killed a wild boar. The carcass was in pretty good nick so the driver decided to offer it to the publican at Cungamilla.

'Yeah, I'll give you 20 bucks for it,' said the publican, 'we're almost out of meat.'

A commercial traveller was stopping at the pub. At dinner the publican offered him the choice of roast pork, grilled pork chops or ham on the bone. 'Fresh killed, local wild boar,' said the publican proudly.

The traveller chose the roast and complimented the publican on the pork. 'Glad you liked it,' said the publican. 'You can have chops, or bacon, or ham, or brawn for breakfast. We don't waste anything out here.'

'Sounds good,' said the traveller, 'could I have a drink of water?'

'Yes, mate, but we've only got bore water.'

'Crikey,' exclaimed the traveller, 'you're right – you don't waste anything, do you?'

A cattle buyer and his mate were travelling back through northern New South Wales late one afternoon. They came across a pub and dropped in for a few well-earned ales. After a few drinks the offsider said to the barman, 'Can a man get a bite to eat around here?'

The barman said, 'Sure, what would you like? Steak and eggs or steak and onions?'

They settled on steak and onions and had one or two more drinks in the interlude. When the tucker finally arrived the buyer, who was hungry, grabbed the dish and started in to eat, only to spit out the first mouthful in disgust and exclaim to the barman, as he threw the plate on the floor, 'That would have to be the worst bloody meal I have ever tasted!'

By this time the pub dog is scurrying around and starting to lap up the food, so the barman retorted in know-all fashion, 'I don't know about the food being crook – the dog's enjoying his, isn't he?'

'Sure, he is eating it,' says the buyer, 'but look at the way he keeps licking his arse to get the taste out of his mouth.'

What's green and red and goes round and round at 100 kilometres an hour?

A frog in a blender.

What's hot, yellow and dangerous?

Shark-infested custard.

A traveller arrives at a country pub hot and very dusty. He orders a meal and a glass of water. After a while the meal arrives but not the water. 'What do you do to get a glass of water in this dump?' says the traveller. The cook replies, 'Well, you could try setting fire to yourself.'

A feller walks into the bar with his mate – an alligator on a chain. He says to the publican, 'Would you serve John Elliott?' 'Blood oath I would,' replies the publican, well aware that John Elliott owned one of Australia's greatest breweries.

'Well, I'll have a schooner for me, and John Elliott for the croc.'

The honeymooners looked at the list of meal times in their hotel.

Breakfast 6 a.m. – 11.30 a.m.
Lunch 12.30 p.m. – 3.30 p.m.
Dinner 6.30 p.m. – 9.30 p.m.

'Kevin,' wailed the bride, 'we'll be kept in eating so long we won't have time to go anywhere.'

A traveller arrives at an outback hotel and orders a meal.

'Only got corned beef, mate,' said the cook.

'That'll do,' said the traveller. He took a seat and when the meal arrived found it consisted of a slab of ancient corned beef and very little else.

'Could I have some tomato sauce to put on it?' the traveller asked. And the cook yelled out to the publican, 'Hey, boss, bastard out here thinks it's Christmas!'

During World War II in North Africa, an officer and twenty diggers were detailed to make a 21-day patrol in the desert. The question of who would be the cook arose. Bluey, who was known to have been a shearers' cook was suggested as eminently suitable. 'Not on your bloody life,' Bluey said, 'pick it out of a hat.' But the others all professed inability to boil water.

After a lot of argument, Bluey agreed to do it, with the provision that 'the first bastard who complains will have to take over the job'. He dished them up all sorts of concoctions and they got all sorts of pain and diarrhoea, but no one complained. Desperate, one morning, Bluey served them up what he said were rissoles.

As one bloke bit into his portion, he cried out, 'Jeez, it's camel shit!' But quickly recovering, he held up a finger and said, 'But mark you, very well cooked.'

The famous artist, Sir Russell Drysdale, is painting away in the Northern Territory thousands of kilometres from nowhere, when he becomes aware of somebody's eyes burning a hole in his back. Sir Russell turns around and there, on the other side of the gully, is an old swaggy. He's watching with fascination as the picture emerges on the canvas. They strike up a very one-sided conversation. Eventually, Sir Russell prevails upon the painfully shy traveller to join him around the campfire later that night.

'I hope you like curry,' he says, 'I've got a really good one simmering away. All I've got to do is get some rice on.'

Later on they're sitting eating by the light of the fire and Sir Russell notices that the old bloke is pushing all the sultanas to one side of his plate. 'Don't you like sultanas?'

'Aww,' says the swaggy, peering closely at his plate in the firelight, 'I thought they were blowies.'

THE DEMON DRINK

A member of the Temperance League was haranguing his audience about the evils of alcohol. Holding two glasses with transparent liquid in front of him, he declared the first glass to be filled with water, aqua pura! But the second contained pure alcohol. He then removed a tin containing worms from his pocket. He put the first worm into the water and it swam around happily. He then put a second worm into the alcohol and it instantly shrivelled up and died.

'There,' he thundered, 'what's the moral of that?'

There was complete silence until an old fellow at the back of the hall called out, 'it looks as if you drink alcohol, you won't have worms!'

The customer, rather the worse for wear, was staggering out of the pub just as a pair of pretty girls, identical twins, was about to enter. Observing his condition, they parted to let him through.

'Now how,' murmured the drunk, 'did she do that?'

A drunk, reeling his way homeward along a country road, came upon a large truck bogged at the side of it. A similar type of vehicle had driven up behind and was endeavouring to push it clear. The engines roared, wheels spun and their chassis quivered. The drunk stood watching in amazement and then became articulate, 'Stone the crows! Them things sure kick up a fuss, and a helluva din, when they're mating!'

A well-dressed man, having overindulged, was wandering alone in the city. He couldn't remember where his car was and couldn't remember where he lived. Floundering along, he was approached by a tall, bearded, distinguished-looking man who said, 'My son, let me help you.'

'Impossible,' said the man. 'I don't remember where I am or who I am.'

'My son, let me take you home.'

'How can you?'

'My son, I know all these things.'

And he did. And it came to pass that he found his home, knew where the key was, unlocked the door and put the man to bed. The man was thankful and though the room was spinning, he recognised it as his room. 'I've got to thank you,' said the man to the kind stranger. 'You've been wonderful. Tell me what is your name?'

'My name is St Paul,' said the stranger.

'That's a nice name – the same name as the bloke in *The Bible*.'

'The same,' said the stranger, 'for I am St Paul.'

The man sat up. 'You're St Paul? That's fantastic. I've always wanted to meet you because I have a question I wish to ask. May I ask you a personal question?'

'Certainly, my son.'

'Tell me, did those bloody Corinthians ever answer your letters?'

Mrs Briggs' hubby, Fred, worked night shift at the CUB. One night, around 1 a.m., a policeman knocked on her door with bad news. 'I'm sorry, Mrs Briggs, but Fred has had an accident.'

'Oh, sweet Jesus, what's happened?'

'I'm afraid he fell into a large barrel of beer and died.'

'The poor darling. Did he suffer a lot, do you think?'

'We don't think so, Mrs Briggs. You see, he got out six times for a pee.'

'I don't like one of the blokes who comes in here after work,' said the barmaid to the boss of the hotel.

'Why?' asked the boss.

'Oh, he orders a beer, drinks it, screws up his face, slams the glass down on the bar and yells out "Piss" very rudely and then walks out. He does it almost every night!'

'Well, you point him out when he next comes in,' said the boss.

The next afternoon, the bloke arrives and the barmaid points him out to the boss who walks up to him and says, 'Ay, you! Piss off!'

'Okay,' says the bloke, 'give us a small scotch then.'

Why did God invent beer?

So ugly girls could get screwed.

It's Dad's 90th birthday, and he and his son are celebrating at the pub. The father says that he will pay for all the drinks that night and says to the barman, 'We'll have double scotches please.' The barman serves them and asks for $10. Whereupon the father hands over a couple of bottle tops.

This outrages the barman who says, 'What the hell's this?' Whereupon the son takes the barman aside and says, 'Look, it's his 90th birthday. Just humour him. Allow him to keep paying with bottle tops and I'll fix you up at the end of the night.' The barman reluctantly agrees and, all night, the father pays for expensive drinks by throwing bottle tops onto the bar. At the end of the night they're walking out the door when the barman yells to the son, 'Come back here!'

'What's up?'

'Look, I've got all these bloody bottle tops and you said you'd fix me up at the end of the night.'

The son says, 'Sorry, I've had a few too many and I forgot. How much do I owe you?'

The barman says, 'Well, 465 bucks.'

'No problem,' says the son. 'Have you got change for a manhole cover?'

A devoted off-roader was showing his buddy the kit and preparations for a venture into the farthest reaches of the Sturt Desert. 'You've forgotten the most important thing,' said the friend.

'How's that?' said the adventurer.

'You've forgotten the gin and the vermouth,' came the reply.

'Gin and vermouth are important? How come?'

'Well, if the worst comes to the worst and your engine's blown up and your water and food are all gone and your radio equipment has failed and you're stuck in the middle of the boiling desert hundreds of kilometres from the nearest help, you get a glass and pour two fingers of gin into it, add one full finger of vermouth and before you get the glass to your lips, faces will pop over every hill and from behind every rock and say, 'That's not the way to make a martini.'

Two women walked into the Ladies' Lounge and ordered a couple of beers. 'Are ya gonna have another, luv?'

'Nah. It's only the way me coat's buttoned.'

A loudmouth Yank, looking for properties to buy around Barcaldine, is in the bar of the Shakespeare Hotel.

'Yeah, ma'am,' he says to the barmaid, 'ah'm looking to buy me a ranch – stations, you call them, they tell me. Ah come from Texas and ah'm looking for a big spread because where ah come from in Texas, everything is big. Why, do you know, mah ranch in Texas is so big, it takes a whole week to ride around it on a horse.'

'Yeah, ' said the wizened little ringer. 'We used to have a 'orse like that. We shot the bastard.'

A man goes into a bar with his wife and, immediately on sitting down, says to the bartender, 'Give me a drink, before it starts.' The bartender pours him a beer. The man drinks it.

'Give me another beer,' he says, 'before it starts.'

The bartender is puzzled. 'There's no entertainment here tonight, sir. The strippers come on Fridays.'

Again the man demands, 'Another drink before it starts.' Whereupon his wife interjects with, 'I think you've had enough to drink, dear.'

And the man says to the bartender, 'See! It's started!'

Two mates meet in a pub, one from Melbourne, one from Sydney. They have an intense debate over the relative virtue of their cities' beers. To settle the question of quality, they decide to send a sample of their favourites to a chemical analyst. After several days the document arrives back from the expert. It reads as follows: 'After exhaustive analysis of the respective properties of both fluids, I and my colleagues have reached the common conclusion that both Clydesdale stallions are too old for work.'

A guide on a coach tour said, 'On my left is the Opera House. On my right is the Town Hall. On my left is Hyde Park. We are now passing Darling Harbour. We are now passing the Rocks. We are now passing the oldest licensed hotel in New South Wales.' And a voice at the back shouted, 'Why?'

LOVE, MARRIAGE AND THE SEX WAR

Bruce enters a chemist shop. 'I want a deodorant.'

'Ball or aerosol,' asks the chemist.

'No,' says Bruce, 'armpits.'

The Bastard from the Bush was in the paddock when he saw the Grim Combine Harvester bearing down on him.

'Just let me have one last root with my wife, and then I'm ready to die!' he begged.

'Okay,' said the GCH, 'you've got ten minutes.'

So the BFTB races home, saying, 'Honey, I'm dying, this is our last root,' leaps on her and comes within minutes.

Then a voice from outside the bedroom window says, 'Your time is up!'

'Goodbye, honey!' says the BFTB, and heads for the door.

'Oh, that's all right for you,' says the wife. 'What about my orgasm?'

A tough-looking bloke turned up at the red light district in Kalgoorlie and said to the Madam, 'Give us the roughest sheila you've got.'

Pretty soon he's ensconced with a great big brassy-looking blonde, and as she slips her dressing-gown off, he strikes a wax match right across her breasts and lights a cigar. He's pleased that she doesn't seem surprised or at all concerned. So he turns away from her with a grin and proceeds to rip off his gear. When he's finished, he turns around, still puffing away and finds her with her back to him, bent double, clutching both her ankles.

'What are you doing?' he says.

She casually replies, 'I just thought you might like to open a bottle of beer before we got started.'

A shearer turns up at a Kalgoorlie brothel and asks the Madam if she's got anything different on offer. 'As a matter of fact, I have,' says the Madam. 'You'll remember that the circus was through here a few weeks ago? Well they sacked the contortionist. So I've given her a job.'

The bloke is enthralled at the possibilities. Once inside the shabby little room, he watches with fascination as the contortionist ties herself into something approaching a Gordian Knot. Whereupon he starts circling her, staring, scratching his head.

'What's wrong, love?' asks the woman in a somewhat muffled voice.

'Look, would you mind farting,' he says, 'just to give me a hint?'

Sheila and Bruce have not been practising safe sex. While Bruce never takes his socks off, he was disinclined to wear a condom. Now the poor girl discovers that she's pregnant and says, 'If you don't marry me, I'm going to jump off Sydney Harbour Bridge.' Bruce's reply is a fond slap on the back. 'You're not only a great root, you're also a good sport!'

'Am I the first girl you ever made love to?'

'You might be. Were you around the back of Rushcutters Bay Stadium at the Everley Brothers' concert in 1960?'

While visiting Sydney a French girl found herself out of money just as her visa expired. Unable to afford passage back to France, she accepted a proposition from a friendly sailor. 'My ship is sailing tonight. I'll smuggle you aboard, hide you down in the hold and provide you with a mattress, blankets and food. All it will cost you is a little love.'

The girl consented and late that night the sailor sneaked her on board. Twice each day he smuggled a few sandwiches below decks and took his pleasure. The days turned into weeks and the weeks might have turned into months if the captain hadn't noticed something going on. He sprang the sailor bonking the girl and said, 'Miss, I feel it's only fair to tell you that this is the Manly Ferry.'

Coming home unexpected, the junior executive finds his wife in bed with a naked bloke. He's about to shoot him when his wife says, 'Don't! Who do you think bought us that condo in Surfers, the BMW, the first-class tickets to London?'

'Are you the bloke?' asks the husband. 'Then get your clothes on. Do you want to catch a cold?'

Nigel and Cedric felt a bit limp, so to cheer themselves up they thought they'd stroll down to Luna Park.

'I'm going to go on the chair-a-planes,' said Nigel.

'Are you sure, Nigel?' said Cedric. 'You're ever so brave.'

So Nigel went on the chair-a-plane. Round and around he went until the chain broke on his seat, sending him hurtling through the air for about 300 metres until he slammed into a brick wall. Cedric ran over to the crumpled heap at the base of the wall and cried, 'Are you hurt, Nigel?'

A dazed Nigel opened his eyes and said, 'Am I hurt? I should say I'm hurt. I went around six times and you never waved once.'

An arrogant red rooster was giving chase to a fluttery little hen. To escape him, she scrambled to the highway and was promptly run over by a truck. Two old maids on a nearby porch witnessed the accident. 'You see,' said one, with an approving nod, 'she'd rather die.'

A girl invited a country boy to her flat for a drink where she introduced him to the ins and outs of carnality. He stayed the night and in the morning she said, 'How about some money?'

'Oh, no thanks. You've been too kind already.'

An old couple arrived at the doctor's surgery with a strange request. 'We want you to watch us making love,' said the man. Puzzled, he obliged. When it was all over he said, 'Well, that was pretty good, particularly considering your age.' And he charged them the standard fee for the consultation.

This happened for week after week. They'd make an appointment, bonk away and pay the bill. The doctor was unable to find anything wrong with the way they screwed and finally asked, 'What exactly are you trying to find out?'

'Nothing,' said the old bloke. 'She's married, so we can't go to her house. I'm married, so we can't go to mine. They charge you $100 at a decent hotel and even a crappy motel charges $30. So we come here for $18 and get $12 back from Medicare.'

Ginger docked at Circular Quay after a frustrating three-month voyage. Unfortunately he'd lost most of his pay playing poker on board ship, so when he eventually found a lady of the night all he could offer her was 50 cents and a pair of plimsolls. She refused with disdain. He wandered around Kings Cross in search of a more accommodating girl, but was refused time and time again. Eventually he found a more sympathetic lady who told him that although she could not possibly accept his offer herself, he could always try Megan down the road. But she warned him not to expect much as she was very unresponsive and would probably just lie there passively.

He eventually found Megan and as times were hard she reluctantly agreed to accept the 50 cents and the pair of plimsolls for her services, but told him not to expect any kind of response from her. Ginger began the amorous act and after a few minutes was pleased to find an arm coming around his back. This was followed shortly after by a leg curling around his rear. Ginger, who had always fancied himself as a bit of a Romeo, gasped, 'I knew you wouldn't be able to resist my charms.'

'Don't worry about me, love,' answered Megan, 'I'm just trying on the plimsolls.'

When's a good time to fake an orgasm?

When a rottweiler's fucking your leg.

There are four kinds of orgasm. Positive, Negative, Religious and Fake. The positive goes, 'Yes, yes, yes, yes!' The negative, 'No, no, no, no!' The religious, 'Oh God, God, God, God!' And the fake, '. . ., . . ., . . ., . . .!' (Fill in the name of your lover in the blank spaces.)

How do you tell if a Mosman woman is having an orgasm?

She puts down her cigarette.

Some time ago a young couple were wed in a small country town. After the wedding they set off for their new home on a pony and trap. The journey went pleasantly enough, and they chatted together enjoying each other's company. After a short while the pony stumbled, but only enough to slightly disturb the newlyweds. The husband said, 'That's one,' and the new bride thought nothing of it. A little later the pony stumbled again which caused the husband to let out a stream of abuse, adding, 'That's twice.'

By now the bride was a little disturbed, but she said nothing, wishing to retain the post-wedding ambience. Unfortunately the pony stumbled yet again which caused the groom to lose his temper. He shouted, 'That's three times!' reined in the pony, jumped off the trap, took out a rifle and shot the pony. The bride was astonished. She ran up to her husband, beat him on his chest and abused him mightily. He pushed her aside and said, 'That's once.'

A young newlywed couple arrived in a rustic hotel in the Victorian high country. The proprietor checked them into the establishment and noticed that the young woman was a matchless beauty. He thought to himself, 'If that bloke is worth his salt he won't surface till dinnertime.'

At about 6 a.m. next day, the proprietor saw the young husband walk through the foyer and out the front door, loaded up with fishing equipment. He thought to himself, 'That's odd, I know what I'd rather be doing.' The husband didn't return until well after dinner that night.

This ritual went on for a few days, with the young bride staying mostly in the hotel room, and the young husband spending all his days fishing. It was too much for the proprietor, he had to know what was going on. So one morning, not long after dawn, he collared the young fellow as he made his way through the foyer. He asked the young man, 'Why do you go fishing all day and leave such a beautiful wife by herself in your room? If I was married to such a woman, I don't think I'd be interested in bloody fishing!'

The young man replied in a whisper, 'My wife has gonorrhoea, so we don't indulge in that sort of thing.'

The proprietor, taken aback by this revelation, was silent for a while then said, 'There are other, um, possibilities, you realise?'

'Yes, I know,' whispered the young man, 'but she also has haemorrhoids and that makes it difficult, you understand . . .' Surprised as he was, the proprietor pressed on, 'But there are further alternatives you must know of!'

The young man whispered in reply, 'Yes, yes I know, but she also has herpes and that makes it somewhat risky.'

The proprietor was stunned and asked the young man, 'With all these complaints and diseases, why the hell did you marry the woman?'

To this the young man replied, 'She also has worms and I love fishing.'

A man and his wife were about to spend their wedding night in a country pub. When the woman had gone upstairs, the bloke asked the barman for a glass of beer, a pot of green paint and a hammer. The barman obliged, but couldn't help asking, 'Look, we've had a lot of strange requests over the years, but never one like this. What's it all about?' To which the man replied, 'I ordered the beer because I like beer. When I get to my room, I'll go into the bathroom and paint my dick green. And if my wife says she's never seen one that colour before, I'm going to thump her with the hammer.'

One of Australia's battleships, containing 300 men, ran aground. Only one sailor survived. He found himself lying on the sands of a deserted island where, fortunately, there was an abundance of fresh water and tropical fruits. As he grew stronger he grew more and more amorous. But the only creature that might provide solace was a very belligerent wild sow. But even when he trapped her, he found that he couldn't possibly keep her still long enough to have his way with her. Flattery didn't work, nor did tying her down. The pig just wouldn't come across. Months passed and his frustrations intensified. The sow would not surrender her honour.

Then, one day, he saw another human being washed up on the beach. It was Elle Macpherson, almost dead from exhaustion and exposure. He dragged her up to his hut, revived her, and spent the next week administering fresh fruit and water until she was feeling much better. Quite her old self. She explained that she'd been on a photographic assignment, posing for her calendar, when the luxury yacht had hit the same reef as the battleship.

'Now I will do anything you desire,' she said. 'You have saved my life and I will be glad to reward you in any way.'

'Well, Elle,' he said, 'there's one thing. Do you think you could hold that fucking pig still?'

In an anatomy class, a young woman is called upon to name the three most important parts of the male body. 'First,' she stammered, 'there's the brain. Second,' she continued, 'there's the heart. The third thing . . . the third thing . . .' She looked hopelessly confused. 'The third thing . . . I've had it on my fingertips . . . I've had it on the tip of my tongue . . . I've had it drilled into me a thousand times . . . but I just can't remember it.'

After trying unsuccessfully for years to have a baby, a young couple went to see their doctor. After examining them both and finding nothing wrong, he suggested they do it 'like the cats do it.'

'Like the cats do it?' asked the husband. And then, with a smile, said, 'Oh, I see what you mean.'

A week later the doctor saw the young man walking down the street with a black band on his left arm. 'Who died?' he asked. 'My wife,' replied the young man. 'You see, we took your advice, but she fell off the roof.'

The various ages and stages of sex:

First, you have bathroom sex where you root in the shower or the bath.

Then you have kitchen sex where you root on the sink or the kitchen table.

Then there's bedroom sex where all your rooting is confined to the bedroom.

Finally, you have corridor sex where you see your wife in the hallway in the morning and say, 'Go and get fucked!'

A bloke approaches a girl and says, 'What about a fuck?'

'No!' she answered indignantly.

'Well how about lying down while I have one?'

At the height of the recession we had to have, a husband is desperate to save money. He tells his wife to learn to cook better. 'That'll save on restaurants.' She must learn to iron his shirts 'to save on the ironing lady'. She'll need to clean the house properly, 'to save on the cleaning lady'.

And she said, 'Why don't you learn to fuck properly, so we can get rid of the gardener?'

A little boy jumps up from the breakfast table and heads for the door. Mum says, 'Where are you going in such a hurry?'

'I'm going to the massage parlour, Mum.'

The mother grabs his arm. 'You won't leave this house until you stop this nonsense. Tell me where *are* you going?'

'Orright, Mum. I'm going to the park to play footy with the kids and Dad can go and get his own hat.'

A man met his ex-wife at a party and after a few drinks asked her if she would spend the night with him 'just for old times sake'.

'Over my dead body,' she said.

'That's right,' he replied, 'let's not change a thing!'

A middle-aged couple was deeply asleep when, about 3 a.m., the doorbell rang. The wife said, 'Percy, go downstairs and answer the door.'

Percy staggered downstairs and said, 'Who's there?'

The voice on the other side said, 'The Boston strangler.'

Percy walked back upstairs and said, 'It's for you, darling.'

Three young fellows from Brisbane were really close mates. They all went to Brisbane State High School, did their apprenticeships together at Evans Deakin and played League for Easts. They met their girlfriends one weekend at the Gold Coast and eventually decided on a joint wedding ceremony and honeymoon at Brampton Island, where they had adjoining units. After checking-in, they went to their units to change for a swim. When the first bloke's wife undressed she revealed herself a bit on the undernourished side. 'Gawd,' cried her husband, 'haven't you got small tits – I didn't realise you were so skinny!'

'What a rotten thing to say,' she cried, 'and on our wedding day, too. Leave me alone. Get out!' So he went out onto the patio and had a smoke.

In the second unit, the wife also undressed, but she was a bit on the generous side. 'Bloody hell,' cried hubby, 'I didn't realise you were fat. You kept that lot covered all right.'

'You beast,' she screamed, 'what a thing to say on our wedding day. Get out!' Husband number 2 joined number 1 on the patio. Shortly, they were joined by number 3. 'Ah,' cried the first two together, 'you must have put your foot in it!'

'No, I didn't,' said number 3. 'But I could have.'

After the first night in a honeymoon hotel the husband went downstairs to the restaurant to order breakfast.

'Egg, bacon and sausages for me, and lettuce for my wife,' he told the waiter.

'Isn't lettuce a rather unusual breakfast choice, sir?' said the waiter.

'Yes,' replied the husband, 'but I want to see if she eats like a rabbit as well.'

The Admiral took his daughter aside on her wedding eve and said gruffly, 'Mavis, I've never advised you on sex since your mother died, but I feel that as you're marrying a sailor I must say just one thing. Let him do anything he likes, but if ever he asks you to do it "the other way" don't let him.' Even though the daughter did not know what he meant, she promised to follow his advice.

The couple were married and had a blissfully happy sex life for six months. But all this time

Mavis had 'the other way' in the back of her mind. One evening she blurted out, 'Please Jack, let's do it the other way tonight.'

Her husband looked at her incredulously. 'What,' he said, 'and risk having babies!'

There was to be a bush wedding and the groom, just a simple country lad, was nervous about having to make a speech, so the vicar gave him a few tips to set him on the right track. The young man's mother had always made sure there was a nice cup of freshly percolated coffee for him whenever he came in from his work on the farm, so she decided to give him a special little coffee percolator so he'd always be able to have the coffee the way he liked it.

When it came the groom's turn to make his speech, he started off just the way the vicar had instructed him – 'I want to thank youse all for comin' along to me weddin' and I want to thank Betty's Mum and Dad for having such a lovely daughter who's now me wife and I specially want to thank me Mum for the perky little copulator she gave me.'

After thirty years of marriage an Italian woman addressed her husband one evening. 'For thirty years I've done everything you expected and asked of me without complaint. Now after thirty years together I wish to ask two things of you so that I may be even happier in my old age.'

'What are they?' asked the husband.

'My love, always you picka your nose,' replied the wife, 'and I wish you would not do that.'

'And the other thing?' enquired the husband.

'Whenever we have sex, always you are on the top and I would really like to be on the top of you sometimes.'

'Well, my dear,' said the husband, 'I have tried, as you have, to make our marriage good, and foremost in my mind I have kept the words of your father when we were betrothed. He said only two things to me. First, he said, "Now you marry my daughter make sure you always keep your nose clean". And second, he said, "And don't fuck up".'

'Yoo hoo, darling, I'm home,' called the man on his return from work. He entered the bedroom and saw a man and a woman just uncoupling. In a vicious voice he demanded, 'What's *she* doing here?'

Bruce returned home late, after boozing with his mates. The house was in darkness. He undressed in the lounge and, as he slipped into bed, remembered that he'd been neglecting his wife of late. Later, he went to the bathroom to clean his teeth and was astonished to find his wife in the bathtub reading a book.

'What the hell are you doing here?' he says.

'What's wrong with relaxing in the bath?'

'Nothing. But who the hell is that in our bed?'

'I told you that my mother was coming to stay!'

At this, Bruce slammed the door, went back to the bedroom and screamed at the recumbent figure, 'Why the hell didn't you tell me it was you!'

'How could I, Bruce, when we haven't been on speaking terms for years.'

What does an Aussie call matching luggage?

Two carrier bags from an offlicence.

What is the definition of an Aussie virgin?

A lamb who outpaces the shepherd.

How do you get an Aussie onto the roof?

Tell him the drinks are on the house.

What's an Aussie intellectual?

Someone who can understand the plot in 'Neighbours'.

What's the difference between an Aussie and a Qantas jet?

The jet stops whining when it gets to England.

Why do Aussies wear short trousers?

To keep their brains cool.

Why do Aussies put XXXX on a can of beer?

They can't spell 'beer'.

What's an Aussie man's idea of foreplay?

Digging his wife in the ribs and saying, 'You awake? Okay, brace yourself'.

Why did the Aussie haemophiliac die?

He tried acupuncture as a cure.

Why do Aussie men give their penises names?

It's because they don't want 95 per cent of their decisions made by a stranger.

What do you call the useless piece of skin on the end of a penis?

A man.

Why are Aussie men like toilets?

They're either engaged or full of shit.

What do you call 100 Aussie men standing in a paddock?

A vacant lot.

Why do Aussie men suffer from premature ejaculation?

Because they can't wait to get to the pub to tell their mates about it.

How do you get an Aussie man to do sit-ups?

Put the remote control between his toes.

What is an Aussie man's idea of a seven-course dinner?

A hot dog and a six pack.

What is the difference between Aussie men and government bonds?

Bonds mature.

Why don't Aussie men get piles?

Because they are perfect arseholes.

Why do Aussies have clear-top lunch boxes?

So they can tell if they're going to work or coming home.

Why wasn't Jesus Christ born in Australia?

Because they couldn't find three wise men and a virgin.

Why does a woman need an arsehole?

Well someone has to put out the garbage.

How many men does it take to put the loo seat down?

None! No men on earth know how it's done.

Why does it take three women with premenstrual tension to change a light globe?

Because it just *does*, all right?!!!'

How many men does it take to change a light globe?

One, and nine to pin the medal on his chest.

How many women does it take to change a light globe?

One, plus two to form a collective, and three to make an application for funding.

What do you call ten blondes standing ear to ear?

A wind tunnel.

How do blondes' brain cells die?

Alone.

What is the blonde's mating call?

I think I'm drunk.

Where would you find a blonde the day his ship comes in?

At the airport.

What did the blonde say to Humphrey B. Bear? Speak to me! Speak to me!

Why do blondes drive BMWs?

Because they can't spell Porsche.

How do you know when a blonde's been using a dishwasher?

When the drain's clogged with paper plates.

What's the difference between a blonde and a shopping trolley?

A shopping trolley has a mind of its own.

What do an intelligent blonde and the Yeti have in common?

No one has seen either of them.

Why do blondes take the pill?

To find out what day it is.

Why did the blonde cross the road?

Who cares? She should have been chained to the bed.

How do you confuse blondes?

Give them a box of M&Ms and ask them to arrange them in alphabetical order.

How do you confuse blondes?

Give them a box of Jaffas and tell them to leave the red ones until last.

How do you confuse blondes?

Sit them in a round room and tell them to find the corner.

Why don't blondes like pickles?

Because they can't fit their heads in the jar.

A blonde and a brunette were walking in a park and the brunette said, 'Oh, a dead bird!' The blonde looked up and said, 'Where? Where?'

How do you kill blondes?
Put spikes in their shoulder pads.

What's a brunette's mating call?
Has that dumb blonde gone yet?

How does a blonde turn on the light after having sex?
She opens the car door.

What's the difference between a blonde and the *Titanic*?
We know how many went down on the *Titanic*.

How do you know when a blonde's been doing a crossword?
Because all the squares are coloured in.

Why was the blonde so pleased when she finished the puzzle in six months?
Because the cover said three to five years.

What do you call six blondes standing in a circle?
A dope ring.

How do you drown a blonde?
You put a mirror on the bottom of the pool.

What do you call a blonde with half a brain?
Gifted.

How do you make a blonde laugh on Monday morning?
Tell her a joke Friday night.

How many blondes does it take to make a chocolate chip cookie?
Thirteen. One to mix the dough, and twelve to peel the Smarties.

How do you give a blonde a brain transplant?
Blow through her ear.

Why do blondes have TGIF printed on their shoes?
So they know their Toes Go In First.

Why do blondes have fur on the hems of their dresses?
To keep their necks warm.

Why do blondes carry ID cards?
To remind them who they are.

How can you tell when a blonde has been using your computer?
There's white-out on the screen.

What do blondes and cowpats have in common?
The older they get the easier they are to pick up.

What does a blonde call a bottle of black hair dye?
Artificial intelligence.

What's the best part of being married to a blonde?
You can park in the handicapped parking space.

What's the first thing a blonde does in the morning?
Gets dressed and goes home.

What do you call a brunette standing between two blondes?
An interpreter.

Why don't blondes order quiche?
Because they can't pronounce it.

How do you know when a blonde's been shoplifting?
Her bag is full of free samples.

How can you tell when a ransom note's been sent by a blonde?
Because of the stamped, self-addressed envelope.

How do you make a blonde's eyes sparkle?
Shine a torch in her ears.

What do blondes wear behind their ears to attract men?
Their ankles.

What do blondes and turtles have in common?
Once they're on their back they are screwed.

What do peroxide blondes and a 747 have in common?
Both have big black boxes.

Why don't blondes like vibrators?
Because they chip their teeth.

What do a blonde and a computer have in common?
You don't know their true value until they go down.

Why did the blonde climb over the glass wall?
To see what was on the other side.

How does a blonde spell blonde?
B-L-oh it doesn't matter anyway.

How does a blonde like her eggs?
Fertilised.

Why can't blondes pass a driving test?
They keep jumping in the back seat at red lights.

How many blondes does it take to change a lightbulb?
Three. One to find a ladder, one to find the bulb and one to find a man to do the work.

How does a blonde kill a fish?
She drowns it.

What did the blonde say when she found out she was pregnant?
I hope it's not mine.

Why are all dumb-blonde jokes one-liners?
So men can understand them.

Three newcomers, a Yank, a Pom and an Irishman, blow into an outback pub and settle down for a quiet ale. They can't take their eyes off a huge bloke with no ears who is sitting across the bar. The publican comes around and warns them not to stare at the bloke as he gets 'real stroppy. He'll come round and barrel you in a minute!' But the Yank has another look at him. Sure enough, round he comes, grabs the Yank around the throat and belts him against the wall.

'What are you lookin' at, stupid?' said the bloke with no ears.

'Why, pardner,' the Yank drawls, 'I was just admiring your hair. You always want to look after that hair or you'll end up wearing a toupee like myself.' And he dips his wig.

Earless drops him and says, 'Sorry, mate,' blushing as he returns to his corner.

They go back to their beers, until the Pom steals a glance over his middy and sure enough around the bar comes Earless. He collars the Pom and whacks him against the wall. 'What are you lookin' at, stupid?'

'Why, old chap, I was just admiring your teeth! You always want to look after those teeth or you'll end up wearing dentures like myself,' he said, demonstrating them with a click.

'Sorry, sport,' said the earless one. He put him back down and straightened him up.

They returned to leisurely sipping on their grog until the Irishman had to have one last look at the space behind the mutton chops. As sure as eggs, around the bar he came. Earless grabbed the Irishman by the shirt, smacked him against the wall and said, 'What are you lookin' at, stupid?'

'Matey, I couldn't help but admire your eyes! You've got beautiful eyes! You always want to look after your eyes or you'll end up wearing spectacles like myself.' And he squinted beguilingly through the lens. 'And that'd be no good because you've got no ears to hang them on.'

One of Alan Jones' players at Balmain has an eye gouged out in a scrum. Inspired by his coach's peptalks he refuses to give up and has a glass eye fitted. But he finds it both socially and professionally limiting. He puts his name down for an eye transplant, but there's a lack of donors. One night, going home from training, his glass eye fails to detect a bloke trying to pass his car on a motorbike. At that very second he decides to change lanes and sends the motorbike flying.

It's late at night and nobody's around and it's clear to the rugby player that the cyclist is dead. He can tell this because both his eyes are wide open and they're pretty good eyes. So he cuts one out with his Swiss Army knife so he can rush to his transplant surgeon and have it popped in his socket. And he replaces the cyclist's missing eye with his glass one.

Everything's fine for a few weeks – his new eye is working wonderfully. But he starts to worry about the cyclist. Perhaps, after all, he wasn't dead. So one arvo he calls into the local pub and asks about the accident.

'Yes, the bloke was dead okay,' says the barman, 'but it's still very mysterious.'

The rugby player feels a chill of fear. 'Mysterious?'

'Yeah, how the hell did he manage to ride his bike all the way down from Surfers Paradise with two glass eyes?'

A man who has had one leg amputated receives an invitation to a fancy dress party. A suitable disguise will take some imagination, he realises, so he goes to a costume hire shop for assistance. The young woman at the counter assures him she has the ideal outfit, and from the storeroom she brings out a velvet coat, tricorn hat, an eye patch and a stuffed parrot. 'There you are, Long John Silver.'

'No, no, no,' despairs the man, 'I'm meant to be in *disguise*. Everyone will recognise me if I wear this.'

The assistant frowns. 'Well, I don't know. Let me have another look.' A minute later she returns with a large sheet. 'Here, I'll cut two eye holes in this and you can go as a ghost. Everything covered.'

'Oh, fabulous,' says the man sarcastically. 'What an imaginative idea.'

The assistant has one more try. Reaching under the counter she whips out a large tin of golden syrup and plonks it on the counter. 'Right, pour this over yourself, stick your wooden leg up your arse and go as a toffee apple!'

Australian troops taken prisoner of war during the Malayan campaign found that they could use bamboo in many ways – as a building material, as a diet supplement, and even as a substitute for toilet paper.

On one occasion troops were paraded to have their rear ends examined by the medic looking for signs of typhoid. While this was in progress, one of their mates was returning to the ranks after visiting the toilet. Noticing that a piece of leaf was still sticking to the tail of the new arrival, a digger broke into uncontrollable laughter. 'Look at that. Just goes to show that that bloody bamboo will grow anywhere!'

The breakdown of the State School dunny obliged the Father at the neighbouring parish school to extend appropriate hospitality. Soon a disgusted Sister was with him to complain about the appalling behaviour of the Protestant boys engaged, it appears, in a competition as to who could urinate the highest. 'What did you do then, Sister?' enquired the Father.

'I hit the roof!'

'Well done, Sister.'

A crim stands before the court on a charge of theft. He was caught standing outside Myer with a handful of expensive necklaces. The window in front of him was part of Myer's and it had been smashed in. A brick was found at the crim's feet. Anyway, he chose to represent himself in court. He argued to the judge that it was not he who committed the crime but rather his left arm. After all, it was his arm that threw the brick and then grabbed the necklaces.

The judge thinks to himself, 'Well, I'll fix this smarty', and proceeds to announce his verdict. He tells the crim that he's decided that he has been persuaded by such an original and eloquent defence and that he has found his left arm guilty, and hereby sentences it to six years' hard labour! The crim smiles, thanks His Honour, twists off his false arm, and hands it to the judge before skipping out of court.

The old bushie staggers across the Simpson Desert, lost and alone but for his faithful dog, Blue. He hasn't eaten for days and his water ran out this morning and, collapsing, he reaches out to pat his loyal friend. Voice breaking with emotion, he says, 'I'm sorry, mate. I've really stuffed it this time, but I'm afraid it's you or me and, well, what I'm trying to say is, I'm going to have to shoot you and eat you, mate.'

Later that night, the old bushie finishes gnawing on his last bone and chucks it on the little pile by the fire. He sits there awhile, wistfully eyeing the flickering flames and then his eyes wander to the little pile of bones and then back to the flames. And he sighs and sadly says to himself, 'Gee, I wish Blue was here. He'd have really loved them bones.'

The old farmer from north Queensland visited the Big Smoke for the first time since WWII. When he came back he told his mates that he'd had his eyes opened and that among other things, he'd bought himself one of those new plastic toilet brushes and was eager to try it.

A few days later his mates saw him in town and asked him how the new bush was working. The old guy replied, 'It does a real good job, but shit it hurts.'

A big young Irish jackeroo from Wellmoringle comes into town for the first time in twenty-two months, makes a beeline for the chemist shop, confronts the pretty young thing behind the counter and makes his requirements known. She goes through a variety of styles and he finally settles on the one he wants.

'How much is that one?'

She says, '92 cents plus tax.'

'Oh, bugger the tacks,' he says, 'I'll wire it on.'

Wally loved Wendy, so he decided to prove it by having her name tattooed on his penis for her birthday. After dinner, he showed it to her in all its glory. WENDY, tattooed along the length of it.

Wendy thought it was beaut. Even when it was detumescent and all you could see was WY.

Later on, Wally was in a public loo when he noticed that the bloke peeing beside him also had WY tattooed on his dick. Wally was at once suspicious and curious. 'Is your girlfriend's name Wendy?'

'No,' said the other bloke, 'I've never had a sheila called Wendy. Why?'

'Well, it's your tattoo,' said Wally as he rather shyly revealed his own.

'Great,' said the bloke. 'Very impressive.'

'You can only see WY,' said Wally, 'but when I get an erection it says WENDY. What does yours say?'

'Well, it's a bit of a mouthful. It says WELCOME TO WOOLLOOMOOLOO AND HAVE A NICE DAY.'

The scene is a country dance. Sitting under a window, the classic wallflower. She has no make-up, wears glasses, has her hair in a bun and very skinny legs. All the other girls are dancing except her. A bloke arrives late and sees that she's the only one available, so asks her for the fox trot. It's not long before she's in his car and they're on their way to his flat. 'I won't waste any time with this sheila,' he thinks to himself. So as soon as they arrive he grabs her hand, opens his fly and places his generative member on her palm. 'Now,' he says, 'that's a penis!'

'Oh,' she says, 'is it? It looks the same as a prick, only smaller.'

What is the difference between white onions, brown onions and a 30 centimetre dick?

None. They all make your eyes water.

The young farmhand was a simple peasant who knew nothing about the facts of life. One day he spotted the dairymaid bending over to milk the cows as her dress rode up. He felt an erection, but did not understand what was happening. Frightened, he ran to show his boss.

'It's perfectly natural, lad, it happens to us all.'

'Well, I don't like it, it frightens me.'

The farmer sighed. 'Okay lad, if it worries you that much get rid of it. Next time it happens grab a couple of handfuls of cow dung and rub 'em on. It'll soon go down.'

The next time it happened the boy rushed into the barn, dropped his trousers and picked up the dung. The maid walked in, saw the erection and her eyes lit up. 'What you doin' then?'

'I'm gonna rub the dung on my cock to make it go down.'

She dropped her knickers, laid in the hay. 'That'd be a terrible waste. Put it up here.'

So he did. Both handfuls.

A male customer approached the counter of the new Body Parts shop, the latest in anatomical technology. 'Would you have any spare penises?' he asked.

'Certainly, sir,' replied the assistant and produced one from under the counter.

'Very nice,' remarked the customer. 'Would you have one a bit bigger?'

'How about this?' suggested the assistant, producing a fair sized member.

'Yes, it is pretty good,' agreed the customer. 'I hate to be a nuisance, but would you have a bigger one, preferably uncircumcised?'

'Feast your eyes on this then,' said the assistant, triumphantly laying out on the counter a huge cock.

'Fantastic!' the customer enthused. 'Exactly the size I'm after. Now, have you got one in white?'

A Regional Development Conference in Sydney was concluded by a banquet at which all the dignitaries made the usual platitudinous speeches. At a table most distant from the podium was a young officer from the Department of Foreign Affairs and Trade. By the time they reached him the food was cold and the wine warm. He was thoroughly pissed off until he noticed an attractive young woman from the New Zealand delegation opposite him. 'Hmmm,' he thought, 'I've never had anything to do with a Kiwi bird. I wonder if we can manage a bit of trans-Tasman cooperation.'

So he knocked a knife onto the floor and, in retrieving it, caressed the girl's ankle. When he sat up, she gave him a little smile. 'Ah,' he said to himself, 'encouraging,' and knocked a fork onto the floor. Retrieving it, he ran his hand up her calf and was rewarded with a broad grin.

'Excellent,' he cried to himself, and down went a spoon. This time, he ran his hand right up under her long gown and massaged the back of her knee. When he sat up, the girl was writing on a scrap of paper. 'Great,' he thought, 'it's on tonight, no worries.' The girl passed the paper across to him and he opened it.

'Evince no surprise when you reach my balls – Evans, ASIO.'

There was an 80-year-old wheat cocky who married a stunningly beautiful 23-year-old blonde. After a month, his mate asked him how married life was. 'Oh, it's terrible, it's terrible,' he says.

'What do you mean?' says his mate.

'Well, I just can't keep my hands off her,' was the reply.

A month later he saw the cocky again and asked him how married life was now. 'Oh it's terrible, it's terrible. I just can't keep my hands off her.'

Two months later he saw him again and asked, 'How's married life now?'

'Fantastic,' came the reply.

'What do you mean?' said his mate. 'What happened?'

To this the cocky replied, 'Well, I sacked all me hands, and bought meself a Combine Harvester!'

Old Danny had been a regular at the old local pub for as long as anyone could remember, and took a poor view of the place being renovated. When the work was completed old Danny frowned his disapproval.

'I suppose it's all right,' he grumbled, 'but I liked things the way they were. Even the old spittoon in the corner has gone. I'm gonna miss that.'

'Yeah,' said the publican, 'you always did.'

Two Welsh miners were working in a shaft in the Hunter Valley. On their way home after a hard day's shift, they fell into conversation with a couple of girls from a local farm. Each finished up escorting a girl in a separate direction. The next day the miners met and one said, 'How did you make out last night?'

'Great, couldn't have been better – what about you?'

'Likewise. Only I got into a hell of a row with the missus.'

'How come?'

'Well, I was having a wash in the tub when my missus noticed my tossle was all clean.'

His mate said, 'You bloody fool – why didn't you do like me? I gave mine a couple of slaps with me cap.'

An eight-year-old child asks Mummy about the origin of babies. Deciding she is now too old for stories of storks or cabbages, mother decides to explain the procreative functions of penis and vagina.

'And when Daddy does that to Mummy, you get a baby.'

'But Mummy,' says the child, 'last night when I came into your bedroom, you had Daddy's penis in your mouth? What do you get that way?'

'Diamonds.'

What's the difference between a clitoris and a pub?

Nine out of ten Aussie blokes know where to find a pub.

Russ Hinze, the immensely fat Queensland Cabinet Minister, was on a fact-finding mission in North Queensland with his minders. They stopped for lunch at a remote café and were surprised to find turtle soup on the menu. After the owner verified that it was fresh turtle soup, Russ said, 'I haven't had that for years.' Off went the owner and while the party had a pre-lunch drink they could hear from the kitchen a continual and vigorous 'chop-chop' sound followd by an increasingly passionate string of invective. Eventually one of the minders went to investigate the delay and found the owner trying to decapitate a live turtle with a cleaver whenever the head appeared. But every time, the turtle was too fast. The minder said to the owner, 'When I say NOW you can get him!' He moved to the rear of the turtle and rammed his finger into the rear apperture of the carapace, upon which the turtle's head appeared, wearing a look of amazement and indignation. And the owner had no difficulty in chopping it off.

Impressed with the efficiency and simplicity of the strategy, the owner asked, 'Where did you learn that trick, mate?' to which the minder replied, 'Oh, that's easy. How do you think we get Russ's tie on each morning?'

A golfer made a terrific drive which everyone complimented. He said, 'Oh, I don't suppose it's too bad for a bloke with a wooden leg.' With that he unscrewed the leg to prove his point. At the next tee he drove even further and again he was complimented. 'Oh, not too bad for a bloke with a wooden arm.' He rolled up his sleeve and unscrewed his arm. At the next, he drove a real beauty straight down the fairway about 400 metres. Again he was complimented, and he said, 'Oh, it's not too bad for a fellow with a wooden heart.' He invited one of the ladies to go behind a bush with him to show her. He was gone for about twenty minutes and one of the others thought they should find out why they were away so long. And there they found the bloke screwing his heart out.

Why does a man have a hole in the end of his penis?

To get a bit of air to his brain.

HISTORY AND THE YARTS

During the French Revolution, a tumbril brings an Englishman, an American and an Irishman to the guillotine and the executioner steps forward, shushes the jeering crowd and sneers at the doomed men. 'So, which of you miserable wretches weel be zee first to die or shall I pick whichever one takes my fancy to face zee blade of doom?' The Englishman steps forward and says, 'No need to be like that, chappie, I'll happily face your blade of doom.'

'Hah!' crows the executioner. 'But how weel you face zee blade of doom? Face up, like a proud Frenchman, or face down like zee snivelling, cowardly English dog you are.'

'Put like that, chappie,' says the Englishman, 'face up it is.'

And so he takes his place at the guillotine, facing the glinting, razor-sharp blade, and the grinning executioner says, '*Au revoir*, miserable English pig-doggie,' pulls the handle and the blade goes whoosh, thunk! And stops a millimetre from the Englishman's neck. '*Sacre bleu*!' cries the executioner, 'it ees a sign from God, you are free to go.' And so the Englishman is freed.

The executioner approaches the American and the Irishman.

'So, who ees eet to bee? Do I drag one of you up here, crying and peesing in your pants, or . . .'

'Ah, shuddup,' says the Yank, shouldering aside the Irishman. 'Let's get this show on the road.'

'*Mais oui*,' says the executioner. 'But how shall you face zee blade of doom. Face down like the miserable snivelling coward you are . . .'

'Face up, and I repeat, shuddup!' says the Yank and he lays down and with an '*Au revoir*, American pig-doggie,' the executioner pulls the handle and, whoosh, thunk! The razor-sharp blade of doom stops a millimetre from the American's throat. '*Sacre bleu*, another act of God! You are free to go,' says the executioner.

Then he turns to the Irishman, but before he can get out a word, the Irishman says, 'If you don't mind, I'd prefer you to keep a civil tongue in your head and in answer to your questions, I'm coming of my own free will and I'll be facing the blade of doom, thank you very much.'

'Hah,' cries the executioner, and when the Irishman is in place, he says, '*Au revoir*, Irish pig-doggie,' but just as he is about to pull the handle, the Irishman stops him.

'Wait a minute!' he calls out, casting an appraising eye up at the guillotine, 'I think I be seeing your problem . . .'

All the Merry Men, and Maid Marion, gathered around Robin Hood's deathbed, waiting for the inevitable end. Manfully, heroically, Robin struggled up and said, 'Friar Tuck, fetch me my long bow. I will fire an arrow out the window and, wherever it lands, that's where you will bury me.'

Deeply moved, they placed the bow and arrow in his trembling fingers, propped him up and faced him towards Sherwood Forest. And with an immense effort, Robin aimed and fired. And so it came to pass that they buried him on top of the wardrobe.

Red Riding Hood is tripping merrily through the forest. Out jumps the big bad wolf, who grabs her and with fangs salivating says, 'Aha, Red Riding Hood. I'm going to gobble you up . . . gobble, gobble, gobble!' To which Red Riding Hood responds, 'Gobble gobble gobble, that's all they think about around here. Doesn't anybody fuck anymore?'

Once upon a time there dwelt, in Fairy Land, a particularly beauteous young man. He was kind of heart and fair of face and form. But, woe and lack-a-day, he also felt accursed, because he had, protruding from his navel, a silver screw. Verily, he could conceal it by adjustment of doublet and hose, yet it did sorely trouble him. So that each day he would go into the deep dark woods and sit in a glade, staring sadly at the silver screw.

Then one day a crone came through the woods carrying a bundle of faggots. The kindly youth adjusted his clothing to conceal his shame and said to her, 'Old crone, those faggots are too heavy for you to carry. Let me lift thy burden.'

The crone was grateful and took him through the woods to her gingerbread cottage where she revealed that she was, in fact, a witch. 'But you have been so kind to me that I will grant you a boon.'

The youth didn't need to consider the boon for a moment. 'Please, please, rid me of this silver screw in my navel.'

The crone bade him go to a distant mountain and to climb to a rocky ledge. There he was to exhort the heavens using a magic spell that she provided. The youth followed her instructions and, struggling through the cruel and stinging woods, came to the ledge. There he began to exhort the heavens, using the crone's magic spell. Suddenly, the blue skies vanished and dark sombre clouds appeared. A great wind sprang up and he heard a sound like angels singing. And from the black clouds came a great shaft of light that focused on him. And down that shaft of light came a giant golden screwdriver.

As the singing reached a crescendo, the screwdriver reached the silver screw, fitting into the groove on its head. The giant golden screwdriver turned once, twice, thrice, then retreated up the shaft of light which, in turn, disappeared. As did the dark boiling clouds and celestial chorus.

The young man looked down at the silver screw and tentatively touched it with trembling fingers. Yes, it was loose! So he turned the screw once, twice, thrice!

And his bum fell off.

Roy Rogers was aseat Trigger as they wended their way home after a most satisfying day at work tending the boundary fences on Roy's large spread. About a mile from the homestead Roy noticed a trail of dust rising from the trail that led from home to the main gate. As he approached, he saw that it was a large squad of cavalry soldiers led by Major Ted. As he came up to the column of troops Major Ted called, 'Whoa!' and addressed the famous cowboy.

'Good evening, Mr Rogers,' he said.

'Good evening, Major,' replied Roy Rogers.

'Are yo' heading home, sir?' asked the Major.

'I am indeed, yessir, I'm looking forward to a real meal.'

'Just before you go, Mr Rogers, there are a few things you should know.'

'Like what, Major?'

'Well, sir, the Indians have been on the rampage over at your homestead.'

'What's happened?'

'There's not much left I'm afraid, Mr Rogers,

they scalped your five children and appear to have raped the girls beforehand. They also raped your wife and mother before killing them. All the cattle are gone and they put an arrow through your dog Pal. Most of the village is burned to the ground and they put poison in your water supply.'

'Christ, I better get over there and see what I can do.'

'Mr Rogers . . .?'

'Yes, Major?'

'Just before you go. Hows about a little song for the boys?'

The Lone Ranger was finally captured by his enemies, the Comanches. As a tribute to his valour, they offered him one last wish. Our hero whistled his loyal and highly intelligent horse Silver, whispering something in his ear. The horse wheeled around and disappeared in a cloud of dust. A few minutes later Silver reappeared with a beautiful, naked and heavy-breasted girl on his back.

She approached the valiant Lone One, and pushed her pussy in his face. But for perhaps the first time in his life the Lone Ranger showed not the slightest interest. Instead he whistled Silver once more. The horse came promptly. The Lone Ranger hooked a finger in Silver's nostril and yelled in his ear, 'I said 'posse' you dumb horse.'

A would-be gunslinger is walking down a street in Texas one afternoon when he hears the music of a honky-tonk piano coming from the local saloon. He decides that it's now or never, and bursts through the swinging doors, stands legs astride, hat pulled down and arms akimbo. No one seems to take much notice as he looks around the room, spots the piano player with a cigar sticking out of his mouth and a lighted candle on each side of the piano. The gunslinger draws a gun, twirls it three times, shoots out the flame of the left-hand candle, and returns the gun to its holster.

Everyone sighs, looks agape and lulls into silence. All except the piano player who just keeps on playing. The gunslinger repeats the performance and shoots out the right-hand candle. Exactly the same response from everyone, but the piano player keeps on playing. So the gunslinger draws both guns, twirls them three times and shoots the cigar out of the piano player's mouth. And the piano player just keeps on playing.

Discouraged, the gunslinger goes to the bar and asks for a drink. The barman pours a drink and comments on the fine piece of shooting. He asks if the gunslinger would mind a bit of advice as he is obviously hankering to become a gunslinger.

'No, not at all,' replies the gunslinger.

'Well,' says the barman, 'firstly, I'd file the sight off the end of the barrel and smooth it right down. You don't need that as you shoot from the hip and it only hinders a fast draw. Then I'd file off the trigger guard and again smooth it right down. You don't need that either, as you could get your finger caught in it one day and it could cost you your life.'

The gunslinger thanks him for his advice and asks if there's anything else he should do.

'Yes,' replies the barman, 'lastly I'd cover both guns in Vaseline.'

'Vaseline?' queries the gunslinger, 'wouldn't that make it slippery?'

'That's the whole idea,' explains the barman, 'because when Wyatt Earp over there finishes playing the piano, he's going to come over here and shove those guns right up your arse!'

A publisher was fishing in the Atlantic, when he caught a rather unusual salmon. 'Please let me go,' begged the fish, and because it was small he threw it back. Later, when fishing again, he caught the same salmon and once more it begged to be released. 'No,' said the publisher, 'no way.'

'Oh,' replied the fish, 'not even if I tell you that I write poetry?'

'What about?' said the publisher, impressed despite himself.

'Oh, the sea and the *Titanic*. I spend a lot of time swimming around the wreck. My name is Rusty and if you let me off the hook, you can publish my first book.'

'Of course,' said the publisher, 'we'll call it Rusty Salmon's *Titanic Verses*.'

Did you hear about the blind man who was given a silver nutmeg grater for Christmas?

Said it was the most violent thing he'd ever read.

Oscar Wilde was reclining, as was his wont, in velour smoking jacket, carnation in button hole, vellum-bound volume of poetry in hand, in his undergraduate rooms, when he heard a great clatter on the stairs below and a door burst open to reveal eight hearty and perspiring rugger players manifestly bent on disturbing his repose.

Wilde rose to his feet and surveyed the scene in a dignified but slightly nervous manner. 'I say, chaps,' he said, 'I may be inverted, but I'm not insatiable.'

What's an innuendo?

An Italian suppository.

How many surrealists does it take to change a light bulb?

Fish.

Just imagine, for a moment, if there were no hypothetical situations.

The Bendigo Players have had a pretty good season. They got good reviews in the *Courier* for their production of *The Fantasticks* and sold out their three-night season of Terence Rattigan's *The Deep Blue Sea*. Their production of *Dimboola* also went pretty well. So they decided to end the year in a blaze of glory with a production of *Hamlet*. Unfortunately the bloke they chose to play the Prince of Denmark was not inordinately talented and kept muffing line after line and missing his cues. Moreover he spoke so badly that he could barely be heard by the audience which began to heckle and boo more and more loudly. Finally the actor strode to the front of the stage and yelled, 'Don't blame me, I didn't write this crap!'

Robert Newton and Wilfred Lawson, both great drinkers, were appearing in an Old Vic Shakespearean season and had to be hauled out of the pub to go on stage. Newton appeared first, and staggered around until a voice in the audience called, 'Hey, you're pissed!' Newton stopped, turned to the audience and said, 'You think I'm pissed? Wait till the Duke of Buckingham comes on.'

Bloke in the bar turns to the guy next to him and says, 'Can I buy you a beer?', and the other bloke replies, 'Look, I'll be perfectly frank with you so we won't waste any of our precious time. See, I'm a genius. And if you buy me a beer you'll want to talk, and what could you say that would interest me, a dead-set genius with an IQ of 196?' And the bloke says, 'An IQ of 196! This is incredible. I'm a genius too, with an IQ of 195 – we can talk! Bartender, two beers.' And so they settle down to discussing quantum physics and the great theories of the cosmos.

Down the bar a bit, a bloke nudges his neighbour and says, 'How about these two? I'm not stupid, in fact, I have an above average IQ of 127 but I wouldn't have a clue what these geniuses are talking about. Quantum what? Theories of where? It's way over my head.' And his neighbour says, 'You have an IQ of 127! I'm above average, too. My IQ is 126 – we can talk! Bartender, two beers.' And so they settle down to discussing feminism's impact on the Australian film industry and the safety features of Volvos.

Further down the bar, a bloke nudges his neighbour and says, 'Check this out, would you? Whatever those genuises are talking about, it's complete gobbledegook to me, and I'm not ashamed to admit that whatever a feminism is, I don't think I need one because I'm a complete moron. I mean all this stuff is way over my head.' And his neighbour says, 'What's your IQ?' The bloke replies, 'I'm stupid, okay. I've got an IQ of 63. You wanna make something of it?' And his neighbour says, 'This is great! I'm a complete moron, too. My IQ is 65 – we can talk! Bartender, two beers. So, been to any auditions lately . . .'

(By a simple adaptation of the punch line, this joke can be made to refer to a variety of professions, e.g. 'Written any good ads lately?')

A man went into a Paddo antique shop and said he'd just found two items in the loft of his old house. And he produced an old fiddle and an even older painting, both in a very tatty condition. He asked the dealer to give them a wipe over and suggest a value for them. The dealer asked the owner to return in a few days. When he did so, the dealer confessed that the examination had turned into one of those good news/bad news stories. So the customer asked for the good news first.

The dealer then said that what he had found was that the items were a Stradivarius and a Rembrandt, which had so amazed him that he had got them authenticated by a valuer of his acquaintance, a man who did regular assessments for Sotheby's.

'What then is the bad news?' asked the customer.

'Well, you see sir, Stradivarius never really made it as a painter . . .'

A young man was collecting money around Wagga for the Murrumbidgee and Murray River Valley Drum and Fife Marching Band. He walked up a long path to a cottage and knocked. An old lady answered the door. 'Madam,' he said, 'I am taking up a collection for the Murrumbidgee and Murray River Valley Drum and Fife Marching Band and I thought you'd like to contribute.'

'What's that you say?' said the old dear, cupping her hands to her ear.

The young man raised his voice. 'Madam,' he shouted, 'I am collecting money for the Murrumbidgee and Murray River Valley Drum and Fife Marching Band and I thought you'd like to contribute.'

'You'll have to speak up,' yelled the old lady.

The young man took a deep breath and roared out: 'MADAM, I AM TAKING UP A COLLECTION FOR THE MURRUMBIDGEE AND MURRAY RIVER VALLEY DRUM AND FIFE MARCHING BAND AND I THOUGHT YOU MIGHT LIKE TO CONTRIBUTE.'

'I still can't get it,' yelled the old girl, her hands cupped to both ears. The young man gave up and started to walk down the path. As he did so the old lady called out, 'Don't forget to shut the gate.'

'Oh, bugger the gate,' said the young man, all but under his breath.

'And bugger the Murrumbidgee and Murray River Valley Drum and Fife Marching Band,' yelled the old girl.

Two men were before the court charged with sodomy. In the course of evidence it was revealed that the man enacting the female role was a trumpet player in the Ashfield Town Band. When he heard this, the Judge immediately said, 'Case dismissed.'

The Prosecutor got to his feet and said, 'But your Honour, this is a proven case.'

'Case dismissed,' repeated the Judge.

'But your Honour,' shouted the Prosecutor, to be interrupted by the Judge who said, 'Have you ever heard the Ashfield Town Band play?'

'No,' confessed the Prosecutor.

'Well, I have,' said the Judge, 'and you can take it from me, they all want fucking.'

On the Mundi Mundi Plains, just north-west of Broken Hill, is a small town called Silverton. The story is told of the old miner who spent most of his time telling stories to tourists in return for a free beer at the local pub. One day, he threw an old sugar bag on the bar, opened up the tied end, and out stomped a large goanna. He bet the tourists that the goanna could play the piano. The goanna jumped off the bar, went over to the piano and started to play. The tourists were amazed.

After a few free beers, the old miner rushed outside to his beaten up FJ ute and started to rummage around in the back. One of the tourists asked him what he was looking for.

'I've got a bloody black snake that can sing in here somewhere.'

The word got around the tourist buses quickly, and everybody stood in the tiny bar. The old miner came in with another sugar bag and emptied it on the bar. Out slithered a long black snake. 'The bugger can sing!' said the old miner. The tourist dollars lined the bar in bets. The old miner was worried. He had only bet for free beers. He picked up the snake and draped it over the piano, the goanna began to play and the snake burst out into song. The tourists all cheered, the old miner picked up the hundreds of dollars in bets. He started to walk out the door when he broke out in uncontrollable laughter.

'I fooled you mob. The bloody snake can't sing. You see, the flamin' goanna's a ventriloquist!'

A man walked into a rough dockside pub in Port Melbourne and bought a pot of beer. Placing the beer on the table, he went across the room to speak to a friend and returned to his seat to find a monkey astride his glass cooling his testicles in the beer. He went over to the landlord to complain but the landlord said, 'The monkey belongs to the pianist, go and tell him.'

Aggrieved, the man went over to the pianist and said, 'Do you know your monkey's testicles are in my beer?'

Looking through his alcoholic haze, the pianist said, 'I don't, mate, but hum a couple of bars and I'll soon pick it up.'

TRAVEL TALES

An Aussie bloke is touring the world and he's in Spain, in a little coffee bar, drinking coffee, funnily enough. On the wall alongside him is a huge bull's head on a wooden plaque. Up close it's enormous. Massive horns, black silky hair, awesome!

The Aussie turns to the bartender and says, 'What's the story behind the bull's head? Excuse me mate . . . you . . . Yeah, it's you I'm talking to. What's the story behind the bull's head. Interesting yarn, is it? Around the bull's head? El Bull's Head? El Head-o de Bullula . . .?'

The bartender has gone very pale. His hand clutching the coffee cup has the shakes and the knuckles are blueish-white.

'Please, Senor,' he says, 'do not espeak to me of thees bull, for thees bull has keelled my brothir.'

The Australian feller, very sensitive to changes in mood, as most Australians are, says, 'Aw, sorry about that. Well, I've only just heard. Your brother was a bullfighter, was 'e, your brother? Bullfighter was 'e? Bullfighter, your brother, was 'e?'

'No,' says the bartender. 'He was sitting there one night and head fell on him.'

Two Australians, with zinc on their noses, were inspecting St Peter's in Rome. 'Gee, look at them Michael Angelo transfers!'

'Not transfers, mate, friezes. Michael Angelo friezes.'

'Well what about them muriels then?'

'Murals, mate, murals.'

At this moment an Italian priest opened the shutter of the confessional and offered to give them a guided tour.

'That's all right sport, you finish your shit in comfort.'

Bluey and Curly, two old Aussie diggers, won the lottery and decided to go on a world tour. In London they go to the Carlton for dinner. After a while Bluey says to Curly, 'I've got to go!' so they whistle up the head waiter and ask, 'Where's the little house, mate?' The head waiter said, 'Little house? Do you mean the lavatory, sir? Across the room, through the archway, across the passage, through the door, down two steps and there you are.' Bluey thanks him and sets off – across the room, through the archway, across the passage, through the door, falls ten metres down the lift shaft, picks himself up, dusts himself off and says, 'Bugger the second step, I'm gonna do it here.'

A businessman rushed into the station and just managed to catch the Brisbane to Rockhampton express. On taking his seat he asked the conductor what time the train reached Gladstone.

'There's no stop in Gladstone, Wednesdays,' replied the conductor.

'What!' exclaimed the businessman.

'There's no stop in Gladstone, Wednesdays.'

'But it's imperative. I have an important meeting there.'

The conductor is adamant. 'This is the weekly express and there's no stop in Gladstone, Wednesdays.'

After much argument a compromise was reached. The conductor agreed to ask the driver to slow down to 60 kilometres an hour as the train went through Gladstone. He would then hold the businessman out of the carriage window, the businessman could get his legs running in thin air as fast as he could and when the conductor thought his leg speed was sufficient he would lower him down onto the platform.

So when the train reached Gladstone this plan was put into action and the businessman hit the platform running at full lick. He ran the full length of the platform, hoping he could stop himself before the end. Just as the last carriage of the train was passing him by, his collar was grabbed by the strong arm of a shearer who heaved him back on board through an open window.

'You were lucky there, mate,' said the shearer, 'there's no stop in Gladstone, Wednesdays.'

A social worker, two children, a lawyer, and a Christian Brother were passengers on an aeroplane when suddenly the door to the cockpit opened and there was the pilot, one parachute strapped on his back and another in his hand.

The pilot says, 'The plane is going to crash, I can't do anything and there are only two parachutes. One is mine and you'll have to decide about the other one.' And he leaps out of the plane. The passengers are terrified. They start sweating and wringing their hands.

The social worker says, 'Perhaps we could strap the children together in the parachute.'

The lawyer screams, 'Fuck the children . . .'

And the Christian Brother says, 'Do you think we have time?'

Two birds were sitting on the roof of an aircraft hangar when an air force jet flew over them, just clearing the hangar roof.

One bird said to the other, 'Shit, he was going fast.'

And the other bird said, 'So would you if your bum was on fire.'

Two typical Australians, wearing blue singlets and thongs, decide to take a trip overseas. Barry and Gary arrive in Rome and are soon caught up in all things Italian – the food, the music, the women. They go into an Italian bar one night and ask the waiter what Italians drink. The waiter informs them that it's usually wine. 'But some people, for example, the Pope, drink other types of liquor.'

'What does the Pope drink?' asks Barry.

'The Pope drinks crème de menthe,' replies the waiter.

'That'll do us,' says Barry and Gary, 'we'll have two pots of this crème de menthe stuff then. '

The next day Barry and Gary wake up very hungover and very ill. Barry says to Gary as they lie near death on the hotel floor, 'If the Pope drinks that stuff all the bloody time no wonder they have to carry the poor bugger around.'

It was the start of the wet season and the English tourist stopped his car at the edge of a stream flowing across the road he was travelling. 'I say, my man, shall I be able to ford this stream?'

'Yeah, mate,' said the cocky, 'she'll be right.'

The Pom drove into the water and sank like a stone. When he spluttered to the surface he shouted, 'I thought you said it was safe to cross!'

'Can't understand it, mate,' said the cocky, 'that water only came halfway up our ducks!'

An Australian tourist was booking into a pub in Killarney.

'Will you have a room with a bath or a shower?' asked the receptionist.

The Aussie, considering his budget, asked what was the difference.

'Well,' said the receptionist, 'with a shower you stand up.'

From the diary of a young girl on her first cruise in the Pacific.

August 14: What a beautiful sunset as we are leaving Sydney Harbour.

August 15: The sea is beautiful and calm. I am slightly bored.

August 16: I met the captain.

August 17: The captain asked me for dinner.

August 18: When I refused the captain's

advances, he threatened to scuttle the ship.

August 19: I saved 2600 passengers and crew.

What's the difference between an English backpacker and a German backpacker?

About 200 metres.

RELIGIOUSLY OBSERVED

Some Brides of Christ were visiting the Taronga Park Zoo. They were all ooohing and aaahing as they gazed down at a huge gorilla. He was gently chewing a banana and reflectively eyeing the crowd. One of the demure young lasses of the cloth reached out a slim arm and beckoned this magnificent beast in a friendly gesture. The wind stirred ever so slightly and blew the hem of the nun's habit up the pit wall and, in a flash, the gorilla leapt the narrow moat, ran up the pit wall, wrenched the habit, beckoning arm and young nun into a screaming bundle under his long, strong arm – and bounded into his bamboo thicket with a look in his eye.

Some considerable time later, the zoo's gamekeepers were able to recover the young and incoherent nun from the grip of the gorilla. She was rushed to hospital and treated for a variety of bodily and mental wounds, which served to put her in a silent and reclusive mood for months.

At last the Mother Superior of the convent could stand it no longer and remonstrated with the numbed nun to the effect that she should put the unpleasantness behind her and get on with His works. She had certainly had a dreadful experience but was fully recovered physically and only through doing Good Works would her mind get well again.

However the young nun just broke down and cried. 'But he never calls, he never writes . . .'

A rabbi and a Roman Catholic priest were alone in a railway carriage. After a while the Catholic priest leaned forward and said to the rabbi, 'I understand in your religion you're not allowed to eat pork.'

'That is correct,' said the rabbi.

'Well, just between you and me, have you ever tasted pork?'

'As a matter of fact, I have.'

After a pause the rabbi said, 'I understand in your religion you're not allowed to have sexual intercourse.'

'That's correct.'

'Well, just between you and me, have you ever had sexual intercourse?'

'As a matter of fact, I have.'

The old Jewish rabbi slapped him on the knee and said, 'It's a damned sight better than pork!'

An Australian hellfire preacher wanted to impress his congregation. He arranged for a boy to get above the pulpit in the loft, instructing him to light a piece of paper and let it flutter down when he reached the great climax of his sermon. 'When I shout "send fire from Heaven" light the paper and let it flutter down.' The great day came and the thunderous sermon was given. The preacher shouted, 'Send fire from Heaven,' but nothing happened. He shouted again, 'Send fire from Heaven'. Still nothing happened. He shouted again and again and again. Finally the voice of the boy could be heard. 'I can't . . . the cat's pissed on the matches.'

During the brief, distinguished reign of Pope John XXIII, a young priest riding his bike in New York was stopped at the traffic lights and saw Christ walking across the pedestrian crossing. Excited by the sight, he rode feverishly to the cathedral and reported the incident to the Monseigneur. The Monseigneur said, 'This is too big for me to handle – you'll have to speak to the Cardinal.'

The Cardinal was then informed of the incident and said, 'This is too big for me to handle – I shall have to ring Rome.' So the Cardinal got out the green phone, dialled Vat 69 and spoke to the Pope. He said to the Holy Father, 'We have a dreadful problem in New York. Christ is here and he's coming to the cathedral. What are we going to do?' There was no reply from the Pope, just heavy breathing.

The Cardinal then said, 'Your Holiness, you'll have to advise us. He will be here at the cathedral in a few minutes.'

There was another long silence at the end of the line. Finally the Pope said, 'You betta lookka very bizzi . . .'

A priest and a minister travelling in a plane sat next to each other. After take off, the hostess asked the priest whether he desired a drink. He replied, 'Scotch and soda, please'. She asked the minister whether he desired the same. 'No thanks,' he said, 'I'd rather commit adultery than drink alcohol.' The priest turned to the hostess and said, 'May I change my order? I didn't know that I had such a choice.'

Two nuns drove to the supermarket in their red Mini Minor to do the weekly shopping. Unable to find a parking spot, one rushed inside the supermarket while the other kept looking. After completing the shopping, the first nun returned to the parking area and asked a man standing nearby whether he'd seen 'a nun in a red Mini?' His reply was, 'Not since I signed the pledge.'

In a country hotel in Queensland the vicar was lunching with his bishop who was undertaking a pastoral tour. The waitress approached and turned to the vicar. 'What will you have, Les?' The bishop raised his eyebrows, mildly surprised at the familiarity. Then it was his turn. 'And what will little Robin redbreast have?'

Jesus was hanging on the cross at Calvary when he saw Peter walking by and yelled out to him. 'Hey, Pete, mate, come up here for a minute. I've got something to tell you!' So Peter started going up the hill, but was intercepted by a guard who cut off his arms. He staggered around from the blow and then heard Jesus calling him again.

'Hey, Peter. Come up here. I've got something to tell you!' So Peter tried again, but this time he got his legs cut off.

'Come on, Peter, it's really important,' cried Jesus. So Peter rolled himself to the top of the hill and gasped, 'Okay, what is it?'

'I can see your house from here!' said Jesus.

Did you hear the one about the nun who was working in the condom factory and thought she was making sleeping bags for mice?

After an exciting sermon, one of the Reverend Nile's parishioners remained seated in an otherwise empty pew, still thrilling to the great man's tirade against the gay and lesbian mardi gras. He noticed that the Reverend had left his sermon on the pulpit. Intrigued, he couldn't help but take a peek. More interesting than the text, which he'd already heard, were the marginal jottings, 'Argument weak here – shout very loudly.'

There was a sizeable graffiti on the wall of Central Railway Station in Sydney. JESUS LIVES! Below it, in smaller lettering, someone had put the question, 'Does this mean we don't get an Easter holiday?'

All the cardinals gather in the Sistine Chapel to elect a new Pope. An assassin plants a bomb and all are killed instantly. So the eighty of them arrive at the Pearly Gates *en masse*. As they're strolling in, Peter stops them and says, 'Where do you think you're going?'

'We have come to collect our eternal reward,' they chorus, 'we are princes of the church.'

'Well, nobody gets straight in without answering this question. Have you committed adultery?'

Suddenly the cardinals look very sheepish and

confused. Then, one by one, they shuffle outside the gates leaving only a single cardinal within.

'Okay, okay,' says Peter to the seventy-nine cardinals. 'Away you go to Purgatory for twelve months. And take that deaf bastard with you.'

It was suggested to a staid and somewhat absent-minded Bishop that he attend a sermon by one of the younger prelates who was attracting surprisingly large crowds with new-style sermons. The Bishop was particularly taken with one of the prelate's anecdotes, 'Some of the happiest hours of my life were spent in the arms of another man's wife. I'm referring, of course, to my mother.'

The bishop decided to borrow this for one of his own sermons a few weeks later. He began, 'Some of the happiest hours of my life were spent in the arms of another man's wife.' Whereupon his face went blank and he said, 'And do you know, I can't for the life of me remember who she was!'

Old Fred worked in the same sawmill for thirty-seven years and on every day of those thirty-seven years he stole a piece of wood. Over the years this amounted to quite a lot of wood. In fact he was able to build himself a house, a shed and even a small place for his daughter when she married. On his retirement the firm threw a big party for Fred, putting on food and a keg and all the trimmings. The Managing Director attended and presented Fred with a gold watch, saying that he'd been such a valued and trusted employee.

Afterwards, Fred moped about the house in a depressed state. When asked by his wife what was wrong, he replied, 'I just can't live with my conscience. There I was being made a fuss of by all those people and they didn't know I'd been pinching wood every day for thirty-seven years.'

'Look,' she said, 'go to confession. It doesn't matter that you haven't been to church since you were a kid. It will ease your conscience.'

Reluctantly Fred trotted off to confession and saw Father Murphy. He said, 'Bless me, Father, for I have sinned. I worked for this firm for thirty-seven years and every day of that thirty-seven years I stole some wood from them. I can't live with myslf. How can I make amends?'

Father Murphy thought for a moment and said, 'Well, Fred, this is a pretty serious matter, so for your penance I want you to make a novena.'

Fred looked at him quizzically and replied, 'I'm not sure what you mean, Father ... but if you've got the plans ... I've got the timber!'

The small outback town had grown a bit and become more scattered so that the local clergy – a Salvation Army captain, a Roman Catholic priest and a Jewish rabbi – were having a hard time keeping each other from stealing their respective flocks. A hasty meeting of the local branch of the Council of Churches was called and, after a good deal of haggling, it was finally agreed they would contribute, equally, to the purchase of a second-hand motor car.

The great day finally arrived and down the main street swung the Army band with the old black A-model rolling behind. At the Post Office the priest stepped out and, midst clouds of incense, sprinkled the ancient chariot with holy water. The rabbi was dumbfounded! What could he do to better these symbolic acts of proprietorship? He racked his brain.

At last inspiration! Down to the beloved acquisition he swept, waving the Star of David and, drawing a pair of tinsnips from the folds of his gown, whipped two inches off the exhaust pipe!

Father O'Flaherty, who was known to like an occasional flutter on the horses, was given a certainty for Saturday by one of his parishioners. But he was told that he had to back it on the course because, if they lost their price, they'd pull it. He thanked the parishioner profusely and began looking forward to Saturday when he remembered that he had scheduled confessions. 'Bloody hell, I can't cancel them,' he cursed. Then he realised he had Michael, a novitiate priest in training with him.

So he approached Michael and said, 'How about doing confessions for me on Saturday.' Michael was shocked. 'I can't do that, Father, I haven't received the sacrament.'

'It's all right, Michael, no one will know and I'll pay you twenty dollars.'

'Twenty dollars is tempting but I wouldn't know what to say, what penances to give,' said Michael.

'It's easy,' said Father O'Flaherty, 'come and look inside the confessional.' He showed Michael inside the priest's side of the confessional and there on the wall was an alphabetical list of sins and their recommended penance. 'See how easy it is,' he said. So Michael agreed to do it.

Confession time arrived on Saturday and the first sinner entered the confessional, 'Bless me Father, for I have sinned ... I have been guilty of telling lies.' Michael ran his finger down the list – A, B, C ... L – Lies – and saw the relevant penance – three Hail Marys, which he gave, and the follow-up blessing. 'Well,' he thought, 'that wasn't too hard,' and began to relax.

In came the next sinner. Same routine, the penance was found and given, and the sinner departed. Then a third sinner entered. 'Bless me Father, for I have sinned ... I have been guilty of having oral sex.' Michael ran his finger down the list – came to O – but there was nothing about oral sex. He began to get agitated and broke out in a bit of a sweat. Just then he looked out the window of the confessional and saw an altar boy walking past. 'Pssst,' he called. The altar boy came over.

'What does Father O'Flaherty give for oral sex?' he asked.

'Oh, usually a can of Coke and a Mars bar.'

A naive young Catholic priest, returning from his rounds, had to walk back through Kings Cross. As he stopped at a corner to cross, one of the ladies of the night approached him and asked, '$200 for a naughty, Father?' Not knowing quite what to make of this, he continued on his way. The same thing happened to him several more times, each time a different girl but asking the same amount. Eventually he arrived back at the seminary and sought an audience with the Mother Superior. 'Mother Superior, what's a naughty?'

'Look, it's $200 – the same as up the Cross. Take it or leave it!'

For many centuries, at Christmas, most of the world's religious leaders paid a visit to the Pope at the Vatican. Each visitor would give a token gift to the Pope, which the Pope blessed and then, unopened, gave back to the giver. For years the Popes had wondered what the Jewish rabbi would have given to the head of the Catholic Church. To settle the question, a recent Pope organised for one of his bishops to intercept the proffered gift, quickly open it and have a look inside, and then hand it back to the Pope.

So the rabbi duly presented his gift to the Pope, wishing His Holiness a happy Christmas. The bishop quickly took the gift behind the throne, opened it and saw what was inside. Then just as quickly he handed it back to the Pope who passed it back to the rabbi with a blessing and his thanks. The Pope could hardly wait to hear what the bishop had found in the 'gift'. Finally the bishop told the Pope what he'd found – a bill for the Last Supper!

A novice went to a monastery where the monks were only allowed to speak two words a year, and those to the abbot. At the end of each year they were given an audience and said their two words. Naturally they were expected to be something along the lines of 'Jesus loves' or some other eternal verity. However at the end of his first year the novice offered, 'Bed hard' and at the end of the second year, 'Food bad' and at the end of the third year his two words were, 'I quit'.

'I'm not surprised,' said the abbot, 'you've done nothing but whinge ever since you came here.'

Two missionaries in the depths of the New Guinea highlands are working hard to convert the local tribe to Christianity. One Sunday, the chief organises a big feast to which the missionaries are invited. As soon as they arrive, they are stripped and bundled into a large cooking pot, already bubbling with vegetables and fragrant herbs. The chief smiles in anticipation. Suddenly, one of his sons rushes forward and spears one of the missionaries.

'Why did you do that?' frowns the chief.

'He was eating all the potatoes.'

When the Queen has a baby, a 21-gun salute is fired.

When a nun has a baby, they fire the dirty old canon.

A nun is in the shower when there's a loud banging at the convent door. All the other nuns are out the back, in the garden.

'Who is it?' she calls out.

'I'm the blind man from the village,' is the reply.

So she runs downstairs in the nude and opens the door.

'Great knockers,' says the visitor. 'Where do you want the blinds?'

Each week the Mother Superior at the convent had a novice drive into town in the Ford to do the shopping. And each week the girl, on her return, would complain that she'd been stopped by police. 'I really don't want to go into town any more,' she implored the Mother Superior. 'Can't you get somebody else to do the shopping?'

'This is really very strange,' said the Mother Superior. 'Are you driving too fast? Are you going through red lights?'

'No, no,' said the novice. 'But no matter how carefully I drive they stop me.'

The Mother Superior decided to accompany the novice on the next trip, to see what was going wrong. She did her best to keep out of sight in the back seat. The novice was driving very, very carefully towards the shopping centre, but lo and behold there was the familiar flashing of blue lights and the sound of sirens. The police car stopped in front of the convent's Ford, and a couple of cops got out. As they walked towards the novice they began unzipping themselves.

'You see, Mother,' said the young girl, 'it's the same every week. Here goes with the bloody breathaliser.'

An old man decided to write a letter to God:

Dear God,

I am nearing the end of my life. The doctors tell me I am dying of cancer and have only a few months to live. In fact, as You know, throughout my entire life I've had nothing but bad luck. But no matter what You have inflicted on me, I have never lost my faith in You.

In return for this loyalty I ask just one thing of You. Please prove Your existence to me by sending $100 in cash, and I will die a happy man.

Yours insignificantly,

An Old Man.

The letter arrived at the local post office where the employees noticed it was addressed To God: Heaven. They all knew the old man and, after reading the letter with tears in their eyes, took pity on him and had a whip around. Ninety dollars was raised and posted to him. The old man was overjoyed and immediately wrote a 'thank you' letter to God. The post office employees received the letter and all gathered around to read it.

Dear God,

I thank You with all my heart for taking time from Your busy schedule and answering my request . . . I am now a happy man.

Yours (in the very near future),

An Old Man.

P.S. I only received $90 of the $100 I asked for. I bet those thieving bastards down at the post office pinched the rest.

When their credibility was at a low ebb, Jimmy and Tammy Bakker decided that a revelation of some sort, a miracle perhaps, was needed to restore their flagging ratings. Somehow, Jimmy managed to contact Jesus. He explained their predicament and asked for divine help.

'Tell you what,' suggested Jesus, 'gather all the faithful and the doubters to the shores of Lake Superior and I'll do my walking-on-water routine. It slayed 'em at Galilee.'

'Fantastic idea,' agreed Jimmy, and sped off to make the arrangements.

On the appointed day a huge crowd – everyone is interested in a second coming – gathered at the lake. Mr Whippy vans and hot dog stands were all over the show. Then, to a deafening cheer, Jesus appeared in pristine white robes. A breathless hush fell over the throng as with theatrical deliberation, arms raised, He stepped slowly onto the lake and walked into the sunset. As the sun sank slowly in the west, Jesus sank slowly into the lake, step by step. Immediately there were enraged cries of 'Fraud!', 'Cheating bastards' and 'Give us our money back.' When the pandemonium subsided, Jimmy was not unnaturally aggrieved. 'Jesus,' he said with some emphasis, 'you've ruined me. I'll never live this down. What the hell happened?'

Jesus was as puzzled as He was wet. 'I can't understand it,' He lamented. 'It went great before.'

Suddenly, the penny dropped. 'Of course!' He cried. 'How could I be so stupid? When I first did this trick I didn't have holes in my feet!'

During a visit to Australia, the Seven Dwarves attended Sunday Mass in Melbourne. They were seated together in one pew, with Grumpy on the aisle. As the service proceeded, the dwarves were talking together, when the dwarf on the seat farthest from the aisle nudged his neighbour with his elbow and whispered in his ear. The message went along to Grumpy, who got up and walked down the aisle to the Mother Superior of the local religious order.

'Mother Superior,' Grumpy asked, 'are there any dwarf nuns in Melbourne?'

'No, Grumpy,' the Mother Superior replied, 'there are no dwarf nuns in Melbourne.'

Grumpy thanked the Mother Superior and returned to his pew, whispering the reply on his return to the dwarf next to him, who passed it onto his neighbour, and so on. When the message reached the end of the pew, the dwarf there thought for a moment and whispered a message to his neighbour, who passed it on, and down the line it went to Grumpy, who got up and walked to the Mother Superior again.

'Mother Superior, excuse me, but are there any dwarf nuns in Victoria?'

'No, Grumpy,' the Mother Superior replied, 'there are no dwarf nuns in Victoria.'

Back in his seat, Grumpy whispered the reply to his neighbour, it travelled along the row, then back came another message, and Grumpy returned to the Mother Superior.

'I'm very sorry to disturb you,' he said, 'but could you please tell me if there are any dwarf nuns in Australia?'

A little peeved by now, the Mother Superior turned to her questioner. 'Grumpy,' she said, 'there are no dwarf nuns in Melbourne, Victoria, Australia, or anywhere else in the world.' Grumpy walked slowly back to the Seven Dwarves' pew, took his seat and passed on the message to his neighbour, as before. It travelled along the row, and there was a brief silence. Then all six of his companions broke into a shrill chorus: 'Grumpy fucked a penguin, Grumpy fucked a penguin . . .'

The scene is Tibet, a few years before the Chinese takeover. A devout young Buddhist wants to be a monk and applies to the leading monastery. He's granted an interview by an ancient lama who says they're willing to give him a try. However, he must try and observe the highest standards of chastity. 'But we understand that, in the beginning, it's very, very difficult. Whatever you do, do not climb over the wall and go down into the town and have anything to do with loose women. We've been in this business a very, very, long time and we make alternative arrangements for the novices. If you must have sex, simply use the yak provided. But if you do, remember to take him a present.'

After a few weeks, the young man feels overwhelming sexual urges but finds the thought of the yak unappetising. So he climbs over the wall and goes into the town. On his return, he is hauled up before the lama. 'This must not happen again! If you feel sexual desire, use the yak. But remember to take it a present.'

A few weeks pass and, once again, the young man is overwhelmed by lust. Once again he ignores the availability of the yak, climbs over the wall and has truck with a lady of easy virtue in the brothel below the monastery. Yet again he is carpeted by the old lama. 'You have had your last warning, my son. Should you disobey me on another occasion, you will be shown the door. And this will have very serious implications for future reincarnation.'

So the very next night the young man feels a quickening of desire and decides to try the yak. He joins the end of a longish queue of novices and monks, each of whom is carrying a beautifully wrapped gift. Finally it is his turn to mount the yak. The yak looks at him and says, 'Where's my present?'

'I didn't bring one,' stammered the young man.

'Typical, typical,' snarled the yak. 'Another case of "fuck you, yak, I'm all right!"'

Every morning the monks filed silently into the great hall. The abbot stood at the front of the hall, watching over them. When the monks were all present, the abbot chanted, 'Good morning,' and the monks reverently replied in unison, 'Good morning.' Prayers then commenced. This went on day after day, year in, year out. A rather spirited monk, small in stature but with a mischievous glint in his eye, decided a change was necessary. One morning, when everything appeared to be following its time-honoured pattern, the abbot chanted, 'Good morning,' and the reply of 'Good morning' was given by all the monks except the mischievous one who said 'Good evening'. The abbot immediately responded tunefully, showing an unexpected familiarity with South Pacific, 'Someone chanted evening.'

A small weatherboard church in North Queensland needed repainting. Tenders were called and naturally the lowest was accepted. The two blokes whose tender was successful realised that they'd under-estimated the cost of the job. But as they were using a water-based paint they managed to cover the church by thinning it down.

'Once it's dry,' they said, 'the congregation will never know the difference!'

When it was completed they stepped back to admire their work, just as a sharp tropical downpour started, leaving a streaky mess on the woodwork.

'Oh, God!' they yelled, 'what are we gonna do now?'

There was a flash of lightning and a voice from the clouds thundered: 'REPAINT! YOU THINNERS!'

Two clergymen, of different racial backgrounds, were arguing whether God was black or white. The argument was getting quite heated when some of their parishioners suggested they hold a combined prayer meeting and ask God in the form of a supplication. 'Tell us, oh God, if your holy presence could be considered black or white!'

There was a pause and then a great voice from the sky filled the church, 'I AM WHAT I AM!'

'Told you so,' said the white preacher.

'What do you mean? How do you get that out of what he said?'

'Well, if he were black he'd have said "I is what I is!"'

A MEDICAL CONDITION

An old bloke, over 90, was brought into Alice Springs for a medical. It was a regular, yearly trip, made by his daughter and her husband from their cattle property about 100 kilometres out of Alice, and the old bloke was getting a bit forgetful. Their regular doctor got him to strip and they went through all the tests. Tap tap, cough, take a deep breath, stick your tongue out, all the usual stuff. The old bloke was all sunburned on his face and hands but the rest of him was blueish white, semi-transparent. You could have held him up to the window if you'd wanted to check the state of his organs.

'Well, Mr Quinn,' said the doctor, 'you are in remarkable physical condition for a man of your age. There's just one more test. But you probably remember the routine from last time.'

The old man said, with a shaky voice, 'how do you mean "routine"?'

'Well, you'll remember that we went through all these tests last year.'

'I've never seen you before in my life,' was his quivering response.

'I assure you you have. But no matter.' The doctor pointed to a shelf containing an array of different shaped beakers and said, 'It just remains for you to fill one of those bottles with a sample of your urine.'

'What?' says the old fella, pointing with a shaking hand across the room. 'From *here*?'

An old man was sitting on the curb outside the pub, sobbing helplessly. A cop asked him what was wrong. 'I'm 75 years old,' he cried, 'and I've got a 25-year-old wife at home who's beautiful, randy, and madly in love with me.'

'So what's the problem?' asked the cop.

'I can't remember my address.'

A doctor had the unenviable task of informing a patient that he had only a few minutes to live. The patient said, 'Isn't there anything you can do for me?'

To which the doctor replied, 'Well, I could boil you an egg.'

A young artist had just had his first exhibition at the Roslyn Oxley Galleries and asked if anyone had shown any interest in his canvasses, vividly expressive of inner torment. 'Well, I've got good news and bad news,' said Ms Oxley. 'The good news is that someone has enquired about your paintings, wondering how much they'd appreciate in value if you died. And he bought all of them.'

'And the bad news?'

'He's your doctor.'

A mother took her 16-year-old to see the doctor because his penis was still the same size as a 10-year-old's. The doctor prescribed plenty of hot buttered toast for breakfast as an aid to normal growth. At breakfast the next morning, the boy was confronted with a huge mound of hot buttered toast. But as he reached for it, his mother slapped his hand away. 'Leave your father's breakfast alone.'

A doctor ended an examination of a pregnant woman and asked, 'Do you smoke after intercourse?'

'Dunno,' she said, 'never looked.'

A young woman is fearful of having a baby because her husband is such an over-achiever on the John Singleton criteria of Australian masculinity, with particular reference to his obsessions with booze and football. So oafish is his behaviour that, when she finds herself great with child, she considers having an abortion. But a friend in Right to Life persuades her to have the child, suggesting that she stroke her tummy whenever possible whilst murmuring, 'Be polite, be polite.' Oddly, the baby never arrives and finally the woman dies at the grand old age of 90. When doctors perform an autopsy, they find two little old men sitting inside her saying, 'After you.' 'No, after you.'

An old miner came into town from the sticks to see a doctor and was greeted at the reception desk by a sweet young thing. She asked his name and address and enquired what it was that ailed him. The miner said, 'I've got a sore cock.' The SYT was shocked and rushed into the doctor to complain. When the miner was admitted, the doctor rebuked him. 'You mustn't use coarse language like that to my receptionist, she's not used to it. If you're asked what's wrong with you in circumstances like this, say that you've got a sore ear or something of that sort.'

Two weeks later the miner returned for further treatment and was again asked to hint at his ailment. The miner said, 'I've got a sore ear.' The SYT asked, 'What's the matter with it?'

'I can't piss out of it,' said the miner.

A bloke went to see his doctor. 'Doctor, I've got a problem. I've got a square dick.'

'Baloney,' said the doctor, 'never seen that in all my years. Whip it out, sport, and let me have a look.' The doctor turned it in between his thumb and forefinger like a piece of limp celery.

'Boy, it's square all right. How did you do that?'

'Putting a crate in the back of the one tonner and my mate dropped his side. Talk about hurt! So I took it to the workshop and tried to squeeze it back into shape in the vice. But the bastard ended up square!'

'Hmmm,' the doctor washed his hands in the basin in the corner of his surgery and started writing out a form on his clipboard.

'What are you doing, doc? Writing me out a script?' His voice was crippled with worry.

'No, I'm giving you three days off work to try and pull yourself round.'

An Australian businessman was in Hong Kong for a few weeks and, after each day's meeting, he'd sneak off to a brothel or a girlie bar. After a few days he began to worry about the appearance of his dick. It was a very strange colour. So he went to an English doctor who specialised in expatriate business executives. 'Oh dear, oh dear,' said the doctor, 'how very sad. That's a classic case of Hong Kong Dong. I'm afraid there's no alternative but to amputate.'

The businessman was appalled and insisted on a second opinion. So he went to a Chinese doctor who specialised in acupuncture and herbal medicine. 'What do you think, doc?' said the terrified Australian. 'The other two doctors I went to see say it's Hong Kong Dong and I'll have to have it amputated.' The Chinese doctor gave him a beatific smile and shook his head. 'Not to worry. Not necessally.'

'You mean you don't have to amputate?'

'No, with Hong Kong Dong it will drop off on its own in just a few days time.'

A bloke went to the doctor to get his sick note signed. The doctor reached into his breast pocket and pulled out a rectal thermometer. 'Damn!' he exclaimed, 'some bum's walked off with my pen again.'

A famous movie star was having a medical by a noted gynaecologist. As he poked and prodded he muttered, 'Ever had a check up there?'

And she replied, 'No dollink, only a Pole and a few Hungarians.'

Two Indian doctors were standing beside the sister's station in a British hospital. One said to the other, 'I don't know whether it's spelt WHOMB or WHOOMB.' The sister stood up and said, 'I couldn't help overhearing you doctor, but it's spelt WOMB.'

'Young woman,' said the doctor, 'I don't think you've ever seen a water buffalo, let alone heard it pass wind under water.'

Did you hear about the girl who swallowed a razor blade? It not only gave her a tonsillectomy, an appendectomy and a hysterectomy, it circumcised her husband, gave the Bishop a hare lip, took two fingers off the hand of a casual acquaintance – and it still had five good shaves left in it.

A Telecom linesman somewhere way out in the outback of Queensland was given a long-haired 'hippy' youth as his assistant. While the linesman was up a pole doing what linesman do, the assistant lay in the long grass at the base of the pole. Suddenly, the assistant screamed out, 'I've been bitten by a snake.'

The linesman quickly connected a portable telephone to a pair of lines and dialled the nearest hospital and reported the incident. After a bit of three-way conversation to establish the identity of the snake, the doctor at the hospital gave detailed instructions on the necessary treatment. 'Put a tourniquet around the limb on the side nearer the heart, make two cuts with a razor blade through the bite marks and suck out the poison.' When he had finished, the linesman asked, 'What will happen if I don't do all that?'

'He'll be dead in half an hour,' replied the doctor.

'What did he say?' asked the assistant.

'You're going to die,' replied the linesman.

A doctor, who had his rooms on the top floor of a Manhattan skyscraper, used to drop into the cocktail lounge on the ground floor on his way home at exactly 5 p.m. every afternoon. Richard, the bar attendant, would always have his favourite drink, an almond daiquiri, which is an ordinary daiquiri with almond nuts sprinkled on top, waiting for him. One afternoon Richard was preparing the doctor's drink and found he was out of almond nuts and so substituted hickory nuts. The doctor arrived, sipped his drink and said, 'Is this an almond daiquiri, Dick?'

Richard replied, 'No, it's a hickory daiquiri, Doc.'

During a divorce case in Adelaide, many years ago. the woman complainant, who was not represented by legal counsel, told the judge that she knew her husband had committed adultery.

'How do you know?' the judge asked.

The woman replied that her husband had contracted Venetian disease.

The judge queried, 'And what is Venetian disease, may I ask?'

The woman looked flustered, but counsel for the defendant stood up and said, 'I think she means a case of gondoliers, Your Honour.'

A doctor made a house call to a dilapidated building on the outskirts of the city to visit a Mrs Jones. There seemed to be a horde of children of all ages and colours and he asked Mrs Jones if they were all hers.

'Yes,' she said.

'Why didn't you go on the pill?' asked the doctor.

'I couldn't afford the pill, all I had was Smarties.'

A patient visited a doctor and said, 'I've been graped.'

'You mean you've been raped,' said the doctor.

'No,' said the woman, 'there were six of them.'

Three surgeons were discussing operations.

First surgeon: 'I like operating on Germans, they are superbly built inside, all pipes are vertical and muscles diagonal, and thus very easy to put together again after cutting.'

Second surgeon: 'I like operating on the Japanese, they are transistorised inside, all their pipes are coloured – so easy to join afterwards. Red to Red, Green to Green, and Blue to Blue.'

Third surgeon: 'I like operating on politicians because they only have two moving parts – their mouth and their arse, and those parts are interchangeable.'

'You've been diagnosed as having syphilis and two highly infectious Asian skin complaints,' said the doctor. 'You'll receive special treatment and a diet of pizza and pancakes.'

'Thanks for the special treatment,' said the patient, 'but why the pizza and pancakes?'

'They're the only foods that can be shoved under the door.'

A young man visits his local doctor and says, 'I don't know what's wrong with me, doctor, but I can't concentrate and life isn't fun anymore.'

'Do you drink?' asks the doctor.

'No,' replies the young man.

'Look,' says the doctor, 'have a couple of wines or whatever you like each evening before your meal. That'll make you feel more relaxed. Do you smoke?'

'No,' says the patient.

'It won't hurt you in small amounts. Have a couple of fags with your drinks – it helps to calm people. Do you have any contact with young ladies – you know, do you ever go to bed with one?'

'Very seldom, doctor.'

'Well, try a little harder. I can assure you that intercourse a couple of times or more a week is good for young men. Try these things and see me in a fortnight.'

The fortnight passes and the patient returns to the doctor's consulting rooms.

'How are you?' asks the doctor.

'A lot better, thank you, doctor.'

The doctor asks if he is having a few drinks each night.

'Yes, doctor, I now have a nice cellar of good wines. It's doing me good,' replies the patient.

'And what about cigarettes?'

'Well, yes, I smoke a pipe now and it is most relaxing.'

Then the doctor says, 'I don't want to be too personal, but what about sex?'

'Well, doctor, I can't arrange it more than twice a week – you know, it's a bit difficult when one is the parish priest in a small country town!'

An 85-year-old has had a triple bypass. He comes back to the doctor saying that his wife is afraid of having sexual intercourse, for fear that it might do him in. The doctor reassures the old chap that he's in fine fettle, that sex cannot possibly hurt him. Delighted, the patient asks the doctor to put it in writing. The doctor happily agrees and scribbles furiously for a few moments. He's then asked to read it aloud.

'Dear Mrs Smith, your husband is in remarkable physical condition. He now has a heart as strong as an Olympic athlete. I wouldn't be at all surprised if he couldn't make love three or four times in a single evening. Yours sincerely . . .'

The old man is delighted, but he asks for a slight amendment.

'Could you please cross out Mrs Smith and make it To Whom It May Concern?'

The gynaecologist completed his examination. 'I'm sorry, miss, but the removal of that vibrator is going to involve a very delicate operation.'

'I'm not sure I can afford it, doc,' sighed the girl. 'Why don't you just replace the batteries?'

A man went to a doctor to have his eyes tested.

'Put your left hand over your right eye and read the top line of the chart,' said the doctor. The man put his right hand over his left eye.

'No, put your LEFT hand over your RIGHT eye and just read the top line of the chart,' said the doctor. The man put his left hand over his left eye.

'No,' said the doctor, 'put your LEFT HAND over your RIGHT EYE and just read the letters on the top line of the bloody chart.' The man put his right hand over his right eye.

'Oh, for Chrissake,' said the doctor and he grabbed a cardboard box, cut a small hole where the man's left eye would be and fitted the box over the man's head.

'Now read me the top line of that chart,' he said.

There was a muffled soft sobbing sound coming from inside the cardboard box.

'Oh, my God,' said the doctor, 'what's wrong now?'

'Well, what I really wanted,' said the man, 'was a pair of those little *round* glasses like John Lennon.'

Two psychiatrists, Dick and Harry, meet twenty years after graduation. Dick says he feels burned out and depressed and is thinking of early retirement.

Harry: 'Let's see. I've got three questions which I try out on my patients to see what shape they're in. Why don't I run them past you, and see how bad it really is.'

Dick: 'All right.'

Harry: 'First, what does a man do standing up, a woman do sitting down, and a dog on three legs?'

Dick: 'That's easy . . . shake hands.'

Harry: 'Right. Second question. What does a dog do in your backyard which, when you step in it, causes you to utter an expletive?'

Dick: 'That's obvious . . . digs a hole.'

Harry: 'That's right too. Finally, where do women have the curliest hair?'

Dick: 'I know. In Fiji.'

Harry: 'Right. Look, there's nothing whatever wrong with you. But you should hear the bizarre answers I get from some of my patients.'

A psychiatrist was concerned that too many of his professional clients seemed incapable of making a decision. To demonstrate this inability he devised a simple experiment. His first patient was a civil engineer. When asked what 2 plus 2 made, the engineer fumbled in his pocket, operated the slide rule and, after some manipulation, looked up in a puzzled way and said, '3.98. No, that doesn't seem right, I'll try again.' Becoming more and more agitated, he thought it might be 4.01.

The next client was a physician of some distinction, and he was posed the same question. What he said was, 'I think it's probably 4, but it could possibly be something else. Perhaps we'd better refer the matter to a specialist.' The lawyer client, who was next, thought that in general it would be considered 4, but that they should have counsel's opinion.

The psychiatrist's last patient was an accountant who, when asked the question 'What does 2 and 2 make?' looked him straight in the eye and said, 'What do you want it to make?'

There are two shrinks, one young and one old, with offices across the hall from each other. Every morning they meet in the lift, both looking pretty good. At the end of the day, when they meet leaving the building, the young shrink looks whacked whilst the older bloke looks on top of the world. One day the young shrink couldn't stand it any longer and said to the old shrink, 'I give up. How do you put up with it? I hear these terrible yarns from my patients all day and just get depressed. What's your secret?'

The old shrink looked at the young shrink and simply said, 'I never listen.'

A gentleman developed a most unfortunate habit. Each Sunday he couldn't resist taking a coin out of the collection plate when it came around. Naturally the parson remonstrated with him and he replied that he found the urge irresistible. 'It worries me, but no matter how much I try I cannot resist taking the money out. It really has me worried.' The parson suggested some psychiatric advice to which the gentleman agreed, also agreeing to stay away from church until he was cured. Six months later, the parson was pleased to see him back in the congregation. But when the time came for the collection, the parson watched in horror as the man, smiling happily, took a handful of coins from the plate. 'I thought you weren't coming back until you were cured,' he said.

'That's right,' said the man, 'I am cured – it doesn't worry me at all now.'

Two psychiatrists pass in a corridor. 'Good morning,' said the first. The second walked on wondering, 'I wonder what he meant by that?'

Neurotics build castles in the air.
Psychotics live in them.
Psychiatrists collect the rent.

The psychiatrist spoke in calm, reassuring tones to his worried looking patient. 'What we're going to do now is . . . I'll draw something on this piece of paper, and I want you to tell me what it means to you. Okay?' Taking his pen, the psychiatrist drew a single, short line on the paper. 'What is that?' he asked.

'That's a clergyman masturbating,' replied the patient, after several seconds.

'All right, now what's this?' said the shrink as he drew two short parallel lines on the paper.

'Those are two lesbian nuns having sex.'

'Well,' said the psychiatrist, as he drew three short parallel lines on the paper. 'What do you see now?'

'Filthy bastards!' exclaimed the patient, staring at the last drawing. 'That's two priests with a nun between them, and they're both having sex with her.'

Looking directly at his patient, the psychiatrist slowly replaced his pen on the desk. 'It's a good thing that you've come to see me. You are badly in need of treatment.'

'I'm in need of treatment?' shouted his patient. 'That's a bloody beauty! You're the one who's going around drawing filthy pictures!'

A psychiatrist was visiting a mental institution and whilst on his rounds noticed one of the inmates stabbing a large watermelon viciously with a knife. He asked him what he was up to. The patient replied that when he left the institution he was going to become a butcher and so was practising on the watermelon. The psychiatrist said this was excellent therapy and encouraged him to continue.

The next patient was making mud pies and explained he was going to be a baker when he got out. Once more, the psychiatrist was pleased and encouraged him to continue 'the good work'. When he got to the next patient, he was surprised to see that he had his prick jammed into a packet of biscuits.

'What are you doing?' he asked.

'Well, I'm never going to get out of here because I'm fucking crackers.'

Why is psychoanalysis a lot quicker for a man than for a woman?

When it's time to go back to his childhood he's already there.

What's a specimen?

An Italian astronaut.

A patient recently came into a psychiatrist's office and told him he had a major problem. When the doctor asked him what the problem was, the man said, 'Well, some mornings I wake up and think I'm a teepee. Other mornings I wake up and think I'm a wigwam.' The psychiatrist responded immediately, 'I know exactly what your problem is.'

'Well, doc, what is it?'

'You're too tense.'

Why don't pygmies use tampons?

They'd trip over the string.

During the war there was a reluctant hero who wanted to fail his medical. He limped in and stated that one leg was shorter than the other. He was passed A1. 'What do you mean, A1? One leg is shorter than the other!'

'That's all right,' said the medical officer, 'where you're going the ground's uneven.'

The sergeant asked a new recruit for his name, to which he replied 'Mack.' The sergeant said, 'I must have the full name.' The recruit replied, 'That is my name.' The sergeant then pointed out that everyone had a Christian name and a surname. To which the recruit replied, 'I was christened John Thomas McDangle originally, but I'm now known simply as Mack.' The sergeant was curious.

'Well, I left school at 16 and, because I was extremely bright, was admitted to medical school. I qualified before I was 21, thus becoming John Thomas McDangle, MD. But I was considered too young to practise medicine, and so decided to do further study. I chose theology. On completion of these studies I became John Thomas McDangle, MD, DD. Then, unfortunately, I got into trouble with a lady of ill repute and got VD. So the medical board removed my MD, the church removed my DD, the VD removed my John Thomas – nothing left to dangle, so just call me Mack.'

GOING, GOING, GONE

Three octogenarians were discussing the plight of the aged. One said, 'I think the worst thing is to lose your hearing. I'm passionately fond of music, but I'm so deaf I can hardly hear a note any more.'

The second said, 'I think it's dreadful to lose your sight. I'm passionately fond of art, but I'm so blind that I can no longer see the paintings in the gallery.'

The third said, 'That's nothing compared to my affliction. On my 80th birthday I married a beautiful young wife of 24. Every morning I wake up and there she is lying beside me. I say to her, "Kylie, let's make love" and she says, "But my darling, we just made love ten minutes ago, before you dropped off again". The worst thing that can happen is to lose your memory.'

A young reporter was interviewing Maggie Mulligan, a spinster lady who had just reached her 100th birthday. 'To what do you attribute your extremely good health?' he asked her.

'Well,' she said thoughtfully, 'I have always eaten moderately and worked hard. I don't drink or smoke, and I keep good hours.'

'Have you ever been bedridden?' he asked.

'Of course,' replied the old lady, 'but don't put that in the paper.'

Kicking and struggling all the way, Dad is carted off to what Dame Edna describes as a 'high security twilight home'. But on his first morning, things take a decided turn for the better. He wakes up to discover that, for the first time in years, he's got a great, thumping erection. On hearing the nurse approach, he covers his proud secret with the sheet. But she's too experienced not to notice and, whipping back the sheet, smiles approvingly.

'Now, isn't that marvellous! And what a pity if it was wasted.' Whereupon she gives the old chap a 'polish'.

'Now, off you go and have a shower,' she says brightly, as she sets off to see the next resident.

The old bloke is in a dormitory block with a shared bathroom and joins several other old codgers for his ablutions. And he's still feeling very, very pleased with himself when he drops the soap and is immediately sodomised by another octogenarian with an erection. That afternoon his son comes to see how Dad's settling in and he describes both sexual encounters, the pleasant surprise and the unwelcome incident. The son says, 'This proves this place is wonderful for the libido.'

'Yes,' says the old codger. 'But I only get an erection once every six months and I'm always falling over.'

An old couple go to the doctor for the husband to have a check up. After a preliminary check the doctor says he wants to do some more tests. He asks for a specimen of urine, a specimen of semen, a blood sample and a faeces sample. The old man, who is hard of hearing, asks his wife, 'What did he say?' She replies, 'He wants to see your underpants!'

Three senior citizens were sitting around talking about their memories. The first said, 'I really have problems. I find myself standing in front of the refrigerator. I don't know whether I just put something in or if I came to get something out.'

The second said, 'I find myself at the foot of the stairs. I don't know if I just came down or if I want to go upstairs.'

The third said, 'I will have to knock on wood

because I do not have these problems.' He gave the table top a vigorous rap. A few seconds later he said, 'Will someone go and see who is at the door?'

There's a new condom on the market. It's designed for men over 60 years old. It's called softwear.

Bill and Daphne have been residents at the Twilight Rest nursing home for some years, during which time they have come to an 'arrangement'. They watch the news and several of their favourite programs together in a discreet corner of the television room each evening. And Daphne gives Bill a 'polish' at the same time.

One evening Daphne comes to join Bill and finds her seat on the couch occupied by another woman. 'Bill, how could you!' she cries. 'You hardly know Bernice, and she's *older* than me! Must be 90 if she's a day!'

Bill smiles, and says sheepishly, 'Yes, but she's got Parkinson's.'

What's grey and hangs out your underpants?
Your grandma.

An old bloke was dying and his four sons, three of whom were priests, and the youngest, Joe, a 'no-hoper' from the bush, were gathered around the bed. In a weak voice the old man said, 'I have a confession to make. Your mother and I were never married.' He then expired. There was a shocked silence eventually broken by Joe, who said, 'Well, I don't know about you three bastards, but I'm going up to the pub for a schooner.'

A young sailor was sitting at The Gap, Sydney's well-known suicide spot. He was telling himself to end it all when a voice said, 'Don't throw yourself off the Gap. I'm a good fairy and I can grant you any three wishes you want.'

Looking around he saw an old crone behind a rock. 'Oh yeah,' said the sailor, 'and what do I have to do to earn these three wishes? Nothing's for nothing in this cruel world.'

'All you have to do is make love to me,' said the crone.

The sailor did this and shortly afterwards, while the old crone brushed her hair, he asked, 'When do I get my three wishes?'

She replied with another question, 'How old are you, sonny?'

'I'm 29,' he said, 'why do you ask?'

And she said, 'Aren't you a bit old to believe in fairies?'

A woman is reading the *Age* on a Melbourne train. She is so astonished by a story on life expectancy that she turns to the stranger beside her and says, 'Do you know that every time I breathe, somebody dies?'

'Fascinating,' he answered, 'ever tried mouthwash?'

How do you tell when a Double Bay woman's husband has just died?

She's the one wearing the black tennis skirt.

Two blokes were talking on the footpath of a small country town, when a funeral cortège went past.

'Who died?' said Bill.

Tom replied, 'The bloke in the back, lying down.'

Two old blokes used to go into the pub every pension day. One day only one came. The publican opened the conversation.

'G'day Bob, how yer goin'? Where's Fred?'

'He got burned last week.'

'Sorry to hear about that. Still, I suppose he'll be back on deck soon.'

'Nah, I don't think so. They don't muck around in them crematoriums.'

When a man died his wife put the usual death notice in the paper, but added that he died of gonorrhoea. No sooner were the papers delivered than a good friend of the family phoned and complained bitterly, 'You know very well that he died of diarrhoea, not gonorrhoea.'

Replied the widow, 'I nursed him night and day so of course I knew he died of diarrhoea. But I thought it would be better for posterity to remember him as a great lover rather than the big shit he always was.'

In Heaven, the police are English, the chefs are French, the industrialists are German, the managers are Swiss, and the lovers are Italian.

In Hell, the chefs are English, the police are

German, the managers are French, the industrialists are Italian and the lovers are Swiss.

A Frenchman, an Englishman and a German all knocked at the same time at the Heavenly Gates. Before admitting them, St Peter asked them to fill out an admission application. The first question asked, 'Have you been unfaithful?' The Frenchman had been unfaithful sixty times. St Peter had a hard look at him and said, 'Well, I suppose we can let you in under these circumstances. But all you'll be able to drive is a battered Volkswagen.'

The Englishman had only cheated twenty times and was given a Peugeot, whilst the German, who had remained completely faithful to his wife, who had never harboured any lustful thoughts, was rewarded with a Rolls Royce.

A few weeks later the three happened to pull up at the same time at a celestial intersection. Both the Frenchman and the Englishman were as happy as larks, but the German had obviously been crying.

When they askd him what was wrong he replied, 'Well, my wife passed me three days ago – and she was on roller skates.'

Lord Olivier arrived in Heaven. 'Who are you?' asked St Peter. 'I'm Laurence Olivier, the world's greatest actor, poet and playwright,' came the reply.

'Well,' said St Peter, 'let's look at the Great Register.' He opened the book and started thumbing through, 'Olivier . . . Fred, Olivier . . . Jim, Olivier . . . Laurence . . . Yes! Here we are! Well, your instructions are to follow that pathway over there until you come to a vine-covered English cottage in which you'll find Lord Byron and William Shakespeare.'

'Right,' said Lord Olivier, and set off. Pretty soon he found the cottage and knocked on the door.

'Come in,' said a voice, 'and identify yourself.' Lord Olivier entered. 'I'm Laurence Olivier, the world's greatest actor, poet and playwright.'

'Aha,' replied Byron, 'I'd heard about the actor and playwright bit – but the world's greatest poet! Indeed, Shakespeare and I would contest that point.'

'Indeed we would,' agreed Shakespeare. 'So why not a small rhyming competition to settle the argument once and for all?'

'I agree,' said Olivier.

'Me too,' said Byron, 'but what shall we rhyme about?'

'How about a bow-legged man standing by a river?' suggested Shakespeare.

'Okay with me,' said Olivier, 'I'll go first.

'Down where the mighty river flowed
There stood a man whose legs were bowed.'

'Very good,' said Byron, 'but methinks far too simple. Try this!

'Where the river to the sea comes out
Stands there a man with legs about.'

'Excellent, Byron,' said Shakespeare, 'but I'm sure I can do better than both those . . . listen!

'Sooth, what manner of man is this
Whose balls hang in parenthesis?'

Just then Banjo Paterson happened to be walking past their window. He stuck his head in and said,

'Well! I've copped some lurks and seen some rackets.
But a bastard, with his balls in brackets?'

A Pope and a lawyer arrived at St Peter's Gate at exactly the same time. The Pope was assigned a modest condo in a gloomy courtyard, whilst the lawyer was given a gleaming mansion overlooking a splendid golf course. 'How can this be?' the lawyer asked St Peter. 'The Father of Christendom gets only a lousy condo and I've been given this joint!'

To which St Peter replied, 'Well, we've thirty-nine Popes here, but you're the first lawyer!'

A young, bedraggled nymphet wandered around the slopes of Mt Olympus at dawn, after an all-night orgy. She was confronted by the imposing, obviously still excited figure of Thor. 'Good morning, my little beauty,' said the deity. 'I'm Thor.'

To which the nymphet replied, 'You're Thor! I'm tho thor I can't even pith!'

St Peter was talking to the Virgin Mary. 'And what's it like being mother of the world's most talked-about prophet?' The Virgin replied, 'Well, actually we were hoping he'd become a doctor.'

There was a carload of nuns (you know the way they always pack about twenty into a Camira) tearing along the highway when they came barrelling around a corner, hit a Mack truck and ended up at the Pearly Gates. 'You can't come in, girls, unless you're pure. We just happen to have a big bowl of holy water here, in case any part of you happens to be impure,' said St Peter, rubbing his hands together.

The first nun bowled up, washed her hands. 'Come on in sister, you're pure.'

The next nun stepped up, stripped off, started splashing under her armpits, across her bosoms and between her legs. 'Gawd, I hope she doesn't pee in there,' said the next nun in line, 'I've got to gargle that!'

St Peter was taking his weekly walk around Heaven checking that all the inmates were happy and contented. He came upon a group of little mice. 'Hello little mice,' said St Peter, 'are you happy here in Heaven?'

'Oh yes, St Peter, we love Heaven. The weather is just lovely, the flowers are beautiful and the sound of the angels singing is wonderful. We just love the sound of the angels singing.'

St Peter said, 'That's just great, little mice. If there's anything I can do to make it even better for you, just let me know.'

'Well,' said the little mice, thinking hard, 'there is something you can do for us. Heaven has such long corridors and we have such little legs that sometimes we get tired walking around. Could we have roller skates?'

'Certainly you can have roller skates,' said St Peter, 'as good as done.'

Next week St Peter was taking his weekly walk around Heaven checking on the inmates and he came upon the cats. 'Hello cats,' said Peter, 'are you happy here in Heaven?'

'Oh yes, St Peter, we love Heaven. The weather is just lovely, the flowers are beautiful and the sound of the angels singing is wonderful. We just love the sound of the angels singing.'

St Peter said, 'That's great, cats. If there's anything I can do to make Heaven even better for you, just let me know.'

'Well, St Peter, we don't think there is anything more you can do for us. Since last week, when you introduced Meals-on-Wheels, life has been just about perfect.'

An old man knocked at the gates of Heaven. 'Yes,' said an angel with a clipboard, 'What can we do for you?'

'I'm looking for my son,' said the old man, 'I'm a carpenter, and it has been a long time since my son and I worked together side by side in my workshop. I was told that I would find him here. They say he has a very important position.'

'Well,' replied the angel, consulting his clipboard, 'we have a few carpenters' sons here, and one or two are rather high up. Does your son have any distinguishing features?' The old man thought for a while. 'Only the holes in his hands,' he eventually whispered.

At that the angel smiled. 'Now I know who you mean. Come with me. We'll find him in the administration area, but I must warn you that he is very busy, and he may simply not remember you. After all,' he said checking his clipboard again, 'you weren't his *real* father, were you?'

The old man sadly shook his head, and they moved on. But as they neared the central high area, a cry went up from one of the great chairs, and a figure rushed towards them.

'Father!'

'Pinocchio!!'

A sailor in the Sydney to Hobart race was washed overboard. After days of being tossed around in the ocean he came to and found himself lying on a golden beach, fringed with palms. Standing over him was a beautiful young woman.

'Gawd, this must be Heaven,' he exclaimed, 'I never thought I'd make it.'

'No, it isn't,' said the girl, 'it's just an island off the trade routes. You must be hungry and thirsty after your ordeal. Let me get you something to eat. You can have anything you like.'

'Come on, this must be Heaven,' said the sailor, but the girl reassured him. 'All right,' he said unconvinced, 'I'll have a pepper steak, rare, with French fries and a side salad and a bottle of champagne.'

'Right,' said the girl, 'give me ten minutes.'

The sailor was still muttering 'this must be Heaven' when she returned with his meal on a silver tray. Hardly able to believe his luck, the sailor devoured his meal and lay back on the sand. The girl lay beside him and threw a leg across him.

'Now that you've eaten and rested, perhaps you'd like to play around with me,' she said.

'Now I know it must be Heaven,' he cried, sitting bolt upright. 'Don't tell me you've got a bloody golf course here as well!'

A new widow attended a séance and was pleased to make contact with her late husband.

'Are you happy, dear?' she whispered, tearfully.

'Very happy,' he replied.

A bit put out at this, she asked, 'What is it like in heaven, then?'

'I don't know, dear – I'm in a lovely field of green grass with a whole herd of beautiful little cows.'

'My poor darling, you must be lonely there without me,' wept the widow.

'Not really,' he answered. 'I'm the only bull here.'

An Australian, a Scotsman and an Aborigine were in a car crash and were all killed. When they arrived at the Pearly Gates, St Peter met them and said, 'Sorry boys, we are full up. You will have to go down below.'

The Australian started to argue saying it was too hot, and he whipped out a $20 note waving it under St Peter's nose and said, 'Will *this* get me in?' St Peter snatched it from his fingers and said, 'It won't get you in *here* but it will get you back where you came from.'

The Aussie agreed. With that he 'came to' and was surrounded by ambulance men. One said, 'Blimey mate, you are lucky. You were clinically dead for half an hour. You're a bloody miracle. What happened?' So the Australian told him how he had given St Peter $20 but still couldn't get into Heaven and had been sent back.

The ambulance man said, 'Well, that's okay for you, but what about these poor devils lying here. They're as dead as dodos.'

'Well,' said the Aussie, 'when I left them up there the Scotsman was trying to beat St Peter down to $5 and the Aborigine was trying to convince him the government would pay for him.'

A poodle in Darwin died and went to Heaven. At the pearly gates he was refused entry by St Peter. 'Why?' asked the dog.

'Because you haven't got a tail. You will have to go back to Earth and get your tail.'

The dog returned to his owner and told him of his plight. 'Well, I can't help you but if you go to the vet who now runs our local supermarket he might be able to help you.'

So the dog trotted down to the local supermarket and, sure enough, there was the vet behind the counter. The vet immediately recognised the dog and asked him what he could do for him. The dog told the vet of his problem. But the vet shook his head and said, 'I am sorry, Rex, but we don't re-tail spirits on Sundays in Darwin.'

And the Last Laugh . . .

It's during the Depression when, late one evening in a country town, an old swaggie knocks on a lonely door. He hears footsteps approaching and it opens, revealing a man with his collar back-to-front. The swaggie says, 'Oh, I'm terribly sorry to disturb you, Father.'

'I'm not a Father,' says the bloke, 'I'm a Church of England clergyman.'

'Whatever, I'll be on my way.'

'No, no. Come on, and tell me what I can do for you.'

Unused to religion, the swaggie's a bit shy. 'I don't want to come in. I'm going around seein' if I can get a meal in return for an odd job or two. I cut wood and stuff like that.'

The clergyman says, 'You are more than

welcome. Sadly, I've just finished cutting our wood. However, if you'd care to stack it at the back of the house I'd be most pleased. And, of course, I'd give you a meal in exchange.'

So the swaggie stacks the wood, washes his hands and stands on the verandah at the back of the house. The clergyman insists that he enters, sitting him down at the kitchen table.

There's not much conversation during the meal. At the end of dinner, the swaggie says, 'Thanks Father, I'll be on my way.'

'No, no relax. Be comfortable. You can sleep out on the verandah tonight if you like.'

'Thanks very much, but I've got to be getting along.'

'Well then, before you go, let me pour you a cup of tea.'

The swaggie pours some into his saucer, blows on the surface and drinks it down. Meanwhile the clergyman has opened his *Bible* and is having a good read.

The swaggie looks at him curiously and says, 'Must be a good book.'

The clergyman lifts his eyes and says, 'As a matter of fact, it's *the* good book.'

'Oh, yes. What's it about?'

'Surely you know what the *Bible* is about?'

'Well, I've *heard* of the *Bible*.'

'You've never read it?'

The swaggie's a bit embarrassed. 'Well, you see, I can't read.'

'That's nothing to be ashamed of, my man. That's why there are people like me involved in the church. We're able to read the word of God and pass it on to our less fortunate brethren.'

'Yeah, well what's it about?'

'Well, it's about quite a number of things. All sorts of stories. Stories of the flood, of our Saviour. This particular part that I'm reading now is about an extremely powerful man of God. A man called Samson who came from a little town called Jerusalem. And he had a woman called Delilah. And these particular verses describe him joining Delilah in the fields whilst she was grinding the corn. Suddenly they were descended upon by 5000 Philistines. Samson called on God, picked up the jaw bone of an ass, slew 3000 of them and completely routed the rest.'

The swaggie looks at the minister in astonishment. 'And would this be a true story?'

'Of course it's true. It's the word of God.'

'He must have been a pretty strong sort of bloke.'

'Oh, an extremely powerful man. As a matter of fact, he was capable of tearing down temples with his bare hands. Simply by pushing over the pillars.'

'Fair dinkum?'

'How could it be anything else. It is, as I've emphasised, the word of God.'

'Yeah, I see.'

The following evening, late, the swaggie's looking for somewhere to camp and sees, in the middle distance, the glow of a campfire. He wanders up. Tentatively, observing the protocol of the bush, trying not to come too close. Beside the campfire is an old rabbiter, brewing up a bunny stew in his 4-gallon kero tin. He sees the swaggie in the shadows and says, 'G'day. Come and get warm and help yourself to the stew.'

The swaggie hops into the bunny stew very appreciatively and the rabbiter says, 'What do you know?'

'Oh, nothing much. Oh, yeah, I did hear something. Terrible story. About this bloke called Simpson. Simpson from Jerilderie. A real bastard. He's going around ripping up the telephone poles. It turns out he was out in the paddock one day giving his girlfriend Delicious a grind in the corn, when all of a sudden 5000 Filipino bastards appeared. So he picks up the arse-bone of a cow, slays 3000 and completely roots the rest. Turned out to be a bit of a poofter.'

INDEX

THE PENGUIN BOOK OF MORE AUSTRALIAN JOKES

collected by Phillip Adams
and Patrice Newell

Penguin Books

To Rory, for all the laughs.

CONTENTS

Life Before Death

'A laugh is the hilarious declaration
made by man that life is worth living.'
Sean O'Casey

'It never cost me a stab nor squirm
to tread by chance upon a worm.
Aha, my little dear, I say
your clan will pay me back one day.'
Dorothy Parker

'It's not that I'm afraid to die. I just don't
want to be there when it happens.'
Woody Allen

'Dust thou art, and to dust shalt thou
return.'
God

1

You're going to die.

Sorry to be the bearer of sad tidings, but it's true. No matter how fast you run, how high you climb, no matter how rich or powerful you are, no matter if you're as encrusted with honours as a pier with mussels, no matter how much of the academic alphabet you can string behind your name, you're going to cark it. Kick the bucket. Shuffle off this mortal coil.

Before this preface borrows too heavily from the Dead Parrot sketch, you may want to know what your death, inevitable if not imminent, has to do with a collection of jokes. The answer is: absolutely everything. Laughter is a life-and-death issue.

These days, an average Australian life span amounts to around 650 000 hours. Well, in 650 000 billion years you'll still be dead. And those billions will be just the beginning of your death sentence, but a fleeting moment in great dollops of eternity.

If we didn't die, if we didn't have to face that endless vista of non-existence, we wouldn't have, wouldn't need, a sense of humour. The issues simply wouldn't arise.

Humans are dignified by doom, defined by an awareness of mortality. As far as we know, no other creature has this essentially tragic awareness. Even those who assuage anxieties by believing in God are confronted by the fact that He's the cosmic comic who, in the greatest of all practical jokes, has provided us with a slapstick fate. Where a handful are condemned to the chair, the gallows, the gas chamber, the garrotte or the fatal injection, God has condemned the entire six billion of us to the hospital, the hospice, the car accident, the plane crash, the stroke.

And not just us human beings, but every living creature. And not just living creatures, but everything that exists. In a catch that makes Catch 22 look reasonable, His Majesty has cursed the entire universe with the Second Law of Thermodynamics, which means that the whole shebang comes to a grinding halt. Shades of those lights are going out all over Europe; the suns, the countless billions of them, will go out all over space-time. And it's not just the solar systems and the galaxies that will be extinguished – it's ditto for the minuscule subatomic particles that cavort in the realms of quantum mechanics.

The end. Finito. Kaput. Facing this awesome and unpleasant fact, human beings, despite the optimism energetically marketed by a plethora of faiths, have every reason to feel just a little depressed. Either that, or an almost orgasmic terror that thrills and chills every atom of our being. So much so that we cry out in rage, in horror, in despair.

Or we laugh.

Laughter is the other way of reacting to the raw deal of our brief existence. Whilst closely related to screaming, it is less shrill and more congenial. And it seems to produce in humans some as-yet undiscovered enzyme that dulls pain and gives a feeling of pleasurable acquiescence. Scientists studying tears of sorrow have recently detected a chemical that cannot be found in tears of joy – it seems that simply by weeping we produce infinitesimal amounts of an internal narcotic that hits receptors in the brain and, in turn, dulls our pain.

The editors of this compilation are convinced that a similar narcotic is produced by laughter, that millions of years of evolution have provided this method of mollifying the melancholia that comes from the prospect of our individual and collective martyrdom – of our inescapable mortality. Until that neuronal narcotic is isolated, synthesised and sold at the supermarket, it's probably a good idea to laugh as often as possible.

Having done death to death, let's now concede that not all jokes directly concern it. Other aspects of our mortal coil come into play, a long list of topics dealing with pains, problems, perils. Nonetheless it is hard to find a joke that doesn't, in some way, focus on the fates.

Almost as much as the grave, we fear the bed where we suffer illness and, even worse, sex. Men fear female sexuality and signal other forms of sexual insecurity by telling homophobic jokes or laughing at the penis. We fear 'the other', what we deem to be foreign or alien, and so tell savage, uncivilised jokes about Aborigines, Jews, migrants. The professions that have power over us are regularly pilloried – politicians, lawyers, priests. Jokes that are bigoted, blasphemous or phobic outnumber all other categories.

If bottoms and genitalia are immensely amusing, then so is constipation, flatulence, premature ejaculation, impotence, pregnancy, defecation, micturition and erections (or the lack of them).

Nuns are funny, because nun jokes combine blasphemy with sexual obscenity, giving you two for the price of one.

The only jokes that seem comparatively free of fear and hatred involve the liberating nonsense of the shaggy dog or pun. All other jokes are, to some extent, tiny acts of exorcism – or at very least, verbal counterparts to the oyster's pearl, wherein an irritant is transformed into something less uncomfortable, more appealing.

Not all laughs are born equal. There are deep, dull laughs like clods of clay falling on coffin lids. There are little shuddering laughs evoking the noise of slipping ropes as the coffin descends. There are screeching laughs, like the sound of unoiled wheels on a hearse. There are last-gasp laughs, death-rattle laughs and laughs like the peals of church bells. There are laughs born in the throat, as guttural as growls, and deep, echoing laughs that come from the belly. There are laughs that barely escape the mouth, which sound wheezy and asthmatic. And laughs that are loud and self-advertising.

And not all laughter is infectious. We know that laughter can be cruel, threatening, intimidating, humourless. And we also know that what provokes laughter in one person may have no effect on another. Whenever people gather together to tell jokes, there's always someone whose response is a bewildered, 'I don't get it'.

Your editors have tried, assiduously, to gather together jokes in every current genre. We have travelled in taxis, hung about in pubs and indecently exposed ourselves to graffiti in public loos, examining it like archaeologists transcribing hieroglyphs. We have appealed for assistance in letters and newspaper columns, and have received and acknowledged over a thousand letters. Consequently, the book you're about to read has more authors than most volumes you're likely to open, and we would like to thank the taxidrivers, the dunny philosophers, the drunks, the accountants and the hosts of helpful correspondents for their generosity of spirit. In doing so we single out elderly ladies for special expressions of gratitude as, almost invariably, the bawdiest and most obscene jokes came from them. We cannot account for this phenomenon. We simply report it.

Having failed to find any jokes that are authentically, unequivocally Australian, we've also failed to find many jokes that are in good taste. They're as rare as rocking-horse manure, as unicorns in gardens, as generous insurance assessors. Like UFOs, good-taste jokes may exist, but there's little hard evidence of them. Perhaps they're being hidden in freezers in the White House, along with the corpses of crashed aliens.

Conversely, whenever we found a joke that might have been regarded as tasteful, it failed another important test – it wasn't funny. It seems that humour is to the disreputable what guilt is to sexual excitement.

At this point it has to be said that we were surprised, indeed shocked, by the community's reception of our previous volume. Conservative estimates suggest that at least a million Australians must have read the previous *Penguin Book of Australian Jokes*, and yet not one complaint was received by us, your intrepid hunter-gatherers, or by Penguin. Whilst advance copies were demanded from us by the Human Rights Commission, whilst notorious wowsers and supporters of anti-vilification legislation demanded review copies, whilst people identified with the pieties of political correctness are known to have looked for trouble, we were neither condemned nor pilloried.

What are we to make of this? Did we sell our book into a moral vacuum? Was our solemn exercise in scholarship deemed unworthy of serious attention? Or were we saved by *The Hand that Signed the Paper* winning the Miles Franklin on our publication date? Did Ms Demidenko/Darville deflect our wrath?

Or was it simply because our readers acknowledged a tendency to bigotry, blasphemy, homophobia and racism? Few of us can claim to be wholly free of such pollutants. And racism is clearly becoming increasingly popular in Australian society, as any analysis of the recent federal election attests.

This is probably a good time to say that we, your editors, find many if not most of the following jokes offensive. Our slim, implausible excuse for collecting them is that we wanted to identify the sorts of jokes that Australians are telling each other at the dawn of the Howard era. It is not the job of an anthropologist to pass judgement on the behaviour of the tribes under observation, but to simply and scientifically record what the hell is going on.

Thus we've decided to repress our sense of outrage at the prejudices your jokes reveal, hoping that the flow of royalties will ease our pain.

For a time we proposed indicating the acceptability of a given joke by employing visual symbols. We wanted something along the lines of the stamps proffered well-behaved students by their primary school teachers, like the little koalas indelibly pressed in one's exercise book, or on the back of one's hand. Many a long, thoughtful meeting was held at Penguin, wondering what icons could be employed. What about a scale of one, two and three plaster ducks for the least offensive jokes? Or tiny portraits of Caroline Jones? To vice the versa, as it were, was a simpler matter. Clearly bad-taste jokes could be identified with stylised images of penises or toilet bowls. In the end, however, we decided that you might prefer to do your own definitional doodles. Hence the provision of generous margins.

We offered a $1000 prize for a great Australian joke we hadn't heard before. No such joke was forthcoming. Rather than returning the money to consolidated revenue, we forwarded a $1000 donation to the literary quarterly *Overland*. Under the motto 'Temper democratic, bias Australian' *Overland* has been plugging away on behalf of Australian culture for decades.

Whilst urging you to proceed with caution, your editors wish to pay tribute to Sandra Blood, who's been forced to type out countless thousands of jokes for these Penguin volumes. This first dulled and finally destroyed Sandra's sense of humour. She has made it clear that she will never listen to another joke as long as she lives, let alone type one. Sandra is now urgently seeking more congenial employment, perhaps as a Hansard reporter or typing up autopsy reports for the City Coroner. People wishing to be voluntarily euthanased need not go to the Northern Territory. Simply say, 'Have you heard the one about . . .?' to Sandra and she'll cheerfully re-enact the famous scene from *Psycho*, stabbing you to death in your shower.

The greatest oxymoron of all is 'life after death'. This notion demonstrates how oxymoronic human beings can be. Whilst a subject of humour, life after death is, of course, beyond humour's power to provide. Nor can it, finally, ward off death. But laughter does provide a great deal of life before death. Which is, after all, when you really need it.

When Dick Met Fanny

13

A couple of gladiators were in the Colosseum in Rome, waiting for their event to begin. They stood waiting in front of the thousands of grinning, salivating spectators.

'Hey, look over there. Is that the emperor?'

'Yep, that's him all right. That's Nero. And that sheila with him, the one with the big knockers, that's his girlfriend. And you'll never guess what happened last night.'

'No, what?'

'Well, she came to my cell downstairs.'

'Nero's girlfriend did?'

'Yep. And she moved towards me.'

'Nero's girlfriend did?'

'Yep, she stroked my hair.'

'Yeah!'

'And kissed me.'

'Yeah!'

'Yeah, with her tongue. And then started lifting up my toga.'

'Yeah!'

'And then she . . . Sorry, I'll tell you later. Here come the lions.'

What does Stevie Wonder's wife do after they've had a fight?

Shift the furniture.

A woman was looking into the window of Raymond Castles admiring a pair of silver shoes when a bloke sidled up beside her. 'Like those shoes? I'll buy them for you if you come to bed with me.'

'Okay. But be warned. I don't like sex very much.'

He bought the silver shoes and took her back to his hotel where, once again, she emphasised her lack of enthusiasm. And, indeed, she just lay there motionless giving him not the slightest encouragement. So much so that he was getting bored himself.

Whereupon she suddenly lifted her legs high in the air and shouted, 'Wow!'

'I thought you didn't like sex,' he said with mounting excitement.

'I don't. But I just love these new silver shoes.'

A little bloke goes into the chemist. 'I want a packet of tampons.'

'Are they for your mother?'

'No.'

'Your sister?'

'No, for me.'

'Why would you want a packet of tampons?'

'Well, on the telly it says if you've got a packet of tampons you can swim, dive, play tennis and ride horseback.'

'Are you the chemist?'

'Yes, I am.'

'But you're a woman.'

'Lots of women are chemists. In fact, this pharmacy is owned by two women, myself and my twin sister. We are devoted to this business. We live it day and night. In fact, we've sacrificed any chance of marriage, any opportunity for a social life.'

'Well, I need advice. I'm desperate.'

'What is it? How can we help?'

'I've got this insatiable urge to fuck, fuck, fuck. And I suffer from a constant, never-ending erection. I'm being driven mad by lust. What can you do for it?'

The chemist consulted her twin sister. 'The best we can offer is $300 a week, and free board.'

'Is it in?'

'Aah, yes.'

'Does it fit?'

'Aah, yes.'

'Does it hurt?'

'No, it feels wonderful.'

'Shall I wrap your old shoes?'

Sid arrived at the family butcher's and confessed that it was his birthday. His 57th. He decided to celebrate it by ordering a pound of steak rather than his usual lamb's fry and snaggers. With cries of 'Happy Birthday, Sid' echoing in his ears, he headed for the bus stop, where a little old sheila asked him why he was looking so pleased with himself. 'Well, it's me birthday. How old do you think I am?'

'Come to the back of the shelter and open yer fly,' she said. After Sid's grin, and another feature, had broadened, he obliged. 'You're 57,' said the old sheila.

'Jeez, howd'ya work that out?'

'Easy, love. I was standing behind yuz in the butcher's.'

'My husband's like a sports car,' said the first woman. 'A fantastic performer.'

'My husband's like a Rolls Royce,' said the second. 'Smooth, powerful, silent.'

'My husband's like a vintage car,' said the third. Only rallies once a year and has to be started by hand.'

Bruce was really sophisticated. He knew how to smooth talk a sheila at a party. 'G'day,' he'd say, or, How ya goin'?'

And at this particular party, it worked. He got a very friendly smile. 'Wanna come back to my place?' he inquired suavely. 'For a root?'

'Oh, I'm very sorry but I can't,' she replied shyly. You see, I'm on my menstrual cycle.'

'No worries,' said Bruce, 'just follow me. I'm on a Yamaha 500.'

A lad from Woolloomooloo
took his girlfriend out to a do.
As he kissed her goodnight
she crossed her legs tight
and broke his glasses in two.

Two blokes and a sheila are marooned on a desert island. After two weeks, the girl is so ashamed with what she's doing with the guys that she kills herself. After another two weeks, the guys are so ashamed with what they're doing with her, they bury her. And after a further two weeks, the guys are so ashamed with what they are doing together, they dig her up again!

It's after hours in the Fitzroy Gardens and a young bloke is lying between the thighs of a girl. 'Christ,' he mumbles, 'I wish I had a torch.'

'So do I,' said the girl. 'You've been munching grass for the past ten minutes.'

'We have two test tubes here,' said the professor of IVF studies from Monash. 'They contain two carefully synthesised ingredients that we can now use to create human life. Solution A is a genetically engineered copy of all the ingredients in the female ovum, while Solution B replicates the active ingredients in male spermatozoa. 'If I mix them in this aseptic glass container a new human life will be conceived. Now, any questions?'

'Could you possibly give us a demonstration?' asked an awed member of the audience.

'I'm sorry, not tonight,' said the professor, 'Solution A has a headache.'

A dirty old man caught the same bus every day because it was packed with office girls. He'd organised to be jammed between the breasts of various attractive women. And there he was, on this particular day, almost wedged between the breasts of a tough feminist.

'Would you like a bust in the gob?' she snarled.

'Oh, you mind-reader, you!' he smiled.

'How can I improve my sex life?'

'Well, you'd better tell me about it for starters.'

'All I do is masturbate. And that gets very, very boring.'

'Okay, here's some advice. Sit on your hand until its numb. Then it will feel like a total stranger's.'

An old sailor, shipwrecked on a desert island, had been masturbating for years. But he was finding it harder and harder. He'd run out of fantasies.

Then, suddenly, he grabbed his old telescope and scanned the horizon. 'My God! A ship!' he said to himself. 'And there, on the deck, a naked blonde. Christ, she's gorgeous. And the ship is heading this way.'

By now he had a great erection. So he flung the telescope away and grabbed it. 'Tricked you, you bastard. There's no bloody ship.'

She arrived at the introduction agency to meet her latest computer-matched date. And was horrified. 'You have to be kidding,' she whispered. 'He's short, he's old, he's fat, he's bald, he is appallingly dressed and he clearly has a problem with personal hygiene.'

'There's no need for you to whisper,' said the agency receptionist, 'he's deaf as well.'

'Can I? Please?'

'No, I don't think we should.'

'Ah, come on, please let me.'

'Well, perhaps. If . . .'

'Anything! Anything!'

'You'll have to buy me a mink.'

'Okay, it's a deal! On one condition.'

'What's that?'

'You'll have to clean out the cage.'

A young couple were breakfasting in the nude in the honeymoon suite at the Sebel Town House. As the woman bent over the tray she tenderly murmured, 'You're so sexy! You make my nipples tingle!'

'Well, no wonder, darling,' he replied. 'You've got one in my tea and the other in the porridge.'

Two blokes down on their luck are boozing in a low-rent pub.

Fred says, 'What do you prefer, Harry, a good root or a wet dream?'

After a thoughtful pause, Harry said, 'I dunno, I'd just as soon a wet dream m'self.'

'Why's that, mate?'

'Well, with a wet dream a man's always inclined to get a better class of sheila.'

A shift worker arrived home to find his wife in bed with three of his mates.

'Hello, hello, hello!' he bellowed.

'What,' she replied, 'aren't you speaking to me?'

What is the best thing about a blow job?

Ten minutes silence.

An Englishman, a Frenchman and an Irishman are discussing lovemaking techniques. In a thick French accent, the Parisian describes taking his wife to a very expensive restaurant, giving her a delicious meal of snail, bouillabaisse and Bollinger, and taking her home to bed. 'She rises two metres from the bed,' he says.

The Englishman describes a delicious dinner at the Dorchester, with roast beef and a fine bottle of wine. 'And when I take her home, she rises ten feet from the bed.'

Not to be outdone, the Irishman talks about

going to the local pub, drinking a dozen pints of Guinness, followed by a visit to the local Indian restaurant for a beef vindaloo. 'And when I get home, she hits the roof!'

Who are the five most important men in a woman's life?

Her doctor, her dentist, her coalman, her interior decorator and her bank manager.

Why?

The doctor gets her to remove her clothes; the dentist tells her to open up; the coalman asks if she wants it in the front or the back; the interior decorator says, 'Now that it's up, do you like it?'; and her bank manager advises against withdrawal for fear of losing interest.

A woman's wedding was rapidly approaching and she was becoming increasingly curious about sex. Matters came to a head when her parents invited the boyfriend to stay and she blundered in on him in the bathroom. There he was, stark naked.

'Mummy,' she whispered later, 'what was that thing hanging down between his legs?'

'It's a penis, my dear. Nothing to worry about.'

'And the knob on the end? Like a fireman's helmet?'

'The glans,' said her mother.

'And what about the two round things about 13 inches back? What are they?'

'For your sake, my dear, I hope they're the cheeks of his arse.'

'Mate,' said Arthur, 'I've got a real problem. I'm on the horns of a dilemma. You see, I've got to choose between two women. One is young and beautiful and I love her very, very much. But she's stone, motherless broke. The other is a much older woman, a widow, with a crook head. But she's a multi-millionaire. What should I do?'

'Follow your heart. Marry the young girl you love. And give me the phone number of the widow.'

After an engine malfunction, a NASA space probe crashed on Venus and the Venusians hauled the survivors, a male and female astronaut, from the wreckage. They saw to their injuries and treated them very, very kindly. And they told them about Venusian biology and culture. For example, they demonstrated how they made baby Venusians –

through the mass production of clones. 'And how do you make humans?' they asked.

The astronauts, feeling 100 per cent after all the care they'd received, gave an energetic demonstration of bonking. When they finished, the Venusians asked, 'Where are the babies?'

'That takes nine months,' said the astronauts.

'Then why were you in such a hurry at the end?'

Three blokes and a woman were in the lift at Australia Square when the cable broke. The lift started plummeting down, down, down. Within a few minutes they'd all be dead. The woman looked at the three men and said, 'Is there one last chance of being a woman?'

Whereupon one dropped his trousers and said, 'Here, love. Iron these.'

A couple were lying in bed together after a bout of lovemaking when she murmured, 'Darling, if I'm pregnant and we have a baby, what will we call him?'

The bloke ripped off his condom, tied it in a knot and chucked it out the window. 'If he gets out of that, we'll call him Houdini.'

'G'day, gorgeous. How 'bout a root?'

'Piss off, ya smooth talkin' bastard.'

Sophie and Eddie were engaged in erotic pleasures of the 69th variety when, despite this particular form of eroticism generally precluding conversation, Eddie embarked on a theme concerning the fatalities caused by volcanoes throughout the ages. He mentioned the number of people killed in Vesuvius, Mt Etna, Gnung Agung and other sundry volcanic operations. Sophie said she was surprised at his depth of knowledge about the subject and asked where he had learned so much about eruptions.

Eddie took a brief respite from his erotic efforts and said, 'Oh, it's nothing, Sophie. I'm just reading it from the page of a *Reader's Digest* that's stuck in your arsehole.'

Two blokes were ambling along the footpath of King William Street in Adelaide when a stunning young woman walked towards them. She had a great figure and a magnificent head of bright-red hair. As she passed them, a delightful zephyr of intoxicating perfume assailed their nostrils. One bloke turned to the other and said, 'Hey, mate, have you ever slept in bed with a beaut bluey sheila like that one?'

'No, mate,' said the other, 'not a bloody wink!'

'You know, I went for 12 years without sex. I was totally celibate.'

'Bothered by it?'

'No, not a bit. Then I had my 13th birthday.'

A bloke was walking along St Kilda Beach one evening at twilight when he accidentally stepped on another bloke's naked bum. And a girl's voice said, 'Thank you!'

The stuttering, scrawny, shy, Woody Allen look-alike entered the Redfern Taxi Club in the wee hours of the morning. Getting himself a beer he sat at a table with one of his taxidriving mates. He had a tale to tell.

'Guess what, mate?' he began. 'Last night I picked up a fare outside the Theatre Royal. The fare was a fantastic-looking woman wearing a full-length mink coat. She just oozed charm and money. Her perfume filled the cab. She even gave me a Darling Point address. She was a 'ten', mate.

'When we got to the address, she found that she had no cash with her, so she invited me to keep the meter running and to come upstairs with her to get the fare and a large tip.

'Well, guess what, mate? We went into the biggest, richest-looking penthouse you'll ever see.

'And guess what, mate? She offered me a drink. I said yes, and she went and brought back a bottle of Chivas Regal.

'Well, guess what, mate? She said that she was hot and slipped her coat and shoes off. She told me I could do the same.

'After a couple of Chivas, she said to me that it seemed to be getting even warmer and she stood up and unzipped her long black gown. She let it fall at her feet. I've never seen a body like it, mate. She was nearly six feet, had huge breasts, long legs and the most creamy skin I've seen. I said yes, it's getting hotter. And I took off my shirt. She had another drink and peeled off her bra and knickers. I took off my trousers and underpants.

'And guess what, mate? She asked me to follow her and we went into another room, her bedroom.

'And guess what, mate? She turned on some soft music and lay down on a huge round bed with black silk sheets.

'And guess what, mate? She had a bottle of

massage oil and she oiled herself all over while I stood there. It was just terrific.

'And guess what, mate? She lay back and stroked her crutch. She moaned and writhed right in front of me. It was fantastic.

'And guess what, mate? I reckon I could have fucked her!'

It was just after sunset and Harry and Bert were enjoying a quiet one in the bar of the local when Harry mentioned that he was starting a new job next week, going on to shift work, he was.

At the mention of shift work, Bert looked at his watch, put his half-finished pot down on the bar and bolted out the pub door.

Harry was very surprised at this unexpected behaviour of his old drinking mate, but drank on regardless.

Exactly an hour later, a stinking, wet, bleeding and very angry Bert staggered back into the bar and joined Harry. 'Jeez, I'm pissed off!' he rasped.

Harry just looked aside at him and said, 'Yairs, I'm not surprised. You left your beer half full. Anyway, why did you bolt?'

'It was partly your fault,' said Bert. 'When you mentioned shift work, I remembered an old girlfriend down the road who had told me her husband was on shift work this evening, and she gave me the nod that I could be in like Flynn.'

'Ah, so that's why you are pissed off, you found out he wasn't at work,' said Harry.

'No,' replied Bert. 'Why do you think I am so wet and stinking – and have a look at me flamin' knuckles! I went round to her place, she opened the door and in pretty short order we were tucked up in her bed. I no sooner thought of what to do next when there was this sound of a car pulling into her driveway and the slamming of a car door. She told me to hide, quick smart, as it must be her husband coming back for his 'lunch' box, which he had left on the kitchen table.'

'Ahah! That's why you are so pissed off – you dipped out and have a bad case of lover's nuts,' interjected Harry.

'No, wrong again,' said Bert. 'I was going to hide under the bed, then in the laundry, and finally I crawled out the bedroom window and hung by my fingertips while the old flame closed the window and dashed into the kitchen. Her husband, the bastard, must have seen the look in her eyes when he ran into the kitchen, or twigged to the way she was dressed for romance, because he galloped into the laundry first, then looked under the bed, and finally caught me hanging on like grim death to the windowsill. He laughed like mad, then ran to the laundry and came back with a bloody mallet which he used on my fingers like a bloody xylophone. I hung on real tight, though, and then the bastard went to the bed and pulled out the half-filled gazunder from underneath it. You know what happened next? He tipped it all over me.'

'So that's why you're pissed off so bad,' commented Harry. 'You got pissed on!'

'No – I'll tell you why I'm so pissed off,' said Bert, as he drained his pot. 'After dipping out on my naughtie, having my hands belted with a mallet and having a piss pot tipped all over me while hanging on for dear life at that bloody window, I looked down and saw that my feet were only three inches from the ground! That's what really pissed me off!'

A married pair of high-school maths teachers had served together all over Queensland, and always took their holidays at Noosa. Eventually they both retired, and the husband said, 'Look, we've always gone away together. Why don't we have a change and go our own ways for a couple of weeks. After all, we've been living in each other's pockets for 40 years.'

'Good idea,' replied his wife. 'We could both do with a real break.'

So, he went up to Cairns and she went to the Gold Coast. After they'd been apart for a week, the husband phoned his wife. 'How's it going, then?' he asked.

'Real good,' she replied. 'What about you?'

'I'm having a great time,' her husband said. 'I've met this girl. She's only 20, lovely figure, blonde hair. We go down to the beach every day. How about you? Getting a bit lonely?'

'No,' answered the wife. 'I'm having a lovely time. I've met this young surfie. Only 19, but tall, bronzed, muscles everywhere and very charming. And he takes me out in his panel van.'

'I see,' her husband said gruffly. 'Well, I'm glad you're enjoying yourself.'

'Yes, I am,' said the wife. 'And I'll tell you something else – 19 goes into 60 more often than 65 goes into 20.'

A millionaire has four girlfriends and can't decide which one to marry. He gives them $250 000 each.

The first one flies off to Paris and spends hers on a Gucci shopping spree.

The second pays off her mother's mortgage and sets up an annuity for her.

The third donates it all to charity.

And the fourth invests it, doubles the money and pays back the millionaire.

Which one does he marry? The one with big tits.

A couple were making love in a 5 Series BMW when the bloke's back seized up. The ambulance men were afraid to move him in case of serious damage to his spine. So the police decided to use the 'jaws of life'. They simply cut the entire top of the car off so the patient could be safely lifted out without bending.

When the ambulance departed the girl sat weeping beside the abbreviated 5 Series BMW.

Feeling sorry for her, a cop patted her on the shoulder. 'He'll be all right,' he reassured her. The girl rounded on him savagely. 'Oh, sod him,' she exclaimed. 'How am I going to explain to my husband what happened to his BMW?'

The newlyweds travelled to a Surfers Paradise hotel and moved into the honeymoon suite. As they were about to undress, the groom remembered that he didn't have any condoms. Excusing himself, he rushed down the steps to the hotel chemist and, in his haste, tripped and hurt his penis. He consulted the hotel doctor who confirmed that the penis was, indeed, broken. He'd have to put a splint on it. The doctor fashioned the splint from a couple of wooden tongue depressers and a bandage.

Returning to the honeymoon suite the groom found his bride was already undressed and lying on the bed. How would he tell her that he couldn't have sex for at least a fortnight? She started to stroke her legs, saying, 'Look at my long smooth, slender legs. They have never been touched by the hand of man.' The she shifted her attention to her breasts. 'Oh, what lovely round breasts I have. And they've never been touched by the hand of man.'

Then she placed both her hands between her legs and said, 'Right here, under my hands, is something else that's never been touched by the hand of man.'

At this moment, the groom decided he had the perfect opportunity to reveal the problem of his broken penis. 'What are you skiting about? Look at my dick! It's still in its packing case.'

Because of a car breakdown after a late reception, a honeymoon couple were forced to spend their first night in an isolated motel that was entirely booked out. The best the proprietor could offer was a single camp stretcher in a small storage room.

Undismayed and with the bloke on top, the couple began to consummate their marriage. Trouble is, camp beds are somewhat unstable. Under the influence of their motion, the bed began to rock, and then to gradually move forward, a couple of inches at a time. A few bumps against the storage room door proved sufficient to open it, and the stretcher began to inch its way down the length of the corridor.

Finally it finished up against the door of Room 17, and began a gentle, rhythmic tapping. A few seconds later, the door was opened by a clergyman in his dressing-gown who, gazing down in shocked disbelief, said, 'Young fellow, that's disgraceful. I forbid you to do that here.'

The young bloke looked up in surprise. 'I'm sorry, mate,' he said. 'I didn't realise where we were. Turn the bed around and I'll fuck off back again . . .'

The girl from the city was fully experienced in carnal matters and had become totally bored with what was available round town. Then she heard there were still some real he-men left in the bush and so set off in search of them. And she came upon a bloke who'd just finished ploughing a huge paddock with a horse team. He was a big, muscular bloke and obviously very, very angry. He unhitched each horse and chucked it bodily over the fence. Then he lifted the six-furrow plough and chucked it over too. The girl had never seen anything so masculine and sexy. She called out to him, 'I need rooting!'

He said, 'So do I. I've just ploughed the wrong bloody paddock!'

The old farmer was on his deathbed. He beckoned his faithful wife to move closer. 'Dearest, you were with me through the Great Depression.'

She dabbed at a tear.

'You were with me through all those droughts.'

She sobbed silently.

'You were with me when we lost the place in the bushfires. And here you are again, by my side when I'm about to kick the bucket.'

Her shoulders were heaving.

'You know, I'm beginnin' to reckon that you brought me a lot of bad luck.'

A cocky drives the 350 km to the nearest town one morning and buys a new pair of riding boots. The best that R. M. Williams can make. They cost him two arms and a leg. He wears them home and clumps up and down the verandah, but no one notices his pride and joys. He puts the feet on the table at tea time. Still no one notices. He polishes them six times whilst playing cards that night. No one says a damned thing.

Feeling very disappointed, he goes to bed early. In any case, he has sheep to crutch in the morning. But he's still determined that somebody will notice his boots. So he clumps into the bedroom where his wife is lying on the bed. Her hair's in curlers and she's got a mud pack on her face because while he's crutching sheep she'll be off to church. She's lying there reading a *Women's Weekly* that can't be more than a month old.

The farmer strips off entirely except for his new boots. He stands at the end of the bed, feet astride, hands on hips. 'Do you notice anything?' he demands.

His wife peeks over the top of her glasses and the *Women's Weekly* and scans the awesome sight.

After what seems an eternity, she replies, 'Your dick is hanging down . . . as per bloody usual.'

The cocky is speechless, lost for words. Not to be outdone, he finally says, 'Too bloody right, woman! It's pointing at me bloody new boots!'

With a twist of the lips and a condescending roll of the eyes, she admires her hubby's new acquisition. Then, very slowly, she looks upwards again and observes with an insight that only 35 years in the bush can provide, 'Pity you didn't get a new Akubra!'

It's a country wedding in Queensland. The MC grabs the microphone and makes the following announcement. 'Sorry, we've had to cancel the reception. The beer hasn't arrived and the bride's been raped.'

The bad news causes considerable distress to those assembled. And just as they're filing out in disappointment, the MC grabs the mike again. 'It's okay! The beer's arrived, the bloke's apologised.'

A truckie is driving along a country highway. Despite signs warning that kangaroos and wombats cross the road for the 'next 5 km' he sees any number of dead bodies on the road. So he slows down. Which is just as well because, suddenly, he spots something moving, right smack bang in the middle of the highway. He slams on the anchors, bringing the truck to a halt a few feet away from a young couple furiously bonking. He winds down the window and starts yelling obscenities at them. The young bloke stands up and apologises. 'Sorry, mate. I was coming, she was coming, and you were coming. But you were the only one that had brakes.'

A travelling salesman finds himself stranded in the tiniest town in Australia. And he knocks on the door of the little pub.

'Sorry, we don't have a spare room,' says the publican, 'but you're welcome to share with a little red-headed schoolteacher if that's okay.'

'Oh, that'll be great,' says the bloke, grinning from ear to ear. 'That'll be bonzer. And don't worry, I'll be a real gentleman.'

'Just as well,' says the publican. 'So is the little red-headed schoolteacher.'

What is 12 inches long and white?
Nothing. If it's 12 inches long, it's black.

How do you make an Australian woman give up sex?
Marry her.

What do motorcycling and sex have in common?
There comes a time when you don't do it any more.

What is the definition of a man?
Life-support system for a penis.

Why is pubic hair curly?
So it doesn't poke your eyes out.

What's the best thing about making love to your wife instead of your lover?
The ten minutes of *absolute* silence!

What do an orgasm and a drum solo have in common?

You know it's coming, but there's nothing you can do about it.

What's the difference between a male chauvinist and a sensitive new-age guy?

Three beers.

What's the difference between a woman and a typhoon?

No difference. It starts with a blow job and you finish up losing your house.

What's the difference between erotic and kinky?

Erotic is when you use a feather. Kinky is when you use the whole chicken.

What's the difference between a condom and a meat pie?

You get more meat in a condom.

Why is an anniversary like a toilet seat?
Men miss both.

How do you stop a woman giving you blow jobs?
Marry her.

What is pink and wrinkly and hangs out your pants?
Your grandma.

Why did the woman cross the road?
More the point, what was she doing out of the kitchen?

What does a Double Bay widow wear to her husband's funeral?
A black tennis dress.

What did the leper say to the prostitute?
Keep the tip.

A randy regular was denied admission to the Touch of Class because of previous bad behaviour. 'I want to come in,' he yelled.

'Okay, then slip $50 through the mail slot.'

He did. Nothing happened. 'Hey, I want to be screwed!'

'What?' said a woman's voice. 'Again?'

A bloke approached his mate at work. 'Look, I've got bad news for you. It's about your wife. I was at the Touch of Class at the weekend and there she was. Mate, I hate to be the bearer of bad news, but your wife is a prostitute.'

'No she's not,' he said. 'She's a substitute. She only fills in at weekends.'

A virgin goes to a knock shop in Elwood for a trial run. He was very, very polite and made a nice impression on the Madam. So she introduced him to one of the nicest of her girls.

A few minutes later he was leaving with a big smile on his face. 'What about some money?' asked the Madam.

'Oh, no thanks. You've been so nice to me already.'

A sailor gets into Sydney after month at sea, desperate for a bonk. He heads straight for the Touch of Class only to discover that there's a Rotary convention in town and all the girls are taken. 'Look, $5000 for one of your girls,' he says to the Madam.

'I'm sorry, sir, but the situation is hopeless. I can't squeeze you in anywhere.'

'Well, how about you?'

'Oh, I'm afraid I couldn't. Really, I haven't done it for ages.'

'Look, I'm really desperate.'

'Sorry, sir, you really wouldn't enjoy it. I'm so out of practice.'

'Look, $5000 plus a pair of Reeboks I bought in Honolulu.'

'Reeboks, eh! All right, but don't blame me if you're disappointed.'

He starts going hammer and tong and is a little bit disappointed because she just lies there. Then, suddenly, she puts an arm around him. And then another!

Encouraged, he renews his efforts and soon she throws a leg around him. And then the other.

When they're finished the sailor smiles with his approval. 'That really wasn't too bad, considering you're out of practice. You really got into it there at the end, arms, legs, the whole bit.'

'Oh, that. No, I was just trying my Reeboks on.'

It was a very expensive brothel but the women all looked like his auntie. There they were, sitting in a row, hair in curlers, fluffy slippers and chenille dressing-gowns. The Madam explained, 'We specialise in clients who suffer from premature ejaculation.'

The bloke went to an S&M parlour and asked the mistress for a woman he could whip. 'You want to do the whipping? We don't usually go in for that sort of thing here. That'll cost you extra. A thousand dollars.'

Insisting on payment in advance, the Madam introduced him to an expert in bondage who copped a few minutes of flagellation before protesting.

'Christ, I've had enough of this. When are you going to stop?'

'When?' screamed the client. 'When you give me my money back.'

A bloke went to a brothel at Kings Cross and it was really busy. So he finished up with an old bird who'd been on the game for decades. Deciding to make the best of it, he went hammer and tong.

'Why the hurry, love?' she asked.

'Sorry, but I haven't had a fuck for months,' he said.

'A sailor, are you?'

'No. I've just got out of the VD clinic.'

'What's the tucker like, love?' said the woman. 'I'm going in tomorrow.'

A bloke goes to a brothel in Kings Cross and is led to a tiny bedroom where a prostitute awaits him. He is about to engage in an act of congress when he notices a cut in the side of her stomach. 'Christ, shouldn't you have that appendix sewn up?'

'No. It's so I can make a bit on the side.'

'You are charged that on the third of June you battered your wife to death with a hammer,' said the clerk of courts.

From the back of the court, a voice yelled, 'You rotten bastard.'

'You are further charged that on the same day you battered your mother-in-law to death with a hammer.'

The voice from the back shouted, 'You filthy rotten bastard!'

The judge had the bloke hauled before him. 'I'm

sorry, your Honour, but I'm his next-door neighbour,' he explained. 'And when I asked him for a loan of the hammer, the rotten filthy bastard said he didn't have one.'

The cops raided a brothel in Kings Cross. In one of the booths they found an Asian bloke bonking like crazy. 'What's your name?'

'My name is Ting.'

In the next room they found another Asian bloke sitting quietly in a shabby armchair. 'And what's your name?'

'My name is Ting.'

'Oh yeah,' said the sergeant suspiciously. 'How come we've just arrested Ting in the room next door?'

'He is Ru Ting. I am Wah Ting.'

A woman decided she wanted a divorce and consulted a solicitor.

'Have you any grounds?'

'Yes, about four acres.'

'Do you have a grudge?'

'No, but we've a lovely carport.'

'Does he beat you up?'

'No, I'm up first every morning.'

'Then why do you want a divorce?'

'Because he cannot carry on an intelligent conversation.'

'Quick! I can hear my husband coming. He's a policeman and he's twice as big as you.'

'Where's the back door?'

'We haven't got one.'

'Okay, where would you like one?'

Rules

1. The Female Always Makes the Rules
   a. The rules are subject to change at any time without notice.
   b. No man can possibly know all the rules. Nearly all females are born with this knowledge.
   c. If the female suspects the males know any of the rules, she may immediately change any or all of the rules.
2. The Female Is Never Wrong
   a. If the female is wrong, it is because of a misunderstanding which was the direct result of something the male did or said wrong.
   b. If rule 2a applies, the male must apologise immediately for causing the misunderstanding.

3. **The Female Can Change Her Mind at Any Given Point in Time.**
   a. The male must never change his mind without written consent from the female.
4. **The Female Has Every Right to Be Upset or Angry at Any Time.**
   a. The male must remain calm at all times, unless the female wants him to be upset or angry.
   b. The female must under no circumstances let the male know whether or not she wants him to be upset or angry.
5. **Any Attempt by the Male to Change Any of the Rules Will Not Be Tolerated.**

A motorist was cruising along the Hume Highway at the normal speed when he suddenly noticed a police car right behind him. He accelerated to 100 km/h and then to 115 km/h, and so on, ever increasingly with the police close behind. Soon the squad car overtook and signalled him to stop. A very irate constable demanded an explanation for his erratic and illegal behaviour. The motorist was most anxious to explain. 'It's like this, Sergeant. Last week one of your officers ran away with my wife, and I was afraid he was bringing her back!'

She was worried about her breasts. 'Do you think I should try silicon implants?'

'Too expensive,' grunted her husband. 'Just get a roll of Sorbent and rub it along your cleavage.'

'Will that make them bigger?'

'Well, it did a great job on your arse.'

After years of marriage they were still hopelessly in love and had a marvellous sex life. But after a mild heart attack his doctor told him that he had to give up sex.

'In your delicate state, intercourse would almost certainly be fatal,' said the doctor.

So husband and wife agreed that they'd sleep apart. She upstairs, he downstairs.

For a week they endured this, tossing and turning and feeling increasingly randy.

Then, next night, they met on the stairs. 'Darling, I was just on my way down to kill you,' said the wife.

'Funny you should say that, dearest. I was just coming up to commit suicide.'

She was looking younger than she'd looked for years. Quite radiant. 'Darling, can you see anything different about me?' she inquired of her husband.

'Yes, dear, you're not wearing a bra.'

'However did you know that?'

'Well, all the wrinkles have gone from your face.'

She: 'Just one more word out of you and I'm going home to Mother.'

He: 'Taxi!'

It was a warm Sunday afternoon, the wife was browsing through a magazine, he was just dozing.

Looking up from her magazine, she said, 'Bruce, do we have sex relations?'

'Of course we do, woman.'

'Then how come they never send us any Christmas cards?'

'I found my wife in bed with my best friend.'

'You bitter?'

'Yeah, and I bit him, too.'

A bloke came home and caught his wife in bed with the next-door neighbour. He shoved him against the wall and aimed his shotgun at his testicles. 'I'm going to blow your balls off.'

'Come on, mate. I'm a sitting duck. How about giving me a sporting chance?'

'Okay, swing 'em!'

'I'm into wife swapping. I'll accept anything in exchange.'

Two blokes were talking about Freudian slips.

'Don't talk to me about them,' said one. 'I made the worst Freudian slip of my life this morning.'

'What happened?' asked the other.

'Well, I was at breakfast and I meant to say to the wife, "Darling, please pass the Corn Flakes". But by mistake, it just slipped out. I said, "YOU'RE RUINING MY FUCKING LIFE, YOU BITCH!!!!".'

A big bloke was working on a construction project in Africa, and while he was there he fell in love with a small, beautifully formed pygmy woman. They married and he brought her back to Australia, proudly introducing her to his boss.

'Good grief, John,' he whispered. 'She's not much bigger than your hand.'

'I know,' he whispered back, 'but she's a bloody sight better.'

It's late, late, late on a foggy, foggy night. And there's a knock at the front door.

The wife said, 'Don't sit there like a beached whale. Go and see who it is.'

The grumbling husband opened the door and there, in the shadows, surrounded by swirling mists, was a terrifying figure in a black cloak.

'Who are you?' the husband whispered.

'Jack the Ripper.'

The husband turned his head and shouted, 'Darling, it's for you!'

'Do you remember, dear,' said the old woman to her husband on their 60th anniversary, 'how, 60 years ago tonight, in this very room, you didn't even give me time to take off my shawl before you started making wild, passionate love to me?'

'Yes, dear, I remember,' the old bloke replied in

a quavery, wavery voice. 'But the way I feel now, you'd have time to knit one.'

She was suing her husband for divorce. The reason: his insatiable appetite for sex. He was at it day and night and night and day. Finally she'd had enough and threw herself on the mercy of the court. 'Very well,' said the judge, 'I'll hear your case, but first you must go over to the clerk and file your petition.'

'File my petition, your Honour? I couldn't even touch it with a powder puff.'

The wife was furious when she arrived home unexpectedly and found her husband bonking a lady midget. 'You promised me weeks ago that you'd never cheat on me again,' she raged.

'Take it easy, darl,' said the husband. 'Can't you see I'm tapering off?'

Sarah is dying. Sam at her bedside looks thoughtful. With a final effort, Sarah lifts her head off the pillow and says, 'Sam, before I go, grant me my dying wish.'

'What is it?' asks Sam.

'Promise me that you'll never marry again.'

'I have to remain alone for the rest of my life?' cries Sam, raising his arms.

'Perhaps that is a bit much to ask,' says Sarah, 'but promise me that if you remarry you won't let her wear my dresses.'

'Sure, my dear. I promise you that,' says Sam. 'They don't even fit her.'

A knight of the realm awoke in his Toorak mansion and was astonished to see that he had a sizeable erection. He called for his butler. 'Yes, a magnificent weapon,' said the loyal serf. 'Shall I inform her ladyship?'

'Christ, no. Bring me my baggy golf trousers and I'll try to smuggle it down to my mistress.'

A bloke was telling his mate that he'd just got a letter from an irate husband. 'He says he'll shoot my balls off if I don't stop screwing his wife.'

'Well, stop screwing her and you'll be okay,' said the mate.

'It's not that simple,' said the bloke. 'The letter was anonymous.'

Staring up at the ceiling during sexual intercourse, the wife yawned and said, 'This room needs decorating.'

The husband snarled in response, 'The bloke who invented decorating needs fucking.'

To which his wife replied, 'How times have changed. On our wedding night you said the bloke who invented fucking needs decorating.'

'I had a funny dream last night,' said the wife at breakfast. 'I dreamt I went to an auction where they were selling willies. There was one there which was fabulous – nine inches and thick, with a fine-skinned head surrounded by a foreskin like a frill-necked lizard.' She sighed, 'Liz Taylor bought it for two and a half million dollars.'

Her husband said, 'Love, did you see any of my size there?'

'Yes,' she said, 'they were selling at a dollar a bundle.'

Next morning the husband came down from bed and said, 'Funny thing, after your dream last night I dreamt I was at an auction where they were selling vaginas.' He smiled dreamily. 'There was one there that was obviously a double-rose, surrounded by the fluffiest pubic hair, and the silkiest clitoris imaginable. Kerry Packer paid five million for it.'

'Did you see anything like mine there, darl?' the wife asked.

'Yeah,' said the husband, 'but I didn't wait to see it sold – the auctioneer was standing in it!'

'I was just thinking, darling, we've had such a marvellous marriage, we've enjoyed a great life together, but one of these days one of us will pass on.'

'True, but don't worry about that now.'

'Well, I was just thinking, when it does happen, I'd like to go and live in Queensland.'

'What the hell do you think you're doing?' yelled the husband when he found his wife in bed with a total stranger.

'There you are,' said the wife to her lover. 'I told you he was thick.'

'Why are you taking so long?' demanded the wife during a protracted bout of intercourse.

'I'm trying, I'm trying,' said her puffing spouse, 'but I just can't think of anyone.'

'How come your marriage has lasted 50 years?'

'Simple. We decided from the beginning that she'd make all the little decisions and I'd decide the major issues.'

'Such as?'

'Well, she decided where I'd work, where we'd live, what school the kids would go to. And I made the major decisions. Like what to do about the ozone hole, the Balkans and sanctions in South Africa.'

'Let's try it a different way tonight.'

'Ooo, let's. What do you have in mind?'

'Back to back.'

'How do we do that?'

'I've invited another couple.'

Though still regarding herself as attractive, the young wife noticed that her husband was becoming less and less interested in their sex lives. So she bought a copy of *Cosmopolitan* and opened the sealed section. It told her to try a few novelty turns, like greeting her husband at the front door wearing nothing but Glad wrap, or high-heeled boots. And there was also a mail-order catalogue that allowed you to order kinky things. But none of it worked. Her husband still seemed bored and listless.

So she persuaded him to visit a psychiatrist and, after a few visits, he was as good as new. And she was enjoying multiple orgasms. But there was a mysterious aspect to his behaviour. Often, during the middle of making love, he'd leap out of bed and rush into the bathroom. She could hear him mumbling something for a minute or two and then he'd return rearing to go.

Finally, she could not contain her curiosity. So when he ran into the bathroom and shut the door, she peeped through the keyhole. And there he was, staring into the mirror, muttering to himself, 'She's not my wife . . . she's not my wife . . . she's not my wife.'

A bloke who was very, very good at Australian history won a pile of prizes on *Sale of the Century*. There were all sorts of things – a new house, a new car, a new boat, a holiday home at Surfers.

Driving up to Queensland, he was stopped by a policeman. 'Did you know you were driving without tail-lights?'

The bloke leapt out of his brand new Lexus looking highly agitated. The policeman recognised him. 'Ah, you're the bloke off *Sale of the Century*. Look, mate, don't worry, it's not a major offence. Nothing to get too upset about.'

'It mightn't mean much to you,' said the bloke, 'but to me I've lost the missus, two kids and my brand new caravan.'

A bloke and his wife went to a family planning clinic.

'We've been married for ten years and we've got no kids,' said the husband. 'And the next-door neighbours say it's because we're stupid.'

'Nonsense,' smiled the doctor. 'It's probably to do with your diet. Or it might be a question of timing. How many times a week do you do it?'

'Do what?' asked the wife.

A Colonel in the Australian Army, stationed in Melbourne, would tell his wife that he had to go away on military manoeuvres every weekend. In fact, he was off bonking a girlfriend in Bendigo. She was really pretty, early thirties, affectionate and energetic. And after their rapturous weekends he'd always offer her a present. 'Would you like a watch? A bangle? A necklace?'

'No, darling,' she'd reply, 'I don't want anything. Just you. Just our weekends together.' But he'd insist that he wanted to buy her something. Whereupon she'd say, 'Well, I would like one of those Swiss Army knives. You know, with the red handle, the little blade, the big blade, the corkscrew, the magnifying glass, the scissors and the thing for taking stones out of horses' hooves.'

Next weekend he was back again for 48 hours of rapturous lovemaking. And, on his departure, he'd ask her what present she'd like. He promised to bring it the very next time they met.

'A little watercolour? A lovely piece of porcelain?'

'No, just the pocketknife.'

The next time he came, he had bad news. 'I'm afraid the Army has posted me to Perth. So I won't be able to see you again, perhaps for years. But I have brought you the memento you asked for.'

Though weeping at the thought of losing him, she smiled bravely as she unwrapped the tissue paper. And there, lo and behold, was the Swiss Army knife, with the red handle, the little blade, the big blade, the nail file, the magnifying glass, the little scissors, the miniature pliers and the thing for taking stones out of horses' hooves. Wiping away her tears, she crossed the room and opened a drawer, which turned out to be full of . . . Swiss Army knives.

'My darling,' said the Colonel, somewhat confused, 'why all the pocketknives?'

'My dear, at the moment I'm an attractive woman. Men desire me. But let's face it, I won't always keep my looks. Time will exact its toll, take its ravages upon me. But when it does, my dearest, there isn't much that a boy scout wouldn't do for a good pocketknife.'

In a pub toilet a couple of blokes are standing side by side having a pee. One spits and says, 'Shit, she could drive.'

The other said, 'Who?'

'This sheila. I was travelling from Geelong to Melbourne when my car broke down and I had to hitchhike. Excuse me, shit she could drive. Now, where was I? Yeah, hitchhiking. Suddenly this souped-up Fairlane 500 pulls up and there's a blonde driving. She leans over and unlocks the door. I climb in and she floors it. I look across at the speedometer and see that, even allowing for parallax, we're doing about 160 km/h. "You're a quick driver, lady", I sez. I see a slight smile on her face. Well, it's not long before we get into traffic on the outskirts of Melbourne. She weaves in and out – doing 120 km/h. I'm a bit concerned at this stage. (He spits.) Shit, she could drive! Somehow we made it to Footscray. She's still doing 100 km/h through thick traffic. Then she pulls on to the wrong side of the road, makes a squeeze between a tram and a semi-trailer coming towards us. By now I'm crouching under the dash with fear. (Spits again.) I said to her, "Lady, if you make it through the gap I'll suck your box dry". Shit she could drive!'

After months at sea, a sailor checked into a waterfront pub and asked reception to 'send up a whore'. Unfortunately he was talking to the new owner, a formidable Catholic lady in her sixties who abhorred adultery and licentiousness. She went upstairs to get her husband to throw the sailor out. He reminded her that he was a regular guest. And as well, he was a pretty big bloke. 'You're too frightened to throw him out? Then I'll do it myself.'

So she marched up the stairs and, pretty soon, there was the sound of breaking furniture, thumps and curses. Finally the sailor came down, shirt torn and exhausted. 'That was quite a whore you sent up,' he said to the publican, 'but it was more like a wrestle than a screw.'

A bloke came into the pub with a huge bruise on his head. 'What happened to you?' asked the barman.

'Well, me and the sheila next door were doing it doggy-style in the back yard. She heard her husband coming and ran under the house.'

A bloke goes into a country pub. Says to the bar lady, 'How about a quickie?' She tells him to behave himself. He says it's worth $100. And, as things are a bit tight, she agrees. This goes on for five nights. She doesn't see him the next week. 'Where have you been?' she asks him when he finally returns.

'Oh, I went back to Brisbane.'

'Oh,' she said, 'I've got a brother in Brisbane.'

'Yeah, I know,' he said. 'He gave me $500 to give you.'

'Quick, barman, give me a drink.'

'Okay, what would you like?'

'Ten whiskies.'

'Ten?'

'Yeah, I've just had my first blow job.'

'And you're celebrating?'

'No. I'm trying to get the taste out of my mouth.'

For months they'd sat side by side on the verandah of the twilight home. Little by little they'd moved their rocking chairs closer together. After this tentative, shy foreplay he said, 'Fuck you.'

And she said, 'Fuck you, too.'

There was a long silence. Finally he said, 'So much for oral sex.'

'I may be 87, but I make love nearly every night of the week.'

'Bullshit.'

'No, I'm dinky-di. I nearly made it on Monday, I nearly made it on Tuesday . . .'

Three old blokes from the twilight home were given, as a treat, a day at the beach. And it turned out to be a nudist beach. They were watching the various young women agog.

When the prettiest of them all walked by, one of the old blokes said, 'I'd like to give her a hug.'

'I'd like to give her a kiss,' said the second.

And the third old bloke said, 'What was that other thing we used to do?'

Bigamy: One wife too many.

Monogamy: Same idea.

'Sir, this is the reception desk. Are you entertaining a woman in your room?'

'Just a minute, I'll ask her.'

Always be sincere even if you don't mean it.

If it floats, flies or fucks, rent it, don't buy it!

If it has tits or wheels you are bound to have trouble with it!

A bachelor is a man who hasn't made the same mistake once!

There were two queues at the Pearly Gates. One, quite long, was ranged behind a sign saying MEN DOMINATED BY THEIR WIVES.

Another read MEN NOT DOMINATED BY THEIR WIVES. There was just one bloke in the queue, and he looked extremely timid. St Peter asked him, 'Are you sure you should be standing here?'

'Yes,' came the reply, 'my wife told me to.'

Two queens got into a heated argument at a party so they went outside and exchanged blows.

This isn't a beer gut – it's a solar panel for a sex machine.

A bloke bought himself a new Schick blade and, after some days of shaving, replaced it. His wife retrieved the discarded blade and used it to shave her armpits. Then his daughter used it to shave her legs. And his mother-in-law, most inadvisably, used the blade to cut some dental floss caught between her teeth.

Unfortunately she swallowed the blade, but that's not the end of the story. Far from it. On its way down, it performed a tonsillectomy, an appendectomy and a hysterectomy. It subsequently circumcised her husband, castrated her lover, gave the bishop a hare lip, amputated the fingers of several close friends – and still had five good shaves left in it.

Two ladies were reclining in deckchairs as the ocean liner crossed the Atlantic. 'I can't believe that I'm here,' said one.

'My husband had to scrimp and scrape to get the money together.'

'Your first trip?' the other asked snootily. 'This is my 30th crossing. You see, my husband works for Cunard.'

'Well, so does mine,' said the first woman. 'I told you that. But there's no reason to swear about it.'

An American tourist pulls over the Hertz car in the middle of nowhere for a pee. Suddenly a bloke jumps out from behind a tree, pointing a shotgun at him. 'Pull yourself off,' he orders.

'What?'

'Masturbate. Right now.'

Nervously, the tourist obliges.

'Now, do it again.'

'I can't do it again.'

'Do it again!'

So the tourist masturbates for a second time.

'Okay, once more.'

'I couldn't do it once more, no matter what. You may as well shoot me.'

'No, that's fine. Now you can give my sister a lift to the next town.'

The captain of a Boeing discovered a very serious fault in the aircraft at 35 000 feet. After breaking the news to the crew he announced to the passengers that the plane would crash in about 15 minutes. He told them that the stewardesses would be available for nooky at the back of the aircraft if anyone was interested. Whereas he, himself, was wondering whether the very beautiful African American woman in 2B would be willing to join him in the cockpit.

Why not? she thought, asking the pilot, 'But why me?'

'Well, when a plane goes down, they always find the black box, and I want to be in it.'

A tourist arrived in a very small town and stopped for petrol. The place seemed deserted. Finally he spotted a funeral procession with a big bloke and a big dog walking behind the hearse. And behind them, in single file, about a dozen blokes trudged in respectful silence.

'Somebody important died?' the tourist asked.

'Yeah, the wife,' answered the bloke with the dog.

'What happened?'

'The dog savaged her.'

Whereupon the traveller asked, 'Do you want to sell the dog?'

'Yeah,' said the big bloke, 'but join the queue.'

The Methodist missionary had been living with the tribe on the Sepik River for a couple of years when the chief took him aside. 'We might be halfway up the Sepik, but you're up shit creek.'

'Why? What have I done?'

'Yesterday a white baby was born to my daughter and you're the only white man for hundreds and hundreds of miles.' The chief started fondling his axe.

'But, Chief, I know it looks bad. But see your pigs wallowing in the mud?'

'Of course I can see them.'

'Well, all of them are white. But there's one black pig and . . .'

'Okay,' said the chief. 'I'll keep quiet if you keep quiet.'

Bill, a blacktracker, never got along with his constable. He resented being called Abo, blackie or nigger. One day, while they were tracking a couple of drunks who'd escaped from the local lock-up, Bill spotted the legendary yellow-belly goanna. Legendary, because traditional belief holds that whoever catches this rare creature is granted three wishes. At the same time, twice as much of the same wish is granted to whomever you hate the most.

So Bill caught the goanna and, twirling it round by the tail, wished aloud, 'I want a big house.' Lo and behold, a big house appeared from nowhere along with two big houses for the constable.

'Shit,' said the constable. 'Girls, Billy, girls. Wish for some sheilas.'

'Okay, okay,' said Bill. 'I want a hundred beautiful girls.' Instantly, 100 pulchritudinous women appeared by Bill's house and 200 beside the constable's houses. Just as the constable was about to go rushing in the front door with some of his girls, Bill gave the goanna another twirl and whispered his third wish.

'I want my sex urge reduced by 50 per cent.'

Family Ties

73

It's still very, very hard for kids to get jobs. So when one woman met another in the supermarket, she said, 'Tell me, how's your son Basil?'

'Basil's getting along fine. He's a scientist, as you know, and just got first-class honours in quantum mechanics at Sydney University.'

'And your daughter?'

'She's smart too. She graduated from the University of New South Wales with degrees in arts, economics and the law.'

'You must be very proud of them. What a talented family. And little Fred? What's he doing?'

'Well, Fred's a drug dealer. If it wasn't for him, we'd all be starving.'

Around lunchtime Fiona left school and headed for home, crying because her first period had started and she had no idea what it was. The teacher, reluctant to get involved, had suggested she talk to her mum.

Between the school and home was a bridge, and as she was halfway across it, a little boy who was wagging school came out from beneath it and said, 'Why are you crying?'

She said, 'Billy, I'm bleeding.'

He said, 'Give us a look.'

She cheerfully obliged.

'Christ,' he said. 'No wonder you're bleedin'. Your cock's been cut off.'

A kid missed the school bus and turned up hours late on his pony. The teacher demanded an explanation.

'Dad went to bed with no pyjamas.'

'And what's that got to do with anything?'

'Well, Dad went to bed with no pyjamas and at 2.30 this morning we heard a noise in the chook shed, so Dad got the shotgun and we went to look. Dad had the gun and no pyjamas and Mum, me and the dog walked behind him. We got outside the chook shed and Dad cocked the gun, pushed the door open and said, 'Who's there?' Just then, my dog put his cold nose on Dad's bum, and I've been cleaning up fuckin' chooks all morning.'

A kid walked out of the toilet into the kitchen where his mum was mixing a cake.

'Can I lick the bowl, Mum?'

'No, you little bugger. Flush it like anyone else.'

What's the difference between street kids and elephants?

Street kids try to forget.

What's the difference between a black baby and a white baby?

Five minutes in a microwave oven.

A little boy woke up crying and ran to see his mother.

'Mummy, Mummy. A voice came to me in my dreams. It said that my grandmother would die today.'

The mother comforted him and told him not to worry, that it was only a dream.

But when he returned from school he found his mother sobbing in the kitchen. She told him that her mother had died just a few hours ago.

That night the voice returned. This time it said that the house on the corner would burn down on Friday night. The mother comforted him, telling him not to worry. But on Saturday morning the whole family was awoken by the sound of the fire engines.

A few days later the voice returned saying, 'Your dog Spot is going to die today.'

His mother tried to comfort and soothe him, but as he returned from school he saw the dog skittled by a car.

A few weeks passed and the voice in his dreams returned. This time it said, 'Your father is going to die at exactly 12 noon today.'

The poor little boy was horrified. So Dad said he'd stay home and help soothe the little lad. He did his best. As they sat at the table for lunch, the hands on the face of the clock reached 12 noon and nothing happened. The child relaxed and became cheerful as the minutes ticked by. But after five minutes there was a great banging at the door. The mother opened it to find the woman from over the road who blurted out, 'Come quick, or let me use your telephone. The milkman dropped dead in the middle of the street about five minutes ago.'

'How did you break your arm?'

'I swerved to avoid a child and fell out of bed.'

The butcher could still remember the day it happened. That young woman, babe in arms, coming into the shop and announcing that the little boy was his. What was he going to do about it?

He tried to hush her up as best he could by promising to supply her with free meat until the kid was 16. And he'd been ticking off the years ever since.

Finally the kid came in to collect the week's supply and announced, 'Guess what? I'll be 16 tomorrow.'

'Yes,' said the butcher with a grin. 'So tell your mum this'll be the last free steak, chops and sausages she'll get. And watch the expression on her face.'

'Mister, she told me to tell you that she's been getting free bread, milk and groceries for the past 16 years. And to watch the expression on your face.'

What's the difference between broccoli and snot?

You can't get kids to eat broccoli.

Grandfather was becoming a pain in the neck. He lived with his grandson and granddaughter-in-law, both very successful professional people who often entertained influential friends and colleagues at dinner parties in their beautiful home. On these occasions, Grandfather was not left out. He attended the dinner parties and, fancying himself as the star turn of the evening, often dominated the occasions with loud and garrulous pronouncements on irrelevant subjects, non-stop from the first martini to the passing of the port, embarrassing everybody in the process.

At last his grandson realised that something had to be done about Grandfather, so he took him aside one day and asked him, kindly and tactfully, if he would tone things down and take more of a back seat in future. Grandfather seemed surprised at this request, to which, however, he finally agreed. His grandson was very relieved, assured his wife that the problem was solved and that Grandfather would turn out to be a paragon of social virtue.

And so Grandfather proved to be. On the next occasion, he sat at the table, quietly eating and drinking, listening attentively to the scintillating table-talk and nodding agreement from time to time – well-mannered, civil and circumspect. His family were delighted.

Towards the end of dinner, Grandfather rose slowly to his feet, put down his napkin, and gave a little bow. 'Turning in?' his grandson enquired, a little hopefully. Grandfather pushed back his chair and walked slowly to the door of the dining room. He opened the door and turned to face the company. He nodded.

'Yes,' he said, 'I think I'll have a quick shit and hit the sack!'

Hire teenagers while they still know everything.

A father-to-be was waiting anxiously outside the labour ward where his wife was hard at it. A nurse popped her head around the door. 'You have a little boy. But it might be an idea to go and have a cup of coffee because we think there might be another.'

Turning pale, he left. An hour later he returned to be told that he was the father of twins. 'But we think there's another one on the way. Come back in a little while.'

This time he went to the pub next door, phoning in to hear that there was a third baby, with a fourth imminent.

After a few stiff whiskies he called the hospital again but was so pissed that he dialled a wrong number – and got the recorded cricket score. Emitting an agonised cry, he collapsed on the floor. As the barman picked him up he heard the voice from the phone, 'The score is 96 all out. And the last one was a duck.'

'My dad's so fast,' said one boy, 'that he can fire an arrow at a tree, run like buggery and catch the arrow before it hits it.'

'My dad's faster than that,' said the second kid. 'He can drop a brick from the tenth floor of a building and run down the stairs and catch it before it hits the ground.'

'My dad's faster than your dads,' said the third kid. 'He works for the Brunswick Council. He knocks off at five and he's always home by two thirty.'

'Mum, where did I come from?'

'From under a cabbage, dear.'

'And where did you come from, Mum?'

'The stork brought me.'

'Grandpa?'

'The stork brought him too.'

'Mum, doesn't it worry you to think that there've been no natural births in our family for three generations?'

The young mum was having coffee with her friends when her three-year-old raced into the room saying, 'I wanna piss. I wanna piss.' Embarrassed, she took him to the toilet and told him, 'Next time you want to do wee-wees, don't use that word. Come in and whisper.'

Shortly thereafter, the child interrupted again by rushing in, hopping from one foot to the other. 'I gotta whisper. I gotta whisper.'

Well, it was something of an improvement, so his mother gave him a slice of tart.

That night he climbed out of his cot and ran into his parents' bedroom. Mum wasn't there but his dad was just dozing off. 'What is it, little fella?'

'I wanna whisper, Daddy, I wanna whisper.'

'Fine, son, fine. Come and whisper in Dad's ear.'

There are two sisters who are Siamese twins, one of whom is a major Tom Jones fan. She sees a poster saying, *Tom Jones. One Night Only in Chicago*.

'We've got to go!' she cries.

'Do we have to?' says the other sister, who's much more into jazz.

'Oh, please, please, please! It'd mean a lot.'

'Oh, okay,' says the other sister, and off they go.

On the night of the concert the sisters have a front-row seat. Tom does a great gig. The joint is jumping. Everyone has a wonderful time. When it's all over, the sisters wait till everyone else has left the auditorium because they hate all the pointing-and-staring-at-the-Siamese-twins routine. Once outside, the sister who's the fan says, 'Wasn't that great! Did you enjoy it?'

'Yeah, as a matter of fact, I did,' replies the other sister.

'Great! Then you won't mind if we hang around the backstage door to see if we can get a glimpse of Tom.'

'Ohhh, do we have to?' says the other sister.

'Yeah, come on, it'll be great!'

'Oh, okay . . .'

So they're hanging around the backstage door and out comes Tom. He can't help but notice the Siamese twins standing there, so he goes over to talk to them.

'Hi,' says Tom. 'I saw you there in the front row. Did you have a good time?'

'Yeah, it was *great*!' the sisters chorus.

Feeling a little uncomfortable with the whole situation, Tom says, 'Look . . . um . . . why don't you two come backstage, have a drink?'

'Great! Love to!' says the sister who's the fan, and off they all go.

So, they drink a few champagnes and, after a while – lo and behold – a bit of a rapport is building between Tom and the sister who's the fan. She says, 'Tom, pardon me for being forward, only, when you're a Siamese twin, you learn not to stand on courtesy. But, have we got a bit of a vibe happening here?'

Tom thinks about this and says, 'Yes . . . yes we have.'

To which she replies, 'Well, Tom. Pardon me for being forward again, but I think you'd like to make love to me, wouldn't you?'

Tom thinks about this even longer, then says, 'Yes, but . . .'

'It's my sister, isn't it, Tom?' says the sister who's the fan.

'No, it's . . .'

'Tom, my sister and I have *grown up* as Siamese twins. We're used to these situations. We have mechanisms for dealing with these sorts of things. If you'd like to make love to me, Tom, and I would dearly like to make love to you, then my sister will do what she always does in such situations. In order to tune herself out, she will play the trombone.'

'She'll *what?*'

'Play the trombone.'

And, sure enough, for the next hour and a half – as Tom and the sister who's the fan make glorious, passionate love – the other sister plays a very commendable selection of jazz, Dixie and some blues trombone.

And at the end of an hour and a half, as the other sister packs away her trombone, Tom and the sister who's the fan kiss each other a starry-eyed goodbye. It's been a wonderful experience. No questions asked. No commitment expected. Once-in-a-lifetime. Goodbye.

Two years later, up go the posters, *Tom Jones. One Night Only in Chicago*.

'Tom's back!' says the sister who's the fan. 'He's on! We've gotta go!'

'Oh, come on,' says the other sister. 'We've done that.'

'Yeah, but we had a great time, didn't we?'

'Yeah . . .'

'Well, let's go!'

'Oh, all right then.'

'*And*,' says the sister who's the fan, 'if we hang around backstage, maybe Tom'll see us. Maybe he'll invite us back for a few drinks. *Maybe* something more could happen!'

'Oh, *come* on!' says the other sister. 'What makes you think he'll remember us?'

What's the definition of confusion?

Father's Day in the western suburbs.

What does *pas de deux* mean?

You're the father of twins.

School of Hard Knocks

87

Two naked professors are sitting on a verandah at the local college talking about life, death, God and general theories of existence.

One turns to the other and says, 'By the way, have you read Marx?' To which the other replies, 'Yes, aren't these cane chairs murder!'

A university lecturer asked her students to describe in a page or less the difference between ignorance and apathy. She was forced to give an A-plus to the student who replied, 'I don't know and I don't care.'

A lecturer in sociology at La Trobe University was touring north-eastern Victoria and called into Glenrowan pub for a beer. He struck up a conversation in the bar with some of the locals and, naturally enough, the topic soon drifted around to that of Ned Kelly. Undeterred by the fact that most of the locals claimed to be related to Ned, even if somewhat remotely, the academic decided to provoke his audience by claiming that a number of psychologists and historians of his acquaintance had put forward the hypothesis that Ned was homosexual.

Springing to Kelly's defence, one of the locals straightened himself up and, with a defiant look at the lecturer, said scornfully, 'I don't know anything about that, mate, but if he was, he would have been a bloody good one!'

A modern fable: An owl hovering in the forest spotted a rabbit in a small clearing. The rabbit was wearing gold-rimmed glasses and was seated at a computer typing away earnestly. Bemused, the owl perched in a tree and watched.

A huge black bear lurched into the clearing and roared, 'I am going to eat you for lunch.'

'No, no!' said the rabbit. 'I'm writing my thesis

on the topic that bears don't eat rabbits – rabbits devour bears.'

The bear guffawed, whereupon the rabbit said, 'Come into this cave and I'll show you.'

Into the cave they went. The owl heard screams and thuds.

After five minutes, the rabbit emerged, brushing a few specks of black fur from his pelt, sat down and resumed his typing.

A large grey wolf appeared. 'I'm going to eat you for dinner.'

'No, no!' said the rabbit. 'I'm writing this thesis on the topic that wolves don't eat rabbits – rabbits consume wolves.'

The wolf sneered, whereupon the rabbit said, 'Come into this cave and I'll show you.'

Into the cave they went. The owl heard screams and thuds. After five minutes the rabbit emerged, brushing grey hair from his pelt, sat down and resumed his typing.

The owl was puzzled. 'May I go into the cave you entered?' he asked.

'By all means,' answered the rabbit.

In the depths of the cave it was very dark, and even the owl had to wait a few moments before he could make out the scene inside. Then he saw an enormous lion, sitting on his haunches, surrounded by cleanly picked bones and a few patches of black and grey fur. Thoughtfully, he flew out.

'What I have witnessed must have a moral,' he told the rabbit.

'Yes,' said the rabbit, 'and here it is. It doesn't matter what the topic of your thesis is – as long as you've got a strong supervisor.'

Three kids were having an experimental smoke behind the school shelter shed.

'My dad can blow smoke through his nose.'

'My dad can blow smoke through his ears.'

'My dad blows smoke through his arse. You can see the nicotine stains in his undies.'

On the first day of school, the children were asked by their teacher what they did in their holidays.

Jasmine said, 'We went to Cairns and saw the rainforest and went on a boat to see the Barrier Reef. We had a lovely time.'

Brittany said, 'We went whale watching at Stradbroke Island. We camped and saw whales and dolphins. We had a top time.'

Aaron said, 'We went to stay on Uncle John's farm and we rode horses and helped with the milking. It was terrific.'

Rhys said, 'We had a great time. We put sticks of dynamite up cane toads' arses . . .'

The teacher said, 'Rhys! The correct term is rectum.'

'That's right, miss. Wrecked 'em! Blew their fuckin' brains out!'

A female teacher stands at the blackboard and says, 'Okay, kids, we're going to have a quiz today. Now, if there were three crows sitting on a fence, and a farmer shoots one, how many will be left?'

A smartarse puts up his hand and says, 'Ooo, me, Miss. I know this one!'

'Not you, Jeff. You're always answering.'

'But I know this one.'

'Okay, okay.'

'There'd be no crows left. One would be dead and the other two would've flown off at the gunshot.'

'No, no, no,' says the teacher. 'This is a maths quiz. If there were three and the farmer shot one, there'd be two left.'

So the smartarse kid says, 'Okay, Miss. I've got a little quiz for you. There are three women eating iceblocks. One of them's sucking it, one of them's licking it and one of them's biting it. Which one of the women is married?'

The teacher doesn't know how to answer. She

thinks a bit. She looks around. She thinks some more. 'Well,' she says finally, 'perhaps the woman who is sucking the iceblock.'

'No,' says the kid. 'It's the one with the wedding ring on her finger. But boy, I *like* the way you're thinking.'

A proud mother prepared her little boy for his first day at school. 'Now, if you want to have a wee-wee, hold up your hand in the class and the teacher will ask you what you want. Tell her you want to go to the toilet and she'll give you permission to leave the room.'

During his first class, the little boy felt the urge and put his hand up. The teacher asked what he wanted. 'I have to go to the toilet,' he said.

'Okay, it's the door on the right at the end of the corridor.'

A moment later he was back at the classroom door looking agitated. 'I can't find it,' he said.

The teacher said, very slowly and carefully, 'Go out, turn left, go to the end of the corridor, and through the door on the right.'

No sooner had he disappeared than he was back again, choking back tears.

'I still can't find it.'

The teacher hailed an older boy walking along the corridor and asked him to show the little lad where the toilet was. They disappeared. When they came back the teacher asked if everything was all right. He said, 'Yes, teacher. He had his underpants on back to front.'

It was a little bush school back o' Bourke. It was the first day for a new teacher, a young woman from the city. She stood nervously at the blackboard.

'Give me a word beginning with A.'

'Arsehole,' said little Mick.

She blushed and said, 'And a word beginning with B?'

'Bastard,' said Freddie.

She decided to give C a miss and asked for a word beginning with D.

'Dwarf,' said Johnny.

Sighing with relief, she asked Johnny to explain what a dwarf was. 'A little cunt about this big,' Johnny said.

The teacher was giving a spelling lesson. She turned to the first boy. 'Now, Tommy, tell the class what your father is, and spell it.'

'My father's a carpenter. C-a-r-p-e-n-t-e-r.'

'Very good, Tommy. Now, Eddie.'

'My father's a butcher. B-u-t-c-h-e-r.'

'Very good, Eddie. This class's spelling is improving.' She turned to the next boy. 'Now, Willie.'

'My father's a shipwright, teacher. S-h-i-t-w-r-i-g-h-t.'

'No, Willie. Try again.'

'S-h-i-t-w-r-i-g-h-t.'

'You are wrong again, Willie. The correct spelling is s-h-i-P-w-r-i-g-h-t. Go and write it on the blackboard. Now, while Willie's doing that, you, Charlie, stand up and tell us what your father is and spell it.'

Charlie jumped to his feet. 'My father's a bookmaker. B-o-o-k-m-a-k-e-r. And six to four Willie writes s-h-i-t on the board!'

'Miss Paterson, as headmaster I must remind you that it's against the rules at this school for teachers to fraternise with students. There's a high level of concern in the community about paedophilia.'

'Yes, sir, headmaster, I know.'

'I'm told that you have a husky young 15-year-old at your home most nights. Ostensibly doing homework.'

'Yes, but it's platonic.'

'Platonic?'

'Yes, it's play for him and tonic for me.'

An art teacher was trying to encourage her young students to approach drawing and painting with freshness, originality. So she drew a circle on the blackboard and asked if anybody could think of a way to use it to represent the theme of poverty.

Little Mildred drew the skeleton of a fish inside the circle. 'You see, a family had only a little fish for dinner. And all that's left on the plate are the bones.'

'Very good, Mildred. But if the people were experiencing real poverty, wouldn't they have boiled the bones to make fish soup?'

She rubbed out the fish, redrew the circle and asked for another suggestion.

Little Fiona stepped up to the blackboard. She drew a series of dots in the circle.

'This family had only a loaf of bread to eat. Those dots are the crumbs left on the plate.'

'But if they were really hungry, wouldn't they have licked the plate completely clean of crumbs, Fiona? Now, that would be real poverty.'

The teacher rubbed out the dots and redrew the circle. 'Anyone else?'

Little Bruce stepped up. He drew a small ring in the centre of the circle and criss-crossed it with thin, spidery lines.

'And what does that represent?' asked the teacher.

'That is a bum covered with cobwebs. And if that isn't poverty, I don't know what is.'

The biology teacher at Ascham was making sure her young ladies had done their homework.

'Angela,' she asked, 'please name for me the organ of the body which, under the right conditions, expands to six times its normal size.'

'I'm sorry, Miss,' said Angela, 'but that's hardly a fit and proper question to ask a nice girl.'

'Denise?' said the teacher, 'can you answer the question?'

'Yes, Miss,' said Denise, 'the pupil of the eye, in dim light.'

'Perfectly correct,' said the teacher. 'And now, Angela, I have just three things to say to you. Number one, you haven't done your homework. Number two, you've a dirty mind. And number three, one of these days you're going to be very, very disappointed.'

A new teacher had taken over the class and she was very pretty.

'How old do you reckon she is?' said young Bruce.

'Dunno. But if we can get her knickers off, we'll know.'

'How come?'

'Well, on the back of mine it says eight to ten years.'

The little boy was having trouble with arithmetic, and whatever the teacher asked him he'd count on his fingers.

'Two plus two?'

'Four.'

'Three and three?'

'Six.'

'Now I want you to stop using your fingers. Put your hands in your pockets and tell me what is five plus five.'

The kid fumbled quietly before he gave the answer.

'Eleven,' he said.

Animal Magnetism

A lady had a very beautiful cat. She utterly adored it. As is the wont of ladies who live alone and adore their cats, she lavished tender care on the truly magnificent animal. One evening as she sat by the fireside stroking his wonderful coat, she dreamed of him turning into a handsome prince. In that instant there was a flash of light. The whole world seemed electrified. And lo and behold, before her stood the most handsome prince anyone could possibly imagine. She was dumbfounded. Whereupon this gorgeous hunk of masculine pulchritude said, 'Aren't you sorry now that you took me to the vet last week?'

A bloke was walking his kelpie along by the river when it slipped and fell in. And although it was a terrific cattle dog, the damn thing couldn't swim. Fortunately a German tourist was taking photos of gumtrees when he saw what happened. Quick as a flash, he dived in, dragged the dog out and gave it mouth-to-mouth.

'Are you a vet?' asked the grateful owner.

'Vet?' replied the German. 'I'm bloody soaking!'

Some drovers were arguing over the relative intelligence of their dogs. 'This mongrel of mine,' said one bloke, 'never, never gets it wrong. And I'm not talking simple commands like "Stay" and "Sit" and "Heel". I'm talking about five-word sentences and instant obedience.'

'Bullshit,' said the others, and collected $50 to back their scepticism. There was soon $100 on the bar so the bloke picked up his dog, threw it in the fire and roared, 'Digger, get out of that fire!'

David Stratton was at the pictures watching *Sense and Sensibility*. There was a blind bloke sitting beside him, and beside him, a labrador. And Stratton couldn't help but notice that the dog seemed to be totally involved in the plot, growling here, giving little yelps there.

'Excuse me,' said Stratton to the blind bloke. 'Your dog is quite astonishing. I just can't get over it.'

'Frankly, it surprises me too,' said the blind man. 'He hated the book.'

A Northern Territory publican was at a loss about what to do with prospectors and ringers who would turn up at his pub after midnight demanding service and then drinking until dawn. He had just about had it, and decided to take a holiday in Sydney, where he stayed with his mate who was the head keeper at Taronga Park Zoo. After discussing his problem with his friend, the mate said, 'We've got an old gorilla we're about to retire, why don't you take him back with you and use him as a bouncer?

The publican thought this a great idea, and the gorilla was duly installed in a room next to the bar at the pub.

Next night, the publican was ready to close up at 11 p.m., when six ringers from out of town arrived and started what was obviously a very serious bout of drinking. After several attempts to get rid of them, the publican eventually released the gorilla at about 2 a.m. A massive brawl developed, which spilled out into the dust outside, accompanied by shouting and screaming. The terrified publican, apprehensive about what he might be responsible for, waited behind the bar. After a while the leader of the ringers staggered back into the bar, covered in blood and with most of his clothing torn off, shouting, 'Who was the bloody idiot who bought that gin a fur coat?'

An ant and an elephant got married despite the advice of their friends. During intercourse, the elephant died of a heart attack and the ant said, 'Damn it, five minutes of passion. Now a lifetime digging the grave.'

The bear and bunny were sitting side by side, both having a crap. 'Do you have any trouble with shit sticking to your fur?' the bunny asked the bear.

'No, not at all.'

Whereupon the bear promptly picked up the rabbit and wiped his arse with him.

A well-to-do matron had long nurtured an ambition to own a talking parrot. So one day she plucked up courage and visited her local pet shop.

When she told the pet shop owner what she wanted he said, 'Madam, I do have a talking parrot, it is the only one I have. But unfortunately it has spent all its life in a bordello, and, as you are obviously a woman of taste, I fear that its language would be likely to offend you.'

'Not at all,' said the woman. 'It would be fascinating to own a parrot with such an interesting background.'

Despite further attempts by the pet shop owner to discourage the woman, she would not be dissuaded and finally bought the parrot.

Now the woman thought she would surprise her family with her acquisition, so she arranged for a cover to be put over the cage, which she then smuggled into her house.

The woman's family consisted of two nubile daughters and a husband. She duly summoned them into the lounge room, announced that she had a surprise for them and whisked the cover from the cage.

The parrot blinked its eyes in the sudden light, looked around, saw the woman and said, 'Ah, a new Madam.' Then it spotted the daughters. 'And new girls.'

Finally the parrot looked at the husband and said, 'But the same old customers.'

A grasshopper hopped into a pub and ordered a G&T. 'Did you know there's a drink named after you?' the barman asked.

'What?' said the grasshopper. 'Bruce?'

An elephant was drinking from the Murray River when he noticed a turtle asleep on a log. He ambled over and kicked it clear across the river.

'What did you do that for?' asked a passing wombat.

'Because I recognised it as the same turtle that took a nip out of my trunk 53 years ago.'

'What a memory,' said the wombat.

'Yes,' said the elephant, 'turtle recall.'

'How did you get on with that giraffe last night?' asked the monkey.

'Well, I'll never take her out again,' said the squirrel. 'She's a nympha. And what with kissing her and screwing her, I was up and down all night.'

A bloke wanted to go to Surfers Paradise for a holiday, but had a problem – his pet cat. So he asked the bloke next door to look after it. At the end of the first week he rang the neighbour from Surfers and asked, 'How's my cat?'

'Dead.'

The bloke was deeply shocked by the news and when he recovered, complained to the neighbour about how he had presented him with the bad news.

'You should have been more subtle, and said, "Your cat's on the roof and we can't get it down. Ring back tomorrow". Then when I rang back the second day you could have said, "The cat fell off the roof and we took it to the vet". And on the third day, you could have broken it to me gently that the cat had died. Then it wouldn't have come as such a terrible, terrible shock. Incidentally, how's my mother?'

'She's on the roof and we can't get her down . . .'

There once was a farmer who had a very sexually active cockerel. This bird was formidable, he stopped at nothing. After serving the hens he would leap into geese, then the turkeys – anything dressed in feathers, he fucked.

One day, after observing the cockerel screwing a duck, the farmer approached the cock and said, 'You silly young bugger. If you keep this up, your vital pieces will be used up in no time and you'll go to an early grave.'

The cockerel just laughed at the farmer and leapt on a passing moorhen. A few days later the farmer noticed a flock of vultures slowly circling in the sky above the farmyard. There, in the centre of the yard, lying on his back, completely still, was the randy cockerel. The farmer, believing the cockerel to be dead, walked over and addressed the corpse. 'You dopey bird, I told you what all that fucking would do for you.'

At that the cockerel slowly opened one eye and pointed a wing at the vultures circling above. 'Shush,' he said. 'Don't frighten them – they're coming down.'

A blind man and his labrador were walking down the street when an old friend approached. So they stopped for a chat.

A codger coming the other way saw the dog and moved to avoid it. 'It's quite all right,' said the blind man. 'He's a friendly dog. He won't bite.'

'I'm not worried about him biting. But the way he lifted his leg, I thought the bugger was going to kick me.'

Somewhere in the saltbush country was an old cocky who had five sheepdogs, all named Fuckya. When asked to explain, the cocky said that he would get up in the morning, step outside and yell, 'Come here, Fuckya.' And the five dogs would come running.

A flea was sitting at a table in a roadhouse cafe, having a cup of coffee, when one of his mates entered. The second flea was wet, cold and shivering so the first flea asked, 'What's happened to you?'

I just got a lift on a bikie's moustache, but didn't know that he'd be driving all through the bloody night through the mountains. It's the middle of winter, and the rain's absolutely pissing down . . .'

The first flea replied, 'That's really dumb. You should do what I do: saunter into the nearest women's toilet, hop up on one of the seats, and when the opportunity comes along, grab a ride in some nice, warm, soft pubic hair.'

The second flea agreed to take his friend's advice, and they went their separate ways.

A week later, the first flea is sitting in the same cafe when his mate comes in wet, cold and shivering, as before.

'Didn't you take my advice?' he asked.

'Look, I did everything just as you told me. I was happily ensconced in some really nice lady's pubic hair, but just my bloody luck. Five minutes later I was back on the bikie's moustache!'

A bloke and his mongrel dog went into a posh restaurant, famous for its gourmet food and its string quartet. The head waiter said, 'I'm very sorry, sir, but we don't allow dogs in this restaurant.'

'But this isn't just any dog,' said the bloke, 'he was trained by that fellow on the ABC. He can speak too. Look, if he tells you the name of the composer who wrote that stuff the string quartet is playing, will you let us stay?'

'Perhaps,' said the head waiter.

'Okay, Blue. Who's the composer?'

'Bach,' went the dog.

'That's nonsense,' said the head waiter, throwing both bloke and dog out of the restaurant.

As they hit the pavement, the dog said, 'Sorry about the mistake. It was, of course, Mozart.'

A penguin decides to shoot down to Phillip Island and visit his rellies, so he hops into his car. It was an automatic – manuals are too hard to operate when you've got flippers. He gets to the crest of the bridge across the island when, *snap*, *bang*, *kerplunk*, the car goes bung. Luckily he sees a service station at the base of the bridge, so he rolls the car down, pulls up by a bowser, hops out and waddles around to the counter. 'Scuse I,' he says, 'but the car's ratshit. Can you have a look at it?'

The mechanic looks down at him from over the counter. 'Yeah, mate, no worries. But I've got a bit of a job on for a moment. It'll be an hour or so before I can have a look and give you any sort of verdict.'

'An hour? What am I going to do here in the middle of nowhere for a bloody hour?'

The mechanic says, 'There's a milk bar over the road. Why don't you just waddle over there?'

The penguin does so and after half an hour waddles back.

'Scuse I,' he says. 'My car, what's the prob?'

The mechanic leans over the counter and sees the penguin. 'Oh, you. Well, it looks like you've blown a seal.'

'No,' says the penguin furiously wiping his beak. 'No, I've just had an ice-cream!'

Three legs. Right ear chewed off. Blind in left eye. No teeth. Recently castrated. Answers to Lucky.

How do you tell which end of a worm is the head?

Bury it in flour and wait till it farts.

How do you titillate an ocelot?

Oscillate its tits a lot.

'Can you give me a lift into town?' asked a bloke leading a cow.

'Yeah, I can give you a lift,' said the motorist, 'but what about your cow?'

'No worries. She'll just follow along.'

So off they went, with the motorist checking in his rear-vision mirror. To his astonishment the cow broke into a trot. They accelerated to 80 km/h but the cow was still there, galloping along like a thoroughbred.

'Amazing,' the motorist muttered, accelerating to 90 . . . 100. And the cow was still there, thundering along.

When he got to 120 the motorist took another decko in the rear-vision mirror. 'I don't like the look of your cow, mate,' he said to the passenger. 'Her tongue's flopping out of the side of her mouth.'

'No worries,' said the bloke, 'that just means she's going to overtake.'

It was the Gundy Agricultural Show and there was a competition for the strangest pet. There was a three-legged dog, a four-legged spider, a one-winged parrot and a calf with two heads. But a kid won second prize with a tin of salmon.

What is the difference between a duck?
One of its legs is both the same.

What do you call a blind dinosaur?
Do you think he saw us?

What do you get when you cross an elephant with a kangaroo?
Big holes all over Australia.

What type of shoes do koalas wear?
Gumboots.

How do you stop a dog fucking your leg?
Give it a blow job.

What do you call a fly without wings?
A walk.

What's the difference between a goldfish and a mountain goat?

One mucks around the fountain . . .

Why did the wombat cross the road?

To see his flat mate.

A horse walks into a bar and the barman says, 'Why the long face?'

An old Afghan in the Northern Territory was showing some tourists how to top up a camel with water. 'That way,' he said, 'you get an extra day out of them between drinks.'

As it bent down to drink, the Afghan picked up two bricks and bashed them over the poor creature's testicles. The camel sucked in its breath and, in doing so, took on three days' extra water.

'Doesn't that hurt?' inquired a tourist.

'Only if you get your fingers caught.'

A Bumpy Playing Field

A city bloke was holidaying at a merino stud. The farmer he was staying with said, 'It's a beautiful morning. Why not take the dogs and do a bit of shooting?'

'Great! Thanks.'

At lunch the farmer inquired, 'How was the shooting?'

'Terrific. Got any more dogs?'

A bloke climbed up the Harbour Bridge and stood teetering high, high above the water. He opened his haversack and pulled out a couple of budgies. He stuck one on his left shoulder and the other on the right. Then he took a great leap into the void, hitting the water at 200 km/h.

'Jesus,' he said, when the police fished him out more dead than alive. 'That budgie jumping isn't what it's cracked up to be.'

A bloke is marooned on a desert island. But he survives as there are plenty of coconuts and fresh water. Months pass and he sees a ripple about a hundred yards off shore. It keeps getting closer and closer until, at last, a tall blonde in full diving gear appears.

'You poor man,' she says. 'How long have you been here?'

He replies that he's lost all track of time and doesn't know. What he does know is that he's dying for a fag.

'No trubs,' she says, unzipping a pocket on the arm of her wetsuit and pulling out a packet of Winnies and a lighter.

Puffing happily, the bloke says he's in seventh heaven and she asks him if he'd like a beer.

'Would I!' So she unzips the other pocket and pulls out a can of Tooheys.

With a fag in one hand and a beer in the other, the bloke reckons he's got it made. Then the blonde starts to unzip the front of her wetsuit.

'Having been here all this time,' she says, 'I guess you'd like to play around.'

And the bloke says, 'How on earth did you fit a set of golf clubs down there?'

At an outback racetrack the stewards had long suspected the owner of doping his horses. So before the main race the chief steward followed him to the stables.

Watching closely, the steward saw the bloke slip something into his horse's mouth.

'Gotcha, you bastard,' he said, grabbing the bloke. 'You'll get rubbed out for life.'

'What are ya talking about?' said the owner. 'These are only homemade lollies the wife makes. Look, I'll show ya.' And he swallowed one. 'Here, you try one. They're beaut.' And he gave one to the steward who, somewhat confused, ate it.

The owner then led his horse to the saddling paddock. 'Get in front from the start and stay there.'

'Is anything likely to pass me?' asked the jockey.

'Just me,' said the owner, 'and the Chief Stipendiary Steward.'

Three gay blokes are having coffee during the Mardi Gras and describing their greatest aspirations.

Bryce explains, 'I want to have a lovely little

hairdretherth shop with perfumeth and shampooth and lots of nithe ladieth to chat to all day.'

'Oooo, how nithe!' the others exclaim.

Bruce says, 'I would like to be a thtar on sthage and lithen to all the applauth when I deliver another great performanth.'

'Oooo, tho good!' the others agree.

Brian isn't to be outdone. 'I would like to be a thtar footballer and play for Canberra against Canterbury in the grand final with the scoreth tied and a minute to go.'

'Be still my beating heart,' chorused the others.

'Canterbury kickth the ball into the air and it comes whithling towards me and I do a mighty leap and take the ball ath all those big bwuteth try to tackle me. But I do a dance and a leap and, with the wind whithling in my hair, run towards the try-line. Other bruteth try to tackle me but I leap and thidethtep and beat them. And the wind ith till whithling through my hair when, finally, there'th no one to stop me . . .'

'What happenth?' squealed his friends.

'Just then, I stop a metre short of the line. Can you imagine?'

The others look puzzled.

'Well, as the thiren goeth, 20 000 Canberra fans are thcreaming "Fuck him!"'

A Pakistani cricket umpire rolls up to the Pearly Gates and finds two signs dividing the crowd. One says 'Heroes' and the other says 'Everyone Else'.

There is a queue in front of the latter sign but the cricket umpire slots himself into the 'Heroes' line. St Peter appears and asks him why he should be classified a hero. The umpire smiles and says, 'I gave Javed Miandad out LBW on his front foot in Karachi, and that's why I should be considered a hero.'

St Peter is quite astonished at the fact that this umpire broke the unwritten rule that *nobody* gives Javed Miandad out LBW on his front foot in Karachi, and asks exactly when the umpire made this heroic call. 'Five minutes ago,' came the reply.

St Peter was standing at the Pearly Gates when Cathy Freeman and Lionel Rose approached, but he told them to go away because heaven did not admit Aborigines. St Peter told God what he had done, but God said to him, 'The Heaven Olympics are coming up. Go back and see if you can get them.' Peter went off but came back yelling, 'They're gone. They're gone!'

God asked him, 'Cathy and Lionel?'

But Peter answered, 'No, the Pearly Gates.'

(Arthur Tunstall, at a meeting of the Commonwealth Gates Association Executive Board in Sydney.)

By the time the building was evacuated, the whole block of flats was ablaze. The fire brigade was losing the battle and everyone was enjoying the excitement. Then a woman appeared at a fourth-floor window, holding a baby and screaming for help. But the fire brigade's ladder wouldn't reach.

Whereupon, Jack Dyer stepped forward and said, 'I'm Captain Blood, once captain of Richmond, member of the AFL's Hall of Fame and greatest ruckman ever. Throw the baby down to me. I've never dropped a mark in my life.'

The mother had no choice. She threw the baby down. Jack jumped into the air, took a screamer of a mark, and kicked a goal.

'Thank you for the swimming lesson,' said the attractive young woman, 'but will I really sink if you take your finger out?'

An Irish Rugby Union player emigrates to Australia and looks around for a rugby club to play with. Nobody's very interested, because he is not much of a player. Eventually, he finds a club willing to give him a go. 'But listen,' the coach says, 'I can't give you a full game. I'll have to pull you off at half-time.'

'That'll be lovely, that'll be lovely,' says the Irishman. 'Back home, we only get oranges at half-time.'

On his very first parachute jump, Harry found himself heading towards terra firma tugging furiously at an unresponsive ripcord. To his astonishment he saw someone rocketing up towards him. Always ready to make polite conversation, he yelled, 'Do you know anything about opening parachutes?'

'Sorry, mate,' came the reply. 'Do you know anything about lighting gas barbecues?'

Who's this an impersonation of?

'Click, how's that? Click, how's that? Click, click, how am I doing? Click, is that right? Click, how's that?'

Give up? A blind bloke with a Rubik's cube.

'Do you play much footy up this way?' the salesman asked the local.

'Yeah, just last week we had a great game against the Snake Gully mob. Blood everywhere. Two multiple fractures. Three broken legs. A couple of broken noses. Busted teeth. Ribs cracked. It was bloody lovely.' He took another sip of his beer. 'And one or two of the players got hurt, too.'

A businessman bought a racehorse. Being a businessman he couldn't afford to take it round the race meetings, so he employed a man called Sam Finnell to cart the horse around the country and race it. So the opposition wouldn't know how it was doing, he said to Sam Finnell, 'Let me know how it's going, but do it in some sort of code.'

So after the first race out, the businessman received a telegram from Sam Finnell, which said, 'SF, SF, SF, SF.' He couldn't understand the telegram so when Sam got back he asked him, 'What's this all about?'

'It's code,' said Sam. 'It stands for Started, farted. Stumbled, fell. See you Friday. Sam Finnell.'

Two loonies go for a pushbike ride. After a few miles one gets off and lets his tyres down. 'What did you do that for?'

'My legs are too short to reach the pedals!'

Whereupon the second gets a spanner and turns his own bike seat around. 'If you're going to fuck around, I'm going home.'

There was a very promising horse which ran away with all the races, so that Tommy Smith wanted him to run in the Melbourne Cup. A marvellous horse, he could do anything, even talk. In fact, he used to grumble at the strict training when he was kept away from mares. By the eve of the Cup he was thoroughly fed up and insisted that unless he had a mare for the night he would not perform on the day. Tommy argued, but the horse was adamant: he must have a mare. Giving in, Tommy said, 'I'll make a bargain with you. If I can find a mare, you must promise me that it will be no more than once.' Pawing and snorting, the horse agreed.

Tommy searched around, but the best he could find was a zebra at the zoo. 'Here she is, mate. Now remember, only once.'

The next morning, Melbourne Cup day, Tommy arrived at the stables to find the horse with head drooping, exhausted, and the zebra much the same. 'You bastard, you promised only once!' Tommy exclaimed.

'Only once!' snorted the horse. 'I've spent all night trying to get the bloody pyjamas off!'

It was a country cricket match. Bill was the club's fast bowler but knew he was going to have a bad day when he discovered that his father-in-law was to umpire the match. Bill's first ball caught the batsman LBW. 'Owzat!'

'Not out,' said the ump.

The second ball snipped the bat to be caught by the wicket-keeper. 'Owzat!'

'Not out.'

Getting really shitty, Bill bowled the fastest ball of his career. It not only hit the middle stump but splintered it, sending the bails into orbit.

'Nearly got him that time,' said Bill.

Pat Cash and Ivan Lendl played an exhibition match at Yalara. After the match they went for a walk together to see Uluru as the sun set. When they were out in the scrub a bit they were confronted by two dingoes. Cash was able to escape, but Lendl was caught by the dingoes, one of which began to eat Lendl as Cash ran for help.

Cash returned soon after with a couple of rangers. They found the dingoes still there, but there was no sign of Lendl.

'Which one was it that ate Lendl?' asked the rangers.

'That one there,' said Cash, pointing to the larger of the two dingoes.

'Now, you're sure? You're sure it was the male one?'

'I'm sure,' said Cash.

So the rangers killed the male dingo and split

open its belly. But there were no bits of Lendl in the dingo's stomach.

Moral: never believe a Victorian when he says the Czech's in the male.

A couple of blokes went fishing in the Gulf of Carpentaria. One had brought the grog and the other was supposed to have brought the bait. But, instead, they both turned up with grog. And no bait.

They were sitting on the beach drinking their grog and wondering about bait when they saw a dirty great carpet snake with a frog in its mouth. So they dribbled some grog on the snake's head and as its fork tongue reached out to lick it, they grabbed the frog. The frog made great bait and they caught a couple of barramundi. Trouble was, the frog was a bit past it, whereupon one of the blokes felt a tap on the shoulder – and there was the snake with another frog.

A duck shooter was banging away at ducks at a billabong between Albury and Wodonga. He'd just shot a couple of birds and was sloshing through the water to retrieve them when a game warden shouted at him from the Victorian bank.

'Hey, the duck season is over in Victoria!'

'So what?' said the shooter. 'I shot these in New South Wales.'

'Doesn't matter,' said the warden. 'They could be our ducks.'

'Come off it,' said the shooter, 'they're bloody wild ducks.'

'Don't argue with me. I'm an expert. Chuck me a duck,' said the warden.

Muttering imprecations the shooter tossed him one of the ducks. The warden caught it, parted its tail feathers and shoved his finger up its bum. He then withdrew his digit and sniffed it. 'Okay, that's a New South Wales duck. Now chuck me the other one.'

'What a load of crap,' said the sportsman. 'They were flying together, side by side. I shot them both with one blast.'

'Don't argue. I'm an expert. Did a three-year course in ducks. Toss me the other one.'

The shooter tossed the second duck.

Once again, the warden caught it, parted the tail feathers, shoved his finger up its bum and, retrieving it, took a long sniff.

'Gotcha,' he said. 'This duck is a Victorian duck.'

'Bullshit,' said the shooter.

'Don't argue with me,' said the ranger. 'I'm an expert and I'm going to write you out a ticket. What's your name?'

'Bill Smith.'

'Where are you from, Bill?'

'Richmond.'

'Richmond Victoria, or Richmond New South Wales?'

Bill undid his belt, dropped his daks, and said, 'You're the bloody expert. You tell me.'

A Fitzroy footballer went one Saturday night to a dance at the Richmond Town Hall, and because the local girls would not be seen dancing with him, eventually got into a conversation with a very beautiful girl in a wheelchair. When the dance had finished, she agreed that he could wheel her home. While walking through the park, she said to him, 'Just because I'm in a wheelchair doesn't mean I don't appreciate the finer things in life, you know – if you want to do something about it.'

The Fitzroy man was amazed. 'Yeah, okay. But how do you manage?'

'It's simple,' she said. 'In the boot of the wheelchair I keep this leather harness. All you've got to do is hang me up in a tree, and you can go for it.'

When he had finished and had put the girl back in the wheelchair, she said to him. 'You are a Fitzroy boy, aren't you?'

'Yeah,' he said, 'but how did you know?'

'Well, the Collingwood and Richmond blokes always leave me hanging in the tree.'

Two blokes decided that they would like a game of golf, and one suggested that it might be nice to invite old Charlie, who was known to like a game, but was a bit frail these days.

Well, old Charlie was delighted with the idea. So off they set. Somewhere approaching the fourth green, one bloke remarked to the other that he hadn't seen old Charlie for a while. The other replied that he had seen him heading for the rough after his tee shot, and that maybe they had better have a look for him, as he'd obviously lost his ball.

They fished around the rough for a while and eventually found old Charlie with the greenkeeper chock-a-block up him.

'What the hell do you think you're doing to old Charlie?' they yelled. And the greenkeeper said, 'He had a heart attack and stopped breathing.'

So the blokes say, 'You're supposed to give a bloke mouth-to-mouth resuscitation when he has a heart attack, not fuck him.'

A dignified English solicitor-widower with a considerable income had long dreamed of playing Sandringham, one of Britain's most exclusive golf courses, and one day he made up his mind to chance it when he was travelling in the area.

Entering the clubhouse, he asked at the desk if he might play the course. The club secretary inquired, 'Member?'

'No, sir.'

'Guest of member?'

'No, sir.'

'Sorry.'

As he turned to leave, the lawyer spotted a slightly familiar figure seated in the lounge, reading the *London Times.* It was Lord Parnham. He approached and, bowing low, said, 'I beg your pardon, your Lordship, but my name is Higginbotham of the London solicitors Higginbotham, Willingby and Barclay. I should like to crave your Lordship's indulgence. May I play this beautiful course as your guest?'

His Lordship gave Higginbotham a long look, put down his paper and asked, 'Church?'

'Church of England, sir, as was my late wife.'

'Education?'

'Eton, sir, and Oxford.'

'Sport?'

'Rugby, sir, a spot of tennis and number four on the crew that beat Cambridge.'

'Service?'

'Brigadier, sir, Coldstream Guards, Victoria Cross and Knight of the Garter.'

'Campaigns?'

'Dunkirk, El Alamein and Normandy, sir.'

'Languages?'

'Private tutor in French, fluent German and a bit of Greek.'

His Lordship considered briefly, then nodded to the club secretary and said, 'Nine holes.'

'It took me bloody hours to play a round with Robbo today. He had a heart attack and died on the fifth hole. And it's bloody hard going drag, hit, drag, hit, drag, hit!'

The club secretary explained to the member that he couldn't play today because the course was fully booked. 'But I've been a member for 30 years.'

'Sorry, sir,' said the club secretary.

'If John Howard lobbed here for a game today, I bet you'd make room for him.'

The secretary conceded the point.

'Well, I just happen to know that the little bastard's in Canberra. So I'll take his place.'

There was a great outcry after Phar Lap's death. The doctors performed an autopsy to see if he'd been poisoned. Among other things, they were surprised to find splinters in the thoroughbred's bum. Finally the penny dropped. The horse had a very close association with young strapper Tommy Woodcock.

Three guys are playing golf. The guys playing ahead of them are so excruciatingly slow that the three are losing their temper. So they walk back to the clubhouse and scream at the manager, 'Can't you get those guys off the course?'

The manager says, 'They're blind.'

So the guy in the pink shirt says, 'Oh, holy Mother, how could I ever have had such thoughts? Everything I believe in. I'll never forgive myself.'

The second guy, a minister, says, 'I taught compassion and understanding and forgiveness all my life.'

And the rabbi says, 'Why can't they play at night?'

Some Australian tourists were in Barcelona for the Olympics and found themselves in a small restaurant in a side street. They were served magnificent meals of rissoles, two to a plate. Having scoffed them, they asked the waiter the name of the dish. 'Gonads,' he said, explaining that they were the testicles of two bulls killed in the Barcelona bullring the previous day. The first reaction of the Australian was to feel somewhat squeamish, but, after all, the dish had been delicious.

So the next day they decided to order it again. However, the waiter apologised, saying that he could only serve one of them. And this time the rissoles were a fraction of the size. 'Sorry, senor. But as you can see, yesterday a bull won.'

What has Princess Diana got in common with Gary Ablett?

They're both fucking good footballers.

A bloke's running a BB rifle range amongst the sideshows at the Royal Melbourne Show. There's a row of very battered tin ducks marching across the back of the tent. A drunk weaves into view and demands a go at the *bing, bing, bing*. After trying to talk the drunk out of it – pointing to the dangers of someone in his state having control of a rifle – the stallholder surrenders. After all, business has been slow.

To his astonishment, the drunk knocks three ducks over – *bing, bing, bing*. 'Shit,' says the stallholder, 'you've won a prize.' And he reaches under the counter and pulls a small live tortoise from a bucket.

'Bewdy,' says the drunk and, taking his prize, he staggers off.

A while later he presents himself, if anything slightly more inebriated, demanding another go. This time the stallholder is even more reluctant to hand over the rifle. But, bugger it, there's not exactly a queue of customers. So he pockets another deener and gives the bloke another go. Once again it's *bing, bing, bing*. Down go three tin ducks. 'Christ,' says the stallholder in astonishment, 'you've won another bloody prize.' And reaching down he presents the drunk with a kewpie doll.

'What's that?' the drunk asks.

'It's your prize. A kewpie doll.'

'I don't want a bloody kewpie doll. I want a meat pie, like last time.'

The local cop calls a mate. 'Bad news, cobber. We've just found your mother-in-law. Her corpse, that is. Wedged in the mangroves. All swollen and horrible, with four dirty great muddies having a go at her.'

'Four muddies! That's terrific. Two for you, two for me . . . and we can put the old biddy back for bait.'

A bloke drove off the first tee at Royal Melbourne and sliced right over the fence on to the road. Without bothering to look where his ball landed, he played another. After the round, the club pro approached him and said, 'You know that drive you sliced off the first tee? It hit a bloke on a motorbike who swerved in front of a truck which ran through the fence on to a railway line and collided with the Southern Aurora. They're still going through the wreckage but the death toll so far is 37, with more than a hundred in hospital.'

'Christ Almighty,' said the golfer. 'What should I do?'

'Turn your right hand over a bit,' said the pro, 'and don't grip so hard with your left.'

Dave, a very strong swimmer, well known to the local lifesavers, was out beyond the breakers when a shark appeared. He began waving frantically to the lifesaver on duty. The lifesaver gave him a friendly wave in return.

Meanwhile, however, the shark had removed one of Dave's legs. *Chompf!* Dave tried waving again. The lifesaver waved back.

Chompf! Off went the second leg. This provoked even more frantic waving, which, once again, elicited a cheerful response.

Chompf! Off went the right arm, leaving only the left arm to wave. He waved it, and the lifesaver, by now getting sick of waving, gave a token response.

Chompf! The last limb had gone. Now, belatedly, the lifesaver noticed a crimson stain surrounding Dave. He charged into the water.

He finally arrived by Dave's torso and told the poor bloke to balance on his back so that both his arms would be free for swimming. And with the shark circling them both, the lifesaver heroically, miraculously made it back to the beach.

'Jeez, I'm buggered,' he groaned.

Dave, still on his back, said, 'Sorry about that. But it was the only way I could hang on.'

In the Political Asylum

Liberal Party. Braille Party.

Labor Party. Rort by a pal.

Coalition. I-anti-cool.

Democrats. Mad sect.

Peter Costello. Lo, elector pest.

Alexander Downer. Wander, axed loner.

Gareth Evans. Hear gas vent.

Cheryl Kernot. Tory hen-clerk.

The cocky went into town and bought a new colour telly. He took it home in the back of his ute and tried it out. Then he rang the electrical store spewing. 'This bloody telly you sold. All I get on it is politicians. No matter what channel I turn to, it's only politicians.'

The store said they'd send a repair man out. When he got back to town the shopowner asked him what happened.

'The poor old bloke really did have a problem,' said the repair man. 'Nothing but politicians on every channel. You see, he was using his windmill for an antenna and had the thing earthed on his manure spreader.'

Why is Ros Kelly like Divine Brown?

Because they both know how to blow huge grants.

As the 1996 federal election campaign neared its end, Paul Keating was trying to remain cheerful and optimistic. 'Look. There are big crowds and they're still waving.'

'Yes,' says an aide, 'but they seem to be holding up less fingers.'

Wycheproof has a train line going right through the middle of town. And right in the middle of the town there is a town hall where a council meeting was going hammer and tong. Suddenly the door opened and a bloke rushed in. 'My mini-bus is stalled on the railroad tracks. I want to ask that it be moved.'

'I say move,' cried a voice from the back of the hall.

'I second it,' said another.

The mayor banged his gavel and said, 'You've heard the motion. All in favour say "aye".'

'Aye,' came the chorus.

'So ordered. Now let's get on with the other business that we were talking about.'

Bob Hawke and John Hewson are standing beside one another at the urinal in Parliament House. Hewson looks over at Bob and says, 'Bob, for such a small man you have a very large member. What's your secret?'

Bob says, 'Every time I go to see my mistress I take the member out, and as I walk up the stairs to where she awaits me in bed, I give it a knock against the wall. It gets big and swollen. It's a bit sore but the pain soon goes.'

That night Hewson decides to try this. As he walks up the stairs he takes out his member and knocks it against the wall. *Thwack! Thwack!*

Mrs Hewson leans out of bed and shouts, 'Is that you, Bob?'

Following the cancellation of a Canberra flight an Ansett ticketer was trying to handle a long queue of passengers when a formidable-looking woman, with a beehive hairdo, pushed her way to the front. 'Get me on this flight. First class.'

'Sorry, madam, you'll have to take your turn. As you can see, there's a long queue of people before you.'

Mrs Bishop was outraged. 'Do you have any idea who you're talking to?'

The ticketer smiled, reached for the PA mike and turned up the volume. 'May I have your attention please? We have a passenger here who doesn't know who she is. If anyone can identify her, please come to the counter.'

When Russ Hinze died, the mortician couldn't find a coffin big enough for the infamous pollie. His anguish was noted by a colleague who said, 'Well, you know what politicians are full of.'

So they gave Russ an enema and buried him in a matchbox.

If you had Idi Amin, Saddam Hussein and Paul Keating in a room with a gun with two bullets, who would you shoot?

Keating. Twice.

In Canberra rectal thermometers were banned when it came to light that they were causing brain damage to politicians.

I'm glad that I'm Australian
I'm glad that I am free
I wish I were a little dog
And Howard was a tree.

In a very small town in northern Queensland a local councillor, who everyone thought was a prick, proposed that a bridge be built over a local creek. It was clear that the bridge would be of little benefit – except to the councillor who happened to be in the bridge-building business.

So another councillor jumped up and said, 'Put a bloody bridge over the silly little creek? It hasn't had any water in it for 20 years. And I could spit halfway across the bugger.'

The first councillor called upon the mayor. 'He's out of order, Mr Chairman. Out of order.'

'I know that,' said the dissenting councillor, 'otherwise I'd spit right across the bloody thing.'

Alexander Downer lands at Washington airport carrying a personal letter for President Bill Clinton from the Prime Minister of Australia. Standing on the tarmac, he hands it to Clinton as the photographers capture the moment. What does the letter say? *Please ignore this man. He's an idiot!*

It was day one of the year at the one-teacher school at Condamine, and two of the new enrolments were twin boys who gave their names as Robert Hawke O'Brien and Paul Keating O'Brien. The teacher wrote a note to the mother:

Dear Mrs O'Brien, these names do not seem correct. Please verify.

Back came the reply: *If you can think of two better names for a pair of bastards, you tell me.*

The late Bob Katter, the father of the current Bob Katter of National Party fame, was once driving through the backblocks of Queensland during a drought. His Land Cruiser got stuck in wheel ruts on a narrow track, and he proceeded to bowl along them. It was the line of least resistance.

Suddenly a cloud of dust appeared on the horizon. It was an approaching vehicle, also stuck in the tracks. Katter decided to stay in his rut, forcing the approaching driver to swerve. It was a woman, who wound down her window and screamed, 'Pig!'

'Bitch!' Katter shouted back.

He accelerated into the cloud of dust only to run smack into the biggest wild pig in Queensland.

Having just died, a man is sitting in the devil's waiting room anticipating his pre-admission interview. He notices that all the walls are covered in clocks – and they're all running at quite different speeds. Wanting to know the significance of the clock arrangement, the dead man approaches the receptionist and asks her for an explanation. The girl explains that there's a clock for every person on Earth, that the more lies the person tells, the faster his or her clock runs. Being impressed by technology, the man wanders through long hallways looking at the names under the countless millions of clocks, and noting the various speeds at which they're running. After a few hours, he returns to the reception desk and tells the girl that he hasn't been able to locate a clock for Peter Costello. The girl looks at him and says, 'Oh, Peter Costello – the devil keeps Peter's clock in his office and uses it as a fan.'

Three blokes are in a boat surrounded by crocodiles. The boat breaks down. People on the shore yell out, 'Don't jump overboard, the crocs will get you.' But the first bloke ignores them. He swims bravely towards the shore and gets eaten halfway. The second bloke has the same fate. The third bloke disappears from sight in the bottom of the boat and re-emerges in the nuddy with something written on his bum. He dives overboard and makes it safely to the shore. 'What did you do?'

'I wrote, *Carmen Lawrence told the truth* on my left buttock . . . and the crocs wouldn't swallow that.'

'Your Majesty, make Australia a kingdom and make me the king.'

'Mr Keating, I'll make it a country and you can be what you are.'

At a political rally a heckler called, 'Clinton should be bloody well hung.'

Whereupon Hillary Clinton said, 'Unfortunately he is.'

'Mr Howard, have you heard the latest political jokes?'

'Heard them? They're all in the Cabinet.'

The Arab sheik asked his sons what they wanted for Christmas. The eldest son wanted a new Lear jet, the second son wanted a Lamborghini, and the third son wished for a cowboy outfit.

On Christmas day the plane and the car were delivered to the palatial tent. But there was no cowboy outfit. The little boy was very, very upset. At last a fax arrived saying that there was a package on the wharf in Kuwait.

So they climbed into the Lamborghini and drove into town. And there, on the wharf, was a big container wrapped in cellophane.

The sheik said to his son, 'Here, at long last, is your cowboy outfit.'

The kid opened the container and inside was the Queensland government.

Prime Minister Howard stood proudly on the dais beside the Governor-General on Anzac Day. Thousands upon thousands of old vets passed, each proffering the official party a snappy salute. They were followed by squadrons of jets, lines of tanks, heavy artillery and columns of infantry. Finally a group of men carrying briefcases, marching out of step, brought up the rear.

'Is that your secret service, Prime Minister?' asked a foreign diplomat.

'No, they're Treasury's economists. And they're more dangerous than the rest put together.'

One day, several years ago, a White House aide approached the President in a state of great agitation.

'Mr President, it pains me to tell you this, but I've just seen the First Lady cavorting naked as a jaybird with a fellow in the Oval Office.'

The President was aghast. 'Who's the guy – I'll kill him!'

'Sir, I can't remember his name, but you know him. The guy with the German name who's a diplomat.'

'You mean he's Kissinger!?'

'No, Mr President, he's fucking her!'

Law and Disorder

What's wrong with the design of police stations? They're above water.

What's 40 cm long and hangs from arseholes? Police ties.

What sort of animal has a cunt halfway up its back? A police horse.

Mr Plod is walking through the local park when he sees a couple bonking near the little Anzac memorial.

''Allo, 'allo, 'allo,' he says, feeling somewhat stimulated. All the more when he recognises the woman as the district's most attractive prostitute.

Looking around to make sure no one's about, he says to the bloke, 'Hey, can I be next?'

'Dunno,' says the bloke. 'I've never fucked a copper before.'

Laurie Connell kicked the bucket in the middle of his trial. He left behind him a grieving family and a great many grieving debtors. At the funeral, the handful of mourners were surprised to see a security truck pull up outside the church and the guards hauling out dozens of gold bars.

The chief security guard explained, 'He stipulated in his will that he wanted to be buried with all the money he had hidden away in the Swiss banks and the Cook Islands. So we're here to load up the coffin.'

They finished putting all the bars in the coffin and the service was held. But when the pallbearers tried to carry it out, it was far, far too heavy to lift, no matter how hard they strained.

Suddenly the first pallbearer, Kerry Packer, opened the coffin and started taking out the gold bars and shoving them into his pockets. The other pallbearers, who were almost as famous, started grabbing gold bars too.

'Just a second,' cried the preacher. 'He wanted to be buried with his money.'

'It's okay,' said Kerry, 'we're leaving him a cheque.'

A pompous bank vice-president from one of the larger city banks was on holidays back of the black stump. Passing through a small country town, he decided to visit the local branch to see how things were going. The one-room bank was completely empty with the front and back doors wide open. Through the back door he could see the bank manager and teller and two stockmen playing cards on the verandah of the bank's residence.

He thought to himself, 'I'll throw a real fright into this sloppy operation', and leaned over the counter and turned on the bank's alarm, which echoed from one end of the town to the other.

The card players did not even look up from their game. But a minute later the publican from the hotel opposite the bank ran across the street into the front door and out the back door carrying four beers for the players.

'We're sacking the accountant.'

'Why?'

'He's too shy and retiring.'

'Is that a reason to sack him?'

'Yes, he's 200 000 shy. And that's why he's retiring.'

The local council decided to plonk a dirty great fountain in the middle of the local park, between the new brick loos and the barbecue area. They put the project to tender and got three quotes, from contractors in Melbourne, Sydney and Brisbane.

They interviewed the Brisbane tenderer first. 'How much?'

'Three thousand dollars.'

'How do you break that down?'

'Well, it's a thousand for the fountain, a thousand for me and a thousand for you.'

The Town Clerk called in the Sydney contractor. 'How much?'

'Six thousand dollars.'

'And how do you break that down?'

'Two thousand for the fountain, two thousand for me and two thousand for you.'

Next the clerk called in the Melbourne bloke who said that his price would be nine thousand dollars.

'And how do you break that down?'

'Well, it's three thousand each and we give the job to the bloke from Brisbane.'

A guy was out bush one day when his four-wheel drive broke down in the middle of nowhere. In keeping with accepted practice he stayed with his vehicle hoping someone would rescue him. After four or five days no one had arrived, and, having run out of food, decided to set off on foot and look for help.

Tired and hungry, he'd walked miles before he stumbled across a bush stream with a log straddled across it. As he attempted to cross the stream the log broke under his weight and landed on a platypus, killing it. Hungry, the man thought he may as well eat it.

Just as he was eating the platypus, a park ranger came along and pinched him for eating a protected species. He was subsequently hauled off to court.

'You are charged with eating an endangered and protected species. Have you anything to say for yourself before I pass sentence on you?' asked the judge.

'Well, as a matter of fact, sir, yes I have,' said the man indignantly. 'There I was, caught out in the bush with my broken-down four-wheel drive. I thought I'd do the right thing like they always tell us and I stayed by my vehicle for fair on nearly a week, but no one came. I thought, blow this, I'm off. So I head off into the scrub, tired and hungry, and suddenly came across this stream with a log over it. As I stepped onto the log it broke and fell into the stream and hit this poor platypus on the head. There wasn't much I could do about it; it was dead. I was hungry, so I thought I'd eat it. Just as I was eating it along came the park ranger – and I don't mind telling you, your Honour, I was very glad to see him.'

'Well, said the judge, 'that sounds like a reasonable story – case dismissed!'

'Thank you, your Honour,' said the man.

As the man was about to leave the courtroom the judge called out to him, 'By the way, tell me, what does platypus taste like?'

'Well, your Honour,' said the man, 'it sort of tastes like a cross between koala and dolphin.'

Three lads were roaring around the backblocks of Queensland in a panel van. They were doing wheelies outside the Town Hall when the cops pulled them over. 'Don't give your real names,' hissed the driver.

A cop asked the bloke sitting in the middle his name. He saw a neon sign over the cop's shoulder. 'David Jones,' he replied.

Now the cop turned to the other passenger. 'And what's your name?'

'Aaah, G. J. Coles.'

Now the cop circled the ute to the driver. 'Okay, name?'

'Aaah. Ken.'

'Ken? Ken what? I suppose you're Ken bloody Myer. What's your last name?'

'Tucky Fried Chicken.'

What's the difference between a lawyer and a leech?

A leech drops off you when you die.

Why is it dangerous for a lawyer to walk on to a building site?

Because they might connect the drain line to the wrong suer.

A group of New Guinean headhunters set up a sales stand in the Sepik River, advertising the following menu:

Sauteed tourist, $20.

Roasted reporter, $25.

Diced diplomat, $15.

Lawyer shashlik, $200.

A customer, noticing the price differential, asked why lawyers cost so much. The headhunter replied, 'Have you ever tried to clean one of those bastards?'

A lawyer returns to his parked BMW to find the headlights broken and considerable damage to the bonnet. There's no sign of the offending vehicle but he's relieved to see that there's a note stuck under the windscreen wiper. *Sorry. I just backed into your Beemer. The witnesses who saw the accident are nodding and smiling at me because they think I'm leaving my name, address and other particulars. But I'm not.*

What's the difference between a vulture and a lawyer?

The vulture doesn't get frequent flyer points.

The local magistrate had had a busy morning fining prostitutes and dealing with domestic violence cases. He was, as usual, dealing with the low-life of the city. So imagine his astonishment when he found himself with the most respectable-looking bloke he'd ever seen in his court.

And indeed he was respectable. He was a JP, Treasurer of the local Rotary Club, and worked as a chartered accountant.

'Sir, why did you climb to the top of the flagpole outside the Town Hall, shout abuse at people passing by and then fart "Advance Australia Fair"?'

The defendant thought about it for a moment or two. 'Well, it's like this, your Honour. If I didn't do something mad once in a while, I'd go crazy.'

'Have you anything to say for yourself?' asked the judge.

'Fuck all,' said the bloke in the dock.

'What did your client say?' asked the judge.

The barrister approached the bench and whispered, 'He said, "Fuck all", your Worship.'

'Odd,' said his Worship, 'I was sure I saw his lips move.'

'I'm looking for a fugitive from the law.'

'Tell me what he looks like.'

'Well, his name is the Brown Paper Kid.'

'The Brown Paper Kid?'

'Yeah, he wears a brown paper Akubra, a brown paper shirt, brown paper jeans and brown paper boots. And he's got a brown paper holster which holds a brown paper gun that shoots brown paper bullets.'

'What's he wanted for?'

'Rustling.'

A Ford Fairlane was driving very erratically through the streets of Brisbane when it attracted the attention of a cop car. They flashed the lights and hit the siren and got the driver to stop. 'Would you mind blowing into this bag?' the police said.

'I can't,' said the driver. 'I'm a chronic asthmatic.'

'Well, sir, how about accompanying us to the station for a blood test?'

'Sorry, officer, I'm a haemophiliac.'

'Well, sir, surely you wouldn't mind stepping out of your vehicle and walking along a straight line?'

'No way. I'm too bloody pissed.'

Criminal in the dock: 'As God is my judge, I am not guilty.'

Judge: 'He's not, I am and you are.'

A young police constable was giving evidence about the defendant's language at the time of arrest. He was having some difficulty in giving the evidence and he hesitated before repeating the words the defendant was alleged to have said.

'Well, go on,' said the magistrate.

'But there are women in court,' replied the constable.

'They won't mind. Go on, tell us what the defendant said.'

'Perhaps I could write it down, sir?'

'He obviously didn't say that, did he, constable? Come on, get on with it . . .'

'Well, sir, he said, "All you coppers are cunts!"'

'Goodness! That's shocking! I didn't know the proportion was *that* high, but keep going,' said the magistrate.

Occupational Hazards

An historian at the War Museum in Canberra was trying to establish why General Monash had been so successful in the First World War, why his troops had been so successful in charging the Germans. Again and again, Australian soldiers had taken far more ground than the pommies. It turned out that Monash always used a special reserve unit made up of accountants. 'When it came time to order them to charge,' Monash wrote in his diary, 'boy, did they know how to charge!'

An accountant arrives at the office and, first thing every morning, unlocks his desk drawer to look at a small piece of paper. He then replaces it and relocks the drawer. He does this, every day, for years.

Eventually he retires and the accountant sitting at the next desk unlocks the drawer and reads the tattered piece of paper. It says, *Debit column is the one nearest the window.*

A hooker went off duty at the Cross and climbed into a cab. 'Would you take me home, please, to Coogee.'

When the cab stopped, she said, 'Bugger, I've forgotten my purse.'

'Well, how are you going to pay for the trip?'

She promptly lifted her skirt. 'With this?'

'Haven't you got anything smaller?'

An old magician who'd worked the vaudeville circuit for years was booked on the Titanic on its maiden voyage. His job was to amuse the first-class passengers during dinner. He was a bit down on his luck and couldn't afford the traditional leggy assistant. He had to make do with a parrot whom he taught to say funny things to the audience like, 'It's under his cloak', or 'It's up his sleeve'. They were halfway through their act one night when the Titanic hit the iceberg. And sank. With an immense death toll.

The magician clung to a piece of flotsam while

the parrot fluttered overhead. He managed to stay afloat all next day, despite the freezing water, and still the parrot fluttered. That night the parrot finally landed on the magician's head.

'Okay, I give up. What have you done with the bloody ship?'

A young actor walks into a famous talent agency determined to be signed up. He bursts into song, tells a few jokes and does a great tap dance.

'You're very good,' says the agent. 'What's your name?'

'Penis van Lesbian,' says the young bloke.

'Sorry, we'll have to change that for a start. We'll call you Dick van Dyke.'

A young guy went to a casting agency to do an audition. While he waited to be called, he saw an assortment of jugglers, fire-eaters and magicians.

When it was his turn, the casting agent said, 'Hurry up now, I'm a busy, busy man. So what is it you do, exactly?'

The boy said, 'Well, actually, I do a bird impersonation.'

The casting agent's face clouded over and he

said, 'Listen, boy, don't you realise this is the 1990s? You'll never get anywhere doing bird impersonations. Get out of here and stop wasting my time.'

So the boy said, 'Stuff you,' and flew out the window.

A couple of blokes from Delhi fronted the employment office to inquire about getting a job.

'Well, what were your previous occupations?' asked the assessment officer.

'I ran a street stall in a market. Did very, very good business selling ladies pantihose.'

'Mmmm,' said the assessment officer, 'you may have some difficulty in Australia. We already have lots and lots of street stalls and market traders. And what about you? What job did you do in India?'

'I was a diesel fitter.'

'A diesel fitter? That's excellent. There's a big demand in Australia for skilled diesel fitters. What company did you work for in India?'

'Oh, I worked with my mate on his stall in the market.'

'I don't understand. He sold pantihose. What role could a diesel fitter play?'

'Well, he'd run around the stall yelling out, "Pantihose! Pantihose!" And I'd yell out, "Diesel fit her. Diesel fit her."'

'The current generation of mobile phones is incredibly old fashioned. They're out of date already. As a matter of fact, I've been electronically wired. So when I want to make a call I simply do this. I talk into my thumb.'

'Fair dinkum?'

'Yes, allow me to demonstrate. "Hello, can you put me through to Frank Blount, the Managing Director of Telstra? G'day, Frank. Sorry to bother you, but I'm just demonstrating the new technologies to some blokes at the pub." Here, say hello to Frank.'

'Is that you, Frank?'

'Yes, this is Frank Blount.'

'Christ, that's amazing.'

'Ouch!'

'What's the problem? Why are you bending over like that?'

'Don't worry, it's just a fax coming through.'

The encyclopaedia salesman wasn't having much luck. No one in central New South Wales seemed all that interested in the 24-volume Britannica with year books and the little 'assemble-it-yourself' bookstand. Not when it cost a couple of thousand bucks.

One Friday night saw him sitting sadly in a country pub, nursing a beer. He realised he was down to his last $50. That was that. After spending that, he'd be flat broke. Then, glancing around at the other blokes in the bar, who looked inbred and stupid, inspiration struck.

'My set of encyclopaedias is worth a couple of grand retail,' he said. 'But if any of you blokes can answer three questions that I select from the information therein, I'll give the whole bloody set to you for a hundred bucks. And if you can't answer all three questions, it's a hundred bucks to me. What do you reckon?'

There was movement amongst the gathering and a few mumbled exchanges. Finally a big, slow-moving bloke moved towards the salesman. 'I'll have a go,' he said. There were any number of approving 'Goodonyas'. And he slapped a $100 bill down on the bar.

This will be money for jam, thought the salesman. 'First question: What's the capital of Liberia?'

The farmer put a finger in his ear, studied the ceiling, frowned for a few moments and, finally, said, 'Monrovia'. The salesman winced. Reassuring himself it was just a lucky shot – perhaps the bloke had been watching *Sale of the Century* – he asked the second question. 'Who was Malaysia's third Prime Minister?'

The young farmer frowned, looked at the ceiling again, looked at the barmaid, looked at his mates and, finally said, 'Jeez, I think it was Tun

Hussein Onn.' The salesman was astonished and leafed desperately through the pages of his encyclopaedia.

'All right, here's question three. How many people attended the closing ceremony of the 1956 Olympic Games in Melbourne and what were their names and addresses?'

The farmer hitched up his trousers, drank a beer, took a deep breath and said, 'Sixty-eight thousand, nine hundred and twenty-two, not including the sheila who had to leave early to have a baby.' Whereupon he began to chant a list of names and addresses.

It took him four days to get to the end of his answer. By then the salesman was devastated. 'How the hell do you know all this stuff?'

'Well,' said the farmer, 'I take smart pills.'

The salesman realised that these must be miraculous preparations. He'd be better off flogging them than encyclopaedias.

'Where can I get some of these smart pills?' he asked.

The farmer scratched his crotch and said, 'Me dad makes them, but he reckons I'm not allowed to tell anyone the recipe. The ingredients are a family secret.'

'But he didn't say you couldn't sell them, did he?' asked the salesman.

The farmer thought for a moment and finally

said, 'I suppose it would be okay if I charged you $50 and you swallowed a couple here and now.'

The salesman eagerly handed over his last $50 bill and watched as the farmer produced a matchbox from his back pocket. 'Take them all now with a midi of beer,' he instructed.

The salesman looked apprehensively at the pills but then, one by one, swallowed them. A look of disgust appeared on his face. 'Christ, these pills taste like sheep shit.'

'See,' said the farmer. 'You're getting smarter already.'

When he was on a roll, John Elliott was making frequent trips to Moscow. With the help of Mikhail Gorbachev he made some marvellous business contacts. Mikhail organised an invitation for Elliott to address a large group of influential Muscovites. He decided that he'd deliver the speech in Russian, by reading from a text that had been translated phonetically. Though he didn't understand the language, he'd give the illusion of speaking it.

But he'd forgotten to get the words for Ladies and Gentlemen. So he rushed through the National Hotel and wrote down the words that were on the two doors. Now he was ready to make the speech. It was a triumph.

But afterwards Mikhail Gorbachev was slightly puzzled. 'It went very well, John. But why did you start your speech by addressing the audience as Water Closets and Urinals?'

The carpet layers had just finished putting in the burgundy Axminster for a rich matron when they noticed a lump in the middle of the room. Taking out his hammer, one of the layers bashed at the lump, attempting to smooth it out. 'Oh, bugger,' he said, patting at his pocket, 'must be me smokes.'

'No, here's your smokes. But have you seen the old girl's budgie?'

A Macleans salesman was on the country run and found himself at a little store in the middle of nowhere. It was dusty, dirty, dilapidated, and he didn't like his chances of making a big sale. Nonetheless he went into his pitch, describing the wonders of Macleans, how the paste worked miracles on your choppers. The store owner watched the performance impassively. Then he said, 'Have a look under me counter.'

The salesman looked and saw shelves packed with Lady Scott toilet tissue.

'Now have a look in me cupboard.'

The salesman looked and there was a mountain of Sorbent toilet tissue.

'Now come and look out the back.' He took the salesman to a backyard shed, opened the door and revealed mountains of Kleenex toilet tissue.

'What's that got to do with me selling toothpaste?' the salesman asked.

'Simple. I've been running this store for 20 years. And if I can't get the locals to wipe their bums, I've got no hope of gettin' them to clean their bloody teeth.'

A Melbourne engineer and his female assistant were working on a new road system in a country area. The engineer told the assistant to go to the other end of the proposed roadway and that he would signal if he wanted anything, as it was very far to walk.

After a while he waved, attracted her attention and then proceeded to signal just what he wanted.

He touched his eye, then his knee and started hitting up and down with his right hand.

The woman at the other end was rather perplexed. Then she nodded her head and replied. She touched her eye. Then her left breast. Then her pelvic region.

The boss was perplexed. Whatever did she mean?

He signalled again. She signalled back exactly as before.

Finally, he waved to her to come towards him. They met in the middle. He said he was quite mystified by her actions.

'Did you understand what I asked?' he inquired.

'Yes,' she said, 'you said, "I need a hammer".'

He said that's exactly what he requested, but he couldn't understand her reply.

'It's very simple,' she said. 'My reply was, "I left it in the tool box".'

His night's work completed, Dan the dunny man was plodding towards the depot when the tumbrel wheel struck a stone and the whole shebang overturned. Unhurt, he stood there surveying the result. A passing motorist stopped long enough to call facetiously, 'Had an accident?'

'No,' yelled Dan, 'I'm stocktaking!'

In 1919 a stockman was taking a mob of cattle to the gulf country when he came across a rabbit-proof-fence man. This lonely fellow hadn't seen anyone for years, so they sat around the campfire catching up with the news. After a lull in the conversation, the stockman said, 'By the way, we won the War.'

'That's good,' said the rabbit-proof-fence man. 'I never could stand them Boers.'

The travelling salesman stopped at a lonely farmhouse and asked for a bed for the night.

'Sorry, I don't have a spare room,' said the farmer, 'but you can sleep with my daughter. Provided you leave her alone.'

The salesman gave the farmer his word and after dinner went to bed. Undressing in the dark, he slipped into the cot beside the farmer's daughter. Next morning, after a big brekkie, he asked for the bill.

'That'll be $5 for the food and $5 for the bed. Seeing as how you had to share.'

'Fair enough,' says the salesman. 'By the way, your daughter wasn't at all friendly. In fact, she was rather cool.'

'Yeah,' said the farmer, 'we're going to bury her today.'

The farmer was taking flying lessons so that he could get part-time work as a cropduster. As he was approaching the local airfield, the radio crackled and a voice said, 'Please give us your estimated height and position.'

'I'm five foot ten, and sitting in the front.'

Why did Dave get the flick from the orange juice factory?

Couldn't concentrate.

What's the difference between a magician's wand and a policeman's truncheon?

The magician's wand is for cunning stunts.

What's the difference between a milkmaid and a stripteaser?

The milkmaid is fair and buxom . . .

Why don't public servants look out of the windows in the morning?

If they did, there wouldn't be anything to do in the arvos.

What's the difference between a farm and a pigeon?

A pigeon can still put a deposit on a tractor.

A bloke was driving a little van very slowly through the city. He was pulled over by a cop. 'Look,' said the policeman, 'it's not that you've broken the law, but I'm curious. Why is it that you keep pulling up, racing round the back of the van and thumping the back door?'

'Well, officer, I've two tonnes of budgies in there and this is only a one-tonne van. And if all the little buggers landed at once, they'd break the springs.'

'Is this the motor pool? How many vehicles are operational?'

'We've got five trucks, five utilities, two scout cars and a tank. And that Bentley the fat-arsed colonel drives around in.'

'Do you know who you're speaking to?'

'No.'

'It's the so-called fat-arsed colonel.'

'Well, do you know who you're talking to?'

'No!'

'Thank Christ for that.'

Dawn. The deserter is being frog-marched to the place of execution. All the way he complains to the members of the firing squad. 'Fancy having to march all this distance in this cold weather just to get shot.'

'And you're complaining,' said one of the squad. 'We've got to bloody well march back again.'

Pacing the poop deck of his proud vessel, Lord Nelson looked up at a lad high in the rigging and called, 'Keep a keen eye out for Spanish sail, m'lad. For today I feel like a fight.'

Soon the boy cried, 'Sir, ten Spanish sail on the starboard bow.'

Nelson turned to his first officer. 'Lieutenant, bring me my red coat. If I'm wounded the blood shall not show. Better for morale.'

Just then the boy in the rigging cried, 'Fifteen Spanish sail on the port bow.'

Nelson said, 'Lieutenant, whilst you're getting my red coat, would you also be kind enough to bring me my brown breeches.'

In the greatest days of the British Empire, a new commanding officer was sent to a jungle outpost to relieve the retiring colonel. After welcoming his replacement and showing the courtesies (gin and tonic, cucumber sandwiches) the protocol decrees, the retiring colonel said, 'You must meet Captain Smithers, my right-hand man. God, he's really the strength of this office. His talent is simply boundless.'

Smithers was summoned and introduced to the new CO. He was surprised to meet a toothless, hairless, scabbed and pock-marked specimen of humanity, a particularly unattractive man less than four feet tall.

'Smithers, old man, tell your new CO about yourself.'

'Well, sir, I graduated with honours from Sandhurst, joined the regiment and won the Military Cross and Bar after three expeditions behind enemy lines. I've represented Great Britain in equestrian events and won a Silver Medal in the middleweight division of the Olympic boxing. I have researched the history of –'

Here the colonel interrupted.

'Never mind that, Smithers. The CO can find all that in your file. Tell him about the day you told the witch doctor to get fucked.'

Bill had been a workaholic all his life and when he kicked the bucket his friends took up a collection for a headstone. It read: ERECTED IN BILL'S MEMORY BY HIS RELATIVES AND FRIENDS.

They installed the headstone before the ground had settled and within a couple of days it had started to tilt. As a temporary measure, the mason looped a piece of fencing wire around it and tied the other end to a nearby tree. Bill's mates visited the grave for the first time since the funeral. 'Christ, that's our Bill,' said one, noticing the wire. 'Work, work, work. Now he's got the bloody phone on!'

A travelling salesman is heading up the Hume Highway towards Albury when he sees a not unattractive young lady thumbing a lift. He pulls over and she tells him she's going to work as a waitress in Wodonga. Seeking to glamorise himself he tells her that he is, in fact, 2AY Albury's top radio announcer. 'A radio announcer!' The girl is wildly excited. 'Are you a disc jockey or do you do talkback?'

'I'm sort of the local John Laws.'

'Oh, I'd love to be in radio. I'd really love to be an announcer.'

'Well, I think I could arrange to get you an audition.'

'Really?' Her excitement is palpable.

Whereupon he unzips his fly and produces his

generative member. And the girl reaches for it, grabs it firmly and bends over it. 'Hello, Mum! Hello, Dad!'

The wharfie had the security guards puzzled. Every day when he left Station Pier at Port Melbourne he wheeled out a wheelbarrow full of rubbish. And every day the guards would sift through the rubbish, certain that he was nicking stuff.

But every day the guards found nothing but rubbish.

Finally the wharfie retired and the guards couldn't bear to say goodbye without knowing. 'Look, we know you've been nicking stuff but we don't know how. What was the secret? What were you stealing?'

As he headed through the gates for the last time, he said, 'Wheelbarrows.'

Just before Prince Charles married Lady Diana, two Australians, being short of a quid to tide them over, answered an advertisement for employment at the palace. The positions were for coachmen to ride on the royal coach to and from Westminster Abbey, and, as the occasion was so auspicious, Her Majesty had decided to do the interviewing herself. So the pair were ushered into the royal presence and she explained that she wanted the wedding to be absolutely perfect, with no faults or flaws, as the eyes and ears of the world would be watching the fairytale wedding.

Now she got down to details. 'Would you mind showing me your legs, as they will be wearing tight-fitting pantihose, and firm legs are important?'

The blokes obliged and the Queen seemed satisfied. She then asked to see their feet as they'd be wearing buckle shoes. Satisfied with the feet, she asked to inspect their manly chests and biceps, and seemed quite impressed.

'Very well, gentlemen, that will be all. Now if you'll just show me your credentials.'

Ten years later, still scratching their heads, the blokes were leaving Wormwood Scrubs and one said to the other, 'You know, I think we would have got that job if we'd been a bit better educated.'

The council's road-building gang had a major problem. They'd gone to work and forgotten to take their shovels. They phoned the foreman to ask advice. 'No need to panic,' he said. 'I'll send the van out with the shovels. But you'll have to lean on each other until they get there.'

Caltex were drilling for oil in northern Australia. They'd freighted in American technicians but had a few Aussies as labourers, one of whom dropped his hammer down the shaft. All drilling had to stop for days on end until, finally, it was removed. It must have cost Caltex a fortune.

The American manager then assembled all the men around the shaft, called the Aussie forward and presented him with the hammer. 'I want you to accept this as a memento,' he told the Australian, 'and hope that it will remind you of the trouble and expense you've caused Caltex through your carelessness. So take it and piss off.'

'Do you mean I'm sacked?'

'Exactly.'

'Well, it's no flamin' use to me,' said the Aussie. And dropped the hammer down the shaft again.

The union talks had gone pretty well and the spokesman emerged from the conference with the boss to deliver the news to his comrades. 'Okay, cobbers. We've won just about everything we wanted. Retrospective salary increases for two years, two months annual leave, fares to Surfers, a two-hour lunchbreak, decent percolated coffee and we only work Friday. Nine to five.'

'What?' one of the workers cried. '*Every* bloody Friday?'

An undertaker was very pleased with himself when he organised for his son to be apprenticed to one of the best. 'You'll learn a lot from him,' he told his boy. 'He's a master of the trade.'

A few weeks later the boy told his dad of a strange experience. 'We got a call from the Hilton to say that a couple had died in bed. Apparently they were lying side by side, naked, dead as doornails.'

'And what happened?'

'Well, the boss got us to put on our poshest gear and we went around to the pub in the best hearse. We introduced ourselves to the manager and then went upstairs. It was all very quiet and dignified.'

'What happened then?'

'We opened the door and entered in a solemn manner befitting the occasion. And there, on the bed, was a naked couple. The boss quietly pointed out to me that the bloke had a gigantic erection. Apparently it's not uncommon in rigor mortis.'

'What happened then?'

'Well, the boss gave it a mighty whack with his umbrella.'

'What happened then?'

'What happened then? A bloody riot. We were in the wrong suite.'

Australia's first astronaut addressed a press conference before blasting off in the shuttle. Yes, he was proud to be included in the NASA team. But he admitted to some disquiet. 'There'll I'll be, sitting on top of 500 000 moving parts, every one supplied by the lowest tenderer.'

A purser on a flight from Cairns to Brisbane asked a passenger in Business Class what he had in his bag.

'Crabs. Caught them this morning. They're still alive and kicking. I'll cook them tonight.'

The purser, a charming young woman, volunteered to keep them in the kitchen until the flight was over.

The flight was full and she was pretty busy. As the plane was circling Brisbane she realised she wasn't quite sure which passenger the parcel belonged to. So she called over the intercom, 'Would the bloke who gave me the crabs in Cairns come forward so that I can give them back to him?'

Toads in the Hole

What's the definition of suspicion?

When your hotdog's got veins.

The little country store had sawdust on the floor and smelt of freshly ground coffee. The scrubbed pine counter contained jars of boiled lollies, boxes of beeswax candles and a shiny bacon slicer. It was the middle of World War II and there was a shortage of commodities. So you had to have your ration coupons.

A domineering local woman walked into the store and began placing an order with the shop assistant. 'I would like three pounds of flour, one pound of butter, half a pound of sugar, a bottle of kerosene, four pounds of potatoes and two pounds of brown Spanish onions – to be delivered by lunchtime.'

The assistant wrote the order in the book but, on reaching the last item, said, 'I'm very sorry, ma'am, but we have no brown Spanish onions, for the time being.'

'Course you have,' said the woman, glaring indignantly. 'I know you keep some under the counter for favoured customers. I insist on having some of those.'

The stand-off continued until the manager made an appearance. 'Good morning, madam. What seems to be the trouble?'

'I have asked for brown Spanish onions and have been told there are none. But I know you keep some for special customers and would like some. *If you please!*'

'Madam,' said the manager, 'you are an intelligent woman. May I ask you a few simple questions?'

'Certainly.'

'Take the word PARSNIP, madam. Without the 'P' and the 'NIP', what have we left?'

The lady replied, 'ARS.'

'Yes,' said the manager. 'Now, without the first four letters of the word BEETROOT, what remains?'

'ROOT, of course.'

'Very good,' said the manager. 'Now, on to the final question. Take the FUGG out of ONIONS and what do we have?'

The woman frowned at him and said, 'But there is no FUGG in ONIONS.'

'Quite right,' said the manager. 'That's what we've been trying to tell you for the last ten minutes.'

'You want salt?' the bloke in the fish shop asked the customer.

'Yeah.'

The bloke reached deep into his hip pocket, pulled out a salt shaker and sprinkled some on the chips.

'Pepper?'

'Yeah.'

The bloke reached into his other pocket, pulled out a pepper shaker and sprinkled some on the chips.

'Vinegar?'

'Yeah. But if you piss on them, I'm not eating them.'

A bloke goes into a cafe for breakfast. He orders a boiled egg and toast. When the egg arrives it falls out of the eggcup and he notices, inscribed on the bottom of the egg in tiny writing, the following: 'I am beautiful, 22 years old, with a perfect figure. And I am looking for a boyfriend.' And there, below the message was a phone number.

So, having finished breakfast, he rings it. 'Thanks very much for calling,' said the young woman, 'but I was married 18 months ago.'

A Jewish bloke in Double Bay wouldn't, couldn't, go to bed without a bowl of mazo ball soup. He loved it and lived for it. One night he sat looking at the plate like a mummy. 'What's the matter? You don't feel good? Something bothers you?' said his wife.

There was no answer.

'Too hot? I'll blow on it.'

There was no reply.

'Too cold? I'll whack it back in the microwave.'

No word.

'For God's sake, what the hell is it?'

Very quietly he said, 'Taste it.'

'Orright, already. Where the hell is the spoon?'

'Exactly.'

It all depends on local custom. In Australia, a fly in one's soup results in it being sent back to the kitchen and a row with the management.

In England, the head waiter quietly, daintily, fastidiously extracts the fly and removes it beneath a serviette.

In France the soup is eaten, the fly left high and dry on the side of the bowl.

In the Orient, the fly is eaten first and washed down by the soup.

In Scotland, the fly is shaken over the bowl and carefully wrung out. Then the soup is consumed.

And there are places where the diner stares into the bowl and complains. 'What's this? Only one fly?'

A young man was standing outside a small suburban coffee shop. He stood there for ten minutes nervously peering through the window. Finally he went into the shop and sat at a table. The waitress asked him what he wanted and he said, very nervously, 'Just a cappuccino.'

When she brought the order to him, he asked if it would be possible for her to help him drink the coffee. The waitress was somewhat puzzled by his request, so he explained that, a few weeks earlier, he'd had a major operation on his intestine and gullet, and as a result was now only capable of drinking liquids through his anus.

'Your anus?'

'Yes, with the help of a funnel and some plastic tubing which I carry with me. All you have to do is pour the coffee slowly down the funnel.' And he inserted the tube into his rectum.

The waitress agreed to help but insisted that he go into the back storage room where no one could see them. Adjusting the tube, he handed the girl the funnel and she started to pour the coffee into it. Ever so slowly.

Suddenly he groaned as if in pain. 'Oh! Oh!'

The waitress became alarmed and said, 'Is it too hot for you?'

'No,' he said. 'Not enough sugar.'

First cannibal, 'I hate her guts.'

Second cannibal, 'Well, just eat the vegetables.'

A bloke went into a seafood restaurant which had been recommended by Leo Schofield, and asked for a lobster tail. The waitress smiled sweetly and said, 'Once upon a time, there was this handsome lobster ...'

A bloke goes into the Chinese restaurant in Bendigo and orders number 43. Chicken with Black Bean Sauce.

'Christ, this chicken is bloody rubbery,' he snarls to the waiter.

He replies, with a charming smile, 'Thank you very much.'

They do a lot of feral-pig shooting at Murrurundi. Half the shops have got stuffed boars' heads on the wall. A tourist calls into the local cafe and checks the menu.

Ham sandwiches, roast pork, pigs' feet, bacon and pork chops.

Being Jewish, he sighs heavily and asks for a glass of water. 'I better warn you, mate,' says the waitress, 'we only have bore water.'

'Bore water!' he replied. 'You don't waste much of a pig!'

The big rugby player was overweight so his coach sent him to the centre for sports medicine.

'Honestly, I've tried every diet under the bloody sun. And nothing shifts the weight.'

'Well, we can help you at the clinic. As a matter of fact we've had immense success with a new method. Mind you, it's not to everyone's taste.'

'Try me.'

'Well, it works like this. You can consume anything you like, anything at all, and as much of it as you like. But you must do so anally.'

'What? Bung it up me bum?'

'Exactly.'

The rugby player was somewhat horrified but agreed to try it. Three weeks later he came back and looked slimmer, stronger and very happy.

'I feel bloody great. No trouble with the tucker. I just it shove it up me arse.'

'Well, it seems to be working.'

A few weeks later he checked in again, even lighter and fitter. 'Doc, you wouldn't believe it, but just before I came in I had a whole pavlova. Just shoved the lot straight up the Khyber.'

The next time he arrived at the clinic he was jiggling up and down and sweating profusely. He seemed to be in considerable distress.

'What's the trouble? You haven't been overdoing it? There shouldn't be this twitching, this hyperactivity. I think we'll have to take you off the diet.'

'No, no, it's fine,' said the rugby player, wiping his brow. 'I'm just eating a packet of Minties.'

An Aussie who lives in Alice Springs wins a trip to Boston. His friends say that they heard that not only is Boston big, but the city sports the best seafood restaurants in the world. Upon arrival in Beantown our dusty friend freshens up at his hotel and then decides to sup. The city's so big he's overwhelmed. He decides to hail a cab and asks the cabby to take him to a good seafood restaurant. (Unbeknownst to him, the cabdriver is a graduate student from Boston College going for his doctorate in linguistics and grammatical syntax.)

'Hey, cabby, where can I get scrod?' asks our bewildered friend. Upon hearing this, the cab driver says, 'Sir, I have heard it asked for in many ways, shapes and forms, but never have I heard it asked for in the past pluperfect.'

What's orange and goes Ho-Ho-Ho?
Fanta Claus.

Villainous Vices

Two bats were hanging upside down in a cave. One turned to the other and said, 'I'm desperate for a drink. Gotta have a drink of blood. So I'm heading off for a while.'

'Well, you better hurry up,' said the other bat, 'it's almost dawn and you won't be able to see a damned thing when the sun rises.'

So the bat goes out like a bat out of hell and is back within a minute, blood dripping from its mouth.

'Well, that was quick. Congratulations.'

And the first bat says, 'Congratulations? Look, you see that dirty great gumtree over there?'

'Yes,' said the other bat.

'Well, I didn't,' said the first bat.

A white horse ambles into a bar and orders a beer. 'Funny thing,' says the barman, 'we've got a whisky named after you.'

'What?' responds the horse. 'Timmy?'

A bloke goes into a bar at Kings Cross and sees a big sign reading: TWO THOUSAND DOLLARS CASH PRIZE. ASK THE BARMAN.

So he goes over and asks the barman what he has to do to win the dosh.

'You have to do three things, and it's all yours,' the barman says.

'Just three?' the bloke asks. He can feel the money in his kick already. 'What are the three things?'

'Well, first you have to go over to that huge bouncer who works outside the Pink Pussycat Club and knock him out. Then we've got a savage dingo in the back room that needs a tooth pulled. Then you have to go upstairs and screw an 80-year-old sheila.'

'No worries,' says the bloke. He wanders over to the bouncer and says, 'Hey, mate, your shoelace is untied.' When the bouncer looks down at his Doc Martens, the bloke flattens him with a solid upper cut.

Then he heads for the back room and the dingo. The barman hears a huge noise – it sounds like the dingo has gone mad.

A few minutes later the bloke emerges from the back room bleeding. His clothes are torn and he's breathing heavily. 'Okay,' he says, 'now where's the old lady that needs a tooth pulled?'

A bloke went to a great party. Smoked some dope, drank a lot of grog. Woke up in the morning and realised he'd lost his watch, a really good fake Rolex. Bugger it. He must have dropped it at the party, but he couldn't remember where the party was, or who'd thrown it. All he could remember was that the house had a red front door and a gold-plated dunny. So he looked all over town, looking for houses with red doors. But none of them had a gold-plated dunny.

Finally, just as he was going to chuck it in, he spotted another house with a red door. And it looked like they'd had a party. There were empty stubbies all over the lawn and a pair of knickers dangling on a rosebush.

He knocked at the front door, which was opened by a woman who obviously had a big hangover. 'Did you have a party here last night?'

'Christ,' groaned the woman, 'did we ever.'

'Well, I think I was here last night. And I lost my watch. All I can remember is this red front door and a gold-plated toilet.'

The woman stared blearily at the bloke, then shouted down the hallway. 'Bruce, here's the dirty bugger who pissed in your saxophone.'

A couple of technicians were fuelling a rocket at Woomera when they noticed that the stuff smelt pretty good. 'And it seems to have a bit of a kick in it,' said one, as he licked a drop off his finger.

'Let's siphon off a couple of gallons for the canteen party,' said the first.

The party was a considerable success.

Next morning the first bloke rang the other, 'How do you feel?'

'All right, so far.'

'Have you been to the dunny yet?'

'No, not yet. Why do you ask?'

'Just to warn you. I'm ringing from Adelaide.'

A drunk at the new Sydney casino stumbled into the loo and started feeding coins into the condom vending machine. Slowly but surely he filled his pockets with them. A bloke was waiting behind him.

'Excuse me, can I have a turn?'

'Not,' said the drunk, 'when I'm on a winning streak.'

Every week a bloke visits the TAB and every week he loses all his money. The woman behind the counter feels sorry for him and decides to help. 'Look, we get some very, very good tips here,' she whispers to the bloke. 'Watch me every week and I'll do something physically to give you a hint.'

That week she scratches her nose. He backs Proboscis and it comes in at ten to one.

Next week she scratches her head. He backs Heir Apparent and it wins by a furlong.

Week three, she scratches between her legs. But he fails to place the winning bet.

'Didn't you see me signal Short 'n Curly?' she says the next time he's at the window.

And he says, 'Yeah, but I thought the cunt was scratched.'

Three blokes are at a country racetrack having a bad day. They've only got $50 left between them. They decide to share a bet, to put all on one horse, in the hope of getting square. But they don't know which horse to back.

The first bloke says, 'Let's go to the toilet, measure the length of our dicks, add them up and back the horse of that number.' They agree and the first bloke comes in at six inches, the second bloke at four inches, and the third bloke at two inches. So they put $50 on number 12 at 100 to one. It wins brilliantly and there's money to burn. Trouble is, they can't decide how to split it up.

The first bloke says, 'I get half because I had six inches of the 12.'

The second bloke says, 'I get a third because I had four inches of the 12.'

And the third bloke says, 'That's not fair. I don't get enough.'

The first bloke says, 'Look, if I didn't have six inches and he didn't have four inches, we wouldn't have backed number 12.'

And the third bloke says, 'And if I hadn't had an erection, we would have backed number 11.'

The colonel didn't drink much, but at a regimental dinner got pissed, stuffed himself and finished up getting the fright of his life when another drunken officer challenged him to a duel. He was rescued by his mates and sent home in a cab.

Next morning he tried to explain to his batman why there was such a mess on his jacket. 'Some bounder bumped into me and I was sick all over my tunic. I'll give him a month's detention when I find him.'

The batman said, 'I'd make it two months, sir. The bastard also shat in your trousers.'

Two blokes are standing at the bar having a glass of beer. 'You look miserable, cobber,' said one. 'What's the matter?'

'Well, my cheese and kisses has just fallen down the stairs and broken both her legs. I just wish it was closing time so that I could go home and pick her up.'

A bloke is standing at the bar having a quiet beer when someone bursts in and belts him across the back of the neck. He feels a blinding pain as he passes out. The assailant tells the bartender, 'When he wakes up, tell him it was a karate chop from Japan.' Then exits.

The following day, the poor bloke is drinking at the bar again when the same yahoo rushes in, kicks him in the neck and, once again, knocks him out. 'When he wakes up,' says the ratbag, 'tell him it was a tae kwon do kick from Korea.' He leaves.

The next day the expert in karate and tae kwon do is sitting at the bar having a beer. All of a sudden his victim bursts in and belts him on the scone. He slips off the bar stool, unconscious. The bloke tells the bartender, 'When the bastard wakes up, tell him it was a piece of four-by-two from the back of the ute.'

A drinker sees a jar full of coins on the bar. 'What's that for?' he asks the barmaid.

'A competition,' she replies. 'Guess how many dollar coins are in the jar and it's yours!'

'Three hundred dollars,' he says. He was right, and won the jar full of money.

Feeling happy, he gets pissed and on the way home trips on his front step and drops the jar. The coins go everywhere. 'Bugger it. I'll clean it up in the morning,' he thinks. In the morning his wife wakes him up. 'Guess what's on the front step?'

Being a smartarse, he says, 'Three hundred one dollar coins.'

'No,' she says, 'two hundred and fifty litres of milk!'

A stuttering drunk approached the barman and said, 'Will you give me a fu, fu, fu ...'

The barmaid glared at him until he completed the sentence.

'A fuff-fuff-few matches. I bub-bub-bub-bet you thought,' the drunk continued, 'I was going to ask you for a fu-fu-fu-fu- ... full box.'

A Melbourne-born man and a Brisbane-born man met one night in a pub. The two found they had much in common, and soon became friends. However, when they offered to shout each other, a dispute broke out as to what beer to order. The Melbourne man wanted to order VB, while the Brisbane man wanted to order XXXX. Eventually they decided to let an impartial judge decide which was the better beer, and so sent a sample of each beer off to the CSIRO. When the results came back, neither was able to claim victory, as they read, 'Sorry to inform you, but both horses have jaundice.'

An old drunk staggers up to a young bloke whose head's under the open bonnet of a car.

'What's wrong?'

'Piston broke.'

'Me too.'

'Listen, mate,' said the drunk to the taxidriver. 'Have you got room in the front for four dozen beers and a couple of pizzas?'

'Sure,' said the driver.

'Thanks, mate,' said the drunk, as he chundered on the front seat. 'Now drive me home to Bondi.'

A drunken punter lifts his head from the bar and notices a sign reading LUNCH 12 to 1. 'Not bad odds. Excuse me, barman, I want to put a tenner on Lunch.'

'Yer pissed. Now bugger off or I'll throw you out.'

So the drunken punter staggers down the street to another pub, where he saw a sign saying LUNCH 11 to 2. 'Christ, the odds are down already. I better hurry up and place a bet. 'Hey, barman, I want $10 on Lunch at 11 to 2.'

'Yer drunk,' said the barman, and threw him out.

The punter staggered down the road to the next pub. Outside there was a sign reading LUNCH 1 to 2. 'Odds on,' thought the punter. 'That's no good. Anyway, I'll go inside and see the race.'

As he walked in the door, the barman shouted out to the cook, 'Sausages, one'.

'Thank Christ,' the punter said. 'I didn't back Lunch.'

A drunk lurched out of a pub and tumbled into the gutter. He woke up a few minutes later with a cop bending over him. 'Where the fuck am I?'

'At the corner of York and George Streets,' said the policeman.

'Never mind the bloody details. Which city?'

A tourist arrives at the Linga Longa pub in Gundy. 'It's a long time since I've seen sawdust on the floor of a pub,' he said approvingly.

'Sawdust? That's not sawdust, mate. That's yesterday's furniture after the whiteants got it.'

Five bikies walked into a country pub and, having ordered their beers, told the lone drinker at the other end of the bar to shout them. When he told them to get stuffed they punched him up and chucked him out the door.

'Not much of a fighter,' said one of the bikies.

'Not much of a driver, either,' said the barman. 'He's just driven his truck over five Harley Davidsons.'

A shearer stopped at a pub with his huge pay cheque. It was a pub used to shearers.

After a couple of rip-roaring days, the shearer was settling up with the publican. 'What's the damage, mate?'

'Well, your room with ensuite down the other end of the hall was 30 quid. You drank 20 quid worth of beer and two quid worth of whisky. You had $25 worth of steaks.'

'Yeah, that's right.'

'And you spent the night with one of the girls. That's another 20 quid.'

'Fair enough.'

'Oh, and there's 25 cents for hay for your horse.'

'That fuckin' horse is gunna ruin me.'

A bloke went into the pub in Murrurundi for a beer, and when he came out there was no sign of his horse. He went raging back into the pub. 'I'm giving youse blokes fair warning. If my fuckin' horse isn't back by the time I finish this beer, the same thing's gonna happen as happened in Gundy.'

When he finished his beer he slammed the glass down and went outside. And there was his horse, just where he'd left it. As he put his boot in the stirrup, a couple of the drinkers came out of the pub. 'By the way, mate, just what did happen in Gundy?'

'I had to walk home,' said the bloke.

A stockman walks into a pub. 'Look, my cobber will be in here soon,' he says to the barman. 'He's a bit of a dill. Short of a few kangaroos in the top paddock. And he'll try to pay for his drinks with bottle tops. So do me a favour, take the tops and I'll come in tomorrow and settle up.'

The barman is not too thrilled but is finally persuaded to go along with it.

A few minutes later, a bloke comes into the pub, orders a beer and plonks down a few bottle tops. And he keeps doing it all afternoon – paying for drinks with bottle tops. He shouts everyone in the pub, hands over more bottle tops and finally staggers off into the darkness.

Next day the stockman returns. 'Did my cobber come in yesterday? Did he pay you with bottle tops?'

'Yep,' says the barman. 'He bought a lot of drinks. It's gonna cost you.'

'No probs,' says the bloke, heaving a hub cup onto the bar. 'Got change for that?'

A little bloke was approaching a pub in Port Melbourne, a bit of a bloodhouse frequented by wharfies. Just as he threw a left to go in the door, he slipped on a pile of dog shit and landed flat on his back. Picking himself up, he staggered to the bar and was having a curative beer when he saw a big docker coming through the door. And he slipped in the same dog shit. As the dazed docker picked himself up, the little bloke walked over and said, 'I just did that.' And the docker punched him right in the face.

'Yes, sir, what's your pleasure?' inquired the barman.

'A scotch and a box of matches,' said the bloke.

He drank the scotch and put ten cents on the counter. 'This is for the matches. I didn't really want a drink, but when you were so nice about it.'

'Don't come the raw prawn. Cough up for the scotch!'

'Get stuffed.'

'Then bugger off!'

A week passes. 'Hey, I told you last week you were barred from this bar.'

'I've never been here before. You must have me mixed up with someone else.'

'Then you must have a double.'

'That's very nice of you. And a box of matches.'

A man was drinking at the bar when the bloke next to him said, 'Tickle your arse with a feather.'

'What did you say?'

'Particularly nasty weather,' said the bloke, with an amiable smile.

He thought this was pretty witty and would try it out. After a few drinks another fellow fronted the bar alongside him – a huge Hell's Angel covered in tattoos. Now somewhat inebriated, the bloke said, 'Stick a feather up your arse.'

The Hell's Angel turned to him, snarling, 'What did you say, you little bastard?'

Whereupon our hero said, 'Cunt of a day, isn't it?'

Two old ladies had been trying to give up smoking for years and used to meet every month or so to check up on each other's progress. Sadly, their habit persisted, until the following conversation took place.

'Well, I've finally done it.'

'Done what?'

'What do you mean, done what? I've given up smoking.'

'I don't believe it.'

'It's true. And it was quite easy. You see, each time I was about to light a cigarette I stopped and sucked a Lifesaver instead.'

'That's easy for you ... You live at Bondi.'

A drunk, having spent all his money, was chucked out of the local pub. Whereupon he walked in front of a ute and was killed instantly.

Next thing he knew he was standing in front of the Pearly Gates being greeted by St Peter.

'Where's the nearest pub, Pete?'

'Fourth cloud to the right,' said St Peter, 'but before you drown your sorrows, let me tell you that up here, we count a million years as a minute, and a million dollars as a cent.'

The drunk thought about this. 'Look, I'm a bit short at the moment, Pete. Could you lend me a cent?'

'Sure,' said St Peter, 'just wait a minute.'

A venerable member of the Melbourne Club had invited the Anglican archbishop to dinner. In preparation he had his butler whiz down to the Toorak Village to fetch a bottle of whisky, a box of Davidoff cigars and a few ounces of snuff. He knew that the bishop enjoyed his snuff.

The butler went to the village, procured the whisky and cigars but forgot the snuff. On arriving back at the gates of the mansion, he realised that he'd had a lapse of memory. But fortunately there were three dry lumps of dog shit on the nature strip which had blanched white in the sun. All he'd have to do was grind it into powder.

The dinner went very well and, afterwards, the businessman and the archbishop were enjoying their whisky and their cigars. But the host could smell dog shit. It was quite distinct.

'Do you smell dog shit?' he asked of the archbishop.

'No, I can't say that I do. But I am having some sinus trouble.'

'In that case, take a pinch of snuff.'

The archbishop took two pinches, sniffing one up each nostril. 'Aah, dear chap, that's splendid snuff. It's absolutely cleared my nasal passages. And you're right – I can smell dog shit.'

A bloke was waiting in the arrivals hall at Mascot Airport. Lots and lots of international passengers were coming through with their luggage. Suddenly a very beautiful woman appeared, and the bloke started calling out, 'F. F., F. F.'

The woman, waving cheerily, shouted, 'E. F., E. F.'

'F. F.' and 'E. F.' were bandied back and forth until a fellow passenger asked the woman what it meant. 'I'm telling him I want to Eat First.'

An old Aussie took his pet giraffe into a country pub and ordered two schooners. In fact, they drank about eight apiece. Then they both staggered to the door. But on the way out the giraffe went arse over head. As the old Aussie reached the door, the barman yelled out, 'Hey, old timer. Don't leave that lyin' on the floor. Take him with you.'

And the old Aussie slurred back, 'That's not a lion, you drongo, that's a giraffe.'

The Body Beautiful?

They were at the pictures. An old bloke sat in front of them and, after a few minutes, there was a terrible odour. They gave him a tap on the shoulder. 'Did you shit yourself, you old bastard?'

'Yep.'

'Then why don't you move?'

'Haven't finished yet.'

How do you make a skeleton?

Hose down a leper.

An Australian executive visits Tokyo. His mission is to sell some Australian components to Toyota.

Unfortunately he's not feeling too well and has an attack of flatulence. So his meeting in the Toyota boardroom becomes an immense embarrassment to all concerned. He can't stop farting. And worse still, his farts sound eerily like a Honda. A Honda at Toyota? There is an immense loss of face.

Worried that he's going to blow the business deal, the bloke goes to the Australian Embassy, who refers him to an English-speaking dentist. The dentist takes one look in his mouth and finds an abscess, which he insists is the cause of the problem. And to the Australian's astonishment, after a simple treatment, the farting stops.

'But I don't understand,' he said to the dentist. 'What has an abscessed tooth got to do with farting?'

'Ah, as you people say, "Abscess makes the fart go Honda".'

'Is your bum asleep?'

'No, why?'

'I thought I heard it snoring.'

A bloke had a very, very bad problem. Smelly feet. He'd tried everything. Nothing worked. It undermined his self-confidence, particularly in romantic affairs. He learned, from painful experience, that no woman would come within a mile of his smelly feet.

So he signed up with a computer dating service and they eventually fixed him up with a girl who described herself as 'absolutely desperate'.

He prepared for the date very carefully. He almost boiled his feet in hot water, covering them with talcum powder, wore clean socks and a big, heavy pair of Doc Martens boots. He laced them as tightly as possible so that no hint of odour could escape.

The girl was very, very quiet. She mumbled a few things but didn't actually say anything and never mentioned his feet. Gaining confidence, he suggested they go to a motel. The girl nodded, and off they went.

Inside the room the girl, still silent, went to the bathroom. He undressed. But when he took off the Doc Martens his feet smelt to high heaven. He threw his socks out the window but it didn't help.

At that moment the girl appeared from the bathroom and the bloke, too scared to face her, ran inside it and slammed the door.

What he didn't know was that the poor girl had a problem as bad as his – the world's worst breath. Which is why she kept her mouth shut.

When he finally came out of the bathroom, she flung her arms around him and started kissing him wildly, passionately, hungrily.

'Darling,' she said, 'there's something I must confess.'

'I know,' he gasped, 'you've eaten my socks.'

A journo is visiting a mental asylum to interview the director. He's running late and as he walks up the driveway passes a patient sitting in his pyjamas and a dressing-gown on a bench in the sunshine. The journo asks the patient the time. He takes out his penis, lays it on the palm of his hand and says, 'Ten to twelve.'

Saying nothing, the journalist goes to his meeting. He leaves an hour later and passes the same man on the same bench. Out of curiosity he asks him the time again. And the man again takes out his penis, lays it across his hand and says, 'Ten to twelve.'

'But you said it was ten to twelve an hour ago,' said the journalist.

The man immediately begins masturbating, saying, 'Damned thing must have stopped!'

A young bloke applies for a job as a salesman. He's interviewed by the manager who can't help but notice that he has a serious stammer.

'Have you had a selling job before?'

'N-n-n-n-n-o. Th-th-th-this will be my fir-fir-fir-first j-j-j-j-j-job.'

'That's a bad stammer you've got. Nonetheless I'll give you a go.'

'Wh-wh-wh-what will I be s-s-s-s-selling?'

'Bibles.'

'B-B-B-B-Bibles?'

'Yes, I'll give you five Bibles, and if you can sell them in a week I'll keep you on.'

A few hours later the stammering salesman comes back.

'I s-s-s-s-sold the five B-B-B-Bibles,' he tells the boss.

'Marvellous. Now I'll give you a box of 50 and if you can sell them in four weeks I'll make you head salesman.'

Three days later he's back. 'I s-s-s-sold the 50 B-B-B-Bibles,' he tells the boss.

'Incredible. What's your sales pitch?'

'What's a s-s-s-s-sales p-p-p-pitch?'

'Well, what do you say to your customers?'

'I just g-g-g-g-go up to the f-f-f-f-front d-d-d-door and when the l-l-l-l-lady comes out, I say "W-w-w-w-would you like to b-b-b-buy a B-B-B-B-Bible off of me, or w-w-w-would you rather me r-r-r-r-read it to you?"'

A couple of furniture removalists were lugging a piano into a Toorak mansion. As they wheezed and gasped their way along the corridor, they heard a voice coming from the cupboard under the stairs. 'When I find you I'm gonna get you, and when I get you I'm gonna eat you.'

Nervously they put down the piano. 'Shit, the place is haunted.'

Whereupon they heard the voice again. 'When I find you I'm gonna get you, and when I get you I'm gonna eat you.'

Slowly, tentatively, they opened the cupboard door – to find the owner's son sitting in the dark picking his nose.

A young bloke, fresh out of a school from the big smoke, has just arrived to begin work as a jackeroo on a cattle station out past Inverell. The truck from town drops him of just after lunch and one of the other jackeroos spends the afternoon with him, showing him round and telling him what has to be done and when.

By the end of the day everything's been covered, he's been fired up with a horse, a saddle and a bunk and he's looking forward to his first full day as he scrubs up for dinner. On his way there, however, he realises that the first-day nerves have cramped his guts up a bit, so he makes a detour to the dunnies: four long-drop holes, side by side, enclosed by three sheets of corrugated iron with a fourth as the roof. A length of old tarp strung across the fourth side acts as the dunny door.

Pulling the tarp aside and stepping in, the young bloke notices another occupant. Squatting over one of the holes is a weather-beaten old cocky with a rollie hanging out of one corner of his mouth. Not being a social situation, the two acknowledge each other with a nod of the head, and the young bloke proceeds to drop his strides and squat over one of the other holes. As he does so, the old bloke finishes, wipes himself with a bit of newspaper and pulls his own strides up. The young bloke can't help but notice a $5 note sticking out of the old bloke's pocket. Before he can say anything, however, the note falls out and flutters down the hole. The old bloke sees this, but being busy tucking in his shirt and buttoning himself up, he's unable to do anything about it.

Without saying a word, he turns around and stands there, staring down the hole. After a while, and with great deliberation, he reaches into his pocket and pulls out his roll. Slowly, he removes a $50 note, puts the rest back in his pocket, then drops the note down the hole to join the fiver.

The young bloke is now staring wide-eyed and open-mouthed at the old cocky. He can't believe what he's just seen.

Without even looking over the old bloke says to him out of the corner of his mouth, 'Well, yer don't expect me to go down there for five bloody dollars, do yer?'

Yorke's Peninsula, although not far from Adelaide, had only a few settlers before 1875 because there are no streams and the ground water is saline. It was originally covered with dense woodland. By 1922 it had been extensively cleared for agriculture, but the country roads all had the original mallee trees on either side.

A Mr Tossell was the editor and proprietor of the newspaper *The Yorke's Peninsula Farmer*. He was also a member of parliament.

One beautiful warm day in early September when the snakes and sleepy lizards were emerging from their hibernation, Tossell was driving his trap along a tree-lined road, calling on farmers to seek their votes.

He had to stop and get down to answer a call of nature, unaware that where he did his business there was a sleepy lizard, which awoke and waddled off.

His companion, sitting in the trap, said, 'Well, Tossell, that's the first time I've ever known one of your motions to be carried!'

What did one tampon say to the other tampon?

Nothing. They were both stuck-up cunts.

Did you hear about the Australian who had a penis transplant?

It didn't take. His hand rejected it.

For years the couples had been playing cards every week, but as they grew older the pace slackened. While the wives were out of the room, one bloke said to the other, 'I usually have to remind you what cards have been played, but tonight I didn't need to. Why not?'

'I've been to memory school.'

'Yeah! What's the name of the school?'

'Let me see ... what do you call that red flower, with thorns on the stem?'

'A rose?'

'Yeah, that's it. A rose. Hey, Rose,' he yelled towards the kitchen, 'what was the name of that memory school I went to?'

During the last war a young digger was posted to a remote part of the Western Desert. Being a dutiful son, he wrote to his mum regularly, and received the following reply. 'John, it is wonderful getting your letters and hearing of your activities, but we've almost forgotten what you look like. Could you send us a photograph.'

Well, there was something of a shortage of photographers in the Western Desert. But he did have a photo that a mate had taken – of him standing starkers except for his slouch hat and desert boots.

He had an inspiration. He'd cut it in half and send mum the top bit. Which he did.

Soon after, another letter from his mother arrived.

'Thank you, darling, for the letter and for the marvellous photo. You do look well. But could you forward one to Granny. She's always asking after you.'

He wondered what to do. He only had the bottom half of the one photograph. Well, the old dear was practically blind and probably wouldn't be able to see the details. So John sent Granny the bottom half.

In due course he got a reply from Granny. 'Dear John, how wonderful of you to send me a photograph. Do you know you're getting to look more like your father all the time. You have bags under your eyes. You need a shave. And what's more, your tie isn't straight.'

The colonel of a commando regiment was forever boasting how tough his men were, to such an extent that the high command got jack of this and decided to send one of their generals to check out his unit.

The general arrived at the army camp one icy-cold day and ordered the colonel to turn out his troops at 6 a.m. next morning for inspection. At 6 a.m. next day, with snow on the ground and an icy wind blowing, he insisted that, because the commandos were so tough, they should parade naked. So that is what they did.

The general strode along the rows of naked men and struck one across the buttocks with his swagger stick.

'Did that hurt, soldier?'

'No, sir!' said the soldier.

'Why did it not hurt?' asked the general.

'Because I am a commando, sir!' replied the lad.

Next soldier was struck a resounding blow to the cheek.

'Did that hurt, soldier?'

'No, sir!'

'Why?'

'Because I am a commando, sir!'

Then the general saw this commando standing to attention with a large erection. *Whack!* went the general's swagger stick, right on the erect organ.

'Did that hurt, soldier?' inquired the general.

'No, sir!' said the lad.

'Why did it not hurt?' asked the general.

'Because it belonged to the soldier behind me, sir!'

Two elderly, retired brigadier-types are in their club having a nightcap, reminiscing on their subaltern days, and their most embarrassing moments.

'It was the First War,' said one, 'and I was in pommyland and invited to the lord of the manor's ball. Tried damned hard not to be an uncouth Aussie. I was dancing with a girl with a very low-cut dress and saw it starting to slip down. I cried out, "Look everybody, out of the window". They did, thus giving the girl a chance to pull her dress up and save her from embarrassment. But damn it, man ... unbeknown to me, there were two dogs fornicating on the lawn. Well, what was yours?'

'Mine? Well, it was when my mother caught me masturbating.'

'But, that's nothing. All us boys got caught sooner or later.'

'Damn it, man, this was last Sunday!'

A bloke went into the pub's dunny and was bitten by a redback on the toilet seat. In the most painful of places. To make matters worse, he knew that the story of his intimate injury would get around the small country town.

Sure enough, when he was in the town a few weeks later he was fronted by an old lady who said she'd heard all about the injury.

'But where exactly did you get bitten?'

There was an embarrassed silence until an old chap sitting at the end of the bar said, 'Well, Edna, if you'd got bit where he got bit you wouldn't have got bit at all.'

Five blokes had been drinking for a while and were starting to get philosophical. One said, 'I wonder if a wink would be the fastest thing in the world?'

The second bloke said, 'I think a blink would be faster.'

The third bloke said, 'What about a think, that's quicker than a wink or a blink.'

The fourth bloke said, 'An electric light switch! You've only got to touch it and the light comes on straight away.'

The fifth bloke said, 'You're all wrong. Diarrhoea.'

'Why diarrhoea?' they chorused.

'Well, I had diarrhoea last night,' he said, 'and before I could wink, blink, think or turn on the light, I shat myself.'

'Jeez, mate,' said the little bloke to the fellow having a piss beside him in the hotel loo. 'You've got a big dick there.'

'And you've got a bloody big arse,' came the response.

'Yeah. It takes a big hammer to drive a big nail.'

'Let me shout you a stout. I hear that drinking stout puts lead in your pencil.'

'I don't know about you, old mate, but I don't have that many women to write to.'

A stranger in a small country town has been breasting the bar for a couple of hours when nature calls. He wanders round the back of the pub and finds a rickety dunny. It is listing slightly to port and the door is held shut with a piece of baling twine. He goes inside and, on finishing the job, looks around for the toilet roll. All he finds is a bare cardboard tube dangling on a piece of fencing wire. Nor is any substitute on offer – no sheets of newspaper hanging from a nail. Finally he sees a sign. 'To our customers. Owing to a shortage of dunny paper, we must ask you to use your finger to clean your bum. However, if you stick it through the knot hole to the left it will be sucked clean.'

The stranger follows the distasteful instructions and sticks a shitty finger through the knot hole. Where upon it is immediately hit by a hammer. Screaming he pulls the finger in – and sucks it!

At 20–30 years	Tri-daily
At 30–40 years	Tri-weekly
At 40–50 years	Try weakly
At 50–60 years	Try oysters
At 60–70 years	Try anything
70 years and over	Try to remember

What to do when you get old:

Never pass a toilet
Never waste an erection
Never trust a fart

His bride was a buxom 20-year-old. But he, despite his millions, was past it. He tried everything to encourage an erection but nothing worked.

Finally he went to a hypnotherapist who, to his astonishment, managed to implant a post-hypnotic suggestion.

'All you have to do is say "Ding!" In that second you'll get a terrific erection. And it will last until you say "Ding, Ding". Then it will go down again. But it will take a huge amount out of your system. I must warn you that you'll only be able to use this approach three times. Now, let's see if it's working. "Ding!"' Instantly a giant erection.

'Ding! Ding!' said the hypnotherapist. Instantly it went down. 'Now you've got two times left,' he said. 'Be very, very careful.'

On the way home the bloke passed the Town Hall clock as it reached 1.30. A giant 'Ding!' rang out and, voila, a huge erection. He swerved his car to the side of the road and sat there palpitating. Half an hour later the clock struck two. 'Ding! Ding!' And his erection disappeared.

He drove the rest of the way home as fast as he could. Rushing inside he said, 'Darling, get your clothes off and jump on the bed.'

Though unconvinced, she obliged. 'Ding!' he yelled. And, there it was, a giant erection.

'Hey, that's really something,' she said. 'But what's all this ding, ding crap?'

The pommy was not long in Australia before he heard that the duck-shooting season was about to start. He decided that he had to join in, so went out and bought all the things he was told he would need: double-barrel shotgun; waders; decoy ducks; hunting cap, etc. You name it, he had to have it.

On the opening morning, he took off into the swamp. He loaded the shotgun just in case he saw something on the way. When he came to a barbed-wire fence he rested the gun on the top strand and proceeded to throw his leg over. The gun was dislodged and went off. His old fellow copped the lot.

He managed to stagger into the nearest town and ask for a doctor. The doctor was horrified at the sight of the multi-holed member, but told the man he would do what he could. On the operating table, the doctor pulled out pellets one by one with tweezers and dropped them into a tray. *Ping, ping, ping.*

Eventually the doctor said that he thought he had the lot out. The pommy asked if he would be all right in his future. The doctor said, 'I think you will be okay, but before you go I suggest you see my brother next door.'

'I sure will, doc. Is he another doctor?'

'No, he's not a doctor, he's a musician. He will show you where to put your fingers so you don't piss in your eye!'

'You show me yours and I'll show you mine,' said the little boy to the little girl behind the shelter shed.

So she pulled down her knickers.

'Look, I'm growing feathers.'

'Then cop this,' said the little boy, as he lowered his pants.

'Christ, you've grown the neck and giblets as well,' she wailed.

Smarten up your act or I'll give you a Blundstone enema.

In fifth dynasty Egypt, a couple of scribes were quilling hieroglyphs onto papyrus, loudly proclaiming the merits of the Pharaoh Cheops. One tapped the other on the shoulder. 'How do you spell macho, mate? One testicle or two?'

'Doctor, I've got five penises.'

'How do your pants fit?'

'Like a glove.'

A bloke went to the doctor. Told him about his farting problem. 'The noise is bad enough,' he says, 'but it's the smell, doc. My farts stink to high heaven. They're ruining my social life.'

'Don't worry,' says the doctor, 'it'll just be a small internal problem. I'll be able to fix you up.'

Just then the bloke lets another one go.

'Christ!' the doctor says, fanning the air with a prescription pad. 'That's the worst-smelling fart I've ever smelt. And that's saying something.' And he gets up, goes to a cupboard, and returns with a long, long bamboo pole, with a sort of metal hook on the end. The patient takes one look and whispers, 'What the fuck are you going to do with that?'

'I'm going to open the skylight.'

Sin-shifters

What's white and hangs off clouds?

The coming of the Lord.

The Morgan Gallop Research organisation was conducting a poll on Australian sexuality. The pollster knocked on the door of a manse. 'Excuse me, sir, how often do you do it?'

'Oh, about seven or eight times a year,' replied the distinguished man who'd half opened the door.

'That doesn't seem very often,' said the researcher.

'Well, it's not bad for a 65-year-old priest without a car.'

Why wasn't Jesus Christ born in Perth?

Because God couldn't find three wise men from the east.

Have you heard of the atheist dial-a-prayer service?

When you phone, nobody answers.

What do you get if you cross a Jehovah's Witness with a Hell's Angel?

Somebody who knocks on your door and tells *you* to fuck off.

A young Irish girl in Dublin went to confession. 'Bless me, Father, for I have sinned. It has been two weeks since my last confession.'

There was a pause. 'Go on, my dear.'

There was silence.

'Come on, come on!'

More silence.

So the priest went out of his side of the confessional and joined her in hers. 'Is it about a boy?'

She nodded.

He kissed her. 'Did he do that to you?'

'Yes, Father. And much worse.'

He fondled her breasts. 'Did he do that to you?'

'Oh yes, Father, and much worse.'

He undressed her and began fornicating in the confessional. When he was finished, he asked, 'And did he do that to you?'

'Oh yes, Father, and much worse.'

The priest yelled, 'What worse can he do to you than that?'

'He gave me the clap, Father.'

A couple of Irishmen were digging up the road outside the local brothel when they saw a C of E vicar approaching. To their astonishment, he ducked through the door. 'That dirty Protestant. What a hypocrite.'

A few minutes later they spotted a rabbi making a sudden detour. 'Did you see what I saw? The Jews are no better.'

And shortly thereafter they spotted a Catholic priest doing the exactly the same thing. 'Mick, take off your hat,' said the other. 'One of the poor girls must be dying.'

One night in an Irish village two revellers were wending their way home when they met the local priest.

'Ah me, lads,' said the priest. 'You look like you've been having a good time.'

'We have, indeed,' said the revellers.

'And what might you have been up to?' said the priest.

'Well, Father,' said one of the revellers, 'we've been down at the pub and everyone has been playing this great game. The women are blindfolded, the men put their willies on the bar and the women have to tell who it is by the feel of their willies.'

'That's disgusting!' said the priest. 'I'll go straight down there and stop that.'

'Oh, I wouldn't do that if I were you, Father,' said the revellers.

'And why not?' asked the priest.

'Because your name has been mentioned a couple of times already.'

The doctor explained to the young patient that he was suffering stress, which, if he didn't do something about, could well lead to depression. 'Take life easier,' was his advice. 'Do you drink?'

'No, I don't.'

'Well, there's no harm in a few drinks. And

although I don't usually recommend smoking, I reckon a few cigarettes wouldn't hurt you. They'd help you relax. As would sex, at least once a week. In fact, given your symptoms, that's essential.'

A few months later the patient returned and was obviously in better health. He told the doctor how much he enjoyed his glass of beer each night and, as well, the odd cigar.

'And what about sex?'

'Hard to find it every week,' said the patient, 'especially for a parish priest in a small country town.'

A prostitute had been visiting a psychiatrist for many, many years, principally to discuss the sexual guilts caused by her profession.

He tried to maintain a professional distance but, suddenly, they were in each others arms and then bonking on the couch.

When it was over they lay quietly, side by side. Then both said simultaneously, 'That'll be $100.'

'Trouble with you, Hymie Goldstein,' said St Peter at the Gates, 'is that you've got a perfect record. Not a blemish. A life of good deeds.'

'So what's the problem?' asked the puzzled Hymie.

'Trouble is, you're too good to be true. We've dozens of popes up here that don't come near you for good deeds. And we'd have to place you above them in the heavenly hierarchy. We follow strict protocol up here, particularly when it comes to good deeds.'

'Sorry,' said Hymie.

'Look,' said St Peter, 'seeing that you're such a good bloke why don't we send you back for another hour or so. Maybe you could do something a little bit naughty in that time. And with your record, you'd still be in the upper echelons. But we wouldn't have the protocol problem with the popes.'

Reluctantly Hymie agreed.

'So here's the deal. You've got an hour, and no more good deeds.'

Instantly Hymie was back in his house as the clock was striking 11. What am I going to do? he thought. I don't drink, I don't gamble. I've never had sex. How am I going to commit even a venial sin? After wasting the first 30 minutes worrying, he thought of the middle-aged lady in the flat next door. And he remembered, decades earlier, lusting after her. Finally he plucked up courage and knocked on the door.

'Oh, how nice to see you. I heard you were ill.'

Plucking up all his courage he rushed at her,

threw her on the couch, ripped off her knickers and put an end to both their virginities. At that very moment, the clock started to strike 12. As the room began to blur and he heard the faint sound of an angel's chorus, he could hear a woman's voice. 'Oh, thank God! Thank God! Only God and I will know what a good deed you've done!'

Two nuns were riding on their bicycles through a French provincial town. 'I haven't come this way before,' said one nun.

'Must be the cobblestones,' replied the other.

The Hare Krishna rushed into a Catholic church in the middle of Mass, calling out, 'My karma has run over your dogma!'

'Excuse me, sir, for interrupting you, but we've a very, very good reason for knocking on your door like this. We want to invite you to become a Jehovah's Witness.'

'No fuckin' way. I didn't even see the accident.'

And old couple were watching the telly one Sunday morning. An American televangelist was jumping up and down, raving and ranting and Bible-bashing, and punctuating proceedings with constant demands for donations. Suddenly he changed tempo and became terribly, terribly sincere. He brought the camera very close to his face and told his viewers that he would transmit some spiritual healing. 'What you must do is place one hand on your heart and the other on the organ that needs a miracle.'

The old lady put one hand on her heart and the other on her arthritic elbow.

The old bloke put one hand on his heart and the other on his withered genitals.

'For God's sake,' said the old lady, 'he said he was going to heal the sick, not raise the dead!'

A bloke was at the Gap, down on his luck, and about to end it all. As he approached the edge, a voice out of nowhere said, 'Don't jump! Don't jump! Cardinal Gilroy will save you!'

The bloke stepped back, looked around, but couldn't see anybody. He approached the edge once more and was about to leap when the voice called out, 'Don't jump! Don't jump! Cardinal Gilroy will save you.'

He jerked back, spun around and looked behind him. No one was there. No one was anywhere in sight. He frowned and once more approached the edge, when the voice once again cried out, 'Don't jump! Don't jump! Cardinal Gilroy will save you!'

And the bloke shouted back, 'Who the hell's Cardinal Gilroy?'

And the voice replied, 'Jump, you Protestant bastard, jump!'

The Archbishop of Canterbury was sitting in the back of St Paul's Cathedral quietly fondling himself beneath his habit. He was so preoccupied that he didn't hear a tourist approach him. But the flash of the camera brought him back to Earth with a jolt.

'Please, please, sell me the film,' he begged. 'In fact, I'll buy the camera.'

Later the Dean noticed that the Archbishop had a new camera. 'How much did you pay for it?'

The Archbishop said, very glumly, 'Two thousand pounds.'

'Christ,' said the Dean, 'somebody saw you coming!'

Taosim:	Shit happens
Protestantism:	Let shit happen to someone else
Catholicism:	If shit happens, you deserved it
Judaism:	Why does shit always happen to us?
Atheism:	No shit
TV Evangelism:	Send more shit
Buddhism:	If shit happens, it is not really shit
Zen Buddhism:	What is the sound of shit happening?
Jehovah's Witnessism:	We can only take so much shit
Hinduism:	This shit happened before

Zen and the office party

Taoist:	Office parties happen
Hindu:	This office party has happened before
Freudian:	I dreamt I had an office party
Hare Krishna:	Partyrama, rama, rama
Cartesian:	I office party. Therefore I am
Protestant:	I've worked hard for this office party
Catholic:	I deserve this office party
Jehovah's Witness:	*Knock, knock.* Where's the office party?
Jungian:	Let's analyse this office party
Zen:	Let's contemplate this office party

Buddhist:	When is an office party not an office party?
Mormon:	Office parties happen again and again and again
Jewish:	Why do office parties always have to happen to me?
Muslim:	Fundamentally, it's an office party
Rastafarian:	Let's smoke this office party

The Council of Adult Education decided to have a series of courses on comparative religion. The most attended course turned out to be on reincarnation, with various would-be Buddhists and local New Agers sitting in rapt attention listening to an account of the Dalai Lamas in Tibet. But there was one bloke in the class who just didn't seem to fit in. During the intense discussion of theological matters he burped, farted and scratched himself. He didn't seem to be paying the slightest attention and, in fact, was disturbing the others.

Finally, the lecturer said, 'Sir, we seem to be boring you. What brought you to a class on reincarnation?'

'Well,' he replied, 'you only live once.'

A really bad bastard who was into drugs, grog, prostitutes and foul language – whose favourite expression was 'fuck the coppers' – was listening to the Salvos in Fortitude Valley. For a while he stood there grinning and chiacking them. But after a while he started listening more seriously. And then he felt tingly and funny all over.

In that moment he decided to mend his ways and join the Salvos.

They were thrilled with their new recruit, and because he was such a big bloke, gave him the big bass drum to bang. After basic training in drumming and oratory, it was his turn to preach. And by an amazing coincidence, the scene took place outside what had been his favourite pub. 'Here I stand before you, ladies and blokes of the Valley. I, too, was like you doing the normal things. I was lecherous, debauched, sodden with booze and dopey with drugs ... and the Salvos showed me the light. And now my days of vice are behind me. I'm swelled up – bursting with the joys of Jesus! I'm so full, I could burst this fucking drum!'

A new priest at his first Mass was so scared he could hardly speak. After the service, he asked the Monsignor how he had done.

'Fine, but next week it might help if you put a

little vodka or gin in your water to relax you.'

The next week the new priest put vodka in his water and really kicked up a storm. After Mass he asked the Monsignor how he had done this time.

'Fine,' he said, 'but there are a few things you should get straight:

1. There are Ten Commandments, not twelve.
2. There are twelve disciples, not ten.
3. David slew Goliath, he did not kick the shit out of him.
4. We don't refer to Jesus Christ as the late JC.
5. Next Saturday there will be a Taffy pulling contest at St Peter's, not a Peter pulling contest at St Taffy's.
6. The Father, Son and Holy Ghost are not Big Daddy, Junior and the Spook.
7. Moses parted the water at the Red Sea. He didn't pass water.
8. We do not refer to Judas as El Finko.
9. The Pope is consecrated, not castrated, and we do not refer to him as the Godfather.'

'You can go home and tell your husband he's going to be a daddy,' said the doctor.

'But, doctor, I'm not married.'

'Well, you can give the good news to your boyfriend.'

'But I haven't got a boyfriend. I have never been out with a man.'

The doctor looked out the window at the night sky. 'Last time this happened there was a big star in the east.'

The bush parson decided to retire from his duties and announced his intention of selling his horse. Knowing that it was a tough little pony, great for the high country, a farmer immediately offered the reverend $200. They shook on it. But when the farmer climbed into the saddle the horse wouldn't budge.

'Oh, I neglected to point out that he's a very, very religious horse. He will only go when you say "Jesus Christ" and will only stop when you say "Amen".'

The farmer thanked the reverend and said, 'Jesus Christ', whereupon the horse took off at a trot. They were travelling back to the high country when a storm started brewing and a bolt of lightning split a nearby tree. The horse bolted and a low branch struck the farmer in the face, momentarily blinding him. As it galloped wildly through the scrub, he tried to think of the word to make it stop. Finally he remembered. 'Amen!' The horse skidded to a halt. And when the farmer regained his vision, he saw that they'd propped right on the edge of a thousand-metre cliff. 'Jesus Christ!!' he said.

A parson, who always read his sermons, placed his carefully prepared text on the pulpit about half an hour before the service. A young member of the congregation thought it would be funny if he removed the last page.

Preaching vigorously, passionately, the minister came to the following words on the bottom of the page '... so Adam said to Eve ...' Trouble was, there was no next page. The minister was horrified to discover that it was utterly and entirely missing. He looked down at his feet, riffled through the other pages, and gained a little time by repeating, 'So Adam said to Eve ...' Then, in a low voice, which the amplifying system carried to every part of the church, he added, 'There seems to be a leaf missing.'

A new Australian lady entered a tram and sat next to a Salvation Army lass. She turned to the Salvo and said, 'Scuse, please. You are vearink a uniform. Vot is it?'

The Salvation Army girl said, 'I work for the Lord Jesus.'

'Very intelesting,' said the new Aussie. 'I'm a verken for the Kraft cheeses.'

A young novice was climbing up the hill towards the grim-looking convent. She carried a little cardboard case in her hand, containing the few items she'd be permitted once inside the walls. Halfway up the hill she stubbed her toe on a rock. 'Oh, shit!'

Standing still she looked around. 'Oh, fuck, I said shit.'

She bit her lower lip. 'Oh, shit, I said fuck.'

Whereupon she turned around and headed down hill. 'Stuff it, I didn't want to be a nun anyway.'

After years of training in the seminary, three young priests were assigned to parishes in and around Tottenham. The girl in the ticket box was uncommonly mammiferous and the priests were somewhat nonplussed.

'Three tickets to Titterston,' stammered the first, prior to blushing and retreating.

'Here, I'll have a go,' said the second priest. 'Three titties to Tockerton.'

'Christ, you're making a real mess of it,' said the third. He snatched the money and approached the window. 'Three tickets to Tottenham, Miss,' he said very, very formally, 'and unless you dress more demurely St Finger will point his Peter at you.'

The Pope was rapidly declining and medical experts, called in from all over the world, argued over the best approach to the crisis. Finally there was consensus – a lifetime of celibacy had built up a huge store of seminal fluid that was choking the Papal arteries. The only cure? An urgent course of intercourse.

The Pope crossed himself and shook his head.

But the physicians were convincing. 'Your Holiness, if you persist in celibacy you'll condemn yourself to death. That is suicide, a mortal sin.'

The Pope asked for three days so that he could pray and consider the theological implications.

On the third day he called the doctors to his bedside. 'I've come to a decision. I will be guided by your advice. But make sure she has big tits.'

A priest was doing the rounds of the Belfast prison. 'What are you in for?' he asked one.

'Murder.'

'And what did you get for that?'

'Life.'

The priest asked a second man what he'd done.

'Forgery. And I got ten years.'

'And what are you in for, my man?'

'Pouring petrol over Protestants and setting them alight.'

'And what did you get for that?' asked the priest.

'About 20 to the gallon,' said the prisoner.

The young novice, on arriving at the convent, was assigned the job of sweeping the steps of the chapel. 'You must keep the entrance immaculately clean,' said the Mother Superior.

Trouble was, the pigeons kept shitting all over them. Every time she got the steps clean, they'd crap on the marble.

'Fuck off! Fuck off!' she'd scream at them.

The Mother Superior said to the novice, 'My dear, your language is unseemly. Just swipe at them with the broom and say "shoo-shoo". Then they'll fuck off.'

Two young nuns went to the supermarket in the convent's mini minor. They couldn't find a parking space so one said she'd keep circling the block while the other ducked into the store.

Returning with a full trolley, the nun could see no sign of her colleague. 'Have you seen a nun in a red mini?' she asked a policeman.

'Not since I stopped drinking,' he replied.

The Mother Superior was addressing the graduation ceremony. 'In the outside world you will be confronted by many temptations. You must remember what you've been taught here. You must cling to your ideals. You must resist all temptation. For example, a man might try to take sexual liberties with you. Remember that one hour of pleasure could ruin your whole life. Any questions?'

'Yes, Mother. How can you make it last an hour?'

The cardinals met in the Sistine Chapel to elect a new Pope. After the first round there was no agreement, so they moistened their ballots and set fire to them, sending the traditional puff of black smoke out of the little vent in the roof. Unfortunately the small fire ignited an old tapestry and within moments the entire chapel was ablaze.

Cut to heaven where the cardinals are lining up for admission. 'Hang on. Don't just go charging in,' roared St Peter. 'You've got to go through the same tests as anybody else. Now, before you're barbecued, how many of you committed sins of the flesh?'

After an awkward silence, 49 cardinals raised their hands. Only one didn't. 'Right,' said St Peter, 'off to Purgatory, you 49. And take the deaf bastard with you.'

At a Catholic school a little girl asks, 'Do angels have babies?'

Whereupon the little boy in front turns around and sneers at her, 'Do they fuck in hell?'

And the nun says, 'Please, please ... one question at a time.'

The vicar prepared a beautiful sermon for his Presbyterian church, describing the plight of the poor. 'Is it the charitable duty of the rich to share their wealth?' he said.

Asked how the sermon went, the vicar replied, 'Well, it was a partial success. I convinced the poor.'

The Pope and Don Juan arrived at the Pearly Gates on the same day. Whilst the Pope lingered near the entrance shaking hands with old friends, Don Juan went straight in. When the Pope finally entered, he bumped into Don Juan. 'My son, I want nothing more than to kneel at the feet of the Virgin Mary. Do you know where I can find her?'

'Yes, holy Father, but you're just a bit late.'

A priest from Brunswick who was suffering from depression went to see a psychiatrist. 'I think you should go overseas, to some place where nobody knows you, and have a very, very good time. Why not try Las Vegas?'

So the priest went to Las Vegas and found himself in the front row of a strip show. And when a pneumatic dancer cavorted past him he leant out and stroked her bum.

'No you don't, Father,' said the dancer.

'How do you know I'm a priest?'

'Because I'm Sister Bridget from Footscray and we've got the same shrink.'

A priest was walking through Sydney's Botanic Gardens when he saw a sad-looking frog sitting on a rock in the middle of a pond. 'Why are you so unhappy?' he asked.

'Well, I wasn't always like this. I used to be a happy, normal boy of eleven, a choirboy at St Patrick's church. But one day I was walking through the gardens and I met a witch. "Go away wicked witch", I said. Whereupon she turned me into a frog.'

'My poor child,' said the priest. 'Can the witch's curse ever be reversed?'

'Yes,' said the frog, 'if a nice, kind person were to take me home and give me a hot meal and put me in a nice warm bed and make sure I was kept warm all night. Then, next morning, I'd wake up as a little boy once more.'

The priest put the frog in his pocket, took him home, gave him a bath and a hot meal and put him into his bed. When the priest woke up the next morning, beside him in the bed was an 11-year-old choirboy.

And that, Royal Commissioner Wood, is why I'm innocent of paedophilia.'

At a Christian Revival meeting the evangelist invites anyone who wishes to be healed to speak up. Way up the back of the hall a hand waves frantically. 'Do you wish to be healed?' asked the preacher.

'Yes, preacher.'

'What is your name?'

'My name is Michael.'

'Well, Michael, come down here to the stage.'

So Michael, with callipers and on crutches, struggles down to the stage.

'Go behind the screen, Michael. Who else wants to be healed?'

And from the audience a voice with a severe cleft-palate impediment says, 'Yeth pleathe, I want to be healed.'

'And what is your name?'

'My name'th Patrick.'

'Well, Patrick, come to the stage and go behind the screen. Now, brothers and sisters, let us pray for Michael and Patrick.' And there's much praying and choral singing.

'Now, Michael,' cries the preacher, 'throw out your crutches.' One crutch comes sailing over the screen and lands on the stage at the preacher's feet. Then the second crutch comes sailing over the screen as well.

'Now, Patrick,' says the preacher, 'speak!'

And we hear Patrick's familiar voice saying, 'Michael'th fallen over.'

An Australian hellfire preacher wanted to impress his congregation. He arranged for a boy to get above the pulpit in the loft and let a lit piece of paper flutter down when the preacher reached the great climax of his sermon. 'When I shout "Send fire from heaven", light the paper and let it flutter down.'

The great day came and the thunderous sermon was given. He shouted, 'Send fire from heaven.' Nothing happened. He shouted again, 'Send fire from heaven!' Nothing happened. He shouted again.

The voice of the boy could be heard, 'I can't. The cat's pissed on the matches.'

What do you get if you cross a Jehovah's Witness with an atheist?

Someone who knocks on your door for nothing.

Jesus Christ was having a great deal of trouble raising money for the cause so he called a meeting of his twelve business advisers for a little supper and commercial input.

'I need ideas,' he said. 'Ideas that must raise money quickly or we all go to the wall.'

'What about the hitting of the rock with the staff and bringing forth the wine?' offered John.

'No, no, no!' JC exclaimed. 'Been done to death all over town.'

'Well, there's the feeding the masses with fish and bread,' said John.

'No, no,' said JC, mildly upset.

'What about the walking on the water bit,' said Luke.

'That's it,' said JC, with gusto. 'Rehearsals tomorrow. Sea of Galilee early morning. Be there!'

So the next morning the 13 were down by the sea to rehearse for the big show. They proceeded to walk out into the water without much trouble, except for one. For him the water came up to his shins, then his hips, then his chest.

John turned to JC and asked, 'Do you think we should tell Judas about the sandbar?'

Two swaggies called in at the presbytery in a country town hoping for a handout. The good father gave them a note and said, 'Take this to the Shamrock Hotel and give it to the proprietor. He'll let you each have a meal and a bath.'

Clutching the note, the swaggies ambled off in the direction of the Shamrock. Then one stopped and said, 'Hey, Bill, what's a bath?'

'How would I know?' replied the other. 'I ain't a Catholic!'

There was a conference of cannibals in New Guinea before they had made progress and learnt how to kill each other with guns. They discussed the different missionaries they had eaten. Some said they liked Methodists. Some said they liked Baptists. Some said they preferred Catholics and some, the socially upward mobile, said they liked the Church of England. One cannibal said they had had a tough one the other day. They had boiled him and boiled him and boiled him, but he was still very tough. They asked what his denomination was. He said he didn't know, but that he was dressed in a brown habit with a cowl and had a fringe of hair round his bald head. The president of the cannibal conference said, 'You should not have boiled him. He was a friar.'

When does life begin?

Roman Catholics say, 'At the moment of conception.'

Anglicans say, 'When the child is born.'

Jews believe differently: 'Life begins when the kids are married, the dog has died and the mortgage has been paid off.'

A couple of teenagers decided it was time to graduate from heavy petting to intercourse.

'Come round tomorrow morning. It's Sunday and my parents will be at church. But don't forget a condom.'

Next morning the boy arrived at the front door just as her parents were leaving for church. 'We're coming with you,' said the boy.

During the sermon the girl whispered, 'I can't believe what you did. Since when have you been religious?'

'Since I discovered that your dad's the chemist.'

A young bloke confessed to the priest that he'd just had sex with a striptease dancer. 'Her name is Pussy Pink, Father, and she's very, very beautiful. But she's also a good Catholic and I'm bringing her to church on Sunday.'

The priest granted absolution and could hardly wait for Mass. The following Sunday he saw a spectacular redhead sitting in a mini skirt in the front pew. He nudged his organist and said, 'Hey, is that Pussy Pink?'

'No, Father,' said the organist. 'It's just the way the sun is shining through the stained-glass windows.'

The young bride sought advice from the priest in the confessional.

'Father, is it all right to have intercourse before receiving communion?'

'Certainly, my dear. Provided you don't block the aisle.'

A drunk lurched into church, meandered down the aisle and then turned left at the confessional. He sat down and immediately started snoring.

After a few minutes he was woken by the priest banging on the partition.

'No use banging,' said the drunk, 'got no paper here either.'

Two mates arrived in a country town. They didn't know a soul. 'So we're going to confession,' said one.

'To confession?'

'Follow me.'

And he squeezed into the confessional and said, 'It's been a week since my last confession, Father, and I'm sorry to say that I've sinned of the flesh again.'

'Was it Mrs Bridges from the general store?'

'No, Father.'

'Was it one of the Briggs twins from the dairy?'

'No, Father.'

'Don't tell me it was that naughty widow Paterson?'

'No, Father.'

'Well, do your usual penance and be off with you.'

'Well, I've got the names,' said the bloke to his mate. 'Now let's look up the phone numbers.'

Two tramps met. One had in his hand a steaming, fresh meat pie. 'Jesus,' said the other, 'where did you get that, and how did you get it?'

'Easy,' said the first. 'This part of Belfast is very strictly religious and I just demonstrate my Bible scholarship. I go to a house and say, "Good morning, missus. I am a God-fearing, Bible-reading beggar. In fact I know my Bible backwards. I know all about Jonah who spent 40 days and nights in the belly of a whale. I know all about Lot's wife who was turned into a pillar of salt. I know all about Esau who sold his birthright for a mess of pottage and I know all about Samson, that strong man, who killed 40 000 Hittites with the jawbone of an ass. Can I have something to eat?" And there you are, it works every time.'

His friend said he would try the same thing. But next day he needed some courage to try it, so only approached a house when suitably fortified.

He knocked on a convenient door and addressed the owner thus, 'Good morning, missus. I'm a God-fearing fucking beggar. I know my Bible arsewise. I know all about Jonah who spent 40 days and 40 nights on the belly of Lot's wife. I know all about Seesaw who sold his wife's afterbirth for a tin of porridge, and I know all about that strong bastard Sando who killed 40 000 Shittites with the arsebone of a giraffe. Give us a pie.'

Black holes are where God divided by zero.

A nun from the Sisters of Mercy was traipsing around the outback in northern New South Wales. It was in the middle of the drought and she was doing whatever she could to help isolated families.

On her way back to Sydney on a lonely bush track she ran out of petrol. She was at her wit's end and as it was growing dark she knelt in the dust and prayed. A few minutes later an old farmer came bouncing along in his rusty Land Cruiser. Having determined the problem, he asked if she had some sort of container – and all she had was a standard-issue, Sister of Mercy bedpan.

The farmer headed for the nearest town to get some petrol. On his return he thumped down the can and apologised that he'd have to leave immediately as he was in the middle of calving. She assured him she'd be all right – she could decant the petrol into the car.

When she'd almost completed her decanting task, and was down to the last few drops, another farmer came along in an equally rusty Land Cruiser. He looked down from his cabin and said, 'I admire your faith, Sister. But, to be perfectly honest, I don't reckon that will work.'

Doctor Crock

It'd been a really tough drought and a drover had mustered cattle up and down the long paddock. And although he was as tough as old boots, he finished up being saddle sore. So a mate told him to try a folk remedy that a bloke from Cooma had told him about. 'Pour the old water out of the billy and shove the tea-leaves up your arse.' So he did.

And it didn't help much. In fact, his backside was hurting so much that he decided to go and see the doctor.

'Hmmm,' said the doctor. 'Hmmm.'

'Something wrong?' asked the drover.

'Not at all,' replied the doctor. 'You're going to take a long trip and you'll meet a tall, romantic stranger.'

What are three good things about Alzheimer's disease?
1. You can hide your own Easter eggs.
2. You make a new friend every day.
3. You can hide your own Easter eggs.

The scene is the nurses' room at St Vincent's, a meeting place for both sacred and secular staff members. An elderly nun whispers to a non-religious co-worker, 'May, do you happen to know the new patient in bed seven?'

'No, I don't, Sister Mary. Why do you ask?'

'Well, when I was giving him a sponge bath I couldn't help but notice that he has your name tattooed on his penis.'

'Really? I'll go and have a look.' Whereupon she heads for the ward. A few minutes later she returns looking a little disappointed. 'I thought it said May at first,' says May, 'but as soon as I touched it I realised it read, "Matrimony".'

The little bloke was born without a penis. 'No probs,' said the doctor, 'thanks to microsurgery we can do a transplant. All we need is three inches – if we can find a compatible donor.'

The family discussed the matter and agreed that Dad would provide an inch, as would Uncle and Grandpa. The operation seemed entirely successful.

Twenty years later, the door of the surgery burst open and in came an enraged young man.

'Excuse me?' the doctor asked.

'Remember that dick operation you did 20 years ago? Well, I was the kid.' And he belted the crap out of the doctor.

'Why did you do that?' said the doctor as he lay bleeding on the floor.

'For putting Grandad's inch in the middle.'

Lacking confidence in traditional medicine to give her much-desired larger breasts, a young woman consulted a faith healer, Dr Sophius. He told her that the treatment was quite simple, but that she would have to follow his instructions implicitly. This she readily agreed to do.

'Well, three times a day, at precisely 9 a.m., 12 noon and 3 p.m., you must say the following words, "Hooby, dooby, dooby. Give me bigger boobies".'

'Is that all? Are you sure it will work for me, Dr Sophius?' she inquired hopefully.

'Yes,' he replied, 'it will work, but only if you say the spell at the exact times. And have faith in me.'

Off she went. The next day at precisely 9 a.m., nobody near, she uttered the words given by the faith healer, and immediately her bustline increased by 5 cm. Delighted, she waited impatiently for 12 noon. Again, completely alone, she spoke the incantation, and again her breasts increased in size.

As 3 p.m. approached she was at a bus stop near a park. Concerned at the presence of others, she walked into the park until she found a quiet spot near a hedge. There, at precisely 3 p.m., she said, 'Hooby, dooby, dooby. Give me bigger boobies.' Two things happened at once. Her breasts popped out another 5 cm, and a bloke bobbed up from the other side of the hedge. Excitedly, he said, 'You beaut! You and I are patients of the great Dr Sophius!'

'How do you know that?' she asked, embarrassed.

'Watch this,' he said, unzipping his fly as he continued with great confidence. 'Hickory, dickory, dock ...'

A bloke goes to see a psychiatrist. 'I've got a problem, Doc. When I go to bed at night I can't sleep because I've got this feeling that there's somebody under the bed. So I get out of the bed to check and while I'm peering under it, I get this strange feeling that somebody's on top of it. That goes on all night. On top. Underneath. On top. I'm going to have a breakdown.'

'I can cure you,' said the shrink, 'but it will take years. Two visits a week at $100 a visit.'

The bloke never returned. But a year later the psychiatrist saw him in the street. 'Why didn't you come back?'

'At 200 bucks a week? Not when the carpenter next door cured me for $5.'

'How did he do that?'

'He told me to saw the legs off me bed.'

A middle-aged cocky went to his doctor complaining, 'The missus and I have a problem. I'm too tired at night to do any good, and only get horny when I'm on the tractor during the day. But by the time I turn off the motor, jump into the ute and drive back to the house, I've gone off again. Can you give me anything for the problem?'

The doctor thought for a while, then said, 'There is nothing I can give you. But I suggest you take a shotgun with you on the tractor, and when you get the hots, fire a few blasts, jump into the ute and meet your wife, who will have heard the shots and who'll come to meet you by car.'

A couple of weeks later, the doctor saw the guy

in the street and remarked on his happy and contented appearance. 'Doc, your suggestion really works. Thank you, thank you.'

Some time later, the doctor ran into the farmer again and remarked on his miserable and unhappy demeanour. 'Isn't it working any more?'

The farmer replied, 'I'll say it's working. But I haven't seen the wife since the duck season started!'

A bloke goes into hospital for a vasectomy. Afterwards the surgeon tells him there's good news and there's bad news. The bad news is that the hospital mixed up the documentation and they've cut off both of his legs. The bloke is horrified. 'Christ! That's dreadful. What's the good news?'

'The chap in the next bed wants to buy your shoes.'

The bloke went to his doctor and said, 'Look, I've got a problem. Every morning at six o'clock I've got to go to the toilet.'

The doctor said, 'Well, it's good to be regular.'

'Yeah, but I don't wake up until seven.'

A doctor is walking the streets of Dublin when he sees two heroin addicts in the process of injecting each other. He goes up to them and says, 'Look, using heroin is bad enough, but you shouldn't be sharing needles these days. Not with AIDS around.'

And one of the heroin addicts replies, 'Oh, we're safe. We're both wearing condoms.'

A man was committed to Callan Park for many years. One day he was taken before a panel of doctors to see if he was fit to be released. 'If you were let out, what would you do?' asked a doctor.

'I'd make a shanghai and shoot little birds,' said the patient.

The doctors looked at each other, shook their heads and locked him up again.

A few years later he was taken before the panel again.

'What would you do if you were released?'

Once again he said he'd make a shanghai and shoot little birds. Once again he was locked up.

A few years later he was taken before the panel for a third time.

'What would you do if you were released?'

'I would walk down the street until I found a pretty girl,' he said.

The doctors looked at each other, venturing

small nods of their heads. Things looked promising. 'Yes, yes. What would you do then?'

'I'd put my arm around her and walk her down to the beach.'

'Yes, yes. What would you do then?'

'I'd lay her down in the sand.'

'Yes, yes! What would you do then?'

'I'd take her pants off.'

'Yes, yes! What would you do then?'

'I'd take the elastic out of them, make a shanghai and go and shoot little birds!'

A bloke arrives at the local surgery and tells the receptionist that he has an appointment with the doctor. He's ushered into a consulting room and, after a few minutes, a rather flustered medico appears. The man says, 'Well, tell me about the tests.'

The doctor replies, 'I've confusing news for you, Mr Jones. We did the test on your wife, and the result was mixed up with another test. Consequently your wife has either AIDS or Alzheimer's.'

'But that's a terrible situation, doctor,' said the bloke. 'What should I do?'

The doctor thought about it for a moment. 'The best solution for you is to go home and send your wife down to the shop for a newspaper,' he said. 'And if she comes back, don't fuck her.'

A female dwarf goes to a doctor complaining of an embarrassing itch in the groin area. The doctor looks her up and down, picks her up and stands her on his desk. He lifts up her skirt and puts his head under. A little perplexed, she hears, *snip, snip, snip, snip, snip*. The doctor emerges from under her skirt.

'How's that?'

'Well, it's a lot better, actually. But ... it's still there.'

Undaunted, he dives back under the skirt. *Snip, snip, snip, snip*. Out he comes.

'How's that?' he asks again, more confident.

'That's wonderful! What did you do?'

'Trimmed the top of your ugg boots.'

'Now, what seems to be the problem?'

'I have this recurring dream about having sex.'

'Well, that's not so unusual.'

'Yes, but I have sex with biscuits.'

'Biscuits?'

'Yeah, biscuits.'

'Wholemeal biscuits?'

'No, not wholemeal.'

'Chocolate biscuits?'

'No, not chocolate.'

'Milk Arrowroot?'

'No.'

'Nice?'

'No, not Nice.'

'Well, what sort of biscuits?'

'Ryvita. Always Ryvita.'

'Then you are fucking crackers.'

After meeting at various IVF clinics in their quest to become pregnant, two women bumped into each other at David Jones. 'My dear, look at you! You must be seven or eight months pregnant!'

'Yes, I finally gave up on science and went to a faith healer.'

'Oh, my husband and I tried that. We went to one for months.'

'That's not how you do it. You've got to go alone.'

'I'm sorry, my old friend. But at this stage of your life I have to advise you of the following. There'll be no smoking, no drinking and no sex.'

'But, doctor, life would be meaningless without smoking, drinking and sex.'

'Okay, but only one cigarette after dinner. That's after dinner, not lunch and breakfast. Dinner only. And no more than one glass of wine a day. No spirits, no beer.'

'What about sex?'

'Very, very occasionally. And only with your wife because it's essential to avoid excitement.'

Princess Di was visiting the repatriation home at Heidelberg. In the first bed she was introduced to a bloke with no arms.

'What a wonderful sacrifice you've made for your country,' said the princess.

'That's nothin', your Majesty,' said the bloke. 'If I'd had four arms, I'd gladly have given them.'

In the next bed there was a bloke with no legs.

'What a wonderful sacrifice you've made for Australia,' said the princess.

'Yep,' said the bloke with no legs, 'and if I'd had ten legs, I'd gladly have given them.'

The next bed had a screen around it. When pulled aside it revealed a head on a pillow. Nothing else, just a head.

'What a wonderful sacrifice one has made for one's country,' said the somewhat dismayed Diana.

'Crap,' said the head.

'We do apologise,' said the doctor accompanying the princess.

'Please excuse him. He's got a bit shitty because he's going to the dentist this afternoon.'

In an attempt to lower medical costs, the Kennett government has introduced a new phone-in strategy for the Department of Health. When you ring up, a voice says, 'If you are an excessive compulsive, press number one. Then press number one again. Then again, then again, then again. If you are a manic depressive, press button one, then button nine, then button one, then button nine, then button one, then button nine. If you are a schizophrenic, press all the buttons. If you are paranoid, don't press any button. We're coming to get you.'

A doctor tells his patient, 'I've got good news and bad news. The good news, you've got 24 hours to live.'

'That's good news? What's the bad news?'

'I forgot to call you yesterday.'

A woman goes to the IVF clinic to be artificially inseminated. She's lying with her legs in the stirrups and the doctor comes in, carrying his trousers over his shoulder.

'I'm sorry, madam, but we're out of the bottled stuff,' he said. 'You're going to have to have draught.'

The doctor placed his stethoscope on the young woman's chest. 'Big breaths, my dear.'

'Yeth, and I'm only thixteen.'

A doctor was trying to write out a prescription, but something was wrong. The fingers moved but no trace was left on the page.

Whereupon he realised that what he had in his fingers was a thermometer.

'Bugger it,' he said to the nurse, 'some bum's walked off with my Biro.'

'I've got bad news for you, Mr Briggs. We've just got the tests back and they confirm that you have a comparatively new illness known as RASH.'

'RASH?'

'Yes, RASH. It combines rabies, AIDS, syphilis, and herpes.' Mr Briggs paled visibly.

'We'll have to put you in strict isolation, Mr Briggs,' the doctor said. 'You'll be locked up in a special RASH ward and fed on a diet of flounder, pancakes and pizza.'

'A diet of flounder, pancakes and pizza? Will that cure me?'

'No. But it's easy to slide under the door.'

A 75-year-old woman decides she wants a baby. She goes to an IVF doctor and asks to be put on the program. The doctor tells her she's too old. She promises to donate $100 000 to further research if he lets her join the program. She gets pregnant and has the baby. Some time later friends call round to see the baby. She tells them to wait until it wakes. So they wait. And wait. Hours pass. They ask again if they can see the baby. She says you'll have to wait until it wakes up. 'I've forgotten where I've put it.'

A bloke who thought he was a dog went to a psychiatrist. When invited to lie down he said, 'But I'm not allowed on the couch.'

The doctor shouts at his hard-of-hearing patient, 'What's it today, Mrs Briggs?'

'Oh, doctor, I'm breaking wind all the time,' she replies. 'It doesn't worry me a lot. In fact, it feels quite nice. But there's no smell and no sound.'

'Take this prescription and come back in a week,' says the doctor.

Seven days later he converses with his patient quite normally. 'How are things now?'

'Oh, doctor, I'm still farting,' she said, 'but at least I can hear it happening.'

'Excellent, Mrs Briggs. That's the ears fixed. Now for the nose! And give your Medicare card to the receptionist on the way out.'

'Doctor, why is the nun in the waiting room crying like that?'

'I just told her she's pregnant.'

'Oh, poor thing.'

'Actually, she isn't pregnant at all. But I've completely cured her hiccups.'

A senior nurse in a Sydney hospital was instructing a new girl in her duties. 'Now go down to bed 12 and give the gentleman there, Mr Wong, a bed bath. Make sure you do him all over. And, dearie, don't you worry when you see it, but he's got his name tattoed on a certain very private part of his anatomy. Just ignore it. Now, off you go.'

Some time later, the senior passed the girl in the ward and asked, 'How did you go with Mr Wong?'

The girl said, 'Fine thanks, sister, but you made a mistake. His name's not Wong, it's Wollongong.'

A new female patient comes into a psychoanalyst's office and he says, 'Take off your clothes and get on the couch.' Surprised, the woman gets undressed and lies on the couch. Whereupon the analyst removes his trousers and climbs on top of her. Afterwards he says, 'You can get dressed now and sit in that chair.' She does so and the analyst says, 'Okay, we've taken care of my problem. What's yours?'

'I'd like to see an outtern.'

'You mean an intern?'

'Whatever you call him, I want a contamination.'

'An examination? In a maternity ward?'

'I don't know what you call it, but I haven't demonstrated for months and I think I'm stagnant.'

A woman rang the family doctor. 'Please come around, doctor. My husband says he's ill.'

'I'm not coming around again, and that's flat. He only thinks he's ill.'

Next day she rang again.

'What is it this time? Does he still think he's ill?'

'No,' she said, 'he thinks he's dead.'

A bloke woke up in a bush hospital and asked why the room was so dark. 'Well,' said the nurse, 'there's a bushfire outside. And we didn't want you to think the operation had been a failure.'

'Quick! I want a tooth pulled. Really fast. We've got to catch a plane. So just rip it out, will ya? Never mind an anaesthetic. We haven't got the time.'

'It will be very, very painful without an anaesthetic.'

'Never mind about the pain. Just do it.'

'Well, that's a very brave attitude. Now, which tooth?'

'Beryl, get in the chair and show the dentist your bad tooth.'

A young bloke goes to his local GP. 'I can't explain very well why I'm here to see you, doctor, but I just feel weak all the time and I've lost interest in all the things I used to enjoy.'

'That's a bit hard to diagnose,' said the doctor, 'but I read only this morning in the *British Medical Journal* that a return to childhood ways and the diet of your early years can work miracles for many people.'

'What's the treatment, doctor?'

'To be brief, you should start drinking mother's milk from its original source.'

'Wherever could I get that?'

'You're lucky, I've just made contact with a young lactating lady who can start your treatment right now. Here is her address.'

The patient knocked at the front door of the apartment and a beautiful young blonde in a diaphanous negligee ushered him into the lounge room. 'Just sit on the couch with me and then lie your poor head on my lap,' she said.

John obeyed, lay his head in her lap and looked up at a descending nipple with a gentle pink areola. He suckled it and blissfully closed his eyes like an infant.

Of course, he rolled his tongue around the nipple and after a few moments the blonde's feelings changed from maternal to amorous. She squirmed somewhat on the lounge and said huskily, 'Is there something else you'd like?'

He pulled his head back and the nipple popped noisily from his lips. 'Yes,' he said dreamily, with his eyes still tightly closed, 'have you got a bikkie?'

An old bloke came gasping into his doctor's surgery. 'I'm frantic, Doc,' he said. 'I've been making love to an old dear at the twilight home and I've got this big erection that won't go away. It's now twice the size it used to be and there's a slight discharge.'

The doctor examined him. 'Congratulations,' he said, 'you're about to come.'

A very old bloke came to see his doctor. 'I'm going to marry a 20-year-old.'

'Well, at your age I think you should take things easy,' said the concerned medico. 'In fact, it might be a good idea for you to take in a young, energetic lodger.'

A year later he bumped into the old bloke. 'How's married life?'

'Wonderful. The wife's pregnant, I'm proud to say.'

'And did you take my advice about the lodger?'

'Yes, I did. She's pregnant too.'

It was visitors' day at the funny farm and all the inmates were standing in the garden singing 'Ave Maria'. And they were singing it beautifully. But the strange thing was that each of them was holding a red apple and tapping it rhythmically with a pencil.

A visitor listened in wonderment to the performance then approached the choir. 'This is one of the best choirs I've ever heard,' he said, 'and I know about choirs. I used to sing with the choir at St Paul's.'

'Yes, I'm very proud of them,' said the conductor.

'You should take them on tour,' said the visitor. 'What do you call them?'

'Surely that's obvious,' said the conductor. 'They're the Moron Tapanapple Choir.'

Struck Dumb

A chemist employed a new girl and left her in charge while he went out for lunch. When he came back he asked if there'd been any customers.

'Yes, a man came in and wanted some Macleans toothpaste. But we didn't have any.'

'Well,' the chemist said, 'you should have sold him something else. You should have tried to get him to buy the Colgate, the Pepsodent or the tooth powder. Make sure that doesn't happen again. If we haven't got exactly what someone wants, try to sell them something else.'

The next day, when the chemist was out at lunch, the same customer came in and asked for some toilet paper.

'Sorry,' said the girl, 'we're right out of toilet paper. Can I interest you in wrapping paper, brown paper, fly paper, sandpaper, or confetti?'

There was a bloke in Sydney who couldn't afford personalised numberplates. So he changed his name to TLX 126.

What's the difference between a magician's act and a bunch of blondes?

The magician's act has a cunning array of stunts.

Why don't blondes breastfeed their babies?

It hurts too much when they boil their nipples.

What do you call a blonde wearing a leather jacket on a motorcycle?

Rebel without a clue.

Why did the blonde want to become a veterinarian?

She liked kids.

What does a blonde do if she's not in bed by ten?

She picks up her purse and goes home.

A blonde and a brunette are skydiving. The brunette jumps out of the plane and pulls the cord. Nothing happens. She pulls the emergency cord and still nothing. Whereupon the blonde jumps out of the plane yelling, 'So you want to race!'

What do you call it when a blonde gets taken over by a demon?

Vacant possession.

What's a blonde's idea of safe sex?

A padded dash.

What do you do when a blonde throws a pin at you?

Run like hell – she's got a hand grenade in her mouth.

Why did the blonde stare at the orange juice can for two hours?

Because it said 'Concentrate'.

Two blondes were driving along a road by a wheatfield when they saw another blonde. She was in the middle of the wheatfield sitting in a rowboat pulling energetically at her oars. One blonde turned to her friend and said, 'You know, it's blondes like that that give us a bad name.'

And the other blonde said, 'Yes, and if I knew how to swim I'd go out there and drown her.'

A blonde rang the local police station. 'We need help. We're three blondes changing a light bulb.'

The policeman said, 'Look, this is not really a police matter. But have you put in a fresh globe?'

'Yes.'

'The power is on?'

'Yes.'

'And the switch?'

'Yes, yes.'

'And the globe still won't light?'

'No, the globe's working fine.'

'Then what's the problem?'

'We got giddy turning the ladder around and fell over and hurt ourselves.'

Two blondes were walking through the woods when one looked down and said, 'Oh, look. Look at the deer tracks.'

The other blonde said, 'Those aren't deer tracks. Those are wolf tracks.'

'No, they're deer tracks.'

They kept arguing and arguing and half an hour later, they were both killed by a train.

How do you plant dope?

Bury a blonde.

What do you call a pimple on a blonde's bum?

A brain tumour.

Why did the blonde keep a coathanger on the back seat?

In case she locked the keys in her car.

Why does a blonde insist on men wearing condoms?

So she can have a doggy bag for later.

How can you tell that it's a fax from a blonde?

There's a stamp on it.

A policeman pulled over a blonde after she'd been driving the wrong way up a one-way street. 'Don't you know where you're going?'

'No, but wherever it is, it must be unpopular because all the people were leaving.'

Did you hear about the blonde who shot an arrow into the air?

She missed.

Did you hear about the blonde who stayed up all night to see where the sun went?

It finally dawned on her.

A blonde was driving up the highway to the Warner Brothers theme park when she saw a sign saying HOLLYWOOD ON THE GOLD COAST LEFT.

After thinking for a minute she said, 'Oh well,' turned round and drove back to Brisbane.

A brunette is drying herself after a shower when, in her full-length bathroom mirror, she notices a single grey pubic hair.

'Good heavens,' she says. 'I know that you haven't been getting much lately, but I didn't know you were worrying about it!'

Why do blondes have see-through lunchbox lids?
So they'll know if it's morning or afternoon.

Why did God create blondes?
Because sheep can't bring beer from the fridge.

What did the blonde name her pet zebra?
Spot.

Did you hear about the blonde dingo?

Got stuck in a trap, chewed off three legs and was still stuck.

What does a blonde say when she gives birth?

Are you sure it's mine?

Why do blondes take the pill?

So they know what day of the week it is.

What happens when a blonde gets Alzheimer's?

Her IQ goes up.

What's the first thing a blonde does in the morning?

Introduces herself.

What's it called when a blonde blows in another blonde's ear?

Data transfer.

How do you know when a blonde reaches orgasm?
She drops her nail file.

Why did blondes vote for the GST?
Because they could spell it.

What did the blonde think of her new laptop?
She didn't like it because she couldn't get Channel Nine.

What do you call it when a blonde dyes her hair black?
Artificial intelligence.

Why don't you give blondes coffee breaks?
It takes too long to retrain them.

How do you get a blonde's eyes to twinkle?
Shine a torch in her ear.

Mick's dog died. So he borrowed Paddy's shovel and went out in the back garden to bury it.

After a while Paddy came out to see how Mick was going, and saw that he'd dug one, two, three holes.

'Why three holes for one dog?'

'Well, you see, the first two weren't deep enough.'

Three builders were working on a Grollo Brothers skyscraper. There was an Australian, an Englishman and an Irishman. The Australian peeled open a sandwich. 'Christ, bloody Vegemite again,' he said. 'If I get Vegemite sandwiches tomorrow I'll jump off this bloody building.'

The Englishman opened his lunch. 'Not cheese again! If I get cheese sangas tomorrow, I'll jump with you.'

The Irishman opened his lunch. 'Not jam again. If I get jam sandwiches again tomorrow, I'll jump too.'

The next day the Australian took one look at his sandwiches. 'Fucking Vegemite,' he said, and jumped off the building.

The Englishman opened his lunch. 'For Christ's sake, cheese!' He jumped too.

Very, very tentatively, the Irishman opened his lunch. 'Bugger me dead, jam again.' And he jumped as well.

At the triple funeral the widows sobbed in each

others' arms. 'If only I'd known that he hated Vegemite,' said the Australian.

'I didn't know he hated cheese so much,' lamented the Englishwoman.

The Irish widow was also deeply shaken. 'I can't figure it out. Paddy always made his own lunch.'

And Englishman, an Irishman and a Scotsman were visiting Luna Park and decided to try the slide. As they lined up to collect their mats, the attendant said, 'Remember that whatever you say on the way down you'll land in at the bottom.'

The Scotsman went first. As he sat on his little mat he began to murmur, 'Money, money, money!' And lo and behold, he landed in a great pile of bank notes.

The Englishman shouted, 'Money, money, money!' too. And he, too, landed in a pile of bank notes.

Then it was the Irishman's turn. He sat on his little mat and launched himself down the long, bumpy slide. 'Weeeee!' he shouted.

An Irishman went ice fishing. He bought himself a hammer, a saw, a stool and a fishing rod. And off he went.

He bashed a hole in the ice with his hammer

and trimmed it with the saw. Then he sat on his stool and started fishing. Whereupon a mighty voice boomed out, 'There are no fish down there!'

The Irishman looked around in astonishment. 'Is that you, God?' he asked nervously.

'No,' boomed the voice. 'It's the manager of the ice skating rink.'

Paddy was very proud of himself. 'I've just finished a jigsaw puzzle, Mick. It was very, very hard and it took me five days to finish it.'

'Five days for a jigsaw puzzle? How many pieces?'

'Forty.'

'Forty pieces. You're telling me that it took you five days to fit 40 pieces together?'

'That's why I'm so pleased with myself,' said Paddy. 'Look. On the box it says five to six years.'

A professional photographer was taking a group photo of workers and machinery in a Belfast factory. He adjusted the tripod and draped the black cloth over the camera and himself. Two factory girls watched with great interest and one said, 'What's he doing?'

The other replied, 'He's going to focus.'

'What? All of us?'

It was a quiz show on telly and the Irish contestant had to complete the following sentence. 'Old McDonald had a ...'

The Irishman yelled out, 'Farm!'

The compere said, 'Great, you're doing very well. Now spell that.'

The Irishman said, 'E-i-e-i-o.'

An Irishman walks into a railway station and presents himself at the ticket counter.

'I'd like a return ticket.'

'Where to?'

'To here!' says the Irishman.

An Irish surgeon has just been admitted to the *Guinness Book of Records*. He was the first medical man to separate a Siamese cat.

An Irishman applied for a job as a strawberry picker. The farmer asked if he had any experience.

'Lots,' said the Irishman. 'I'll show you how good I am. Just lend me a ladder.'

The Irishman went to a brothel, and, seeing a BYO sign on the door, went home to get his wife.

An Irishman was having sex with a Scottish lass and when it was all over she expressed some dissatisfaction. 'Aren't Irishmen supposed to be big and thick?'

'Aren't Scots meant to be tight?'

An Englishman, an Irishman and an Australian were being conscripted into the army. None of them liked the idea.

The procedure began with a medical exam. The Australian was first to be called in, and after a few minutes, returned with a huge grin. 'They've rejected me! They won't have me because I've got FF.'

'What's FF?' asked the Irishman.

'Flat feet,' said the Aussie.

Next it was the pom's turn. And he came out grinning from ear to ear. 'They won't take me. I've got KK.'

'What's KK?' asked the Irishman.

'Knock knees.'

It was the Irishman's turn. After an hour he came out looking very, very pleased.

'I can't go either. They told me I've got TC.'
'TC? What's TC?'
'Terminal cancer,' said the Irishman.

Mick entered the pub, proudly fronting the bar with a handful of dog shit. 'Look what I nearly trod in,' he said.

An Irishman opened a factory in Dublin – to bottle goldfish farts for spirit levels.

An Irishman lost a hundred dollars on the Melbourne Cup. And another hundred on the replay.

An Irishman on Anzac Day: 'Was it you or your brother who got killed in the war?'

An Irish duck overflew his mark and ended up in Australia. He was exhausted from the trip but made extra effort when he saw a pair of native ducks on the horizon. He flew and joined them. However, they travelled a good half hour before anyone broke the silence.

'Quack!' said the first duck.

'Quack!' said the second duck.

'Give us a break,' the Irish duck puffed. 'I'm goin' as quack as I can!'

Two Irishmen from a little village went to Dublin for the first time and decided to go to the cinema, also for the first time. When they got inside, the film had started, so they had to fumble their way down the dark aisle. Seeing their plight, an usher with a torch approached to help them. 'Watch out,' said one to the other. 'Here comes a bike!'

A large Irishman was holding up a telegraph pole while a little Irishman stood on his shoulders with a tape measure. A passer-by said, 'Wouldn't it be easier to lay it on the ground to measure it?'

And the big Irishman said, 'Look, we already know its length.'

And the little Irishman said, 'Now we want to find its height.'

Reilly always slept with a gun under his pillow. Hearing a noise at the foot of the bed, he shot off his big toe. 'Thank the Lord I wasn't sleeping at the other end of the bed,' he said at the pub. 'I would have blown my head off.'

The attendant at the car wash chatted to an emerging customer. 'I bet you're Irish.'

'Now how on earth did you guess that?' said the customer.

'Well, to tell the truth, we don't get too many people coming through here on motorbikes.'

An Irishman is on a quiz show, and the compere, in his very best Kenneth Williams accent, asks him, 'Can you name three famous people from history?'

And the Irishman is there thinking and thinking. 'Ah, tree famous people from history, eh? Oh dat's a hard one? Oh, yes. Joan of Arc, Alfred da Grate, und Dick da Shit.'

The audience is aghast. The compere is beside himself, and just as the studio manager is about to eject the Irishman from the set, his mate in the back row stands up and yells, 'I tink he means Richard da Turd!'

An Irishman decides to go on a quiz show and the compere asks him, 'Tell me, can you give the first names of these three famous people from history: Churchill, Hitler and Gandhi?'

'Ah, Churchill, eh? Arr, Winston. Yus, dat's it, Winston. Now, Hitla. Oh, dat's a hard one. Hitla. Yus. Oh! A-dolf. Yus, dat's it, A-dolf. And Gandhi, eh. Gandhi. Oi know, oi know. Goosey Goosey.'

Irish aphrodisiac: a crate of Guinness and a housebrick.

'You know,' said the Irish farm labourer to his boss, 'I feel very guilty working for you.'

'How so?' asked the farmer, surprised.

'Sure, I have the feeling that I'm doing a pair of horses out of a job.'

'The train for Edinburgh will leave from platform three at 20 minutes to four,' said the fella over the intercom at Victoria Station. 'The Birmingham express will leave from platform two at half past five. And those of you who are going to Dublin, listen closely. Keep an eye on the clock and when the big hand's pointing straight to the top and the little hand's right at the bottom, then you go and get on your train, which is the big green one.'

'Paddy', said the farmer, 'go out and see if it's raining.'

'Aw, Da,' answered his son, 'can't you call in the dog and see if it's wet?'

The new police officer found a dead horse in Chichester Street, Belfast. 'How do you spell Chichester?' he asked the group of onlookers, but no one knew, or was game to assist a policeman in front of witnesses.

'All right then. Some of you give me a hand to pull the animal into Mary Street.'

An Irishman, an Englishman and an Australian are at the local pub, lamenting their woes. The Englishman says, 'Old chaps, I think my wife is having an affair. I came home yesterday to find the room in disarray, and when I checked under the bed I found a whole lot of pipes and wrenches. I think she's having an affair with a plumber.'

His companions feel his pain, and the Australian takes a swill of his beer before telling his own sorry story. 'That's nothing. I think my wife is having an affair too, but with an electrician. I checked under the bed and found a tangle of insulation wires. She's doing the dirty on me.'

They sit in silence for several minutes, before the Irishman confesses, 'My wife, I'm sure, is having an affair with a horse, and I'm right upset about it. I came home one evening and found our bedroom all messed up. And when I checked under the bed, I found a damned jockey!'

Identity Crises

In many outback cattle properties, stock work would have been impossible without a ready supply of cheap Aboriginal labour. And cattlemen, given the opportunity, liked to breed a few extra stockmen for themselves.

During the worst of a hot summer, Missus went down to Brisbane until the temperature dropped. Her husband would go down for a few days at Christmas but spent most of his time with the herd.

On return in the autumn, Missus would resume command of the household and smarten up the domestic staff, mostly lubras, questioning old Betty on how things had gone in her absence. And Missus was determined to obtain all the facts. All of them.

'When Missus away, boss muck about a bit?' she would ask.

'No, Missus,' came the sing-song response. ''E no muck about. 'E fair dinkum.'

A black-faced bloke is sitting at the bar in a pub in Surfers Paradise. The local drinkers have never seen an Abo there before and can't help but notice that he has a very white middle finger. Later the black-faced bloke goes into the gents' for a piss, and one of the other drinkers follows him. He notices that the blackfella has a white penis – and comes out and tells his mate. 'He's got a white finger and a white dick,' he whispers to the barman.

'No worries, mate,' the barman says, 'he's just another bloody Cessnock coalminer up here on his honeymoon.'

Why are local Abos migrating to Thailand?

They want to be Thai coons.

An Aborigine goes to heaven. St Peter is pretty impressed to see a blackfella from Australia. 'I'm so impressed that I'm going to send you back to Earth so you can spread the glad tidings to other

Aborigines. What would you like to be reincarnated as?'

'A piece of dog shit.'

'Why a piece of dog shit?'

'Well, you lie around in the sun and go whiter and whiter and the cops don't pick you up.'

Captain Cook arrives in Australia and is astonished by the flora and fauna. Seeing a native standing on one leg, leaning on his spear, he asks, 'What's that funny animal jumping around, going boing, boing?'

'Kangaroo,' comes the reply.

'What did you just tell that pommy bloke?' asks another Aborigine who'd been watching the scene.

'Kangaroo. Which means, as you know, I haven't the foggiest idea what you're fucking well talking about!'

Jacky is walking down the main street when he spots another well-known Aborigine leaning against a light pole. He walks over and says, 'Hey! You jist the fella I wanna see. I need some advice from yuh.'

'Yeh, what's the problem, mate? Tell uz all 'bout it.'

'Well, last month I bought a colour TV and

yesterdy I got this here bit of peper in the mail an it sez I owe them munney for the TV. I got the munney, what I got to do wit it?'

Wilf takes the piece of paper from Jacky, glances at it, and says, 'Whitey calls this thing a beel but you dun hav to worry 'bout it cos wese on weelfahr and the guvmint look after us blackfellas. You got the munney, eh? Good, we can go and get a coupler phaglons uv red and hev a party.' Which they proceed to do.

Some two months later Jacky is in town again and sees Wilf, walks up to him and says, 'Eh, Wilfey, I got another pise of peper in the mail yesterdy. This wun called a summens as they wan more munney. I got the munney, what I do, Wilfey?'

Wilf takes the paper and says, 'Gise a look at it. I tol you last time that wedon hev to wurry 'bout things like this cos wese on weelfahr the guvmint look after us. Got the munney, eh! This time we can get tree phaglons uv red and hev a bigger party than las time!'

Some three months later Jacky spots Wilf in the community store and says, 'Some mate you are. Your advice ain't worth a piece uv crow shit. I now go anudder pise uv peper this wun called a subpena. It's for a lot more munney. What the hell is a subpena?'

Wilf takes the subpoena from Jacky and scans it. 'Eh, Jacky, this in Letin. I dun read Letin. Hey hang on. Member wen we wuz goin to the coven and them nuns wuz tring to learn uz them things at the beginnin and end uv words. Well, they wuz Letin. Well, sum uv it coming bek. Let me tink. If I remember right now. Sub mean under. Pena, dat probably mean penis. Sub, under, penis. Under penis. Hey, Jacky, I tink dey got you by the balls und you bitter pey.'

A blackfella goes to a doctor. He's got a parrot sitting on his head and the parrot looks at the doctor and says, 'Hey, how can you remove this blackhead I've got on my foot?'

An Aborigine goes into his local employment office. Says he wants a job. Bloke checks the cards. 'Got one here – Managing Director of Grace Brothers, just down the road.'

The Abo looks at him with astonishment, bewildered.

'And what about this? Chief of the Reserve Bank. Or Managing Director of the Nine Network?'

'Oh, stop bullshitting,' says the Abo.

'You started it,' says the employment officer.

How do we know that Adam and Eve weren't Aboriginal?

Because if they were they'd have eaten the bloody snake.

How do we know that The Man from Snowy River was Aboriginal?

If he was white, people would have remembered his name.

What do you call ten Aborigines in one cell?

A chandelier.

An elderly Aboriginal couple were on a pedestrian crossing in Darwin when a drunken hoon in a four-wheel drive, doing a good 100 km/h in the 60 zone, skittled them. One was thrown violently into the air and landed metres away in a bush. The other crashed through the windscreen, finishing up on the Toyota's back seat.

'Will there be any charges, mate?' slurred the tattooed redneck driver when the cops arrived.

'Bloody oath,' said the cops, 'we'll charge the

one in the bush with leaving the scene of an accident without giving his name and address, and we'll get the other on breaking and entering.'

A tourist goes up to an Aborigine in the Kimberleys. 'They're very nice sunglasses,' he says.

'They're not sunglasses. They're my nostrils.'

Two Aborigines were discussing the new Northern Territory government's policy on Aborigines. 'They're paying us to have these injections. You only need one and it turns you white. And they give you 500 bucks in return.'

'Well, let's get them.'

'No, let's one of them try it and see if it works. Then we can meet later, have a beer and talk about it.'

So one had the injection, got the $500 and met his mate at the pub.

'Cripes, it works. You've gone all white, man. Come on, let's have a drink.'

'Wait a minute. You don't expect me to be seen drinking with a blackfella!'

It was a hot day in north Queensland and a traveller came to an inlet where there was an Aborigine sitting on the bank. The traveller asked, 'Are there any sharks in here, mate?'

'No sharks, boss.'

So the white joker stripped off and dived in. After a while he asked the Aborigine why he wasn't swimming.

'Too many crocodiles, boss.'

The boss and the Aboriginal stockman go shooting. They agree to share the bag. They shoot a turkey and a crow.

Back at the station the boss says, 'Well, Albert, we agreed to share the bag so I'll let you decide. Either I'll take the turkey and you take the crow, or, if you prefer, you take the crow and I'll have the turkey.'

Albert thought for a while and said, 'Funny thing, boss, but which ever way we share, I seem to cop the crow.'

A whitefella is driving in the outback. He gets utterly, hopelessly lost. He sees an old Aboriginal bloke sitting under a tree. He pulls over and asks, 'Hey, mate, can I take this road to Sydney?'

'Might as well. You've taken every other bloody thing.'

A hungry Kakadu crocodile was waiting on a bank of a river for a boatload of plump American tourists. Days passed, no tourists. Finally an Aborigine came down to the river to spear barramundi, and although he was pretty skinny, the crocodile decided that he'd be better than nothing. So he lunged at him, grabbed his feet and began to gulp him down, bit by bit. Whereupon the long-awaited boat of American tourists came into view. One of them spied the head sticking out of the croc and said, 'Look! Look!'

Another tourist, a woman, said, 'I thought they said Aborigines were poor. Well, there's one with a Lacoste sleeping bag.'

An Aborigine went to the doctor and explained that no matter how many times he and his wife had intercourse, they couldn't conceive. Could the doctor possibly help?

'Well, the best thing for you to do is bring me a specimen of your semen. Here's a container for that very purpose.'

Two days later the Aborigine returned to the

surgery and plonked the specimen container down on the table. The doctor stared at it and said, 'But there's nothing in it. It's empty.'

'I couldn't manage it,' said his patient. 'You don't know the trouble we had, trying to do what you told me to do.'

'What happened?' asked the doctor.

'Well,' said the Aborigine, 'I held it in my right hand, then I held it in my left hand. Then my wife held it in her right hand, then her left hand. Then my mother-in-law tried it with her teeth in. And then with her teeth out.'

'And, and . . .?'

'And we still couldn't get the bloody lid off!'

A large Aboriginal lady went to the doctor and told him of the aches and pains she had all over her body. The doctor told her to go behind the screen, remove all her clothes and squat under the window. He then told her to move to one corner of the room and squat there. Looking thoughtful, he asked her to move to another corner of the room and squat down. 'Can you tell what's wrong if I squat down?' asked the extremely large lady.

'No,' said the doctor, 'but I'm thinking of buying a black leather sofa and was wondering where the best place to put it was.'

Two women, one black and one white, were standing outside Long Bay Prison. The white woman said, 'My son got life for rape and murder.'

The black woman said, 'My son got death for drunk and disorderly.'

A whitefella went fishing with an Aboriginal mate who caught all the barramundi while he didn't get any. 'How come you're catching all the fish and I'm not?' he asked.

'Well, it's an old Aboriginal custom. This morning I woke up and my wife was sleeping on her right side, so I've been fishing on the right side of the boat. Yesterday I fished out of the left side of the boat because she'd been sleeping on her left side.'

'And what happens if she's been sleeping on her back?'

'I don't go fishing.'

An old Aborigine was explaining the origin of the term 'boong'. 'It started off a while back when it was still legal to run us over, and the noise off the roo bar was "boong".'

An Abo was walking down the Swan River near the power house when he found a flagon. He dusted it off and there was a big puff of smoke. 'I'm your genie. I grant you two wishes.'

'Okay, I wish I was white.'

So she made him white, adding, 'Hurry up, I haven't got all day. What's your second wish?'

'I wish I was rich and never had to work any more.'

And puff, he was black again.

What three things can't you give an Aborigine?

A fat lip, a black eye and a job.

An Aborigine went to the supermarket and asked the checkout lady, 'Excuse me, where can I get two dozen cans of cat food?'

She said, 'Get out of here. I know what you're like, you coloured people. You're going to feed that to your kids.'

'No, no, no,' he said. 'I've got a cat.'

And she said, 'Well, you're not getting the cat food until I see your cat.'

So he went off and came back with a cat. And she said, 'All right then, here's half a dozen cans.'

Next day he came back and said he wanted some dog food.

'No, you can't pull that on me. I know you're going to feed that to your kids.'

He said, 'Look, I've got a dog.'

She said, 'Bring it in.'

So he went home and brought in his big kangaroo dog, Blue. So she gave him the dog food.

The next day he walked in and presented the checkout lady with a heavy plastic rubbish bag. She said, 'Christ, this smells disgusting.'

'Yeah,' he said, 'could I have half a dozen rolls of toilet paper?'

An Aborigine was driving down the highway in his four-wheel drive when a cop pulled him over. 'Look, you shouldn't be driving in your drunken condition, but I'm only going to give you a caution.' So the Aborigine took off. Only to discover that the copper was alongside him again. 'Bugger this,' said the Abo, 'I'm not going to talk to this bloke again.' So he really put his foot down. But there was the copper alongside him still. So he slammed on the brake and said, 'What's the matter this time?'

And the copper said, 'I've got my handcuffs caught in your door handle.'

An Aborigine went into a whitefella butcher shop and said, 'Crikey, look at those funny things there! What are those legless lizard things?'

The whitefella butcher said, 'They're sausages.'

'Well, I'd better have some of them. How do you cook them?'

'Just like fish,' said the butcher. 'You fry them in the frying pan.'

'So give me a kilo of those things called sausages.'

He came back an hour later and said, 'Boss, give me another ten kilo of them sausages.'

'By God, that's a lot of sausages,' said the butcher, 'you must have a very big family.'

'No, it's not that. But by the time I cleaned and gutted them, there wasn't much left.'

Two Aborigines got married and went to a motel room. He took off his trousers and she said, 'Crikey, you sure got some small knees.'

'Yeah, I know. When I was a kid I got kneemonia and my knees ain't grown since.'

With this he took off his shoes. 'Crikey, you sure got small toes.'

'Yeah, I know. When I was a kid I got toemain poisoning and my toes ain't grown since.'

Next he took off his underpants. 'Crikey, I'm glad you never got dicktheria!'

What do you call two Abos in an overturned car?
Tenants.

'I've got an identity crisis,' announced the eight-year-old, coming home after school.

'What do you mean?' said his mum. 'You're only bloody eight.'

'Yeah, but Mum, you know the problem. You're Aboriginal and Dad's Jewish.'

'So what?'

'I'm confronted by an ethical dilemma,' said the kid. 'You see, there's this terrific bike at school that a kid wants to sell me for $20. And I don't know whether to offer him $10 – or to pinch it.'

A group of English cabinet makers were in Australia looking for interesting timbers. At a timber mill in Victoria they were inspecting some newly sawn timbers and asking for information.

'Now this,' said the Aussie, 'is hardwood, and it's used for makin' kegs for beer.'

'He means barrels for ale,' a posh voice announced from the back of the group.

'And this one is hard, hardwood, and it's used for makin' coffins for stiffs.'

'He means caskets for corpses,' said the posh voice up the back.

The Aussie let the remark pass and pointed to a third example of local timber.

'And this one is hard, hard, *hard*wood and it's used for makin' piles for piers. And for the benefit of the bloke up the back, I don't mean haemorrhoids for aristocrats.'

A Kiwi farmer counting his sheep: '303, 304, 305, hello darling, 307, 308 . . .'

A Welshman and an Englishman were arguing politics in the pub. The pommy, a left-winger, said, 'Margaret Thatcher has a face like a sheep's arse.'

Whereupon the Welshman punched him in the moosh.

'Christ, I didn't know you were a Conservative,' said the pom, spitting out a broken tooth.

'I'm not,' said the Welshman. 'I'm a shepherd.'

Two women were standing outside a little supermarket in Alice Springs wondering what to do with their noisy kids. The white woman decided to plonk hers in the kids' seat on the trolley and went into the supermarket. The black woman's trolley didn't have a kids' seat so she called her son over. 'What am I going to do with you?' she asked.

A white redneck was walking past. 'Why don't you lick his lips and stick him to the shop window?'

A New Zealand couple had been living in a *ménage à trois* but it was creating serious tensions. So they ate the sheep.

Why do seagulls have wings?
To beat the Abos to the tip.

Why do Abos have big nostrils?
Big fingers?

What do you call an Abo with dandruff?
A lamington.

How does an Irishman have a bubble bath?

Sits in a puddle and farts.

How do you get a pom out of the bath?

Turn on the water.

What did the Irish dingo do?

It ate the pram.

What do you call an Abo with a gun?

Sir.

An Italian man fishing on Port Phillip Bay found that his aluminium dinghy was sinking. He grabbed the radio and yelled, 'Maya Daya, Maya Daya, I sink. Quick, help! The little bambinos hava no papa ifa no one helpa!'

'No worries, mate,' said a crackly voice. 'We've received your call and are immediately despatching our Fokker Friendship to assist you.'

'I no want your fokker friendship. I want your fokker help!'

How do you stop Fijians from jumping on your bed?

Stick velcro on the ceiling.

A migrant, just off the boat from Italy, walks into a country pub. He tells the drinkers, 'My name isa Luigi. I'm a new Australian and prouda to be here.'

Whereupon he walks to the bar and asks for an empty glass. He pees into it and drinks the lot. He then leaves the pub and heads for the cattleyards with a number of puzzled fellow drinkers wandering behind.

To everyone's astonishment, he squats on the ground and starts talking to some cow manure.

He then hops over a side fence, grabs a chook from a backyard pen, and attempts to have sex with it.

Finally one of the drinkers says to Luigi, 'Whaddaya think ya doin'?'

Luigi says, 'I wanta be a good Australian. I wanta be justa like you. I wanta drinka the piss, talka the bullshit, fucka the chicks.'

An Italian started work on a building site and his foreman said, 'We've lots of ethnics here so we give everyone a nickname, according to their country of origin. Since you're from Italy, we're going to call you Wog.'

Noticing that the Italian bloke was insulted, the foreman said, 'Look, I'll introduce you to the other fellas and you'll get the picture. This is our Greek. We call him Nick the Greek. Nick the Greek, meet Wog the Italian.

'This bloke's from Edinburgh. He's called Mack the Scot. Mack the Scot, this is Wog the Italian.

'This bloke's from Dublin. He's Paddy the Irishman. Paddy, meet Wog the Italian.

'Finally, this is our one home-grown Australian. We call him Whacker the Australian, or Whack for short. Whack, meet Wog.'

Having finished the introductions, the foreman left them to get on with it.

On his return he was horrified to see the others kicking the shit out of the Italian. He yelled out, 'Nick, Mack, Paddy, Whack, leave the Wog alone.'

A new Australian, with a reasonable command of English, starts his first job. It's on a building site, and within a few minutes, he's offended when a co-worker, albeit in a friendly tone of voice, calls him a bastard. The new Australian complains to the foreman, proclaiming his legitimacy. In an attempt to build a bridge of understanding, the foreman calls out, 'Okay, which one of you bastards called this bastard a bastard?'

A businessman in India visits the local store and buys a few groceries. Pappadams, curry, rice, vindaloo paste. He then asks the bloke behind the counter for a roll of toilet paper. He presents him with a lovely 600-sheeter, Lady Scott two ply, with a very discreet design deriving from the Willow pattern.

'How much?'

'Ten rupees.'

'Too much, too much. Something cheaper.'

Out came a roll of Sorbent. 'Heavenly soft and most absorbent,' said the shopkeeper.

'How much?'

'Six rupees.'

'Too much, too much. Waste of money. Got anything else?'

'Well, only the house brand.' And he reached under the counter to produce a rather bleak-looking roll of paper, somewhat off-white in colour and unevenly rolled on the spindle.

'How much?'

'Two rupees.'

The businessman hands over the coins and departs. He returns the next day with what was left of the roll.

'Lady Scott, Sorbent, what do you call this?'

'It doesn't have a name,' says the shopkeeper.

'You should call it John Wayne.'

'Why John Wayne?'

'Because John Wayne, he take no shit from no Indian.'

Did you hear about the New Zealander who thought the Canning Stock route was an annual event?

Two Englishmen, two Scotsmen, two Welshmen and two Irishmen were stranded on a desert island. The Scotsmen started the Caledonian Club to celebrate all things Scottish – tossing the caper, playing the bagpipes. The two Welshmen started an eisteddfod. The two Irishmen formed the IRA and agreed to blow up anything built by the English. The two Englishmen went to opposite ends of the island and would not talk to each other as they had not been introduced.

In Italy a poll was taken to determine why men got up at night. Here are the results:

10% to raid the fridge;
15% to have a pee;
75% to go home.

Soon the Japanese will own so much of Queensland that visitors will have to leave their shoes at the New South Wales border.

A New Zealander was wandering along Bondi Beach when he saw an Australian bloke jumping up and down on a manhole cover.

He was shouting, 'Twenty-nine, twenty-nine, twenty-nine.'

'Uxcuse me,' says the Kiwi, 'bit why are you doing thet?'

'Exercise,' the Australian said. 'Stress relief. Great for getting rid of the tension. You should try it.'

So the Kiwi starts jumping up and down on the manhole cover. And just when he's got himself going, the Aussie yanks the manhole cover away and the Kiwi disappears.

The Aussie slides the manhole cover back into position and starts jumping up and down again. 'Thirty, thirty, thirty.'

A Chinese couple were having a mildly inventive bout of sexual intercourse when he asked his wife for a sixty-niner. She indignantly replied, 'If you think

I'm getting out of bed at this hour to cook you Beef and Black Bean Sauce, you've got another thing coming.'

A Kiwi living in Sydney walked into a shop and said, 'Fush and Chups.'

The shopkeeper replied, 'You'd be a Kiwi, wouldn't you, mate?'

Disgusted, the Kiwi stormed out of the shop, muttering to himself, 'U've gotter git some ilocution lissons so these blddy Ozzies wull live me ulone.' Which he duly did, practising every day, saying over and over, 'Fish and Chips' until he had it word perfect, the vowels no longer strangulated.

Right, he thought, entering the same shop, now I'll show this Aussie bastard. 'Fish and Chips,' he demanded of the shopkeeper in his best Ocker.

'You'd be a Kiwi, wouldn't you, mate?' replied the shopkeeper.

'How the bloody hell did you know?' howled the distraught Kiwi. 'I've just had six months of elocution lessons to get rid of my Kiwi accent.'

'Nothing to do with your accent, mate,' said the shopkeeper. 'It's just that this is a furniture shop.'

An Australian bloke's definition of foreplay:
'You awake love?'

Why is the Australian bloke like a wombat?
Because he eats, roots and leaves.

Why do Australian blokes make love with their eyes closed?

Because they can't stand to see women enjoying themselves.

Australian foreplay: 'I'll make you a cuppa after.'

Australian foreplay: 'Brace yourself, Raelene.'

A young English migrant's first job in Australia was on a cattle station in the far north. After a few months he asked the blokes what they did for female company. They said, 'We use a goat.'

He was horrified, but after another three months found the thought acceptable. So he joined the other blokes as they went in search of a goat herd. Selecting one, the Englishman was taking his pleasure when he realised that the other blokes were laughing their heads off.

'Why are you laughing?'

Still pissing themselves, they said, 'You picked the ugly one!'

How do you know when a Vietnamese robs your house?

Because your dog is missing and your homework's done.

The shearers had been giving the Chinese cook buggery. They'd put snails in his boots, spiders under his pillow and a dead snake in his coat pocket. Finally they felt a bit sorry for the poor bloke and said that they wouldn't do it any more.

'No more spiders?'

'No,' they promised.

'No more snails? No more snakes?'

'No, no more tricks,' they said.

'Okay, then I stop pissing in soup.'

How can you tell when an Australian's getting better?
He tries to blow the froth off his medicine.

How can you pick a Kiwi in a shoe store?
He's the one standing at the ugg boot display with an erection.

Why is British beer like bonking in a boat?
They're both fucking close to water.

Why did the Arabs shoot down the Concord?
Because with a nose like that, it had to be Jewish.

How do you get a one-armed Irishman down from a tree?
Wave to him.

What's the difference between a pommy cricket team and a 747?
The 747 stops whining when it gets to Sydney.

What's the difference between an Australian wedding and an Australian funeral?

One less drunk.

Why do Queenslanders call their beer XXXX?

Because they can't spell beer.

What's the difference between making yoghurt and making an Australian baby?

With yoghurt you have to start with a bit of culture.

What words are written on the walls of an English brothel?

PLEASE TELL THE GIRL WHEN YOU'RE FINISHED.

An Irishman walked into a pub in Sydney and asked the barman for a pint of Guinness for himself and a thimbleful of whiskey for his friend. He then pulled a tiny little bloke out of his breast pocket and plonked him on the bar.

'Is that a leprechaun?' asked the barman.

'No,' said the Irishman. 'It's an Australian with all the bullshit squeezed out.'

How do you get a hundred Vietnamese refugees into a Vegemite jar?

Tell them it floats.

The Nine Network decides that Ray Martin should host a weekly quiz. The contestants are required to guess the identity of a particular object by asking no more than 20 questions, to which the answers must be either Yes or No.

For week after week there's one woman who invariably wins. She becomes the Barry Jones of 20 Questions. No matter how obscure the object, she nails it down in four or five questions. It's like watching a demonstration of Einstein's 'intuitive leap'.

Martin insists there must be a way to catch her out. So he chooses an object himself. 'A nigger's cock,' he says to the studio audience while the champion is out of earshot in a special soundproof room. 'I will repeat that: a nigger's cock.'

The champion is brought into the studio confident and smiling. 'Okay,' says Mr Australia, 'you have 20 questions and three minutes to guess the object starting . . . now!'

'Is it animal?'

'Yes.'

'Is it alive?'

'Usually.'

'I know. A nigger's cock.'

It was a quiz program where contestants were required to answer three questions on chosen topics. An expert could squeeze into the booth with the contestant and assist with the last answer if the contestant had got that far.

Not unexpectedly, one contestant had chosen the topic of sex, and had a Frenchman in the booth with him as his adviser. The first question was, 'You're in bed with a 20-year-old virgin. Where do you kiss her first?'

The man advanced the correct answer, 'On the mouth.'

The second question was where he would kiss her next, and he again tentatively proffered an answer, 'On the breast.'

'Now for $60 000,' demanded the quizmaster, 'where do you kiss her next?'

The man turned eagerly to the French expert and demanded, 'What's the answer?'

'Don't ask me,' quipped the Frenchman. 'I got the first two wrong.'

During the Pacific War a wealthy Melbourne hostess phoned the American military command in Melbourne and offered to entertain several American officers for dinner. Being of racist leanings she added that she would prefer it if there were no Jews among the officers.

On the appointed evening, her butler ushered in three coal-black army captains.

'It's very good of you to invite us over for dinner like this, ma'am,' one of them said.

Clutching a chair for support, the hostess said, 'I'm awfully afraid that there must have been some mistake.'

'Oh surely not, ma'am,' the captain replied, 'Colonel Cohen never makes mistakes.'

An Australian, a Jew and an Irishman were so broke they were sitting in a rubbish tip where they'd been scavenging, even though a cold southerly was blowing. The Aussie touched a bottle of the grog beside him. Out came the magic bunyip and granted them one wish each.

The Australian said he never wanted to be without a beer for the rest of his life. The Jew said he never wanted to be without money. The Irishman thought, then whispered something in the bunyip's ear. 'Granted,' said the bunyip and dissolved back into the bottle. They headed for the pub to celebrate their luck.

The Aussie ordered a schooner, and glugged it in one go. As he banged the glass down, it miraculously refilled itself. The Jew went to the door, took his last $5 note from his tattered coat and held it up to the wind. The wind plucked the note away. He put his hand in his pocket and found the note replaced. He did this several times, then closed the door, delighted that he would always have money in his pocket.

There was a pounding at the door, and it burst open. Standing there were two men in white nighties and funny pointed white hoods.

'Okay, y'all,' drawled one of the hooded figures, 'which one of you guys wanted to be hung like a nigger?'

An Englishman was driving through the backblocks of Australia. As he passed a paddock he noticed a little girl running from a huge Herefordshire bull. Despite her best efforts the bull was rapidly gaining on her. The Englishman jumped out of the car, and, ignoring the agonising shocks, clambered over an electric fence. He then ran like mad towards the bull. Unbeknown to him, a journalist from the local paper was driving by and witnessed his courage. The Englishman reached the bull, grabbed it by the horns and stopped its charge just inches from the child. He flipped the bull over and, wrenching at the horns, broke its neck.

'Christ, that was great, mate,' said the journo. 'I've never seen a bloke with so much strength and courage. It makes me proud to be an Australian. Look, this story's going right on the front page of the *Gundy Advocate*. Now, just give me a few details about yourself. I take it you're a local?'

Next day the *Gundy Advocate* had a big headline on the front page. POMMY BASTARD KILLS CHILD'S PET.

A Barry McKenzie-type arrives in London and starts a pub crawl. He finishes up in a posh pub in Knightsbridge. The barman was quite impressed with his drinking capacity. He downed beer after beer after beer. Even though he kept complaining that it was 'warm as piss'.

After a while the barman suggested that he might need to go to the toilet. 'Nah, I'll be apples. Pour me a few more.' And he continued to drink, showing not the slightest desire to point Percy at the porcelain.

Finally it was closing time. 'Last orders, please,' said the barman. The Bazza-type ordered three more and downed them in a flash.

He was the last to leave the pub, and, as the barman ushered him out the door, he saw Bazza pause on the pavement and undo his fly. 'Sir,' the barman said, 'you can't do that here!'

'I ain't gonna do it here,' said Bazza, 'I'm gonna do it wa..a..a..a..a..ay over there!'

An Englishman is looking for the subway. He walks up to an Australian and, looking at him somewhat fastidiously, says, 'I say, excuse me – would you tell me how I can get underground?'

The Australian says, 'Sure thing. Drop dead, you pommy bastard.'

An Englishman, a Scot and an Irishman were on the Titanic the night she struck the iceberg. As she started to sink, the chaplain shouted, 'We are doomed. We're about to meet our maker. I urge you to do something religious.'

So the Englishman murmured a prayer. The Irishman sang a hymn. The Scot took up a collection.

A Scot met a Scottish doctor on the street and hoping for some free medical advice asked, 'What should I do for a sprained ankle?'

'Limp.'

A Scottish gentleman is one who gets out of the bath to piss in the handbasin.

The Scot went for his annual check-up and, as usual, proffered the doctor a large bottle of urine.

After the test, the doctor announced that the analysis had been reassuring. There was absolutely nothing abnormal in the specimen. The Scot returned home to tell the family the good news. 'My dear, you and I and the kids and Grandpa are all in good health.'

The Scot had been sitting beside his dying wife for days and nights. Having looked more and more uncomfortable for some time, he finally leaned over and said, 'I have to go for a while. I have to go to the toilet. But I'll be back as soon as possible. However, my dear, if you feel yourself slipping away while I'm out of the room, would you mind blowing out the candle.'

A Scot went to a clinic for a check-up and was told that he was pre-diabetic. 'You've got too much sugar in your urine.' Next morning he pissed on his porridge.

'Is this your first time in Sydney?' the taxidriver inquired of a Scotsman wearing the full cossie of kilt and sporran.

'Ai,' he said, 'and not only that, I'm on my honeymoon.'

'Then where's your wife?'

'Oh, she's been here before.'

A Scotsman was touring Australia, and a bloke invited him to the Leagues Club. He watched the people playing the pokies for a while and realised that he needed to piss. Trouble was that you needed 20 cents to get in. His friend gave him the coin but just as the Scot was about to use it he saw someone leaving the loo, grabbed the door and got to pee free.

So he decided to put the 20 cents in one of the pokies. And to everyone's astonishment, won the $20 000 jackpot. 'If it hadnae been for you, laddie,' the Scot said to his friend, 'I'd not ha' won. You deserve to be rewarded. Here, have your 20 cents back.'

Two Jews had planned to assassinate Hitler. They learned that he drove by a certain corner at noon each day so they waited for him there with their guns well hidden. At exactly noon they were ready to shoot, but there was no sign of Hitler. Five minutes later, nothing. Another five minutes went by but no sign of the fuhrer. By 12.15 they'd started to give up hope. 'My goodness,' said one of the men, 'I hope nothing's happened to him.'

During the early days of the Hitler regime, Goebbels maintained that Jews were, in reality, clever people and that Hitler was making a mistake in being so tough on them. Hitler said, 'On the contrary, they're stupid.'

To settle the argument the two men disguised themselves and went shopping. They first entered a china shop run by a German, where Goebbels asked for left-handed teacups. The poor German had never heard of such a thing. He stammered, apologised and finally admitted that he hadn't any.

Next Goebbels and Hitler went into a shop run by a Jew. The Jew scratched his head, smiled and cried, 'What a lucky thing. I have just six left-handed teacups left. Naturally I carry them in stock, although they're very hard to get. And, you understand, being so rare, they're a little more expensive than ordinary teacups.' Goebbels paid up and picked up the package.

'Any time you want more I'll be very glad to order them,' the Jew called after them.

When they reached the street, Goebbels turned to Hitler. 'There, didn't I tell you? The Jews are a lot smarter.'

'What do you mean smarter?' snarled Hitler. 'He was just lucky. He had some in stock.'

Not being a religious man, Hitler was inclined to consult his astrologers about the future. As the tide for war worsened, he asked, 'Am I going to lose the war?' Answered affirmatively, he then asked, 'Well, am I going to die?' Consulting their charts, the astrologers again said yes. 'When am I going to die?' was Hitler's next question.

'You're going to die on a Jewish holiday.'

'But when? On what holiday?' he asked in agitation.

The reply, 'Any day you die will be a Jewish holiday.'

Rosenblum was on his way to the market in Munich with a chicken under his arm. He was accosted in the street by a Nazi bully who demanded, 'Jew, where are you going?'

'I'm going to the market to buy some feed for my chicken.'

'What does he eat?' the Nazi snarled.

'Corn,' replied Rosenblum.

'Corn? The nerve of you Yids. German soldiers go hungry while you Jews feed your chickens on native German corn.' He then belted Rosenblum and continued on his way. A moment later another Nazi stopped Rosenblum. 'Where are you going, Jew dog?'

'To the market to buy some feed for my chicken.'

'What does he eat?'

'Wheat.'

'Wheat? Of all things, the Jew's chicken eats wheat while German children go hungry.' And he promptly knocked Rosenblum to the ground.

He picked himself up and continued on his way but he was approached by yet another Nazi.

'Where are you going, kike?'

'To the market to buy some feed for my chicken.'

'Feed for your chicken? What does he eat?'

'Look,' said Rosenblum, 'I don't know. I figure I'd give him a couple of pfennigs and he'll buy whatever he wants.'

Hitler sometimes disguised himself to visit public places in order to hear the people's reaction to his appearances and speeches. One day he shaved off his moustache, donned a hat and a long coat, and went to the pictures. Every cinema had to flash Hitler's photo on the screen and everyone would rise and proclaim, 'Heil Hitler'. When the fuhrer's likeness appeared and the crowd saluted, Hitler remained in his seat. The man next to him prodded Hitler and said, 'Look, friend, we all feel the way you do. But you're taking your chance by not standing up.'

A Jew arrives in hell. He wants to learn about his new surroundings and looks around. In the corner there's a writing table, looking cool and comfortable. And there, leaning over some papers, is Hitler.

The Jew asks, in horror, 'Isn't this supposed to be hell?'

'Take it easy,' another Jew reassures him. 'He has to translate *Mein Kampf* into Hebrew.'

An old Jew in Berlin is surrounded by a group of raucous Nazis who knock him to the ground and ask him, derisively, 'Jew, who was responsible for the war?'

The old Jew is no fool. 'The Jews,' he replies, 'and the bicycle riders.'

'Why the bicycle riders?' asks the Nazis.

'Why the Jews?'

A couple of Australian tourists are wandering through Vienna, marvelling at the art nouveau architecture. They come upon a little old coffee shop and go inside for a break and a slice of cake. Sitting in the corner they see a bloke who looks uncannily like Goebbels. He's watching a bloke playing darts. He is a dead-ringer for Hitler.

Fascinated, the Australians order their cakes and coffees and sit at a nearby table. They watch the two men very, very carefully. The resemblances to Hitler and Goebbels are absolutely eerie. They look exactly the same as the fuhrer and his offsider looked in the early 1940s, over half a century ago. They try to eavesdrop on their conversation but don't understand German.

Finally one of the Australians goes over to the bloke playing darts, the one who looks uncannily like Hitler, and says, 'You look uncannily like Hitler.'

'That's because I am Hitler,' comes the snarled reply.

'And you, you look exactly like Goebbels.'

'And why wouldn't I look like Goebbels? I am Goebbels.'

The Australians are astonished. 'How could this be? I mean, you've both been dead for 50 years.'

The bloke who looks like Hitler says, 'We are the embodiment of the finest German science. We are clones, created from surviving pieces of tissue.'

'Tissue taken from us at the time of our death,' adds Goebbels.

'And what are you going to do?'

'We're going to start all over again. We are going to establish a Fourth Reich.'

'Are you going to do all the same things?'

'Almost exactly,' says Hitler. 'We will, for example, kill six million Jews.'

'And two tennis players,' adds Goebbels.

The Australians look at each other in horror and astonishment. And one of them asks, 'Who are the tennis players?'

Whereupon Hitler turns to Goebbels and says, triumphantly, 'I told you no one cared about the Jews.'

A salesman calls on a business with three partners. Cohen, Goldberg and Lipschits. He steps up to the information window and addresses a woman sitting on a stool.

'Good morning, my dear. I want to talk to Mr Cohen.'

'He's out of town.'

'I'll talk to Mr Goldberg.'

'He's away.'

'What about Mr Lipschits?'

'He's tied up.'

The salesman comes back in the morning.

'I want to talk to Mr Cohen.'

'He's out of town.'

'I'll talk to Mr Goldberg.'

'He's away.'

'What about Mr Lipschits?'

'He's tied up.'

The same sequence of events occurs five days in a row. The same questions, the same answers. 'I demand the truth!'

'Sir, every time Cohen and Goldberg leave town they tie up Lipschits.'

A Jewish guy's got a parrot. It talks fluently. He goes into a pub and bets everyone that the parrot can talk. Gets odds of 25 to one. Ready to clean up. The parrot won't talk. He has to pay out all the money. He goes home determined to kill the parrot. As he wraps his fingers around its neck, the parrot says, 'Hey, just think of the odds you'll get tomorrow night.'

How many Hassidics does it take to change a light globe?

The question is irrelevant. We Hassidic Jews never change anything.

Mrs Cohen was bragging to her friends about her son. 'Ladies,' she said, 'you don't know what it means to have a good son. My boy lives in a penthouse and he's built on three rooms with a kitchen specially for me. He takes me out to dinner every night. We go to the theatre three times a week. Last month he took me on a cruise of the South Pacific. He don't do nothing without talking to me first.

'And ladies,' added Mrs Cohen, 'my son goes to a psychiatrist five times a week. And who do you think he spends the whole time talking about? Me!'

Two Jews were lined up before a firing squad in Poland when the officer asked if they had any last requests.

One said he'd like a cigarette. When the Nazi came close enough, he spat in his face.

'Please, Moishe,' said his mate, 'don't make trouble.'

Two Americans, one Jew and one Chinaman were sitting on a park bench in New York reading their newspapers.

Suddenly the Jewish bloke jumped up and started beating the crap out of the Chinese man. As he lay on the ground he looked up and said, 'What you do that for?'

To which the Jewish bloke replied, 'Pearl Harbour!'

As he got up and dusted himself off, the Chinese bloke replied, 'But I Chinese, not Japanese.'

The Jewish bloke said, 'Chinese, Siamese, Japanese – they're all the same to me!'

They recommenced reading their newspapers. Suddenly the Chinese bloke jumped up and started to karate chop the Jewish man. As he looked up, very dazed, he asked, 'What did you do that for?'

The Chinese bloke replied, 'The Titanic.'

'But that was an iceberg.'

'Goldberg, Steinberg, iceberg – they're all the same to me!'

A young Effie goes to Hollywood and after three months phones his momma. 'I'm married, Momma.'

'No! Next you'll be telling me you've married a goy.'

'No, Momma.'

Then what's her name?'

'Goldberg, Momma.'

'Thank goodness. And her first name?'

'Whoopi, Momma.'

A couple of blokes were standing side by side in a public loo when the shorter of the two said, 'Are you Jewish?'

'Yes.'

'And do you come from around Elwood?'

'Yes.'

'And at your circumcision, were you cut by the cock-eyed Liebler?'

'Yes. How do you know all these things?'

'Because Liebler always cuts with a left bias, and you're pissing on my shoes.'

When the young couple returned from their honeymoon, the bride went straight home to mum and dad. She explained that her husband was not doing his marital duties. Concerned, the family consulted a rabbi who promised to talk to the young man.

'My boy, when you're in bed tonight, you must put the longest part of your body into the hairiest part of hers.'

He promised he would.

A few days later, the bride returned to her parents, still feeling unloved.

Once again the rabbi was called in and once again he spoke to the young man.

'But, Rabbi, I've been putting my nose into her armpit just like you told me to.'

A Scot, an Englishman and a Jew were eating together in Acland Street. As a waiter cleared away the coffee, he heard the Scot ask for the bill.

Next day the *Herald Sun* headline read JEWISH VENTRILOQUIST SHOT IN ST KILDA RESTAURANT.

To celebrate their 30th anniversary, Mrs Cohen takes her husband to Double Bay and points to a block of flats. 'It's ours, darling.'

'Ours? How?'

'Well, all these years I've been charging you $20 each time we made love. I saved all those dollars and bought this block of flats.'

'Oh, dearest, if only I'd known. I would have given you all my business.'

An American tourist arrived at Bondi Beach and approached an old bloke sitting by the water.

'Excuse me, I'm a stranger here. But is this a good time of the year for swimming?'

'Lukewarm,' said the bloke.

So the American dived in and was immediately afflicted by hypothermia.

'Christ, it's freezing! Why the hell did you tell me it was lukewarm?'

'Vell, it luke varm to me.'

'Now, let me get this straight, Ms Goldfarb. First the water turned to blood, then there were frogs, lice, flies and a murrain on all the cattle, followed by boils, hail, locusts, darkness all over the land and the death of the first born. Now, why do I get the feeling you're about to ask for the day off?'

It's a Sydney Symphony Orchestra concert at the Opera House. A subscription ticket holder is concentrating on a violin concerto when an old Jewish bloke sits beside him. 'The violinist is Jewish,' he says. After a few seconds he adds, 'Also the conductor. And the cellists. And the harpist. There is a marvellous solo from a flautist, also Jewish.'

'Oh, Jesus,' said the concert-goer in exasperation.

'Also Jewish!'

An Irishman returns to Belfast after an Australian holiday. His family ask for a report.

'Australians? The most hospitable people I've ever met. They'll share their house, their food, they share everything. It's those white bastards you have to watch.'

Cultural Cringe

A famous ophthalmologist performed a cataract operation on an old, greatly venerated Australian painter. To express his gratitude, the painter insisted on painting a huge mural across the front of the hospital.

When the ophthalmologist saw the great work – depicting a vast eyeball surrounded by lashes – he said, 'Thank Christ I decided not to be a gynaecologist.'

Two marble statues, one depicting a naked man, the other a naked woman, had been poised on their plinths in a park for many years. They were positioned so that they faced each other, and each was enchanted by the beauty of the other. But being statues precluded hanky-panky.

Whereupon an angel appeared and told them that because they'd stood there so steadfastly through an endless succession of hot summers and harsh winters, they'd be rewarded by half an hour of human life. This would allow them to do whatever they'd been wanting to do.

Brought to life, the statues clambered off their pedestals, looked at each other and said, 'Shall we?'

'Yes, let's.' And they disappeared into some bushes where passers-by might have heard a lot of rustling. After a while they emerged from the foliage all hot, flustered and happy. The angel observed that they'd only used a small part of their allotted time.

'Why not start all over again?'

The statues giggled and the marble man said to the woman, 'Yes, let's do it again. Only this time the other way round. I'll hold down the fucking pigeon and you can shit on it.'

Two old mates meet in the pub.

'G'day, Arthur,' said Fred. 'Haven't seen you for yonks. How's the family?'

'Fine,' said Arthur. 'We've all taken up music. I play the violin, my wife plays the triangle, one of the kids plays the flute and the other plays the saxophone. Come around one night and we'll play you some Mozart. Now, what about your mob?'

'Oh, pretty much the same said Fred. 'We're into martial arts. I've taken up judo, my wife does karate, and the kids do tae kwon do. Come round one night and we'll belt the shit out of you.'

'You're not one of those fuckin' hypnotists, are you?' asked the doorman of the Leagues Club.

'No,' said the bloke. 'I'm a singer.'

'Okay,' said the doorman. 'You want to see the secretary. His office is the second door on the right.'

So the singer went in and fronted the club secretary.

'You're not going to tell me you're a fuckin' hypnotist,' said the secretary.

'No! I'm a singer.'

'Okay,' said the secretary. 'You can go and see the pianist and he'll arrange your music.'

Whilst he was rehearsing 'I Did It My Way', the pianist said, 'You don't do anything else in your act, do you? Fuckin' hypnotism, for example?'

'No,' said the bloke. 'I keep telling everybody that I'm a singer. That's it. Why all this bullshit about hypnotism?'

'Well, it's like this,' said the pianist. 'Last Saturday we had a hypnotist, and he was pretty bloody good. Got the entire audience in a trance. Hundreds of them.'

'What's wrong with that?'

'Well, halfway through the act he tripped over the microphone cable and went arse over tit down those little stairs. Got a blood nose and yelled "shit!". Well, the cleaners were at it all Sunday.'

A couple were sitting in an opera box above the stage when during Mahler's Fifth Symphony, the woman gave her boyfriend a hand job. He ejaculated vigorously, right into the orchestra pit hitting a violinist right in the middle of his bald head.

'Shit,' he said. 'I've been hit by a flying fuck.'

'And so you should be,' said the conductor. 'You've been playing like a cunt all night.'

The Newcastle Symphony Orchestra was holding a fundraising night, but unfortunately, Roger Woodward couldn't make it. So they hired an old local pianist who, 30 years before, had been a stand-in pianist for the Berlin Philharmonic.

Since moving to Newcastle he'd fallen on hard times and hard drink. He wasn't in the best of shape. But he was the best available. So he trundled out on stage in his stained tuxedo and lowered himself onto a wicker chair that he had insisted on bringing.

Unfortunately there was a split in his trousers, and a gasp of horror from the audience.

'Do you know your knackers are hanging through the old wicker chair?' hissed the first violinist.

'No,' the old bloke said, 'but if you hum the tune I'll soon pick up on the melody.'

In the wee hours of the morning a once-famous scriptwriter staggered towards his bed after yet another three-day drug and booze binge, but just before he lapsed into unconsciousness he heard . . . *Tap, tap, tap, tap*. It sounded like the typewriter in his study. Too bombed to do anything about it, he passed out.

A day later he woke, and as he stumbled past his study he saw, sitting on his desk by his typewriter, a pile of A4 paper. Bewildered, he took a closer look and found a script, 120 pages long with his name on it. He read it and marvelled at how fantastic it was. 'My God, I don't even remember writing this,' he muttered, before sending it to his agent. The film went on to become a great success. And so, overcome with delight, the writer went back to bingeing and boozing and womanising. Years passed and not another word was written. Then, one night, as he stumbled drunkenly towards his bed, he heard . . . *Tap, tap, tap, tap*. This time he forced himself to his study door and saw an elf perched on his chair, happily typing away. 'It was you, wasn't it? You wrote that last script,' he said.

'That's right,' said the elf, as he tap, tap, tapped away.

'Are you going to finish this one?' asked the excited scriptwriter.

'Maybe,' said the elf, 'maybe not.'

'What'll it take to make you finish?' the scriptwriter demanded. 'I know! Cocaine! I'll go out and buy you the best cocaine. I always find that helps me.'

'No, thank you,' said the elf, 'I don't do drugs.'

'Okay, I know! Booze! I'll buy you the best cognac and champagne money can buy.'

'No, thank you,' said the elf, typing away, 'I don't drink.'

'Women, then,' said the desperate writer. 'Surely a bevy of beautiful models will excite you enough to finish it.'

Tap, tap, tap. The elf continued writing. 'No, thank you. I'm happily married.'

'Well, what then?' exploded the scriptwriter. 'What do you want to finish the script? Surely there's something I can give you.'

Tap, tap, tap. Then the elf paused, looked at the scriptwriter, and said, 'Well, there's one thing.'

'Yes! Yes! What? Just name it!'

'Well, this time I'd like a co-writing credit.'

The scriptwriter looked down at the elf, his

nostrils flared, his eyes opened wide, and he screamed, 'Oh, get fucked!'

A bloke takes his wife to the Opera House for the first night of *Nambucco*. It is a very eccentric production, combining all sorts of odd, unlikely visual elements. The bloke is bored silly and, even worse, needs a piss. So he extricates himself from the row, apologising as he squeezes past scores of knees. But out in the foyer he can't find the loo. He pushes at this door and that and finally hears tinkling water. Desperate, he rushes inside to find a fountain. It's too much. He can't bear it. So he has a quick piss into the ornate bowl. Finally he apologises his way back to his seat, surprised by various slaps on the back and sporadic bursts of applause.

'Have I missed much of the second act?' he whispered to his wife.

'Missed it?' she says, indicating the stage where the singers are bellowing around the fountain. 'You were the star.'

A couple are trying to enjoy the movie but there's a bloke sitting a few seats in front of them moaning and groaning.

They call an usher. 'You obviously need medical help. Where are you from?'

'The balcony,' came the agonised reply.

An artist was commissioned to paint a mural to celebrate Governor Phillip's landing. He took the job on, on the understanding that no one was to see it until it was completed. When the time came for the unveiling – shock, horror. The wall was a mass of pictures illustrating, in most biological detail, all the positions from the Kama Sutra, and up in the top right-hand corner a fish with a halo. The first man to recover his breath cried out in rage.

'That's art!' declared the painter.

'But what has it go to do with Captain Phillip's landing?'

'Holy Mackerel, look at all them fucking Kooris!'

The daughter of a well-known Shakespearian scholar, after her first-year examination in English at university, took home the questions to her father. He looked at the exam paper and said, 'This first question is easy. It asks you to name the four great plays of Shakespeare. What did you write?'

'I wrote, "Three inches, Six inches, Nine inches and Twelve inches".'

'But that's nonsense. Shakespeare wrote no such plays.'

'But he did, Father. The terms I used are the new verbal shorthand used by students at universities these days. You see, three inches is the shorthand for *Much Ado About Nothing*. Six inches means *As You Like It*, Nine inches is *Midsummer Night's Dream* and Twelve inches is *The Taming of the Shrew*.'

A history teacher was testing the knowledge of his new class. 'Which British explorer discovered Australia? And in what year?' he asked. Row after row of silent, blank faces. Finally a little Japanese boy, the son of a Toyota executive, waved his hand.

'Please, sir,' he cried excitedly. Trouble was that this kid knew all the answers, irrespective of the subject, so the teacher turned desperately to the rest of the class. 'Surely one of you must know when Australia was discovered.'

No takers, only the Japanese kid.

'Please, sir, please, sir.' His little arm was flailing in the air. 'All right, tell us.'

'Please, sir, it was Captain James Cook. And the year was 1770.'

Infuriated by the other dunderheads, the teacher roared at them. 'Aren't you ashamed of yourselves? Look how it takes a visitor to our country to know the answer.'

He turned to the little Japanese boy. 'Thank you for showing these idiots their idiocy. You may go home at three o'clock but all the other kids will stay in and write an essay on . . . Captain Cook.' Whereupon a voice piped up from the rear of the classroom. 'Fucking Japs!'

'Who said that?' roared the teacher.

'Please, sir,' came the reply. 'Douglas Macarthur. In 1942.'

'I don't like to talk about the war,' said Helen Demidenko, 'because my grandfather died in a concentration camp. He fell out of a watch tower.'

When Burke and Wills set out on their great journey, they had an Afghan to drive the camels, a German to read the maps and they put a Chinaman in charge of supplies. On the dawn of the beginning of their great trek, the Afghan was in position, leading the long line of camels. The German, with his monocle polished, was sitting in his dray poring over the maps. But there was no sign of the Chinaman. Worse still, there was no sign of any supplies.

But they headed off anyway, convinced that he'd be coming along behind them.

But he never came. And the trip turned into a catastrophe. Finally, when Burke and Wills were almost dead from exposure and starvation, in the middle of nowhere, the Chinaman jumped out from behind a tree and said, 'Surplise! Surplise!'

Heard of the bloke who's half Japanese and half black?

Every year on December the seventh he attacks Pearl Bailey.

Two Iraqi generals were sitting sweating in a bunker in the middle of the desert, awaiting the full force of Desert Storm. And they passed the time by discussing their Russian weapons.

'Our Russian tanks are really good,' said one general. 'Lots of thick armour and big, loud, powerful guns.'

'Yes, the new tanks are very good. But I'm worried by the operating instructions.'

'Why?'

'Well, under the heading "Tactics", it says, "When attacked, retreat, and draw the enemy forces deep into your territory. Then await the snows of winter".'

Mark Anthony returned to Egypt after years of war with the Hittites and the Babylonians. 'Where's Cleopatra?' he demanded of the servant.

'My lord, she's in bed with hepatitis.'

Mark Anthony unsheathed his sword and yelled, 'I'll kill that Greek bastard!'

After the Gulf War, the Americans had to put out hundreds upon hundreds of burning oil wells, deliberately set ablaze by the retreating army of Saddam Hussein. Finally, only one was left, but it proved intractable. There was nothing they could do to put it out. And they tried everything.

They called for Red Adair, offering him two million dollars if he'd dash over and do the job. But Red was busy putting out an oil rig fire in Siberia.

'Why not Green Adair?' someone suggested.

'Who?'

'Green Adair. He's Irish. Works cheaper than Red.'

So they phoned him in Dublin and offered him one million dollars.

A few hours later the blokes from Caltex were astonished to see a giant helicopter hovering over them. They were even more astonished when, after it landed and the nose opened, a truck driven by Green Adair and his crew went charging at the fire. Instead of stopping as it neared the flames, it went right into the middle of them, and for a while they lost it from sight. Then they glimpsed Green Adair and his offsider leaping out, jumping up and down on the flames.

It took them the best part of an hour but they emerged badly singed but triumphant. Three cheers rang out across the desert.

'And what will you do with the million dollars?' asked the bloke from Caltex.

'The first thing?' said Green Adair. 'Get some brakes for that fucking truck.'

It was Anzac Day and an old digger climbed on the bus. He found himself opposite a Salvation Army officer. He stared blearily at the uniform and finally inquired, 'What's your regiment? I don't seem to recognise it.'

'I'm a soldier of the Lord,' said the Salvo. 'I go to Townsville to fight the devil, then to Brisbane to fight him and then down to Newcastle, Sydney and Melbourne.'

'Good on ya, mate,' said the digger. 'Keep on headin' the bastard south.'

Displaying a lot more enthusiasm than worldliness, the young education officer arranged to address a company of diggers just back from a search-and-destroy patrol in Vietnam. A gnarled old sergeant called the troops to order with, 'Righto, youse lot, quieten down. The lieutenant has come all the way from Saigon to give youse a talk, and the least youse can do is listen to him.'

He then turned to the education officer and asked quietly, 'What will you be speaking about, sir?'

Just above a whisper, the lieutenant replied, 'Well, sergeant, after what they've been through, I thought a little talk about some of the finer things of life might be appropriate. What if we have a little chat about Keats?'

'Yes, certainly, sir,' said the sergeant, as he turned to address the muttering, disgruntled troops. 'Quiet there in the ranks!' he began. Then, as the troops became silent, he continued. 'Now, listen, youse ignorant lot. The lieutenant is going to talk to youse about Keats. And you'd better shut up and listen, because half youse mob wouldn't know one end of a bloody keat from the other!'

It was Anzac Day and an old digger, obviously the worst for wear, was lolling back in the tram. A woman was shocked to notice that his fly was open and his penis was in full view. What to do? Should she just avert her eyes and pretend not to have noticed? No. It was Anzac Day, he'd fought for his country and she must do her duty. So she leant over, tapped him on the knee and said, 'Excuse me, sir, but do you know that your John Thomas is sticking out?'

He looked down, pondered for a second, and replied, 'Don't kid yourself, lady, it's only hanging out!'

'I shall return.' – General Douglas Macarthur

'We will fight them on the beaches.' – Winston Churchill

'Fuck, what was that?' – The mayor of Hiroshima

Ned Kelly was holding up the mail coach. He lined up the passengers and ordered his men to hang the women and fuck the men. A passenger corrects him, saying, 'Mr Kelly, you mean hang the men and fuck the women?'

Whereupon a man up the back of the coach cried out, 'Who'th robbing thith coach, you or Misther Kelly?'

An English economist, a don at Cambridge, had been visiting Australia to study the influence of Thatcherism on government policies. On his return, he addressed a local community group about what he'd seen in the colonies.

At question time, an audience member commented that while there'd been much emphasis on Australia's primary production and mining sector, there'd been absolutely no mention of cultural matters.

The questioner recognised that the speaker was an economist, but, nonetheless, felt he might have something to say about the state of the arts in Australia.

The economist said that despite its many and varied achievements, Australia remained a non-event in the artistic and cultural areas. 'Indeed,' he said, 'Australians are, in this regard, absolute barbarians.'

Whereupon a voice could be heard from the rear of the room. 'Pig's fucking arse we are!'

'King Arthur, I have raped and pillaged all the Saxons to the south.'

'You idiot, Lancelot. I told you to rape and pillage the Saxons to the north. I don't have any enemies in the south.'

'I'm afraid you do now.'

Graffiti is for people who can't write books.

If you've got water on the knee, you're not aiming straight.

Why are waterbeds cutting down on adultery?
Ever tried to crawl under one?

John Wayne is dead.
The hell I am!

Bronwyn Bishop kick-starts jumbos.

Being a member of a union is like using a franger – you get a false sense of security while being screwed.

But for Venetian blinds it would be curtains for all of us.

Tutankhamen has changed his mind – he wants to be buried at sea.

Transcendental meditation is better than sitting around doing nothing.

Before the Howard government came to power we were on the edge of an economic precipice. Since then we've taken a great step forward.

A stitch in time would confuse Stephen Hawking.

Teenagers are God's punishment for having sex.

I'm pink therefore I'm spam.

Things may be bad but they're better than next year.

Cigarettes cause statistics.

Cancer cures smoking.

What do you say to a sociology student with a job?

A cheeseburger, a coke and fries.

End violence to women now.
Yes, dear.

Sex is just one damp thing after another.

Ignore this sign.

Roses are reddish
Violets are bluish
If it wasn't for Jesus
We'd all be Jewish.

Religion is man's attempt to communicate with the weather.

Is reincarnation making a comeback?

Due to Paul Keating's deficit, the light at the end of the tunnel will be turned off at weekends.

Reality is for people who can't cope with drugs.

Racism is a pigment of the imagination.

I'm bisexual. When I can't get it, I buy it.

Elvis is dead.
Good career move.

Power corrupts – absolute power is even more fun.

Politically correct graffito:
Ethnics out!

Help the cops – beat yourself up.

The best-laid plans of mice and men are lost in the files.

'A piano is a piano is a piano.' – Gertrude Steinway.

Just because you're paranoid doesn't mean they're not out to get you.

Aural sex gives eargasms.

Save money on obscene calls – reverse charges.

What did we do before we discovered nostalgia?

If you notice this notice you will notice that this notice is not worth noticing. So don't notice it.

Nervous breakdowns are hereditary. You get them from your kids.

Necrophilia means never having to say you're sorry.

Necrophilia is dead boring.

Beam me up, Scotty. There's no intelligent life down here.

Masturbation is the thinking-man's television.

The meek shall inherit the Earth, but not the mineral rights.

Marriage is a fine institution. But who wants to live in an institution?

I'd rather have a full bottle in front of me than a full frontal lobotomy.

Jesus is alive and well and signing copies of the Bible at readings.

Jesus saves – with St George.

The first three minutes of life are very dangerous.
So are the last.

Jesus lives!
Does this mean no holidays at Easter?

On the tits of a barmaid from Sale
Were tattooed the prices of ale
And on her behind
For the sake of the blind
Was the same information in braille.

Bo-peep did it for the insurance.

Keep incest in the family.

My inferiority complex isn't as good as yours.

Keep Australia green.
Have sex with a frog.

This door will shortly appear in paperback.

God is dead.
Oh, no I'm not!

'God is dead.' – Nietzsche.

'Nietzsche is dead.' – God.

I like sadism, necrophilia and bestiality. Am I flogging a dead horse?

Archduke Franz Ferdinand found alive. First World War a mistake.

Feudalism: your count votes.

Avoid the end of the year rush – fail your exams now.

Don't drink and drive. You'll spill it.

Diarrhoea is hereditary. It runs in your jeans.

The decision is maybe and that's final.

All men are cremated equal.

I used to be conceited. Now I'm perfect.

We want new clichés.

Australians are living proof that Aborigines screw kangaroos.

Art is what you can get away with.

I couldn't care less about apathy.

Be alert. Your country needs lerts.

My wife's an angel.
You're lucky. Mine's still alive.

Paparazzi with the Lot

A lion was drinking from a pool with its bum in the air when a chimpanzee passed by. Mistaking the gender of the big cat, the chimp crept up behind it to play hide the sausage.

The lion let out an agonised roar and the chimp rapidly departed. Infuriated, the lion chased it through the jungle. The chimp dashed into a safari camp, snatched a pith helmet, sat in a chair and pretended to read a copy of *The Times*.

The lion arrived in the clearing and asked, 'Have you seen a chimp around here?'

'You mean the chimp that rooted the lion down by the stream?'

'Christ,' said the lion, 'don't tell me it's in the papers already!'

Elvis Presley knock-knock joke:

Knock, knock.
Who's there?
Wurlitzer.
Wurlitzer who?
Wurlitzer one for the money, two for the show . . .

Prince Charles has to go to Glynbourne-on-Sea to judge the local flower show. It's a particularly distinguished affair and has been staged very successfully for 200 years, stopping only during the Boer War and the First and Second World Wars. He arrives beautifully dressed in his Jermyn Street suit, but is wearing a fox hat which looks somewhat out of place.

Finally the Anglican vicar of Glynbourne-on-Sea cannot contain his curiosity. He's asks him to explain how someone who looks as smart as a rat with a gold tooth can be so silly as to wear a fox hat.

The prince attempts an explanation. 'This morning Mother heard I was coming to Glynbourne-on-Sea and she said, "where the fuck's that?"'

The bloke couldn't believe his luck. There he was, shipwrecked with Elle Macpherson. But they realised they'd have to behave themselves because he was married and she was very famous. And it was only a matter of time until they'd be rescued. They agreed to stay on opposite sides of the island and to meet once a week to check on provisions.

But when they met a week later they yielded to their sexual appetites. Afterwards, they felt somewhat ashamed of themselves and decided to go their separate ways. They would scan the horizon for signs of ships and meet in a week's time.

A week later, they met on the same lonely beach. But this time the bloke had brought a change of clothing. 'Could you dress up as a man?' he asked Elle. 'I found these on the shore.'

Elle looked at him suspiciously. 'Are you telling me you're kinky?'

'No, not a bit.'

She reluctantly agreed and no sooner had she climbed into the clobber than he put his arm around her and said, 'G'day, mate. You'll never guess who I fucked last week!'

Her Majesty invited a distant cousin, Prince Ludwig, to stay at Buckingham Palace, only to discover that he couldn't keep his hands off the pageboys.

'Ludwig,' her Majesty said to the prince, 'you

must stop this. I've got enough trouble with the tabloids without this. We cannot have these goings on at Buckingham Palace.'

'Sorry, ma'am,' said the prince. 'I'll turn over a new leaf.'

But next day Ludwig saw a pageboy leaning out a palace window. He raced over, slammed the window down on the boy's neck to trap him and was just removing his trousers when the Queen walked in.

'Ludwig! And you said you were going to turn over a new leaf!'

'And I will, ma'am, I will. Just as soon as I get to the bottom of this page.'

Princess Di was asked to launch a ship at Newcastle dockyards. After busting the bottle of Bollinger, she expressed the desire to meet some of the men who'd built the proud vessel. 'And this, your Highness, is our Dave. Dave is one of the strongest blokes on the waterfront. Tell her Highness how much you can lift, Dave.'

Dave shuffled his feet, looked at the ground and said modestly, 'Aw, about a fuckin' ton.'

'Break it down!' whispered the shocked official.

'Well, about half a fuckin' ton.'

The late actress Tallulah Bankhead is leaving Harrods wearing her new full-length sable coat. As she's about to climb into her limousine, a beggar woman approaches her, saying, 'Please, Miss Bankhead, help me. I haven't eaten in three days.'

Ms Bankhead smiles understandingly and says, 'Well, my dear, you must *force* yourself!'

In happier days the Queen and Lady Di went on a tour of Northern Ireland. They left their hotel and went for a ride in the Rolls Royce, but took a wrong turn in Belfast and got hijacked by the IRA. The leader, Paddy, said to Di, 'Give us all those diamonds Prince Charles has given you.'

And Di said, 'I'm sorry, I didn't bring any of my jewels with me.'

Whereupon the IRA searched the car and Lady Di but couldn't find any diamonds.

They then turned to her Majesty and said, 'All right, give us the crown jewels.' But the Queen said, 'I'm sorry, but I didn't bring any of my crown jewels with me.'

Whereupon they searched the Queen and the car and couldn't find any crown jewels.

So Paddy said, 'Right, we'll just have to steal the car.' And they evicted the royals and drove off.

After they'd gone, the Queen turned to Lady Di

and said, 'Di, my dear, you were wearing your diamonds when we left the hotel. Where did you hide them?'

Diana said, 'As soon as I saw the IRA I quickly hid them in that little secret place only Prince Charles knows about. But, ma'am, you were wearing your crown jewels when we left the hotel. Where did you hide them?'

And the Queen said, 'As soon as I saw the IRA I hid them in that little secret place only Prince Philip knows about.'

Then Lady Di said, 'Jeez, we should have brought Princess Margaret. We could have saved the Rolls Royce.'

Kerry Packer was playing polo when he went arse over tit off the horse. And lay very, very still. The ambulance arrived, found he was dead, connected their defibrillator and gave him a few thousand volts. The tycoon stirred. Opening his eyes he said, 'You saved my life. What can I do for you?'

'Well, Mr Packer,' said the ambulance driver, 'I'm a keen golfer. You might like to buy me a couple of clubs.'

Packer went out and bought him Royal Melbourne and Huntingdale.

Lady Renouf was being chauffeured home when the Rolls Royce got a puncture. The car wobbled to a dignified halt and the chauffeur got out. There was a long delay. Lady Renouf wound down the window.

'Do you want a screw, driver?' she asked.

The chauffeur said, 'Might as well, Lady Renouf. 'I can't get this bloody hubcap off.'

The new Australian ambassador to the English court had opened his term with a splendid afternoon garden party. All the VIPs were there, including the Queen herself.

After the formalities were finished, the ambassador approached the Queen. After the requisite small talk, the ambassador enquired whether the lady would care for a drink.

'A sherry or a port, your Majesty?' he asked.

'Ah, sherry,' she sighed. 'Ambrosia, the nectar of the gods. The colour redolent of English autumn, the sylvan settings, the Turner landscapes. The fragrance enchanting, bouquet at its best, transporting me to heights of pleasure. The flavour so pleasing, it sets me awash with the joy of tasting truly.'

'And port, your Majesty?'

'Port? No, Mr Ambassador. For some unknown reason it always gives me an itchy twat!'

Bob and Blanche were on a second honeymoon in the Sahara. Blanche had planned a moonlight ride on a camel. The evening was balmy and they glided across the silver sands. When they came to an oasis they dismounted and Blanche produced a bottle of Bollinger. They sat and toasted their future together. Clutching their white robes, they remounted the camel to return to their far-off tent. But the camel refused to budge. After much walking around, pleading, kicking, promising that no camel would be deprived by the year 2000, Bob still hadn't managed to budge the beast.

Blanche got down on her hands and knees to examine the brute. With a snort and a lunge, the huge animal got to its feet and pounded off into the distance.

'Jeez, Blanche, what did you do?'

'Well, I saw this swelling between his legs,' said Blanche, 'and I bit it.'

'Well, for God's sake, bite mine. I've got to catch him,' said Bob.

What ends with -u-n-t and smells fishy?

Rex Hunt.

What's brown and runs around Ayers Rock?
A dingo doing a lap of honour.

What's a test tube baby's worst enemy?
A dingo with a straw.

What's the difference between driving a Volvo and putting your hand down the front of Bob Hawke's pants?
You feel a bigger dick driving a Volvo.

What's fat, blonde and lives in Florida?
Salman Rushdie.

What do you call Bob Hawke's balls?
Blanched hazelnuts.

What's fe-fi-fo, fe-fe-fi-fo?

Ita Buttrose's phone number.

How many Arthur Tunstalls does it take to change a light bulb?

None. He's from the Dark Ages.

Arnold Schwarzenegger was tired of being battered and bruised in action sequences. Even though his double did the major stunts, there were still scenes to be shot in which Schwarzenegger could be clearly identified.

So he spent some of his vast fortune on developing a clone. And when it was delivered from the lab, it was absolutely remarkable. Every detail of Schwarzenegger's face and physique was perfectly replicated, down to the last mole. There was even a scar on the left elbow Arnie had got in his weightlifting days.

But there was one problem. The clone had an enormous penis. And it was given to huge, prolonged erections. As well, the clone got more and more ambitious and tried to push the original Arnie out of scenes. Finally, the two of them got to fighting. The LAPD got a phone call from Schwarzenegger asking them to come to his suite at the Beverly Hills Hotel. By the time they arrived, horrified crowds had gathered to watch Schwarzenegger and his naked clone struggling on the roof of the building. To make matters worse, the clone had a huge erection.

Finally, desperately, Schwarzenegger grabbed the clone by the penis and threw him off the building.

'Sorry, Mr Schwarzenegger,' said the LAPD, 'we're going to have to arrest you and charge you with Murder One.'

'Murder One? But it was in self-defence.'

'Nonetheless, it was you who made the obscene clone fall.'

A bloke is walking through Hyde Park in Sydney where he sees a couple of tickets for Channel Nine's *Midday Show* nailed to a tree. Terrific, he thinks as he rushes over to the tree, and steals the nails.

Brian Johns is desperate for ratings and so insists that the ABC have a quiz show to rival *Sale of the Century*. One segment has a contestant think of a four-letter word, spell it and put it in a sentence in order to win a prize, which, like all ABC prizes, is really boring. It's a book token you can redeem at an ABC Shop.

In the first episode, there's a contestant who answers every question, just about the brightest quiz contestant since Barry Jones. And they get to the four-letter-word segment.

'Okay, what's your word?'

'GARN. G-A-R-N,' says the contestant.

'Garn? What sort of word is that?' says Quentin Dempster, who's managed to land the quizmaster gig.

'GARN GET FUCKED!' shouts the contestant.

The switchboard is jammed with complaints, and Johns cancels the show.

Six months later they decide to give it one last chance. In the first episode there's a bearded bloke who looks uncannily like Barry Jones and who turns out to be as brilliant as his predecessor. He gets a perfect score, and, then, it's four-letter-word time.

'SMEE. Capital S, capital M, double E!!'

'What do you mean SMEE?' says Quentin.

Whereupon the bloke rips off his false beard and yells, 'SMEE AGAIN. GARN GET FUCKED!'

The Nine Network decided to bring back *New Faces*. Bert Newton was lured back to his old job, and, pretty soon, it was rating like a beauty. Nonetheless truly original, imaginative acts were few and far between. But then, one night, Bert introduced a woman who astonished the audience by simply dropping a mouth organ into her knickers. Whereupon they heard, somewhat muffled, a thoroughly professional rendition of 'Advance Australia Fair'.

After the program Bert decided to introduce her to Paul Dainty. He rang Paul up and said, 'Paul, I've got a great act. You'll be able to make a fortune out of her.'

'What does she do?'

'Just listen to this.'

And he handed the woman her mouth organ which she promptly dropped down the front of her knickers. He brought the phone close as she started to play, 'Australians all, let us rejoice'.

When the performance was over, Bert said, 'There, Paul. What do you think of that?'

Paul said, 'It just sounds like some cunt playing the mouth organ.'

Steven Spielberg dies and goes to heaven where he's met by St Peter. 'Stevie, baby. Great to see you. You're looking good. Now, have I got a project for you!'

'Are you crazy?' says Spielberg. 'I'm dead. I had a heart attack from over-work. I want heaven's version of Hawaii, and I want it now.'

'Come on, Steve, lighten up,' said St Peter. 'This is a dream deal. The script is by William Shakespeare.'

'I don't care,' says Spielberg. 'I want a holiday.'

'Just listen to the concept,' says St Peter. 'It's a musical, and the score is by – wait for it, you're going to love it – Beethoven!'

'Okay, it sounds terrific, but the answer's still no.'

'But, Steve, the sets are going to be by Michelangelo.'

St Peter's eyes glisten as Spielberg considers the deal. 'Okay, I'll do it.'

'Fantastic! Wonderful!' says St Peter, as he throws an arm around Spielberg's shoulders and walks him through the gates of heaven. 'Now, we only have one small problem. You see, God's dating this chick and she thinks she can sing . . .'

Given her religious proclivities, Blanche Hawke was very, very worried whether her late husband, Bob, would make it into heaven. So she made a telephone call.

'This is the Virgin Mary,' said the receptionist, 'can I help you?'

'Yes, has Mr Hawke arrived as yet?'

'No, he hasn't.'

A little later Blanche repeated the call.

'This is the Immaculate Mary, Mother of God. May I help you?'

Blanche called heaven the next day and the call was answered slightly differently. 'This is Mary, may I help you?'

She turned to her friends and said, 'Bob's in heaven.'

Some time before achieving fame as a cameraman for *Dances with Wolves*, Dean Semler was being presented to Queen Elizabeth in a line-up of notables at a Royal Command Performance. Not recognising him – as he works behind the camera rather than in front of it – Queen Elizabeth asked him what he did. 'I'm a photographer, ma'am,' he replied.

'Oh, how interesting!' she said. 'I had a brother-in-law who was a photographer!'

'Well, isn't that a coincidence!' he said. 'I had a brother-in-law who was a queen!'

Shortly after Evel Knievel's attempt to jump over the Grand Canyon on a rocket-powered motorbike, some tourists were gazing down at the great fissure, marvelling at its depth, width and emptiness. 'It's a mile wide, a mile deep and not a thing living in it,' said the guide.

'Hang on,' said one of the tourists, who was studying the bottom of the canyon with his binoculars. 'There's a dead donkey down there. And there seems to be someone stuck under it.'

The guide reported the sight to the park guards who journeyed to the bottom of the canyon and found a tragic sight. Beneath the dead donkey was a skeleton wearing a T-shirt reading 'PADDY KNIEVEL'

Sydney or the Bush!

A farmer was standing on the verandah farewelling a couple of visitors. When they were about 30 metres away he called out, 'Oo'roo.' The couple turned, waved and called, 'Oo'roo' back. A few yards further on, the farmer called, 'Oo'roo' again. And again the couple responded, waving and calling, 'Oo'roo'. A few yards further down the track the farmer called, 'Oo'roo' for the third time. And this time they turned giving a half-hearted wave and a less enthusiastic, 'Oo'roo'. Whereupon the farmer yelled out, 'For Christ's sake, will you shut up! That's the name of me bloody dog.'

Dad and Dave were hunting for wild pigs with their dogs when they heard some piglet squeals coming from beneath a fallen log. While Dad kept watch in case the parents came back, Dave squeezed right underneath the log into what turned out to be a large burrow. Whilst he was grabbing at the piglets, everything turned black. 'Dad, what's blocking the light?'

'Son, you'll find out if the sow's tail breaks.'

Dad won the lottery. Next day Snake Gully was full of people coming to congratulate him. Dave and Mabel drove over with the grandkids, and neighbours who hadn't spoken to him for years turned up for a beer.

After they'd all left, Dad and the missus sat at the kitchen table having a cuppa. She said, 'What do you think we should do now we've got all this money?'

Dad thought for a while. 'I reckon we might just keep farming till it's all gone.'

Dave took Mabel to Paris and while she was having an afternoon nap at the hotel, he wandered off to look at the Eiffel Tower. He stood staring up at it, full of wonderment and awe. There was nothing like it in Snake Gully.

After a few minutes a pretty young woman came up to him and whispered, ''Ello, mon cher. Would you like a bit?'

'Why? Are they pulling it down?'

It was Mabel's birthday and Dave asked her what she'd like for a prezzo. She said, 'Dave, I'd like you to get circumcised.' So he went into town and asked the doctor.

'That'll cost you $500.'

'Too much,' said Dave, so he went across to the vet's. They told him they'd do the job for $100.

'Too much,' said Dave.

So he went home and decided on do-it-yourself. He sharpened his axe and went around to where he beheaded chooks. And he whacked his dick on a bloodstained stump. And then he lifted his axe and went *whack*. 'Too much,' said Dave.

Early one morning the phone rings at Dave and Mabel's in Snake Gully. 'Is that Snake Gully 127?' a voice asks.

'No, it's Snake Gully 271,' says Dave, sleepily.

'Oh, sorry to disturb you. I must have the wrong number.'

'No trubs,' says Dave, 'the phone was ringing anyway.'

Dad and Dave decided to diversify into chooks but were having teething troubles. They knew it was important to have high-quality roosters and felt that the old one they'd bought probably wasn't up to it. So they kept buying others, with unfortunate results.

Whenever they let a young rooster into the pen it would swagger up to the old rooster and say, 'All them hens are mine. And you can piss off.'

'I'll tell you what, I'll race you round the chook shed,' the old rooster would say, 'and if I win, I keep half the hens. If I lose, you can have the lot.'

'Okay,' the young rooster would say, 'and because of your age, I'll give you a head start.'

And off they'd go. The old rooster was racing for all he was worth, but the young rooster was catching up fast. Then Dave would come out with his shotgun and blast the young rooster.

'Dad, that's the third poofter rooster we've had in a row.'

Dad was charged with bestiality by the Snake Gully police. Dad visited his son whilst he was awaiting his court appearance in the cells.

'Tell me about it, son,'

'Well, Dad, Mabel wasn't talking to me. And I got really, really lonely. And I noticed our pet emu was bending over and I just couldn't resist it.'

'The pet emu?' said Dad incredulously. 'Wasn't that a bit difficult?'

'Oh, for the first 200 metres,' said Dave, 'then we got in step.'

Dave announced his intention of enlisting in the army. When Ma heard the news she asked Dad to speak to him. So he took his son out on the verandah and began to lecture him.

'Dave,' said Dad, 'you must beware the demon drink.'

'Don't worry, Dad,' said Dave, 'I've never touched the stuff. Never will.'

'And Dave,' said Dad, 'you must avoid gambling.'

'No worries, Dad. I've never bet in my life. Never will.'

Dad took a deep breath and continued. 'And son, I have to warn you about women. The temptations of the flesh!'

'No trubs, Dad,' said Dave, 'I'll never go out with women. I'm going to keep myself nice for Mabel.'

Dad walked into the kitchen. 'No need to worry, Ma. The army won't take him. He's a bloody half-wit.'

Dave and Mabel received an invitation to the Snake Gully Fancy Dress Ball. They were wondering what they could wear when Dave remembered that he'd slaughtered a cow a couple of weeks earlier and had hung the skin over the fence to cure. So they decided they'd go as a cow, with Dave playing the front half and Mabel the back.

The ball was a great success and Dave and Mabel won the prize for the most original cossie. It was well after midnight when they took their leave and, as it was a fine moonlit night, they decided to take a short cut home across the paddock. Off they went, still dressed as a cow, with Dave in front and Mabel behind. Halfway across the paddock they were startled to hear a loud snorting and a stamping of hooves.

'Christ,' called out Mabel. 'It's the bull! What'll we do?'

'You better brace yourself, Mabel,' said Dave. 'I'm gonna start chewin' grass.'

In the good old days, before wool prices crashed, a cocky went to London to order another Rolls Royce. He went to see the dealers in Berkley Square and turned down the first two or three models. It seemed they just weren't good enough.

Finally, they unveiled the latest, greatest Rolls Royce priced at £250,000.

'Yeah, that'll do. But I want one of them press-button glass windows between the front and back seats.'

'Of course, sir,' said the salesman. 'But do you mind me asking you something? Sliding glass windows like that aren't very popular these days. They're regarded as old fashioned, even a bit elitist. And we didn't think Australians went in for that sort of thing.'

'Then none of you buggers have ever had the back of your neck licked by a sheep on the way to market.'

Two cobbers had been humping their blueys out back o' Bourke for months. One morning, through the heat haze, they see something big and black and very dead. As they approach they also realise that it's in an advanced stage of decomposition. A few hours later, trudging on in silence, one bloke says to the other, 'Did you see that dead ox?'

Come evening, when the campfire was blazing,

the other replied, 'That wasn't no ox, that was a 'orse.' Then he rolled himself up in the blanket and went to sleep.

Next morning the first bloke had decamped. He'd disappeared, leaving only a scrap of paper under a stone where his swag had been. On it he'd scribbled the following words: *There's too much bloody argument in this camp*.

The old bushie decided to visit the big smoke, but he had never travelled by train, so he didn't know what to do.

'Just go up to the ticket window,' his mates told him. 'They'll put you right.'

So the old bushie got a lift into town, found the railway station and joined the queue at the ticket window. The young woman in front gave some money to the booking clerk, saying, 'Alice Springs, single.'

When the bushie's turn came, he plonked a $50 note down and said, 'Mick O'Brien, married with two kids.'

'Tough? Where I come from, tough? Christ, the ground's so stony we have to blast the seed in with shotguns. And harvest it with search warrants.'

It's late at night in the middle of the bush. A bloke in an FJ hears a bang and feels the car swerve. Bugger it, a blow out. But it's okay, he's got a spare. But what he doesn't have is a jack. Bum, bum, bum.

Then, across the paddocks, he glimpses a light. Yes, it's from a farmhouse window. 'He'll be able to lend me a jack,' mutters the bloke, and sets off towards the farm.

He steps into some cow shit, tears his coat climbing through a barbed-wire fence, and has to kick at a couple of barking kelpies. And he's not sure what sort of welcome he's going to get. 'It's late. He's probably had a real bastard of a day. He's gone to bed early and is dead to the world. And I'm going to have to wake him up.'

As he got closer to the farmhouse he thought, 'He's now climbing out of bed. He's really cranky.'

When the farmer opened the door with a friendly smile, the bloke was already turning away. 'Get fucked, you miserable bastard. And stick your jack up your arse.'

A census official arrives in a small town in north Queensland. 'What's the population of the place?' he asks of the local undertaker.

'One thousand and sixteen.'

'Is it growing or declining?'

'Neither. It's always been one thousand and sixteen.'

'It can't always be the same. It's got to go up or down.'

'No,' said the undertaker, 'always one thousand and sixteen.'

'But aren't any babies ever born here?'

'Of course,' said the undertaker. 'Lots. And every time there's a baby, some young bloke has to leave town.'

A man lies dying of thirst in the middle of the Nullarbor when he sees a kangaroo approaching with a salesman on its back. The salesman dismounts and attempts to sell him a paisley tie. The man rasps, 'Christ, a bloke's dying of thirst and you want to sell him a bloody tie.'

The salesman remounts and goes bounding off on his kangaroo. The parched man drags himself along until he sees a restaurant shimmering in the distance. As he crawls closer he is delighted to see hoardings advertising all types of cold drinks. He crawls to the door. 'Please let me in to buy something to drink.'

'Sorry,' says the doorman. 'No one's admitted without a tie.'

A bloke was looking around the goldfields at Bendigo and found an open mineshaft that seemed to go down and down and down forever. He pulled a coin out of his pocket and dropped it down the hole. And though he listened very carefully he didn't hear it touch the bottom. So he threw a large rock that was lying close by. Once again, he didn't hear it hit the bottom.

He then spied a railway sleeper so he dragged it towards the hole and dropped it down. As he did this, a billy goat came thundering up behind him and threw itself down the hole. 'Shit!' he said. 'I wonder why the goat did that?'

Whereupon an old man appeared on the scene and said, 'Excuse me, have you seen a goat anywhere around here?'

And he said, 'Funny you should say that. A dirty great goat just came charging up behind me and threw itself down the mineshaft.'

'Oh,' said the old man, 'it couldn't have been my goat. I had it tethered to a railway sleeper.'

'Is that the train for Hay pulling out?' the young jackeroo yelled as he dashed to the barrier at Central Station.

'Either that,' said the guard, 'or the station's backing up.'

A couple of swaggies were making camp one night, under a coolibah tree near a billabong. While one rolled a smoke, the other went down to fill the billy. 'There's a chap down there,' he said on his return.

'Gettin' fish, is he?'

'Nope.'

'Gettin' rabbits then?'

'Nope.'

'What's he gettin'?'

'Drowned.'

An old swaggie was trapped on the wrong side of a flooded river and, after a few weeks, ran out of food. He tried to stuff a jumbuck in his tuckerbag but the ground was so slippery he couldn't catch one. So he had to kill his dog – a faithful pooch that had been his only companion for almost ten years. And after he'd eaten all the meat, he sat staring sadly into his campfire. And he noticed how the flames were lighting bits of the dog's skeleton. And he said, 'My old dog would have liked them bones.'

A rugged old bushwhacker in a pub is scoffing at tales of present-day hardship and telling how things were really tough in his day. He caps every story with,

'You blokes, you talk about 'ard times.' At last he comes to the time when he was out in the middle of the Gibson Desert, all his water gone and left with only a handful of flour which he could make into a damper if only he had water. So he squats, holding the flour in his cupped hands between his legs so that he can piss on it. But before he can piss, he farts and blows all the flour away. 'You blokes, you talk about 'ard times.'

A Tasmanian discovered a flock on the roadside outside Launceston and stopped for a chat with the drover. 'Where are you from?'

'Up Coonabarabran way,' drawled the drover.

'Christ, how did you get your flock across Bass Strait?'

'Aw, I didn't come *that* way.'

While driving around the backblocks, an English tourist ran over a rooster and killed it. Being an honest chap he stopped and knocked on the farm door. 'I'm afraid I've killed your cock, madam, but I'd very much like to replace him.'

'Whatever you want,' said the farmer's wife. 'Go around the side there and you'll find the hens in the back.'

A bloke knocked on the door of a farm and offered to do some fencing.

'How much fence do you reckon you can put up in a day?' asked the farmer.

'Aw, about a mile.'

'Not enough. I've got a local fella who puts up so much fence in one day that it takes him two days to walk back.'

A bloke was tramping through the wheatbelt during the Depression looking for work. He called into a farm and asked the cocky if he had any jobs. The farmer said, 'Done any ploughing?'

'On a small scale,' the bloke replied.

'Have you done any furrowing?'

'On a small scale,' the bloke said.

'What about sowing? Have you done any?'

'On a small scale,' came the reply.

The cocky was becoming jack of this and said, 'Listen, mate, is there anything you've done on a big scale?'

'Yeah, I fucked a pig on a weighbridge once.'

There was a country dance and the young jackeroo invited the farmer's wife to waltz. After a couple of circuits of the floor she whispered in his ear, 'Come outside.'

Feeling a bit scared, he declined. Only to feel her holding him tighter. 'Come outside,' she said again.

Finally, fearfully, he agreed. Outside it was pitch dark so he pulled the torch from his pocket. 'Did you have that torch in your pocket while we were waltzing?' said the farmer's wife. 'Yeah,' said the jackeroo.

'Well, let's go back to the dance.'

A farmhand from out the back o' Bourke rode into Sydney on his camel to live it up and spend his big pay cheque. He'd really tried one on this day, and had ridden across the Harbour Bridge and decided to have just one last drink in North Sydney before sleeping it off. When he staggered out of the pub, he couldn't find his camel where he'd left it, so weaved into the police station to report its theft.

Officer: 'Now, sir, that you've given us your name and address and reported the theft of your camel, we'll take down a few details and a description of your camel for our records please. Did the camel have one hump or two?'

Farmhand (after some consideration): 'Aw, I think it had one . . . no, two humps. Ah, Jeez . . . no, one. I'm a bit hazy about that.'

Officer (restraining his irritation): 'Well then, sir, could you please tell us the colour of the camel?'

'Aw, sort of black. No, more brownish-black. Then again, perhaps greyish-beige. Ah, Jeez, hard to describe the colour exactly, officer.'

'Well then, sir, what about its height – how many hands was it?'

'Oooh,' said the farmhand, lifting his arms and squinting his eyes in concentration, 'about up to here. Then again,' lowering his arms, 'more about this high. Bit hard to tell ya, officer.'

'Well then, sir, I suppose it'd be impossible for you to be able to tell us the sex of this camel?' the officer asked.

'No, no, officer. It's female.'

'Look, sir. How can you be so sure? You couldn't tell us how many humps your camel had, you couldn't tell us the colour it was or even give us a fair idea of how high it stood. How come you're so sure of its sex?'

'Oh, that's easy, officer,' said the farmhand proudly. 'As I rode over the bridge this mornin', I heard some blokes call out from a passing car, "Look at the silly cunt on that camel!".'

There was a single bloke who won the lottery and bought himself a huge property in the Northern

Territory. He'd just settled in and was relaxing one evening on his porch, sipping a cup of tea and watching the sun going down. He saw a speck of dust on the horizon, which grew and grew. It materialised into another bloke on horseback.

'G'day! Welcome to the district!' said the bloke on the horse.

'G'day!' said the new owner, 'and thanks.'

'There's a bit of a party at my place Saturday night. Wanna come?'

'What'll it be like?'

'Oh, you know. Plenty of grog, plenty of tucker, plenty of rootin' and plenty of fightin'.'

'Sounds all right. Will I need to dress up?'

'Nah. It's just the two of us.'

Four Sydneyites were lost out back o' Bourke. They'd been driving around for hours on dirt roads and not getting anywhere. They came to an old codger leaning on a gate. 'Excuse me,' said the driver of the car, 'which road can we take to get back to Sydney?'

The bloke said nothing in reply.

'Listen, mate,' said the driver, 'should we go straight ahead?'

'I dunno.'

'Well, should I go left?'

'Dunno.'

'Or right?'

'Dunno.'

'You don't know much, do you?' said the driver.

'No,' said the codger, 'but I'm not bloody lost.'

A young bloke from outback Queensland, who'd never been away from his small country town, found himself the holder of the winning ticket in a raffle, first prize being a return trip to London with lots of spending money.

Within days he found himself in London. He was in a wonderful room in an upstairs flat in Chelsea with the best-looking sheila he had ever seen. Things had gone exceedingly well for him. She was naked on a four-poster king-size bed waiting for him. He stripped.

To her amazement, he didn't come directly to her but began to throw the furniture out of the French doors onto the road below. When he'd finished, tens of thousands of pounds worth of fine antiques had vanished out the doors. He turned to her at last.

'What did you do that for?' she whimpered.

'Well, I've never fucked a woman before. But if it's anything like a kangaroo, I'm gonna need all the room I can get!'

Out near Uluru the flies were dreadful. A tourist spotted an old bloke there. 'How do you find the flies here, mate?'

'You don't have to,' he replied, 'they find you.'

'But don't you want to do something for them?'

'No, I let 'em fend for themselves.'

'But don't you shoo them?'

'No, I let 'em run round barefoot.'

'But I don't like all these flies here, mate.'

'Well, let us know the ones you do like and I'll hunt the rest.'

'But seriously, do you know the progeny of a single fly can number thousands?'

'Strewth,' said the old-timer, 'what would the progeny of a married one be?'

Things were crook in the bush and the farm, like the sheep, was on its last legs. One day a bloke knocked at the door and announced that he worked for an oil company and was seeking permission to sink an exploratory hole. Yes, there'd be a few bob in it, even if they didn't find anything.

The farmer agreed, and a huge rig was dragged in and drilling began. But after they'd past the 500 m mark without a trace of oil, the company gave up and moved out. Whereupon the farmer decided to use some of the money he'd made from the oil company to build himself a little dunny right over the 500 m shaft. Why waste a good hole?

A year later the farmer decided that he was sick of hard seasons and put the place up for sale. The first to inspect were a city couple with dreams of being hobby farmers. While the wife looked over the house, the husband asked if he could use the dunny. The farmer showed him to the new building and the city bloke stepped inside.

Time passed and he didn't return. Worried, the farmer and the wife pushed the door open and found the husband collapsed on the dunny seat. Very dead.

'Did your husband have a heart condition?'

'No, no,' sobbed the wife. 'He was very fit and healthy.'

'Did he do anything . . . odd, when he was on the loo?'

'Well, he did have this silly habit of holding his breath until he heard the splash.'

At a family farm way out in the bush a farmer was down behind the chook shed repairing some wire as night approached.

'Tea's ready, love,' called the wife from the back door. 'You'd better come in now!'

'Not yet,' came the distant reply.

An hour later she called out, 'You'll miss the news on the telly, love. You'd better come in now.'

'Not yet!'

Another hour passed. 'I'm going to bed! Now will you come in?'

'Not yet!'

The wife called into the darkness. 'It's dark, it's late, it's getting cold. Give me three good reasons why you won't come in.'

'I'll give you four. One, I'm not hungry. Two, I don't feel like watching the telly. Three, I'm not sleepy. And four, I can't get my foot out of this bloody dingo trap.'

An old cocky has lost his best cow. He checks the neighbours' paddocks, takes a trip into the local pound and alerts the local constabulary just in case it's been nicked.

Finally he asks the rector if he would make an announcement during the Sunday service. As is the outback custom, a wedding had been arranged in conjunction with the service so the cocky had to sit right up the back.

Being a bit deaf he finds it hard to hear what the rector is saying, and fails to realise that, in fact, he is uniting a Reg Dow and a Mary Jones in holy matrimony. At this point the cocky mumbles to himself, 'Ah, here it comes now,' the appeal for information about his red cow.

He waits politely until, at the end, the priest concludes, 'Therefore, if anyone knows any reason why these two persons should not be joined in matrimony, he should now declare it.' Whereupon the cocky sings out, 'Don't forget to tell 'em she's got one blind tit and all the hair scratched off her belly.'

In a shearing shed back o' Bourke a new arrival asked, 'What do you do for sex around here?'

'Well, on Friday nights we fuck the cook for $33.'

'Why so much?'

'Well, the cocky's manager doesn't approve, so we slip him 20 bucks and the cook doesn't like it. So we pay $2 each for four blokes to hold him down.'

After a long drought it had begun to rain. And it rained for days and days. The river had swollen, broken its banks, and the whole district was flooded.

Not to be outdone by the weather, a travelling salesman rowed a boat across to the homestead, where a farmer, his wife and children were sitting on the galvo roof.

'Pretty bad, eh?' called the salesman, clambering

up into the gutter. As he sat chatting he noticed a battered old Akubra moving round and round in circles on the floodwater.

'Do you see that?' asked the salesman.

'Oh, that,' said the farmer. 'That's Grandpa. Last week he said that come hell or high water, he was going to mow the lawn today.'

A female bureaucrat from the Department of Agriculture was addressing a meeting of farmers on the subject of animal pest control. 'It is no longer permissible to kill dingoes,' she said, 'but male dingoes can be legally trapped, castrated and released.'

An exasperated cattle farmer jumped to his feet and said, 'Will someone tell this bloody woman that the dingoes are eating my calves, not rooting them.'

A bloke who had a cattle stud in Queensland was telling a friend from the city that he could weigh bulls without using scales. 'It's easy. An ancient skill handed down in my family for generations. I tell their weight by just feeling their testicles.'

'Bull,' said the bloke from the city. 'I don't believe a word of it.'

So the farmer went over to one of his bulls, felt its balls and announced, 'Fifteen hundred kilos.'

They pulled the bull onto the scales and it was exactly 1500 kilos. 'Christ, that's amazing! Can anybody else do it?'

'Well, as a matter of fact, the wife can. She's better at it than me.'

'Okay, here's a hundred bucks that says she can't find me a 2000 kilo bull just by feeling its balls.'

Whereupon the farmer told his son to fetch Mum.

He came back without her. 'Sorry, Dad, Mum's busy.'

'Busy? What's more important than winning $100?'

'I dunno,' said the boy, 'but I think she's weighing the milkman.'

A young jackeroo picked up the new governess from the railway station. Driving her back to the property they passed a bull fucking a cow. 'How do they know when it's the right time to do that?' inquired the governor.

'Sense of smell,' said the jackeroo.

Then they saw a stallion mounting a mare and a ram attending a flock of ewes.

'How do they know when it's the right time to do that?'

'Sense of smell.'

When they reached the homestead the jackeroo unloaded the young woman's luggage from the horse and cart and plonked it on the verandah. 'See you around,' he said.

'Yes,' said the governess, 'come over when your cold gets better.'

There was an agricultural show in a country town and the spruikers were going hammer and tong. The Jimmy Sharman Boxing Troupe was the big drawcard and all the young blokes were listening to Sharman bellowing through his megaphone. 'Who's gonna have a go? No, not with one of the boxers. We've got matches for all of them. I want someone to wrestle my wrestler. The Masked Monster from Murrurundi. Is anyone game to wrestle the Masked Monster?'

No takers. No surprise – the Masked Monster was built like a brick dunny.

'How about you, young fella?' Sharman said to a young stockman. 'Five bucks if you have a go, and ten bucks if you win.'

'I don't know nuthin' about no wrestlin',' said the kid. 'Only wrestlin' I've done is throwin' the big poddies at brandin' time.' But after much urging he agreed to take on the Masked Monster from Murrurundi.

'You'd better take your belt off,' said Sharman, pointing to a belt with a knife pouch.

'Nah. If I take me belt off, me daks'll fall down.'

'Okay then. Leave it on,' said Sharman.

And the two of them began wrestling, sending up a huge cloud of dust. Suddenly there was an agonised scream and the stockman emerged from the cloud. He looked at his watch. 'Not bad,' he muttered. 'Threw him, earmarked him and castrated him in eight seconds.'

A Collins Street cocky bought a farm in the Western District, just down the road from Malcolm Fraser's Nareen. He paid through the nose for it, mainly because of the really great tree growing by the homestead. A huge old gum said to be around 500 years old. He was really proud of the tree and showed photographs of it to all his mates in Melbourne. He even got Arthur Boyd to do a painting of it.

But his mates refused to believe the tree was 500 years old. So he phoned the farm manager to get more details. He said he'd find out what he could.

A couple of days later he called his boss. 'That tree by the homestead, it's exactly 553 years old.'

'Five hundred and fifty-three,' said the grazier proudly. 'And how can you be so sure?'

'No probs,' said the manager. 'We just chainsawed the bastard down and counted the rings.'

It was on the black soil plains of Queensland during the wet. The cocky was riding his horse very, very carefully through the mud when he spotted a familiar Akubra. Reaching out with his stock whip he lifted it up. And there, beneath it, was his bullocky, up to his ears in mate.

'Christ,' said the cocky, 'you're really in it.'

'I'm okay,' said the bullocky, 'but the team's in pretty deep.'

The squatter hired a new hand and sent him out to the back paddock to dig 20 post holes. At the end of the day he drove out in the four-wheel drive to inspect the work and found the hand lying under a tree smoking a cigarette.

'Hey, I told you to dig 20 holes and there are only 18.'

'Well, boss,' said the new hand, taking another drag on the fag, 'I dug 20. Some bastard must have pinched a couple.'

Two young blokes are backpacking their way around outback Queensland and get caught in the floods. So they ask for help at a nearby cattle station. The owner, a widowed lady, welcomes them as if they are her own sons and gives them a good, hearty meal. But she thinks it's inappropriate that they sleep in the house. The hay barn, however, will be perfectly comfortable.

The pair leave the next day and, after having traipsed around much of Australia, separate.

Years later, meeting in Brisbane, they go off to a local pub and start reminiscing.

'Remember the floods, and the hay barn?'

'Of course I do.'

'We always used to be truthful to each other, didn't we?'

'I hope we still are.'

'Okay, when I was asleep, did you creep in and kip down with the widow?'

'Yeah, I did.'

'And did you give her my name and address instead of yours?'

'Yeah, I did. Sorry, mate.'

'Don't be. Two years back she died and left me the whole 100 000 acres.'

A couple of boundary riders from the north-west came down to Perth. After years of hard yakka they felt like a bit of fun. But after a couple of weeks of boozing, their money ran out. So they applied for jobs with a local council where they were told to see the foreman in his office at the works yard.

The first boundary rider went into the office to be interviewed. The foreman said, 'If I was to poke you in the eye with my finger, what would you be?'

He replied, 'Half blind.'

'And if I was to poke you in both eyes?'

'Totally blind.'

'Fine. You can start on Monday. And when you go out, send your mate in.'

Outside, the boundary rider said to his mate, 'Look, you only get asked two questions. The answers are easy. Half blind, and totally blind.'

Feeling confident, the second boundary rider sat opposite the foreman. 'If I cut your left ear off, what would you be?'

'Half blind,' said the boundary rider with a broad grin.

The foreman looked at him incredulously. 'And if I cut both your ears off?'

'Totally blind.'

'How the hell do you make that out?'

'Well, me hat would fall over me eyes.'

A young bloke had been working on a sheep station for a few months when he felt an insistent stirring in the loins. So he spoke to an old hand. 'What's a fella do if he wants a fuck around here?'

The old hand told him where to find the prettiest wethers. But the young bloke didn't think much of that.

A few months later, however, he changed his mind. But he couldn't get the sheep to cooperate. So he went back to the old bloke, who was well into his seventies, for help.

The old bloke grabbed the best-looking ewe and, despite his age, undid his fly buttons and got stuck into it.

The young bloke was very impressed and couldn't wait for his turn. But he had a question. 'Before you started rooting the wether, you looked all around the place. Why?'

'Well,' said the old bloke, 'I've been keeping company with an emu.'

At Nar Nar Goon, they grow very, very big pumpkins. So big that they carve them out and use them for weekenders. One bloke was hacking away at a giant pumpkin when he dropped his axe down the hole. So he threw down a knotted rope and began, very carefully, to lower himself down into the gloom. After a while his eyes adjusted to the darkness and he saw a faint light. It turned out to be an old-timer holding a hurricane lamp. 'Have you seen my axe?' he asked.

'No,' said the codger. 'Have you seen a team of horses?'

'The drought up here is so bad that the council's had to close two lanes of the swimming pool.'

The drought seemed to be getting worse and worse. There was no feed on the properties and bugger all on the long paddock.

The drought got worse. A sympathetic tourist asked a farmer, 'Do you think it'll rain?'

'Hope so,' said the farmer, peering sadly at the sky. 'Not so much for my own sake as for the boys'. I've seen it rain.'

How do you get rid of a boomerang?

Throw it down a one-way street.

Why do they bury cockies only three feet deep?

So that they can still put their hands out.

A couple of battlers from the bush, who'd been through everything together, finally won millions in the lottery. They celebrated with a beer in the local pub and agreed that a few million dollars wouldn't change things. Except for the flash cars they'd always wanted.

Leaving the pub somewhat unsteadily, they went straight to a showroom where they astonished the salesman by buying two Rolls Royces. One each.

One codger produced his cheque book and reached for his pen. The other said, 'No, no, mate. Fair go. You paid for the beers.'

A yuppie parks his Porsche outside a country pub and wanders in for a beer. A local farmer is sitting at the bar and the yuppie inquires after his health.

'Not . . . too . . . bad,' comes the slow, measured response.

'You from around here?' asks the yuppie.

'Yeah . . . got a place . . . down the . . . road a bit.'

'Excuse me saying this,' said the yuppie, 'but you speak very, very slowly.'

'Do yer . . . reckon? Around . . . here . . . I'm . . . regarded . . . as a . . . bit of a . . . sparkling . . . conversationalist. My brother . . . Arthur . . . speaks . . . really . . . slowly. And . . . my sister . . . speaks . . .

slower . . . than him. So when . . . a bloke . . . put the . . . hard . . . word . . . on her . . . and . . . before she could . . . say she . . . wasn't . . . that kind . . . of a . . . girl . . . she bloody-well . . . was.'

The barman at the bush pub was one of the toughest guys you've ever seen; muscles, tattoos, unshaven, sweaty and pulling beers in a black singlet. The shearer couldn't take his eyes off him. 'What the hell d'yer think yer staring at?' said the barman eventually.

'I just can't get over the likeness. It's a truly remarkable resemblance,' said the shearer. 'You're a dead-ringer for my wife. In fact, if it wasn't for the moustache . . .'

'I haven't got a moustache,' interrupted the barman.

'No, but my wife has!'

A pommy tourist arrives in Australia, hires a car and drives into the outback. He looks out the window and is deeply shocked to see a bloke bonking a kangaroo.

Hoping to steady his nerves, he stops at the next pub and orders a Pimms. No sooner has he raised it to his lips than he notices a one-legged bloke masturbating at the other end of the bar.

He turns to the barman. 'What's the matter with you people? Are all you Australians depraved? I've been here a few hours and I've already seen one guy having intercourse with a kangaroo and another masturbating in public.'

'Fair go, mate,' says the barman, 'you can't expect a bloke with one leg to catch a kangaroo!'

An intrepid Englishman, a teacher by profession, booked himself a cycling holiday in outback Queensland during the big wet. It was 90 degree heat and 100 per cent humidity. Inevitably he became lost; his maps were all soggy; he had to push his bike along dirt roads with the wheels up to the rims in mud. Despite his pith helmet and stiff upper lip, he was soaked to the skin and unhappy. Being hot, he was thirsty; not sweating, he needed to relieve his bladder; being a self-perceived English gentleman, he was averse to going behind or even in front of the nearest tree.

He was feeling exhausted and anxious when, through the teeming rain, he saw a fingerpost. When he came to it, he removed his glasses, carefully wiped them on his damp handkerchief, replaced them, and, before they were misted, managed to read the sign – TIP. Believing it to be some form of civilisation, he followed the road, and to his relief came upon a country hotel.

After hitching his bike to the horse-rail, he staggered through the door marked BAR. It was a stark room with a wooden floor and a few dilapidated tables, at one of which sat four men in heavy-duty clothes. Each was wearing a bush hat with corks suspended from the brim. They were drinking from straight ten-ounce glasses. Dripping his way to the bar, he asked the barman, who stared at him rather suspiciously, for a beer. As it was served he whispered, 'Do you have a loo?'

The barman stared even more intently, but made no response.

'The loo? The John? The toilet? Oh, for God's sake, the lavatory – please?'

The barman pointed silently to a dark door at the far end of the room. Thankful, our hero nursed his bladder to the door and opened it to the pouring rain and a paddock. There, on the left, was a pile of shit about 40 foot high, dripping and leaning thixotropically. On the right was another pile, this one only ten foot high, also dripping but looking much more stable.

'Thank God someone had the sense to start a new pile,' he muttered, as he braved the rain to the smaller pile.

He was in the middle of relieving himself when

he was stopped mid-stream by a bullet thudding into the pile next to his ear. Desperately trying to get back into his trousers and turn at the same time, he saw one of the corked-hatted men standing in the doorway with a smoking .22 in his hand. The man removed his cigarette from his mouth and said, 'Get outta the Ladies', yer pommie bastard!'

An Australian was on the piss in Earl's Court where, despite his crude behaviour, he found himself being eyed warmly by the barmaid. She confessed that she was partial to Aussies and invited him back to her flat. It turned out to be about 20 flights up a narrow, rickety staircase. First she gave him a few extra beers – she had some cans of Fosters in the fridge – then heated him a meat pie in the oven and doused it in Rosella tomato sauce. Finally she said there were other indoor pastimes they could enjoy. Would he like to come into the next room? The Aussie clambered enthusiastically to his feet. 'Christ, how did you get a pool table up here?'

The scene is a urinal at the back of a pub. An Aussie and a pom enter for a pee. The Aussie finishes and heads straight back for the bar. The pom finishes, washes his hands and, as he re-enters the bar, complains in a loud voice, 'Don't they teach you colonials to wash your hands?'

To which the Aussie replies, 'Nah, mate, they teach us not to piss on them.'

A bus full of tourists arrived in Kakadu. Everyone piled off, except for one old bloke. 'Don't you want to see the Aboriginal carving?'

'No thanks,' he said. 'I've lived on a farm all my life and I've seen plenty of cows calving. So I don't suppose it'd be much different.'

Grab Bag

Phonetic Dictionary

Ad Hoc:	Cooking with wine
Adder:	Tally clerk
Adenoid:	Irritated by adverts
Alimony:	Arab coins
Alpaca:	Kerry's brother
Anemone:	Foe
Antelope:	Absconding insect
Aphrodisiac:	Trapeze artists from Zaire
Arable:	Islamic
Armada:	Which art in heaven
Badinage:	Memory, six, teeth
Barbecue:	Awaiting haircut
Blackguard:	Negro sentry
Bulletin:	Loaded
Canteloupe:	Chaperoned
Capsize:	Seven and three-quarters

Carrion:	Continue
Castanet:	Go fishing
Castrate:	Theatre review
Chinchilla:	Aftershave
Condescending:	Greek Paratrooper
Copulate:	Tardy policeman
Counter-culture:	Retailing
Curlicue:	Friendly dog
Cyclamate:	Tandem
Divest:	Princess's garment
Dragster:	Transvestite
Emulate:	Dead bird
Equilibrium:	Sedative for horses
Equivocal:	Duet
Farthing:	Distant object
Felonious:	Monk
Flatulent:	Borrowed apartment
Fodder:	Male parent
Foolhardy:	Stan Laurel
Forensic:	Ill migrants
Foreplay:	Bridge
Foresight:	Saga
Forfeit:	Quadruped
Frigate!:	Angry exclamation
Frontispiece:	Penis
Gangplank:	Political platform
Gangrene:	IRA hitsquad
Grateful:	Enough firewood
Gunwale:	Harpoon

Handicap:	Useful hat
Homophone:	Gay hotline
Huguenot:	Large tangle
Ideal:	You shuffle
Infantry:	Seedling
Injury:	Empanelled
Innuendo:	Italian suppository
Inquire:	Member of chorus
Intercourse:	Sorbet
Internee:	Cartilage
Jargon:	Lost container
Jaywalker:	Whisky
Juniper:	Hebrew child
Lactose:	Ungulate
Lieutenant:	Vacant apartment
Littoral:	Precise
Lobotomy:	Sagging arse
Macabre:	Scottish tree
Malefactor:	Sperm
Manifold:	Origami
Masturbator:	Accomplished fisherman
Matelot:	Promiscuous
Moorish:	Habit-forming
Musket:	Sweet wine
Napkin:	Short sleep
Nobility:	Thirsty swagman
Nomad:	Sane
Notice:	Melted
Opine:	Irish tree

Palindrome:	Friend at airport
Palliasse:	Friendly donkey
Paradox:	Two hounds
Pasturage:	Older
Picnicker:	Select underwear
Pique:	Mountain top
Polygon:	Dead parrot
Propaganda:	True goose
Racketeer:	Tennis player
Ramparts:	Sheep's balls
Ruminant:	Hungry insect
Rumour:	Boarder
Sari:	So am I, very!
Scatology:	Jazz speak
Scintillate:	Nocturnal orgy
Semen:	Sailors
Signet:	Young swan
Silicon:	Dumb trick
Slapstick:	Teacher's cane
Sorghum:	Pyorrhea
Support:	Imbibe fortified wine
Surcingle:	Unmarried baronet
Sycamore:	Chronically ill
Syntax:	Fred Nile's ambition
Tartar:	Goodbye
Thinking:	Slender monarch
Truculent:	Borrowed lorry
Undertake:	Bury
Vicarious:	Clergyman's debts

Wedlock: Chastity belt
Yataghan: Once more

A bloke arrives at Australia Square and asks where he can find Harry Siedler's office.

'Top floor. But the lift's on the blink, so you'll have to use the stairs.'

Just as the bloke was beginning his long trudge, the guard calls out. 'And if you see the gorilla on the way up, for Christ's sake don't touch him!'

The gorilla? the bloke thought to himself. Don't touch the gorilla?

Up and up he climbs. Up and up and up. And somewhere near the 39th floor he finds himself confronted by a dirty great gorilla – with its back to him.

Despite the warning of the guard, he can't resist reaching out and touching the gorilla on the shoulder.

The gigantic creature spins around, the bloke screams and starts running downstairs, with the gorilla close behind him. Down the stairs they go – down, down, down. In and out of doors, along corridors. Finally the bloke can't go on. He collapses on the floor, sobbing helplessly. And the gorilla looms over him, touches him on the shoulder and says, 'You're it!'

There was a horse sale in Scone. They'd knocked down a few yearlings from Segenhoe and a few polo ponies from Kerry Packer's place at Ellerston. They rounded the auction off with a few cheap horses for cattle work and, finally, there was only one left. A broken-down hack that nobody wanted. Whereupon a timid-looking bloke in a suit – he might have been a local accountant – bid $100. And the horse was knocked down to him. He then asked for help to get the horse home. So one of the kids who'd been helping at the sale loaded the horse on to a float and took it through the town to a neat, fussy little house on the outskirts. But there was no paddock. No stable. Not even a big garden.

'Just do what I ask,' said the little bloke, 'and I'll give you $50.'

'Okay, mate.'

'In here,' said the little bloke, opening the front door.

With considerable difficulty, the kid got the horse into the hall.

'Now, up there,' said the little bloke, pointing to a flight of stairs.

Finally they got the horse upstairs.

'In here.'

'The bathroom?'

'Yes, stand him in the bath.'

This took considerable time. At last the horse was standing in the bath.

'Now shoot him.'

'Shoot him?'

'Fifty dollars. Shoot him.'

Later, downstairs, the bloke gave the kid the $50.

'Look here, Mister. Before I leave, what's going on?'

'Well, my brother is coming to stay. He's a know-all. Every time I open my mouth he butts in and says, "I know, I know". He always knows. And I'm determined to get my own back. After dinner he'll go up to the bathroom for a piss. Then he'll come down shouting, "There's a dead horse in your bath!" And I'll say, "I know, I know".'

A sailor, an ostrich and a cat walked into a pub. They climbed on to one, two, three bar stools. The ostrich shouted a round. The sailor shouted a round. But the cat simply looked the other way when it was his shout.

'Why doesn't the cat buy a round?' asked the barman.

'It's a long, sad story,' said the sailor. 'I was alone on a desert island when a bottle came bobbing through the surf. When I opened it, a genie appeared and he granted me one wish. And all I asked for was a long-legged bird with a tight pussy.'

A fellow walked into a shoe shop one day wanting to buy a pair of shoes. A lady served him and asked what size he was.

'Size five', was the reply.

'Oh!' said the lady. 'You look like a size ten to me.' But the customer insisted on a size five. So the lady got them and the guy tried to squeeze into them without much luck, so he asked for a shoe horn and after another 15 minutes, finally got them on and said, 'No, too big. I'll take a size four.'

So the lady came back with a size four, and the guy tried for 20 minutes with no luck. He asked for a crowbar and after another 15 minutes finally got them on and said thanks, then paid for them and walked out in obvious pain.

Two weeks later the shop lady saw this guy walking down the street. He was almost doubled over in pain, and as he shuffled his feet you could see the agony on his face. She stopped him and asked why he insisted on wearing these shoes.

'Well,' he said, 'last month my mother and father died in a tragic accident. A week after that I had the winning numbers in the lottery but forgot to register them. Then my wife ran off with another man, and my daughter announced she's pregnant and her brother is the father. The taxman is hassling me, a weird religious sect has moved in next door and the council has just put my rates up. The only joy I get in life these days is when I go home and take these bloody shoes off!!!'

A young bloke applies for a job in a menswear shop in a country town.

'Listen, son,' said the manager, 'we've had a drought here for the last ten years and the local abattoir's closed down. So times are tough. I could only afford to hire you if you're a really, really good salesman.'

'Ooh, but I am, I am!'

'Okay, I'll give you a go. I'm going out to lunch and by the time I get back I want you to have sold these pink hotpants. They're identical to the ones that that Don Dunstan bloke wore to Parliament in the early '70s and I've never been able to sell them. You flog those and you're hired.'

When the owner returned from lunch he found that the pink hotpants had, in fact, disappeared from stock. But the young salesman was in bad shape, his trousers ripped and his face was covered in scratches.

'What happened?'

'Well, I sold the hotpants. The bloke was really pleased with them. But his seeing-eye dog gave me buggery.'

Little Red Riding Hood was skipping through the forest on her way to Grandma's house when out jumped the Big Bad Wolf.

'I'm going to eat you all up,' he snarled.

'What's the matter?' said Little Red Riding Hood. 'Doesn't anybody fuck any more?'

A bloke started talking to Captain Hook in a bar and said, 'Gee, you've been in the wars. What happened to your leg?'

'Well,' said Captain Hook, 'I got into this battle, see, with Peter Pan, and the cannon goes off and the ball cuts my leg clean off. And I had to get this wooden one put on.'

'How about the hook? What happened to your hand?'

'Well, see, I got into this fight with Peter Pan, this big sword fight and – *swish!* – the blade takes off my whole hand and I had to have this hook put on.'

'And the patch on your eye? What happened there?'

'Well, I'm out on the boat and I look up to the sky and this seagull craps right into it. Lost the whole eye.'

'Hang on,' said the bloke, 'you can't lose an eye because a seagull craps in it.'

'You can,' says Captain Hook, 'if you've only had your hook for one day!'

Once upon a time, there was a very handsome young prince, and he was as good and kind as he was handsome. One day when he was out hunting unicorns, he came across a very old lady sitting crying on the banks of a creek, as if her heart would break. Getting off his charger, he asked her what ailed her. She said she had to cross the creek to get back home. There was too much water in the creek; it was very cold and muddy, and she couldn't find a bridge. He told her to dry her tears and he would carry her across. This would be very difficult, given that she weighed a great deal and smelt something awful.

On putting her gently down on the other side, the old woman suddenly turned into a fairy godmother (not a princess). She told him that she had heard how good looking he was, and that this was exceeded by his great care and kindness for others. She would now grant him anything he wished.

Looking at his magnificent stallion, the prince said he would like to have the genitals of his horse. She said his wish was granted, and vanished into thin air.

Back at the court the prince had a wonderful time, besieged by all the ladies. News of this reached the king's ear, so he decided to go in search of the fairy godmother. Next day he was out hunting and came across the old woman sitting on the banks of the creek. He again carried her across the creek and once again she changed into a fairy godmother. She told the king that she would grant him anything he wanted. Excitedly the king asked for the genitals of his horse, and she told him his wish was granted. However, the king had been riding a mare that day. So, of course, the king and the prince lived happily ever after!

A UFO lands in the Rundle Mall just as a garbage truck comes along. Spotting the UFO, the driver tries to do a wheelie and one of the bins falls off and rolls across to where the extraterrestrial is standing. It doesn't hesitate for a second. The extraterrestrial picks up the bin and runs after the speeding truck.

'Madam! Madam!' he calls. 'You've dropped your handbag!'

Having waddled to the bus stop in a very tight mini skirt, the young woman was finding it hard to board the high step. She reached round, loosened the zip but still couldn't get her leg up. So she reached behind and unzipped it a little further. But she still couldn't quite make it.

Whereupon she was suddenly lifted onto the bus by a pair of hands on her bum. She turned around, determined to slap the bloke's face. 'How dare you!'

'I thought you wouldn't mind,' he said, 'not after you opened my fly twice.'

A battered Volkswagen was stopped at the traffic lights. A luxurious stretch limo slowed to a halt beside it. The bloke in the VW opened his window and banged on the window of the limo. The chauffeur touched a button and the window slid silkily down.

'Got a TV in there?' asked the bloke in the VW.

'Of course,' said the limo driver, 'and a phone and a fax, a cocktail cabinet, and a CD player.'

'Yeah,' said the VW driver, 'I've got all them too. Have you got a spa, but?'

'No,' said the limo driver.

'Well, I've got a spa in here,' said the bloke in the VW.

The lights changed and the limo driver roared off, leaving the VW floundering.

Next day the limo driver went to Stretch Limos Pty Ltd and had a spa fitted. Not just a spa, but a double spa.

A few weeks later he saw the VW again, parked by the side of the road. The chauffeur pulled up, got out and approached the old car. Its windows were all steamed up, so he had to bang on the roof to attract attention.

The window of the VW came down an inch or so, rather shakily.

'It's me,' said the chauffeur. 'I just wanted you to know that I've got a spa in my limo. A double spa.'

The bloke in the VW looked really angry. 'Shit!' he snarled. 'You got me out of the shower just to tell me that?'

Mr and Mrs Merchant Banker returned to their mansion to find that they'd been robbed – in a big, very systematic way. Obviously the naughties had backed a removal truck into the driveway leading to the triple garage and loaded up the lot. The Bang and Olufsen tellies and hi-fi sets had gone, the Brett Whiteleys, the microwave oven, the Miele appliances and the Braun rechargeable razor. They'd taken the leather lounge suite, the Armani clothes, the antique Persian rugs and the autographed photo of the Merchant Banker with President Reagan. The only thing left was, astonishingly, the very, very expensive Nikon camera and a couple of toothbrushes.

Not to worry. Everything was insured. And the couple joked about the kindness of the robbers in at least leaving them their toothbrushes. Oh, and the Nikon.

A few weeks later they completed the roll in the

camera and sent it off for processing. It came back showing a couple of blokes in balaclavas bending over with toothbrushes shoved up their arses – the toothbrushes Mr and Mrs Merchant Banker had been using ever since the robbery.

It was the Melbourne Motor Show at the Exhibition Buildings and one of the centrepieces was a gleaming Rolls Royce. Beside it stood a salesman, wearing a white tie, a dinner jacket and striped trousers.

A little old lady toddled up to him and said in a tiny voice, 'Please, sir, could you tell me where the loo is?'

Whereupon the salesman took the old lady by the arm, walked her to the loo, put a coin in the slot for her and then used his silk handkerchief to wipe her backside.

'Oh,' she said, 'thank you so much. You've been so kind.'

'Not at all,' said the salesman. 'Yours was the only genuine inquiry I've had all day.'

A laconic cow cocky was sitting over a beer listening to his mate who had just returned from working in the outback.

'. . . then I rolled the car bloody miles from nowhere. When I came to, I was trapped, couldn't move. Do you know that I was stuck in there for two days! Not a truck, not a car, nothin' came along that bloody road.'

'Yeah,' the cocky drawled, 'I'd believe that.'

'And then, blow me down, but two cars came along within five minutes!'

'Oh yeah?'

'Yeah, was I bloody glad to see them – the Johnstons and the Balls.'

'Yeah?'

'Yeah.'

The cow cocky thought for a moment. 'Hope you were dragged out by the Johnstons.'

Some years ago this old Tumbarumba drover gets a telegram to say his daughter in Wagga Wagga has just given birth to his first grandson. He decided he must pay her a visit, so gets out his old pushbike and sets off. The bike hasn't been used in years and the front wheel squeaks with each revolution. 'Only one thing to fix that,' he says to himself. 'Gotta get meself some goanna oil.'

So he props his bike against a gumtree, ambles off into the bush and comes back ten minutes later dragging a four-foot goanna by the tail, which he cuts off. And, with a motion similar to wringing out a wet towel, squeezes the oil out of the goanna's tail into the hub of his front wheel.

Back in the saddle, the bike fairly takes off down the slight slope. What a difference! But now the slope gets steeper and the bike really rockets, with the old feller hanging on for his life. They come to a bend halfway down the hill, he loses control, leaves the road and wakes up in Wagga Hospital with a fractured pelvis, two dislocated shoulders and three broken ribs. Upon his release three weeks later, having seen his daughter and grandson, he begins the long walk back in search of his bike.

When he reaches the spot, he can't see the bike anywhere . . . until he pushes back the brim of his Akubra to scratch his head. He looks up and there, way up in the tree, hanging from a branch, is the old bike. And would you believe it – that flamin' front wheel's still going around!

The Ku Klux Klan guy drives into a service station in Kalgoorlie and orders $20 worth of petrol. The attendant says, 'Shall I check under the hood?'

The travelling salesman's car broke down and he stumbled over a paddock to the farmhouse. He explained his predicament and asked if he could stay the night. 'Of course,' said the farmer, 'but I must warn you that I don't have daughters. I'm a bachelor and you'll have to share my bed.'

'Bugger it,' said the salesman, 'I'm in the wrong joke.'

Did you hear what happened when the fuses blew at the contortionists' club?

It was so dark you couldn't see your bum in front of your face.

What's the difference between an angry audience and a mad cow?

One boos madly and the other moos badly.

Knock, knock.

Who's there?

Ken.

Ken who?

Ken I come in?

Knock, knock.
Who's there?
A little old lady.
A little old lady who?
I didn't know you could yodel.

Knock, knock.
Who's there?
Ammonia.
Ammonia who?
Ammonia a little boy who can't reach the doorbell.

What has four wheels, five doors and hangs around French cathedrals?

The hatch-back of Notre Dame.

An amateur archaeologist rings up the National Museum and tells them that he's unearthed a 4000-year-old mummy that died of a heart attack.

Whilst impressed with the find, the museum people doubted that the mummy had had a coronary. But they decided to conduct a post mortem.

'You were absolutely right,' they reported to the archaeologist. 'The mummy did die of a heart attack. But how did you know when you hadn't unwrapped the bandages?'

'Well, when I dug him up he was holding a bit of papyrus in his hand. And when I deciphered the hieroglyphs it said, "Ten thousand shekels on Goliath".'

The Accident Appreciation Squad was grilling a young woman who'd been involved in a collision. 'What gear were you in?'

'What gear? This simple, black chiffon number from Sportsgirl.'

A judge in petty sessions was having trouble with the witness's name. 'You say your name is Peach?' he said. 'Well, how do you spell it?'

'P-i-e-t-z-c-h-e, your Worship,' replied the man.

'Tell me then,' said the judge. 'How would you spell "apricot"?'

Fetherstonhaugh, the young subaltern posted to a dangerous area of India, asks the experienced colonel for his chosen safety priorities. Says the colonel,

'Watch out for the dreaded wishband snake . . . protect your men at all costs. When you see its long, banded body slithering through the undergrowth, go fearlessly forward, run your hand quickly up from the tail area, and *snap*! Break its neck.'

A month later the colonel visits the outpost and calls on Fetherstonhaugh. The subaltern is in a sickbed, swathed from head to toe in bandages. 'My God! What happened?' asks the colonel.

'Sir,' chokes out Fetherstonhaugh, 'Do you recall telling me to beware of the dreaded wishband snake?'

'Yes,' replies the colonel.

'And advising me to tackle it by running my hand quickly up its long, banded body?'

'Of course, my boy.'

'Sir, have you ever shoved your thumb up a tiger's bum?'

A bloke was sitting in front of Young & Jackson's, his head in bandages and crutches on his lap. One arm was in a sling and the other held his hat.

'You poor fellow,' said a matron, dropping a few coins in the hat. 'But things could be worse. After all, you could be blind.'

'That's right, lady. When I was blind I kept getting foreign coins.'

Vietnam. A wounded GI arrives in an Australian field hospital. He looks up at the Aussie nurse and faintly inquires, 'Did I come here to die?'

'No, love, yer came here yesterdie,' she said reassuringly.

A flash bloke from the coast drove his Mercedes sports out to a little mud pub at Bedourie. He then started boring the locals with facts – zero to 100 in five seconds, a top speed of 300 km/h, worth $300 000.

'Well, mate, we've got a bloke here who can top that.'

Bets are placed. 'Call Jim,' they shout, and the race is on. Flash Jack is off like the clappers – first gear, second gear – when he hears a thumping on his car door.

'Oi, can't you go any faster?' shouts Jim.

'Of course I bloody well can.' And the Merc tears away.

Third gear, through fourth to fifth and the Merc hits 300 km/h. Suddenly he hears a hell of a thump on the car door and Jim, like bloody Superman, screams past – off into the blooming scrub, smashing small trees en route.

That sundown, Jim, ripped to bits, his T-shirt gone, ears, nose and lips split, hobbles quietly into the mud pub at Bedourie. 'Good on ya, mate,' the blokes in the bar chorus. 'But you're a bit scratched, eh, cobber?'

'Strike me fuckin' dead. How would you feel if you got a blow-out in your left sandshoe doing 350 kilometres?'

'I'm telling you, mate, that Murray cod I caught last week was six foot long.'

'Well, where is it then?'

'Oh, it broke the line and got away.'

'Well, I fished that same stretch of river last week and was casting near where that old paddle-steamer sank. And I hooked the old lantern. And when I pulled it up, it was still burning.'

'Fair go. You don't expect a bloke to believe that.'

'Well, chop three feet off your Murray cod and I'll blow out the candle.'

An old codger with a bald head and a wooden leg wanted to go to the fancy-dress party at the twilight home but was too mean to spend much on a costume. He went to a couple of fancy-dress shops but wouldn't pay the $20 for even the cheapest costume. There was, finally, only one shop.

'I haven't got much money,' he told the manager. 'What have you got for $5?'

The manager looked at the old codger, focused on his bald head then had a decco at his wooden leg. Finally he reached under the counter and produced a tin of treacle. 'That'll be five bucks.'

'That's not a fancy-dress outfit,' protested the codger. 'That's just a cheap tin of treacle.'

'Look, it's the best I can do for five bucks. Pour the treacle over your bald head, stick your wooden leg up your arse and go as a toffee apple.'

An old farmer turned 90. The local cops sent him a letter saying that he'd have to hand in his driver's licence. That is, unless he could pass a short written test and a medical, as well as demonstrate his driving skill to the local sergeant.

Well, he passed the medical with flying colours and got all the answers right in the written test. So he started driving the sergeant around the town in his Land Cruiser. And to the sergeant's surprise, he did very well indeed. Outside the station the sergeant said, 'Oh, by the way, can you make a U-turn?' The farmer sat quietly for a moment and then, with a sly, sidelong glance at the copper said, 'Nah, but I can sure make their eyes water!'

An old loony went to the post office to send a telegram. The postmaster read out the telegram as he counted up the words. It was 'Foozle, foozle, foozle, foozle, foozle, foozle'.

'Do you really want to send this?' he asked the loony. 'It doesn't make sense.'

'Yes,' said the loony, 'that's what I want to send.'

'Oh well,' answered the postmaster, entering into the spirit of the thing, 'but for the same money you could put in three more foozles.'

'No,' said the loony firmly, 'that would be silly!'

A drunk climbed on board the number 48 tram and spoke to the bloke sitting opposite. 'Hey, what's your name then?'

'Paul,' said the man, intensely embarrassed by becoming the focus of attention of the other passengers.

The drunk was silent for a few moments, then asked, 'Say, did those Thessalonians ever write back to you?'

Reality is for people who can't handle computers.

Too many cooks make the phone book heavy.

Two missionaries in Papua New Guinea were captured by a group of tribesmen wearing lots of bird of paradise feathers and those interesting little cone things on their dicks.

They were tied to a tree and were approached by the chief who spoke pretty good English. 'You have two choices. You can either choose death or oogabooga.'

The first missionary decided that death didn't sound too good so he'd take a punt on oogabooga.

On hearing this, the tribesmen became very excited and yelled 'oogabooga, oogabooga' a lot. Then they took the cone devices off their dicks and pack-raped the missionary.

The chief now approached the second missionary. 'I am a good Christian and, rather than suffering the shame of your heathen practice, I shall practice martyrdom. Give me death.'

'Fine,' said the chief, 'death by oogabooga!'

A salesman from Harvey World Travel had just won a sales competition. The prize was a trip for two to Bali. But he was sick and tired of travel and his idea of a holiday was to stay at home. He was sitting at his desk feeling sorry for himself when he saw an old man and an old woman looking through the window of the shop. Their noses were pressed against the glass and their eyes were focused on photographs of . . . Bali.

He made up his mind in an instant. Rushing outside, he dragged them into his office and said, 'I know that on your pension you couldn't hope to afford a holiday, let alone one in Bali. Well, you're going to have one. And I won't take no for an answer.'

He asked his secretary to present them with the two flight tickets and details of the hotel bookings in Denpasar. They left the shop astonished.

Some months later he saw the little old lady in the street. 'And how did you like Bali?' he asked her.

'Oh, everything was wonderful. The flight was marvellous and the room was lovely and the beach was beautiful. I don't know how to thank you. But one thing has puzzled me. Who was that old bloke I had to share the room with?'

A Qantas jet was about to leave Mascot for Singapore, en route to London. The passengers were all on board, then the pilot appeared. He was wearing a pair of very dark glasses and carrying a white stick. To general astonishment, he tapped his way up the aisle to the flight deck.

'Christ,' a woman whispered to her husband, 'the pilot's blind.'

'Crap,' he said.

'But he is blind. The dark glasses! The white stick! You must go and speak to him, see what's going on.'

So the husband went to the flight deck and spoke to the pilot. 'Excuse me, but are you really blind?'

'Yes, I am.'

'But how can you possibly fly the plane if you're blind?'

'It's easy. Look at the instrument panel. You'll see that everything's in braille – the controls, the dials, the levers.'

'But, for Christ's sake, you can't see! How do you know when you pull back on the joystick?'

'That's easy. Do you see the Hilton Hotel at the end of the runway?'

'Of course.'

'Well,' said the pilot, 'I start the engines, roar down the runway and when I hear everyone screaming "Shit!" *then* I pull back on the joystick.'

The *Sydney Morning Herald's* travel writer was touring America and he decided to visit one of the newly opened casinos on the Indian reservation. It was a Mohawk casino, and sitting in the lobby was a marvellous old bloke with a feathered headdress. 'That's Big Chief Forget-Me-Not,' said the manager. 'Because this is Indian territory, he's allowed free use of the hotel for the rest of his life.'

'Why is he known as Big Chief Forget-Me-Not?' asked the writer.

'Because of his memory. Although he's almost a hundred he can remember every detail of his life.'

The travel writer decided to test the chief's memory. 'Okay, what did you have for breakfast on your 18th birthday?'

'Eggs,' came the reply.

The travel writer checked out the next day and happened to return to the hotel after another four weeks. There, in the foyer, was the old Indian chief. 'How?' said the Australian.

'Scrambled,' said the chief.

Index

C

H

I

Q

T

THE PENGUIN BOOK OF JOKES FROM CYBERSPACE

collected by Phillip Adams and Patrice Newell

Penguin Books

THE PENGUIN BOOK OF JOKES FROM CYBERSPACE

collected by Phillip Adams
and Patrice Newell

Penguin Books

To Sandra Blood, who once again gave hers that others might laugh. And to John Glenn, who cast his net very wide indeed.

I am the very model of a modern teenage cyberpunk
I rent my own apartment and it's full of electronic junk.
I own a Vax, a 486, I've even got a PDP
I finished Myst and Doom but I'm stumped by Wing Commander Three.
I'm very well acquainted with matters pornographical
I have a list of image sites, both overseas and national.
I'm totally an anarchist the government I'd like to wreck,
Though if they were to get blown up, who'd give to me my welfare cheque?
When I've learnt what progress has been made upon the Internet,
When I know something more than just a smattering of netiquette,
In short when I can have a worldwide soapbox on which to stand,
I've got no time for other things, like beer and trips to Disneyland.
My life outside the Internet is very, very sad, you see
I cannot get my spots to fade, my social life's a tragedy.
But still, if you need answers that concern your electronic junk
I am the very model of a modern teenage cyberpunk.

A cybersong, to the tune of 'A Modern Major General'

CONTENTS

An Electronic Epidemic

Influenza. Billions have caught it, tens of millions have died from it. Again and again it appears, invading country after country. Unable to treat it, even to explain it, desperate doctors have conferred with astrologists who insist its dread cycles synchronise with the approach of comets. First came the cosmic visitor, astrologists insisted, then the epidemic. The doctors accepted the comet's influence, its 'influenza'. And that became the name of the contagion.

Now, as we approach the end of a century and of a millennium, we confront a contagion far deadlier than the flu. Instead of being transmitted from person to person through the respiratory tract, by such old-fashioned means as inhalation of infected droplets resulting from coughing and sneezing, we have an electronic epidemic with a transmission rate approaching the speed of light. It is called the Internet, and within a few short years 30 million people have been afflicted. Thus far the majority of victims have been the male offspring of the middle class, whose immune systems have been repressed by spending too many hours sitting alone gazing at computer screens or fondling their laptops. However, there are grim signs that the Internet is beginning to infect/afflict females as well.

Searching for an explanation of the outbreak, we looked for the influenza of comets. Halley's was a recent visitor but an unlikely culprit, given that it was a nocturnal display and somewhat feeble. Now, thanks to two amateur astronomers, Mr Hale and Mr Bopp, we know the truth. Coinciding with the launch of William Gates's Windows 95, with the public listing of Netscape, the astronomers discovered a comet a thousand times greater in size and brilliance than Halley's. Suddenly appearing from behind mighty Jupiter it seemed, at first, to be heading straight towards Earth where it would do us in like the dinosaurs. Recent calculations by astronomers – using computers with Internet connections – suggest a near-miss. In about a year's time.

Clearly this comet has been conjured by the epidemic, rather than the epidemic by the comet. Though, if the Internet continues to spread, the gravitational pull of cyberspace will draw the visitor from outerspace and our planetary software, namely human beings, will be emphatically Hale-Bopped.

Not that those infected by the Internet show much concern. As soon as they catch the disease they quarantine themselves in close proximity to their computer and, bathing themselves in the seance-glow of cathode, start showing the familiar symptoms of gee-whizzery and unbridled optimism. Just as many of those who contract multiple sclerosis become pathologically cheerful – 'euphoria' is regarded as a symptom of MS – those caught in the Internet become delirious with joy. While the luddite sees every cog and microchip as a personal threat, those who surf the Internet see their technology as delivering, among other laudable things, an end to the dangerous anachronism of nationalism – marking the dawn of a new age in democracy, of global citizenship in a world without walls, without boundaries, without hierarchies.

Feverish, bright-eyed, the innocent victims of the Internet speak wildly about its promise. Currently connected via keyboard, it's only a matter of time, they insist, before voices replace fingertips. Then instantaneous translation of the spoken word will banish forever the curse of the Tower of Babel, and all the world will be able to communicate instantly. Others insist that barriers of gender will fall as well, since here is a form of communication that, for the moment at least, blurs the issue. Many males create feminine personae for the Internet, whilst women can present themselves as males. Even when the system becomes multi-media, vocal *and* visual, the technologies will allow people to camouflage themselves, to create any voice or face they wish to present to the wider world. Techno-transvestisism, if you will.

Meanwhile, the disabled community hopes that programmers will recognise their special needs, so that they too will be full participants in an electronic world which, unlike the real one, will not deny them access or acceptance.

The Net is deemed to be anarchic, ready to subvert the powers of the powerful, to undermine the monoliths, to mock the secrecy of government and corporation. Experience the ecstasy. Hear the hubris. The tens of millions caught up in this contagion sing its praises louder than all the church choirs in history sang in praise of the Saviour.

But then, the Internet *is* the saviour. How appropriate, at the end of a millennium, that we should be welcoming this microchip Messiah. (Last time a carpenter, this time a laptop.) And the yearnings of the faithful have a poignant beauty, a multi-orgasmic excitement, a transcendental fervour. Verily we say unto you, the information superhighway forms a clover leaf with the road to Damascus.

There are people who go even further, who talk of a synthesis, a fusion of human and artificial intelligence. It is not the meek who will inherit the world in this scenario, but the nerds.

Imagine the planet as a giant brain, with everyone on the Internet a neuron, using their modems as synapses; linked in a vast, collective intelligence; forming, finally, a mighty, unified consciousness. That metaphor is only the beginning. Now that the New Age intersects with the New Physics, you hear another, even more astonishing argument. It goes like this: the death sentence of the second law of thermodynamics is being challenged by the growth of intelligence, of consciousness. It is blossoming on our planet, via technologies like the Internet, and will inevitably, finally, fill the cosmos. So while God didn't exist and doesn't exist, He, She, or It is coming into existence.

There's little room for devil's advocacy, for the doubting Thomas, in these rapturous extrapolations. Try as you might to mop their fevered brows and calm them down, the sufferers of the contagion, the devotees of this cathode cult, cannot be soothed or persuaded. The suggestion that there's a dark side to every moon, that no technology has ever lived up to its promoters' promises, falls on deaf ears.

One would wish the new technology a sacred destiny but know that it will be profane. 'Twas ever thus and ever will be. Virtual reality, that oxymoronic term, could deliver imagined experiences of unimaginable beauty and may, for the odd philosopher or artist, do so. But we already know that for most it will be a tawdry and salacious experience; a three-dimensional, tactile computer game of butchery, lechery or both.

Film was to be a great force for good, doing for the human imagination what Esperanto would do for language. Silent movies became the first global medium, the likes of Chaplin and Pickford the most famous people the world had ever known. Then, slowly but surely, cinema became a charnel house, and now most people most of the time troop along to films that are essentially fascist, in which the likes of Willis, Schwarzenegger or Stallone engage in egomaniacal one-upmanship, examples of American triumphalism.

Another small problem was, of course, the cultural dominance of Los Angeles, its great voice drowning out other voices, making (for example) Australian feature films rarities in their own culture, strangers in their own cinemas. Even after Australian governments, state and federal, spent hundreds of millions of dollars in either direct subsidies or foregone revenue supporting local production, box office figures still demonstrate the total dominance of the US, of LA. For every $100 spent at the Australian box office, $94 goes to American films, leaving $6 to be shared amongst all the rest. And when you factor in the video stores, let alone television viewing habits, America achieves a share of market, a share of mind unprecedented in human history. Not even the Roman Catholic Church, at the height of its powers, could claim the reach of the major studios.

Television. It was to be 'the meeting place of strangers', the greatest force for democracy, the greatest educative tool the world had ever known. True, from time to time there was a glimmering of evidence that its contribution was benign, magnanimous. Some held, for example, that it was televised images of carnage that forced Washington to retreat from the Vietnam War. (Just for the record, this happens to be piffle. War and Vietnam got on wonderfully for many, many years, just as war and television get on wonderfully today, as the high ratings and enthusiastic response to Desert Storm remind us.) There were some who said that, without television, the Berlin Wall wouldn't have crumbled and communism wouldn't have collapsed. But you've only to look at the outpourings of America's 5000 channels – a number that's rising by the hour – to realise that the stuff it pumps out would earn you a fine as a polluter should you try to pour it down the drain.

Thirty-three years ago, we argued that we hadn't had 15 years of television but one year's television 15 times. Much the same needs to be said about those 5000 channels. Given the poverty of original programs, the paucity of quality, the predominance of endlessly repeated movies and series, America doesn't really have 5000 channels at all. It has 50 channels 100 times.

Not even literacy has proved to be the triumph it was touted. Comparatively few people use literacy for literature. Most use the skill to look up the TV programs for the 5000 channels, or to read their astrological charts or the magazines chocker with celebrity stories about Michael Jackson, Princess Di and O.J. Simpson. Whilst the Bible remains a best-seller, millions have preferred *Mein Kampf*, Mao's *Little Red Book* or the latest novel by Jeffrey Archer.

Nuclear power promised us infinite supplies of cheap energy, and instead gave us Hiroshima, Nagasaki, the Cold War and Chernobyl. Show us a technology and we'll show you a two-edged sword, a broken promise.

A world without walls? Without boundaries? Without hierarchies? Not if Bill Gates can help it. Let his name be a warning. Microsoft intends building tollgates all over the infobahn, and any number of other gatekeepers are muscling in. On Friday, 11 August 1995, Wall Street celebrated the Internet with a 600 per cent rise in the shares of a newly listed, 15-month-old, loss-making company called Netscape Communications. Within minutes they'd valued it at $3.8 billion, more than enough to rank it among the top 30 Australian enterprises, and outranking the likes of Woolworths, Mayne Nickless and the second-string banks.

Netscape Communications produces the navigator point-and-click Internet browser software to facilitate cyberspace exploration. Within a nanosecond, the new company was giving Bill Gates a run for his money and reminding us that the free and easy, anarchistic days of the Internet are ending.

In the late '60s, boffins working for the US Defence Department's Advance Research Projects Agency (ARPA) called the Internet into being. The first network, small and secret, started operation in 1969. It was intended to help researchers build networks that could survive technical problems or wholescale attacks. It was hoped that the new system might remain viable even after nuclear war. Because it had no centre, no nexus, the Internet was, and remains, resilient.

Over the next 20 years the Net grew steadily as more and more institutions linked in, hooked up. Soon there was a plethora of interlinked networks, many of them financed by the US government and others by semi-government agencies. And slowly but surely, commercial organisations moved in.

Between the ideal and the reality falls the shadow. Already the idealism of the Internet is being debauched by carpetbaggers, advertisers, marketers, pornographers, conspiracy theorists, paranoid right-wingers, racists, bigots and would-be entrepreneurs. It's no longer the nerds who are the problem.

Online gambling is shaping up as the next big Internet challenge (after pornography) for regulatory authorities, with an absence of safeguards to prevent access by children and lack of security for financial transactions the main concerns. The Caribbean Casino provides a warning at the beginning of its Internet site that it is off limits to people under the age of 18, but it has no mechanisms to enforce this rule. There are concerns that Internet casinos could pose a serious threat to government revenue from legalised forms of gambling. The casino is the brainchild of a 34-year-old Canadian, Mr Warren Eugene, who has evaded US laws by setting up his operation in the tax haven of the Turks and Caicos Islands, part of the Bahamas. Mr Eugene told the *Wall Street Journal* that he believed the cybercasino could be a 'trillion dollar worldwide business'.

Every day the system, so all-at-once and urgent, so full of possibilities, grows. And with it grow the abuses. As libertarians, we abhor censorship and are reluctant to join the ranks of control freaks. Despite the efforts of Microsoft, Netscape, et al, the Internet remains free of a centre, a backbone, a controlling nexus. There's no transmitter to turn off, no presses that can stop rolling.

It's true that the Internet is the largest, most powerful and efficient network for the storage and transmission of information that we've seen. Only a few years back, it had a guiding philosophy that seemed to guarantee its integrity. Then it became a juggernaut, and now it's a bandwagon. And because anything goes on the Net, it is already being blamed for social problems in the way we previously blamed television.

The Net was recently blamed, in effect, for the Oklahoma City bombing – it was alleged that bomb-building advice, from ultra-right sources, was on the Net. The fact is that any number of paranoid publications and survivalist mags – not to mention a couple of official government publications – explain how to use diesel fuel and fertiliser for explosive purposes. It makes no more sense to blame the Net for our social problems than it does to suggest it's responsible for the Hale-Bopp comet.

Recently it's become patently, painfully obvious that the New Age has been infiltrated by the hard right. The Australian magazine *Nexus* (*Noxious* might be more appropriate) began its life by recycling conspiracy theories, promoting alternative therapies and listing UFO sightings. Latterly it's been giving space to the most rabid right-wingers in the US, and suggesting that the Oklahoma City bombing was the work of ASIO. Slowly but surely Shirley MacLaine has given way to the Michigan Militia, and the same phenomenon has been observed in alternative journals in the UK and Europe. Similarly, Australia's green movement has been subverted by white supremacists, using ecological arguments to camouflage racist immigration policies. So we shouldn't be surprised that the Internet has been embraced by skinheads and neofascist crazies. You can hardly blame the Net for that – any more than you can blame the telephone directory for listing the names and addresses of bigots. Or the roads for encouraging Eric Butler to buy a car.

Nonetheless, the likelihood is that the meretricious will drown out the worthy. While we're told that the Internet will put us in touch with the Uffizi, the Prado, the Louvre, and the cave paintings of Lascaux, James Gleick, the author of *Chaos*, says, 'It's a wave, and no wave is complete without its backwash.' And Gleick sees in the cyberspace democracy the same stresses and undercurrents that assail real-world society. He's discovered you can get anonymous, threatening letters by e-mail even quicker than you can get them in the post. 'Angry teenagers screech at one another from behind pseudonymous masks,' says Gleick. 'Just the other day a young man I've never met posted a public message expressing the desire to see my hands blown off in an explosion.'

Luddites like Kirkpatrick Sale, who likes to smash computers with sledgehammers in front of audiences in American halls, see the Net turning the world into a society of loners, devastating the warp and weft of communities and substituting a mess of electronic pottage.

The other criticism is, of course, elitism – that the Net is only for the affluent. Jon Katz, critic for *Wired* magazine, admits to this danger but points out that 'low income earners don't read serious daily papers or magazines either. They'll probably have access to computers when digital technology fuses with television and becomes easier and cheaper . . . Everything has a price tag – the car makes us mobile and pollutes; airplanes get us places but are noisy and crash; medicine prolongs life and causes most people to die alone and in hospital. I think the world has never sorted out its feelings about technology. We fight it every time.'

Recently a University of Michigan sophomore was arrested on charges of transmission of a threat by electronic means, and thus became the first person to be charged with a federal crime for behaviour on the Internet. Needless to say, enthusiasts of cyberspace took close note. The Internet is speech driven – albeit a hybrid form of speech combining elements of talk, broadcast and print publication – and wants to be left as free and unfettered as possible.

The Michigan case was dismissed. For good or ill, cyberspace would remain ungoverned and ungovernable, an electronic Wild West. Like real live speech, Internet speech can incorporate behaviour that is legally actionable by civil or criminal means: fraud, transmission of threats, libel, copyright violation, and the like. Lawyers and users are still trying to work out the ways in which existing laws may be applied to the Net. Software has progressed a little faster. There are 'bozo filters', which roam the Net and cancel things people find obnoxious, and the NetNanny, which filters out adult or other material at the terminal. Meanwhile, commercial services such as Compuserve and American On Line regularly cancel the accounts of users who break sometimes restrictive house rules – as do universities, many of which have banned, for example, pictorial pornography, not only because it may cause offence but because, frequently, it involves violation of copyright.

In Australia the federal government is looking at ways to clean up the Internet and block objectionable material, such as child pornography. Attorney-General Lavarch is proposing that operators of computer networks be self-regulating under a broad industry code of practice, and that a complaints body be set up for the public.

But a very big imp is out of the bottle, and you can already download a service offering nearly one million porno images which have been downloaded 8.5 million times by consumers in over 2000 cities in over 40 countries. Then there's the guy in Antarctica who's set up a service that sends pictures of imaginary pizzas. Australian columnist Peter Goers made contact and ordered, from the available categories, a 'pizza with kittens, baseballs and green lollies'.

While still chuckling over that, he surfed the categories: Anal Sex, Assassins, Baptist Bible Study, Bifem Sex, Big Tits, Christ, Cricket Talk, Depressed, Dog Sex, Hottub, Gay Sheep. But it was hard to be amused by the considerable amount of information he found under Bombs. How to make explosives from all manner of freely available household products, and 'how to kill teachers and other people you don't like'.

Nonetheless, provided you don't play with it too much – because you'll go blind – the Internet is no more likely to destroy society than it is to save it. It's probably sensible to remember our favourite aphorism: data isn't information, information isn't knowledge, and knowledge isn't wisdom. People seeking wisdom on the Net will face immense frustrations because it seems to contain an infinity of dumpbins full of data, whereas nuggets of wisdom, as in the real world, are few and far between.

There are many who will surf the Net seeking answers to the most tantalising questions that humans have ever asked. Where do we come from, why are we here? Others, like us, are more interested in humour. Where do the flies go in the winter time? What happens to the picture when you turn off the television set?

We've often wondered where jokes came from. Some years ago we discovered that many were coming from the Internet. For example, when a space shuttle exploded, killing all on board, it was an Internet wit who immediately proffered the suggestion that NASA stood for 'Need Another Seven Astronauts?' So we went searching and found that, indeed, a great many members of the Internet, mostly American, mostly young and mostly male, are exchanging or creating jokes in little collectives, by raising a topic and asking for contributions.

Take a phenomenon like the Blonde joke. Someone types a few examples on the screen and issues an open invitation. Soon you can scroll through thousands of them, of varying quality, as people desperately try to top each other. Ditto for Polish jokes which, rather than Irish jokes, tend to represent America's favourite form of racial bigotry.

It was once observed that the world would one

day be thrown off its axis by the weight of *National Geographic* magazines accumulating in North America. According to our investigations, the accumulated weight of light bulb jokes represents a more urgent threat. As long as they stay in the Net we may survive, but God help us if too many people print hard copies.

Years ago, an American documentary film on automation revealed that all the light globes in America are manufactured by a total of four people. Now the Internet demonstrates that a great many people are employed, if not gainfully, on the manufacture of light bulb jokes. Whilst only four people might make the bulbs, millions are involved in changing them.

If you judge the unpopularity of a profession by the number of jokes on the Net, lawyers have a major image problem. It would be possible to fill a far thicker book than this with nothing but lawyer jokes, closely followed by attacks on economists and, inevitably, on politicians. And particularly on the Clintons. The anti-Clinton jokes are legion and, by and large, unfunny. Surprisingly, many more are directed at Hillary than at Bill, confirming that right-wingers tend to be misogynists. Sadly, almost as many are aimed at the hapless Chelsea. Whilst the mother is accused of everything from lesbianism to murder, the jokes at the expense of the child emphasise her alleged ugliness and almost invariably involve incest in or around the Oval Office.

We are astonished by the number of attacks on, of all things, viola players. Why this harmless, if not mellifluous-sounding instrument is deemed so vile, we do not know. But the weight of evidence – a total of 2000 jokes, at last count, attacking the instrument and those who play it – reveals a new dimension of bigotry. A popular folksong tells us that there will soon be ten million lawyers in the US, so there are plenty of opportunities for unhappy, abrasive encounters with the profession. But viola players? One doubts that there could be more than 10 000 viola players in the US. After all, if you were to multiply the number of viola players in your average symphony orchestra by the number of symphony orchestras in the US, you'd get, at best, a few hundred. In per capita terms, therefore, viola players are many times less popular than attorneys.

Other popular targets include engineers, IBM and Bill Gates. Presumably a majority of cyberpunks are Apple users, which explains why they get so acrimonious about IBM's acronym. The initials are held to signify many a dangerous notion: Insolence Breeds Mediocrity, Institute of Broken Minds, Incredible Bunch of Muffinheads, etc. Microsoft comes a close second, with Bill Gates more demonised than Saddam Hussein.

Mostly, however, Internet jokes are just jokes. They represent the usual attempts to exorcise the normal range of fears and anxieties. Jokes are principally a method of coping with things that embarrass or frighten us – women, sex, race, religion, mortality, flatulence, old age, the penis. Tell a joke and you're almost certainly revealing an anxiety. They confirm what we discovered when compiling *The Penguin Book of Australian Jokes* – that most jokes are global jokes, endlessly localised. Thus a Clinton joke becomes a Keating joke becomes a Major joke becomes a Yeltsin joke.

Yes, there are daily updates on the O.J. Simpson trial, but these tend to have a half-life of a half-hour. Whilst they can be noted, there's not much point in including them. In any case, almost all of them, like almost all the Hugh Grant jokes, are libellous.

More interesting are the little get-togethers of electronic tribes, sub-cultures who tell jokes in secret languages. We discovered a number of jokes being circulated by pilots, airline and private, concerning air traffic controllers, aviation authorities, and cockpit error. Apart from being highly alarming to nervous fliers, they're often so jargon-ridden as to be incomprehensible.

Nuns, penguins and gorillas retain their popularity on the Internet, but we hadn't expected tens of thousands of jokes about elephants, and particularly the social relationships between elephants and ants. Nor had we expected the Net to be such a rich source of aphorisms and canonical lists.

More in line with the known demographics of Net users are the thousands of pages on *Star Trek*. The numbers of Internet users who double as trekkies is astonishing.

Given that America is a born-again culture, that a majority – indeed a moral majority – of Americans are regular churchgoers, we shouldn't have been surprised by the popularity of Heaven jokes. We're not sure how difficult it is for a camel to pass through the eye of a needle – or how hard it'd be for the very rich Bill Gates to pass through the

Pearly Gates – but it's easy to find hundreds of jokes about St Peter vetting new arrivals. We were reminded of the recent rumour on the Net that Microsoft had bought the Vatican – a story so persistent that the corporation had to issue a denial. The Vatican chose to remain silent.

Perhaps this preoccupation with Heaven links back to the aesthetics of *Star Trek*, a program that always looked a tad Pearly-Gatish. Here was the future imagined in terms of a classical past. How odd that so many distant galaxies were populated by people dressed in togas who wandered amongst plaster rocks and doric columns whilst orating like bad Shakespearean actors. Perhaps Heaven is just another cosmic destination for trekkies to visit.

Access, Auspac, Bandwidth, Bulletin board, Chameleon, Click, cracking, cross post, domain name, downstream, e-mail, incription, file, finger, format, freeware, hacking, hypertext, interface, internaut, load, log in, modem, MOO, navigate, password, ping, port, route, scrollback, server, session, site, tyre-kicker, upstream, vandal, vehicle, visit, WWW, zip, zippie: the Internet already has its own language, thousands of words used as code or shorthand by its passionate citizens. This langauge is rapidly invading Australian English and will soon add to the 10 000 Americanisms that have recently found their way into *The Macquarie Dictionary*.

So, like television, like cinema, like rock 'n' roll, like rap, like country and western, like the jargon of the junkie, the Internet is, thus far, just another north American culture that is busy colonising the planet. And us. Let us hope that in time the Net does become truly global. But for the time being this global phenomenon, like Marshall McLuhan's Global Village, has an American address. Whatever the Internet's strength, that remains, for us, its weakness.

does become truly global. But for the time being this global phenomenon, like Marshall McLuhan's Global Village, has an American accent. Whatever the internet's strength, that remains, for us, its weakness.

DUMB AND DUMBER

A painting contractor was discussing a job with a woman. In the first room she said she'd like a pale blue. The contractor wrote this down, went to the window, opened it and yelled out, 'Green side up.' In the second room she told the painter she'd like a soft yellow. He wrote this on his pad and went to the window, opened it and yelled, 'Green side up.' In the third room she asked for a warm rose colour. The painter wrote this down, walked to the window, opened it and yelled, 'Green side up.' The lady then asked him why he kept yelling green side up. 'I'm sorry,' came the reply, 'but I have a crew of blondes laying turf across the street.'

There was a middle-aged man called Steve who decided to return to college to pursue a degree. Not being sure of what he wanted to take, he began to look around campus at all the different colleges. He saw the college of physics, the college of sociology, the college of psychology and the college of assuming. Having never heard of a college of assuming, Steve was puzzled.

While he stood there pondering what it was, the Dean of the college happened by and inquired if he could help. Steve replied, 'I've never heard of the college of assuming. What is it?'

'Well, I'm the Dean of the college. Here in the college of assuming, we take assumption to a new art form,' said the Dean.

'I still don't understand,' replied Steve.

'Let's try this. Can I assume you have a dog?' asked the Dean.

'Why, yes, I do have a dog,' replied Steve.

'And can I assume that you have a backyard for your dog to play in?' inquired the Dean. 'Why yes, I do have a backyard for my dog,' said Steve.'

'Okay, and can I further assume that because you have a backyard you also have a house?' said the Dean.

'Why yes, I do have a house,' said Steve, beginning to be amazed.

'Now, because you have a house and a dog, and a backyard, can I then assume that you have a wife?' said the Dean flatly.

'That's amazing! Yes, I do have a wife,' said Steve.

'Then because you have a wife, can I assume you are not gay?' inquired the Dean.

'No, I'm not gay,' replied Steve.

'There you see,' stated the Dean. 'From the simple fact of assuming you had a dog, I was able to assume you had a house with a backyard, a wife, and you are not gay.'

Clearly amazed, Steve enrolled in the class of assumptions. One day about three weeks later, while waiting for class to start, Steve saw a very puzzled man in the halls. 'Can I help you?' inquired Steve.

'Why yes,' replied the man. 'What is the college of assuming?'

Delighted, Steve replied, 'The college of assuming takes assumption to a new art form.'

'I'm not sure I understand,' replied the man.

'Well, let me give you an example,' said Steve. 'Do you own a dog?'

'Well no,' replied the man.

Steve quickly stepped back and said, 'You fag!'

The heaviest element known to science was recently discovered by university physicists. The element, tentatively named Administratium (Ad), has no protons or electrons, which means that it has an atomic number 0 and falls outside the natural patterns exhibited by other elements. However, it does have one neutron, 125 assistants to the neutron, 75 vice neutrons and 111 assistants to the vice neutrons. This gives it an atomic mass of 312. The 312 particles are held together by a force involving the continuous exchange of meson-like particles, called 'memos'. Because it has no protons or electrons, Administratium is inert. Nonetheless, it can be detected chemically, in that it seems to impede every reaction in which it is present. According to one of the discoverers, even a small amount of Administratium makes one reaction which normally lasts less than a second take more than four days. Administratium has a half-life of approximately three years. It does not actually decay. Instead, it undergoes a reorganisation in which a vice neutron, assistants to the vice neutron and certain assistants to the neutron exchange places. Some studies have indicated that its mass actually increases after each reorganisation, although this is yet to be explained. Another phenomenon which has been observed, as expected from the mechanics of minute particles, is that the more one tries to pin down the positions of vice neutrons within the structure of Administratium, the more uncertain those positions become.

Within a short time of the discovery being announced, the existence of the element was confirmed in laboratories around the world. In addition, a team at the University of Utah told a press conference they had been able to create Administratium in fusion experiments conducted at room temperature. Using highly sophisticated probability detectors, the team had Polak-monitored a stream of memos from a fax-mounted device. Dr May B. No and her associate, Dr May B. Yes, said the details of their experiment were being kept confidential, pending further development of the data. But, they claimed, there were definitely more memos that came out of the device than went in!

A city fella takes a ride in the country and heads

along the highway in his soft-top BMW. He turns off and drives along a dirt road in the middle of nowhere and, after a while, comes across a farmer driving a tractor. And the darndest thing – the farmer wasn't wearing any pants.

'Hey, how come you're not wearing trousers?'

'Well, city boy, the other day I went out aworking in the fields and I plum forgot t' wear me shirt. Got back home that night and m' neck was stiffer than an oakwood board. So this here's my wife's idea.'

A student walks into a car showroom and after a long talk with a salesman, he picks the car he wants to buy.

'Do you have the cash to pay for it, sir, or will you be making a hire-purchase agreement?'

'I'll buy it on HP, thanks.'

So the student dictates his details to the salesman, who fills in the HP application. Then, to the salesman's astonishment, he signs at the bottom of the form with a big cross and a little cross.

'What're these crosses?'

'Well, the big cross is my name and the little cross is "BSc Agriculture".'

A guy walks into a bar, approaches the bartender and says, 'I've been working on a top secret project on molecular genetics for the past five years and

I've just got to talk to someone about it.'

The bartender says, 'Okay, but before we talk about that, just answer me a few questions. When a deer defecates, why does it come out in little pellets?' The guy doesn't know. The bartender then asks, 'Why is it that when a dog poops, it lands on the ground and looks like a coiled rope?' The guy has no idea. So the bartender says, 'You don't know shit! And you want to talk about molecular genetics?'

Smitty is interviewing for a new bartender. He asks one guy applying for the job how he became interested in tending bar.

'Actually,' says the guy, 'I learned to appreciate the value of mixing drinks when I was a forest ranger. Before I went off into the wilderness on my first assignment, my fellow rangers gave me a farewell party. As a going-away gift, they gave me a martini-making kit, a bottle of gin, vermouth, a mixer, a stirrer, and a bottle of olives. I was confused. Why would I need a martini set in the woods? A more experienced ranger set me straight: you'll find this to be the most important piece of equipment you have. You might be out there in the wilderness totally alone for weeks, maybe months. Soon you'll remember your martini set. You'll take it out and begin to make yourself a martini, and within 30 seconds there will be someone at your side saying, 'That's not the way to make a martini . . .'

A man walks into a pub with a giraffe on a lead. 'I'll have a pint of Guinness,' says the man, 'and ten pints for the giraffe.'

The man then starts to down his pint in one go. The giraffe sees this and starts banging down the ten pints like there's no tomorrow. The race is on, the man gets halfway down and the giraffe's only on number four. Then, with an amazing burst of speed, the giraffe just manages to scrape ahead. But on pint number ten the giraffe gets halfway then collapses dead on the bar. The man promptly finishes his pint and starts to leave. 'Hey,' says the barman, 'you can't leave that lyin' there!' Says the man, 'It's not a lion, it's a giraffe.'

A blonde walked into a hair salon and insisted that the stylist cut around the earphones of her Walkman. The stylist did as she asked.

About a month later, the blonde returned to have her hair styled again. Again, the stylist was told to cut around her earphones.

This happened for months on end. Finally, the hairstylist couldn't contain his curiosity so, while giving the blonde a haircut, he pulled the earphones off. Whereupon the blonde fell to the floor stone dead. The paramedics arrived and took the body away. The hairstylist lifted the earphones to hear what she'd been listening to. He put them on and heard: 'Inhale ... exhale ... inhale ... exhale ...'

Why were blondes made 10 per cent smarter than cows?

So when you squeeze their tits they don't shit on your face.

Three blondes were walking along a beach when they found an old oil lamp made of brass. They rubbed it and, lo and behold, a genie appeared. 'I am the genie of the lamp. I can give each of you as much intelligence as you desire,' said the genie.

'Oh my,' cried the first blonde, 'I guess I would like to be 100 times smarter than I am now!' ZAP. The genie turned her into a brunette.

'Well,' said the second blonde, 'I don't think I need to be that smart. I'd like to be about ten times smarter than I am now.' ZAP. The genie turned her into a redhead.

'Gee,' said the third blonde, 'I think I'm just about okay the way I am. I get a lot of attention and men seem to like me. I guess if anything I'd like to be ten times dumber than I am now.' ZAP. The genie turned her into a *man*.

Why did the blonde get fired from the M&M factory?

She kept throwing away all the Ws.

What's black, blue, red and brown and lies in a gutter?

A brunette who's told too many blonde jokes.

A blonde was tired of hearing blonde jokes and decided to prove people wrong. She spent weeks studying a map of the United States, memorising all the capitals for all the states. The next time someone started telling a blonde joke she said, 'Hey, not all blondes are stupid. I can prove it. Give me the name of any state and I'll tell you its capital.'

'Vermont,' someone suggested.

'V.'

How do you change a blonde's mind?

Blow in her ear.

How do you measure a blonde's intelligence?

Stick a tyre pressure gauge in her ear.

How do you keep a blonde busy all day?

Put her in a round room and tell her to sit in the corner.

How do you get a blonde to marry you?
Tell her she's pregnant.
What will she ask you?
'Is it mine?'

How can you steal a blonde's window seat?
Tell her the seats that are going to London are all in the middle row.

Why is a blonde like Australia?
They're both down under, and no one cares.

What do you give the blonde who has everything?
Penicillin.

Why do blondes wear panties?
To keep their ankles warm.

What's the difference between a blonde and a brick?
When you lay a brick it doesn't follow you around for two weeks whining.

How can you tell when a blonde reaches orgasm?
She drops her nail file.

How does a blonde commit suicide?
She gathers her clothes into a pile and jumps off.

How does a blonde get pregnant?
And I thought blondes were dumb.

What's the difference between a chorus line of blondes and a magician?
A magician has a cunning array of stunts.

Why do blondes hate M&Ms?
They're too hard to peel.

What job function does a blonde have in an M&M factory?
Proof-reading.

Why can't blondes make Coolade?

Because they can't fit eight cups of water into the little packet.

How do you keep a blonde in suspense?

I'll tell you tomorrow.

What happens when a blonde gets Alzheimers?

Her IQ goes up.

Why can't blondes make ice-cubes?

They forget the recipe.

Did you hear about the blonde whose boyfriend said he loved her?

She believed him.

Did you hear about the blonde who robbed a bank?

She tied up the safe and blew the guard.

How many blondes does it take to play hide and seek?

One.

What's the difference between a blonde and a trampoline?

You take off your shoes before using a trampoline.

Why do blondes like lightning?

They think someone is taking their picture.

Why do blondes drive BMWs?

Because they can spell them.

What does the postcard from a blonde on holiday say?

'Having a wonderful time. Where am I?'

Why don't blondes make good pharmacists?

They can't get the bottle into the typewriter.

What do you get when you offer a blonde a penny for her thoughts?

Change.

What do a blonde and President Gorbachev have in common?

They both got fucked by ten men whilst on holiday.

What's the difference between a blonde and President Gorbachev?

He knows who the ten men were.

Why does a blonde keep a coathanger on her back seat?

In case she locks her keys in the car.

What did the blonde call her pet zebra?

Spot.

Why are there no dumb brunettes?

Peroxide.

What's a blonde's favourite nursery rhyme?
Humpme Dumpme.

A blonde went to a library and checked out a book called *How to Hug*. She got back home and found it was volume seven of the encyclopaedia.

A cop stops a blonde woman who's driving down a motorway.

'Miss, may I see your driver's licence please?'

'Driver's licence, what's that?'

'It's a little card with your picture on it.'

'Oh, duh! Here it is.'

'May I have your car insurance?'

'What's that?'

'It's a document that says you're allowed to drive the car.'

'Oh, this! Duh! Here you go.'

The cop then unzips his trousers and the blonde goes, 'Oh no, not another breathalyzer test.'

Two blondes are walking through the woods. One looks down and says, 'Look at the deer tracks.' The other blonde looks and says, 'Those aren't deer tracks, those are wolf tracks.' 'No, those are deer tracks.' They keep arguing and arguing and ten minutes later they're both killed by a train.

A blonde is telling a priest a joke that is both dirty and Polish. Halfway through the priest interrupts her. 'Don't you know I'm a priest? And that I'm Polish?'

'Oh, I'm sorry,' the blonde apologises, 'do you want me to start over and talk slower?'

A young blonde is asked out on a date. The boy picks her up and they go to a nearby carnival. They ride a few rides, play a few games and seem to be hitting it off. During a sort of romantic lull, the boy says, 'What do you want to do now?'

'I want a weigh,' she says. Well, okay, thinks the boy. They walk over to the fortune scales and weigh her. They play a few more games and stop for food. 'What do you want to do now?' asks the boy again.

'I want a weigh,' she says. Mmm, a little odd, but I'll go along with it, the boy thinks. Again they get her weight and fortune.

After a few more games and a marvellous fireworks show, the boy repeats, 'What do you want to do now?'

'I want a weigh,' she says. Damn, thinks the boy, she's just too weird for me. They get her weight and fortune again and the boy drives her home.

As she walks into the house her sister says, 'How did your date go?'

'Wousy,' says the girl.

A young businessman rented a beautiful office and furnished it with antiques. But no business was coming in. Sitting there, worrying, he saw a man come into the outer office. Wanting to look busy, he picked up the phone and pretended he was negotiating a big deal. He spoke loudly about big figures and huge commitments. Finally he hung up and asked the visitor, 'Can I help you?'

The man said, 'I've come to install the phone.'

Jack and Jill have both been perfect employees, much valued by the company. Owing to the downturn in business, one of them has to go. But which one? The boss decides on a plan. He'll watch Jack closely for a day and, having monitored his performance, will similarly monitor Jill's. Then he'll make the decision.

The next day, Jack arrives early, works hard all morning and doesn't even take time off for a pee. He skips lunch and works very, very hard all afternoon. There are no private phone calls, no coffee breaks, and he leaves around 7 p.m.

'If they're both such diligent workers,' thinks the boss, 'the choice will be very hard indeed.'

Next morning, Jill comes in half an hour late complaining of a headache. She pops some aspirin, hangs around the water fountain talking to her friends, takes a very long coffee break, leaves early for lunch, comes back late, makes lots of private phone calls, and bores all her colleagues by telling them how miserable she feels. Then she takes some more aspirin and leaves around 4 p.m.

Next morning the boss calls her into his office. He says, 'Jill, you know I have to either lay you or Jack off.'

She says, 'Well, you're going to have to jack off because I've got a headache.'

Three blondes were attempting to change a light bulb. One of them decided to call 911.

BLONDE: We need help. We're three blondes changing a light bulb.

OPERATOR: Hmm. You put in a fresh bulb?

BLONDE: Yes.

OPERATOR: The power in the house is on?

BLONDE: Of course.

OPERATOR: And the switch is on?

BLONDE: Yes, yes.

OPERATOR: And the bulb still won't light up?

BLONDE: No, it's working fine.

OPERATOR: Then what's the problem?

BLONDE: We got dizzy spinning the ladder around and we all fell and hurt ourselves.

A young man gets a job as a circus roustabout. The circus owner, thinking he might be able to recruit him as an assistant lion tamer, takes him to the practice cage. The head lion tamer, a beautiful young woman, was just starting her rehearsal. As she entered the cage, she removed her cape with a flourish and, standing in a gorgeous abbreviated costume, motioned to one of the lions. It crept towards her, licked her knees and rolled over twice.

'Well,' said the owner to the young man, 'think you could do that?'

'I'm sure I could, sir,' said the young man, 'but you'll have to get that lion out of there.'

A young bloke started work in a supermarket. First day, a customer asked him if she could buy half a grapefruit. He excused himself to ask the manager. 'Some ratbag out there wants to buy half a grapefruit,' he began, only to see that the customer had entered the office behind him, 'and this lovely lady would like to buy the other half.'

Impressed with the way the clerk had resolved the problem, the manager later asked him, 'Where are you from?'

'Lancaster, Pennsylvania,' replied the clerk, 'home of ugly women and great hockey teams.'

'Yes? My wife is from Lancaster,' said the manager menacingly. And the clerk asked, 'What team was she on?'

Two male engineering students meet on campus. One says, 'Hi, where'd you get the new bike?'

'Well, I was walking to class the other day when a

pretty co-ed rode up, jumped off it, took off all her clothes and said, "You can have anything you want!"'

'Right,' said his friend, 'her clothes probably wouldn't have fit you anyway.'

One morning Daddy Bear came down to breakfast, to find his porridge bowl empty. 'Somebody's been eating my porridge,' said Daddy Bear.

'Someone's been eating my porridge!' said Baby Bear.

At that moment Mummy Bear came out of the kitchen and said, 'You stupid bastards. I haven't made it yet!'

On his first date with a beautiful woman, a bloke decided to impress her with his abilities in wine tasting. He told the wine steward to bring a bottle of 1985 Sterling Cabernet Sauvignon from the Carneros district vineyard. Upon tasting it, the young man berated the wine steward. 'No, no, no! This is a 1987 vintage from the North Coast vineyards near Calistoga. Please bring me exactly what I ordered.'

The second bottle was poured and, once again, the man was very annoyed. 'No, no, no! This is 1985 all right, but it's from the Mount Helena vineyards!'

Watching the drama from the bar, an old drunk

staggered over to the couple's table and said, 'Wow! That's an impressive ability you've got. Can you tell me what's in this glass?'

Not wanting to pass up an opportunity to impress, the man sipped at the drunk's glass. 'Christ, that tastes like piss,' he yelled as he spat the mouthful out.

'That's right!' exclaimed the drunk. 'Now tell me where I was born and how old I am.'

A girl comes home from her first semester at college. She yells, 'Mom, Mom, I've got a case of VD.'

'Put it in the cellar,' says her mother, 'your old man will drink anything.'

A piece of bacon and a sausage are in a frying pan being cooked. The sausage says, 'It's hot in here, isn't it!' and the bacon replies, 'Wow! A talking sausage!'

A bloke walks into a very expensive cake shop, goes up to the counter and asks for a donut. The assistant picks up a pair of elegant silver tongs, retrieves a donut and places it on a doiley.

The customer is impressed. 'That's very hygienic – using a pair of tongs.'

'Oh yes sir, this is a very clean shop.'

'Well, in that case I'll have a chocolate éclair as well.'

Once again the assistant picks up the silver tongs and retrieves a chocolate éclair, placing it on a paper doiley. While he's doing this the customer notices a piece of string sticking out of the assistant's trousers. 'What's the string for?'

'Well sir, it's such a hygienic shop that when I go to the toilet I mustn't touch my penis. So I pull it out with the string.'

The customer thinks about this for a moment and asks, 'How do you put it back again?'

'Oh, that's easy,' says the assistant, 'I use the tongs.'

A guy in a restaurant says to the waiter, 'I'd like the fried lobster with french fries and broccoli.' The waiter says, 'Sorry, sir, we have no broccoli.'

'Never mind,' says the bloke, 'I'll have the roast duck, roast potatoes, cabbage and broccoli.'

The waiter says, 'Sir, we have no broccoli today.'

'In that case, I'll have the chicken, sprouts, the carrots and broccoli.'

'Listen sir, how do you spell dog, as in dogmatic?'

'D-O-G.'

'How do you spell cat, as in catastrophe?'

'C-A-T.'

'How do you spell fuck, as in broccoli?'

'There's no FUCK in BROCCOLI!'

'That's what I've been telling you for the past ten minutes, you stupid git.'

A guy was stuck on a desert island for years. Then, from the depths of the ocean, came a stunning dark-haired beauty equipped with scuba gear. She walked slowly, voluptuously, up to the guy and asked very softly, 'Would you like a cigarette?' His eyes filled with wonder as he answered, 'Sure.' She unzipped a pocket on the sleeve of her wetsuit, pulled out a pack of cigarettes and a light. She offered him a cigarette, took one herself and lit them both.

As they smoked their cigarettes, she asked, 'Would you like a martini?' 'Wow! Yes,' he responded with immense enthusiasm. So she unzipped another pocket, pulled out a shaker of martinis, a couple of glasses and poured them both a drink.

She watched him as he sipped the drink and, with a breathtakingly beautiful smile, whispered into his ear, 'Would you like to play around?'

Amazed at his good fortune, he said, 'You've got to be kidding! You've got golf clubs in there, too?'

After a long day on the course the exasperated golfer turned to his caddy and said, 'You must be the absolute worst caddy in the world.'

'No, I don't think so,' said the caddy. 'That would be too much of a coincidence.'

A lady goes into a hardware shop and asks for a hinge. The man at the counter gets one and asks, 'Do you want a screw for that hinge?'

The lady says, 'No, but I'll blow ya for that toaster over there.'

Juan and Jose were shopping for horses. When they'd each found the horse they wanted, they were in a quandary.

'How will we tell which horse is yours and which is mine?' asked Jose.

'I know. You crop your horse's ears and I'll leave mine as they are,' answered Juan.

'No, that would hurt the horse.'

'Okay. I'll cut my horse's tail and you keep your horse's tail long.'

'Nooo! Horses need their tails long to brush flies off.'

'I know. Branding! I'll put a big X on the rear of my horse. And you put a big Y on yours.'

'No, no. My horse is too beautiful to mark up like that.'

'I've got it,' said Jose. 'You take the black one. I'll take the white one.'

A guy walks into a bar and sits down on the barstool. 'Hey, barthendther, gifth me a beer.' The bartender walks over with a tall cool one. 'Here'sth your beer.'

The other guy sits up straight. 'Heey, you're imithating mee.'

'No, I talk thith way too.'

'Okay, I guesth itth okay.'

Later, a big burly guy walks in and sits down at the other end of the bar. 'Yo, bartender. Gimme a beer.' The bartender responds, 'One beer comin' up, man.'

The little guy gets ticked off and yells, 'Heey, you were imithathing mee!' The bartender comes over close and replies, 'No, I wasth imithathing the other guy.'

Why do farts smell?

For the benefit of the deaf.

Do you know what mothballs smell like?

Yes.

Really. How do you get their little legs apart?

Why did the couple stop after three children?

Because they read that every fourth child born is Chinese.

What is bright orange and sounds like a parrot?

A carrot.

What's the difference between a university and a polytechnic.

At a polytechnic they teach you to wash your hands after going to the toilet. At a university they teach you not to piss on your hands in the first place.

Many an American tourist around Windsor Castle has been heard asking, 'Why did they build it so close to the airport?'

ENGLISH TOURIST: Hello. Do you farm around here?

CORNISH FARMER: Aye.

ENGLISH TOURIST: Fantastic day, isn't it?

CORNISH FARMER: Aye.

ENGLISH TOURIST: Have you lived here all your life?

CORNISH FARMER: Not yet.

Going through his wife's bedroom drawers, a farmer discovered three soya beans and an envelope containing $30 in cash. He confronted his wife, who promptly confessed. 'Darling, over the years I haven't been completely faithful to you. But when I do fool around, I put a soya bean in the drawer to remind myself of my indiscretion.'

The farmer admitted that he hadn't always been faithful either and, therefore, was inclined to forgive and forget a few moments of weakness. 'Where did the $30 come from?' he asked.

'Oh that,' his wife replied. 'When soya beans hit $10 a bushell, I sold out.'

A ham sandwich walked into a bar, ordered a drink and the bartender said, 'No, we don't serve food here.'

A man entered a barber shop and said, 'I'm sick of looking like everyone else. I want to be different. Give me a part from ear to ear!'

'Are you certain?'

'Absolutely,' said the man.

The barber did what he was told and the satisfied customer left the shop.

Three hours later he came back. 'Put it back the way it was,' he said.

'What's the matter?' asked the barber, 'are you tired of being a non-conformist already?'

'No,' he replied, 'but I'm tired of people whispering in my nose.'

An English tourist is on holiday in a Cornish village when he spots what is obviously the village idiot sitting next to the horse trough. In his hand is an old stick, and tied to the end is a piece of string which is dangling in the water. The tourist decides to humour the fellow and asks, 'Have you caught anything yet?' The village idiot looks up and studies the stranger before saying, 'Aye, you be the seventh today.'

Three vampires walk into a bar and order drinks. The first vampire asks for Blood. The second vampire asks for a Blood Light. The third vampire asks for some hot water. The bartender is baffled. 'Why don't you want Blood, like everyone else?' 'Because,' says the vampire, pulling out a tampon, 'I'm making tea.'

INTERSEX

How do you know when a female yuppie achieves orgasm?

She drops her briefcase.

A woman decides to buy a new cupboard, one of those you have to assemble yourself. Back home she reads the instructions very carefully and manages to assemble the cupboard in the bedroom. It looks great. Then a train passes and the damn thing collapses. Undaunted, she rereads the instructions and reassembles the cupboard. Another train passes and the cupboard collapses again. Convinced she's doing something wrong, she rereads the instructions and reassembles the cupboard. A train passes and the cupboard collapses for the third time. Finally, fed up, she calls the store and is told they'll send along a technician to have a look.

The technician arrives and assembles the cupboard. Whereupon a train passes and the cupboard collapses. Baffled by this unexpected event, the techo decides to reassemble the cupboard and sit inside it, to see whether he can find out what causes the cupboard to collapse.

About an hour later the woman's husband comes home, sees the cupboard, says, 'That's a nice looking cupboard,' and opens it. 'You won't believe this,' says the technician, 'but I'm standing here waiting for the train.'

A strikingly handsome man and a very beautiful dark-haired woman were having dinner in a fine restaurant. Their waitress, taking an order at a table a few steps away, noticed that the man had stopped smiling and now had a rigid facial expression. Moreover he was slowly sliding down his chair and under the table. Strangely, his dinner companion seemed unconcerned. The waitress watched fascinated as the man slid all the way down his chair and out of sight under the tablecloth. The woman remained calm and unruffled, apparently unaware that her dining companion had disappeared.

After the waitress had finished taking the order, she approached the table and said to the woman, 'Pardon, M'am, but I think your husband just slipped under the table.'

The woman looked up at her and calmly replied, 'No, he didn't. He just walked in the door.'

A bloke goes into a bar carrying a small box. He asks the bartender. 'If I show you the neatest thing you've ever seen, will you give me a free beer?'

The bartender says, 'Sure, but I've got to warn you, I've seen a *lot* of things in my time.'

'Yeah, but you've never seen anything like this,' says the man, opening the box to reveal a tiny little person at a piano, jamming away. 'He plays Bach, he plays Stravinsky, he plays John Cage, he plays it all.' The bartender is mightily impressed.

'That *is* the neatest thing I've ever seen. Where did you get him?'

'Well, I was walking on the beach, found this brass lamp and rubbed it, and a genie came out and granted me a wish.'

'Do you think I could have a wish, too?' the barman asks.

'Sure,' says the man, producing the lamp from his coat pocket. The bartender gives it a rub, the genie pops out and the bartender says, 'I want a million bucks.' POOF! The bar is full of ducks. They're flying around. They're crapping on everything. They're everywhere.

The bartender screams at the man, 'Why didn't you tell me your genie was defective?'

'Yep, hard of hearing. I didn't ask for a 12-inch pianist, either.'

A prostitute goes into a bar and spots a koala on a stool. They talk, they flirt, and the koala takes her home. After a night of passion the koala climbs out of bed and ambles towards the door. 'Where are you going?' yells the prostitute. 'I haven't been paid.' Suspecting that a koala mightn't understand the nature of her profession, she reaches for a dictionary and shows him the definition. 'Prostitute: n. a woman who performs sexual services for money.' Whereupon the koala grabs the dictionary and shows her a definition: 'Koala Bear: n. a furry marsupial. Eats bush and leaves.'

Elvis, Liberace and John Belushi are sitting around in Heaven bored out of their heavenly lives. They go to Gabriel and ask if there's any way they can get out. Apprehensively he agrees to let them return to Earth for a short while, telling them that if they even think of committing a sin, they'll go straight to Hell.

So, zap, they're on Hollywood Boulevard. As they're walking, Elvis sees a bar. He heads towards the door and the moment he touches it, poof! He's gone. The others realise that Gabriel was serious.

A little while later John Belushi sees a little packet of white powder lying in the gutter. He thinks for a moment and bends over to pick it up. Poof! Liberace disappears.

Why does Mike Tyson cry after sex?

The mace.

Three women were sitting in a bar talking about their lives. The first one said, 'My husband is an architect. When we make love it has power, it has form, it has function. It is incredible!'

The second one said, 'My husband is an artist. When we make love it has passion, it has emotion, it has vision. It's wonderful!'

The third woman sighed and, sipping a marguerita, said, 'My husband works for Microsoft. When we make love, he just sits at the end of the bed and tells me how great it's going to be when it gets here.'

What do you get when you cross a computer with a prostitute?

A fucking know-it-all.

Once upon a time an explorer in a distant land was granted an audience with the king, who was an impressive figure except for one unusual feature – his head. It was tiny, about the size of a grapefruit. After talking with his majesty for some time, the explorer couldn't contain his curiosity a moment longer and asked the royal personage about the size of his cranium.

After a pause, the king explained that he hadn't always been a king and that, in fact, he'd once been a fisherman. One day, whilst pulling in his nets, he found he'd caught a mermaid.

'From the waist up, she was a very beautiful woman. From the waist down, a fish. I was preparing to take her to market to sell as a curiosity when she spoke to me and said that she was a magic mermaid. And she said that if I let her go, she would grant me three wishes. I agreed to this and asked for gold, jewels and other riches. Immediately these appeared. Next, I asked to be made a king and have a kingdom to rule, with a great castle. As you can see, this wish was granted.

'The mermaid then asked me what my third wish was. I said I found her very beautiful and that I wanted to make love. She replied that as she was only half woman, this wasn't possible. That's when I made my mistake. "Well, in that case,' I said, 'can you give me a little head?"'

A man rushes into his house and yells at his wife, 'Brenda, pack your things. I've just won the State Lottery.'

Brenda replies, 'Shall I pack for warm weather or cold?'

'I don't care,' says the man, 'just as long as you're out of the house by noon.'

'Well, I was playing golf with my wife. I'd been having a great game but unfortunately she wasn't. On the 15th tee I hit a beautiful shot, 270 metres straight down the fairway. My wife steps up and hits a tremendous slice that leaves the course and lands in the pasture out of bounds. We both went looking for the ball and just as we were about to give up I spotted a glint of white coming from a cow's behind, just under its tail. I lifted the tail to make sure, and then called to my wife saying, 'Here, honey, this looks like yours.' That's the last thing I remember.'

What did the leper say to the prostitute?
You can keep the tip.

Why was the leper caught speeding?
Because he couldn't take his foot off the accelerator.

Two guys want to buy two tickets to Pittsburgh. They go to the ticket counter and notice that the ticket agent is very, very beautiful, with large breasts and prominent nipples. Fixating on them they say, 'We'd like two pickets to Tittsburgh.' Overwhelmed with embarrassment, they run away and don't know what to do. Then they see a priest walking by and explain that, for reasons they can't articulate, they're unable to buy two tickets to Pittsburgh. Can he help them?

He immediately agrees, walks up to the counter

and, like the boys, can't help but notice the magnificent mammary glands and the prominent nipples. Nonetheless he manages to say, 'I'd like to buy two tickets to Pittsburgh.'

The woman behind the counter asks, 'And how would you like your change?' He says, 'In nipples and dimes.'

The old couple were on a car trip. They stopped at a roadhouse for lunch and the old woman left her glasses on the table. She didn't miss them until they'd been driving for half an hour. The old man complained all the way back to the restaurant. When they finally arrived, as she was climbing out of the car to retrieve her specs, the old man said, 'While you're in there, you may as well get my hat, too.'

The new bride was a bit embarrassed to be identified as a honeymooner. So when she and her new husband pulled up at the motel, she asked him if there was any way they could make it appear they'd been married a long time. 'Sure,' he said, 'you carry the suitcases.'

She left him in bed when the phone rang, and was back in a few seconds. 'Who was it?' he asked.

'My husband,' she replied.

'I better get going,' he said, 'where was he?'

'Relax. He said he was downtown playing poker with you.'

PURSER: I'm sorry Mr Jones, but we left your wife behind in New York.

MR JONES: Thank goodness, I thought I was going deaf.

A young man said to his girlfriend's father, 'I realise this is only a formality, but would you mind if I married your daughter?'

'Who says it's only a formality?' asked the father angrily.

'Her obstetrician,' replied the young man.

A hubby comes home early and finds his wife in bed with another man. 'Who the hell is this?' he demands.

'Good question,' answers the wife. 'Say, fella, what's your name?'

Marriage teaches you loyalty, patience, understanding, perserverence and a lot of other things you wouldn't need if you'd stayed single.

A woman had an artist paint a portrait of her dripping with jewels. 'If I die and my husband remarries,' she explained, 'I want his next wife to go crazy looking for the diamonds.'

A husband and wife go to the fairground. She wants to go on the ferris-wheel but he's too scared, so she goes on it by herself. The wheel goes round and round and suddenly the woman is thrown out and lands in a heap at her husband's feet. 'Are you hurt?' he asks.

'Of course I'm hurt. Three times round and you didn't wave once!'

One evening a husband comes home to his apartment very roughed up. When his wife sees him she asks, 'What happened to you?'

'I got into a fight with the apartment manager.'

'Whatever for?'

'He said he had slept with every woman in the complex except one!'

'Hmmm. I bet it's that snooty Mrs Green on the third floor.'

A businessman called home at noon one day, but the maid answered. When the man asked to speak to his wife, the maid replied, 'She's upstairs in the bedroom entertaining her boyfriend.' After sputtering and fuming for a minute, the businessman asked the maid if she would like to make $100 000 for a few minutes' work. She said, 'Of course. What do I have to do?' He answered, 'Take my shotgun from the closet and shoot the both of them.'

The maid put the phone down. He heard footsteps proceeding upstairs, then two shots rang out. The maid picked up the phone and said, 'Okay, it's done. What shall I do with the bodies?'

The man said, 'Take them out back and throw them into the pool.'

'What pool?' the maid asked.

After a moment of silence, the man said, 'Is this 555 3724?'

MAN A: So, how was your honeymoon?

MAN B: Very good until the morning after waking up. I forgot and said to my wife, 'You are wonderful. Here's $100.'

MAN A: It's not that bad, she might not know that you thought of her as a hooker.

MAN B: I know, but my wife then gave me back $50 and said, 'Here's your change.'

HE: Your birthday is coming up, so I'd like some idea of what you'd like.

SHE: I want a divorce!

HE: I'm really sorry, but I hadn't planned to spend that much.

A young bloke goes on a date with his girlfriend. After some heavy petting in the back of the car, he asks her for oral sex. 'No,' she says, 'you won't respect me.'

After a few months, the young man asks again. Again she says, 'No, you won't respect me.'

Eventually the two get married and the husband says to his bride, 'Okay, we're married now. You know I love you. You know I respect you. Now, please, can I have oral sex?'

'No,' she says, 'I just know that if I do, you won't respect me.'

So he waits and waits and waits. Until, after 30 years of marriage, he says, 'Honey, we've been together for decades. We've raised three fine children. You know that I respect you utterly and completely. So please, please, PLEASE, how about oral sex? Just once.' And she finally gives in.

Afterwards they're lying in bed when the telephone rings. The husband turns to his wife and says, 'Answer that, you cocksucker.'

A bloke gets a rise and decides to buy a new scope for his rifle. He goes to the gun dealer and asks the assistant to show him one. The assistant says, 'This scope is so good that you can see my condo all the way up on that hill.' The man takes a look through the scope and starts laughing.

'What's so funny?' asks the assistant.

'Well, I see a naked man and a naked woman running around the bedroom.'

The assistant grabs the scope from the man and looks through it. Then he hands the customer two bullets and says, 'I'll give you the scope for nothing if you can take these two bullets, shoot my wife's head off and shoot the guy's dick off.'

The customer takes another look through the scope and says, 'You know what? I think I can do that with one shot.'

Two women were walking down the street. One said to the other, 'There's my husband coming out of the florist with a dozen roses. Damn! That means I'm going to have to keep my legs up in the air for three days.'

'Well, why don't you get a vase?'

A husband and wife with small children employed a coding system when discussing sex. The term for intercourse was 'washing machine'.

They were lying in bed one night when the husband turned to his wife and said, as seductively as he could manage, 'Washing machine.' She, being a working parent, was tired and murmured, 'Not tonight, dear.' He rolled away.

Five minutes later he rolled back and murmured, 'Darling, washing machine . . . washing machine.' She said, 'I've got a headache.' He rolled away again.

Ten minutes later the wife, feeling guilty, turned to her husband and said, 'Okay, washing machine.'

'That's okay,' he replied, 'it was a small load and I did it by hand.'

Why do men like love at first sight?

It saves them time.

What do you give to a man who has everything?

A woman to show him how to work it.

Why don't men have mid-life crises?

They stay stuck in adolescence.

How does a man show he's planning for the future?

He buys two cases of beer instead of one.

What makes men chase women they have no intention of marrying?

The same urge that makes dogs chase cars they have no intention of driving.

What do you do with a bachelor who thinks he's God's gift?

Exchange him.

Why are husbands like lawnmowers?

They're hard to get started, emit foul odours, and don't work half the time.

What's the difference between a new husband and a new dog?

After a year, the dog is still excited to see you.

What is the thinnest book in the world?

What men know about women.

How many does it take to screw in a light bulb?

One. Men will screw anything.

What's a man's idea of foreplay?
A half-hour of begging.

How can you tell if a man is sexually excited?
He's breathing.

What's the difference between men and government bonds?
Bonds mature.

How do you save a man from drowning?
Take your foot off his head.

What do men and beer bottles have in common?
They're both empty from the neck up.

How many men does it take to change a roll of toilet paper?
We don't know. It's never happened.

The three stages of sex life of a man:
Tri-weekly. Try-weekly. Try-weakly.

The TV is on the blink, so a woman calls a repairman. Just as he's finished, the woman hears her husband's key in the lock. 'Sorry,' she says to the repairman, 'but you'll have to hide. It's my husband and he's insanely jealous.'

The repairman hides inside the TV console. The husband plops down in his favourite chair to watch some football. Inside the TV, the repairman is all squished up and getting hotter and hotter. Finally, on the verge of suffocation, he climbs out, marches across the room and out the front door.

The husband looks at the TV set, looks at his wife, looks back at the set again and says, 'I didn't see the referee send that guy off the field, did you?'

A man returns early from a business trip to find his wife making passionate love to a total stranger in their bedroom.

Goggle-eyed, he asks, 'What on earth are you doing?'

The wife turns to the other man and says, 'See, I told you he was as dumb as a post.'

God created man before creating woman, because you need a rough draft before you create a masterpiece.

Man says to God, 'God, why did you make woman so beautiful?'

God says, 'So you would love her.'

'But God,' the man says, 'why did you make us so dumb?'

God replies, 'So she would love you.'

A woman was chatting with her neighbour. 'I feel really great today. You see, I started out this morning with an act of unselfish generosity. I gave a $5 bill to a bum.'

'You gave a bum $5? That's a lot of money to give away like that. What did your husband say about that?'

'Thanks.'

'I heard you just got married again.'

'Yes, for the fourth time.'

'What happened to your first three wives?'

'They all died.'

'How did that happen?'

'My first wife ate poison mushrooms.'

'How awful! And your second?'

'She ate poison mushrooms.'

'And your third? She ate poison mushrooms, too?'

'No, she died of a broken neck.'

'An accident?'

'Not exactly. She wouldn't eat her mushrooms.'

A semi-trailer driver stops to pick up a woman hitchhiking. The driver opens the door and says, 'Climb in. I'm not like the other truckies that only let the good-looking girls have a ride.'

'My boyfriend and I aren't compatible. I'm a Virgo and he's an arsehole.'

A man parked his car in a supermarket carpark and was walking past an empty cart when he heard a woman ask, 'Mister, are you using that cart?'

'No,' he answered, 'I'm only after one thing.'

As he walked towards the store, she murmured, 'Typical male.'

A priest and a nun were returning from the church convention when their car broke down.

They had it towed to a garage and faced the fact that they'd have to spend the night in a motel. There was only one motel in town and it only had one room available. So they had a problem.

'Sister,' said the priest, 'I don't think the Lord would mind, under the circumstances, if we spent the night together in this one room. I'll sleep on the couch and you take the bed.'

'I think that would be okay,' said the nun.

They prepared for bed and each one took their agreed place. Ten minutes later the sister said, 'Father, I'm terribly cold.'

'Okay,' said the priest, 'I'll get up and get you a blanket from the closet.'

Ten minutes later the nun said, 'Father, I'm still terribly cold.'

'Okay, Sister,' said the priest, 'I'll get up and get you another blanket.'

Ten minutes later, the nun said, 'Father, I'm still terribly cold. I don't think the Lord would mind if we acted as man and wife for just this one night.'

'You're probably right,' said the priest. 'Get up and get your own damn blanket.'

A bloke was walking his pet duck when he decided to go and see a new Bruce Willis movie. But the lady at the box office said that he couldn't take the duck inside, so he walked around the corner and put the duck inside his raincoat. Safely inside, he squeezed into the only vacant seat, beside a married couple. About half an hour later the wife whispered to her husband, 'Funny, this guy next to me . . . his fly's open.'

Her husband replied, 'Well, is that the first time you've seen a man's pants unzipped?'

'No, honey, but . . . his thing is sticking out!'

Her husband said, 'Well, is that the first time you saw a man's penis?'

'No,' she screamed, 'but it's the first one I ever saw eating popcorn.'

A woman is in bed with her boyfriend while her husband's at work. Suddenly she hears his car in the driveway. She yells at the boyfriend, 'Quick! Grab your clothes and jump out the window.'

The boyfriend looks out the window and says, 'I can't jump out the window! It's raining like hell!'

She says, 'If my husband catches us in here, he'll kill both of us.'

So the boyfriend grabs his clobber, jumps out the window and finds himself in the middle of a charity marathon. He starts running alongside the others, in the nude, carrying his clothes on his arm. One of the runners asks him, 'Do you always run in the nude?'

He answers, 'Oh yes, it feels so free having the air blow over your skin.'

Another runner then asks the nude man, 'Do you always run carrying your clothes on your arm?'

The nuddy answers breathlessly, 'Oh yes, that way I can get dressed at the end of the run, climb in my car and go home.'

A third runner then asks, 'Do you always wear a condom when you're running?'

The nuddy answers, 'Only if it's raining.'

An old bloke is interested in joining a nudists' colony and gets permission to just wander around the grounds to decide if it's right for him. So he strips and goes for a walk. After a while he gets tired and decides to relax on a bench. A beautiful woman walks by and the sight of her causes him to become excited. The woman, noticing his erection, goes over and performs oral sex. The man is thrilled. He hurries back to the office and says he wants to join immediately and pays the first year's dues. He then lights up a cigar and goes out for another walk. While walking, he drops his cigar, bends over to pick it up and a young man runs up and performs anal sex. The old bloke immediately returns to the office and cancels his membership. 'But why?' asks the reception. 'You just said this was one of the greatest places you'd ever visited.'

'Yes,' says the old bloke, 'but at my age I only get excited once every three months, and I'm always dropping my cigar.'

The French Health Ministry invested a million francs in a research project to find out why the male penis has a head on it. They concluded that it gives the woman more pleasure.

The Germans, not to be outdone, spent five million deutschmarks on their own research. They concluded that the shape is intended to give the man more pleasure.

The Americans decided to lay the issue to rest. They spent ten dollars and concluded that the head is there to keep your hand from sliding off.

A bloke walks into a doctor's office complaining about a little bump on his forehead. It started small but it's getting bigger by the day. 'I don't know what it is, we'll scan it and in two weeks you can phone me for the results,' says the doctor.

He phones the doctor two weeks later, who tells him that he'd better come into the office because the prognosis isn't great. The man drags himself there with shoes of lead and asks the doctor to give it to him straight.

'You're growing a dick on your forehead.'

The man asks the doctor if it can do any harm.

'No,' the doctor continues, 'of course it's not cosmetically attractive but don't worry. In eight weeks you won't be able to see it any more.'

'Do you mean it will fall off by then?'

'No, it won't fall off. But by then your scrotum will be hanging over your eyes.'

A young man went into a drug store to buy a condom. The pharmacist told him that condoms come in packs of three, nine or 12 and asks which the young man wants. 'Well,' he said, 'I've been seeing this girl for a while and she's really hot. I want the condoms because I think tonight's the night. We've having dinner with her parents and then we're going out. And I've got a feeling I'm going to get lucky. So you better give me the 12-pack.'

The young man paid for his purchase and left. Later that evening he sat down to dinner with his girlfriend and her parents. He asked if he might give the blessing, and they agreed. He began the prayer and continued praying for about ten minutes. The girl lent over and said, 'You never told me you were such a religious person.' He lent over to her and said, 'And you never told me that your father was a pharmacist.'

A golfer encountered a genie and was granted a wish. He thought a while and said, 'Well, I've always been embarrassed by being rather small, if you know what I mean. Could you make me large?'

'Done,' said the genie, and disappeared.

Continuing his game, the man noticed an immediate change in his generative member. Within several holes, it was down to his knee, and by the 18th, it had crept into his sock. After holing his final putt, the man hurriedly returned to where he'd met the genie.

'Problem?' enquired the genie.

'Yes. Do you think I could trouble you for one more wish?'

'And what might that be?' asked the genie.
'Could you make my legs longer?'

After three months in the Far East, a businessman arrives home to discover that he's contracted a strange disease in the genital region. The doctor gives him the news that his penis will have to be amputated.

'I demand a second opinion,' the businessman says. So he sees numerous doctors all over Europe and North America but all advocate the same form of surgical intervention. Despairing of western medicine, the businessman decides to consult an Oriental doctor. After all, it seems that he's contracted an Oriental disease. The doctor, whose office is full of snakes in bottles and strange herbal remedies, gives the man and his member an examination. 'No, amputation isn't necessary.' The patient is elated.

'Brilliant! I saw so many western doctors and they all said amputation was the only way.'

'Western doctors!' snorts the Chinese gentleman. 'What do they know? Any Oriental herbalist or acupuncturist could tell you that it'll drop off by itself in four to six weeks.'

What's 12 inches long and white?
Nothing.

Johnny and Jim are walking through the desert. Suddenly, a snake bites Jim's prick.

Jim panics and Johnny panics. 'What can we do? We should call for a doctor,' screams Jim.

WHAM! Suddenly, in the middle of the desert, there's a telephone box. Johnny goes in, calls a doctor.

Johnny: My friend has been bitten by a snake. What do I do?

Doctor: What kind of snake?

Johnny: A one-metre, green and yellow one.

Doctor: Aye, aye. They're very dangerous.

Johnny: What can we do?

Doctor: The only thing you can do is suck the poison out. Otherwise your friend will be dead within half an hour.

Johnny hangs up. Jim, looking pale, asks what the doctor said.

'He said you'll be dead within half an hour.'

A man is driving his Porsche along Hollywood Boulevard when he's flagged down by an attractive hooker. She says, 'I'll do whatever you tell me to for $100.'

'Okay,' says the bloke as he hands over the money, 'paint my apartment.'

Homer hired a hooker and they met in his hotel room. 'I've got a little ... little tiny favour to ask.'

'Okay, but you'll have to pay extra,' said the prostitute. Homer took all his clothes off, went into the shower and said, 'Now, take the hairdryer, turn it on and blink the lights.' The prostitute turned the hairdryer on and when she started blinking the lights, Homer moaned with pleasure. 'Ooo, oooh, man this is great!'

'Now, I'm standing in the middle of a forest, it's raining cats and dogs and lightning's lit up the sky. The wind is blowing and in the distance you can hear thunder.'

'Okay, okay,' said the prostitute, 'isn't it time to make love now?'

'Are you crazy?' said Homer. 'In this weather?'

A man at a bar, deep in private thoughts, turned to a woman just passing by and said, 'Pardon me, Miss, do you happen to have the time?'

The woman screamed, 'How dare you make such a filthy, lewd, disgusting proposition to me.'

The man snapped to attention in surprise and was uncomfortably aware that every pair of eyes in the bar had turned in their direction. 'I was just asking for the time, Miss,' he mumbled, terrified. Whereupon the woman shrieked, 'I'll call the police if you say another word!'

Grabbing his drink, and feeling terribly embarrassed, the man crept to the far end of the room and huddled at a table, holding his breath and wondering how soon he could sneak out the door. A few moments later, the woman joined him. In a very quiet whisper she said, 'Sir, I'm terribly sorry to have embarrassed you, but I'm a psychologist and am studying the reaction of human beings to shocking statements.'

The man stared at her for five seconds, and then leaned back and bellowed, 'You'd do all that for me for just $2? And you'd do it to every other guy in the bar for another ten?'

A slightly drunk man walked into a bar, went up to the bartender and said, 'I'll bet you $50 I can bite my right eye!' Noticing the man had had a few to drink, the bartender took him up on it. The drunk then proceeded to pop out a glass eyeball and bite it. The bartender paid, and the man left.

The next day the man returned, a little drunker than the previous day, and he said to the bartender, 'I'll bet you $50 I can bite my left eye!' Knowing that the man couldn't have two glass eyes, the bartender again took him up on it. This time the man pulled out his false teeth and 'bit' his eye. The bartender paid up.

The next day, the man came in stone drunk. He went to the bartender and said, 'I'll give you a chance to get your money back. I'll bet you $100 that you can put a shot glass on the other end of the bar, and I can stand on this end and piss in it without getting a single drop outside the glass.'

The bartender just couldn't pass up the chance to get his $100 back, and the guy was very drunk, so he took the drunk up on his bet. He put the shot glass on the other end of the bar, and the drunk simply pissed all over the bar. The bartender smiled and said, 'You lost!' The drunk just smiled and gave him the $100.

The bartender said, 'You're not too unhappy about losing all your money. Why not?' The drunk explained, 'Because I just bet this guy $2000 that I could piss all over your bar and you wouldn't care!'

What's the difference between Madonna and Christopher Reeve's horse?

Madonna will jump anything.

How do you make a hormone?

Don't pay her.

What's the definition of an orgy?

A party where everyone comes.

What does a man with a 10-inch dick have for breakfast?

Well, this morning I had bacon, eggs, juice ...

What do you get when you cross PMS with ESP?

A bitch who thinks she knows everything.

What are the three words you don't want to hear while making love?

Honey, I'm home.

The scene was the Garden of Eden. God called Adam to him and said, 'Now I will teach you how to kiss.'

'Lord, what is kiss?' asked Adam.

'I will show you,' said God, and taught Adam everything he needed to know about kissing. Whereupon Adam went to Eve and kissed her for a while.

Then God called Adam back and said, 'Now I will teach you how to make love.'

'Lord, what is make love?'

'I will show you,' said God, and he taught Adam everything about making love. Adam went to Eve but came back almost immediately.

'Lord,' he asked, 'what is a headache?'

Soon after a girl started working at the local bank she noticed a very handsome man walking by her office. A co-worker told her that he was the bank's president and that he made a great deal of money.

She was determined to get to know him but wasn't quite sure how to go about it.

She sought the advice of her analyst. While she was around this man, he suggested, she should pretend she had a string attached to the top of her head and that it hung down her left side to her waist. She should pretend that a penny was attached to the end of the string. Then, when walking near the president, she should pretend to hit the penny with her left hip. This, stated the analyst, would provoke his interest.

Next day, she passed the man in the hall and began moving her left hip whilst in her head she was thinking, Hit the penny, hit the penny, hit the penny. And, as predicted, the man noticed her and stopped to chat.

A few days later, the man still hadn't asked her out. She went to the analyst again and this time he told her to pretend she had another string attached to the top of her head, that it hung down to her right hip. And attached to this string was a nickel. As she walked near the man, she was now to use her hips to hit first the penny and then the nickel.

The next day, she approached the man and began moving her hips according to the analyst's directions. In her head she was thinking, Hit the penny, hit the nickel, hit the penny, hit the nickel. And this time the man stopped and asked her out.

After a few weeks and many dates the girl decided she wanted to marry him. She talked to her analyst, who suggested that she pretend she had yet another string attached to the top of her head, and that it hung down her back to her bottom. Attached to this string was a dime. She was now to use her hips to hit all of these imaginary coins.

On her next date, she began moving her hips according to instructions. And in her head she was thinking, Hit the penny, hit the nickel, hit the dime, hit the penny, hit the nickel, hit the dime. And that night, just as the analyst promised, the man asked her to marry him, whereupon she began making wedding plans.

Being a virgin, she was worried about the honeymoon. She told her analyst that she was unversed in the art of making love, and he told her to pretend that one more string was attached to the top of her head, and that it hung down in front of her to her private parts. And attached to this string was a quarter. He told her that everything would be all right on the honeymoon if she hit the coins while making love.

Finally, the wedding day arrived and after the ceremony the couple went off on their honeymoon. That night, in the bathroom of her hotel, she practised moving her hips. Hit the penny, hit the nickel, hit the dime, hit the quarter. Hit the penny, hit the nickel, hit the dime, hit the quarter. Soon they were in bed and began making love for the first time. She started moving her hips. In her head she was thinking, Hit the penny, hit the nickel, hit the dime, hit the quarter. Hit the penny, hit the nickel, hit the dime, hit the quarter. Oh fuck the small change. Hit the quarter, hit the quarter.

The six most important men in a woman's life

1. The doctor, because he says, 'Take your clothes off.'
2. The dentist, because he says, 'Open wide.'
3. The hairdresser, because he says, 'Do you want it teased or blown?'
4. The milkman, because he says, 'Do you want it in the front or back?'
5. The interior decorator, because he says, 'Once it's in you'll love it.'
6. The banker, because he says, 'If you take it out too soon you'll lose interest.'

What is worse than being raped by Jack the Ripper?

Being fingered by Captain Hook.

Two gay men are walking by a morgue on a very hot day. One of them turns to the other and says, 'Want to stop in and suck down a cold one?'

A woman is talking to her best friend about getting a tattoo done for her husband's birthday. The friend recommends a popular tattoo artist who can tattoo just about anything. The woman visits the tattoo parlour the next day and asks for two butterflies to be tattooed on her butt. She wants the butterflies because her husband calls her his 'little butterfly'. The tattoo artist says he can't do such a large tattoo in such a short time and suggests that he puts two bees on her butt instead. The woman's a little disappointed, but agrees.

The next day she invites her husband into the bedroom and says, 'Sweetie, your birthday present is under my housecoat.'

He proceeds to undress his wife, lifting up her bottom so that he can have a good look.

'And who the hell is Bob?'

A young man joins the Foreign Legion, and is sent to live deep in the heart of Africa, surrounded by desert. After a few months with no female contact, he visits his commander. 'I haven't had sex for ages. Can you help me?'

'Well,' says the commander, 'you can borrow my camel any time you like.' The man declines, not wishing to seem that desperate. Six months later, feeling increasingly frustrated, he goes to the commander again, who says, 'The offer of my camel is still there.'

A year goes by and the poor man can stand it no longer. He goes to the commander one more time, his hands shaking. 'It's no use – I haven't had sex for a year. I must use your camel.' The commander agrees, the man takes the animal around the back of the compound and relieves his frustrations.

On returning, the man thanks the commander who says, 'Any time, young man. It's much quicker to the local brothel by camel, isn't it?'

One day a little boy went to his mother and asked, 'Mummy, what's a pussy?' A little shocked, his mother remained composed, went to the encyclopaedia, opened to the Cs and showed her son a picture of a cat. 'That is a pussy.'

'Oh,' replied the boy. 'Well, Mum, what's a bitch?' Again the mother went to the encyclopaedia, opened to the Ds and showed her son a picture of a dog. 'Son, this is a dog. A female dog is called a bitch.'

The little boy sought confirmation from his father. 'Dad, what's a pussy?' His father went to the dresser drawer, pulled out an issue of *Penthouse* and drew a circle. 'Son, that is a pussy.'

'Oh,' replied the boy. 'Well, what's a bitch?'

'Everything outside of the circle,' replied his father.

Two businessmen working in New York decided to get themselves a mistress. They set her up in her own apartment and agreed to split all expenses 50/50. The men alternated evenings with her, and things went fine for a few months.

One day the mistress announced to the two men that she was pregnant. They decided to do the right thing, and split all expenses 50/50.

When the mistress went into labour, one of the men was out of town on a business trip, so the other man went to the hospital with her. When the traveller returned, he headed for the hospital and saw his friend looking very glum outside the maternity ward.

'Is she all right? Were there problems with the birth?' he asked his friend.

'Oh, she's fine, but I've got some bad news for you. She had twins, and mine died.'

A man and a woman lived in a nursing home and over a period of years became best friends. They did everything together – they ate together, played chess together, went for walks together. One night after dinner the gentleman leaned over the table and said, 'Let's have sex together.' The woman protested that it had been 15 years since her last attempt. She wasn't sure if she could. But after further consideration, she decided that you only live once. 'What the heck,' she told him. 'Meet me at my room at 9 tonight.'

Arriving all excited, he began to undress, but the woman said there was something she had to say. 'I've lived a full life and have no complaints. Please don't let what I'm about to say make you think I don't want to do this, but I feel I have to tell you this. I have acute Angina.'

The old man reflected for a while, then continued to undress himself. 'Well, that's good, because the rest of you ain't so hot.'

A couple from Fresno, a real hick town, were on their honeymoon in a hotel. They were getting ready to get to know each other in the biblical sense when the wife looked over at her new husband and said, 'I've never done this before. So please be gentle.'

The husband got a scared look on his face and said, 'Wait a minute.' He ran outside to a phone booth where he called his father. 'Dad, she's a virgin. What'll I do?'

'Come home, son. If she's not good enough for her family, she's not good enough for our family.'

A very, very old man was staying at an expensive hotel. As he walked through the lobby he saw a most attractive older woman. Knowing that his life was short, he decided to take a chance and proposition her. He walked over and said, 'I have never done this before, but I find you very attractive, and wonder if I paid you $1000 would you come up to my room and have sex with me?' The woman was surprised, but considering the man's age, she figured that he'd be quite harmless and unable to perform. So she agreed. To her astonishment, the old man's performance truly amazed her. He put everything he had into it.

As he paid her the $1000 he said, 'Had I known you were a virgin, I would never have propositioned you. Or I would have offered you more money.'

The woman replied, 'That's okay. Had I known you were able to get it up, I would have pulled my pantyhose down.'

A marine, long stationed overseas, was contemplating his return home. He sent his wife an e-mail message. 'When I get home, there's going to be a lot of lovemaking going on. If you want in on it, you better meet me at the gang plank.'

She e-mailed back. 'You're so right. And if you want in on it, you'd better be the first guy down the gang plank.'

A guy goes to the doctor and discovers he has only one night to live. He tells his wife and they decide to get into some serious sex. After about an hour, they both fall asleep, but soon the guy awakes and decides he hasn't got much time left, so he tries some more foreplay.

After a while, she begins to respond and soon they're going at it like wild animals. Again they fall asleep. But, shortly, the husband wakes up and thinks he could do with one final round. He grabs his wife but she just ignores him.

He tries everything to get her excited, but she just gets pissed off, saying, 'That's enough. I know you want to do it again, but you don't have to get up in the morning.'

Abe, an 84-year-old New Yorker, is complaining to his old friend Sam that his sex life 'ain't so good any more'. Sam suggests that Abe goes to see a porno movie – that way he'll learn all the new techniques and enhance his sex life. Abe goes to Times Square and watches *Deep Throat* and *Debbie Does Dallas*. When he gets home, his wife, Golda, also in her 80s, asks where he's been and he tells her.

'You went to a porno movie, for heaven's sake why?' she asks.

'So I could learn the new ways and improve our sex life.'

'And did you learn anything useful?'

'Yes, I learnt that you should moan during sex. They moan a lot when they do it nowadays.'

'You want me to moan?' Golda asks.

'That's right, I want you should moan when we do it.'

That night they begin making love and Golda asks, 'Now you want I should moan, Abe?'

'Not yet Golda.'

Fifteen minutes she asks again if she should start moaning, and he again replies, 'Not yet.'

A half hour passes and the lovemaking is now really intense. 'You want I should moan now Abe?'

He pants, 'Yes, yes, now!'

'Oiyev, the crowds at Macy's today. I couldn't stand it . . . and the prices at the market . . . terrible. And the subway was stuck for 15 minutes . . . and . . .'

A woman walked into the drug store and said, 'I want to buy a vibrator.' The druggist waggled a finger and said, 'Come this way.'

The woman replied, 'If I could come that way, I wouldn't need a vibrator.'

Two sailors are on shore leave. They're walking down a busy street when one sees a beautiful blonde. He asks his buddy if he's ever slept with a blonde. 'Yeah, I've slept with a blonde before,' replies his friend.

They continue walking on down the street, taking in the sights, when the sailor sees a gorgeous brunette. 'Oh, what a babe!' he exclaims. 'Have you ever slept with a brunette?'

'Sure,' replies his buddy, 'I've slept with brunettes several times.'

They continue along and after a while the first sailor sees a beautiful redhead. He can't get over how lovely she is. 'How about a redhead?' he asks his buddy. 'Have you ever slept with a redhead?'

'Not a wink!'

As a truck driver came flying over the top of a steep hill, he spotted two figures in his path rolling around in the middle of the road. The driver blew his horn and braked frantically, but the couple continued their lovemaking in spite of his warnings.

The truck finally slid to a halt barely three inches

from the pair. 'Are you crazy?' the driver shouted at them. 'You could have been killed!'

The man stood up and faced the driver. 'Well, I was coming, she was coming and you were coming,' he panted, 'and you were the only one with brakes.'

Back in the good old days when Dudley Fuzz was in the habit of whooping it up, he was standing at a bar when a lady of enticing appearance approached him and suggested that they have a drink. Dudley said, 'Well, I'm no John D. Rockefeller, but I'll buy.'

After developing a slight buzz, she suggested a dance. Dudley smiled and said, 'I'm no Fred Astaire, but I'll give it a whirl.'

Later, she suggested that they go up to her room. 'I'm no Cary Grant,' he replied, 'but I'll follow you up there.'

They then went to the lady's apartment, where they had another drink, then did what had been on their minds all evening, anyway. Afterwards, the lady said, 'What about some money?'

Dudley shot back, 'Well, I'm no gigolo, but I'll take it.'

'Sangfroid' is when you find your lover in bed with someone else and you shoot them both in cold blood. 'Savoire faire' is when you find your lover in bed with someone else but you laugh because today's your turn with the hamster.

Three married couples want to join a new movement – the Orthodox Church of Sexual Repression. The first couple are in their 20s, the second in their 30s, the third in their 40s. Near the end of the introductory interview the priest tells them that they have to pass one small test, which entails abstaining from sex for a month. The three couples agree to try.

A month later they're having their final interview. The cleric asks the 40-year-old couple whether they'd managed to abstain. 'Well, it wasn't too difficult,' says the man, 'I spent hour after hour in my workshop and she loves gardening, so we had plenty of distractions. We did okay.'

'Very good, my children, you are welcome in our anti-fornicative faith. And how well did you manage?' he asks the 30-year-olds. 'Frankly, it was very difficult,' the husband says. 'We thought about sex all the time and we had to sleep in different rooms. And we prayed and prayed and prayed. However, we have been celibate for the entire month.'

'Very good, my children, you are welcome amongst the ranks of the spiritual and celibate. And how about you?' he asks the 20-year-old couple. 'Father, not too good at all. Oh, we did fine for the first week. But by the second week we were going crazy with desire. Then, one day during the third week, my wife dropped a head of lettuce, and when she bent over to pick it up, I weakened and took her right then and there.'

'Verily I say unto you, my son, you are not welcome in our church.'

'Yeah? Well, we're not too welcome at the greengrocer's either.'

What's the difference between hard and light?

You can get to sleep with a light on.

King Arthur was heading off for the Crusades when he called one of his squires and said, 'Here is the key to Guinevere's chastity belt. If in ten years I haven't returned you may use the key.'

His Majesty crossed the drawbridge and set off along a long dusty road. He stopped, turned his horse and took one last look at his castle. Whereupon the squire rushed towards him yelling, 'Stop! Your majesty! Thank goodness I was able to catch you. This is the wrong key!'

Mrs Jones woke up one night to discover her drunk husband trying to fill her mouth with aspirin.

She screamed, 'What in hell do you think you're doing?'

'Don't you have a headache?' he asked.

'No, I bloody well don't.'
'Great, let's fuck.'

A man picks up a girl in a bar and convinces her to come back to his hotel room. When they're relaxing afterwards he asks, 'Am I the first man you ever made love to?'

She looks at him thoughtfully. 'You might be,' she says, 'your face looks familiar.'

Two fellows were sitting in a coffee shop when the town's fire alarm went off. One jumped up and headed for the door. His friend shouted, 'Tom, I didn't know you were a fireman.'

'I'm not,' said Tom, 'but my mistress's husband is.'

A reverend gentleman decided it was time to tell his triplet daughters about the birds and the bees. At the same time he would test their innocence. Thus, he approached his first daughter, dropped his trousers and pointed to his generative member. 'Do you know what this is?'

'That's your cock,' she replied.

'You foul-mouthed hussy. Go and rinse your mouth out with soap,' he ranted.

Still fuming, he approached his second daughter,

pointed to his generative member and asked if she knew what it was.

'That's your dick.'

'Be gone, you daughter of Jezebel. Ye scarlet woman. Go and stick your tongue in boiling vinegar.'

Finally, he sought his third daughter and, dropping his trousers, pointed to his manhood and asked if she knew what it was. 'I've no idea,' she replied.

'Oh my chaste darling,' he said, 'that is my penis.'

To which she responded, 'You call that a penis?'

A tired traveller pulled into a three-star hotel around midnight and asked reception for a single room. As the clerk filled out the paperwork the traveller looked around and saw a gorgeous blonde sitting in the lobby. Asking the clerk to wait, he went over and talked to her. A few minutes later he came back with the girl on his arm and said, 'Fancy meeting my wife here! Guess I'll need a double room.'

Next morning, he came to settle his bill. Handing over his Amex card, he was appalled to be confronted with an account for $3000. 'What's the meaning of this?' he yelled at the clerk, 'I've only been here one night.'

'Yes,' said the clerk, 'but your wife has been here for three weeks.'

Have you heard Hugh Grant's next movie is called *Nine Months, Four Weddings and a Blow Job*?

Nine Months had a great opening weekend. Took $13 million at the box office. Pretty good, given that Hugh spent just $60 on the advertising.

What's pink and hard in the morning?

The *Finance Times* crossword.

What's pink, wrinkled and hangs out your trousers?

Your gran.

A bunch of guys are hanging out in their usual bar after work one day when a very attractive woman walks in and sits down right in the midst of them. After about two minutes of amazed looks, one of the men manages to ask the woman her name.

'Don't you recognise me, guys? It's me, Bernie. I had a sex change!'

Well, the men are all amazed at how their old drinking buddy, Bernie, looks with all his new equipment. So they buy some more drinks and get to talking about old times with Bernie/Bernice. After a few hours, the conversation rolls around to the subject of Bernice's operation. One of the guys says,

'Tell me, Bernice, what was the most painful thing about the operation? Was it when they cut your dick off?'

'No. That was painful, but that wasn't the most painful thing.'

Another man pipes up, 'I bet I know! I'll bet the worst part was when they cut your balls off, right?'

'No,' Bernice says, 'that really hurt, too, but that wasn't the worst part either.'

Finally, one of the men asks, 'Well, just what was the worst, most painful part of the operation?'

'When they cut my skull open and removed half my brain.'

A Freudian critique of Dr Seuss's *The Cat in the Hat*:

The Cat in the Hat is a hard-hitting novel of prose and poetry in which the author re-examines the dynamic rhyming schemes and bold imagery of some of his earlier works, most notably *Green Eggs and Ham*, *If I Ran the Zoo*, and *Why Can't I Shower with Mommy?* In this novel, Theodore Geisel, writing under the pseudonym Dr Seuss, plays homage to the great Dr Sigmund Freud in a nightmarish fantasy of a renegate feline helping two young children understand their own frustrated sexuality.

The story opens with two youngsters, a brother and a sister, abandoned by their mother, staring mournfully through the window of their single family dwelling. In the foreground, a large tree/phallic symbol dances wildly in the wind, taunting the children and encouraging them to succumb to the sexual yearnings they undoubtedly feel for each other. Even to the most unlearned reader, the blatant references to the incestuous relationship the two share set the tone for Seuss's probing examination of the satisfaction of primitive needs. The cat proceeds to charm the wary youths into engaging in what he so innocently refers to as 'tricks'. At this point, the fish, an obvious Christ figure who represents the prevailing Christian morality, attempts to warn the children, and thus, in effect, warns all of humanity of the dangers associated with the unleashing of the primal urges. In response to this, the cat proceeds to balance the aquatic naysayer on the end of his umbrella, essentially saying, 'Down with morality; down with God.'

After pooh-poohing the righteous rantings of the waterlogged Christ figure, the cat begins to juggle several icons of western culture, most notably two books, representing the Old and New Testaments, and a saucer of lacteal fluid, an ironic reference to maternal loss the two children experienced when their mother abandoned them 'for the afternoon'. Our heroic Id adds to this bold gesture a rake and a toy man, and thus completes the Oedipal triangle.

Later in the novel, Seuss introduces the proverbial Pandora's box, a large red crate out of which the Id releases Thing One, or Freud's concept of Ego, the division of the psyche that serves as the conscious mediator between the person and reality, and Thing Two, the Super-ego which functions to reward and punish through a system of moral attitudes, conscience, and guilt. Referring to this box, the cat says, 'Now look at this trick. Take a look!' In this, Dr Seuss uses the children as a brilliant metaphor for the reader, and asks the reader to re-examine his own inner self.

The children, unable to control the Id, Ego and Super-ego, allow these creatures to run free and mess up the house, or more symbolically, control their lives. This rampage continues until the fish, or Christ symbol, warns that the mother is returning to reinstate the Oedipal triangle that existed before her abandonment of the children. At this point, Seuss introduces a many-armed cleaning device which represents the psychoanalytic couch, and proceeds to put the two youngsters' lives back in order.

With powerful simplicity, clarity, and drama, Seuss reduces Freud's concepts on the dynamics of the human psyche to an easily understood gesture. Seuss's poetry and choice of words is equally impressive and serves as a splendid counterpart to his bold symbolism. In all, his writing style is quick and fluid, making *The Cat in the Hat* impossible to put down. While this novel is 61 pages in length, and one can read it in five minutes or less, it is not until after multiple readings that the genius of this modern-day master becomes apparent.

One sunny afternoon Superman was out flying around. Crime was slow that day so he decided to go over to Spiderman's house.

'Hey Spidey,' said Superman, 'let's go get a burger and a beer.'

'No can do,' said Spiderman. 'I've got a problem with my web-shooter. Can't fight crime tomorrow without it.'

So Superman went over to the Batcave. 'Hey Batman,' said Superman, 'let's go get a burger and beer.'

'Not today, Supe,' said Batman. 'My Batmobile has a flat tyre and I've got to fix it today. Can't fight crime tomorrow without it.'

A somewhat disgruntled Superman took to the air, cruised around the skies and found himself over a penthouse apartment. And what did his super vision see? None other than Wonder Woman, lying on the deck, spread-eagled, stark-naked.

Superman had a brilliant idea. 'They've always said I'm faster than a speeding bullet. And I've always wondered what she'd be like.' He zoomed down, did the deed, and flew off in a flash.

All of a sudden Wonder Woman sat up and said, 'What the hell was that?' and the Invisible Man climbed off her replying, 'I don't know, but it hurt like hell.'

GOD, I DON'T KNOW

Why God never received tenure at any university:

1. He had only one major publication.
2. It was in Hebrew.
3. It had no references.
4. It wasn't published in a referee journal.
5. Some even doubt he wrote it himself.
6. It may be true that he created the world, but what has he done since then?
7. His co-operative efforts have been quite limited.
8. The scientific community has had a hard time replicating his results.
9. He never applied to the Ethics Board for permission to use human subjects.
10. When one experiment went awry he tried to cover it up by drowning the subjects.
11. When subjects didn't behave as predicted he deleted them from the sample.
12. He rarely came to class, just told students to read the Book.

13. Some say he had his son teach the class.
14. He expelled his first two students for learning.
15. Although there are only ten requirements, most students failed his test.
16. His office hours were infrequent and usually held on a mountain top.

What do you get when you cross a nun with a PC?

A computer that will never go down on you.

An electrical engineer, a mechanical engineer and a civil engineer were having a discussion about what kind of engineer God was. The electrical engineer insisted God was an electrical engineer because the brain, the most important part of the body, employs electrical impulses.

The mechanical engineer insisted that God was a mechanical engineer because of the design of the world's best pump, the heart.

The civil engineer just laughed and said that she knew for a fact that God was a civil engineer. 'After all,' she said whilst pointing to their private parts, 'who else but a civil engineer would put a waste-water system through a recreation zone?'

A Catholic, a Baptist and a Mormon were sitting together one Sunday bragging about the size of their respective families.

The Catholic said, 'I've got a pretty big family. In fact I've now got four kids, all boys. One more and I could have a basketball team.'

The Baptist said, 'That's nothing. I've got eight boys, one more and I could have a baseball team!'

The two looked at the Mormon. After a moment of contemplation, he said, 'Well guys, I now have 17 wives. One more and I could have a golf course.'

A doctor, an architect and a computer scientist were arguing about whose profession was the oldest. In the course of their arguments, they got back to the Old Testament. The doctor said, 'The medical profession is clearly the oldest, because Eve was made from Adam's rib, and that was a simply incredible surgical feat.'

The architect didn't agree. 'In the beginning there was chaos and a void, and out of that the garden and the world were created. So God must have been an architect.'

The computer scientist said, 'Yes, but where do you think the chaos came from?'

A man walks along a lonely beach. Suddenly he hears a deep voice shout, 'DIG!' He looks around, but nobody's there. I am having hallucinations, he thinks.

Then he hears the voice again. 'I SAID DIG!' So he starts to dig in the sand with his bare hands and, after some time, he finds a small chest with a rusty lock. The deep voice says, 'OPEN!' So the man opens it and he sees lots of gold coins.

The deep voice says, 'TO THE CASINO!' The man takes the chest to the casino and the deep voice says, 'ROULETTE!' So he changes all the gold into a huge pile of roulette tokens and goes to one of the tables, where the players gaze at him with disbelief. The deep voice says, '27!' He takes the whole pile and drops it at 27. The table nearly bursts. Everybody is quiet when the croupier throws the ball. The ball stays at 26. The deep voice says, 'SHIT!'

Jesus and Moses are bored stiff in Heaven. 'Hey Moses,' says Jesus, 'why don't we disguise ourselves, go down to Earth and play 18 holes?' Moses agrees. So after donning appropriate clobber and renting clubs and carts, they arrive on the tee of the first hole. A long par-four with trouble down both sides.

They flip a coin and Moses wins the honour. He gets up over the ball and takes a mighty swing. The ball sails 300 metres down the middle of the fairway, coming to rest in a perfect position. 'Nice shot,' says Jesus grudgingly.

Jesus tees up a ball and hits a hard duck hook, which ends up on the side of a hill, not 100 metres away.

A squirrel spots the ball, picks it up in his mouth

and takes off running. A snake curled up on the rocks strikes at the squirrel and swallows it, ball and all. An eagle spots the snake, swoops down and carries it away in its talons. As it flies over the first green, a bolt of lightning flashes from the sky and hits the eagle. The eagle drops the snake, the snake regurgitates the squirrel, the squirrel lets the ball drop from its mouth, the ball rolls five metres across the green and into the hole. Moses lifts an eyebrow and asks Jesus, 'Are we going to play golf, or just screw around?'

Jesus and Moses were sitting up in Heaven, talking about Earth and some of the things they never got to do there. Jesus said to Moses, 'Man, I really want to go and play just one game of golf. Maybe God will let me go and play a game.' So Jesus went and asked God if he could play a game of golf. 'Well, I suppose,' said God, 'but Moses has to go with you as your caddy.' Jesus and Moses agreed, and soon found themselves at Pebble Beach, with golf shoes, and a bag of clubs, and one ball.

Jesus had been playing a good game, when he came to the ninth hole and saw a plaque. It read: 'The only person to ever score a hole-in-one on this hole was Arnold Palmer.' 'Well,' said Jesus, 'if Palmer could do it, why can't I? I'm Jesus Christ.' Moses gave him his ball and tee, and stood back to watch. Jesus adjusted his robe and halo, fixed his stance and exhaled deeply. He shouted, 'Fore!' and whacked the ball. It sailed into the air, hooked a little to the left, and splashed nicely into the water trap.

'Oh, no!' said Jesus. 'That was my only ball! Hey Moses, could you go and get it for me?' Moses went down to the water trap, parted the water, and walked in to get the ball back. Jesus teed off. 'Fore!' It sailed down into the water trap again. 'Hey Moses ...' But Moses was already on his way to get the ball. Moses came back, but before he returned the ball he said, 'I'm tired of getting your ball. If you hit it in the water again, you can get it yourself.'

Jesus took the ball and, sure enough, hit it straight into the water. He went down to the water, looking for the ball while walking on top of the water. Some other golfers started to play through and noticed this guy walking around on the water. One of them said to Moses, 'Who's that guy think he is? Jesus Christ or something?'

'No,' replied Moses, 'Arnold Palmer.'

A man finds a corked bottle on the green. He opens it and a genie appears to grant him one wish. After thinking about it for a while, the golfer says, 'I'd like to shoot par golf regularly.'

'No problem,' says the genie, 'but understand that your sex life will be reduced as a side effect.'

'Fine by me,' the man says. And POOF, the deed's done.

A few months later the genie reappears on the same golf hole and asks the man how his golf game is going.

'Great,' says the man, 'I'm now carrying a scatch handicap.'

'And what effect has it had on your sex life?'

'I can still manage to have relations two or three times a month.'

'Two or three times a month!' the genie says. 'That's not much of a sex life.'

'Well,' the golfer responds, 'I don't think it's too bad for a middle-aged priest with a very small parish.'

Sitting on the train with a young curate, the bishop was doing *The Times* crossword. 'Three across,' he said out loud, 'exclusively female, four letters, ends in U-N-T.'

'Aunt,' suggested the curate.

'Shit,' said the bishop, 'have you got an eraser?'

The scene is the confessional. A sinner murmurs to the priest, 'Forgive me, Father, I used the f-word this week.' 'Dear oh dear. Tell me, my son, the circumstances in which you used the f-word. Perhaps you suffered extreme provocation?'

'Well, I was golfing. And I hit a beautiful shot that sailed straight as an arrow for 300 metres. But then it suddenly detoured into the woods.'

'And that is when you used the f-word? I can appreciate your frustration, my son. I am a golfer myself.'

'No, not at that point Father. I then hit a perfect shot out of the woods. Only to see it land in the sand trap.'

'Now, I can understand you saying the f-word at that moment.'

'No, Father, I remained calm even then. I got out my sand wedge, hit a perfect shot right at the pin. But the ball stopped an inch from the cup.'

'How frustrating. And that, of course, is when you used the f-word.'

'No, Father, I was still calm.'

'YOU MEAN YOU MISSED THE FUCKING PUTT?'

Jew dies, goes to Heaven. Meets St Peter at the Pearly Gates. Gets guided tour of Heaven. At one point they come to a huge wall. St Peter says, 'Ssshh.' The Jew asks why. St Peter says, 'On the other side of the wall are the Christians, and they think they're the only ones here.'

St Peter has a day off and Jesus is standing in for him. Whilst booking in the new arrivals, Jesus notices an old man in the queue who seems familiar. When he gets to the front of the line, Jesus asks him his name.

'Joseph.'

Jesus is now more inquisitive. 'Your occupation?'

'Carpenter.'

By now Jesus is getting quite excited. 'Did you have a little boy?'

'Yes.'

'Did he have holes in his wrists and ankles?'

'Yes.'

Jesus looks at the old man and with a tear in his eye shouts, 'Father! Father!'

The old man looks puzzled and, after a moment, replies, 'Pinocchio?'

Three men were standing in line at the Pearly Gates. It had been a pretty busy day so Peter told the first one, 'We're just about full up at the moment, so I've been asked to admit only people who've had a particularly horrible death. What's your story?'

The first replies, 'Well, I'd suspected my wife of cheating on me. So today I came home early to try to catch her. As I came into my 25th-floor apartment, I could tell something was wrong. But all my searching around didn't reveal where this other guy could have been hiding. So I went out onto the balcony and, sure enough, there was this bloke hanging off the railing. I was really mad, so I started beating him and kicking him, but he wouldn't fall off. So I went back into the apartment, got a hammer and started bashing his fingers. He let go and fell. But he fell into the bushes, stunned but okay. I was so angry I rushed into the kitchen, grabbed the fridge and threw it over the edge. It landed on him, killing him instantly. But all the stress and anger got to me, and I had a heart attack and died on the balcony.'

'That sounds like a pretty bad death to me,' said Peter, letting the man in.

'It's been a very strange day,' said the second man. 'You see, I live on the 26th floor of my apartment building and every morning I do exercises out on my balcony. Well this morning I slipped and I fell over the edge. I got lucky and caught the railing of the balcony on the floor below me. But suddenly this man burst onto the balcony and started beating me and kicking me. Then he got a hammer and started bashing at my hands. Finally I let go but again I got lucky and fell into the bushes. I was stunned but okay. Whereupon a refrigerator came falling out of the sky and crushed me. And now I'm here.'

Once again, St Peter conceded it was a pretty horrible death.

Then the third man told his story. 'Picture this,' he says, 'I'm hiding naked inside a refrigerator . . .'

A bloke applies for admission at the Pearly Gates. St Peter says that there's a test consisting of three questions.

'For the first question, tell me which two days of the week begin with the letter T.'

'That's easy,' said the bloke, 'today and tomorrow.'

'Hmm,' said St Peter. 'Okay, just. Now for the second question. Tell me how many seconds there are in a year.'

'Twelve.'

'Twelve!' exclaimed St Peter. 'How twelve?'

'There's January 2nd, February 2nd, March 2nd, etc.'

'Okay,' said St Peter, 'for the third question, tell me God's first name.'

'Andy.'

'Andy?'

'Yeah, it's there in the song. "Andy walks with me, Andy talks with me, Andy tells me I'm His own ..."'

A busload of priests have an accident and all of them are killed instantly. On arriving at the Pearly Gates, they find there's a terrible queue. St Peter is there looking at a big book, jotting down notes, mumbling occasionally. There's a person standing in front of his desk being processed. There is an enormous number of people waiting, and the wait seems to take forever.

People are arriving all the time, some in mangled states, some famished and some looking normal. Then a dishevelled man comes in, cigarette hanging from his lips like it has taken root. The stubble on his chin looks as though it could sand diamonds. He stands at the back of the queue like everyone else. St Peter spies him, stands up and goes over to him. 'Oh, come in. Come in! Welcome. No need to queue, we have you already processed. Special treatment for you.'

'Hey,' says one of the priests. 'How come he gets special treatment? We are, after all, men of God.'

'That man,' says St Peter, 'was a taxi driver. He has scared the hell out of a lot more people than any of you.'

A political activist named Colin had just arrived in Hell and was told he had to make a choice. He could go to Capitalist Hell or Communist Hell. Wanting to compare the two, he wandered over to Capitalist Hell where, outside the door, Adam Smith stood looking bored.

'What's it like in there?' asked Colin.

'Well,' replied Adam, 'in Capitalist Hell they flay you alive, boil you in oil, chain you to a rock, and let a vulture tear your liver out. Then they cut you up into small pieces with sharp knives.'

'That's awful,' said Colin, 'I'm going to check out Communist Hell.' He went over to Communist Hell, where he discovered a long line of people waiting to get in. The line went round and round seven times and then receded towards the horizon. Colin pushed his way to the head of the line where, lo and behold, Karl Marx was busily signing people in. He asked Karl what Communist Hell was like.

'In Communist Hell,' said Marx impatiently, 'they flay you alive, boil you in oil, chain you to a rock, and let vultures tear out your liver. Then they cut you up into small pieces with sharp knives.'

'But isn't that the same as Capitalist Hell?' Colin asked.

'Yes,' sighed Marx, 'but sometimes we don't have oil, sometimes we don't have knives ...'

A guy dies and goes to Hell. The Devil greets him warmly at the gates and they enter a long corridor. As they walk along the Devil explains, 'Now that you're in Hell, you must choose the manner in which you will spend all eternity. I will show you some rooms and you must choose one.'

They get to the first room. The door opens and the man peers in. An endless circle of the damned with weights strapped to their backs walk around barefoot on hot coals. 'Oh, I don't think I like that,' says the man. They continue on to the second room.

In the second room, the damned walk around listening to elevator Muzak, walking on broken glass. 'Oh, I don't think I could stand that,' says the man.

In the last room, the man is surprised to find the damned standing around up to their armpits in shit, drinking coffee. 'That doesn't look so bad!' says the man. 'I'll stay here for eternity.'

'Very well,' says the Devil, closing the door behind him.

'Hmm, this isn't so bad,' thinks the man, as a demon gives him a cup of coffee. Suddenly the room supervisor calls out on his megaphone, 'All right everybody, coffee break's over! Back on your heads!'

Jesus walks into a hotel, tosses three nails on the front desk and says, 'Hey, can you put me up for the night?'

Jesus, hanging on the cross, spots Peter in the crowd at the bottom of the hill. 'Peter,' he calls, 'Peter.' Peter hears his name and replies, 'I hear, Lord. I'm coming,' and starts up the hill towards the cross. A Roman guard blocks Peter's way and says, 'Stop, or I'll cut off your arm.' But Peter says, 'I must go on, my Lord is calling me,' and tries to pass the guard, who cuts off his arm with a sword.

Jesus calls again, 'Peter, Peter . . .' Peter continues, bleeding and in terrible pain, up the hill towards the cross. Another guard blocks his way and says, 'Stop, or I'll cut off your other arm.' Peter ignores this, saying, 'I must go on, my Lord is calling me.' As Peter tries to pass, the second guard cuts off his other arm with his sword.

Jesus calls again, 'Peter . . .' Peter, getting weak from the pain, continues up the hill. A third guard blocks his way and says, 'Stop, or I'll cut off your leg.' Peter says to the guard, 'I must go on, my Lord is calling me.' As Peter tries to continue up the hill, the guard cuts off his leg. Peter falls in a heap of pain and blood, but still manages to push and drag himself up the hill towards the cross with his one remaining leg.

Jesus calls again, 'Peter, Peter . . .' Peter replies, 'I hear Lord, I'm coming.' Another guard steps in front of Peter and says, 'Stop, or I'll cut off your other leg.' Peter squirms to try to pass the guard, and the guard cuts off Peter's other leg. In excruciating pain, Peter uses sheer willpower to drag his mutilated body to the base of the cross. Panting, he raises his eyes towards Jesus and says, 'I am here, Lord. I have answered your call.'

Jesus looks down at Peter and says, 'Peter . . . I can see your house from up here.'

What was the last thing Jesus said to Mary as he was hanging from the cross?

'Mary, bring me my pumps, these spikes are killing me!'

Why doesn't Jesus eat M&Ms?

They fall through his hands.

A crowd of people has collected around a harlot, preparing to stone her. Jesus walks through the crowd, saying, 'Whosoever is without sin, let them cast the first stone.' Over the crowd comes a rock and, POW, it hits the harlot square on the head and kills her. Jesus says, 'Mother, sometimes you just piss me off!'

What's the difference between Jesus and a painting?

It takes only one nail to hang a painting.

A man was trapped on a desert island and it was sinking into the sea. As the water lapped round his feet a motorboat suddenly approached. 'Come on man, get in,' said the boatman.

'No,' the man said, 'I have faith in Jesus. He will save me.'

So the boat went off and the water continued to rise. When it was up to his chest another boat appeared. 'Get in the boat or you're going to drown,' said the boatman.

Again he said, 'No, I have faith in Jesus. He will save me.'

The boat went off and the water continued to rise. When it was up to his chin, a third boat appeared. 'This is your last chance, get in!'

'No, Jesus will save me.'

The boat departed, the water continued to rise and the man drowned. Arriving in Heaven he was greeted by Jesus. 'Hey Jesus, I trusted in you all my life and you let me down. You let me drown! I don't believe it.'

'*You* don't believe it!' said Jesus. 'I sent three fucking boats to save you.'

There was a wealthy Jew who owned a nail company. His only son had just graduated from college and the father wanted to get him involved in the company. So he placed his son in charge of the new advertising campaign. He told him that he would have no supervision and that any and all resources he needed would be at his disposal. The son was elated and immediately set off to make his father proud.

Four weeks later the son proudly proclaimed, 'I have finished!' He took his father out to examine the first product of the new campaign: a billboard portraying Christ on a cross with the caption, 'Even Then They Used Goldberg Nails'.

The father explained to the son that they couldn't portray Christ on a cross as it might offend their Christian clients. Dejected, the son said that he would fix the problem and report back to his father.

One week later the son took his father to see the billboard. Christ was no longer on the cross; he was lying at the base of the cross and the caption read, 'This Wouldn't Happen With Goldberg Nails'.

Have you heard of Salman Rushdie's new book?

It's called *Buddha, You Fat Fuck.*

One day a nun was fishing and caught a huge fish for supper. A man was walking by and said, 'Wow, what a goddamn fish!' The sister said, 'Sir, you shouldn't talk to me like that, I'm a nun!' and the man said, 'But that's the name of it: a goddamn fish.'

So the sister took the fish back to the rectory and said, 'Mother Superior, look at the goddamn fish I caught.' The Mother Superior said, 'Sister, you shouldn't talk like that!' And the sister said, 'But Mother Superior, that's the name of it: a goddamn fish.'

The Mother Superior said, 'Well give me the goddamn fish and I'll clean it.' While she was cleaning the fish the Monsignor walked in and she said, 'Monsignor, look at the goddamn fish that Sister caught.' The Monsignor said, 'Mother Superior, you shouldn't talk like that!' and the Mother Superior said, 'But that's the name of it: a goddamn fish.' So the Monsignor said, 'Well, give me the goddamn fish and I'll cook it.'

That evening at supper there was a new priest at the table, and he said, 'Wow, what a nice fish.' The sister said, 'I caught the goddamn fish.' And Mother Superior said, 'I cleaned the goddamn fish.' And the Monsignor said, 'I cooked the goddamn fish.' And the new priest said, 'I like this fucking place already!'

Two nuns are bicycling down a cobblestone street. The first one says to the other, 'I haven't come this way before.'

The second one says, 'I know, it's the cobbles.'

How do you get rid of a nun's hiccups?

Tell her she's pregnant!

What is the definition of suspicion?
A nun doing press-ups in a cucumber field.

What is the definition of innocence?
A nun working in a condom factory thinking she's making sleeping bags for mice.

What do you call a nun who walks in her sleep?
A roaming Catholic.

How do you get a nun pregnant?
Dress her up as an altar boy.

What's black and white and red and has trouble getting through a revolving door?
A nun with a spear through her head.

Two nuns in a bath. The first one says, 'Where's the soap?'
The second one replies, 'Yes it does, doesn't it?'

'I would like to have 120 bananas for the convent,' says Mother Superior at the grocery store.

'If you buy such a large quantity, it is more economic to buy 144 of them,' says the shopkeeper.

'Oh well, we could always eat the other 24.'

MOTHER SUPERIOR: Sister Maria, if you walk through town at night and you're accosted by a man with bad intentions, what would you do?'

SISTER MARIA: I would lift my habit, Mother Superior.

MOTHER SUPERIOR (shocked): And what would you do next?'

SISTER MARIA: I would tell him to drop his pants.

MOTHER SUPERIOR (even more shocked): And what then?'

SISTER MARIA: I would run away. I can run much faster with my habit up than he can with his pants down.

A priest asks a nun if he can walk her back to the convent. She says, 'Just this once.' Upon arriving, he asks if he can kiss her. She replies, 'Well all right, as long as you don't get into the habit.'

Two nuns are walking down an alley at night. Two guys jump out and start raping them. The first nun looks to Heaven and says, 'Forgive them, Father, for they know not what they're doing.' The second nun looks up and says, 'This one does!'

It was Friday, and four nuns went to the priest at the local Catholic church to ask for the weekend off. They argued back and forth for a few minutes. Finally the priest agreed to let them leave the convent for the weekend. 'However,' he said, 'as soon as you get back Monday morning I want you to confess to me what you did over the weekend.' The four nuns agreed, and ran off.

Monday came, and the four nuns returned. The first nun said to the priest, 'Forgive me, Father, for I have sinned.' The priest asked, 'What did you do, Sister?' She replied, 'I watched an R-rated movie.' The priest looked up at Heaven for a few seconds, then replied, 'You are forgiven. Go and drink the holy water.'

The first nun left, and the fourth nun began to chuckle quietly under her breath.

The second nun said to the priest, 'Forgive me, Father, for I have sinned. I was driving my brother's car and I hit a neighbour's dog and killed it.' The priest looked up to Heaven for half a minute, then said, 'You are forgiven. Go and drink the holy water.'

By this time the fourth nun was laughing quite audibly.

Then the third nun said, 'Forgive me, Father, for I have sinned. Last night, I ran naked up and down Main Street.' The priest looked up at Heaven for a full five minutes before responding. 'God forgives you. Go and drink the holy water.'

The fourth nun fell on the floor, laughing so hard, tears ran down her cheeks.

The priest asked her, 'Okay, what did you do that was so bloody funny?'

The fourth nun replied, 'I peed in the holy water.'

The nuns at the local convent had their daily announcement session. The Mother Superior walked out in front of the 100 nuns with a very serious frown on her face.

MOTHER SUPERIOR: There was a sinful deed committed here yesterday.

99 NUNS: Oh, no!

ONE NUN: Hee, hee, hee.

MOTHER SUPERIOR: Today I found a pair of men's underwear.

99 NUNS: Oh, no!

ONE NUN: Hee, hee, hee.

MOTHER SUPERIOR: And I also found a condom.

99 NUNS: Oh, no!

ONE NUN: Hee, hee, hee.

MOTHER SUPERIOR: And it has been used!

99 NUNS: Oh, no!

ONE NUN: Hee, hee, hee.

MOTHER SUPERIOR: And there was a hole in it!

ONE NUN: Oh, no!
99 NUNS: Hee, hee, hee!

Four nuns were standing in line at the gates of Heaven. Peter asks the first if she has ever sinned.

'Well, once I looked at a man's penis,' she said.

'Put some of this holy water on your eyes and you may enter Heaven,' Peter told her.

Peter then asked the second nun if she had ever sinned. 'Well, once I held a man's penis,' she replied.

'Put your hand in this holy water and you may enter Heaven,' he said.

Just then the fourth nun pushed ahead of the third nun.

Peter asked her, 'Why did you push ahead in line?' She said, 'Because I want to gargle before she sits in it.'

The seven dwarfs are in Rome and they go on a tour of the city. After a while they go to the Vatican and meet the Pope. Grumpy, for once, seems to have a lot to say. He keeps asking the Pontiff questions about the church and, in particular, nuns.

'Your Holiness, do you have any really short nuns?'

'No, my son, all our nuns are at least five feet tall.'

'Are you sure? I mean, you wouldn't have any

nuns that are, say, about my height? Maybe a little shorter?'

'I'm afraid not. Why do you ask?'

'No reason ... you're positive? Nobody in a habit that's about three feet tall, two and a half feet tall?'

'I'm sure.'

'Okay.' Grumpy looks dejected at this news, and the Pope wonders why, so he eavesdrops on the dwarfs as they leave the building.

'What'd he say?' What'd he say?' chants the other six dwarfs.

Grumpy says, 'He said they don't have any.'

And the other six start chanting, 'Grumpy fucked a penguin! Grumpy fucked a penguin! Grumpy fucked a penguin!'

A nun is undressing for a bath when there's a knock at the door. The nun calls out, 'Who is it?' A voice answers, 'A blind man.'

The nun decides to get a thrill by having the blind man in the room while she's naked, so she lets him in. The man walks in, looks straight at the nun and says, 'Corrrrr, and can I sell you a blind, dearie?'

A nun and a priest were travelling across the desert and realised halfway across that the camel they were using for transportation was about to die. They set up a makeshift camp, hoping someone would come to their rescue, but to no avail. Soon the camel died.

After several days of not being rescued, they agreed that they were not going to be rescued. They prayed a lot, and discussed their predicament in great depth.

Finally, the priest said to the nun, 'You know, Sister, I am about to die, and there's one thing I've always wanted here on Earth – to see a woman naked. Would you mind taking off your clothes so I can look at you?'

The nun thought about this request for several seconds and then agreed to take off her clothes. As she was doing so, she remarked, 'Well, Father, now that I think about it, I've never seen a man naked either. Would you mind taking off your clothes, too?' With little hesitation, the priest also stripped.

Suddenly the nun exclaimed, 'Father! What is that little thing hanging between your legs?'

The priest patiently answered, 'That, my child, is a gift from God. If I put it in you, it creates a new life.'

'Well,' responded the nun, 'forget about me. Stick it in the camel.'

Three nuns who had recently died were on their way to Heaven. At the Pearly Gates they were met by St Peter. Clustered around the gates was a collection of lights and bells.

St Peter stopped them and told them that they would each have to answer a question before they could enter.

ST PETER: What were the names of the two people in the Garden of Eden?

1ST NUN: Adam and Eve.

The lights flashed, the bells rang and in she went through the Pearly Gates.

ST PETER: What did Adam eat from the forbidden tree?

2ND NUN: An apple.

The lights flashed, the bells rang and in she went through the Pearly Gates.

And finally it came the turn of the last nun.

ST PETER: What was the first thing Eve said to Adam?

Afer a few minutes thinking she said, 'Gosh, that's a hard one!'

The lights flashed, the bells rang and in she went through the Pearly Gates!

A man is driving down a deserted stretch of highway when he notices a sign out of the corner of his eye. It says SISTERS OF MERCY HOUSE OF PROSTITUTION 10 MILES. He thinks it is just a figment of his imagination and drives on without a second thought. Soon he sees another sign which says SISTERS OF MERCY HOUSE OF PROSTITUTION 5 MILES and realises that these signs are for real.

When he drives past a third sign saying SISTERS OF MERCY HOUSE OF PROSTITUTION NEXT RIGHT his curiosity gets the best of him and he pulls into the drive.

On the far side of the parking lot stands a

sombre stone building with a small sign next to the door reading SISTERS OF MERCY. He climbs the steps and rings the bell. The door is answered by a nun in a long black habit who asks, 'What may we do for you, my son?' He answers, 'I saw your signs along the highway and was interested in possibly doing business.'

'Very well, my son. Please follow me.'

He is led through many winding passages and is soon quite disoriented. The nun stops at a closed door, and tells the man, 'Please knock on this door.' He does as he is told and the door is answered by another nun, holding a tin cup.

'Please place $50 in the cup, then go through the large wooden door at the end of this hallway,' she says. He gets $50 out of his wallet and places it in the second nun's cup. He trots eagerly down the hall and slips through the door, pulling it shut behind him. As the door locks behind him, he finds himself back in the parking lot, facing another small sign: GO IN PEACE. YOU HAVE JUST BEEN SCREWED BY THE SISTERS OF MERCY.

Sister Catherine is asking all the Catholic school children in fourth grade what they want to be when they grow up.

Little Sheila says, 'When I grow up, I want to be a prostitute!'

Sister Catherine's eyes grow wide and she barks, 'What did you say?'

'A prostitute!' Sheila repeats.

Sister Catherine breathes a sigh of relief and says, 'Thank God! I thought you said a Protestant.'

A nun gets on a bus and sits behind the driver. She tells the bus driver that she is very ill and wants to experience sex before she dies. The bus driver agrees to accommodate her, but the nun explains that she can't have sex with anyone who is married, as that would be a sin. The bus driver says he's not married. The nun says she also has to die a virgin, so she will have to take it in the arse.

Being the only two on the bus, they go to the back and take care of business. When they are done, and he has resumed driving, he says, 'Sister, I have a confession to make. I am married and have three children.'

The nun replies, 'That's okay. I have a confession, too. My name is Dave, and I'm on my way to a costume party.'

An old nun is walking home from the convent one day, when a man jumps out from the bushes and has his way. Then the man says, 'What will you tell the Holy Father now, Sister?'

She says, 'I must tell the truth! I will say I was walking home from the convent when a man jumped out from the bushes and raped me twice, unless you're tired!'

Did you hear the one about the man who opened a dry cleaning business next door to the convent?

He knocked on the door and asked the Mother Superior if she had any dirty habits.

Three nuns are walking down the street, when a man jumps out and flashes at them. The first nun has a stroke, the second nun has a stroke, but the third one doesn't touch him.

There was an Irish nun sitting on the curb, sipping a bottle of stout, and obviously drunk out of her mind. The town constable walked up to her and said, 'Sure now, Sister Colleen, and why'd ya be doing a thing like this?'

The sister replied, 'Oh now, it's not fer meself I done it, sir. I done it fer the Mother Superior, to cure her constipation.'

The perplexed policeman looked askance at this and asked, 'And how might it be that yer present state could have anything to do with the Mother Superior's constipation?'

To which Sister Colleen said, 'When she sees me this way, she'll be shittin' a brick.'

A priest decides to pay a visit to a nearby convent which is in a rundown neighbourhood. As he walks down the street, several prostitutes approach and proposition him.

'Twenty bucks a trick!'

These solicitations embarrass the priest, who lowers his head and hurries on until he gets to the convent. Once inside he displays his naivety by asking the Mother Superior, 'What's a trick?'

She answers, 'Twenty bucks – just like on the outside!'

A nun is driving through some very lonely countryside. The car stops and she notices there is no petrol left, so she walks to the nearest filling station. But, of course, being a nun, she is a little unworldly, and she forgets to take along a jerrycan for the petrol. The nice guy at the filling station doesn't have one either. He thinks for a while, then hands her a chamberpot full of petrol. The nun walks back to her car and starts pouring the petrol into the tank. A bypassing car stops, and the driver looks out and says, 'Sister, how I would like to have as much faith as you!'

A guy gets on a bus and sees a nun sitting in the corner. Under her wimple he spots a glimmer of her face, which is remarkably beautiful. When she moves, her vestment cannot hide the fact that she has a gorgeous figure. He gets more and more excited until, finally, he approaches her and says, 'Sister, I don't normally do this sort of thing, but I think I love you. Can we get together some time?' Enraged, the nun gets off the bus.

The bus driver asks him why he was bothering the nun. The guy apologises, insisting that he has never done this sort of thing before. But the bus driver says, 'Don't apologise, I was checking her out myself. In fact, let me do you a favour. Did you see where she got off? There's a little park there, and every day she goes to pray, at the same time. If you go there tomorrow, maybe you'll get lucky.' The guy thanks him and leaves.

Next day, he goes to the park and there is the nun in a secluded spot by some trees. So he walks off into the bushes and comes back a few minutes later dressed in a long white robe, with a long blonde wig, a blonde beard and a crown of thorns. The nun is overwhelmed. She asks what he wants her to do. He explains that every few thousand years he likes to come to Earth and get laid. Blushing, the nun says it would be an honour, but insists on turning her back on him.

Afterwards, he is suddenly overcome with a blast of guilt and says, still panting, 'Sister, I have to confess. I'm not really Jesus. I'm actually the guy who was annoying you on the bus yesterday.'

The nun says, 'That's okay. In fact, I'm not really a nun. I'm actually the bus driver.'

A pale-faced nun, still in shock, enters the office of the Mother Superior and reports, with a profound blush, 'Mother Superior, we've discovered a case of syphilis.'

'Wonderful!' says the old nun. 'I was getting sick of the Chablis.'

The Mother Superior is praying in the chapel when she hears an inordinate amount of laughing and giggling outside. Looking through a chink in the stained glass, she sees all the sisters riding around on their new bikes, and having a great deal of fun. However, they're making so much noise, she can't concentrate on her praying. So she goes out and says, 'Sisters, please! A bit more quiet or you'll all have to put the saddles back.'

During his visit to the US, Pope John II had a meeting with a senator. The senator asked the Pope, 'Your Holiness, how do you find our country?'

The Pope replied, 'I love it! It's a wonderful country! Friendly people, blessed with an abundance of natural resources . . .' and so on and so forth. The senator asked, 'Is there anything about our country that you don't like? I am, after all, a United States senator, and maybe I could change some things.'

The Pope thought a while and said, 'Now that

you mention it, there are two things about your country that I do not like.' The senator asked, 'What are they? Maybe I can help.'

'The first thing I don't like about your country is the large number of Polish jokes told. They make my countrymen out to be a bunch of idiots!'

The senator said, 'I have a solution for that! When I get back to Washington, I'll get together with some of my Senate colleagues and we'll pass a bill, which I'm sure will become law, that will make it a federal crime to tell a Polish joke, and anyone caught telling a Polish joke will be fined $50. How do you like that?'

The Pope replied, 'Great idea! I love it!'

The senator asked, 'Now, why don't you tell me the second thing you don't like about the US? Maybe I can do something about it as well.' The Pope answered, 'M&Ms.'

The senator, a bit confused, asked, 'M&Ms? What's not to like about M&Ms?'

The Pope replied, 'They're hard to peel.'

The Pope died. Like all good Christians he went to Heaven and knocked on the door. Peter opened the door and lifted an enquiring eyebrow. The Pope said, 'I'm the Pope.' Peter picked up the phone and rang Jesus. 'I have someone here who says he's the Pope. Do you know him?'

'No, never heard of him. Send him to Hell,' Jesus answered.

'That can't be true. Ring God himself,' the Pope

said. So Peter rang God and said, 'We've got someone who says he's the Pope. Do you know him?' God answered, 'No, never heard of him, send him to Hell.'

'The last chance I have is the Holy Spirit,' the Pope said. Peter rang him and said, 'I have someone here who says he's the Pope. Do you know him?'

'Yes,' he said, 'I know him. He's the one who told everyone I got Maria pregnant. Send him to Hell.'

A rich American tourist holidaying in Rome was intent on seeing the Pope. He waited in a long queue, wearing a rather expensive suit and hoping the Pope would notice how smart he was and perhaps exchange a few words with him.

As the Pope made his way slowly down the queue, he walked right passed the American without noticing him. The Pope then stopped next to a tramp, leaned over and whispered something in his ear, and made his way on again.

This pissed off the American, so he agreed to pay $1000 to the tramp for his suit in the hope that the Pope would speak to him the next day.

The next morning, the Pope made his way slowly up to the American. When he finally reached him, the Pope leaned over and spoke softly in his ear, 'I thought I told you to fuck off!'

What happened to the Pope when he went to Mount Olive?

Popeye beat the shit out of him.

The Pope is on his 1988 tour of America, in the middle of a three-day bash in New York. On the second day, he is driving back to his motel after a heavy day's bible bashing. It suddenly occurs to him that he is a little peckish and so he decides to go for something to eat. Out of the corner of his eye he notices Mel's Diner and immediately pulls over.

He hops out, kisses the ground a couple of times and then goes in and sits down. A sleazy waitress wanders over, notices who he is and then straightens herself up. 'Yes, your Holiness, what would you like?' The Pope thinks for a while. 'Well, daughter, I have this terrible craving for a nice steak.'

'Sure Mac, er, I mean your Holiness. Would you like it well done, medium or rare?'

'Oh, I think I'd like a very rare one please.' The waitress raises her arm. 'One bloody steak, Mel!' she shouts. The Pope is horrified. 'Oh no, my daughter, you mustn't swear. There's no call for that!'

'But you don't understand – "bloody" describes how the steak is cooked. Very rare.' The Pope smiles. 'I understand, how stupid of me.

A little later, the Pope's steak arrives and he gets stuck in. It's delicious, and he goes to bed that night feeling satisfied. The next day, the Pope has an even bigger God-squadding session, in which he is assisted by 31 of his cardinals. Afterwards he calls his cardinals together. 'Right lads, as you've done a really good job today, I'll treat you to a bit of nosh at this place I know. You'll like it, I'm sure.'

So the Pope takes his cardinals to the diner and calls to the waitress, 'Can I have 32 bloody steaks please?'

Immediately, one of the cardinals slaps his knee. 'Hey, yeah! And plenty of fucking chips, okay?'

The Pope is travelling along in the Popemobile, beside a large river in South Africa. He catches sight of a black man struggling and screaming in the river as he tries in vain to fight off a huge crocodile. Suddenly, two white men leap into the water, drag the man and the croc to land, and then beat the crocodile to death with sticks.

The Pope is really impressed by this. He goes over to where the two men are standing next to the bleeding and unconscious black man and says, 'Congratulations. That was the most wonderful thing to do, and I can see that it is men like you who will rebuild this country as an example of racial harmony.'

The Pope then goes on his way. One of the white men says, 'Who was that?' and the other replies, 'That was the Pope, he is in direct communication with God. He knows everything.'

The first man says, 'Maybe, but he knows fuck all about crocodile fishing.'

A fellow was visiting the Vatican and became separated from his tour group. Desperately needing a pee, he found a bathroom and walked in and, to his horror, discovered the Pope sitting on the toilet, masturbating. He promptly snapped a couple of pictures. The Pope, recovering his composure, offered the photographer ten million lira for his camera, which the fellow accepted.

After disposing of the film, his Holiness decided he'd take the camera on his travels. One day, whilst visiting the US, a bishop was admiring his Holiness's camera. 'How much did you pay for it?'

'$10 000.'

'Wow! The guy that sold you that must have seen you coming!'

One day, a young priest is instructed by his elders that he must hear confessions. He has never done this before, and so he is given a list of what to give out as penance.

A woman comes into the confessional and begins. 'Forgive me Father, for I have sinned.' The priest replies, 'What is your sin, my child?'

'I have told lies,' she says. The priest consults his list and sees that the required penance is two Hail Marys.

'Anything else, my child?' he asks. 'Father, I've committed fellatio,' she replies. The priest scans the list and panics because he cannot find fellatio! He sticks his head out of the door of the confessional and sees an altar boy passing by. 'Quick, what does

Father Brown give for fellatio?' he asks. 'Ten dollars' the boy replies.

One day, the old man in charge of ringing matins at the local monastery died, so the abbot decided to advertise for a new bellringer. After running an ad for several days in the local newspaper, an applicant finally showed up. Much to the abbot's dismay, this man had no arms.

'I'm afraid,' said the abbot, 'that you don't have much of a career as a bellringer ahead of you.'

'Nonsense,' said the man, 'let me show you what I can do.'

They climbed up the bell tower, and the man proceeded to run full-speed across the tower, throwing himself face-first into the bells. A lovely pealing sound resulted, and the abbot decided then and there to hire the man.

The man acted as the monastery's bellringer for several months until, while ringing the evening meal, he missed the bells and plummeted from the tower, killing himself. In the resulting investigation, the chief of police called over the abbot and pointed out the dead man. 'Do you recognise this man?' asked the police chief.

'Hmmm,' said the abbot, 'I don't recall his name, but his face rings a bell.'

What is red and full of feathers?

A fallen angel.

What's an atheist's favourite Christmas movie?
Coincidence on 34th Street.

An old man was unhappy because he'd lost his favourite hat. Instead of buying a new one, he decided to go to the local church and pinch one out of the vestibule. But when he tried, an usher saw him and forced him to sit in the pew and listen to the entire sermon on the Ten Commandments.

After church, the old man went to the preacher, shook his hand and said, 'I want to thank you for saving my soul today. I came to church to steal a hat and after hearing your sermon on the Ten Commandments, I decided against it.'

'You mean the Commandment "Thou shalt not steal" changed your mind?' asked the preacher.

'No,' said the old man. 'The one about adultery did. As soon as you mentioned it, I remembered where I'd left my hat.'

Two clergymen were discussing the present sad state of sexual morality. 'I didn't sleep with my wife before we were married,' one clergyman said self-righteously. 'Did you?'

'I'm not sure,' said the other, 'what was her maiden name?'

A preacher is buying a parrot. 'Are you absolutely certain it doesn't swear?' asked the preacher. 'Oh absolutely. It is a very religious parrot,' the storekeeper assured him. 'Do you see those strings on his legs? If you pull the right one he'll recite the Lord's Prayer. And if you pull the left one, he'll recite the 23rd Psalm.'

'That's wonderful,' said the preacher. 'But what happens if you pull both strings?'

'I fall off my fuckin' perch, you goddamn shit-for-brains,' screeched the parrot.

A monastery was perched high on a cliff and the only way to reach it was to ride in a basket which was hauled to the top by several monks. Obviously, the ride up the steep cliff in the basket was terrifying. One visitor got exceedingly nervous. About halfway up he noticed that the rope by which he was suspended was old and fraying. With a trembling voice, he asked the monk who was riding with him how often they changed the rope. The monk thought for a moment and answered, 'Whenever it breaks.'

A drunk gets on a bus, staggers up the aisle and sits next to an old lady, breathing fumes all over her. She looks at him with withering contempt and says, 'I've got news for you. You're going straight to Hell.' The drunk jumps out of his seat and shouts, 'Christ! I'm on the wrong bus!'

An Irish priest and a rabbi found themselves sharing a compartment on a train. After a while, the priest opened a conversation by saying, 'I know that in your religion, you're not supposed to eat pork. Have you actually ever tasted it?'

The rabbi said, 'I must tell the truth. Yes, I have, on the odd occasion.'

Then the rabbi had his turn of interrogation. He asked, 'Your religion, too. I know you're supposed to be celibate. But . . .'

The priest replied, 'Yes, I know what you're going to ask. I have succumbed once or twice.'

There was silence for a while. Then the rabbi peeped around the newspaper he was reading and said, 'Better than pork, isn't it?'

Above a monastery on Mount Athos, there's a cave that particularly spiritual monks choose to spend some years sitting inside. It's very difficult to get up there. Very dangerous.

A monk was told that once he had entered the cave, his only contact with the world would come every six years, when he'd be allowed to speak just two words. Six years later the head monk asked the novice what his two words were. 'More food,' said the novice. 'Okay,' the head monk said, 'I'll leave you a couple of extra loaves of bread.'

Six years later the head monk asked again. 'I'm cold,' said the novice. 'No problem,' said the head monk, 'I'll leave you this blanket.'

Six years later the head monk inquired of the

novice if there was anything else he wanted to say. 'I quit,' said the novice. To which the head monk testily responded, 'Fine by me. Good riddance. All you've ever done since you got here is complain.'

One day a mum and her eight-year-old daughter were walking along the beach, just at the water's edge, when a huge wave crashed on the beach, sweeping the child out to sea. 'Oh God,' lamented the mother, looking up at the heavens and shaking her fist. 'She was my only child. I can't have more. She was the love and joy of my life and I've cherished every moment she's been with me. Give her back to me and I'll be in church every day. Forever!'

Suddenly an even bigger wave deposited the girl back on the sand. The mother looked up to Heaven and said, 'She was wearing a hat!'

In the beginning was the Plan.

And then came the Assumptions.

And the Assumptions were without form.

And the Plan was without substance.

And darkness was upon the face of the Workers.

And they spoke amongst themselves, saying, 'It is a crock of shit, and it stinketh.'

And the Workers went unto their Supervisors and said, 'It is a pail of dung, and none may abide the odour thereof.'

And the Supervisors went unto their Managers, saying, 'It is a container of excrement, and it is very strong, such that none may abide by it.'

And the Managers went unto their Directors, saying, 'It is a vessel of fertilizer, and none may abide its strength.'

And the Directors spoke amongst themselves, saying to one another, 'It contains that which aids plant growth, and it is very powerful.'

And the Vice Presidents went unto the President, saying unto him, 'This new plan will actively promote the growth and vigor of the company, with powerful effects.'

And the President looked upon the Plan, and saw that it was good.

And the Plan became Policy.

This is how Shit happens.

Where did Prince Charles spend his honeymoon?

Indiana.

Why did Jesus cross the road?

He was nailed to the chicken.

Deciding that the time had come, God calls Boris Yeltsin, Bill Clinton and Bill Gates into his office and says, 'The world will end in 30 days, go back and tell your people.'

So Bill Clinton goes on TV and tells the American people, 'I have good news and I have bad news. The good news is that the basic family values upon which we have based our lives are right. Yes, there is a god. The bad news is that the world will end in 30 days.'

Boris Yeltsin goes to the Russian people and says, 'I have bad news and I have worse news. The bad news is that we were wrong. There is a god. The worse news is that the world will end in 30 days.'

Bill Gates goes to his executive committee and says, 'I've great news and I've got fabulous news. The great news is that God thinks I'm important. The fabulous news is that we don't have to ship Windows 95 after all.'

What's the difference between *Jurassic Park* and IBM?

One is a high-tech theme park dominated by dinosaurs. The other is a Steven Spielberg film.

SHAGGY DOGS

A farmer purchased 20 pigs. On arriving back at the farm, he found he'd bought all females. He asked his neighbour if he could bring them over to mate with his boars and the neighbour was willing to oblige.

So he took his female pigs next door to frolic all day with the males. When he came to take them home, he asked, 'How will I know if they're pregnant?' The neighbour answered, 'Tomorrow morning. If they're agrazin', they're pregnant.'

The next morning the pigs weren't agrazin', so the farmer loaded them back on his truck and took them to the neighbour. He didn't mind, and the male pigs didn't. They were waiting by the gate when they heard the truck coming.

The next day, same thing. So he put them on the truck and took them back to the neighbour.

On the fourth day the farmer was feeling discouraged, and tired of loading all the pigs and driving to the neighbour's with them. So he said to his wife, 'Honey, I just can't bear it. Would you look at the pigs and tell me if they're agrazin'.' She looked out, smiled, turned to him and said, 'Honey, they're not agrazin', but they're all lined up at the truck, and one's up on the front seat, honkin' the horn.'

Flopsy Bunny had never been out to see the real world. One day he escaped from his parents' home and was bouncing along when he came across a snake. Flopsy Bunny had never seen a snake; the snake had never seen a bunny rabbit.

Said the snake, 'Hello, you have lovely fluffy ears, a lovely little white tail and lovely brown fur – you must be a bunny rabbit.'

Said Flopsy Bunny, 'That's very good. Let me see, you have horrible scaly skin, nasty little slitty eyes, and a horrible rasping voice. You must be Nikki Lauda.'

Tonto and the Lone Ranger were lost on the prairie one day. The Lone Ranger says to Tonto, 'Use your Indian instincts and get us out of this mess.'

Tonto bends down and puts his ear to the ground. He turns and says to the Lone Ranger, 'Buffalo come.' The Lone Ranger says to Tonto, 'How do you know?'

Tonto says, 'Ear sticky.'

A cowboy rides into town, hitches up his horse and walks into a bar. He gets a beer, drinks it, and walks out. Half a second passes and he bursts back into the bar and says, 'ALL RIGHT, WHICH ONE OF YOU MOTHERS PAINTED MY HORSE'S FACE YELLOW?' A huge man-mountain stands up, looks down at the cowboy and says, 'I did.' The cowboy looks up at him and whispers, 'The first coat's dry.'

A cowboy goes into a bar, has a beer, walks outside and finds his horse has been stolen. He walks back into the bar, and fires his gun through the ceiling. 'WHICH ONE OF YOU MOTHERS STOLE MY HOSS?' he yells. No one answers. 'ALL RIGHT, I'M GONNA HAVE ANOTHA BEER, AND IF MY HOSS AIN'T OUTSIDE BY THE TIME I FINISH, I'M GONNA DO WHAT I DUN IN TEXAS.'

He gets another beer, walks outside, and his horse is back. So he gets on it and makes to ride out of town. The bartender wanders out of the bar and asks, 'Say pardner, what happened in Texas?'

The cowboy turns to him and says, 'I had to bloody walk home.'

It was a boring Sunday afternoon in the jungle so the elephants decided to challenge the ants to a game of soccer. The game was going well, with the elephants beating the ants ten goals to nil, when the ants gained possession.

The ants' star player was dribbling the ball towards the elephants' goal when the elephants' left-back came lumbering towards him. The elephant trod on the little ant, killing him instantly.

The referee stopped the game. 'What the hell do you think you're doing? Do you call that sportsmanship, killing another player?'

The elephant replied, 'Well I didn't meant to kill him – I was just trying to trip him up.'

A man went to a doctor to have his penis enlarged. This particular procedure involved splicing a baby elephant's trunk onto the man's penis.

Overjoyed, the man went out with his girlfriend to a very fancy restaurant. After cocktails, the man's penis crept out of his pants, felt around the table, grabbed a roll and quickly disappeared under the tablecloth. The girl was startled and exclaimed, 'What was that?'

Suddenly the penis came back, took another roll and just as quickly disappeared. The girl was silent for a moment, then finally said, 'I don't believe I saw what I think I just saw. Can you do that again?'

With a bit of an uncomfortable smile, the man replied, 'Honey, I'd like to, but I don't think my ass can take another roll.'

An elephant is walking through the jungle when she gets a thorn in her foot. She is in absolute agony until an ant strolls by. So the elephant says, 'Help me, help me.'

But the ant refuses unless the elephant agrees to let the ant have his wicked way with her. Replies the elephant, 'Anything! Anything!' So, out comes the thorn and up gets the ant and proceeds to enjoy himself.

Meanwhile, in a tree directly above them, a monkey who is witnessing the whole episode is in knots of laughter. Consequently he falls out of the tree on top of the elephant.

Says the elephant, 'Ouch!'

Says the ant, in his own little frenzy, 'Suffer bitch, *suffer*!'

An elephant is walking through the jungle. All of a sudden he falls into a pit and starts screaming. By chance a chicken hears the screaming and decides to investigate. He sees the elephant in the pit and shouts, 'Don't worry, I am going to save you.' The chicken then calls on the King of the Jungle.

The King of the Jungle promptly arrives in his red Porsche. He throws a rope from the Porsche into the pit, the elephant ties it around himself and the King of the Jungle pulls him out of the pit. The elephant is saved.

So grateful is the elephant to the chicken that he promises him he will one day do the same for him.

As chance would have it, the next week the

elephant is walking through the jungle and hears the screaming of a chicken. He wanders over and sees that his friend the chicken is stuck in a pit. The elephant shouts, 'Don't 'worry, chicken. I will save you.'

So the elephant throws his tail into the pit. However the tail is too small and the chicken cannot reach it. Undeterred by this, the elephant throws in his trunk but, alas, this also is too small. As a last desperate effort the elephant throws in his penis.

Success! The chicken grabs the elephant's enormous penis and climbs out to safety.

Moral of the story: if you have a big dick you don't need a red Porsche to pull a chick.

Father, mother and son decide to go to the zoo. At the elephant enclosure the boy looks at the elephant, sees its willy, points to it and says, 'Mummy, what is that long thing?' His mother replies, 'That, son, is the elephant's trunk.'

'No, at the other end.'

'That, son, is the tail.'

'No, Mummy, the thing under the elephant.'

A short embarrassed silence after which she replies, 'That's nothing.'

The mother goes to buy some ice-cream and the boy, not being satisfied with her answer, asks his father the same question. 'Daddy, what is that long thing?'

'That's the trunk, son,' replies the father.

'No, at the other end.'

'Oh, that's the tail.'

'No, no Daddy, the thing below,' asks the son in desperation.

'That is the elephant's penis. Why do you ask, son?'

'Well, Mummy said it was nothing,' says the boy.

Replies the father, 'I tell you, I spoil that woman.'

How do you get four elephants into a Volkswagen?

Two in the front and two in the back.

What do you get when you cross an elephant with a kangaroo?

Bloody great holes all over Australia.

How do you know if there is an elephant under the bed?

Your nose is touching the ceiling.

Why do elephants paint the soles of their feet yellow?

So that they can hide upside down in bowls of custard.

Did you ever find an elephant in your custard?
No? Well, it must work.

What do elephants use for tampons?
Sheep.

How do you stop an elephant from charging?
Take away his credit card.

Have you heard about Hannibal crossing the Alps with elephants?
None of the offspring survived.

What do you do if an elephant comes through your window?
Swim for your life!

Why are elephants wrinkled?
Have you ever tried to iron one?

Why does a duck have flat feet?
To stamp out fires in the woods.

Why does an elephant have flat feet?
To stamp out burning ducks.

After the flood when the ark came to rest on Ararat, Noah released all the animals, and held a meeting and explained to them that the Lord wanted them to be fruitful and multiply and repopulate the Earth.

In a week he went around to check on things. The place was humming with activity: the insects had all reproduced and there were flies, mosquitoes, bees, and so on; the mice and hamsters were pregnant, the birds were building nests, and the other animals were going about the courting process. All except two snakes down by a stream in a swampy bit that no one else wanted. They were just lying there, curled up on rocks in the sun. 'Hey, be fruitful and multiply!' Noah told them.

The male snake raised his head and said, 'Don't sweat it!' So Noah went back to his business.

A couple of weeks later Noah made another trip around. The insects were into the third generation already, and the place was fairly hopping with baby hamsters, mice, bunnies, and so on. The cat and the dog were both pregnant, and the birds were all sitting on eggs. Even some of the larger animals were showing signs of mating. All but the snakes. The only sign of activity was that the two had changed rocks. Noah again enjoined them to get with it. 'We're cool!' the male snake assured him.

A few weeks later, Noah again made the rounds. Almost all the large animals were pregnant by now, and many birds had hatched. There was a litter of kittens, and the dog was expecting her litter any minute. Noah hurried down to the stream to see the snakes. He found them chopping down trees, sawing the wood into logs and building furniture!

'Will you two get with it!' he said. 'Don't sweat it, everything is under control!' the male snake replied.

Well, a few weeks later Noah again took a look around. By now even the elephant was pregnant, and the place was alive with baby animals. And when Noah hurried down to check on those snakes, the area around the stream was positively wriggling with baby snakes. Which, of course, proves that anybody can multiply with log tables!

Once there was a marine biologist who loved dolphins. He spent his time trying to feed and protect his beloved creatures of the sea. One day, in a fit of inventive genius, he came up with a serum that would make dolphins live forever. Of course, he was ecstatic. But he soon realised that in order to mass produce this serum he would need large amounts of a certain compound that was only found in nature, in the metabolism of a rare South American bird.

Carried away by his love for dolphins, he resolved that he would go to the zoo and steal one of these birds. Unbeknown to him, as he was arriving at the zoo an elderly lion was escaping from its cage. The zookeepers were alarmed and immediately began combing the zoo for the escaped animal, unaware that it had simply lain down on the sidewalk and gone to sleep.

Meanwhile, the marine biologist arrived at the zoo and procured his bird. He was so excited by the prospect of helping his dolphins that he stepped absentmindedly over the sleeping lion on his way back to his car.

Immediately, 1500 policemen converged on him and arrested him for transporting a myrna across a staid lion for immortal porpoises.

One afternoon there was a good witch who was flying along, when all of a sudden she heard a soft crying from down below. When she landed, she saw a yellow frog. Touched by his sadness, the witch asked why he was crying. 'None of the other frogs will let me join in all their frog games. Boo hoo.'

'Don't cry, little one,' replied the witch, and with a wave of her magic wand, the frog turned green. All happy now, the frog was checking himself over when he noticed that his penis was still yellow. He asked the embarrassed witch about this, and she told him there were some things that she just couldn't do. But if he saw the wizard, he'd fix things up for him. So, happily, the little green frog hopped along his merry way.

Feeling quite happy about herself, the witch once more took to the skies. And once more she heard crying. But this time of a thunderous sort. So down to the ground she flew, only to discover a pink elephant. The witch asked him why he was crying. 'None of the other elephants will let me join in their elephant games. Boo hoo.'

Now, if you have ever seen an elephant cry, you know it's a pathetic looking sight, but a pink elephant crying is just downright heart-breaking. So once again the witch waved her magic wand and POOF, the elephant was grey.

All happy now, the elephant was checking himself all over when he noticed that his penis was still pink. He asked an embarrassed witch about this, and she told him that there were some things that she just couldn't do. But if he saw the wizard he would fix things up for him.

At this point the elephant started wailing. 'I don't know where the wizard is,' he sobbed.

'Just follow the yellow prick toad.'

Bilbo Backens was sitting in his hobbit hole one day when a group of young hobbits known for causing trouble in the village began harassing young Frodo, calling him names. Bilbo, sick and tired of these young ruffians and their untame ways, began throwing bricks at them from his window. However, try as he might, he couldn't seem to hit a single one. Why? Because, of course, everyone knows bad hobbits are hard to brick!

Hank had a problem with flatulence. No matter what he ate, he farted. So he dreaded his new girlfriend's invitation to have dinner with her parents.

It was a very formal occasion and after he'd been sitting at the table for a while, he felt an incredible pain in his stomach and just had to fart. Just then, the family's dog Fido, which was sitting under the table, let out a growl. His girlfriend's mother yelled, 'Fido!' Hank was relieved. It didn't matter if he farted, they'd blame the dog.

So he let go a bigger fart and, sure enough, the father yelled at the dog. 'Fido!' But the pressure was still building up so Hank lets out a huge, ripping fart and the mother yelled at the dog again. 'Fido, get out from under the table before he shits all over you!'

Dave, out caught in the rain, ducked into a pub. There he met some old friends, had a few drinks and a few more, and at midnight started to stagger home through the rain. Feeling cold, he decided to get himself an Indian curry, so he headed for his local Taj Mahal take-away and ordered an extra hot vindaloo.

Arriving home, he placed the curry on the table and went upstairs for a pee. Whereupon the cat approached the curry and, feeling neglected and hungry, decided to have a go at it. Nibble nibble, chomp chomp, lick lick. The vindaloo vanished.

Dave returned and was appalled to discover the

cat licking the plate. He grabbed it by the neck and dragged it outside. 'You dreadful little moggie. I hate you. You're dead,' he ranted. Filling a dustbin with water, he threw the hissing cat into it and slammed the lid down. He then put a few bricks on top, just to be on the safe side.

Dave returned to his sitting room feeling very sorry for himself. A few minutes later he heard a knock on the window and, lo and behold, there was the cat. The cat looked at him and said, 'You wouldn't happen to have any more water, would you?'

A woman buys a parrot only to find that it says nothing but, 'My name is Mary and I'm a whore.' She tries to teach the bird more acceptable phrases but, after weeks, has failed utterly. 'My name is Mary and I'm a whore,' it says over and over again, often at the most inopportune moments and much to the lady's embarrassment.

One day her parish priest dropped by and, sure enough, the parrot squawked out the only words it would say. She apologised to the priest, explaining that the bird resisted all efforts at reform. The priest offered to take the bird to visit the two birds he had, as all his birds would say were Hail Marys while clutching rosaries in their talons. Perhaps they'd have a good influence on the lady's parrot.

So he took her parrot to his house and put it in the cage with his parrots. 'My name is Mary and I'm a whore,' said the lady's parrot. Whereupon one of the priest's birds said to the other, 'Throw that damn rosary away, our prayers have been answered.'

In Africa a camera crew has been assigned to get footage of the World Famous Gorilla Wrestler at work. The camera crew is in the truck with him and his dog, and they come across a small tree. The wrestler says to them, 'Just wait here, I'll be right back.'

He climbs the tree, wrestles with a gorilla for a while, then throws it to the ground. Quick as a flash, the man's dog jumps on the poor animal and has sex with it until it faints. The man throws it in the back of the van, and they drive on to a medium-sized tree with a medium-sized gorilla. And the same thing happens.

Then they're driving along, and there's a huge tree with an absolutely massive gorilla in it. The man hands the cameraman a gun. 'What's this for?' the cameraman asks.

'Well, there's a small chance that I might lose the battle here. And if I do, shoot the dog!'

The animals were bored. Finally the lion had a great idea. 'Let's play the game the humans play. Football. I've seen it on TV.'

The lion's team received. They got their two firsts down and then had to punt. The mule punted and the rhino was back deep for the kick. He caught the ball, lowered his head and charged. First he crushed a road-runner, then two rabbits. He gored a wilderbeast, knocked over two cows, and broke through to the daylight, scoring six. Unfortunately they lacked a place kicker and the score remained 6-0.

Later in the first half the lion's team scored a touch-down and the mule kicked the extra point. The lion's team led at half-time.

The lion gave a pep-talk in the locker room. 'Look you guys, we can win this game. But we've got to keep the ball away from the rhino. He's a killer. Mule, when you kick off, be sure to keep it away from the rhino.'

The second half began. Just as the mule was about to kick off, the rhino's team changed formation and the ball went directly to the rhino. Once again, the rhino lowered his head and was off running. He stomped two gazelles, skewered a giraffe, bulldozed an elephant out of the way. It looked like he was home free when, suddenly, at the 20-yard line, he dropped down dead. There were no other animals in sight.

The lion went over to see what had happened. Right next to the dead rhino he saw a small centipede.

'Did you do this?' he asked the centipede.'

'Yeah, I did,' the centipede replied.

The lion yelled, 'Where the hell were you during the first half?'

'Get off my back. I was putting on my shoes!'

A tiger woke up one morning feeling magnificent. He felt so great he went outside and cornered a small monkey and roared at him, 'Who is the mightiest of all the jungle animals?' The terrified little monkey replied, 'You, of course. No one is mightier than you.'

A little while later it was a deer's turn. 'Who is the greatest and strongest of all the jungle animals?' roared the tiger. The deer just managed to stammer a reply. 'Oh great tiger, you are by far the mightiest animal in the jungle.'

On a roll, the tiger swaggered up to an elephant who was quietly munching on some weeds and roared at the top of his voice, 'Who is the mightiest of *all* the animals in the jungle?' The elephant grabbed the tiger with his trunk, picked him up, slammed him down, picked him up again and shook him until the tiger was just a blur of orange and black. Finally it threw the tiger into a nearby tree. The tiger fell out of the tree, staggered to his feet, looked at the elephant and said, 'Man, just because you don't know the answer, no need to get so pissed off!'

A blind man was waiting to cross the road when his guide dog peed on his leg. He reached into his pocket, took out a biscuit and gave it to the dog. A passerby who'd seen everything was very touched. 'That's very tolerant of you after what he just did.'

'Not really,' came the reply. 'I'm just finding out where his mouth is, so I can kick him in the nuts.'

A newly married couple inherited a parrot from an aged uncle. The parrot was very talkative and forever informing visitors as to what went on in the newly-weds' home. One evening after an embarrassing comment from the bird, the husband had had enough and said to the parrot, 'That's it. You're going to be covered up much earlier in future and if you take your cage cover off or embarrass us again, you're off to the zoo.'

A few days later the couple were preparing for a short trip and, as usual, the suitcase was too full to close. The husband said, 'I'll get on the top and jump up and down and see if you can get it.' After a bit the wife said, 'This is no good, I'll get on top and you see if you can get it.'

This still didn't work so the husband said, 'Tell you what, let's both get on top and bounce up and down – that'll get it.' With this, the parrot pulled off the cage cover and said, 'Zoo or no zoo, this I've gotta see!'

A man took his dog into a pub, bought a pint and settled down to watch football on the TV set above the bar. As luck would have it, it was a Fulham home game. After a one-sided match, Fulham lost, and the dog said, quite clearly, 'Oh, no – not again!'

The barman, startled, walked over to the owner and said, 'Did your dog just say "Oh, no – not again"?'

'Yes,' replied the owner blandly, 'he always says that when Fulham lose.'

'What does he say when Fulham win?'

'Don't know. I've only had him five years.'

A man goes into a pub with a pig under his arm. The barman spots him and says, 'That's the ugliest looking animal you've got there. Where on earth did you get it?

'Won it in a raffle,' says the pig.

A man was driving through the country, got thirsty and entered a pub. After a few minutes a large brown horse came clip-clopping in, sat down at a table, crossed its legs and ordered a coffee. Astonished, he asked the pub keeper if this wasn't just a little strange.

'Very,' he said. 'Normally it drinks a pint of beer.'

A pheasant was standing in a field chatting to a bull.

'I would love to be able to get to the top of yonder tree,' sighed the pheasant, 'but I haven't got the energy.'

'Well, why don't you nibble on some of my droppings?' replied the bull. 'They're packed with nutrients.'

The pheasant pecked at a lump of dung and found that it gave him enough strength to reach the first branch of the tree. The next day, after eating some more dung, he reached the second branch. And so on. Finally, after a fortnight, there he was proudly perched at the top of the tree. Whereupon he was spotted by a farmer who dashed into the farmhouse, emerged with a shotgun and blew the fuck out of the pheasant.

The moral of this story? Bullshit might get you to the top, but it won't keep you there.

Where do you find a tortoise with no legs?

Where you left it.

A horse walks into a bar and the bartender says, 'What a long face you have!'

A guy walks into a bar and puts his alligator on the counter. The bartender says, 'You can't bring that alligator in here.'

'It's a pet alligator. Watch,' says the guy, tapping it on its head. The 'gator opens its mouth wide. The guy unzips his pants, pulls out his penis and puts it in the alligator's mouth. He then taps the alligator on the head and it closes its mouth gently on the vulnerable member. Everyone in the bar is aghast.

He then taps the 'gator on the head again, it opens its mouth and he puts his penis back in his pants.

The guy says, 'I'll give anyone in the bar $50 to do the same thing.' The patrons are very, very quiet. Suddenly a drunken voice yells out, 'I . . . I . . . I'd like to do that. But I don't think I could keep my mouth open that long!'

A baby harp seal walks into a bar. The bartender says, 'What will you have, baby harp seal?' And the baby harp seal says, 'Anything but Canadian Club on the rocks.'

Two tall trees are growing in the woods. A small tree begins to grow between them and one big tree says to the other, 'Is that a son of a beech, or a son of a birch?' The other says that he cannot tell.

A woodpecker lands on the small tree. One of the tall trees says, 'Woodpecker, you're a tree expert. Can you tell if that is a son of a beech or a son or a birch?' The woodpecker takes a taste of the small tree and replies, 'It is neither the son or a beech nor son of a birch. That, gentlemen, is the best piece of ash I've ever had my pecker in!'

A police dog responds to an ad for work with the FBI. 'Well,' says the personnel director, 'you'll have to meet some strict requirements. First, you must type at least 60 words per minute.' Sitting down at the typewriter, the dog types out 80 words per minute. 'Also,' says the director, 'you must pass a physical and complete the obstacle course.' This perfect canine specimen finishes the course in record time. 'There's one last requirement,' the director continues, 'you must be bilingual.' With confidence, the dog looks up at him and says, 'Meow!'

A farm family were gathering in the kitchen for breakfast. As the youngest son sat down, his mother told him he wasn't going to get anything to eat until he'd fed the animals. Angry, he thumped out the door and headed for the chicken coop. As he fed the chooks, he kicked each one in the head. Then it was off to the paddock to feed the cow. As she bent down to start on some fresh hay, he kicked her in the head. He poured slops into a trough for the pigs and, as they started eating, kicked them in the head. He then headed back to the kitchen and sat down. His mother was outraged. 'I saw what you did. Since you kicked the chickens you'll get no eggs for breakfast. And since you kicked the cow you'll get no milk. And no bacon or sausages because you kicked the pigs.'

His father came down the stairs and, nearly tripping on the cat, kicked it. The boy looked up at Mum and said, 'Are you gonna tell him or should I?'

Tired of driving, a salesman parked his car beside a paddock. Immediately a horse came to the fence and began to boast about his career. 'Yes, I'm a great horse. I've run in 25 races and won over $5 million. I keep my trophies in the barn.'

The salesman considered the value of owning a talking horse, found the farmer and started negotiations.

'Aah, you don't want that horse,' said the farmer.

'Yes, I do,' said the salesman, 'and I'll give you $100 000 for it.'

Without hesitation the farmer said, 'He's yours.'

Whilst writing out the cheque, the salesman asked, 'By the way, why wouldn't I want your horse?'

'Because,' said the farmer, 'he's a liar. He hasn't won a race in his life.'

Two devout churchgoing women were chatting in front of the store when a dusty old cowboy rode up, tied his horse in front of the saloon, walked around behind it, lifted its tail and kissed it full on the rectum.

Disgusted, one of the women said, 'That's sickening. Why did you do that?'

To which the cowboy replied, 'I've got chapped lips.'

'Does that make them feel better?'

'No, but it stops me from licking them.

At a conference on the supernatural, one of the speakers asked, 'Who here has seen a ghost?' Most hands went up. 'And how many of you have had some form of interaction with a ghost?' About half the hands remained up. 'Okay, now how many of you have had physical contact with a ghost?' Three hands stayed up, and there was a slight murmur in the crowd.

'Well, that's very interesting. Let me ask if any of you have, how shall I put this, been intimate with a ghost.' One hand stayed up. The speaker was astonished. 'Sir, are you telling us that you've actually had sexual liaison with a ghost?'

The guy with his hand up suddenly looked embarrassed and said, 'Oh, I'm sorry. I thought you said goat.'

Two dogs are in a vet's waiting room. Each eyes the other with a combination of suspicion and sympathy.

'What are you here for?' the first dog asks.

'Well, I was feeling really bad the other day. And my master's six-year-old started bugging me. I tried to ignore the little shit, but was feeling so rotten that I bit his hand off.'

'I know exactly how you must have felt. So why are you here?'

'Well, they reckon I'm too vicious so I'm going to be . . . you know . . . I'm going to be desexed.'

'Oh dear, I'm sorry.'

'So, what are you in here for?'

'Oh, nothing really.'

'Go on, tell me. It'll take my mind off the operation.'

'Okay, well it's like this. The bitch next door was in heat and I was feeling really randy. Then my mistress came into the kitchen wearing a short skirt and no underwear and when she bent over to put some dog food in my bowl I just couldn't resist.'

'So you're here for the operation too?'

'No. I'm here to have my nails clipped.'

A society lady had a miniature schnauzer which was suffering from an ear infection. The vet told her that this was due to an ingrown hair and the best treatment would be to remove the hair with a depilatory cream. The woman went to a chemist and asked for assistance in selecting the best product. He explained that some were better for legs, while others were better for facial hair. He then asked, 'May I ask where you intend to use it?'

She replied, 'It's for my schnauzer.'

He said, 'Okay, use this brand. But don't ride a bike for two weeks.'

Air Force One crashes, instantly killing President Clinton, Vice President Gore and their wives. St Peter greets them personally at the Pearly Gates and informs them that they've been granted an audience with God. They are led by St Peter to a tremendous throne room and there, lo and behold, is the supreme being. 'And who might you be?' God asks the Vice President. 'I'm Albert Gore junior, Vice President of the United States of America.' 'Ah, yes, you've done much for the environment. Love your work. Come sit on my left.'

'And you there, who are you?' 'Your Holiness, I'm William Jefferson Clinton, President of the United States.' 'Right, you are a brave man who has confronted some difficult issues. Come sit on my right.'

'Now, who might you be?'

'My name is Hillary Rodham Clinton and *you* are sitting on *my* seat.'

Bill, Hillary and Al are flying from DC to the West Coast. Al says, 'Boy, I would like to drop a $100 bill out of the plane and make one person very happy.' Hillary replies, 'I would rather drop ten $10 bills out and make ten people very, very happy.'

Bill replies, 'I would drop 100 $1 bills and make 100 people really happy.'

The pilot, listening to all this, turns around and says, 'Why don't all three of you jump out and make 250 million people very happy?'

Why doesn't Hillary wear mini-skirts around the White House?

Because her balls would show.

What are the two worst things about Bill Clinton?

His face.

It's been discovered that Clinton was a test-tube baby. Apparently he wasn't worth a fuck back then either!

What did the band play at Clinton's inauguration?

Inhale to the chief.

Why is Bill Clinton apprehensive about going to the movies?

Because he's afraid the usherette will ask to see his stub.

Hillary came into the room with a big smile and a spring in her step. 'My, you're in a good mood,' said Bill, 'why are you so happy?'

'I just got back from my annual physical exam and the doctor said I had the breasts of a 25-year-old woman,' Hillary gushed.

'Did he say anything about your 46-year-old ass?' Bill asked. 'No,' said Hillary, 'your name wasn't mentioned.'

Clinton is out jogging in a seedy area of Washington DC. He notices a good-looking prostitute. She calls out, '$50.' He's tempted but the price is a little high, so he calls back, 'Five!' She turns away in disgust and Bill continues his jog.

A few days later he finds himself jogging in the same area and, as luck would have it, the prostitute is still there. But she won't come down on her price. 'Fifty,' she shouts, and Bill answers her, 'Five.' No sale.

About a week later, Hillary has decided she wants to get into shape and goes jogging with Bill. They get to the seedy part of town and the same prostitute is still there. She eyes Bill and Hillary together and yells, 'See what you get for $5.'

I'm glad I am an American, I'm glad I'm free. I wish I were a dog and Clinton was a tree.

Three high-school boys are walking down the street in Washington. Suddenly they see Bill Clinton go jogging by, and he's about to be hit by a car. They pull the President out of the way and save his life. Bill says, 'Thank you for saving me. I'll grant each of you a wish.'

The first boy says, 'I want to go Georgetown.' Bill pulls some strings and the boy gets admitted.

The second boy says, 'I want to get into West Point but it normally requires a congressional appointment.' So Bill calls up his Democratic friends in congress and gets the boy his appointment.

The third boy says, 'I want to be buried in Arlington National Cemetery.' Bill says, 'That's an odd request for a 17-year-old.' The boy says, 'Yeah, but when my father finds out I saved your life he's going to kill me.'

Hillary's being driven around Washington DC when she spots a little boy sitting in a park with a wagon. She thinks, A great press opportunity, and has her driver pull over. She gets out to talk to the boy and discovers that he has six little puppies in the wagon. She comments on how nice they are and the little boy says, 'Thank you, m'am, they're Democrats.' Of course Hillary is extremely pleased.

A few days later Bill decides to take one of his jogs down to McDonald's, which is close to the park, and Hillary mentions that if he should see a little boy with a wagon he should stop and talk to him. Bill sees the little boy with the wagon and puppies and says, 'What nice puppies those are.' The boy says, 'Thank you, sir, they're Republicans.' 'Wait a minute,' said Bill, 'Hillary told me they're Democrats.' The boy responds, 'Yes sir, but now their eyes are open.'

Bill Clinton is considering changing the Democratic Party emblem from a donkey to a condom, because it stands up to inflation, protects a bunch of pricks, halts production, and gives you a false sense of security while being screwed.

Bill Clinton's new revelations about his sex life: he's finally admitted to having sex with Gennifer Flowers a couple of times ... but he didn't come.

Why are people in Arkansas having peanut butter and jelly for Thanksgiving this year?

Because they sent their turkey to the White House.

Potential presidential candidates were meeting the Wizard of Oz. President Bush went first to see the Wizard and said, 'Everyone says I have no compassion or feeling. I wish to have a heart.' The Wizard said, 'So be it.'

The second was Dan Quayle. He said to the Wizard, 'People think I'm unintelligent and have no commonsense whatsoever. I wish to have a brain.' The Wizard said, 'So be it.'

The third was Ross Perrot. 'People say I have no confidence and lack conviction. I wish to have some courage.' The Wizard said, 'So be it.'

And then Bill Clinton approached. The Wizard looked at him and said, 'Well, what do you want?' To which Clinton replied, 'I'm here for Dorothy.'

Bumper sticker on an Arkansas car: If you can read you this you're not from here.

How did Bill and Hillary Clinton meet?

They were dating the same girl in high school.

Why do they put Clinton's picture on the inside of toilet bowls?

So the arseholes can see who they voted for.

If Bill and Hillary and Al and Tippa took a boat ride and the boat capsized who would be saved?

The United States of America.

Why is Bill Clinton diverting federal funds from improving schools to improving jails?

Because when his term is through, he won't be going to school.

A man goes into a bar in Montana. He's watching TV over the bar and Bill Clinton comes on. He says out loud to no one in particular, 'If that guy isn't the biggest horse's arse I've seen, I don't know who is.'

A big cowboy comes down the bar and knocks him off his stool. He gets back up and starts watching TV again. This time Hillary comes on. He says, 'I thought Bill was bad, but Hillary is definitely the biggest horse's arse in the world.'

Another cowboy comes and knocks him off his stool. The guy's perplexed. He gets back on his stool and says to the bartender, 'Excuse me, I thought I was in a conservative state. Where am I? Clinton country?' 'No,' said the bartender, 'you're in horse country.'

Clinton is giving a speech. A member of the audience wakes up momentarily and asks, 'Has he finished yet?' A neighbour replies, 'He finished an hour ago, but he hasn't stopped.'

Chelsea asks Hillary, 'Mom, what did you have at the state dinner?'

'Some beef, some asparagus, and 7374 green peas.'

'Don't bullshit me, Mom. When did you count the peas?'

'While your father was giving his speech.'

Bumper sticker seen in Scotsdale, Arizona: Where the hell is Lee Harvey Oswald now that we really need him?

What's the difference between the Panama Canal and Hillary Clinton?

The Panama Canal is a busy ditch.

Clinton's walking his dog around the White House lawn. He walks it past the guards' post, and a marine says, 'Mr President, is that a new dog?' Clinton smiles and replies, 'Why yes, I got it for my wife.' The marine inspects the dog, looks up with a smile and says, 'Good trade.'

If called to testify in a trial, how long will it be before Clinton commits perjury?

When he's sworn in.

President Clinton and Vice President Gore were coming back from a health-care meeting in their limo when Gore asked, 'Hey Bill, what are you gonna do when you get back to the White House?'

The slickster replied, 'Well, I'm gonna tear off Hillary's panties.'

'Wow!' exclaimed Gore, 'I didn't know you and Hillary were so passionate.'

Clinton replied, 'We're not. It's just that the damn things are starting to cut into my waist.'

Hillary Clinton dies and goes to Heaven. St Peter approaches her and says, 'Hillary, I know you're Somebody down on Earth, but up here you're just another person and I'm swamped right now. So have a seat and I'll get back to you as soon as I can.'

Hillary sits down and begins looking around. She notices a huge wall that extends as far as the eye can see, and on that wall there are millions and millions of clocks. She can't help noticing that on occasion some of the clocks jump ahead 15 minutes. When St Peter returns she asks, 'What's the deal with the clock?' St Peter replies, 'There's a clock on the wall for every married man on Earth.'

Hillary asks, 'What does it mean when the clock jumps ahead 15 minutes?' St Peter replies, 'That means that the man that belongs to that clock has just committed adultery.'

'Hillary asks, 'Well, is my husband's clock on the wall?'

St Peter replies, 'Hell no. God has it in his office and is using it for an electric fan.'

A little old lady arrives at US Immigration. The official's question is, 'Do you advocate the overthrow of the government by violence or subversion?' She pauses for thought and says, 'Violence, I think.'

A bloke's been through a terrible divorce and as he leaves the courthouse says under his breath, 'It's about time I had some good luck.'

Whereupon, POOF! A genie appears. The genie says, 'You may have three wishes, but whatever you wish for your wife will get double.'

The man says he's agreeable and asks for $20 million. The genie points out that his wife will get $40 million. The man asks to be ten years younger. The genie points out that, now, his wife will be 20 years younger.

'And what is your third wish?' asks the genie.

'Beat me half to death.'

A man walking along a road in the bush comes across a shepherd with a huge flock of sheep. 'I'll bet you $100 against one of your sheep that I can tell you the exact number in this flock,' he says. The shepherd thinks it over and, because it's a big flock, takes the bet. The man says, '973.' The shepherd is astonished because that's exactly right. He says, 'Okay, I'm a man of my word, take an animal.' The man picks up a sheep and begins to walk away.

'Wait!' cries the shepherd. 'Give me a chance to get even. Double or nothing that I can guess your occupation.' The man agrees. 'You're an economist for a government think-tank,' says the shepherd. 'Amazing,' says the man, 'you're exactly right. But how did you work it out?' 'Well,' says the shepherd, 'put down my dog and I'll tell you.'

A mathematician, an accountant and an economist apply for the same job. The interviewer calls in the mathematician and asks him, 'What does 2 + 2 equal?' The mathematician replies, 'Four.' The interviewer asks, 'Four exactly?' 'Yes, four exactly.'

The interviewer then calls in the accountant and asks the same question. The accountant says, 'On average, four, give or take 10 per cent, but on average, four.'

Then the interviewer calls in the economist and poses the same question. 'What does 2 + 2 equal?' The economist gets up, locks the door, closes the shades, sits down next to the interviewer and says, 'What do you want it to equal?'

Three econometricians go hunting and come across a huge deer. The first econometrician fires, but misses, by a metre to the left. The second econometrician fires, but also misses, by a metre to the right. The third econometrician doesn't fire, but shouts in triumph, 'We got it! We got it!'

A civil engineer, a chemist and an economist are travelling in the countryside and, feeling weary, stop at a small inn. 'I've only two rooms, so one of you will have to sleep in the barn,' says the innkeeper.

The civil engineer volunteers to do so, and goes outside while the others go to bed. But in a short time he's knocking at the door. He says, 'There's a cow in that barn. I'm a Hindu and it would offend my beliefs to sleep next to a sacred animal.'

So the chemist says, 'Okay, I'll sleep in the barn.' Soon there's another knock – it's the chemist saying, 'There's a pig in that barn. I'm Jewish and cannot sleep next to an unclean animal.'

So the economist is sent to the barn. Soon there's even louder knocking. They open the door and see that it's the cow and the pig.

A party of economists were climbing the Alps and after several hours got hopelessly lost. One of them studied the map, turning it up and down, trying to identify distant landmarks, consulting his compass, squinting at the sun. Finally he said, 'Okay, see that big mountain over there?'

'Yes,' said the others.

'Well, according to the map, we're standing on top of it.'

Albert Einstein dies and meets three New Zealanders in the queue outside the Pearly Gates. To pass the time he asks their IQs. The first replies, '190.'

'Great,' says Einstein, 'we can discuss the contribution by Ernest Rutherford to atomic physics and my theory of general relativity.'

The second answers, '150.'

'Good,' says Einstein. 'I look forward to discussing the role of New Zealand's nuclear-free legislation and quest for world peace.'

The third New Zealander mumbles, '50.' Einstein pauses and then asks, 'So what is your forecast for the budget deficit next year?'

Why did God create economists?

In order to make weather forecasters look good.

Why did the economist cross the road?

It was the chicken's day off.

Two economists meet on the street. One enquires, 'How's your wife?' The other responds, 'Relative to what?'

Economists have forecast nine out of the last five recessions.

A totalitarian head of state asks for an economist with one arm to advise his government. Why? Because he was tired of economists who says, 'Well, on the one hand ... but on the other hand ...'

Three leading economists hired a Cessna to go hunting moose in northern Canada. The pilot reminded them that it was a small plane and they'd only be able to bring back one moose.

But the economists killed one each and, come Sunday, talked the pilot into letting them bring all three dead moose on board. Shortly after the takeoff, the plane stalled and crashed. In the wreckage, one of the economists woke up, looked around and said, 'Where the hell are we?'

'Oh, just about 100 metres east of the place we crashed last year.'

An economist:

Someone who didn't have enough personality to become an accountant.

Someone who knows a hundred ways to make love, but doesn't know any women.

An economist returns to his old university. He expresses interest in the current exam questions, and his old professor shows him some. To his astonishment, they're the same ones that he answered ten years ago. How come? The professor explains, 'The questions are always the same – only the answers change.'

Economics is extremely useful as a form of employment for economists.

A central banker walked into a pizzeria to order a Hawaiian. When the pizza was ready, the clerk asked him, 'Should I cut it into six pieces or eight pieces?' The central banker replied, 'I'm feeling really hungry. You'd better cut it into eight pieces.'

The first law of economists: For every economist, there exists an equal and opposite economist.

The second law of economists: They're both wrong.

An economist is an expert who will know tomorrow why the things he predicted yesterday didn't happen today.

A study of economics usually reveals that the best time to buy anything is last year.

It was the final May Day in the Soviet Union with Gorbachev reviewing the tanks and the troops and the planes and the missiles. Finally ten men marched by dressed in black. 'Are they spies?' asked Gorby. 'They are economists,' replied the KGB director. 'Imagine the havoc they will wreak when we set them loose on the Americans.'

If an economist and a tax inspector were both drowning and you could only save one of them, would you go to lunch or read the paper?

Why do economists carry their diplomas on their dashboards?

So they can park in the handicapped parking.

An economist died in poverty and many local futures traders donated to a fund for his funeral. The CEO of a bank was asked to donate a dollar. 'Only a buck?' he said. 'Only a buck to bury an economist? Here's a cheque. Go bury 1000 of them.'

A physicist, a chemist and an economist are stranded on an island with nothing to eat. Miraculously, a can of soup washes ashore. The physicist says, 'Let's smash open the can with a rock.' The chemist says, 'Let's build a fire and heat the can first.' The economist says, 'Let's assume that we have a can opener ...'

An Australian, an Englishman and a Japanese were discussing their respective countries over a drink. The Englishman mentioned that British medicine had progressed so far that doctors had recently taken a single liver, cut it into six pieces and then transplanted it into six separate men. This had resulted in six new workers in the job market.

The Japanese guy said that in his country doctors

had cut a lung into 12 pieces, transplanted these into 12 people in need of healthy lungs, thereby putting 12 new people in the job market.

Not to be outdone, the Australian said, 'That's nothing. In my country, we took one arsehole, made it Prime Minister, and now there are five million people in the market for a job.'

A priest, a psychologist and an economist are playing golf. They get behind a very slow twosome who, despite having a caddy, take all day to line up their shots. To make matters worse, they're four-putting every green. By the eighth hole the three men are complaining loudly about the slow players ahead. The priest says, 'Holy Mary, I pray that they should take some lessons before they play again.' The psychologist says, 'There are some people who just like to play golf slowly.' The economist says, 'I really didn't expect to spend this much time playing a round of golf.'

By the ninth hole, they've had it. The psychologist goes to the caddy and demands that they be allowed to play through. The caddy explains that his two golfers are blind, that both are retired firemen who lost their eyesight saving people in a fire.

The priest is mortified. 'Here I am a man of the cloth and I've been swearing at the slow play of two blind men.' The psychologist is also embarrassed. 'I'm a man trained to help others with problems and I've been complaining about the slow play of two blind men.' The economist ponders the situation. Finally he goes to the caddy and says, 'Listen, next time they should play at night.'

Margaret Thatcher died and arrived at the Pearly Gates where she was confronted by St Peter with his clipboard.

'Name?' asked St Peter.

'Baroness Thatcher,' she replied.

Peter checked through all the names on the clipboard but couldn't find the baroness's. 'I'm sorry, you can't come in. Your place is downstairs in Hell.'

The imperious baroness turned and walked down the stairs. A short time later the phone rang. 'Hello, Pete, it's the Devil speaking. You'll have to take that bloody woman. She's only been here ten minutes and she's closed half the furnaces to reduce capacity.'

President Clinton has, as we all know, a deep commitment to marriage. Ever anxious to be politically correct, he recently rewrote the vows for a staffer's nuptials. He circled 'till death us do part' and wrote 'too morbid – do you want to alienate every sick person in America?'

When he got to 'I take you to be my lawful wedded wife', he deleted 'wife' and inserted 'partner', warning 'do not use sexist expressions'. And next to 'for better, for worse, for richer, for poorer', he wrote 'polarising – how about the middle ground?'

A man goes into hospital for a vasectomy. Prior to the operation, he's led into an exam room by a nurse who immediately drops to his knees and goes down on him.

He's astounded and, afterwards, asks, 'Why did you do that?'

'Well, we found it's the most efficient way to empty the seminal ducts,' she replies.

She then has him laid on a trolley, and wheels him towards the operating theatre. On the way he is astounded to see a ward full of men, all vigorously masturbating.

'What's this?'

'Oh, they're on Clinton's new health plan,' she explains.

Three men were telling stories around the campfire. Their conversation turned to medical miracles.

First man: 'There's a guy who lives just up the street from me. He used to work in construction. One day he got his hand run over by a bulldozer. Crushed it flat. Yet today, thanks to the doctors, he's a concert pianist.'

Second man: 'That's nothing. I knew a guy in college, the laziest bum on Earth. Very fat, out of shape. He was trying to bum a ride one day and got hit by a truck. Broke just about every damn bone in his body. But they managed to put him back together and now he's been chosen to run in the marathon in the Atlanta Olympics.'

Third man: 'Well, I knew this poor retarded kid. Couldn't do a whole lot. But someone at the munitions factory took pity on him and gave him a job as a stock boy. He was working in the warehouse one day and got locked in. It was pitch black and he couldn't find the door. And not being very bright, he lit a match. The whole joint went sky high. All they could find of him was his arsehole and his eyebrow. From those little bits they were able to put him back together and today that kid is the Governor of Massachusetts.'

A guy was lost in the mall by the Washington Monument. He stopped a cop and asked, 'What side is the State Department on?' The cop answered, 'Ours, I hope.'

A stockbroker in New York gets tired of his colleague's stories of going duck hunting each year. They boast of their prowess in the hunt and how many ducks they bag. Not to be outdone, he decides he's going hunting and buys the most expensive shotgun available. He spends a fortune on hunting clothes and gear, gets his licence and sets off.

After an exasperating day of tromping through the marshes and briars without seeing a single duck, he heads back to his car. On the way he sees a duck fly overhead. He raises his gun, blazes away at it and actually hits it. The duck falls into a nearby farmyard.

As the hunter starts to climb over the fence to retrieve his kill, he's confronted by a farmer who says, 'Where in the hell do you think you're going, city boy?'

'I'm going to get my duck.'

'My property, my duck,' says the farmer.

'Oh come on, I've been out here all day and that's the only duck I've seen. I shot it. It's my duck.'

The farmer again says, 'My property, my duck.'

They argue for a few minutes and finally the farmer says, 'I'll tell you what. We'll settle this country-style.'

'What's that?' the stockbroker asks warily.

'Well, I'll kick you in the balls as hard as I can and then you kick me in the balls as hard as you can, and we keep this up and the last man standing keeps the duck.'

Not wanting to return empty-handed, the stockbroker finally agrees. The farmer, wearing heavy workboots, kicks the guy in the balls with all his might. The stockbroker's eyes roll back in his head as he coughs and wheezes and struggles to stay on his feet. Composing himself somewhat, he says to the farmer, 'Okay, now it's my turn.'

The farmer replies, 'You can have the duck.'

GROOVE NET

What do Ethiopians and Yoko Ono have in common?

They're both living off dead beetles.

Have you heard about Michael Jackson's new book?

It's called *The Ins and Outs of Child Rearing.*

What's the difference between Michael Jackson and a grocery bag?

One is white, made out of plastic, and dangerous for kids to play with. And the other you carry your groceries in.

How can you tell if Michael Jackson has company?

There's a ferris wheel parked outside his house.

The world's best and most famous conductor made a small mistake while conducting the New York Symphony Orchestra. The audience didn't notice, the orchestra didn't notice either, but he knew he'd made the mistake and decided that he should retire. Once the performance had finished, he turned and faced the audience and said, 'Ladies and gentlemen, this is my last performance as a world-class conductor. I'm now announcing my retirement.'

After a few minutes' silence from the shocked audience and orchestra, he was greeted with boos and hisses. He walked from the stage, only to be met by his manager, standing in between two gorilla-sized bodyguards. 'Oh no, you don't,' his manager said, 'you're not retiring.'

Forced back to work by his manager, he endured week after week of conducting he no longer wanted to do. While lying in bed one night with his wife of many years, he turned to her and said, 'Dear, would you be able to get me a small handgun?'

'Yes, dear,' she said, and he rolled over and went to sleep.

Sure enough, at his next performance, the conductor had a small handgun concealed in his jacket. Once the concert had finished, he turned to the audience and said, 'I'm announcing my retirement for the second time. This is my last performance.'

The tuba player from the orchestra stood up and shouted, 'You can't be serious!' and the conductor whipped out his handgun and shot the tuba player dead. It wasn't long before the police arrived and the conductor was taken away.

Days later, the conductor was taken to court. 'How do you plead to the charge of first-degree murder?' the judge enquired. 'Guilty, your Honour,' the conductor replied. 'Do you realise the sentence for first-degree murder in this state is death by electrocution?' the judge asked. The conductor thought for a moment, but came to the conclusion that death would surely be better than continuing on like he was. 'Yes, your Honour,' the conductor said.

While being strapped into the electric chair, one of the guards came to the conductor and said, 'You may have one last request before we terminate your life. What would you like?' After pondering a few seconds, the conductor replied, 'A silver platter with a dozen bananas.' His request was granted, and the conductor scoffed the bananas.

The room was emptied, and the switch was flicked. The conductor's hair stood on end, but he survived! As one guard was about to flick the switch again, he was stopped. 'He survived the chair and the law says we have to let him go.'

The conductor left the building, only to be greeted by his manager and the two gorilla-sized bodyguards. 'Back to work,' his manager said.

More weeks of forced conducting went by. Lying

in bed again one night with his wife, he asked, 'Dear, could you get me a grenade?'

'Yes, dear,' she replied.

At his next performance, the conductor waited until the end of the concert, the grenade tucked neatly in his undies. 'For the third time, I'm announcing my retirement!' he yelled. He took out the grenade, pulled the pin, and threw it into the audience. The grenade exploded, killing 23 members of the crowd. The police arrived, and he was taken away again.

'You again?' asked the judge. 'I thought I'd sentenced you to death not long ago.' The conductor shrugged. 'Okay, how do you plead to 23 counts of first-degree murder?' the judge asked. 'Guilty to all counts,' replied the conductor.

While the settings were changed to triple the voltage of the current going to the chair, the conductor was granted another last request.

'A silver platter with two dozen bananas,' was his answer. He scoffed the bananas, the room was evacuated and the switch was flicked. It appeared that they'd manage to kill him this time, but the conductor regained consciousness when they were about to remove his body. His manager and the two gorilla-sized bodyguards were waiting for him as he left the building. 'Back to work!'

The weeks dragged on, and the conductor couldn't take it any more. 'Dear, could you get me a missile launcher?' he asked his wife as they lay in bed.

'Yes, dear,' she replied.

He didn't even wait for the concert to start. 'Fuck

yas all!' he screamed, and launched a missile into the New York Symphony Orchestra, killing all 190 band members. The army was called in this time, and he was dragged away.

'Jesus Christ, you again? You're supposed to be DEAD!' the judge roared. The conductor just shrugged. 'May I ask how you plead for 190 counts of first-degree murder?'

'Guilty as sin!' the conductor screamed. 'The bastards deserved it!' He was hauled away.

A public announcement was issued to all local residents warning that there would be a short out in the power. Meanwhile, the city's electrical engineers were busy rerouting a massive dose of voltage into the electric chair. Once again, the conductor was granted a last request. 'Three dozen bananas on a silver platter,' he said. He scoffed the bananas, the building was completely vacated, and the electric chair was activated by remote control, some two kilometres away. The building exploded, reducing it to rubble. They fished through the ruins to find the conductor's ruined body.

His funeral was held some days later and as the casket was being lowered into the grave there was a knock on the coffin lid. Women fainted as the conductor crawled out of the coffin – alive!

He was taken to a large press conference. One reporter stood up and asked, 'You've survived three visits to the electric chair. How did you do it?'

'I've tried telling people before,' he said. 'I'm just a bad conductor.'

A violist is sitting in the front row crying hysterically. The conductor asks the violist what's wrong. The violist answers, 'The second oboe loosened one of my tuning pegs.' The conductor says, 'Well, that does seem a bit childish. But it's nothing to get so upset about. Why are you crying?' To which the violist replies, 'He won't tell me which one.'

How many musicians does it take to screw in a light bulb?

I don't know, big daddy, but hum a few bars and I'll fake it.

What did the drummer get in his IQ test?

Drool.

What's the difference between a violin and a viola?

There's no difference. The violin just looks smaller because the violinist's head is so big.

Why are viola jokes so short?

So violinists can understand them.

How do you tell the difference between a violinist and a dog?

The dog knows when to stop scratching.

How many second violinists does it take to change a light bulb?

None. They can't get up that high.

Why is a violinist like a scud missile?

Both are offensive and inaccurate.

Why don't viola players suffer from piles?

Because arseholes are in the first violin section.

How do you make a cello sound beautiful?

Sell it and buy a violin.

Two bass players were engaged for a run of *Carmen*. After a couple of weeks they agreed to each take an afternoon off so that they could watch the matinée performance from the front of house. Joe duly took his break. Back in the pit that evening, Mo asked how it was. 'Great,' said Joe. 'You know that bit where the music goes BOOM boom boom boom? Well there are some guys up top singing a terrific song about a bullfighter at the same time.'

Why are harps like elderly parents?
Both are unforgiving and hard to get in and out of cars.

How do you get piccolos to play in unison?
Shoot one.

Why is a bassoon better than an oboe?
The bassoon burns longer.

What is a burning oboe good for?
Setting a bassoon on fire.

Why did the chicken cross the road?
To get away from the bassoon recital.

Why is an 11-foot concert grand better than a studio upright?

Because is makes a bigger kaboom when dropped over a cliff.

What is the definition of 'nerd'?

Someone who owns their own alto clarinet.

What do you call a bass clarinetist with half a brain?

Gifted.

What's the difference between a saxophone and a lawnmower?

Lawnmowers sound better in small ensembles. The neighbours are upset if you borrow a lawnmower and don't return it. The grip.

What's the difference between a trumpet player and the rear end of a horse?

I don't know either.

In an emergency, a jazz trumpeter was hired to play solos with a symphony orchestra. Everything was great through the first movement when she had some really hair-raising solos, but in the second movement she started improvising madly when she wasn't supposed to play at all. After the concert the conductor came round looking for an explanation. She said, 'I looked in the score and it said 'tacit' – so I took it.'

What's the difference between a bass trombone and a chainsaw?

Vibrato, plus it's easier to improvise on a chainsaw.

How do you know when a trombone player is at your door?

The doorbell drags.

What is a gentleman?

Someone who knows how to play the trombone, but doesn't.

What do you call a trombonist with a beeper?

An optimist.

What's the difference between a dead trombone player lying in the road and a dead squirrel lying in the road?

The squirrel was on his way to a gig.

What kind of calendar does a trombonist use for his gigs?

Year-At-A-Glance.

What's the difference between a French horn section and a '57 Chevy?

You can tune a '57 Chevy.

A woman had gone a long, long time without so much as the hope of a relationship. When she finally picked up a good-looking guy and went out with him, her friends were curious as to how it went.

'What's he like?' a friend asked.

'Oh, he's fine I guess. He's a musician, you know.'

'Did he have class?'

'Well, most of the time, yes. But I don't think I'll be going out with him again.'

'Oh, why not?'

'Well, he plays the French horn, so I guess it's just habit, but every time we kiss, he sticks his fist in my rear!'

Why are orchestra intermissions limited to 20 minutes?

So you don't have to retrain the drummers.

What do you call someone who hangs out with musicians?

A drummer.

How do you know when a drummer is knocking at your door?

The knock always slows down.

Why do bands have bass players?

To translate for the drummer.

What's the difference between a drummer and a terrorist?

Terrorists have sympathisers.

What do drummers use for birth control?

Their personalities.

If you threw a violist and a soprano off a cliff, who would hit the ground first?

The violist. The soprano would have to stop half-way down to ask directions. Still, who cares.

What's the difference between a soprano and a terrorist?

You can negotiate with a terrorist.

What's the difference between a soprano and a pirahna?

The lipstick.

What's the difference between a soprano and a pit bull?

The jewellery.

How many sopranos does it take to change a light bulb?

Just one. She holds the bulb and the world revolves around her.

What's the difference between a Wagnerian soprano and the average All-Pro offensive lineman?
Stage makeup.

What is the difference between a soubrette and a cobra?
One is deadly poisonous, and the other is a reptile.

How do you tell if a Wagnerian soprano is dead?
The horses seem relieved.

What's the first thing a soprano does in the morning?
Gets up and goes home.

What's the difference between a soprano and a Porsche.
Most musicians have never been in a Porsche.

A jazz musician dies and goes to Heaven, where an angel takes him by the hand and says, 'Hey man, welcome! You've been elected to the Jazz Allstars of Heaven – right up there with Satchmo, Miles, Django, all the greats. And we've got a gig tonight! Only one problem – God's girlfriend gets to sing.'

What do you see if you look up a soprano's skirt?

A tenor.

How do you put a sparkle in a soprano's eye?

Shine a flashlight in her ear.

Where is a tenor's resonance?

Where his brain should be.

What's the definition of a male quartet?

Three men and a tenor.

What's the difference between a World War and a high school choral performance?

The performance causes more suffering.

Why do high school choruses travel so often?
Keeps assassins guessing.

There's nothing I like better than the sound of a banjo, unless of course it's the sound of a chicken caught in a vacuum cleaner.

What's it mean when a guitar player is drooling out of both sides of his mouth?
The stage is level.

How do you get a guitar player to play softer?
Give him some sheet music.

Why do bagpipe players walk while they play?
To get away from the noise.

How many country and western singers does it take to change a light bulb?
Three. One to change the light bulb and two to sing about how great the old one was.

What happens if you play blues music backwards?
Your wife returns to you, your dog comes back to life, and you get out of prison.

What does it say on a blues singer's tombstone?
I didn't wake up this morning.

How many sound men does it take to change a light bulb?
One, two, three. One, two, three ...

Two musicians are driving down the road when they glance into the rear vision and, to their horror, see the Grim Reaper sitting in the back seat. He informs them that they've had an accident and have both died. But before he takes them off into Eternity, he'll grant each musician one last request – something to remind them of their past life on Earth.

The first says that he was a country and western musician and would like to hear eight choruses of 'Achy-Breaky Heart' as a last hurrah. The second musician says, 'I was a jazz musician ... kill me now.'

What's the difference between a bull and a symphony orchestra?

The bull has the horns in front and the arsehole in the back.

A conductor and a violist are standing in the middle of the road. Which one do you run over first, and why?

The conductor. Business before pleasure.

Why are conductors' hearts so coveted for transplants?

They've had so little use.

What's the difference between a conductor and a sack of fertiliser?

The sack.

What's the difference between a symphony conductor and Dr Scholl's Foot Pads?

Dr Scholl's Foot Pads buck up the feet.

What's the difference between a pig and a symphony orchestra conductor?

There are some things a pig just won't do.

What's the ideal weight for a conductor?

About two and a half pounds, including the urn.

A musician calls a symphony orchestra's office to talk to the conductor. 'I'm sorry, he's dead,' comes the reply. The musician calls back 30 times, always getting the same reply from the receptionist. At last she asks him why he keeps calling. 'I just like to hear you say it.'

A musician arrives at the Pearly Gates. 'What did you do when you were alive?' asks St Peter.

'I was the principal trombone player of the City of Birmingham Orchestra.'

'Excellent, we have a vacancy in our celestial symphony orchestra for a trombonist. Why don't you turn up at the next rehearsal?'

So when the time for the next rehearsal comes, our friend presents himself with his heavenly trombone. As he takes his seat, God moves, in a mysterious way, to the podium and taps his baton to bring the players to attention. Our friend turns to the angelic second trombonist and whispers, 'So what's God like as a conductor?'

'Oh, he's okay most of the time, but occasionally he thinks he's von Karajan.'

It was the night of a grand concert and all the celebrities and notables had turned up to hear it. But around 8 o'clock there was still no sign of the conductor. The theatre manager was desperate, fearful of refunding everyone's money. He went backstage and asked the musicians if any of them could conduct. None of them could. He went around and asked the staff if any of them could conduct. No luck. He started asking people in the lobby, in the hope that maybe one of them could conduct the performance. No luck.

He went outside and started asking everybody passing by if they could conduct. No luck whatsoever. By now the concert was 20 minutes late in starting and the crowd were getting restless and would soon be demanding their money back.

The desperate manager looked around and spied a cat sitting on a fire hydrant, a dog peeing on a tree and a horse standing in the street. 'Oh, what the heck,' he exclaimed, 'what do we have to lose?'

So the manager went up to the cat and asked him, 'Mr Cat, do you know how to conduct?' The cat meowed, 'I don't know. I'll try.' But although it tried really hard it couldn't stand upright on its hind legs.

The manager sighed and thanked the cat and

then asked the dog, 'Mr Dog, do you think you can conduct?' The dog woofed, 'Let me see.' But although it managed to stand on its hind legs and wave its front paws around, it couldn't keep upright long enough to last through an entire movement. 'Nice try,' the manager told the dog, and turned in utter desperation to the horse.

'Mr Horse, how about you? Can you conduct?' The horse looked at him for a second, and without a word turned around, presented its hind end and started swishing its tail in perfect 4-4 time.

'Thank Christ!' yelled the manager. 'The concert can go on.' However, the horse then dropped a load of plop onto the street. The assistant manager was horrified and told the manager, 'We can't have this horse conduct. What would the orchestra think?'

The manager looked first at the horse's rear end and then at the plop lying in the street and replied, 'Trust me – from this angle, the orchestra won't even know they have a new conductor.'

Once upon a time there was a blind rabbit and a blind snake. One day the blind rabbit was happily hopping down the path towards his home when he bumped into someone. Apologising profusely, he said, 'I'm blind and didn't see you there.'

'Perfectly all right,' said the snake. 'I'm blind too, and couldn't see to step out of your way.'

They conversed in a friendly fashion and finally the snake said, 'This is the best conversation I've had with anyone for years. Would you mind if I felt you to see what you're like?'

'No,' said the rabbit, 'feel away.'

So the snake wrapped himself round the rabbit and snuggled his coils and said, 'Ummmm, you're soft and warm and fuzzy and cuddly and those ears! You must be a rabbit.'

'That's right,' said the rabbit. 'May I feel you?'

'Go right ahead.'

And the snake stretched himself out full-length on the path. The rabbit stroked the snake's body and then drew back in disgust.

'Shit,' he said, 'you're cold, and slimy, you must be a conductor!'

'Mummy,' said the little girl, 'can I get pregnant by anal intercourse?'

'Of course you can,' her mother replied, 'how do you think conductors are made?'

There were two people walking down the street. One was a musician, the other didn't have any money either.

What's the first thing a musician says at work?

Would you like fries with that?

St Peter is checking people at the Pearly Gates. The first is a Texan. 'Tell me, what have you done in your life?' asks St Peter.

'Well, I struck oil,' says the Texan, 'so I became rich, but I didn't sit on my laurels. I divided all my money among my entire family in my will, so our descendants are set for about three generations.'

St Peter says, 'Very good, come in.'

The second guy in line says, 'I struck it big in the stock market, but I didn't just provide for my own like that Texan guy. I donated $5 million to Save the Children.'

'Wonderful,' says St Peter. 'Who's next?'

A third guy has been listening, and says timidly with a downcast look, 'Well, I only made $5000 in my entire lifetime.'

'Heavens,' said St Peter, 'what instrument did you play?'

St Peter's checking people into Heaven. He asks a man, 'What did you do on Earth?'

The man replies, 'I was a doctor.'

St Peter says, 'Fine, go right through the Pearly Gates.'

'Next. What did you do on Earth?'

'I was a schoolteacher.'

'Go right through those Pearly Gates. And what did *you* do on Earth?'

'I was a musician.'

'Go round the side, up the freight elevator, through the kitchen.'

What's the difference between a seamstress and a violist?

The seamstress tucks up the frills.

What's the difference between a seamstress and a soprano?

The seamstress tucks and frills.

Definition of a string quartet: A good violinist, a bad violinist, an ex-violinist and someone who hates violinists, all getting together to complain about composers.

How is lightning like a violist's fingers?

Neither one strikes in the same place twice.

How do you keep a violin from getting stolen?

Put it in a viola case.

What's the difference between a viola and a coffin?

The coffin has the dead person on the inside.

What do you do with a dead violist?
Move him back a desk.

What's the difference between a viola and a trampoline?
You take your shoes off to jump on a trampoline.

What's the difference between a viola and an onion?
No one cries when you cut a viola.

What's the definition of 'perfect pitch'?
Throwing a viola into a dumpster without hitting the rim.

Why do violists stand for long periods outside people's houses?
They can't find the key and they don't know when to come in.

How can you tell when a violist is playing out of tune?
The bow is moving.

Why is playing the viola like peeing in your pants?

They both give a nice warm feeling without making any sound.

Why is a viola solo like premature ejaculation?

Because even when you know it's coming, there's nothing you can do about it.

Why don't violists play hide and seek?

Because no one will look for them.

What do a viola and a law suit have in common?

Everyone is happy when the case is closed.

A violist and a cellist were standing on a sinking ship.

'Help,' cried the cellist, 'I can't swim.'

'Don't worry, said the violist, 'just fake it.'

A violist came home and found his house burned to the ground. When he asked what happened the police told him, 'Well, apparently the conductor came to your house and – ' The violist's eyes lit up and he interrupted excitedly, 'The conductor? Came to *my* house?'

A viola player decides he's had enough of being a viola player, the butt of all jokes. So he decides to change his instrument. He goes into a shop and says, 'I want to buy a violin.' The man behind the counter looks at him for a moment and then says, 'You must be a viola player.'

The viola player is astonished. 'Well, yes I am, but how did you know?'

'Well, this is a fish and chip shop.'

A man went on a safari in darkest Africa. The native guides took him deep into the jungle where they could hear the screeching of birds and the howling of wild animals. After a few days of travel he was being driven crazy by the constant drumming noise in the background. He asked the leader of the guides what the drumming was. He got no answer. Just a stony silence. They travelled deep into the jungle and the drumming got louder. But nobody would explain it.

Finally, one morning, after days of ever-louder drumming, there was a sudden silence. Whereupon the native guides screamed and hid in the undergrowth. 'What's wrong? Why have the drums stopped?' the man asked.

The native guides chorused, 'Very bad.'

'Why?'

'When drum stops, very bad. Next comes viola solo!'

SEEING THE LIGHT

How many Windows programmers does it take to change a light bulb?

Four hundred and seventy-two. One to write WinGetLightBulbHandle, one to write WinQueryStatusLightBulb, one to write WinGetLightSwitchHandle . . .

How many managers does it take to change a light bulb?

'We've formed a task force to study the problem and why light bulbs burn out, and figure out what, exactly, we as supervisors can do to make the bulbs work smarter, not harder.'

How many Tech Support folk does it take to change a light bulb?

We have an exact copy of the light bulb here, and it seems to be working fine. Can you tell me what kind of system you have? Okay, now exactly how dark is it? Okay, there could be four or five things wrong ... have you tried the light switch?

How many Microsoft technicians does it take to change a light bulb?

Three. Two to hold the ladder and one to screw the bulb into a faucet.

How many Microsoft vice presidents does it take to change a light bulb?

Eight: one to work the bulb and seven to make sure Microsoft gets $2 for every light bulb ever changed anywhere in the world.

How many testers does it take to change a light bulb?

We just noticed the room was dark; we don't actually fix the problem.

How many developers does it take to change a light bulb?

The light bulb works fine on the system in my office.

How many C++ programmers does it take to change a light bulb?

You're still thinking procedurally. A properly designed light bulb object would inherit a change method from a generic light bulb class, so all you'd have to do is send a light bulb change message.

How many shipping department personnel does it take to change a light bulb?

We can change the bulb in seven–ten working days; if you call before 2 p.m. and pay an extra $15, we can get the bulb changed overnight. Don't forget to put your name in the upper right-hand corner of the light bulb box.

How many Microsoft engineers does it take to change a light bulb?

None, Bill Gates will just redefine Darkness (TM) as the new industry standard.

How many monkeys does it take to change a light bulb?

Two. One to do it, and one to scratch his bum.

How many Californians does it take to screw in a light bulb?

Five. One to screw in the light bulb, and four to share the experience.

How many New Yorkers does it take to change a light bulb?

None of your fucking business. Get owta my way!

How many Englishmen does it take to change a light bulb?

What do you mean change it? It's a perfectly good light bulb! We've had it for 100 years and it's worked just fine.

How many Ukrainians does it take to screw in a light bulb?

They don't need to. They glow in the dark.

How many African-Americans does it take to screw in a light bulb?

Two. One to hold the bulb, and one to drive the pink Cadillac in sight circles.

How many Iranians does it take to change a light bulb?

One hundred. One to screw it in and 99 to hold the house hostage.

How many Israelis does it take to screw in a light bulb?

Sixty-four to storm the room and take control of it, one to forcibly eject the old bulb and another to screw it in.

How many Australians does it take to screw in a light bulb?

Sixteen. One to change the bulb and 15 to stand around saying, 'Goodonya mate.'

How many dead politicians does it take to change a light bulb?

As many as possible.

How many Bill Clintons does it take to change a light bulb?

None. He'll only promise change.

How many Dan Quayles does it take to screw in a light bulb?

One, but it has to be a pretty dim bulb.

How many libertarians does it take to screw in a light bulb?

None. If you want to sit in the dark, that's your business.

How many Russian leaders does it take to change a light bulb?

Nobody knows. Russian leaders don't last as long as light bulbs.

How many Marxists does it take to change a light bulb?

None. The seeds of revolution and change are within the light bulb itself.

How many Maoists does it take to change a light bulb?

One to screw in the bulb and 1000 to chant, 'Fight Darkness!'

How many Apple employees does it take to change a light bulb?

Seven. One to screw it in and six to design the T-shirts.

How many Apple programmers does it take to change a light bulb?

Only one. But why bother? The light socket will be obsolete in six months anyway.

How many editors does it take to change a light bulb?

Two. One to screw in the bulb and one to issue a rejection slip to the old bulb.

How many cafeteria staff does it take to change a light bulb?

Sorry. We closed 18 seconds ago, and I've just cashed up.

How many librarians does it take to change a light bulb?

Don't know, but I could look it up for you.

How many supermarket cashiers does it take to change a light bulb?

Are you kidding? They won't even change a $5 bill.

How many Mafia members does it take to change a light bulb?

Three. One to change the light bulb and one to kill the witness.

How many Teamsters does it take to change a light bulb?

Eighteen. You got a problem with that?

How many bureaucrats does it take to change a light bulb?

Two. One to screw it in and one to screw it up.

How many astronomers does it take to take change a light bulb?

None. Astronomers prefer the dark.

How many university professors does it take to change a light bulb?

Just one. But once they get tenure, they don't change any more.

How many football players does it take to change a light bulb?

The entire team. And they all get a semester's credit for it.

How many psychologists does it take to change a light bulb?

Just one. But the light bulb has to really *want* to change.

How many chiropractors does it take to change a light bulb?

Just one, but it takes 30 visits.

How many jugglers does it take to change a light bulb?

One, but it takes at least three light bulbs.

How many magicians does it take to change a light bulb?

Depends on what you want to change it into.

How many circus performers does it take to change a light bulb?

Four. One to change the bulb and three to sing, 'Ta da!'

How many actors does it take to change a light bulb?

Nine. One to climb the ladder and replace the bulb, eight to stand around grumbling, 'That should be *me* up there!'

How many actresses does it take to change a light bulb?

One. But you should have seen the line outside the producer's hotel room.

How many movie directors does it take to change a light bulb?

Just one, and when he's done, everyone thinks that his last light bulb was much better.

How many screenwriters does it take to change a light bulb?

Why do we have to change it?

How many mystery writers does it take to change a light bulb?

Two. One to screw it in almost all the way and another to give it a surprise twist at the end.

How many poets does it take to change a light bulb?

Three. One to curse the darkness, one to light a candle and one to change the bulb.

How many fishermen does it take to change a light bulb?

Five. And you should have seen the light bulb! It must have been *this* big!

How many Einsteins does it take to change a light bulb?

That depends on the speed of the change and the mass of the bulb. Or vice versa, of course. It just might be easier to leave the bulb in and change the room. It's all relative.

How many heterosexual males does it take to screw in a light bulb in San Francisco?

Both of them.

How many gay men does it take to screw in a light bulb?

Three. One to screw in an Art Deco bulb and two to shriek, 'Fabulous!'

How many lesbians does it take to change a light bulb?

Two. One to do it and one to make a video documentary about it.

How many evolutionists does it take to change a light bulb?

Only one, but it takes eight million years.

How many pessimists does it take to change a light bulb?

None. Why bother? It's just going to burn out anyway.

How many Carl Sagans does it take to change a light bulb?

Billions and billions.

How many Jewish mothers does it take to change a light bulb?

'That's all right, I'll sit in the dark.'

How many *real* men does it take to change a light bulb?

None. Real men aren't afraid of the dark.

How many Christians does it take to change a light bulb?

Three, but they're really only one.

How many Christian Scientists does it take to change a light bulb?

None, but it takes at least three to sit and pray for the old one to come back on.

How many pro-lifers does it take to change a light bulb?

Six. Two to screw in the bulb and four to testify that it was lit from the moment they began screwing.

How many Pygmies does it take to screw in a light bulb?

At least three.

How many auto mechanics does it take to screw in a light bulb?

Six. One to force it with a hammer, and five to go out for more bulbs.

How many bankers does it take to screw in a light bulb?

Four. One to hold the bulb and three to try and remember the combination.

How many investment brokers does it take to screw in a light bulb?

'My God, it burnt out! Sell all my G.E. stock now!'

How many Zen Buddhists does it take to screw in a light bulb?

Two. One to screw in the bulb, and one to not screw in the bulb.

How many cops does it take to screw in a light bulb?

None. It turned itself in.

How many database people does it take to screw in a light bulb?

Three. One to write the light bulb removal program, one to write the light bulb insertion program, and one to act as a light bulb administrator to make sure nobody else tries to change the light bulb at the same time.

How many disarmament folk does it take to screw in a light bulb?

They won't because:

1. If we change our bulb, they will just change theirs to a brighter one, so where will it all end?
2. We already have enough bulbs to illuminate the entire world three times over.
3. We shouldn't spend money for light bulbs as long as anyone is hungry anywhere.
4. We don't know what effect all of this artificial light will have on the future of mankind.
5. Nature provides us with all the light we need, we just haven't learned to husband it yet.
6. Artificial light isn't aesthetically correct.
7. The candle is more traditional, and it uses no electricity.
8. It is the responsibility of the federal government to provide light to all Americans, without regard to race, age, creed, colour, sex, religion, socio-economic status, national origin or need.

How many doctors does it take to screw in a light bulb?

That depends on whether it has health insurance.

How many existentialists does it take to screw in a light bulb?

Two. One to screw it in and one to observe how the light bulb itself symbolises a single incandescent beacon of subjective reality in a netherworld of endless absurdity reaching out towards a maudlin cosmos of nothingness.

How many fatalists does it take to screw in a light bulb?

What does it matter? We're all gonna die anyway.

How many feminists does it take to screw in a light bulb?

1. That's not funny!
2. Two. One to change the bulb and one to write about how it felt.
3. Three. One to screw it in and two to talk about the sexual implications.
4. Four. One to change it, and three to write about how the bulb is exploiting the socket.
5. Three. One to change the bulb, and two to secretly wish they were the socket.
6. Two. One to screw in the light bulb and one to kick the balls off any man trying to help the first one.

How many fundamentalists does it take to screw in a light bulb?

The Bible doesn't mention light bulbs.

How many junkies does it take to screw in a light bulb?

'Oh wow, is it like dark, man?'

How many lesbians does it take to screw in a light bulb?

Three. One to screw it in and two to talk about how much better it is than with a man.

How many modern artists does it take to screw in a light bulb?

Four. One to throw bulbs against the wall, one to pile hundreds of them in a heap and spray-paint it orange, one to glue light bulbs to a cocker spaniel, and one to put a bulb in the socket and fill the room with light while all the critics and buyers are watching the fellow smashing the bulbs against the wall, the fellow with the spray gun, and the cocker spaniel.

How many netheads does it take to tell yet another light bulb joke?

One thousand, six hundred and twenty-two. One to tell the original joke, and the rest to give some minor variation of it.

How many psychoanalysts does it take to screw in a light bulb?

How many do you think it takes?

How many Reaganists does it take to screw in a light bulb?

Two. One to screw it in, and one to send the bill to the next generation.

How many Roman Catholics does it take to screw in a light bulb?

Two. One to screw it in, and another to repent.

How many Russians does it take to screw in a light bulb?

That's a military secret.

How many lawyers does it take to change a light bulb?

Such number as may be deemed necessary to perform the stated task in a timely and efficient manner within the strictures of the following agreement:

Whereas the party of the first part, also known as 'the lawyers' and the party of the second part, also known as 'the light bulb' do hereby and forthwith agree to a transaction wherein the party of the second part (light bulb) shall be removed from the current position as a result of failure to perform previously agreed upon duties, i.e. the lighting, elucidation, and otherwise illumination of the area ranging from the front (north) door, through the entry way, terminating at an area just inside the primary living area, demarcated by the beginning of the carpet, any spillover illumination being at the option of the party of the second part (light bulb) and not required by the aforementioned agreement between the parties. The aforementioned removal transaction shall include, but not be limited to, the following steps:

1. The party of the first part (lawyer) shall, with or without elevation at his option, by means of a chair, step stool, ladder or any other means of elevation, grasp the party of the second part (light bulb) and rotate the party of the second part (light bulb) in a counter-clockwise direction, said direction being non-negotiable. Said grasping and rotation of the paty of the second part (light bulb) shall be undertaken by the party of the first part (lawyer) to maintain the structural integrity of the paty of the second part (light bulb), notwithstanding the aforementioned failure of the party of the second part (light bulb) to perform the customary and agreed upon duties. The foregoing notwithstanding, however, both parties stipulate that structural failure of the party of the second part (light bulb) may be incidental to the aforementioned failure to perform and in such case the party of the first part (lawyer) shall be held blameless for such structural failure insofar as this agreement is concerned so long as the non-negotiable directional codicil (counter-clockwise) is observed by the party of the first part (lawyer) throughout.

2. Upon reaching a point where the party of the

second part (light bulb) becomes separated from the party of the third part ('receptacle'), the party of the first part (lawyer) shall have the option of disposing of the party of the second part (light bulb) in a manner consistent with all applicable state, local and federal statutes.

3. Once separation and disposal have been achieved, the party of the first part (lawyer) shall have the option of beginning installation of the party of the fourth part ('new light bulb'). This installation shall occur in a manner consistent with the reverse of the procedures described in step one of this self same document, being careful to note that the rotation should occur in a clockwise direction, said direction also being non-negotiable and only until the party of the fourth part ('new light bulb') becomes snug in the party of the third part (receptacle) and in fact becomes the party of the second part (light bulb).

Note: The above described steps may be performed, at the option of the party of the first part (lawyer), by said party of the first part (lawyer), by his or her heirs and assigns, or by any and all persons authorised by him or her to do so, the objective being to produce a level of illumination in the immediate vicinity of the aforementioned front (north) door consistent with maximisation of ingress and revenue for the party of the fifth part, also known as 'The Firm'.

How many Chicago school economists does it take to change a light bulb?

None:

1. If the light bulb needed changing, the market would already have done it.
2. The darkness will cause the light bulb to change by itself.
3. If the government would just leave it alone, it would screw itself in.
4. There is no need to change the light bulb. All the conditions for illumination are in place.
5. They're all waiting for the unseen hand of the market to correct the lighting disequilibrium.
6. Because, look! It's getting brighter! It's definitely getting brighter!

Or:

Just one, but it really gets screwed.

Or:

A thousand: ten theoretical economists with different theories on how to change the light bulb, and 990 empirical economists labouring to determine which theory's the correct one, while everyone is still in the dark.

How many MBAs does it take to change a light bulb?

'Only one if you hire me. I can actually change the light bulb myself. As you can see from my resumé, I've had extensive experience changing light bulbs in my previous positions. My only weakness is that I'm compulsive about changing light bulbs in my spare time.'

How many doctoral students does it take to change a light bulb?

'Should have an answer for you in about five years.'

LAWYERS AND OTHER CRIMINALS

As the highway patrolman approached the accident site, he found that the entire driver's side of the BMW had been ripped away, taking with it the driver's arm. The injured yuppie, a lawyer obviously in shock, kept moaning, 'My car, my car,' as the officer tried to comfort him. 'Sir,' the patrolman said gently, 'I think we should be more concerned about your arm than your car.'

The driver looked down to where his arm should have been, then screamed, 'My Rolex! My Rolex!'

A little old lady walked into a branch of Chase Manhattan Bank holding a large paperbag. She told the teller that she had $3 million in the bag and wanted to open an account. But first, she insisted on meeting the president of the bank. After looking into the bag and seeing a huge amount of money that might well have amounted to $3 million, the teller called the president's office.

The lady was ushered into the president's presence. She explained that she liked to know the people that she did business with. The president asked her how she'd come into such a large amount of cash. 'Was it an inheritance?'

'No,' she replied, 'I bet.'

'You bet?' repeated the president. 'On horses?'

'No,' she replied, 'on people.'

Seeing his confusion, she decided to demonstrate. 'I'll bet you $25 000 that by 10 a.m. tomorrow your balls will be square.' The bank president immediately accepted the bet and for the rest of the day was very, very careful. He decided to stay home that evening and take no chances.

Next morning he checked himself in the shower to make sure that everything was okay. Everything was. He went to work and waited for the little old lady to come in at 10 and give him his $25 000.

At 10 a.m. sharp she was escorted into his office with a younger man whom she introduced as her lawyer. 'Well,' she asked, 'what about our bet?'

'I don't know how to tell you this,' he replied, 'but I'm the same as I always have been, only $25 000 richer.'

The lady requested that she be able to see for herself and the president, thinking this was reasonable, dropped his trousers. She then instructed him to bend over and grabbed hold of him. Yes, everything was normal. As the president adjusted his clothing, he noticed her lawyer banging his head against the wall. 'What's wrong with him?' the president asked.

'Oh him,' she replied, 'I bet him $100 000 that by 10 this morning I'd have the president of Chase Manhattan Bank by the balls.'

Mickey Mouse was trying to convince the judge to give him a divorce from Minnie. 'I'm sorry, Mickey,' said the judge, 'but your claiming Minnie is crazy is not a valid reason for me to grant a divorce.'

'I didn't say she was crazy,' said Mickey, 'I said she was fucking Goofy.'

A burglar breaks into an apartment on Fifth Avenue, opposite the Met. He's sure that nobody's home but, just in case, keeps the lights off. While he searches for the wall safe he hears a voice saying, 'I can see you! Jesus can see you too!' He freezes in his tracks. Doesn't move a muscle.

A couple of minutes pass. The voice repeats, 'I can see you! Jesus can see you too!' The burglar takes out his flashlight, switches it on, looks around the room. He sees a birdcage with a parrot in it. 'Did you say that?'

The parrot says again, 'I can see you! Jesus can see you too!'

'Ah, so what. You're just a fucking parrot,' says the burglar.

'I may be just a parrot,' replies the bird, 'but Jesus is a fucking doberman!'

The three bears returned from a stroll in the woods to find the door of their little house wide open. Cautiously they went inside. After a while Daddy Bear said, 'Somebody's been eating *my* porridge.'

Mummy Bear yelled, 'Somebody's been eating *my* porridge!'

Little Baby Bear rushed in. 'Bugger the porridge. Someone's nicked the video.'

A big city lawyer was called in on a case between a farmer and a large railroad company. The farmer had noticed his prize cow missing from the field through which the railroad passed and filed suit against the railroad company for its value. The case was to be tried before a JP in a backroom of the general store, and the attorney immediately cornered the farmer and tried to have him settle out of court. Finally the farmer agreed to take 50 per cent of what he was claiming.

After the farmer signed the release and took the cheque, the young lawyer couldn't help but gloat a little. He told the farmer, 'I hate to tell you this but I put one over on you in there. I couldn't have won the case. The engineer was asleep and the fireman was in the caboose when the train went through your farm that morning. I didn't have a single witness to put on the stand.'

The farmer replied, 'Well, I tell you. I was a little worried about winning that case myself. Because that damn cow came home this morning.'

A golfer sets up for a tee shot with a row of trees and an out-of-bounds on the right side. He slices wildly and the ball heads off in the direction of the trees. About 15 minutes later, a highway patrolman approaches him. 'Is this your ball?'

'Yes, I think it is.'

'Well,' says the officer, 'it went over the trees and through the window of a house. It hit a cat and the cat ran out the front door. A school bus was driving by at the time and the driver, trying to miss the cat, hit a tree. The bus exploded into flames and there were no survivors.'

'Oh my god, that's terrible,' said the golfer. 'Is there anything I can do?'

The policeman replied, 'Well, you might try keeping your left arm a little straighter and start your down swing with your hips.'

PROSECUTOR: Did you kill the victim?

DEFENDANT: No I didn't.

PROSECUTOR: Do you know what the penalties are for perjury?

DEFENDANT: Yes I do. And they're a hell of a lot better than the penalty for murder.

Lawyers are people who can write a 10 000-word document and call it a brief.

What's the difference between a lawyer and a prostitute?

A prostitute will usually quit screwing you when you're dead.

What's black and brown and looks good on a lawyer?

A doberman.

What do you call 1000 lawyers chained together at the bottom of the ocean?

A good start.

Why do they always bury lawyers 12 feet deep?

Because deep down, lawyers are okay.

A tourist wandered into an antique shop in San Francisco's China Town. It was poorly lit and the shelves were groaning with fascinating and intriguing objects. Picking through them he discovered a marvellously detailed life-size bronze sculpture of a rat. It was so lifelike, so vividly detailed, that he couldn't resist it. He asked the shop owner for the price. '$12 for the rat, sir,' said the shop owner, 'and $1000 more for the fascinating story behind it.' 'You can keep the story, old man,' the tourist replied, 'but I'll take the rat.'

He left the store with the bronze rat under his arm and as he crossed the street, two live rats emerged from a sewer drain and fell into step behind him.

The tourist looked over his shoulder and began to walk faster. But with every step there seemed to be yet another rat following him. By the time he'd walked a few blocks, there were hundreds of them at his heels. People began to point and shout. And he began to panic.

He walked faster and faster and soon began to run as multitudes of rats swarmed from sewers, vacant lots, basements and abandoned cars. Finally, he panicked and ran full tilt towards the waterfront at the bottom of the hill.

The rats kept up squealing hideously. There must have been millions of them so that by the time he reached the water's edge there was a trail blocks long behind him – and a deafening squeaking and squealing filled the air.

Gathering his last skerrick of strength, he climbed up on the lightpost, and hurled the bronze rat into the bay, as far as he could heave it. Whereupon the seething tide of rats surged over the breakwater into the sea, and drowned.

When he gathered himself together, he made his way back to the antique shop. 'Ah, so you've come back for the rest of the story,' said the shop owner, with a wise smile.

'No,' replied the tourist. 'But I was wondering if you happened to carry bronze lawyers?'

How can you tell when a lawyer is lying?

His lips are moving.

Why won't sharks attack lawyers?

Professional courtesy.

What do you have when a lawyer is buried up to his neck in sand?

Not enough sand.

What's the difference between a lawyer and a bucket full of shit.

The bucket.

What is the definition of a shame?
When a busload of lawyers goes off a cliff.
What's the definition of a crying shame?
There is an empty seat.

What do you get when you cross the Godfather with a lawyer?
An offer you can't understand.

Why is it that many lawyers have broken noses?
From chasing parked ambulances.

Where do you find a good lawyer?
In the cemetery.

What's the difference between a lawyer and a gigolo?
A gigolo only screws one person at a time.

What's the difference between a lawyer and a vampire?
A vampire only sucks blood at night.

Why do lawyers wear neckties?
To keep the foreskin from crawling up their chins.

How many law professors does it take to change a light bulb?
You need 250 just to lobby for the research grant.

If you see a lawyer on a bicycle, why wouldn't you swerve to hit him?
It might be your bicycle.

A little boy asks his mother, 'Mum, do prostitutes have babies?'
'Of course, sweetie, where do you think all the lawyers come from?'

A customer visits a brain store. 'How much for engineer brain?'
'$3 an ounce.'
'How much for doctor brain?'
'$4 an ounce.'
'How much for lawyer brain?'
'$100 an ounce.'

'Why is lawyer brain so much more?'

'Do you know how many lawyers you need to kill to get an ounce of brain?'

A grade school teacher was asking students what their parents did for a living. 'Tim, you're first,' she said. 'What does your mother do all day?'

Tim stood up proudly and said, 'She's a doctor.'

'That's wonderful. How about you, Annie?'

Annie shyly stood up, shuffled her feet and said, 'My father is a mailman.'

'Thank you, Annie,' said the teacher. 'What about your father, Billy?'

Billy proudly stood up and announced, 'My daddy plays piano in a whorehouse.'

The teacher was aghast and promptly changed the subject to geography.

Later that day she went to Billy's house and rang the bell. Billy's father answered the door. The teacher explained what his son had said and demanded an explanation. Billy's father said, 'I'm actually an attorney. But how can I explain a thing like that to a seven-year-old?'

A lawyer died and arrived at the Pearly Gates. To his dismay, there were thousands of people ahead of him in the line to see St Peter. To his surprise, St Peter left his desk at the gate and came down the long line to where the lawyer was, and greeted him warmly. Then St Peter and one of his assistants took the lawyer by the hands and guided him up the front of the line and into a comfortable chair by his desk. The lawyer said, 'I don't mind all this attention, but what makes me so special?'

St Peter replied, 'Well, we've added up all the hours for which you billed your clients, and by my calculation you must be around 193 years old.'

A lawyer and a physician had a dispute over precedence. They referred it to Diogenes, who gave it in favour of the lawyer as follows: 'Let the thief go first and the executioner follow.'

'How can I ever thank you?' gushed a woman to Clarence Darrow, after he had solved her legal troubles.

'My dear woman,' Darrow replied, 'ever since the Phoenicians invented money there has been only one answer to that question.'

The Pope and a lawyer find themselves together before the Pearly Gates. After a small quantum of time which is spent discussing their respective professions, St Peter shows up to usher them to their new Heavenly station. After passing out wings, harps, halos and such, St Peter decides to show them to their new lodgings. After only a brief flight from the gates, Peter brings them down on the front lawn of a palatial estate with all sorts of lavish trappings. This, Peter announces, is where the lawyer will be spending eternity. 'Wow!' says the Pope, 'if he's getting a place like this, I can hardly wait to see mine!' They take flight once again and, as Peter leads on, the landscape below begins to appear more and more mundane until they finally land on a street lined with brownstone houses. Peter indicates the third on the left as the Pope's new domicile and turns to leave, wishing the pontiff his best. The Pope, in a mild state of astonishment, cries out, 'Hey, Peter! What's the deal here? You put that lawyer feller in a beautiful estate home and I end up in this dive?'

Peter looks at the pontiff amusedly and replies, 'Look here, old fellow. This street is practically encrusted with spiritual leaders from many eras and religions. We're putting you here so you guys can get your dogma together. That other guy gets an estate because he's the first damned lawyer to make it up here!'

Carlson was charged with stealing a Mercedes Benz and, after a long trial, the jury acquitted him. Later that day Carlson came back to the judge. 'Your Honour,' he said, 'I wanna get out a warrant for that dirty lawyer of mine!'

'Why?' asked the judge. 'He won your acquittal. What do you want to have him arrested for?'

'Well, your Honour,' replied Carlson, 'I didn't

have the money to pay his fee, so he went and took the car I stole.'

'You seem to have more than the average share of intelligence for a man of your background,' sneered the lawyer at a witness on the stand. 'If I wasn't under oath, I'd return the compliment,' replied the witness.

A judge in a small city was hearing a drink-driving case and the defendant, who had both a record and a reputation for driving under the influence, demanded a jury trial. It was nearly 4 p.m. and getting a jury would take time, so the judge called a recess and went out in the hall looking to impanel anyone available for jury duty. He found a dozen lawyers in the main lobby, and told them that they were a jury. The lawyers thought this would be a novel experience and so followed the judge back to the courtroom. The trial was over in about ten minutes and it was very clear that the defendant was guilty. The jury went into the jury room, the judge started getting ready to go home, and everyone waited.

After nearly three hours, the judge was totally out of patience and sent the bailiff into the jury room to see what was holding up the verdict. When the bailiff returned, the judge said, 'Well, have they got a verdict yet?'

The bailiff shook his head and said, 'Verdict? Hell, they're still doing nominating speeches for the foreman's position!'

Diogenes went to look for an honest lawyer. 'How's it going?' someone asked. 'Not too bad,' said Diogenes. 'I still have my lantern.'

A woman and her little girl were visiting the grave of the little girl's grandmother. On their way back to the car, the little girl asked, 'Mummy, do they ever bury two people in the same grave?'

'Of course not, dear,' replied the mother. 'Why would you think that?'

'The tombstone back there said "Here lies a lawyer and an honest man".'

The defendant who pleads his own case has a fool for a client, but at least there will be no problem with fee-splitting.

Two guys, George and Harry, set out in a hot air balloon to cross the Atlantic Ocean. After 37 hours in the air, George says, 'Harry, we better lose some altitude so we can see where we are.'

Harry lets out some of the hot air in the balloon, and the balloon descends to below the cloud cover. George says, 'I still can't tell where we are. Let's ask that guy on the ground.'

So Harry yells down to the man, 'Hey, could you tell us where we are?' And the man on the ground yells back, 'You're in a balloon, 100 feet up in the air.' George turns to Harry and says, 'That man must be a lawyer.' Harry says, 'How can you tell?'

'Because the advice he gave us is 100 per cent accurate, and totally useless.'

For three years, a young attorney had been taking his brief vacations at a country inn. The last time, he'd finally managed an affair with the innkeeper's daughter. Looking forward once again to an exciting few days, he dragged his suitcase up the stairs of the inn, then stopped short. There sat his lover with an infant on her lap!

'Helen, why didn't you write when you learned you were pregnant?' he cried. 'I would have rushed up here, we could have got married, and the baby would have my name!'

'Well,' she said, 'when my folks found out about my condition, we sat up all night talkin' and talkin' and decided it would be better to have a bastard in the family than a lawyer.'

God decided to take the Devil to court and settle their differences once and for all. When Satan heard this, he laughed and said, 'And where you think you're going to find a lawyer?'

Santa Claus, the Tooth Fairy, an honest lawyer and an old drunk are walking down the street together when they simultaneously spot a $100 bill. Who gets it? The old drunk, of course. The other three are mythological creatures.

A lawyer named Strange was shopping for a tombstone. After he had made his selection, the stonecutter asked him what inscription he would like on it.

'Here lies an honest man and a lawyer,' responded the lawyer.

'Sorry, but I can't do that,' replied the stonecutter. 'In this state, it's against the law to bury two people in the same grave. However, I could put "Here lies an honest lawyer".'

'But that won't let people know who it is,' protested the lawyer.

'Certainly will,' retorted the stonecutter, 'people will read it and exclaim, "That's Strange!" '

At a convention of biological students, one student remarks to another, 'Did you know that in our lab we have switched from mice to lawyers for our experiments?'

'Really?' the other replied. 'Why did you switch?'

'Well, for three reasons: first, we found that lawyers are far more plentiful; second, the lab assistants don't get so attached to them; and thirdly, there are some things even a rat won't do. However, it's far more difficult to apply our findings to human beings.'

What do you call a lawyer with an IQ of 50?

Your Honour.

What do you call a lawyer who's gone bad?

Senator.

In front of you stand four men: Adolf Hitler, Idi Amin, Saddam Hussein and a lawyer. You're holding a gun which contains only three bullets. Who do you shoot?

Use all three bullets on the lawyer.

What is the difference between a lawyer and a vulture?

The lawyer gets Frequent Flyer miles.

How many lawyers does it take to roof a house?

Depends on how thin you slice them.

How do you get a lawyer out of a tree?

Cut the rope.

What is it that a goose can do, a duck can't and a lawyer should?

Stick his bill up his arse.

What's the difference between a catfish and a lawyer?

One's a bottom-crawling scum sucker, and the other's just a fish.

Why did the lawyer cross the road?

To get to the car accident on the other side.

Did you hear about the terrorist who hijacked a 747 full of lawyers?

He threatened to release one every hour if his demands weren't met.

What does a lawyer and a sperm have in common?

Both have about a one in three million chance of becoming a human being.

Why does California have so many lawyers and New Jersey so many toxic waste dumps?

New Jersey got to pick first.

Why did the post office recall the new 'lawyer' stamps?

Because people couldn't tell which side to spit on.

Did you hear about the lawyer from Texas who was so big when he died that they couldn't find a coffin big enough to hold the body?

They gave him an enema and buried him in a shoe box.

How many lawyers does it take to change a light bulb?

Sixty-five: 42 to sue the power company for failing to prevent the surge that took the bulb out in the first place, 14 to sue the electrician who wired the house, and nine to sue the bulb manufacturer.

Why has the Baptist Church quit baptising lawyers?

Because they can't get the ring out of the baptismal tub.

A defence attorney in a Northern California murder case says he believes Max the parrot may hold the answer to who smothered Jane Gill to death in her bedroom two years ago. But an attempt to get the African grey parrot's testimony into evidence last week was blocked by the judge. Max was found dehydrated and hungry in his cage two days after Gill's murder. After the parrot was coaxed back to health at a pet shop, the shop's owner said the bird began to cry out, 'Richard! No, no, no!' The man charged in the case is Gill's business partner, and his name is not Richard. He says he is innocent. Gary Dixon, a private investigator working on the case, surmised that the bird is now in a witness protection program. 'Max's identity has been changed and he is now a macaw.'

ATTORNEY: At the scene of the accident, did you tell the constable you had never felt better in your life?

FARMER: That's right.

ATTORNEY: Well then, how is it that you are now claiming you were seriously injured when my client's auto hit your wagon?

FARMER: When the constable arrived, he went over to my horse, who had a broken leg, and shot him. Then he went over to Rover, my dog, who was all banged up, and shot him. When he asked me how I felt, I just thought that under the circumstances it was a wise choice of words to say I've never felt better in my life.

The lawyer is standing at the gates to Heaven and St Peter is listing his sins:

1. Defending a large corporation on a pollution suit when he knew they were guilty.
2. Defending an obviously guilty murderer because the fee was high.
3. Overcharging fees to many clients.
4. Prosecuting an innocent woman because a scapegoat was needed in a controversial case.

And the list goes on for quite a while. The lawyer objects and begins to argues his case. He admits all these things but argues, 'Wait, I've done some charity in my life also.'

St Peter looks in his book and says, 'Yes, I see. You once gave a dime to a panhandler and you once gave an extra nickel to the shoeshine boy. Correct?'

The lawyer gets a smug look on his face and replies, 'Yes.'

St Peter turns to the angel next to him and says, 'Give this guy 15 cents and tell him to go to Hell.'

It's been discovered that lawyers are the laval stage of politicians.

A small town that cannot support one lawyer can always support two.

The trouble with the legal profession is that 98 per cent of its members give the rest a bad name.

Four surgeons were taking a coffee break and discussing their work. The first one said, 'I think accountants are the easiest to operate on. You open them up and everything inside is numbered.'

The second said, 'I think librarians are easiest to operate on. You open them up and everything inside is in alphabetical order.'

The third one said, 'I like to operate on

electricians. You open them up and everything inside is colour coded.'

The fourth one said, 'I like to operate on lawyers. They are heartless, spineless, gutless, and their heads and their arses are interchangeable.'

The scene is Heaven, with three men standing at the Pearly Gates. St Peter says to the first man, 'Let's see, you're Mr Jones, the engineer. We've been expecting you. Please follow me.' St Peter leads him down a hall to a door marked 101. 'This is where you'll be staying, Mr Jones,' says St Peter. Inside is a dank, dark, cold, musty room. Water is dripping from the walls where torture equipment is dangling. And chained to the centre of the floor is a growling, savage dog. Mr Jones nervously steps in as a loud voice cries from above, 'Mr Jones, you have sinned!' St Peter slams the door and returns to the remaining two men.

'And you are Mr Smith, the doctor,' says St Peter. 'You are in room 102. Please follow me.' A door opens into a room which is dark and dank with water dripping down the walls and horrible torture equipment hanging everywhere. And, once again, a growling, snarling dog is chained to the centre of the floor. As Mr Smith enters weeping, a voice from above cries, 'Mr Smith, you have sinned!' St Peter slams the door and returns to the last man.

'And you must be Mr Brown, the lawyer. We've been waiting for you. You are in room 103. Please follow me.' When they get to room 103, St Peter opens the door to reveal another dark, musty, gloomy room with torture equipment hanging from the slimy walls. But in the centre of the room stands Bo Derek. As the lawyer steps into the room, the voice cries out, 'Bo Derek! You have sinned!'

The lawyer died having not lived a wholly admirable life. He found himself at the gates of Hell. 'Welcome,' announced the Devil, greeting him warmly. 'Glad you could join us. As this is your last taste of free will, you're allowed to choose which of three possible places in which to spend Eternity.' There were three doors behind the Devil. He opened the first. Flames shot into the room and the lawyer could see thousands of people amidst the fire. 'No,' said the lawyer, 'not this one.'

The Devil opened the second door. The lawyer could see an infinity of people working at an immense rock pile. They were all being whipped as they hammered the large boulders into smaller ones. 'No, again,' said the lawyer.

Finally the Devil opened the third door which showed vast numbers in a lake with vomit up to their chins. All of them were chanting, 'Don't make waves! Don't make waves!'

'That's awful,' commented the horrified lawyer.

'You think that's bad,' asked the Devil. 'You should see it when the angels spend the weekend here with their motorboats!'

A dying man gathered his lawyer, doctor and clergyman to his bedside and handed each of them an envelope containing $25 000 in cash. He made each promise that after his death they would place the three envelopes in his coffin. He told them that he wanted to have enough money to enjoy the afterlife.

Next week the man died. At the wake the lawyer, doctor and clergyman each placed an envelope in the coffin and bid their friend farewell.

Three months later the three met by chance. The clergyman, feeling guilty, confessed that there was only $10 000 in the envelope he'd placed in the coffin. Rather than waste all the money, he'd sent $15 000 to a mission in South America. He asked for their forgiveness.

Moved by the gentle clergyman's sincerity, the doctor confessed that he, too, had kept some of the money for a worthy medical charity. His envelope, he admitted, had only had $8000 in it.

The lawyer was seething with self-righteous outrage. He expressed his deep disappointment in the felonious behaviour of two of his oldest and most trusted friends. 'I am the only one who kept his promise to our dying friend. My envelope contained my personal cheque for the entire $25 000.'

In the middle of the night, in the middle of nowhere, two cars collide and a fair amount of damage is done, although neither driver is hurt. It's impossible to assess blame for the accident. One driver is a doctor and the other a lawyer. The lawyer calls the police on his cellular phone. They'll be here in ten minutes.

It's cold and damp and both men are shaken. The lawyer offers the doctor a drink of brandy from a hip flask. The doctor gratefully accepts and hands it back to the lawyer, who puts it away. 'Aren't you going to have a drink?' the doctor says. 'After the police get here,' replies the lawyer.

A truck driver used to amuse himself by running over any lawyer he saw walking on the side of the road. Every time he saw a lawyer walking, he'd swerve to hit him. And there'd be a loud thump. Then he'd swerve back on the road. He found this immensely enjoyable.

One day the truck driver was driving along when he saw a priest hitchhiking. He pulled the truck over and asked the priest, 'Where are you going, Father?'

'I'm going to the church in the next town.'

'No problem, Father, I'll give you a lift. Climb in.'

The happy priest climbed in to the passenger's seat and the truck continued on its way. Suddenly the driver saw a lawyer walking down the road and swerved to hit him. But remembering there was a priest in the truck, he swerved back at the last minute. However, even though he was certain he'd missed the lawyer, he still heard a loud thud.

Not understanding where the noise came from, he glanced in his mirrors and when he didn't see anything, turned to the priest and said, 'I'm sorry, Father. I almost hit that lawyer.'

'That's okay,' replied the priest, 'I got him with the door.'

An airliner was having engine trouble and the pilot told the cabin crew to have the passengers prepare for an emergency landing. A few seconds later he asked the flight attendant if everyone was buckled in and ready. 'All set back here, captain,' came the reply, 'except for one lawyer who's passing out business cards.'

A very good man dies and as a reward for an honourable, charitable life, goes to Heaven. When he arrives, St Peter meets him with a warm welcome. 'Since you were such a good person in life,' says the saint, 'you may enter.'

'Thank you. But before I come in, could you tell me what to expect? What kind of people are here?'

'All kinds,' replied St Peter.

'Well, are there any convicted criminals in Heaven?'

'Yes, some.'

'Are there any communists in Heaven?'

'Yes, there are.'

'Are there any Nazis in Heaven?'

'Just a few.'

'Well, are there any lawyers in Heaven?'

And St Peter said, 'What? And ruin it for everyone else?'

A monster was on trial, facing a possible life sentence. So his lawyer bribed a juror to hold out for a lesser charge. After hours of deliberation the jury returned a verdict carrying a maximum of ten years in prison. Afterwards, the lawyer approached the corrupted juror. 'You had me so worried. When the jury was out so long I was afraid you couldn't pull it off.'

'I was worried, too,' answered the juror. 'The others all wanted to acquit him.'

A man went into a Chamber of Commerce in a small town. Obviously distressed, he asked the man at the counter, 'Is there a criminal attorney in town?'

The man replied, 'Yes, but we can't prove it yet.'

A farmer walks into an attorney's office wanting to file for divorce.

'May I help you?'

'Yes, I want to get one of those day-vorces.'

'Do you have any grounds?'

'Yeah, I've got about 140 acres.'

'No, you don't understand, do you have a case?'

'No, I've got a John Deere.'

'No, you don't understand, I mean do you have a grudge?'

'Yeah, I've got a grudge. That's where I park my John Deere.'

'No, sir, I mean do you have a suit?'

'Yes sir, I've got a suit. I wear it to church every Sunday.'

'Well sir, does your wife beat you up or anything?'

'No sir, we both get up at 4.30 a.m. Together.'

'Well, is she a nagger or anything?'

'No, she's a little white gal, but her last kid was a nagger. That's why I want this day-vorce.'

I broke a mirror in my house. I'm supposed to get seven years of bad luck. But my lawyer thinks that he can get me five.

Undistinguished and often shabby in appearance, Ulysses S. Grant did not recommend himself to strangers by looks. He once entered an inn in Galena, Illinois, on a stormy winter's night. A number of lawyers in town for a court session were clustered around the fire. One looked up as Grant appeared and said, 'Here's a stranger, gentlemen, and by the looks of him he's travelled through Hell itself to get here.'

'That's right,' said Grant cheerfully.

'And how did you find things down there?'

'Just like here,' replied Grant, 'lawyers all closest to the fire.'

A mature woman was discussing her forthcoming and fourth wedding with a priest. 'Father, how am I going to tell my husband that I'm still a virgin?'

'Child, you've been a married woman for many years. Surely that cannot be.'

'Well, Father, my first was a psychologist and all he wanted to do was talk about it. The next one was in construction and he always said he'd get to it tomorrow. The last one was a gynaecologist and all he did was look. But this time, Father, I'm marrying a lawyer, and I'm sure I'm going to get screwed.'

A devout couple were about to get married when a tragic car accident ended their lives. When they got to Heaven they asked St Peter if he could arrange for them to be married, since it was what they'd hoped for in life. He thought about it and agreed but said they'd have to wait.

About 100 years later St Peter sent for them and they were married in a simple ceremony.

Thirty years later, they discovered that, perhaps, it would be better not to spend all eternity together. They returned to St Peter and said, 'We thought we'd be happy forever but now believe we have irreconcilable differences. Is there any way we can get divorced?'

'Are you kidding?' said St Peter. 'It took me 100 years to get a priest up here to marry you. I'll never get a lawyer.'

Three persons arrive at Heaven and St Peter greets them before the Pearly Gates. 'Welcome to Heaven. We have just one last thing to do before you enter. Are you ready for your last test?'

The first person says, 'I've prepared for this moment for 80 years.'

'Okay,' says St Peter, 'spell God.'

'G-O-D.'

'Very good. Enter your eternal reward.'

The second person says, 'That was easier than I thought. I'll take my test now.'

'Okay,' says St Peter, 'spell love.'

'L-O-V-E.'

'Excellent. Enter your eternal reward.'

The third person, a lawyer, says, 'Boy, this is gonna be a snap. Give me my test.'

'Okay,' says St Peter, 'spell "prorhipido-glossomorpha".'

There was a terrible accident at a railroad crossing. A train smashed into a car, pushed it almost a kilometre down the track. Fortunately no one was killed but the driver took the train company to court. At the trial the engineer insisted that he'd given the driver ample warning by waving his lantern back and forth for nearly a minute. He stood up and convincingly demonstrated how he'd done it. The court believed his story and the suit was dismissed.

'Congratulations,' the lawyer said to the engineer afterwards. 'You did superbly under cross-examination.'

'Thanks,' he said, 'but he sure had me worried.'

'How's that?' the lawyer asked.

'I was afraid he was going to ask if the damn lantern was lit.'

A lawyer had a jury trial in a difficult business case. The client was out of town when the jury came back with its decision. The lawyer immediately sent a telegram to his client reading: JUSTICE TRIUMPHED.

The client wired back: APPEAL AT ONCE!

A lawyer was asked if he'd like to become a Jehovah's Witness. He declined, as he hadn't seen the accident, but said that he would still be interested in taking the case.

Two young women who hadn't seen each other for a long time met shopping. One said to the other, 'Chloe, it's been so long. I heard you got married.'

'Yes,' the second woman said, 'I married a lawyer, and an honest man too.'

'Hmm,' said the first woman, 'isn't that bigamy?'

A lawyer was doing a cross-examination of a defendant. The lawyer said, 'Now, isn't it true that on the fifth of November last year you rode naked through the streets on top of a dust cart, letting off fireworks and singing 'I Did It My Way' very loudly?'

The defendant asked, 'What was that date again?'

A lawyer was approached by the Devil. The Prince of Darkness said he could fix it so that the lawyer would win all of his court cases, make twice as much money, work half as hard, be appointed to the Supreme Court by the age of 49 and live to be 90. All he had to do was promise the Devil his soul, the soul of his wife, of his children, and the souls of all his ancestors. The lawyer thought for a minute before asking, 'So, what's the catch?'

There were two brothers. One went to business school and became a banker, the other went to law school and became a lawyer. They drifted apart, completely losing touch with each other. The banker did very well, becoming vice president of a large bank with many branches. One day the banker realised the lawyer's 50th birthday was coming up. He felt he should try to locate his missing brother. He sent letters off to various bar associations and finally his efforts were rewarded. He received a letter that his brother was vice president and general counsel for a small circus in Kansas. No phone number – the circus didn't have a telephone.

So the banker flew to Kansas City and took a bus to Topeka. There he asked a cabdriver for help. The cabdriver drove the banker to the outskirts of town and then to a smaller town and then to a little village. At the far end of the village was a sad, dilapidated little circus covered with dust. All the trucks and trailers needed a paint job. The circus wasn't second-rate. Not even third-rate. And there he found his brother's trailer, with his name on the door, and, in wobbly lettering, 'Vice President and General Counsel'.

The banker knocked on the door. The lawyer opened it. The brothers tearfully embraced and each told the other what they'd been doing over the last 25 years. After 30 minutes of this the lawyer consulted his watch and said, 'Time to give the elephant an enema.'

'What?' asked the banker as the lawyer dressed himself in a rain slicker. 'Time to give the elephant his enema,' repeated the lawyer.

'What are you talking about?' asked the banker.

'Well,' said the lawyer, 'the circus has fallen on hard times. We didn't have the money for liability insurance. Last year, after the circus had its parade through a small town, an old man slipped on some shit the elephant had left on the street. He broke his leg. We were sued. We lost. And the payment to the old man just about wiped us out. We couldn't afford another claim like that. It would ruin us. And there's a parade this afternoon.'

With that, the lawyer walked outside, grabbed a fire hose, inserted the nozzle in the elephant's bum and turned on the hydrant. Almost immediately, after a deep abdominal rumble, the elephant sprayed the lawyer from head to toe with shit.

The banker watched these proceedings in utter disbelief. At first he couldn't speak. But then he said to his brother, 'Please, please, PLEASE. You don't have to do this. Come with me. I have a good position with the bank. I can get you a clean job as a teller. Maybe even as a loan officer.'

The lawyer, wiping the shit off his face, shouted: 'What! And give up the practice of law?'

A lawyer and an engineer were fishing off the Barrier Reef. The lawyer said, 'I'm here because my house burnt down and everything I owned was destroyed by the fire.'

'That's a coincidence,' said the engineer. 'I'm here because my house and all my belongings were destroyed by a flood, and my insurance company also paid for everything.'

The lawyer looked puzzled. 'How do you start a flood?'

A Russian, a Cuban, an American and a lawyer are in a train. The Russian takes a bottle of the best vodka out of his pack, pours some into a glass, drinks it and says, 'In Russia, we have the best vodka in the world. Nowhere in the world can you find vodka as good as the one we produce in Ukraine. And we have so much of it, that we can just throw it away.' With that, he opens the window and throws the rest of the bottle through it. All the others are quite impressed.

The Cuban takes a pack of Havanas from his pocket, lights one and says, 'In Cuba we have the best cigars in the world: Havanas. Nowhere in the world are there so many and so good cigars and we have so much of them that we can just throw them away.' Saying that, he throws the pack of Havanas through the window. Once again, everybody is impressed.

The American takes a deep breath, stands up, opens the window and throws the lawyer through it.

What was O.J.'s favourite play when he was in the Buffalo Bills?

Cut left, then slash right!

Knock, knock.
Who's there?
O.J.

O.J. who?
That's fine, you're on the jury.

O.J. was seen running through the airport, jumping over seats and babies and strollers, to catch his plane to Chicago. A rental agent was frantically running after him yelling, 'Mr Simpson, Mr Simpson, you forgot your bloody glove.'

Did you hear about O.J.'s new movie? It's called *Sex, Knives and Athletic Tape*.

Why did O.J. do it?
He was practising for a part in the new movie, *Jock the Ripper*.

Why do they call him O.J?
Because he beats the pulp out of his women.

There's a new drink about in the bars now, called the Bloody Nicole. It's the same thing as a Bloody Mary, but instead of adding tomato juice, you add O.J.

O.J. wants the jury to come to his golf club and see how bad his slice is.

The defence claims that O.J. was acting on the advice of his marriage counsellor. After the last attempt at reconciliation failed, the counsellor told O.J. to take another stab at it.

O.J. Simpson gets sent to jail and is laying in his cell, depressed. His cellmate says to him, 'Hey, it's not all that bad. We've a lot of activities around here. Do you like sports?'

'Hell, yes,' says O.J.

'Do you like football?'

'Hell, yes,' says O.J.

'You'll like Mondays then. Do you like baseball?'

'Hell, yes,' says O.J.

'Great, you'll love Wednesdays then. Are you gay?'

'Hell, no,' says O.J.

'Pity. You're going to hate Fridays.'

O.J.'s introduced to his new cellmate, a huge, nasty looking guy doing consecutive life sentences. He says to O.J., 'Look here, we're gonna get somethin' straight off da bat. Are you gonna be the husband oh da wife?'

O.J. says, 'What?'

The guy gets real mad and says, 'Are you gonna be da husband oh da wife?'

O.J. thinks fast and says, 'I'll be the husband.'

The guy then says, 'Okay. Now get down on yo' knees and suck your wife's dick!'

What do O.J. Simpson and Michael Jackson have in common?

They are both missing a glove.

What did Michael Jackson say to O.J. Simpson?

'Don't worry, I'll take care of the kids.'

Did you hear that John Wayne Bobbitt called O.J. last night? He wanted O.J. to know that he knows what it feels like to be separated from a loved one.

What do you get when you put Lorina Bobbitt, Tammy Faye and O.J. Simpson in the same room?

A butcher, a Bakker and a licence plate maker.

Why did O.J. sit in the Bronco for so long?

Because Rodney King told him not to get out of the car.

What would you have if O.J. was put in the cell with David Koresh and Jeffrey Dahmer?

You'd have a complete breakfast: cereal, toast and O.J.

The greatest marketing idea of the century: His and Her knives endorsed by O.J. Simpson and Lorina Bobbitt.

What's the only thing worse than being married to Lorina Bobbitt?

Being divorced from O.J. Simpson.

What does O.J. stand for?

Obdurate Jerk
Obligatory Jokes
Obsessively Jealous
Odourous Journalism
Out Joyriding
Outlook: Jail

What are the three worst words to hear from O.J. Simpson?

I love you.

Did you hear about the new O.J. breakfast special?

It's eggs, steak and prune juice. First, you beat it, then you stab it with a knife, then you get the runs.

It's one thing to kill your ex-wife, but another thing to take a victory lap around the city afterwards.

After looking all over LA, they finally found 12 people who had never seen O.J. Simpson, never heard of O.J. Simpson and had no idea who O.J. Simpson is or was. They're all professors at USC.

O.J. went into the hospital for a biopsy. When the doctor pulled out his scalpel, O.J. said, 'You call that a knife?'

Imagine someone walking round with his hands together behind his back, wiggling his fingers. Someone asks, 'What's this?'

'O.J. Simpson signing autographs.'

'O.J. my man, haven't seen you in a while. How's Nicole?'

'I think she's dead.'

'What do you mean, you think she's dead?'

'I dunno. The sex is still the same, but the dishes are piling up in the sink.'

Did you hear that O.J. is merchandising to help pay for his defence?

But there's a problem with the O.J. watches. There seems to be an hour missing, from 10 p.m. to 11 p.m.

What do Nicole Brown Simpson and the Australian yacht in the America's Cup have in common?

They both went down in under two and a half minutes.

O.J. Simpson's lawyers report to their client, 'We have good news and bad news. The bad news is that your blood has been DNA tested as being the blood at the murder scene. The good news is that your cholesterol's fine.'

Police are now saying that O.J.'s no longer a suspect because they found a Superbowl ring at the murder scene.

Why did O.J. go to Chicago?
To find a clean towel.

A certain wealthy lawyer had a summer house in the country, to which he retreated for several weeks of the year. Each summer, he would invite a different friend to spend a week or two at the house, which was in a backwoods section of Maine.

On one particular occasion, he invited a Czechoslovakian friend to stay. The friend, eager to get a freebee off a lawyer, agreed. Early one morning, they decided to pick berries for their breakfast. As they gathered berries, along came two huge bears, a male and a female. The lawyer, seeing the two bears, immediately dashed for cover. His friend, however, wasn't so lucky, and the male bear reached him and swallowed him whole.

The lawyer ran back to his Mercedes, tore into town as fast as he could, and got the local sheriff.

The sheriff grabbed his shotgun and rushed back to the berry patch with the lawyer. Sure enough, the two bears were still there. 'He's in that one!' cried the lawyer, pointing to the male, while visions of lawsuits from his friend's family danced in his head. He just had to save his friend.

The sheriff looked at the bears and, without batting an eyelid levelled his gun, took careful aim and shot the female. 'What did you do that for?' exclaimed the lawyer. 'I said he was in the other!'

'Exactly,' replied the sheriff, 'and would you believe a lawyer who told you the Czech was in the male?'

Reports today indicate that O.J. Simpson has told his Defence Attorney, Johnny Cochrane, 'I'll kill that fucking dog with my bare hands if they bring it to court!'

What's the difference between Christopher Reeve and O.J.?

At least O.J. will walk.

Did you hear that Jeffrey Dahmer escaped from jail?

He was last seen heading towards Oklahoma City in an A-1 steak sauce truck.

What did Ron Goldman say to Nicole Simpson as they were going to Heaven?

Here are your fucking sunglasses.

A doctor, a lawyer and an architect were arguing about who had the smartest dog. They decided to settle the issue by getting all the dogs together and seeing whose could perform the most impressive feat. 'Okay, Rover,' ordered the architect, and Rover trotted over to the table and in four minutes constructed a complete scaled model of a cathedral out of toothpicks. The architect slipped Rover a cookie, and everyone agreed that it was a pretty impressive performance.

'Hit it, Spot,' commanded the doctor. Spot lost no time in performing an emergency Caesarian on a cow. Three minutes later the proud mother of a healthy little heifer was all sewn up and doing fine. Not bad, conceded the onlookers, and Spot got a cookie from the doctor.

'Your turn, Fella,' said the lawyer. Over went Fella, humped the other two dogs, took their cookies, and went out to lunch.

PADDIES AND POLAKS

A man walks into a bar and orders a glass of Polish vodka. A man sitting next to him remarks, 'That's a coincidence. I, too, am enjoying a Polish vodka. Since I arrived from the old country, this is the only bar in which I have found it.' To which the first replies, 'Old country! I'm from the old country. Let me buy you another!'

As the drinks are being poured, one of the men asks, 'What part of the old country are you from?'

'Krakow,' replies the other.

'This is weird,' said the first. 'I, too, am from Krakow! Let's get another shot.'

After the new round arrives, the first asks, 'So, pal, what did you do back in Krakow?'

'Not much, really. I came here right out of high school. I graduated from the Lech Walesa Technical Academy in '81.'

'This is eerie,' replies the other. 'I'm Walesa Tech. '81. Let's get another shot.'

But the bartender says, 'Slow down fellas, I gotta

make a call.' The bartender calls his wife and tells her that he'll be late getting home. When she inquires as to the cause, he replies, 'Oh, the friggin' Liszjewski twins are here again!'

A pigmy went to his first cricket match and was describing it to his witch-doctor on his return. 'It was a beautiful sunny Sunday,' he said. 'A big crowd of people had gathered around this big field of grass. In the middle there was a thin strip of mowed grass. And there were three sticks at either end. And a man in a long overcoat came out with two men in sweaters. And he tossed something silvery into the air. They went out and in came 11 men in sweaters and white pants. One of them was padded and had great big gloves. Then out came two men with pads on their legs and small gloves holding big sticks. They took positions at either end of the strip and another man came running towards them and threw a red ball at the person holding the stick. And at that very minute it started to pour. Those white men sure know how to make rain.'

A Pole, a Brit and an American rob a bank. Afterwards, each hides in a different tree. The cops go to the American's tree and say, 'Who's up there?' The American guy says, 'Tweet, tweet.' The cops say, 'Oh, just a bird.' They go to the British guy's tree and say, 'Who's up there?' The British guy says, 'Meow, meow.' 'Oh, that's just a cat,' the cops say. So they go to the Polish guy's tree and say, 'Who's up there?' The Polish guy says, 'Mooooooo!'

An Oregonian, a Californian and a Texan were out camping. They were lazing around the campfire when the Texan pulled out a bottle of Tequila and, after taking a couple of swallows, threw the bottle up in the air, pulled out his six-shooter and neatly shot the bottle. The Californian noted that there'd still been some Tequila left in the bottle, but the Texan replied, 'That's okay, we have plenty of Tequila where I come from.'

The Californian promptly brought out his bottle of White Zinfandel, took two swallows, threw it up in the air and shot it with a 9mm semi-automatic Glock pistol with a 15-shot clip, stating, 'We have plenty of this where I come from.'

The Oregonian took all this in and finally opened a bottle of Henry's Blue Boar Irish Ale. He downed the entire bottle, threw it up in the air, shot the Californian with a 12-gauge shotgun and deftly caught the bottle. The Texan's jaw dropped nearly to his silver buckle and his eyes widened. The Oregonian seemed puzzled at the reaction. 'It's okay, we've plenty of Californians where I come from and I can get a nickel for the bottle.'

An Englishman, an American and a Scot were in a café drinking tea. A fly came up and landed in the Englishman's tea. The man scooped the fly out, called the waiter and said, 'I say, there's a fly in my tea.'

As the waiter came back with a fresh cup of tea for the Englishman, a fly landed in the American's tea. 'Damn!' the American shouted, standing up. 'There's a fly in my @*#&$! tea!' Again the waiter headed off for a fresh cup.

Just as the waiter was coming back with the American's tea, a fly landed in the Scot's tea. 'I notice there's a fly in your tea,' the waiter said hurriedly. 'Do you want me to get you another cup?'

'No,' said the Scot, who scooped the fly out of his cup and, holding it by its wings, shook it and said, 'Spit it out, ye wee bugger!'

An American, a Russian and an Israeli are waiting to order in a restaurant. The waiter says, 'Excuse me, but I've got bad news. There's a shortage of meat.' The Russian asks, 'What's meat?' The American asks, 'What's a shortage?' The Israeli asks, 'What's excuse me?'

A Frenchman and an Italian were sitting next to an American on an overseas flight. They began discussing their home lives. 'Last night I made love to my wife four times,' the Frenchman bragged. 'This morning she made me delicious crêpes and told me how much she adored me.'

'Last night I made love to my wife six times,' said the Italian. 'This morning she made me a wonderful omelette and told me she could never, never love another man.'

The Frenchman turned to the silent American. 'And how many times did you make love to your wife last night?'

'Once,' he replied.

'Only once!' said the Italian. 'And what did she say to you this morning?'

'Don't stop.'

An American tourist went into a restaurant in a Spanish provincial city for dinner, and asked to be served the specialty of the house. When the dish arrived, he asked what kind of meat it contained.

'Sir, these are the *cojones*,' the waiter replied.

'The what?' exclaimed the tourist.

'They are testicles of the bull killed in the ring today,' explained the waiter.

The tourist gulped but tasted it anyway and found it to be delicious. Returning the following evening, he asked for the same dish. After he finished the meal, the tourist commented to the waiter, 'Today's *cojones* are much smaller than the ones I had yesterday.'

'True, sir,' said the waiter. 'You see, the bull, he does not always lose.'

A zoo acquires one of an endangered species of gorilla. Right from the outset she's very bad tempered, very difficult to handle. The zoo's vet announces she's in heat. But what to do? There's no male of her species available. Whereupon the zoo administrators remember that one of their zookeepers, an Irishman called O'Reilly who is responsible for cleaning animals' cages, is notorious for his ability to satisfy females. Perhaps they could persuade him to satisfy the gorilla.

So they approach O'Reilly with a proposition. Would he be willing to screw the gorilla for $500? O'Reilly asks for the night to think things over and on the following day says that he'll accept the offer on three conditions. 'Firstly, I don't want to have to kiss her. Secondly, I want any offspring to be raised Roman Catholic.'

The zoo administration quickly accedes to these conditions. But what could be third? 'Well,' says O'Reilly, 'you've got to give me some time to come up with the $500.'

Two retired English officers were sitting in their armchairs in a London club reading their respective papers. 'By jove,' said one, looking over the top of *The Times*, 'do you remember old Carruthers during the War? I thought he'd died, but it turns out they've found him after 40 years living up a tree with a gorilla.'

'I say. Male or female gorilla?'

'Female of course. Nothing queer about old Carruthers.'

A young man of the upper class took a walk in Soho on a very windy day. As he passed a young woman, the wind caught her skirt and lifted it above her head. The man said, 'Oh, it's airy, isn't it?' The young woman replied, 'Yeah, what the 'ell did you expect? Feathers?'

Mulligan and Sean were taking a little stroll. 'At my funeral,' said Mulligan, 'I want you to pour a bottle of Irish Whisky over me grave.'

'I'll be glad to,' said Sean. 'But would you mind if it passes through me kidneys first?'

Paddy and Mick landed themselves a job at a sawmill. Just before morning tea, Paddy yelled, 'Mick! I lost me finger!'

'Have you now?' says Mick. 'And how did you do it?'

'I just touched this big spinning thing here like thi– Damn! There goes another one!'

O'Connell was staggering home with a pint of booze in his back pocket when he slipped and fell heavily. Struggling to his feet, he felt something wet running down his leg. 'Please, God,' he implored, 'let it be blood.'

'Ah, Sean,' said Michael McStain, 'how'd ye be comin' by that glorious black eye, me lad?'

Sean O'Malley shook his head and replied, ''Tis the damndest thing. I was over at Molly's house, dancin' with the lovely lass, when her father walked in.'

'An' old Master Callahan is thinking that dancin' is an evil thing, cured by a black eye, is that it?'

'Na, na, Michael. The old man's deaf, an' couldn't hear th' music.'

'Hello, Pan American Airlines?' said Big Mick Lonegan. 'Could ye be tellin' me how long it takes to fly from Boston to Dublin?'

The voice on the telephone said, 'I'll see sir, just a minute.'

'Ahh, 'tis fast, to be sure. Thank ye,' Mick said as he hung up.

Paddy O'Shea got friendly with some of the local Boston Irish, and they took him to an upscale Irish pub.

'Amazin', just amazin', that's what America is,' he said, looking with delight into his glass. 'Never have I been seein' an ice cube with a hole in it!'

'Oi sure have,' said his host, Michael Sullivan. 'Bin married to one fer 15 years.'

An Irishman buys a packet of peanuts. He hands one to his wife. After a while, she asks for another. 'What for? They all taste the same.'

Two Irishmen were working on a building site digging a ditch. The foreman was at them all the time to keep busy. No breaks, just work, work, work. Finally one of the Irishmen noticed that the foreman left around 3.00 every afternoon. So they started leaving at 3.15.

The next day when the foreman left at 3.00, the workmen left at 3.15. One of them, Pat, arrived home, walked into the house, opened the bedroom door, and discovered the foreman in bed with his wife. He immediately ran back to the building site and dug like mad until 5.00.

The next day Pat told his mate, 'Listen, we can't knock off work any more at 3.15. I almost got caught.'

Paddy is on holidays with his girlfriend in Las Vegas. After paying a fortune for tickets they go to a night club where Paddy has been assured they'll be able to mingle with the stars. Sure enough the place is full of them and the conversation is very exciting.

'Hi ya, Madonna!'

'How do, Clint?'

Far from being impressed, Paddy's girlfriend is

annoyed that Paddy doesn't know any of the stars, and that nobody's interested in talking to them. On a visit to the toilet Paddy finds himself standing beside Frank Sinatra. Paddy explains the problem, tells him he's been a fan ever since 'On The Town' and has all his records. Would Mr Sinatra please help him out? All he has to do is walk past Paddy's table and say, 'How ya Paddy?' For once, Frank is in a good mood and agrees.

Twenty minutes later Frank walks up to the table where Paddy and his girlfriend are sitting talking. 'Hey Paddy,' shouts Frank. Paddy looks up and says, 'Fuck off, Frank, can't you see I'm talking to my girlfriend?'

Two women are walking down the Falls Road in Belfast. One says to the other, 'Don't them soldiers look stupid wearing camouflage in the middle of the city?' To which the other replies, 'What soldiers?'

Two IRA volunteers are waiting in ambush for an English patrol. It's due to pass at midday but hasn't arrived by 1.00. Then it's 2.00, and finally 3.00. Seamus is getting worried. 'God, Sean, they're awful late. I hope nothing's happened to them!'

Paddy heard that a fortune could be made by working as a lumberjack in Canada. So off he goes. After some weeks, he arrives at a lumberjack camp and asks the foreman for a job.

'Okay sonny, but you'll have to do a test first. If you can chop down 100 trees tomorrow, you're hired.'

So next day, Paddy gets his chainsaw and happily saws away all day. When the trees are counted Paddy only has 98. 'Oh, well,' says the foreman, 'you'll get another chance tomorrow.'

Next day, same story, 99 trees. 'I don't believe this,' says the foreman, 'a big strong fella like yourself should be able to cut down 100 trees in a day. You get one more chance, and I'll join you to show you the trick of it.'

Next day, Paddy and the foreman go into the forest. Upon arrival at a nice spot the foreman puts the chainsaw on the ground and starts the engine. Says Paddy, 'Holy Jesus! Where's the noise coming from?'

Paddy visits the hospital. 'I want to be castrated!' he demands cheerfully.

'Are you sure about this?' the doctor asks. 'Have you discussed it with your wife?'

'Yes, yes! I've thought about this for a long time. Let's get it over with!'

So the operation is performed. On his way home from hospital Paddy meets Mick.

'Well, hello Paddy! I haven't seen you for a

couple of days,' Mick says as they shake hands.

'No, I've been in hospital.'

'Well, that's funny. I'm on my way there right now!'

'Really? What's up?'

'I'm going to be vaccinated.'

'Oh shit! That's what it's called!'

How do you get a one-armed Irishman out of a tree?

You wave to him.

A bloke pulls up to a petrol station in Ireland and asks for five litres of petrol. The attendant replies they don't sell petrol.

'Don't sell petrol? What sort of garage is this? Well, check the oil for me.'

The attendant says they don't sell oil.

'What? Top up the radiator for me then.'

The attendant says they don't have any water, that in fact the garage is just a front for the IRA.

'Okay, then blow my tyres up.'

A young man was living on one side of London but his job was on the other. After a few years he bought himself one of the most expensive cars on the market. It was dazzlingly duco'd, had a very loud horn, went extremely fast, and all the girls watched as he drove by.

But living in London had its problems. He rarely had the chance to drive the car at top speed. So he decided to ferry the car to Ireland where, he thought, he could get away with a bit of high-speed driving.

Just out of Dublin he pressed down on the accelerator and sent the car rocketing to 140, 150, 160 kph. Then suddenly, as if they'd appeared from nowhere, he saw a man and a donkey crossing the road. They were so unused to traffic that they hadn't bothered to look. He swerved the car to the right missing them both but couldn't stop. He crashed through a fence and hit an old oak in a nearby field. The old man said to the donkey, 'Sure, an' we just got outta that field in toime, didn't we!'

How do you tell the Italians at a cock fight?

They're the ones betting on the duck.

And how can you tell if the Mafia's involved?

The duck wins.

A gondolier was floating down a canal singing 'O Solo Mio'. God looked down and wondered what would happen if he took half the gondolier's brain away. He did and the gondolier sang *O so, o so*. So God wondered what would happen if he took away the rest of the gondolier's brain, and he started singing 'When Irish Eyes Are Smiling.'

Guido goes to the godfather. Could he find a job for his nephew, due to arrive from Sicily? 'No problems,' says the godfather.

'Sir, I should tell you that the boy is deaf and dumb.'

'That's okay,' said the capa. 'We'll give him a job as a bagman and he won't need to talk.'

The boy had been working for several months picking up numbers-game receipts when the Don called Guido into his office. 'That little scumbag nephew of yours has been skimming from the collections,' he roared. 'I figure he's stolen about $600 000 by now and I want it back.'

Guido found his nephew and in sign language warned the boy of the godfather's rage. 'He's very upset with you and wants to see us both right away.' The boy followed his uncle to the Don's office and Guido signed to the lad, 'The godfather wants to know where the money is you stole from him.'

The boy shrugged his shoulders as if he knew nothing about it. Whereupon the don pulled a .357 magnum from the drawer, pointed it at the boy's head and bellowed, 'Tell that little puke he's got ten seconds to tell you where the money is or I'll blow his head off.'

The boy's eyes widened and he quickly signed to his uncle, 'I stashed the money under the basement stairs at your house.'

'Well,' the don demanded, 'what did the little shit say?'

Guido replied, 'He says he doesn't think you have the guts to pull the trigger.'

One day I'ma gonna Malta to bigga hotel. Ina morning I go down to eat breakfast. I tella waitress I wanna two pissis toast. She brings me only one piss. I tella her I want two piss. She say go to the toilet. I say, you no understand, I wanna piss onna my plate. She say you better no piss onna plate, you sonna ma bitch. I don't even know the lady and she call ma sonna me bitch!

Later I go to eat at a bigga restaurant. The waitress brings me a spoon and a knife, but no fock. I tella her I wanna fock. She tell me everyone wanna fock. I tell her you no understand, I wanna fock on the table. She say you better not fock on the table, you sonna ma bitch.

So, I go back to my room inna hotel and there is no shits onna my bed. I call the manager and tella him I wanna shit. He tell me to go to toilet. I say you no understand. I wanna shit on my bed. He say you better not shit onna bed, you sonna ma bitch.

I go to the checkout and the man at the desk say, peace on you. I say piss on you too, you sonna ma bitch, I gonna back to Italy!

Sam makes a confession to his wife. 'Sadie, the doctor says I've got disherpes.' Sadie looks it up in her home medical dictionary. 'Sam, not to worry,' she says. 'It says here that disherpes is a disease of the Gentiles.'

Schwartz and Goldstein decide to set up business but are told they'll do better if they have less foreign-sounding names. Schwartz thinks about this for a long, long time and decides to go for Smith. Goldstein also goes for the name of Smith and they call their business Smith & Smith.

First day, first phone call: 'May I speak to Mr Smith,' to which the receptionist replies, 'Which Mr Smith do you want? Schwartz or Goldstein?'

A young Jew and an old Jew are travelling on a train. The young Jew asks, 'Excuse me, sir, what time is it?' The old Jew doesn't answer.

'Excuse me, sir, what time is it?' The old Jew keeps silent.

'Sir, forgive me for interrupting you all the time, but I really want to know what time it is. Why won't you answer me?'

The old Jew says, 'Son, the next stop is the last on this route. I don't know you, so you must be a stranger. If I answer you now, according to Jewish tradition I have to invite you to my home. You're handsome and I have a beautiful daughter. You will both fall in love and you'll want to get married. And tell me, why would I want a son-in-law who can't even afford a watch?'

Moshe goes to a tailor to try on his new bespoke suit. But the arms are too long. 'No problems,' says the tailor, 'just bend them at the elbow and hold them out in front of you. See, now it's fine.'

'But the collar's up around my ears.'

'Nothing, nothing. Just hunch your back up a little. No, a little more. Per'

'But I'm stepping on my cuffs!'

'Bend your knees a little to take up the slack. Look in the mirror – the suit fits perfectly.'

Twisted like a pretzel, Moshe lurches out of the store and Rebecca and Florence see him go by.

'Look,' says Rebecca, 'that poor man.'

'Yes,' says Florence, 'but what a beautiful suit.'

It's Yom Kippur, the holiest day of the Jewish calendar. As it draws to a close in a small synagogue, the Rabbi is praying fervently. 'God, oh God, I am nothing before you.' The cantor joins in, 'God, oh God, I am nothing before you.' Whereupon the beadle, inspired by their piety and fervour, cries out, 'Oh God, I am nothing before you.'

The cantor raises his eyebrows, looks at the Rabbi and says, 'Look who thinks he's nothing!'

A Polak returns from work and finds his wife in bed with a friend. He raves, he rants, he pulls a pistol out of his pocket and holds it up to his own head. Whereupon his wife starts laughing uncontrollably. 'Don't laugh, bitch,' he yells. 'You're next!'

How did the Polak burn his face?

Bobbing for French fries.

Men will go to extraordinary lengths to prove their manhood. Witness Frenchman Pierre Pumpille of Lyon, who recently shunted a stationary car two metres by head-butting it. 'Women thought I was a god,' he explained from his hospital bed. But he was a sissy compared to Polish farmer, Krystof Azninsky, who staked a strong claim to being Europe's most macho man by cutting off his own head.

Azninsky, 30, had been drinking with some friends when it was suggested they strip naked and play some 'men's games'. They began by hitting each other over the head with frozen swedes, but then one man seized a chainsaw and cut off the end of his foot. Not to be outdone, Azninsky grabbed the saw and, crying, 'Watch this then,' swung at his own head and decapitated himself. 'It's funny,' said one companion, 'because when he was young he put on his sister's underwear. But he died like a man.'

A young Polak wants to try out for his high school's football team. He seeks out the coach, who asks him if he can block.

The Polak runs into a telephone pole and shatters it.

The coach asks the Polak a few more questions before throwing him a football. The coach asks, 'Can you pass that?'

The Polak replies, 'You bet, sir. If I can swallow it, I can pass it.'

The Polak apprentice, assisting in building a house, takes a nail from the box and looks at it. He tosses it over his shoulder and picks up another one which he nails into the board in front of him. He picks up the next nail, looks at it and throws it over his shoulder. His boss says, 'What the hell are you doing? Those were all brand new nails. Why are you throwing half of them away?'

'Boss, I know they're new. But some of them are pointing in the wrong direction.'

To which the boss says, 'You Polish idiot. Those are for the other side of the house!'

Polish loan sharks lend out all their money and skip town.

A Polish firing squad stands in a circle.

The new Polish navy has glass bottom boats, to see the old Polish navy.

Have you seen a Polish mine detector? He puts his fingers in his ears and starts stamping on the ground with his foot.

Why did the Polak cross the road?
He couldn't get his dick out of the chicken.

Two Polish guys rent a boat and go fishing on a lake. They're amazed by the number of fish they catch, so one says to the other, 'We'll have to come back here tomorrow.'

'But how will we remember where the spot is?'

The first guy takes a can of spray paint, paints an X on the bottom of the boat, and says, 'We'll just look for this X tomorrow.'

The other guy says, 'You idiot. How do you know we'll get the same boat?'

A 747 recently crashed in a cemetery in Poland. So far Polish officials have retrieved 2000 bodies.

An English guy is driving with a Polish guy as a passenger. He pulls over because he's worried that his turn signal isn't working, and asks the Polish guy to step out of the car and check the lights while he tests them. The English guy turns on the turn signal and says, 'Is it working?' To which the Polish guy responds, 'Yes, it's working. No, it's not working. Yes, it's working. No, it's not working.'

Three men are travelling in the Amazon: a German, an American and a Polak. Unfortunately, they are captured by some Indians. The head of the tribe says to the German, 'What do you want on your back for your whipping?' The German responds, 'I will take oil.' They put oil on his back and a large Indian whips him ten times. When he's finished the German has huge welts on his back and can hardly move.

The Indians haul him away and say to the Polak, 'What do you want on your back?'

'I'll take nothing!' says the Polak, and stands there straight, taking his ten lashings without a flinch.

'What will you take on your back?' the Indians ask the American, who says, 'I'll take the Polak.'

A Polak wanted to join an amateur basketball team. The coach decided to give him a chance. 'I'll give you three questions. If you come back in a week and answer them all correctly you're on the team.'

'Great,' said the Polak.

'Here are your questions. First, how many days are there in a week that begin with the letter T? Second, how many seconds are there in a year? And third, how many Ds are there in the Rudolph the Rednosed Reindeer?'

Next week the Polak came back.

'So how many days in the week start with T?'

The Polak said, 'Two.'

'Very good,' said the coach, 'and what are they?'

'Today and tomorrow.'

'Hmmm, okay,' said the coach. 'How many seconds in a year?'

'Twelve.'

'Twelve! How the hell did you come up with 12?'

'Well,' said the Polak, 'there's the 2nd of January, the 2nd of February, the 2nd of – '

'Okay, okay,' said the coach. 'Now how many Ds in Rudolph the Rednosed Reindeer?'

'That's easy. Three hundred and sixty-five.'

'What!' cried the coach. 'How did you get that figure?' To which the Polak sang, 'De-de de-de de-de-de.'

A Polak goes to a carpenter. 'Can you build me a box that's two inches high, two inches wide and 50 feet long?'

'Well,' said the carpenter, 'it could be done, I suppose, but what would you want a box like that for?'

'Well,' said the Polak, 'a neighbour moved away and forgot some things. So he's asked me to send him his garden hose.'

A Polak is learning how to skydive. The instructor tells the Polak to jump out of the plane and pull his ripcord. The instructor explains that he himself will jump out right behind him so that they can go down together.

The time comes. The instructor reminds the Polak that he will be right behind him. The Polak jumps from the plane and, after a few seconds, pulls the ripcord. Then the instructor jumps too. He pulls his ripcord but the parachute doesn't open. The instructor, frantically trying to get his parachute open, plummets past the Polak. The Polak, seeing this, undoes the straps to his parachute. 'So you wanna race, eh?'

An Englishman, a Frenchman and a Polak were captured by the Germans and thrown into prison. Fortunately the guard is kindly and says, 'I'm going to lock you away for five years but I'll let you have anything you want now. Before I lock you away.'

The Englishman said, 'I'll have five years' supply of

beer.' His wish is granted and they lock him away with his beer.

The Frenchman says, 'I'll have five years' supply of brandy.' His wish is granted and they lock him away with his brandy.

The Polak says, 'I'll have five years' supply of cigarettes.' His wish is granted and they lock him away with his cigarettes.

Five years later the war is over, and the Americans arrive. They release the prisoners. The Englishman staggers out totally drunk. Then the Frenchman rolls out, rather inebriated. Then they release the Polak, who comes out and says, 'Has anyone got a light?'

A Polish guy is walking along the beach at Cannes. There are many beautiful women lying in the sun and he wants to meet one. But try as he might, the women don't seem interested. Finally he walks up to a French guy who is surrounded by adoring women. 'Excuse me,' he says to the Frenchman, 'I've been trying to meet one of these women for about an hour now and I can't seem to get anywhere. You're French, you know these women. What do they want?'

'Maybe I help you a leetle beet,' says the Frenchman. 'What you do ees, you go to zee store, you buy a leetle bikini sweeming suit, you walk up and down zee beach, you meet a girl very qweekley zees way.'

'Thanks,' says the Polish guy and goes off to the

store. He buys a skimpy red bathing suit, puts it on, goes back to the beach. He parades up and down but still has no luck. So he goes back to the Frenchman. 'I'm sorry to bother you again, but I went to the store, got a swimsuit and I still haven't been able to meet a girl.'

'Okay,' says the Frenchman, 'I tell you what you do. You go zee store, you buy potato. You put potato in sweeming suit and walk up and down zee beach. You will meet girl very, very qweekley zees way.'

'Thanks,' says the guy. He goes to the store. Buys a potato. Puts it in the swimsuit. But after marching up and down for an hour, the women are still avoiding his gaze. So he goes back to the Frenchman. 'Look, I got the suit, I put the potato in it. I walked up and down the beach. Still nothing. What more can I do?'

'Well,' says the Frenchman, 'maybe I can help you a leetle beet. Why don't you try moving zee potato to the front of the sweeming suit?'

A man goes to a brothel. The madam is out of women, but since the guy is Polish, she thinks she can get away with an inflatable doll. He'll never know the difference. But because she's never tried this before, she waits outside the door. After five minutes the Polak comes out. 'How was it?' asks the madam.

'I don't know,' says the Polak. 'I bit her on the bum and she farted and flew out the window.'

How do you know if a Polak has been using a computer?

There's white-out on the screen.

A Polish guy is walking down the street carrying a brown paper bag. He runs into one of his friends who asks, 'Hey, what do you have in the bag?'

The man tells his friend that he has some fish in the bag.

His friend says, 'Well, I'll make you a bet. If I can guess how many fish you have in the bag, you'll have to give me one.'

The Polish man says, 'I'll tell you what. If you can tell me how many fish I have in this bag, I'll give you both of them.'

Who wears a dirty white robe and rides a pig?

Lawrence of Poland.

Did you hear about the tragedy in Poland?

In Poland's largest shopping mall there was a terrible outrage. People were stuck on the escalators for four hours.

A Polak, an African-American and a white guy were driving through a desert when they ran out of gas. They decided to start walking to the nearest town, 50 miles back, to get some help.

A rancher was sitting on his front porch that evening when he saw the white guy top the horizon and walk towards him. The rancher noticed that the white guy was carrying a glass of water. The rancher said, 'Hi, there. What are you doing carrying a glass of water through the desert?'

The white guy explained his predicament and said that as he had a long way to go, he might get thirsty, so that's why he was carrying the water.

A little while later the rancher noticed the African-American walking toward him with a loaf of bread in his hand. 'What are you doing?' asked the rancher.

The man explained the situation and said that as he had a long way to go, he might get hungry, and that's why he had the bread.

Finally, the Polak appeared, dragging a car door through the sand. More curious than ever, the rancher asked, 'Hey, why are you dragging that car door?'

'Well,' said the Polak, 'I have a long way to go, so if it gets too hot, I'll roll down the window.'

Polish Airlines Flight 113 was descending for a landing at an airport unknown to the pilot, who suddenly exclaimed to the co-pilot, 'Holy cow! Look how short the runway is! I've never seen one that short!'

The co-pilot yelled, 'Wow! You're right! That's incredible! Are you sure we can make it?'

'Well, we better, we're almost out of fuel.'

The pilot got on the intercom and notified the passengers to put their heads between their knees and prepare for an emergency landing. Then he set the flaps down and slowed the plane to just over stall-speed. The jumbo jet came screaming in, on the ragged edge of control. The pilot's hands were sweating, the co-pilot was praying. They touched down and came screeching to a halt just before the edge of the runway, the tyres smoking. 'Whew! That was close!' yelled the pilot. 'That runway was short!'

'Yeah!' said the co-pilot, 'and wide too!'

A Polak was suffering from constipation, so his doctor prescribed suppositories. A week later the Pole complained to the doctor that they didn't produce the desired results. 'Have you been taking them regularly?' the doctor asked. 'What do you think I've been doing,' the Pole said, 'shoving them up my arse?'

How do you know you're flying over Poland?

There's toilet paper hanging on the clotheslines.

Did you know that Poland has just bought 10 000 septic tanks?

As soon as they learn how to drive them, they're going to invade Russia.

Did you hear about the Polak who thought his wife was going to kill him?

On her dressing table he found a bottle of Polish Remover.

Three men applied for a job as a detective. One was Polish, one was Jewish and one was Italian. Rather than ask the standard questions during the interview, the chief decided to ask each applicant just one question and base his decision upon that answer.

When the Jewish man arrived for his interview, the chief asked, 'Who killed Jesus Christ?' The Jewish man answered without hesitation, 'The Romans killed him.' The chief thanked him and he left.

When the Italian man arrived for his interview, the chief asked the same question. The Italian replied, 'Jesus was killed by the Jews.' Again, the chief thanked the man, who then left.

When the Polish man arrived for his interview, he was asked the same question. He thought for a long time before saying, 'Could I have some time to think about it?' The chief said, 'Okay but get back to me tomorrow.'

When the Polish man arrived home, his wife asked, 'How did the interview go?' He replied, 'Great, I got the job, and I'm already investigating a murder!'

A Polak was jumped by two muggers. He fought desperately but was finally subdued. The muggers went through his pockets. 'You mean you fought like that for 57 cents?' asked one of the muggers incredulously.

'Is that all you wanted,' moaned the Pole, 'I thought you were after the $400 in my shoe.'

Kowalski and Lisjewski are hard at work cleaning out the sewer on a sweltering day in July, beneath the streets of the Bronx. Kowalski says, 'I really hate this crummy, smelly job, shovellin' shit!'

Lisjewski says, 'Yeah, me too. I hate it!'

Kowalski says, 'How come you and me is down here underground shovelling shit and breaking our backs, when Rafaelli is up there sittin' in the truck with the air-conditioner on, smokin' cigarettes and readin' the newspaper? That's what I'd like to know!'

Lisjewski says, 'You know what I'm gonna do? I'm going up there and I'm gonna say to that Rafaelli just like I said it to you, and then we'll see what he's got to say.'

Lisjewski says, 'Yeah, go up there and tell 'im what you said.'

So Kowalski brushes the muck off his pants, climbs up the ladder to the street and goes over to the truck. Rafaelli says, 'Whaddaya want, Kowalski? And hurry up, it's hot out here.'

Kowalski says, 'Well, I just wanna know one thing, Rafaelli. How cum me 'n Lisjewski is down there underground shovellin' shit, and yer up here in the air-conditionin', smokin' cigarettes all day? How come?'

Rafaelli smiles and says, 'Is that all you wanted to know? That's real easy, Kowalski.' He holds his hand out in front of the heavy iron truck bed and says, 'Okay, Kowalski, hit my hand real hard.'

Kowalski unloads a huge haymaker of a punch and, of course, Rafaelli pulls his hand away quickly. Kowalski smashes his fist against the truck.

'Okay, Kowalski,' says Rafaelli, 'that's the reason why I get to stay up here in the truck, and you and Lisjewski gotta shovel shit in the sewer. Do you get it now?'

Kowalski nods and returns to the ladder, rubbing his hand. When he gets back down into the tunnel, Lisjewski is waiting for him. 'What'd he say, Kowalski? How come izzit that Rafaelli gets to sit up there in the truck, and we gotta come down here and shovel shit?'

Kowalski says, 'I don't know if you're gonna be able to undertand this, but I'll try to explain it just like Rafaelli told me. Now, hit my hand real hard.' and Kowalski holds his hand up in front of his face . . .

An Italian, an American and a Polak are captured by the French and are taken to the guillotine. The executioner places the Italian on the block and asks if he has any last words. The Italian replies, 'I pray to the Virgin Mary that I may live.' The blade drops, and stops a mere inch from the Italian's neck. Amazed, the French let him go.

Next, the American is put in position and asked if he has any final words. He replies, 'In the name of Jesus Christ, please have mercy.' They drop the blade, and again it stops, just an inch from the American's neck. In disbelief, they let him go free.

Then the Polak is placed on the block, and they ask if he has any last words. He says, 'Yeah, you've got a knot in your rope.'

A Polak is hired to paint the lines on the road. On the first day he paints ten miles, and his employers are amazed. But, the second day he painted just five, and on the third day, he painted only a mile of the road.

Disappointed, his boss asks what the problem was. The Polak replies, 'Well, sir, every day I have to walk farther and farther to get back to the paint bucket.'

There are three construction workers eating lunch on top of a building. An Italian, a Polak, and an Asian. The Italian has a meatball hero, the Asian has noodles, and the Polak has knockwurst. The Italian and the Asian are tired of having the same lunches every day. The Italian says that if he gets a meatball hero the next day he will throw it off the building. The Asian says that if he gets noodles tomorrow he will also throw it off the building. The Polak says that if he gets knockwurst tomorow he will throw it off the building.

Sure enough, the Italian and the Asian open their lunchboxes the next day and find they have a meatball hero and noodles respectively, and both throw their lunches off the building. Without opening his lunchbox, the Polak throws his sandwich off the building, too. The other guys ask him how he knew it was knockwurst again without even looking. He responds, 'Because I pack my own lunch.'

Why did the Polak sell his waterskis?

Because he couldn't find a lake with a hill in it.

Two Polaks are flying across Europe in a three-engined 727. The pilot announces, 'Folks, we just had one engine go out. But don't worry, this plane can fly just fine on two engines, but we're going to be about an hour late getting into Warsaw.'

An hour later the pilot gets on the intercom again. 'Sorry, but a second engine just went out. But please don't worry. This plane is designed to fly safely on one engine. But we will be about two hours late getting into Warsaw.'

After that announcement one Polak looks at the other and says, 'Well, I sure hope the third engine doesn't go out. Otherwise we'll be up here all night.'

Did you hear about the Polish airliner that crashed?

It ran out of coal.

What is 200 yards long and eats cabbage?

A Polish meat queue.

Two Polish peasants are loitering by the side of the road one day when a tourist pulls up in his car. He winds down the window and asks, 'Do you speak English?' The peasants both shrug their shoulders. The tourist then tries, '*Parlez vous Francais*?' Again the peasants plainly don't understand. The tourist then shows off his skill by trying German, Russian, Italian and Spanish, but to no avail. Finally he drives off in disgust. One peasant comments in Polish, 'It must be wonderful to be able to speak so many languages.' The other retorts, 'Pah! Look how far it got him!'

What did the Polish people light their houses with before they used candles?

Electricity.

An American, a Frenchman and a Polak are lined up in front of a firing squad, awaiting execution. The American is first. He points behind the firing squad and shouts, 'Flood!' When the soldiers turn to look, he escapes.

The Frenchman quickly devises his plan and shouts, 'Tornado!' He escapes as well.

The Polak, thinking he has caught on, yells, 'Fire!'

A tribe of Native Americans named all women according to the animal hide with which they made their blanket. So one woman was known as Squaw of the Buffalo Hide, while another was Squaw of the Deer Hide. And there was a particularly strong woman who was known as Squaw of the Hippopotamus Hide. She was as large and powerful as the animal from which her blanket was made.

Year after year, the woman would enter the tribal wrestling tournament and easily defeat all challenges from the Squaw of the Buffalo Hide, the Squaw of the Deer Hide, the Squaw of the Horse Hide and the Squaw of the Bear Hide. One year, two of the squaws petitioned the chief to allow them to enter their sons as a wrestling tandem in order to defeat the Squaw of the Hippopotamus Hide.

When the match began, it became clear that the squaw had finally met an opponent that was her equal. The two sons wrestled and struggled vigorously. The match lasted for hours without a clear victor but finally the chief intervened and declared that, in the interests of the health and safety of the wrestlers, he would declare a winner.

He retired to his tepee, contemplated the great struggle and found it extremely difficult to decide a winner. After much deliberation, he came out and announced his decision.

'The Squaw of the Hippopotamus Hide is equal to the sons of the squaws of the other two hides.'

A missionary was sent to spread the good word in Bongo Bongo, but found little success. He approached the king to see what would be necessary to engender co-operation. The king had seen pictures of European kings and queens sitting on thrones, and told the missionary that he would have the entire tribe converted if only he could have a golden throne. The missionary wrote to the Home Mission Board to tell them of this marvellous opportunity, and they sent him a throne. No, it wasn't solid gold, but the king liked it very much, and the whole tribe converted. The missionary was regarded as a hero by fellow evangelists.

In his later years, however, the king got arthritic and decided that sitting on his hard, golden throne was exacerbating his aches and pains, so he stashed the throne up in the attic of his grass shack.

Trouble is, one day the throne came crashing through the ceiling and squashed the old king.

Which only goes to show that people who live in grass houses shouldn't stow thrones.

Who killed more Indians than Custer?

Union Carbide.

What's the difference between yoghurt and Australia?

Yoghurt has a real live culture.

How many South African policemen does it take to break an egg?

None. It fell down the stairs.

It's the first day back at school after the summer holidays and all the little children are fidgeting about with excitement.

TEACHER: Okay, kids, we'll begin the year by discussing what we did over the holidays. Joey, what did you do?

JOEY: Well, Miss, I had a wonderful time. Every morning I would go down to the beach and play in the sand.

TEACHER: Very good Joey, if you can spell 'sand' I'll give you a Mars Bar.

JOEY: Mmmmh . . . s-a-n-d.

TEACHER: Very good Joey, here's a Mars Bar. Sally, what did you do over the holidays?

SALLY: Well, Miss, I would go down to the beach and play in the sand too. Sometimes Joey and I would go for a paddle in the sea.

TEACHER: Lovely. If you can spell 'sea' you can have a Mars Bar.

SALLY: S-e-a.

TEACHER: Good Sally, have a Mars Bar. Now what about you Leroy? What did you get up to?

LEROY: Well, Miss, I also went down to the beach, but none of the other kids would play with me 'cause my skin's a different colour.

TEACHER: Oh, poor, poor Leroy. How dreadful. That's racial hatred for you. If you can spell 'prejudice' you can have a Mars Bar.

What's black and eats bananas?

Half of London.

President Reagan visited India and was touring the countryside with Rajiv Gandhi. Reagan couldn't help but notice people shitting in the open. Wanting to help, he produced his cheque book and offered a donation to build a few toilets. This embarrassed

Ghandi enormously, but he felt it was undiplomatic to refuse.

A few months later, Ghandi visited the US and he hoped to see someone shitting out in the open, so that he could put Reagan in a similarly embarrassing position. Finally, fortunately, he found one man squatting in public view. Delighted, Ghandi offered Reagan a donation for building a toilet.

'Oh, he has his own toilet,' Reagan said, 'but he insists on shitting like this. He's the Indian Ambassador.'

An Eskimo has a broken snowmobile, so he brings it in to be serviced. After checking it out, the service mechanic says, 'It looks like you blew a seal.'

The Eskimo looks at him and says, 'No, that is just frost on my moustache.'

CYBERKIDS

One of Johnny's favourite pastimes was hiding in the wardrobe while his mother entertained her lover. One day Johnny's dad came home early, so his mum shoved her lover into the wardrobe and Johnny struck up a conversation.

JOHNNY: Sure is dark in here.

MAN: Yeah kid, it sure is.

JOHNNY: Wanna buy a football?

MAN: I don't think so, kid.

JOHNNY: You really should buy this football.

MAN: What the hell for?

JOHNNY: It might make me forget I saw you here.

MAN: Okay, kid, how much?

JOHNNY: A hundred bucks.

MAN: What! Okay, but keep your mouth shut.

The guy paid and left as soon as the coast was clear. Next week Johnny was in the wardrobe again, Mum's lover was pounding away again, when Dad came home early again. So the man winds up in the closet again, and Johnny starts talking to him.

JOHNNY: Sure is dark in here.

MAN: Yeah kid, it sure is.

JOHNNY: Wanna buy a football helmet?

MAN: Let me guess. A hundred bucks and you'll forget you saw me. Right?

JOHNNY: Right.

The guy pays up and takes off as soon as he can.

Later that week Johnny's dad tells Johnny to get his football and helmet so that they can play some ball. 'I can't Dad, I sold them for two hundred bucks,' says Johnny. Dad says, 'Johnny, you're a lying little cuss and you're going to pay for that one.' And sends him off to confession.

Johnny sits in the confessional, the door shuts, and the window opens to the priest. 'Sure is dark in here,' Johnny says.

The priest replies, 'Listen kid, I'm out of money and I don't even like football.'

A father was walking with his young son in the park when they came upon two dogs having sex. The boy asked his dad what the dogs were doing. He said they were making a puppy.

A couple of days later the boy walked in on his parents who were having sex on the couch. He asked his father what they were doing. He said that they were making a baby.

The boy replied, 'Can you turn Mummy over? I'd much rather have a puppy.'

It was obvious to Mum and Dad that the only way to pull off a Sunday afternoon quickie without their ten-year-old son hanging around was to send him out on the balcony. So they ordered him to report on all the neighbourhood activities.

The boy began his commentary. 'There's a car being towed from the parking lot,' he said.

'An ambulance just drove by.'

'It looks like the Andersons have company,' he called out.

'Max is riding a new bike and the Coopers are having sex.'

Mum and Dad shot up in bed. 'How do you know that?' the startled father asked.

'Their kid is standing out on the balcony too.'

A priest was walking down the street when a small boy approached from the other direction carrying a bottle of acid. The priest was afraid that the child might injure himself, so he offered to trade a bottle of holy water for the dangerous fluid. 'What will holy water do?' asked the boy.

'Well,' replied the priest, 'I rubbed this on a woman's belly and she passed a baby.'

To which the boy replied, 'That's nothing. I rubbed this on a cat's arse and it passed a motorcycle.'

'Dad, what is politics?'

'Politics? Well, consider our home. I am the wage earner, so let's call me Capitalism. Your mother is the administrator of the money, so we'll call her Government. We take care of you and your needs, so we'll call you the People. We'll call the maid the Working Class, and your baby brother the Future. Do you understand so far?'

'I'm not really sure, Dad, I'll have to think about it.'

Late that night, the boy's sleep was disturbed by the crying of his baby brother. He got up and found that the baby had soiled its nappy. He went to his parents' room and found his mother fast asleep, and then discovered that his father was bonking the maid so vigorously that they didn't hear his knocks on the door. He returned to his bed and went to sleep.

Next morning he reported to his father, 'Dad, I now think I understand what politics is.'

'Good, my boy. Explain it to me in your own words.'

'Well, while Capitalism is screwing the Working Class and the Government is sound asleep, the People are being completely ignored and the Future is full of shit.'

There was a kid who hung around the local grocery store where the bigger boys always teased him. They said he was two bricks shy of a load, two pickles shy of a barrel, dumber than a box of rocks, that his belt didn't go through all the loops, that the lights were on but no one was home, that his elevator didn't go all the way to the top, or that his elevator did go all the way to the top but no one got off.

To prove the kid's stupidity, the bigger boys frequently offered him a choice between a nickel and a dime. He'll always take the nickel, they said, because it's bigger.

The grocer took the kid aside and said, 'Those boys are making fun of you. They think you don't know a dime is worth more than a nickel. Are you grabbing the nickel because it's bigger? Or what?'

The kid looked at the grocer and whispered, 'No. But if I took the dime they'd quit doing it.'

'Jimmy, did your mother help you with your homework last night?' the teacher asked.

'No, she did it all.'

Little Johnny was sitting in class one day. All of a sudden he needed to go to the bathroom. He yelled out, 'Miss Jones, I need to take a piss.'

'Now, Johnny, that is *not* the proper word to use in this situation. The correct word you want to use is "urinate". Please use the word "urinate" in a sentence correctly, and I will allow you to go.'

Little Johnny thinks for a bit. 'You're an eight – but if you had bigger tits you'd be a ten.'

I like kids, but I don't think I could eat a whole one.

Five-year-old Johnny is running around the house making life miserable for his mother. She says, 'Johnny, why don't you go across the street and watch them build the house. Maybe you can learn some new things.'

Johnny disappears for about four hours and when he returns his mother asks, 'Did you learn anything interesting today?'

'I learned how to hang a door,' Johnny replies.

'That's great! How do you do that?'

'Well, first you get the son of bitch. Then you slap the piece of shit up there but it's too fucking small. So you shave a cunt hair off here and a cunt hair off there and put the goddamn thing up.'

Johnny's mother is floored by his language. 'You go to your room and wait until your father gets home!'

Later, Johnny's dad goes into his room and says, 'I understand you got in a little trouble today.'

'All I did was tell Mom how to hang a door.'

'Why don't you tell me?' Dad asks.'

Well, first you get the son of bitch. Then you slap the piece of shit up there but it's too fucking small. So you shave a cunt hair off here and a cunt hair off there and put the goddamn thing up.'

Dad screams, 'That's it, young man. You go get a switch from the backyard.'

Johnny looks at his dad and says, 'Fuck you, that's the electrician's job.'

There were two young brothers talking in their backyard waiting for their mother to make them lunch. One was four, the other three.

FOUR: I'm getting pretty old now, I think I can start cussing.

THREE: Oh yeah?

FOUR: Yeah, I think I'm going to start saying damn whenever I feel like it.

THREE: You know what?

FOUR: What?

THREE: I think I'm getting pretty old, I'm going to start cussing too.

FOUR: Oh yeah? What are you going to say?

THREE: I'm going to say arse.

Their mother calls them in for lunch and asks the four-year-old, 'What do you want for lunch?'

'Oh damn, I think I'll have some spaghetti-o's.'

The mother was aghast. She took the four-year-old by the ear to the bathroom, washed his mouth out with soap, spanked him and put him in his room and slammed the door.

She returned to the kitchen and asked the three-year-old, 'What do you want for lunch?'

'I don't know, Mom but you can bet your arse it won't be spaghetti-o's.'

A bright, well-behaved little boy lived with his parents and grandparents in suburbia. One evening, the boy's father passed outside his bedroom window and was pleased to hear him kneeling beside his bed saying his prayers. He finished off with:

God bless Mummy
God bless Daddy
God bless Grandma
Ta ta Grandpa.

The father thought this form of prayer a little strange, but was so pleased that his son was praying of his own accord that he thought nothing more of it. Until, that is, Grandpa passed away with a stroke during the night.

A few weeks later, he again overheard his son's prayers:

God bless Mummy
God bless Daddy
Ta ta Grandma.

Sure enough, the next morning they found the little boy's grandmother had had a heart attack in the middle of the night and passed away.

Several weeks later the father overheard his son say:

God bless Mummy
Ta ta Daddy.

The father was stricken with grief. What had he done to deserve such a short life! He was still in the prime of life.

So great was his turmoil, that he didn't get a wink of sleep all night. He got up in the morning expecting disaster to strike at any time. He drove extra carefully to work that morning, and stayed in his office all day.

On his return home, he poured out his worries to his wife. He'd had an awful day, grief-stricken, worried, and he just wanted to get it over with. But his wife had no time for him. 'You think *you've* had a bad day. I've been waiting for you to get back to help me out. I've had a terrible day today. I got up this morning and opened the front door to find the milkman lying dead on the porch ...'

IS THERE A DOCTOR IN THE MOUSE?

The other day Ray Charles went to the doctor for a check-up. After the examination, the doctor told Ray, 'I have some good news and some bad news.' Ray said, 'Give me the bad news first.'

The doctor said, 'I'm afraid we got some bad results from one of your tests, and we are going to have to operate and cut off your left testicle.'

Ray sort of winced, pondered a bit and said, 'Well, what's the good news?'

To which the doctor replied, 'You still got the right one baby, uhh huhh.'

Did you hear about the gynaecologist who quit his job and went into interior decoration?

He could wallpaper the whole house through the keyhole.

Two gynaecologists meet at a conference. As usual, they tell each other what cases they have had during the past year:

'Well, I had a patient with breasts just like melons.'

'Incredible! So big?'

'Yes.'

'But I had a patient with a clitoris just like a lemon.'

'Wow. So big?'

'No, so sour.'

A young mother had just given birth to a baby, and the nurse was congratulating her when the doctor came in bouncing the baby from hand to hand. The mother looked startled. The doctor then said, 'Here, catch!' and promptly tossed the baby to the mother, but it landed on the window ledge and fell out the window.

The lady shrieked, 'You bastard, you've killed my baby!'

The doctor replied, 'April Fool! It was dead already!'

Twins are born.

Mother happy.

Father happy.

Mother: 'Just look at the lovely babies ...'

Father takes one by the head, and the little neck breaks.

Doctor rushes in. 'How could you DO that?'
Father: 'It was easy. Look!'

Dave's office insisted that he go to the doctor's for a complete physical. Worried that the doctor might notice that his hearing was getting worse, Dave asked his wife to come along. After a long wait they finally got to see the doctor, who checked Dave's pulse, heart rate and blood pressure. 'Dave, I'll need to do some additional tests. I'll need a urine sample, a stool sample and a sperm sample.'

Dave turned immediately to his wife and whispered, 'What? What did he say?'

'Don't worry about it,' she said, 'just leave your underpants.'

A world-famous urologist believed he could diagnose any disease simply by looking at a urine sample. To test his prowess, a friend with tennis elbow peed into a jar and then got additional donations from his wife, daughter and his dog. The next morning, he jerked off in it as well.

He gave the bottle to the famous urologist and was told he'd be called in a few days with the results.

Finally the urologist called and said, 'It was a tough case but I think I've solved it.'

'What's wrong with me?' the man asked.

'Well, your wife has the clap, your daughter is

pregnant, your dog has worms and if you quit playing with yourself, you wouldn't have tennis elbow.'

A guy goes to his doctor for a check-up. After a lot of tests the doctor says, 'I've got some bad news and some good news. After going over all your tests, I've discovered that you've a latent homosexual personality.'

'Oh, my God, that's awful,' says the guy. 'So what's the good news?'

The doctor says, 'Well, I think you're kinda cute.'

A nurse in the maternity ward asked the young med student why he was so enthusiastic about obstetrics. 'When I was in medical rotation,' he said, 'I thought I was suffering from heart attacks, asthma and itch. In surgery I was sure I had ulcers. In the psychiatric ward I thought I was losing my mind. Now, in obstetrics, I can relax!'

A fellow goes to the doctor and says, 'Doctor, I have this problem that I'm always farting all of the time. Although they don't smell, they do make loud noises, and it's affecting my social life.' The doctor gives him some pills and asks him to return next week.

He returns and says, 'Those pills did no good. In fact they made things worse. I still fart as much, but now they smell terrible.'

To which the doctor replied, 'Good! Now that we have your nose working again, let's work on your farting.'

There was a businessman, and he was feeling really crook, so he went to see the doctor about it. The doctor said to him, 'Well, it must be your diet. What sort of greens do you eat?' And the man replied, 'Well, actually, I only eat peas. I hate all other green foods.'

The doctor was quite shocked at this and said, 'Well, man, that's your problem. All those peas will be clogging up your system, you'll have to give them up!'

The businessman said, 'But how long for, I mean I really like peas!'

And the doctor replied, 'Forever, I'm afraid.'

The man was quite shocked by this, but he gave it a go and sure enough, his condition improved and he pledged that he would never eat a pea again.

One night years later, he was at a work convention and getting quite sloshed. One of his workmates said, 'Well, ashually, I'd love a cigarette, cozi avint ad a smoke in four years. I gave it up.'

The barman said, 'Really? I haven't had a game of golf in three years because it cost me my first marriage. So I gave it up!'

And the businessman said, 'Thash nuvving. I haven't ad a pea in six years.'

The barman jumped up screaming. 'Okay, everyone who can't swim, grab a table.'

An elderly couple went into a doctor. They told the doctor, 'We're having some trouble with our sex life. Could you watch and offer some suggestions?'

The doctor replied, 'I'm not a sex therapist. You should find someone else.'

The couple said, 'No, no, we trust you.'

After watching them have sex, the doctor said, 'You don't seem to be having any troubles. I wish my sex life was as good. I can't give you any suggestions.'

This was repeated the next week and the following week. The exasperated doctor finally said, 'You aren't having any trouble. Is this your idea of kinky sex?'

The man replied, 'No, actually the problem is if we have sex at my house, my wife will catch us. If we have sex at her house, her husband will catch us. The motel charges us $50, and we can't afford that. You only charge $35, and Medicare pays half of that.'

Bill and Bruce were cutting wood when Bruce cut his arm off. Bill wrapped it in a plastic bag and took it to a surgeon who said, 'I'm an expert at reattaching limbs. Come back in a few hours.'

So he came back in a few hours and the surgeon said, 'I finished faster than I expected. Bruce is down at the local pub.'

Bill went to the pub and saw Bruce throwing darts. A few weeks later, Bill and Bruce were cutting wood again and this time Bruce amputated his leg. Bill put it in a plastic bag and took it back to the surgeon who said, 'Legs are a bit more difficult. Come back in six hours.'

Six hours later Bill returned and the surgeon said, 'No worries, Bruce is down playing soccer.' And lo and behold, so he was, kicking goals.

A few weeks later, Bruce had an even worse accident and cut off his head. Bill put the head in a plastic bag and took the rest of his friend to the surgeon who said, 'Well, I don't know. Heads can be really tough. But come back in 12 hours.'

Twelve hours later the surgeon said, 'I'm sorry, your friend died.' Bill said, 'That's okay, I understand. As you said, heads are tough.'

To which the surgeon replied, 'Oh no. The surgery went fine. But Bruce suffocated in the plastic bag.'

A fellow had been suffering from terrible headaches. Finally he went to the doctor, who gave him a thorough examination. 'Well, I'm not sure exactly what's causing the problem, but we've found a cure. You'll have to be castrated.'

The man, needless to say, was horrified. 'No, doctor, I prefer to suffer the headaches.'

But as time passed, they got worse and worse and finally he was driven back to the surgery. 'Okay, I'll have the operation.'

Afterwards the man was very depressed and his doctor told him, 'I recommend you begin a new life – start fresh from this point.'

Taking the advice, the man went to a men's shop for new clothes. The salesman said, 'Let's start with the suit. Looks like you'd take about a 38-regular.'

'That's right,' said the man. 'How did you know?'

'Well, when you've been in the business as long as I have, you get pretty good at sizing a man up. Now for the shirt, looks like a 15-long.'

'Exactly,' said the man.

'And for underpants, I'd say a size 36.'

'Well, there's your first mistake,' said the man. 'I've worn 34s for years.'

'No, you're a size 36 if ever I've seen one,' said the salesman.

'I ought to know,' the man replied. 'I take 34.'

'Well, if you insist,' said the salesman. 'But they're going to pinch your balls and give you headaches.'

A woman went to her physician for a follow-up visit after he'd prescribed testosterone for her. She was a little worried about some of the side effects. 'Doctor, the hormone you've been giving me has been a help but I'm afraid you're giving me too much. I've started growing hair in places I've never grown hair before.'

The physician said, 'A little hair growth is a perfectly normal side effect of testosterone. Just where has it appeared?'

'On my balls.'

A woman was going to marry one of those chauvinists who wanted a virgin, so she went to a physician and asked him to reconstruct her hymen. He told her it would cost around $500 but there was another way that would cost only $50. She agreed to try the cheap way, paid her money and the doctor went to work on her for some time.

After the honeymoon, she returned to the doctor and told him everything was perfect. It had hurt a lot and there'd been a little bleeding. She asked him how he'd done it. 'I tied your pubic hair.'

A woman goes to a doctor's office for a check-up. As she takes off her blouse he notices a red H on her chest. 'How did you get that mark?' asks the doctor.'

'Oh, my boyfriend went to Harvard. He's so proud of it that he never takes off his Harvard sweatshirt, even when we make love.'

A couple of days later another girl arrives for a check-up. As she takes off her blouse the doctor notices a blue Y on her chest. 'How did you get that mark?'

'Oh, my boyfriend went to Yale. He's so proud of it, he never takes off his Yale sweatshirt. Not even when we make love.'

A couple of days later a third girl comes in for a check-up. As she takes off her blouse he notices a green M on her chest. 'Do you have a boyfriend at Michigan?' asks the doctor.

'No, but I have a girlfriend at Wisconsin. Why do you ask?'

A woman goes to the doctor and says, 'I've got a bit of a problem. But I'll have to take off my clothes to show you.' She goes behind the screen and disrobes.

'Well, what is it?' asks the doctor.

'It's a little bit embarrassing,' she replies. 'See, two green circles have appeared on the inside of my thighs.'

The doctor examines her, consults his text books but is just about to give up. Then, suddenly, he says, 'Have you been having an affair with a gypsy?'

The woman blushes and confesses, 'Well, actually I have.'

'That's the problem,' says the doctor. 'Tell him his earrings aren't gold.'

A mute was walking through the city one day when he came upon a friend who'd been similarly afflicted. In sign language he enquired how his friend was doing. His friend spoke to him. 'Oh, can that hand-waving shit. I can talk now,' he said.

Astonished, the mute asked for details. It seems his friend had gone to a doctor who, seeing no physical damage, had put him on a treatment program.

Gesturing wildly, the mute asked his friend to ring the specialist and make an appointment for the very next day.

After an examination, the specialist confirmed that there was no permanent damage. The mute was essentially in the same condition as his friend, and there was absolutely no reason why he couldn't be helped as well.

'Let's have the first treatment right now,' signed the excited mute.

'Very well,' replied the specialist. 'Go into the next room, drop your pants and lean over the examination table. I'll be right in.'

The mute did as instructed and the doctor sneaked in with a broomstick, a mallet and a jar of Vaseline. A brief procedure resulted in the mute jumping from the table, screaming, 'AAAAAaaaaaaa!'

'Very good,' smiled the specialist. 'Next Tuesday we move on to B.'

A guy walks into a shrink's offices and says, 'Doctor, doctor, please help me. I'm convinced I'm a dog.' The shrink replies, 'Well, why don't you just get on the couch and we'll talk about it.'

The guy says, 'Can't. I'm not allowed on the couch.'

Two psychiatrists met in the corridor of the hospital. One says, 'Good morning.'

'What exactly did he mean by that?' the other wonders.

A man started a new job in a pickle factory, but after a week he had to visit the psychiatrist. 'I've got to leave the pickle factory,' he said, 'every time I start work I have an inexplicable desire to put my prick in the pickle slicer.'

The psychiatrist told him to relax and go back to work. But after a week the man came back, saying his urge had got worse. Once again, the psychiatrist calmed him down and sent him back to work.

The next week the man came back looking really dejected and said, 'I finally did it. I put my prick in the pickle slicer.'

'What happened?' asked the psychiatrist.

'The boss came in and caught me and I got the sack.'

'What about the pickle slicer?' asked the psychiatrist.

'Oh,' said the man, 'she got the sack as well.'

A patient thinks he's George Washington. He finishes up one session by telling the psychiatrist, 'Tomorrow we'll cross the Delaware and surprise them when they least expect it.' As soon as he's gone, the shrink picks up the phone and says, 'King George, this is Benedict Arnold. I have the plans.'

A woman with a problem goes to a psychologist, but she's very hesitant about describing it. Eventually he manages to glean that she thinks she might be sexually perverted.

'What kind of perversion are we talking about?'

'Well. I like to be ... no, no. I'm sorry, doctor, but I'm too ashamed to talk about it.'

'Come, come, my dear. I'm a psychologist. I've been dealing with these problems for decades. So just tell me what's the matter.'

The woman tries to explain, but gets so embarrassed that she blushes furiously and looks on the verge of collapse. At this point the psychologist has a bright idea. 'Look, I'm a bit of a pervert myself. So if you show me what your perversion is, I'll show you what mine is.'

The woman considers the offer for a few moments and agrees. 'Well, my perversion is ... my perversion ... I like to be kissed on the bottom!'

'Shit, is that all!' says the psychologist. 'Look, go behind the screen, take off all your clothes and I'll come round and show you what my perversion is!'

The woman obeys and after undressing behind the screen, gets down on all fours in the hope of having her bottom kissed. After 15 minutes, nothing has happened so she peers around the screen to see the psychologist sitting behind his desk, with his feet on the table, reading a newspaper and whistling.

'Excuse me,' says the woman, 'I thought you said you were a pervert.'

'Oh, I am,' says the psychologist. 'I've just shat in your handbag.'

An anthropologist came home after spending a year on a South Sea island. His friends asked him if he had anything unusual to report. He replied that one tribe had invented palm leaf suppositories to cure constipation. 'How good are they?' he was asked.

'Well,' he said, 'with fronds like that, who needs enemas?'

What do you call three people in wheelchairs on top of each other?

A vegetable rack.

CRUISING THE SUPERHIGHWAY

As a little girl is coming out of school, a man pulls up in his car, winds down the window and says to her, 'I'll give you a sweet if you'll get in the car with me.'

The little girl says, 'No, I'm not getting in the car.'

The next day the man pulls up again, winds down the window and says, 'I'll give you two sweets if you'll get in the car with me.'

The little girl says, 'No, I'm not getting in the car.'

The third day the man pulls up and offers her a whole bag of sweets if she'll get into the car.

'No, Dad,' replies the girl, 'there's no way I'm getting into the Lada!'

Having troubles with her VW Beetle, a woman pulled over to the side of the road and opened the hood. To her astonishment, there was nothing there. Another woman with a VW Beetle stopped to see if she could help. The first woman said, 'Well, it seems I don't have an engine.'

The second woman replied, 'That's okay. I've got a spare one in the boot.'

A driver tucked this note under the windshield wiper of his automobile. 'I've circled the block for 20 minutes. I'm late for an appointment, and if I don't park here I'll lose my job. Forgive us our trespasses.'

When he came back he found a parking ticket and this note: 'I've circled the block for 20 years, and if I don't give you a ticket, I'll lose my job. Lead us not into temptation.'

A man in a Porsche 911 stops at a stoplight and a guy on a scooter pulls up next to him. The guy on the scooter leans over and takes an admiring look at the inside of the Porsche and tells the driver that he has a really hot car. Well, the light turns green so the driver of the Porsche decides to show off and he peels out and leaves the guy on the scooter in the dust. Then, all of a sudden, he sees the scooter zip past him. So, being a little cocky, the Porsche driver floors it again and blows past the guy on the scooter. A few seconds later, he again sees the scooter zip past him. By now he's a little irate as well as a little miffed that the scooter keeps passing him. So he floors it until he is going over

160 kmh. He thinks to himself there's no way the scooter could catch him now. But then he looks in the rearview mirror and sees the scooter starting to catch up. He then decides to find out what that scooter really is, and slams on his brakes. The scooter crashes into the Porsche. After the dust has settled, the Porsche driver sees the scooter driver lying on the road and goes over to him and asks how he could go as fast as the Porsche on a little wimpy scooter. The dying man replies, 'I can't really, but my suspenders were caught in your side mirror . . .'

A Lada stops suddenly on a highway. A Jaguar crashes into it. And behind that, a Rolls Royce crashes into the Jag. The Rolls Royce driver steps out of his car, and complains, 'You fool, my radiator grille is broken. It will cost me one day of income!'

Complains the Jaguar driver, 'The front of my car is squeezed, it will cost me one month of salary!'

Says the Lada driver, 'My car is completely smashed. I will have to work one year to buy myself a new one!'

Answers the Rolls Royce driver, 'Fancy anyone buying such an expensive car!'

What's the difference between a Lada and AIDS?

You can still palm AIDS off to someone else.

How can you double the worth of a Lada?

By filling its gasoline tank.

Why is a Lada so handy during the Finnish winter?

You don't need seatbelts – you freeze tightly to the seat.

Why do they give away free TVs with Ladas?

So you've got something to do while waiting for the mechanic to come and fix it.

What do you call a Lada with a turbo?

A Skoda.

What do you call someone who buys a secondhand Lada?

A scrap dealer.

What does a Lada buyer do to look sophisticated?

Wears dark glasses.

But how do you tell the Lada buyer from all the other people with dark glasses?

He's the one with the white stick.

What's the difference between two Jehovah's Witnesses and a Lada?

You can shut the door on two Jehovah's Witnesses.

Man walks into a service station and asks the mechanic, 'Do you have a windscreen wiper for a Lada?'

The mechanic scratches his head, thinks for a bit and replies, 'Well, it seems to be a reasonable swap – yes, I do.'

In the middle of Spain, a Lada is driving along and meets a donkey. The donkey, never having seen a Lada before, asks, 'What are you?'

The Lada says, 'I'm a car, what are you?'

The donkey says, 'I'm a horse.'

What do you call a Lada at the top of a hill?

A miracle.

Three guys die and are awaiting admission into Heaven. St Peter says to them, 'I've only one question before you enter. Were you faithful to your wives?'

The first guy answers, 'Yes, I never even looked at another woman.' St Peter says, 'See that Rolls Royce over there? That's your car to drive while you're in Heaven.'

The second guy says, 'Once I strayed, but I confessed to my wife and she forgave me and we worked it out.' St Peter says, 'See that new Buick over there? That's your car to use in Heaven.'

The third guy says, 'I have to admit, St Peter, I chased every bit of tail I could and was with a lot of women.' St Peter says, 'That's okay. You were basically a good guy. So that old VW Bug over there is yours to use while you're in Heaven.'

The three guys climb into the cars and drive through the Pearly Gates.

A few weeks later, the second and third guys are driving along in the Buick when they see the first guy's Rolls Royce parked outside a bar. They stop and go into the bar and find him with empty bottles all around him, face buried in his hands. 'Buddy, what could possibly be so bad?' they say. 'You're in Heaven, you drive a Rolls Royce, and everything is great.'

He says, 'I saw my wife here yesterday.'

The other two say, 'But that's great! What's the problem?'

'She was driving a Lada.'

The atomic scientist was so exhausted from the lecture circuit that he let his chauffeur give one of his lectures while he dressed as the chauffeur. During the question and answer period there came a very difficult question. Holding his composure, the chauffeur-turned-atomic-scientist responded, 'That question is so ridiculously simple to answer, I'm going to have my chauffeur answer it for you.'

A very dignified man enters a Swiss Bank and enquires about taking out a loan for 2000 Swiss francs.

'What security can you offer?' the banker enquires.

'Well, my Rolls Royce Silver Ghost is parked out front. I'll be away for a few weeks. Here are the keys.'

Four weeks later the dignified man returns to the bank and pays off the loan. 2024 francs, including interest.

'Pardon me,' the banker says, 'But I can't help wondering why you bothered with a 2000 franc loan – a man of your obvious means.'

'Very simple,' he replied, 'Where else could I have stored a Rolls for a month for 24 francs?'

The atomic scientist was so exhausted from the lecture circuit that he let his chauffeur give one of his lectures while he dressed as the chauffeur. During the question and answer period, there came a very difficult question. Holding his composure, the chauffeur turned atomic scientist responded, "That question is so ridiculously simple to answer, I'm going to have my chauffeur answer it for you!"

A very dignified man enters a Swiss Bank and enquires about taking out a loan for 2000 Swiss francs.

"What security can you offer?" the banker enquires.

"Well, my Rolls Royce Silver Ghost is parked out front. I'll be away for a few weeks. Here are the keys."

Four weeks later the dignified man returns to the bank and pays off the loan: 2024 francs, including interest.

"Pardon me," the banker says, "But I can't help wondering why you bothered with a 2000 franc loan — a man of your obvious means."

"Very simple," he replied. "Where else could I have stored a Rolls for a month for 24 francs?"

LOGGING OFF

Why did Maria Schriver marry Arnold Schwarzenegger?

They're trying to breed a bullet-proof Kennedy.

Bill Gates died and went to Heaven. On arrival, he had to wait in the reception area. This was the size of Massachusetts with literally millions of people milling about, living in tents with nothing to do all day. Food and water were being distributed from the backs of trucks; staffers with clipboards were fighting their way through the crowd. Booze and drugs were being passed around. Fights were commonplace. Sanitation conditions were appalling. It looked like Woodstock gone metastatic.

Bill lived in a tent for three weeks until, finally, one of the staffers approached him – a young man in his late teens with acne scars wearing a blue T-shirt with the words TEAM PETER on it.

'Hello,' said the staffer, in the bored voice of a bureaucrat. 'My name is Gabriel and I'll be your induction co-ordinator.'

Bill started to ask a question but Gabriel interrupted him. 'No, I'm not the Archangel Gabriel. I'm just a guy from Philadelphia named Gabriel. I died in a car wreck at the age of 17. Now, give me your name, last name first. Unless you're Chinese, in which case it's first name first.'

'Gates, Bill.' Gabriel checked his clipboard.

'What's going on here?' asked Bill. 'Why are all these people here? Where's St Peter? Where are the Pearly Gates?'

Gabriel ignored the questions until he located Bill's entry. 'It says here that you were the president of a large software company? Is that right?'

'Yes.'

'Well then, do the massive chip-head! When Heaven opened for business, only 100 people or so died every day. Peter could handle it all by himself, no problems. Now there are over five billion people on Earth. Jesus, when God said to go forth and multiply he didn't mean like rabbits! Now 10 000 people die every hour, over a quarter of a million people every day. Do you think Peter can meet them all personally?'

'I guess not.'

'You guessed right. So Peter had to franchise the operation. He's now the CEO of Team Peter Enterprises Inc. Just sits in the corporate headquarters and sets policy. Franchisees like me handle the actual inductions. Your paperwork seems to be in order and with a background like yours, you'll be getting a plum job assignment.'

'Job assignment?'

'Of course. Did you expect to spend the rest of eternity sitting on your arse and drinking ambrosia? Heaven's a big operation. You have to pull your weight.' Gabriel had Bill sign a triplicate form, then tore out the middle copy and handed it to him.

'Take this down to Induction Centre #23 and meet up with your Occupational Orientator. His name is Abraham.' Bill started to ask a question, but Gabriel interrupted. 'No, he's not *that* Abraham.'

Gates walked down a long, muddy trail until he came to Induction Centre #23. After a mere six-hour wait he met Abraham.

'Heaven is centuries behind in its data processing infrastructure,' explained Abraham. 'We're still doing everything on paper. It takes us a week to process new entries. Your job will be to supervise Heaven's new data processing centre. We're putting in the largest computing facility in creation. Half a million computers connected by a multi-segment, fibre-optic network, all running into a back-end server network with a thousand CPUs on a gigabyte channel. Fully fault tolerant. Fully distributed processing. The works!'

'Wow!' said Bill, 'what a great job! This really is Heaven!'

Abraham and Bill caught the shuttle bus and went to Heaven's new data-processing centre. It was a truly huge facility, a hundred times bigger than the Astrodome, with workmen crawling all over it. And in the middle, half a million computers, arranged neatly, row-by-row. Half a million.

'Macintoshes!' said Bill, horrified.

'All running ClarisWorks software! Not a single byte of Microsoft code!' said Abraham.

The thought of spending the rest of Eternity using products he'd spent his life working to destroy was too much for Bill. 'What about PCs?' he exclaimed. 'What about Windows? What about Excel? What about Word?'

'This is Heaven,' explained Abraham. 'We need a computer system that's heavenly to use. If you want to build a data processing centre based on PCs running Windows, then GO TO HELL!'

In Hollywood, every producer has his yes-man whose job is to follow the producer around and say, 'Yes, CB, Right CB,' and so on. Well, one of these yes-men got depressed, so down in fact that he was unable to function. So he consulted a psychiatrist. The psychiatrist quickly determined the problem, and told the yes-man that he just had to find a release for his negative feelings, and say no.

'But if I said no I'll get fired!' the yes-man protested. The psychiatrist said, 'Oh, I don't mean on the job, I mean go out to the Grand Canyon and find a ledge off the trail, and there you can yell no to your heart's content and no one will be any the wiser.'

Well, the yes-man decided to try it. He went to the Grand Canyon and found a spot off the trail, stood there and very timidly said no. It felt good, so he tried it a little louder. 'No!' Even better! Soon he was shouting, 'NO, NO, NO, NO!' at the top of his lungs and feeling great.

He went back to work a changed man, and said yes with all the proper enthusiasm, because on the weekend he could escape to the Grand Canyon and say no.

Other yes-men decided to try this also, and soon every weekend the Grand Canyon was crammed with yes-men shouting no.

A new yes-man came to Hollywood and he too felt the need for such a release, but when he tried to find a ledge in the Grand Canyon all of them seemed to be taken. He hunted and hunted, but every place he found was already taken by another yes-man. Finally he found a small ledge which had been overlooked because of its size. Thankfully he scurried out on it and stood there and said no. It felt great! So he wound up and released an enormous no and in so doing lost his balance and fell to his death.

Which just goes to prove that a little no ledge can be a dangerous thing.

There once was a little pink lady. She had a little pink house and a little pink dress and a little pink dog. This lady sold Avon.

One day the lady was walking down a street selling her Avon when she came across a little red house. She pressed the doorbell. In the little red house lived a little red man. He was having a bath in his little red bathtub when he heard his little red doorbell ring.

'There goes my doorbell!' he said to himself as he clambered out of his little red bath. He grabbed a little red towel and put it around his waist and walked down his little red stairs to his little red door.

But, when he opened the door, his little red towel slipped and fell off. The little pink lady screamed and ran out across the street. A car coming down the road hit her and she died.

Moral: never cross the street when the little red man is flashing.

As a part of a funeral package, an undertaker agreed to provide a seven-word notice in the local paper for a frugal woman who was making arrangements for her recently deceased husband. She was asked what she'd like to say. She thought about it for a while, and then said, 'John is dead.'

The undertaker reminded her that she had paid for seven words.

The woman pondered a bit more, then with a very serious expression said, 'John is dead. Pickup truck for sale.'

A very old man was walking the grounds of a retirement home. He staggered up to another resident and said, 'Hello, my name is Charlie. How old do you think I am?' The resident looked him up and down and said, '80.' Charlie said, 'Nope, 95,' and staggered on.

He approached another resident. 'Hello, my name is Charlie. How old do you think I am?' The second resident looked him over and guessed 86. Again Charlie said, 'Nope, 95,' and walked on.

He approached an elderly woman and asked her how old she thought he was. The woman unzipped his fly, reached into his pants, felt his private parts for a few minutes and said, '95.' Amazed, Charlie exclaimed, 'How can you tell?'

The old woman said, 'I heard you tell those other guys.'

The old age pensioners' club of a small English town are boarding a coach for the annual trip to the seaside at Whitby. As the last old chap is walking along the aisle to his seat, the vehicle lurches into motion. He stumbles and lands in the lap of an octogenarian lady. During the resultant struggle, his elbow pokes the old woman in the left breast.

Back on his feet he says, 'I'm sorry about that, my dear, but if your heart is as soft as your breast, I'm sure I'll see you in Heaven.'

To which she replies, 'And if your dick is as hard as your elbow, I'll see you in Whitby.'

A couple of dear old ladies were sitting on a patio in their twilight home. Both were very, very bored. One turned to the other and said, 'Nothing happens here. All the men are half dead. There's no fun.'

The other said, 'Okay, let's do something to liven the place up.'

So they agreed to streak along the verandah to attract the attention of the old blokes who were sunning themselves.

One of them looked up and said to the other, 'Did you see that?'

The other said, 'I think so. Couldn't say for sure. My eyes aren't too good these days. What were they wearing?'

'Couldn't say for sure. But whatever it was, they needed ironing.'

Finally, Fred's family has had it. They take him out to the retirement home and install him. After a few hours a lovely young nurse comes and asks if he'd like to spend some time on the verandah. Fred says, 'Sure.'

Fred and the nurse are on the verandah enjoying the sun when Fred begins to lean to his left. The nurse, thinking he's going to fall, pushes him back upright. A few moments later Fred begins to lean, this time to his right. The nurse pushes him back upright. After a few minutes the scene is repeated. Finally she takes Fred back to his room. The next day Fred's friend Bob comes to visit. 'How do you like it here?' asks Bob.

'Well,' says Fred, 'it's fine, I suppose. The bed's not too soft and it's not too hard. The food is reasonable. The people are pleasant, but they won't let you fart on the verandah.'

'I finally stopped grandma from sliding down the bannisters.'

'How?'

'I wrapped barbed wire around it.'

'That stopped her?'

'Not entirely. But it sure slows her down.'

Three old blokes are sitting on the porch of a retirement home.

'Fellas, I've got a real problem,' says the first. 'I'm 70 years old, and every morning at 7 a.m. I get up and try to pee. All day long I try to pee. They give me all kinds of pee medicine but nothing helps.'

The second old man says, 'You think you've got problems. I'm 80 years old. Every morning at 8 I get up and try to move my bowels. I try all day long. They give me all kinds of laxatives but nothing helps.'

Finally the third old man speaks up. 'Fellas, I'm 90 years old. Every morning at 7 sharp, I urinate. Every morning at 8 sharp, I move my bowels. And every morning at 9 sharp, I wake up.'

Why is it good to have Alzheimer's Disease?

You can hide your own Easter eggs.

RUBBER BULLETS, PAPER PLANES

'Men,' says the sergeant to the new recruits, 'you've been placed under my supervision so I can teach you sissies how to do one of my favourite things. Kill! Unfortunately the army is under-funded these days, so I'll have to furnish you with these high-quality broomsticks. What I want you to do with them is point at your target and yell, Bangety-bang.'

The men did this for the rest of the week.

'Now you'll be taught how to kill close up. I don't have the money to buy you bayonets so I'm providing you with these plastic combs. What you need to do with them is to tape them to the end of your broomsticks and practice using them by yelling, Stabbety-stab!'

They practised this for a week and became quite good at it.

Suddenly training was over and they were told it was time to defend their country. Though they were afraid, they followed their sergeant into battle.

Eventually they worked their way up to the front line. With nothing but a comb taped on a broomstick in their trembling hands and fear and doubt in their hearts, they pointed at the oncoming enemy and yelled, 'Bangety-bang.' Surprisingly, it worked. They fought fiercely and their enemies dropped like flies. When the enemy got too close, they used their combs and yelled, 'Stabbety-stab.'

The battle raged on and the loss of life on both sides was significant.

Finally it was down to only two men. One from each side. The man from the USA raised his comb-broomstick and pointed it at the unarmed man shuffling towards him and yelled as loud as he could, 'Bangety-Bang!' It didn't work. Finally the man got so close that the US soldier could use his comb directly on him. He jabbed at the enemy and yelled, 'Stabbety-Stab!' That didn't work either.

Indeed, the enemy knocked him down and ran right over him. The fallen US soldier couldn't figure it out until he heard the enemy repeating, 'Tankety-tank, tankety-tank.'

A senior pilot was explaining his emergency equipment to some cadets touring a US Air Force base. He showed them his parachute, emergency radio, signal mirror and other survival items. A cadet noticed a pack of playing cards and asked what they were for.

'Oh,' replied the pilot, 'these are my last resort. If nothing else works and nobody comes to the rescue, I take these, lay out a game of patience and wait. In a few minutes someone will be looking over my shoulder saying, "No – put that card over there."'

Two heavily bemedalled gentlemen are sitting in a hotel bar late at night reminiscing over the old days. The first had been in the army, and insisted that that service had the greatest reputation when it came to womanising, that he'd slept with hundreds during the war. The other had been an admiral, and insisted that the navy had a greater tradition of virility.

'Crap,' said the general, 'I just know Iza slept with mow women than youse!'

'Sheeet, no!'

'Okay, when did you last sleep with a woman?'

'About 1945.'

'You call that virile!'

The admiral looked at his watch. 'Well, it's only 2130 now.'

A young soldier lost his bayonet. Rather than face the consequences of this misdemeanour, he carved an excellent imitation of the missing blade. For months he went about his duties with the wooden weapon in his scabbard. Finally the inevitable order came. 'Fix bayonets!' He could do nothing but stand there, his scabbard untouched. The sergeant demanded an explanation. 'Sir, it's a promise I made to my dad,' said the soldier, 'as he lay on his death bed. I told him I would never bear a bayonet on the anniversary of his death.'

'That's the damndest story I've ever heard,' roared the sergeant, 'let me see that bayonet!'

'For breaking a solemn promise,' said the soldier as he drew it out, 'may the Lord turn this to wood!'

The captain and several of his officers were returning to the ship after an evening ashore. As they climbed the gangway the captain threw up all over his uniform. Pointing to a young seaman at the head of the gangway he shouted, 'Give that man five days in the brig for vomiting on his captain.'

Next morning the captain was checking the log and saw that the young seaman had been sentenced to ten days. He asked the chief mate why. 'Well, Cap'n, when we got you undressed we found he'd also shat your underpants.'

'Well,' snarled the marine sergeant to the cowering private, 'I suppose when you get discharged from the army you'll just be waiting for me to kick the bucket so that you can come and spit on my grave.'

'Not me, Sarge,' the private replied, 'once I get

out of this man's army, I ain't ever going to stand in line again.'

A navy squid returned home to visit his father the day after he was supposed to have had his first parachute jump. 'Dad, I was real scared up there. Everyone was going out before me and I just couldn't bring myself to jump out of that plane! So finally my commander comes up behind me as I'm looking out the plane door and says, "Son, if you don't jump right this instant, I'm going to fuck you up the ass!"'

His father asks, 'Well, did you jump?'

The son replies, 'A little, at first.'

The Central Intelligence Agency ran a Help Wanted ad for new recruits. Three men answered the advertisement and were invited to the office for an interview. After filling out their applications, they were taken, one at a time, into another room. Here an interviewer told them, 'One of the requirements for joining this organisation is that you prove your unswerving loyalty to us. We want you to take this gun, go into the other room and shoot your wife.'

The first job-seeker refused. 'Sorry, I can't do that. We just got married.' The interviewer asked him to leave.

The second applicant was then taken into the room and given the same instruction. 'I can't do that,' he protested, 'we've been married ten years and have two lovely children.' So he was rejected as well.

The last applicant was presented with the ultimatum in the same monotone, to which he replied, 'Sure, I'll do it.' And he marched into the other room.

Shots were fired. Then all sorts of noises came from the room as if a brawl were ensuing. There were screams, kicking and thumping. Finally the third applicant returned and was asked what had happened. He said, 'Some jerk put blanks in the gun. So I had to strangle her.'

World War III. The USA have succeeded in building a fantastic computer that is able to solve any strategical or tactical problem. The military leaders are assembled in front of the new machine. They describe the situation to the computer and then ask it, 'Shall we attack? Shall we retreat?'

The computer computes for an hour and then comes up with the answer, 'Yes!'

The generals, rather stupefied, look at each other. Finally one of them asks the computer, 'Yes, what?'

After another 15 minutes the computer replies, 'Yes, sir!'

A British officer spotted a busker at the bottom of the escalators of a London underground station.

The busker had a sign which read: VETERAN SOLDIER OF THE FALKLANDS WAR. The officer thought, Poor chap. I was there and it was hell. Feeling sorry for his fellow veteran, he took £20 out of his wallet and gave it to the busker, who responded with a hearty, '*Grazias, señor.*'

Did you know the Shuttle commander was on the radio when the shuttle blew up?

And on the walls, and on the windscreen, and on the ceiling.

How do you fit 11 astronauts in a VW Bug?

Two in the front, two in the back, and seven in the ashtray.

A 747 is flying over the Atlantic and the pilot finishes a routine announcement over the intercom. When he puts the mike down he forgets to hit the off switch. 'Take over for a while, Dave,' he says to his co-pilot. 'I'm going to take a shit and then bang that new stewardess.'

Needless to say, the passengers are enormously amused and intrigued by this revelation. The stewardess is so embarrassed and indignant that she hurries towards the cockpit. In her haste, she trips and falls to her knees in the aisle. The sweet old lady in 7F says, 'Don't rush dear. He said he had to take a shit first.'

A man travelling by plane was in urgent need of the toilet. But each time he looked up the illuminated sign proclaimed that it was occupied. The stewardess, aware of his predicament, suggested that he use the plane's new prototype women's loo. But he mustn't press any of the buttons inside. They were labelled WW, WA, PP and ATR.

The man's curiosity got the better of him and he started pressing the buttons. When he pressed WW, warm, fragrant water was sprayed all over his entire bottom. He thought, Wow, the women really have it made. Still curious, he pressed the button marked WA, and a gentle breeze of Warm Air quickly dried his hindquarters. He thought this was fantastic and reached for the button marked PP. This yielded a large Powder Puff that delicately applied a soft talc to his rear. Naturally he couldn't resist the last button marked ATR.

When he woke up in the hospital, he buzzed for the nurse. 'What happened to me? The last thing I remember is that I was in the new ladies' room on a plane.'

'Yes. Apparently you were having a great time until you pressed the ATR button, which stands for Automatic Tampon Removal. Your penis is under your pillow.'

Sue and Bob, a pair of tightwads, lived in the Mid-West and had been married for years. Bob had always wanted to go flying. The desire deepened each time a barnstormer flew into town to offer rides. Bob would ask, and Sue would say, 'No way, $10 is $10.'

The years went by, and Bob figured he didn't have much longer, so he got Sue out to the show, explaining that it was free to watch. And once he got there his desire became even stronger. Sue and Bob started to argue. The pilot, between flights, overheard, and said, 'I'll tell you what, I'll take you guys up flying, and if you don't say a word the ride is on me, but if one of you makes one sound, you pay $10.'

So off they flew, the pilot doing as many rolls and dives as he could. Heading for the ground as fast as the plane could go, he pulled out of the dive at the very last second. Not a word. Finally, he admitted defeat and went back to the field. 'I'm surprised, how could you not say anything?'

'Well, I almost said something when Sue fell out, but $10 is $10!'

You are one of a group of people on a malfunctioning aeroplane with only one parachute.

PESSIMIST: You refuse the parachute because you might die in the jump anyway.

OPTIMIST: You refuse the parachute because people have survived jumps just like this before.

BUREAUCRAT: You order a feasibility study on

parachute use in multi-engine aircraft under code red conditions.

LAWYER: You charge one parachute for helping sue the airline.

INTERNAL REVENUE SERVICE: You confiscate the parachute along with their luggage, wallet, and gold fillings.

ENGINEER: You make another parachute out of aisle curtains and dental floss.

MATHEMATICIAN: You refuse to accept the parachute without proof that it will work in all cases.

PHILOSOPHER: You ask how we can know the parachute actually exists.

PSYCHOANALYST: You ask what the shape of a parachute reminds them of.

DRAMATIST: You tie them down so they can watch you develop the character of a person stuck on a falling plane without a parachute.

ARTIST: You hang the parachute on the wall and sign it.

REPUBLICAN: As you jump out with the parachute, you tell them to work hard and not expect handouts.

DEMOCRAT: You ask them for a dollar to buy scissors so you can cut the parachute into two equal pieces.

LIBERTARIAN: After reminding them of their constitutional right to have a parachute you take it and jump out.

SURGEON GENERAL: You issue a warning that skydiving can be hazardous to your health.

ASSOCIAITON OF TOBACCO GROWERS: You explain

very patiently that despite a number of remarkable coincidences, studies have shown no link whatsoever between aeroplane crashes and death.

NATIONAL RIFLE ASSOCIATION: You shoot them and take the parachute.

ENVIRONMENTALIST: You refuse to use the parachute unless it is biodegradable.

OBJECTIVIST: Your only rational and moral choice is to take the parachute, as the free market will take care of the other person.

BRANCH DAVIDIAN: You get inside the parachute and refuse to come out.

The Greatest Lies in Aviation:

I'm from the FAA and am here to help you.
We'll be on time, maybe even earlier.
I only need glasses for reading.
If we get a little lower, I think we'll see the lights.
I'd love to have a woman co-pilot.
All you have to do is follow the book.
Sure I can fly – it has wings, doesn't it?
I'm *sure* the gear was down.

An experienced skydiver is about to jump when he notices that he's sitting next to another guy, obviously outfitted to dive, but wearing dark glasses, carrying a white cane, and holding the leash of a seeing-eye dog.

After some hesitation, he speaks to the blind guy,

expressing his admiration for his courage. He then asks him how he knows when the ground is getting close. The blind guy replies, 'When the leash goes slack!'

Once upon a time there were three brothers who were knights in a certain kingdom. Now there was a princess in a neighbouring kingdom who was of marriageable age. The three brothers decided to travel there and see if one of them could win her hand. They set off in full armour, with their horses and their page. The road was long and there were many obstacles along the way, robbers to be overcome, hard terrain to cross. As they coped with each obstacle they became more and more disgusted with their page. He was not only inept, he was a coward, he could not handle the horses, he was in short a complete flop. When they arrived at the court of the kingdom, they found that they were expected to present the princess with some treasure. The two older brothers were discouraged, since they had not thought of this and were unprepared. The youngest however, had the answer: Promise her anything, but give her our page.

What lies at the bottom of the sea and whimpers?

A nervous wreck.

Someone scrawled the following on a wall at a university.

Is there intelligent life on Earth?

A week or so later someone else tacked on: Yes, but we're only stopping to refuel.

A man is on a package tour of the USA. On day one, the bus goes to Mexico. He's looking forward to wild, decadent times but the bus drops him at a sleepy pueblo with a population of three people and one tumbleweed. The bus departs with the driver shouting something about returning in three hours.

The man decides to make the best of it. Surely he can amuse himself for three hours. The man heads for a bar and tries to talk to the patron, who turns out to be the most boring person on earth. Five minutes feels like three hours, so the man makes his excuses and departs. Next he sees a sleepy hombre sitting against the wall in his sombrero. '*Quel estas 'l'hora?*' he asks in his best Spanglais.

'You want man?' replies the hombre.

'No, no. The time, what is it?'

The hombre reaches out to a mule, lifts its scrotum and then lets it drop. 'About 2.30,' he says.

'Astonishing,' says the tourist, 'how did you manage that?'

Once again the hombre reaches out and lifts the donkey's scrotum. 'You see that clock tower over there?'

'Yes.'

'So can I, now.'

A spaceship from the planet Zong lands in Farmborough in the middle of the night. The town is deserted as the aliens descend from their ship. They wander around for a while until they come across a garage and what they perceive to be intelligent life – a petrol pump. The chief Zong greets the petrol pump. 'Greetings, I am Zong, a Zong from the planet Zong. We have come in our spaceship, the Zong, to meet Earth people. Take me to your leader.'

The Zong receives no reply, so he repeats his demands using shorter words: 'Take me to your leader.' The petrol pump, unsurprisingly, says nothing. By now, the short-tempered captain of the Zong is getting a bit annoyed at being ignored. He levels his ray gun at the petrol pump, much to the distress of his first mate, and demands, 'Take me to your leader, insolent scum, or I will blow you to pieces!'

Of course, the petrol pump remains silent. His Zongian shipmates try to restrain him, but the leader fires. There is an almighty explosion as the petrol pump bursts into a huge ball of flames and the crew are hurled hundreds of metres into the air. They land in a nearby field with a bump. 'What the hell happened?' shouted the Zong captain. 'I tried to warn you,' said the first mate, 'You just don't mess with a guy who can wrap his penis around his waist and stick it in his ear.'

GIGGLE-BYTES

IBM:

I Beg Mercy
I Blame Microsoft
I Bought Macintosh
Idiots Become Managers
Idiots Bewilderment Machines
Idiots Bought Me
Illustrative of Bad Marketing
Immense Bins of Money
Immense Bucket of Manure
Imperialism By Marketing
Impractical But Marketable
In a Befuddled Manner
In Business for Money
Incredible Bunch of Muffinheads
Incredibly Big Machine
Industry's Biggest Mistake
Insipid Brainless Monster
Insolence Breeds Mediocrity

Installed By Masochists
Institute of Broken Minds
Intensely Boring Machines
Intergalactic Brotherhood of Motherfuckers
International Bureaucracy Merchants
Involuntary Bowel Movement
It Beats Mattel
It's Broken Mummy
I've Been Misled

Aphorisms

I bet I can quit gambling.
A closed mouth gathers no feet.
A journey of a thousand miles begins with a cash advance.
A king's castle is his home.
A penny saved is ridiculous.
All that glitters is a high refractive index.
Ambition is a poor excuse for not having enough sense to be lazy.
Anarchy is better than no government at all.
Any small object when dropped will hide under a larger object.
Be moderate where pleasure is concerned, avoid fatigue.
Of the choice of two evils, I pick the one I've never tried before.
Death is life's way of telling you you've been fired.
Do something unusual today – accomplish work on the computer.

Don't hate yourself in the morning – sleep till noon.
Earn cash in your spare time – blackmail friends.
Entropy isn't what it used to be.
Familiarity breeds children.
Health is merely the slowest possible rate at which one can die.
History doesn't repeat itself – historians merely repeat each other.
It's a miracle that curiosity survives formal education.
It works better if you plug it in.
Life is what happens to you while you're planning to do something else.
Quoting one is plagiarism. Quoting many is research.
Reality is the only obstacle to happiness.
The attention span of a computer is as long as its electrical cord.
The only difference between a rut and a grave is the depth.
The only way to get rid of temptation is to yield to it.
The road to success is always under construction.
To be, or not to be, those are the parameters.
To err is human – to really foul things up requires a computer.
Blessed are they that run around in circles, for they shall be known as wheels.
Charity: the thing that begins at home and usually stays there.
Drawing on my fine command of language, I said nothing.
Every absurdity has a champion to defend it.
Everything you know is wrong.

Take care of the luxuries and the necessities will take care of themselves.
The universe is laughing behind your back.
To think is to be human, to compute divine.
There are no saints, only unrecognised villains.
The light at the end of the tunnel is an oncoming freight train.
Nothing is true. Everything is permitted.
Just because everything is different doesn't mean anything has changed.
The opposite of a correct statement is a false statement. But the opposite of a profound truth may well be another profound truth.
Never invest your money in anything that eats or needs painting.
Tip the world over on its side and everything loose will land in Los Angeles.
Any smoothly functioning technology will have the appearance of magic.
I think that in creating man, God somewhat overestimated his ability.
We are what we pretend to be.
Time is an illusion perpetrated by the manufacturers of space.
A physicist is an atom's way of knowing about atoms.
We don't know who discovered water, but we are certain it wasn't a fish.
I either want less corruption, or more chances to participate in it.
If the Aborigines drafted an IQ test, all of western civilisation would flunk it.

The meek shall inherit the earth, but not its mineral rights.

A man without religion is like a fish without a bicycle.

The unnatural – that too is natural.

I used to be indecisive: now I'm not so sure.

I'd give my right arm to be ambidextrous.

Science has proof without any certainty. Creationists have certainty without any proof.

Logic is an organised way of going wrong with confidence.

An intellectual is someone whose mind watches itself.

A little caution outflanks a large cavalry.

The only remedy for sex is more sex.

Everyone is entitled to my opinion.

He who laughs last didn't get the joke.

Atheism is a non-prophet organisation.

Gravity brings me down.

Help stamp out and abolish redundancy.

Where there's a will, there's an inheritance tax.

If everything is coming your way, you're in the wrong lane.

While money can't buy happiness it certainly lets you choose your own form of misery.

Two is company, three is an orgy.

Xerox never comes up with anything original.

As much use as:

A one-legged man in an arse-kicking contest.
A chocolate teapot.
Milk shoes.
A nuclear-powered computer controlled intercontinental ballistic duck.
A flammable fire extinguisher.
A glass cricket bat.
A gelignite suppository.
A coal-powered frog violin.
Granite sugar cubes.
Pasta audio wire.
A pastry telephone.
Ice-cream gloves.
A sugar surf board.
Span windscreen wipers.
A blind lifeguard.
Wooden soap.
Shortbread tyres.
A whipped-cream jet engine.
A knitted light bulb.
A plate-steel trampoline.
An invisible traffic light.
A bread boat.
Plasticine wire cutters.
A neon pink secret door.
Chocolate staples.
A lead balloon.
A latex multi-storey car park.
A margarine turbocharger.
Custard floorboards.
Gravy ceiling tiles.

A fried motor boat.
A mud monitor.
A silent telephone.
A velvet TV set.
A concrete engine.
An exploding bassoon.
A stone cigarette.
Syrup underwear.
A plastic oven.
A wax truss.
A licquorice suspension bridge.
Soap false teeth.
Asbestos water wings.
A lemonade roof.
A pair of jelly wellingtons.
A jam cardigan.
A paper bicycle pump.
Non-stick cellotape.
A sponge radar.
Anti-matter sun-tan lotion.
A soluble drain pipe.
A cubic ball bearing.
An inflatable dartboard.
A glass hammer.
A packet of rubber nails.
Elevator Earth shoes.
Heat'n'eat popsicles.
A see-through mirror.
A revolving basement restaurant.
A G-rated porn flick.
Roll-on hairspray.
Braille speedometers.
A screen door on a submarine.

An ejector seat in a helicopter.
Waterproof teabags.
Solar-powered torches.
A pocket in a pair of underpants.
A chocolate dick.
An ashtray on a motorbike.
A sodium submarine.
Tits on a bull.
A condom with a hole in it.
A box of matches in the desert.

Collectibles

Why do you need a driver's licence to buy liquor when you can't drink and drive?
Why isn't phonetic spelled the way it sounds?
Why are there interstate highways in Hawaii?
Why are there flotation devices under plane seats instead of parachutes?
Have you ever imagined a world with no hypothetical situations?
How does the guy who drives the snowplough get to work in the mornings?
If 7-eleven is open 24 hours a day, 365 days a year, why are there locks on the doors?
If you're in a vehicle going the speed of light, what happens when you turn on the headlights?
Why do they put Braille dots on the keypad of the drive-up ATM?
Why is it that when you transport something by

car, it's called a shipment, but when you transport something by ship, it's called cargo?

You know that little indestructible black box that is used on planes – why can't they make the whole plane out of the same stuff?

Why is it that when you're driving and looking for an address, you turn down the volume on the radio?

PC:

Piece a Chit
Primitive Calculator
Pseudo Computer

Condom slogans

Before you attack her, wrap your whacker.
Don't be silly, protect your willy.
Cover your stump before you hump.
Don't be a loaner, cover your boner.
If you're not going to sack it, go home and whack it.
Before you bag her, sheath your dagger.
You can't go wrong if you shield your dong.
It'll be sweeter if you wrap your peter.
Wrap it in foil before checking her oil.

Elephant books

The French book: *100 Ways to Cook Elephants*
The English book: *Elephants I have Shot on Safari*
The Welsh book: *The Elephant and its Influence on Welsh Language and Culture. Or, Oes ysgol tocynnau eleffant llanfairpwll nhadau coeden*
The American book: *How to Make Bigger and Better Elephants*
The Japanese book: *How to Make Smaller and Cheaper Elephants*
The Greek book: *How to Sell Elephants for a lot of Money*
The Finnish book: *What Do Elephants Think About Finnish People?*
The German book: *A Short Introduction to Elephants, Vols 1–6*
The Icelandic book: *Defrosting an Elephant*
The Swiss book: *Switzerland: The Country Through Which Hannibal Went With His Elephants*
The Canadian book: *Elephants: A Federal or State Issue?*

Forty-six things that never happen in *Star Trek*

1. The *Enterprise* runs into a mysterious energy field of a type that it has encountered several times before.
2. The *Enterprise* goes to check up on a remote outpost of scientists, who are all perfectly all right.

3. The *Enterprise* comes across a Garden-of-Eden-like planet called Paradise, where everyone is happy all the time. However, everything is soon revealed to be exactly as it seems.
4. The crew of the *Enterprise* discover a totally new lifeform, which later turns out to be a rather well-known old lifeform, wearing a silly hat.
5. The crew of the *Enterprise* are struck by a strange alien plague, for which the cure is found in the well-stocked sick-bay.
6. An enigmatic being composed of pure energy attempts to interface with the *Enterprise's* computer, only to find out that it has forgotten to bring the right leads.
7. A power surge on the Bridge is rapidly and correctly diagnosed as a faulty capacitor by the highly-trained and competent engineering staff.
8. A power surge on the Bridge fails to electrocute the user of a computer panel, due to a highly sophisticated 24th century surge protection feature called 'a fuse'.
9. The *Enterprise* ferries an alien VIP from one place to another without serious incident.
10. The *Enterprise* is captured by a vastly superior alien intelligence which does not put them on trial.
11. The *Enterprise* separates as soon as there is any danger.
12. The *Enterprise* gets involved in an enigmatic, strange and dangerous situation, and there are no pesky aliens they can blame it on in the end.
13. The *Enterprise* is captured by a vastly inferior

alien intelligence which they easily pacify by offering it some sweeties.

14. The *Enterprise* is involved in a bizarre time-warp phenomenon, which is in some way unconnected with the 20th century.
15. Somebody takes out a shuttle and it doesn't explode or crash.
16. A major Starfleet emergency breaks out near the *Enterprise*, but fortunately some other ships in the area are able to deal with it to everyone's satisfaction.
17. The shields of the *Enterprise* stay up during a battle.
18. The *Enterprise* visits the Klingon Home World on a bright, sunny day.
19. An attempt at undermining the Klingon-Federation alliance is discovered without anyone noting that such an attempt, if successful, would represent a fundamental shift of power throughout the quadrant.
20. A major character spends the entire episode in the Holodeck without a single malfunction trapping him/her there.
21. Picard hears the door chime and doesn't bother to say, 'Come.'
22. Picard doesn't answer a suggestion with, 'Make it so!'
23. Picard walks up to the replicator and says, 'Coke on ice!'
24. Councillor Troi states something other than the blindingly obvious.
25. Mood rings come back in style, jeopardizing Councillor Troi's position.

26. Worf and Troi finally decide to get married, only to have Kate Pulaski show up and disrupt the wedding by shouting, 'Did he read you love poetry? Did he serve you poisonous tea? He's MINE!'
27. When Worf tells the bridge officers that something is entering visual range no one says, 'On screen.'
28. Worf actually gives another vessel more than two seconds to respond to one of the *Enterprise's* hails.
29. Worf kills Wesley by mistake in the Holodeck.
30. Wesley Crusher gets beaten up by his classmates for being a smarmy git, and consequently has a go at making some friends of his own age for a change.
31. Wesley saves the ship, the Federation and the Universe as we know it, and EVERYONE is grateful.
32. The warp engines start playing up a bit, but seem to sort themselves out after a while without any intervention from boy genius Wesley Crusher.
33. Wesley Crusher tries to upgrade the warp drive and they work better than ever.
34. Beverly Crusher manages to go through a whole episode without having a hot flush and getting breathless every time Picard is in the room.
35. Guinan forgets herself, and breaks into a stand-up comedy routine.
36. Data falls in love with the replicator.
37. Kirk (or Riker) falls in love with a woman on a

planet he visits, and isn't tragically separated from her at the end of the episode.

38. The Captain has to make a difficult decision about a less advanced people which is made a great deal easier by the Starfleet Prime Directive.
39. An unknown ensign beams down as part of an away team and lives to tell the tale.
40. Spock or Data is fired from his high-ranking position for not being able to understand the most basic nuances of about one in three sentences that anyone says to him.
41. Kirk's hair remains consistent for more than one consecutive episode.
42. Kirk gets into a fistfight and doesn't rip his shirt.
43. Kirk doesn't end up kissing the troubled guest-female before she doesn't sacrifice herself for him.
44. Scotty doesn't mention the law of physics.
45. Spock isn't the only crew member not affected by new weapon/attack by alien race, etc. due to his darn green blood or bizarre Vulcan physiology and thus he cannot save the day.
46. The episode ends without Bones and Kirk laughing at Spock's inability to understand the joke, and he doesn't raise his eyebrow.

Medical terminology for the layman

ARTERY: The study of fine paintings

BARIUM: What you do when CPR fails

CAESAREAN SECTION: A district in Rome
COLIC: A sheep dog
COMA: A punctuation mark
CONGENITAL: Friendly
DILATE: To live longer
G.I. SERIES: Baseball games between teams of soldiers
GRIPPE: A suitcase
HANGNAIL: A coat hook
MEDICAL STAFF: A doctor's cane
MINOR OPERATION: Coal digging
MORBID: A higher offer
NITRATE: Lower than the day rate
NODE: Was aware of
ORGANIC: Musical
OUTPATIENT: A person who has fainted
POST-OPERATIVE: A letter carrier
PROTEIN: In favour of young people
SECRETION: Hiding anything
SEROLOGY: Study of English knighthood
TABLET: A small table
TUMOR: An extra pair
URINE: Opposite of you're out
VARICOSE VEINS: Veins that are close together

A code of ethical behaviour for patients

1. DO NOT EXPECT YOUR DOCTOR TO SHARE YOUR DISCOMFORT: involvement with the patient's

suffering might cause him to lose valuable scientific objectivity.

2. BE CHEERFUL AT ALL TIMES: your doctor leads a busy and trying life and requires all the gentleness and reassurance he can get.
3. TRY TO SUFFER FROM THE DISEASE FOR WHICH YOU ARE BEING TREATED: remember that your doctor has a professional reputation to uphold.
4. DO NOT COMPLAIN IF THE TREATMENT FAILS TO BRING RELIEF: you must believe that your doctor has achieved a deep insight into the true nature of your illness, which transcends any mere permanent disability you may have experienced.
5. NEVER ASK A DOCTOR TO EXPLAIN WHAT THEY ARE DOING OR WHY THEY ARE DOING IT: it is presumptuous to assume that such profound matters could be explained in terms that you would understand.
6. SUBMIT TO NOVEL EXPERIMENTAL TREATMENT READILY: though the surgery may not benefit you directly, the resulting research paper will surely be of widespread interest.
7. PAY YOUR MEDICAL BILLS PROMPTLY AND WILLINGLY: you should consider it a privilege to contribute, however modestly, to the well-being of physicians and other humanitarians.
8. DO NOT SUFFER FROM AILMENTS THAT YOU CANNOT AFFORD: it is sheer arrogance to contract illnesses that are beyond your means.
9. NEVER REVEAL ANY OF THE SHORTCOMINGS THAT HAVE COME TO LIGHT IN THE COURSE OF TREATMENT BY YOUR DOCTOR: the patient-doctor relationship is a privileged one and you

have a sacred duty to protect your doctor from exposure.

10. NEVER DIE WHILE IN YOUR DOCTOR'S PRESENCE OR UNDER HIS DIRECT CARE: this will only cause him or her needless inconvenience and embarrassment.

Mistakes made by Adolf Hitler

Leaving his little moustache.
Not buying lifts for his shoes.
Chose the swastika as the party symbol rather than the daisy.
Lost the Ark to Indiana Jones.
Chose unfashionable blacks and browns rather than trendy plaids.
Referred to Stalin as 'that old Geogian fart'.
Bad toupé.
Chose Italy as ally.
Made pass at Eleanor Roosevelt during 1936 Olympics.
Always got Churchill out of bed for conference calls.
Never had fireside mass rallies.
Told Einstein he had a stupid name.
Used SS instead of LAPD.
Admired Napoleon's strategy.
Strong fondness for saukraut and beans made staff avoid him.
Failed to revoke Rudolph Hess's pilot licence.
Pissed off Jesse Owens at 1936 Olympics.

Passed in Finnish 'tanks with snowshoes' offer before invasion of USSR.

Blew nose on Operation Barbarossa maps, forcing extemporaneous invasion of Soviet Union.

Took no steps to keep Neville Chamberlain in power.

Came off as poor loser when *Triumph of the Will* failed to win Oscar for Best Foreign Film.

Got drunk on schnapps and told Tojo to attack the US, saying, 'The US has only 20 times your industrial power. What are you, a wimp?'

Listened to too much Wagner and not enough Peter, Paul and Mary.

Being born.

Kept Colonel Klink in command.

Used same astrologer as the Reagans.

Not the full quid

A couple of slates short of a full roof.

A couplet short of a sonnet.

A day late and a dollar short.

A few beers short of a six-pack.

A few ears short of a bushel.

A few feathers short of a duck.

A few peas short of a pod.

A few straws shy of a bale.

A few tiles missing from his space shuttle.

A few yards short of the hole.

A kangaroo loose in her top paddock.

A pane short of a window.

A semi-tone flat on the high notes.
A span short of a bridge.
Airhead.
Bubble brain.
All foam, no beer.
All hammer, no nail.
All hat and no cattle.
All the lights don't shine in her marquee.
All wax and no wick.
An experiment in Artificial Stupidity.
Answers the door when the phone rings.
As focused as a fart.
Bad spot on the disk.
Batteries not included.
Bright as Alaska in December.
Bubbles in her think tank.
Can't count his balls and get the same answer twice.
Cart can't hold all the groceries.
Cheats when filling out opinion polls.
Chimney's clogged.
Clock doesn't have all its numbers.
Couldn't organise a piss-up in a brewery.
Couldn't pour water out of a boot with instructions on the heel.
Couldn't write dialogue for a porno flick.
Cranio-rectally inverted.
Deep as her dimples.
Defective hard drive.
Dock doesn't quite reach the water.
Doesn't just know nothing; doesn't even suspect much.

Doesn't know whether to scratch his watch or wind his balls.
Elevator doesn't go all the way to the penthouse.
Elevator goes all the way to the top but the door doesn't open.
Elevator is on the ground floor and he's pushing the DOWN button.
Enough sawdust between the ears to bed an elephant.
Goalie for the dart team.
Got into the gene pool while the lifeguard wasn't watching.
Has all the brains God gave a duck's arse.
Has an IQ one point lower than it takes to grunt.
Has his brain on cruise control.
Has no upper stage.
Has the personality of a snail on Valium.
Having a party in his head, but no one else is invited.
He's so dense, light bends around him.
Her modem lights are on but there's no carrier.
His head whistles in a cross wind.
His IQ is a false positive.
His spark can't jump the gap.
If brains were taxed, he'd get a rebate.
If his brains were money, he'd still be in debt.
If his IQ was two points higher he'd be a rock.
If you stand close enough to him, you can hear the ocean.
In the shopping mall of the mind, he's in the toy store.
Informationally deprived.
Inspected by #13.

IQ lower than a snake's belly in a wagon-rut.
It's hard to believe he beat 100 000 other sperm.
Knitting with only one needle.
Left the store without all of his groceries.
Levelled off before reaching altitude.
Lights are on but nobody's home.
Lives in La-la-land.
Living proof that nature does not abhor a vacuum.
Missing a few buttons on his remote.
Mouth is in gear, brain is in neutral.
Moves his lips to pretend he's reading.
Nice house but not much furniture.
No coins in the fountain.
No grain in the silo.
No hay in the loft.
No one at the throttle.
Not the brighest bulb on the Christmas tree.
Oil doesn't reach his dipstick.
One bit short of a byte.
One board short of a porch.
One bun short of a dozen.
One hot pepper short of an enchilada.
One node short of a network.
One pearl short of a necklace.
Ready to check in at the Ha-Ha Hilton.
Running on empty.
Serving donuts on another planet.
She wears a ponytail to cover up the valve stem.
Short-circuited between the earphones.
Sloppy as a soup sandwich.
Slow as molasses in January.
Slow out of the gate.
Smarter than the average bear.

Smoke doesn't make it to the top of his chimney.
So boring, his dreams have Muzak.
So dim, his psyche carries a flashlight.
So dumb, blondes tell jokes about him.
So dumb, he faxes face up.
So dumb, his dog teaches him tricks.
So slow, he has to speed up to stop.
So stupid, mind readers charge half price.
Someone blew out his pilot light.
Suffers from Clue Deficit Disorder.
Switch is on, but no one's receiving.
Takes her 1.5 hours to watch *60 Minutes.*
The cheese slid off his cracker.
The wheel's spinning but the hamster's dead.
Thick as pig dung and twice as smelly.
Thinks cellular phones are carbon-based life forms.
Thinks Moby Dick is a venereal disease.
Three chickens short of a henhouse.
Toys in the attic.
Travelling without a passport.
Two chapters short of a novel.
Uses his head to keep the rain out of his neck.
Warranty expired.
Wasn't strapped in during launch.
Whole lotta choppin', but no chips a flyin'.
Zero K memory.

Top 17 children's books not recommended by the National Library Association

Bob the Germ's Wonderous Journey Into and Back Out of Your Digestive System.

The Little Engine that Became Intoxicated and Killed Civilians.

Rudolph the Rednosed Reindeer's Games of Revenge.

Clifford the Big Red Dog Accidentally Eats His Masters and is put to Sleep.

Valuable Protein and other Nutritional Benefits of Things from your Nose.

A Pictorial History of Circus Geek Suicides.

Charles Manson Bedtime Stories.

Daddy Loses His Job and Finds the Bottle.

Babar Meets the Taxidermist and Becomes a Piano.

Controlling the Playground: Respect Through Fear.

David Duke's World of Imagination.

Curious George and the High-Voltage Fence.

The Boy Who Died from Eating All His Vegetables.

Teddy: The Elf With the Detached Retina.

The Pop-up Book of Human Anatomy.

Things Rich Kids Have, But You Never Will.

Let's Draw Betty and Veronica Without Their Clothes On.

The Care Bears Maul Some Campers and are Shot Dead.

Useful phrases for Arab travel

AKBAR KHALI-KILI HAFTIR LOFTAN:
Thank you for showing me your marvellous gun.

FEKR GABUL GARDAN DAVAT PAEH GUSH DIVAR:
I am delighted to accept your kind invitation to lie down on the floor with my arms above my head and my legs apart.

SHOMAEH FEKR TAMOMEH OEH GOFTEH BANDE:
I agree with everything you have ever said or thought in your life.

AUTO ARRAREGH DAVATEMAN MANO SEPAHEH-HAST:
It is exceptionally kind of you to allow me to travel in the trunk of your car.

FASHAL-EH TUPEHMAN NA DEGAT MANO GOFTAM CHEESHAYEH MOHEMARA JEBEHKESHVAREHMAN:
If you will do me the kindness of not harming my genital appendages, I will gladly reciprocate by betraying my country in public.

KHREL, JEPAHEH MANEH VA JAYEII AMRIKAHEY:
I will tell you the names and address of many American spies travelling as reporters.

BALLI, BALLI, BALLI:
Whatever you say!

MATERNIER GHERMEZ AHLIEH, GHORBAN:
The red blindfold would be lovely, Excellency.

TIKEH NUNEH BA OB KHRELLEH BEZORG VA KHRUBE BOYAST NO BEGERAM:
The water-soaked breadcrumbs are delicious, thank you. I must have the recipe.

Why did the chicken cross the road?

PLATO: For the greater good.
KARL MARX: It was a historical inevitability.
MACHIAVELLI: So that its subjects will view it with admiration, as a chicken which has the daring and courage to boldly cross the road, but also with fear. For whom among them has the strength to contend with such a paragon of avian virtue? In

such a manner is the princely chicken's dominion maintained.

HIPPOCRATES: Because of an excess of light pink gooey stuff in its pancreas.

JACQUES DERRIDA: Any number of contending discourses may be discovered within the act of the chicken crossing the road, and each interpretation is equally valid as the authorial intent can never be discerned, because structuralism is dead, dammit, dead!

THOMAS DE TORQUEMADA: Give me ten minutes with the chicken and I'll find out.

TIMOTHY LEARY: Because that's the only kind of trip the Establishment would let it take.

DOUGLAS ADAMS: Forty-two.

NIETZSCHE: Because if you gaze too long across the Road, the Road gazes also across you.

OLIVER NORTH: National security was at stake.

B.F. SKINNER: Because the external influences which had pervaded its sensorium from birth had caused it to develop in such a fashion that it would tend to cross roads, even while believing these actions to be of its own free will.

CARL JUNG: The confluence of events in the cultural gestalt necessitated that individual chickens cross roads at this historical juncture, and therefore synchronicitously brought such occurrences into being.

JEAN-PAUL SARTRE: In order to act in good faith and be true to itself, the chicken found it necessary to cross the road.

LUDWIG WITTGENSTEIN: The possibility of 'crossing' was encoded into the objects 'chicken' and 'road', and circumstances came into being which caused the actualisation of this potential occurrence.

ALBERT EINSTEIN: Whether the chicken crossed the road or the road crossed the chicken depends upon your frame of reference.

ARISTOTLE: To actualise its potential.

BUDDHA: If you ask this question, you deny your own chicken-nature.

HOWARD COSELL: It may very well have been one of the most astonishing events to grace the annals of history. An historic, unprecedented avian biped with the temerity to attempt such a Herculean achievement formerly relegated to homo sapien pedestrians is truly a remarkable occurrence.

SALVADOR DALI: The Fish.

DARWIN: It was the logical next step after coming down from the trees.

EPICURUS: For fun.

RALPH WALDO EMERSON: It didn't cross the road; it transcended it.

JOHANN FRIEDRICH VON GOETHE: The external hen-principle made it do it.

ERNEST HEMINGWAY: To die. In the rain.

WERNER HEISENBER: We are not sure which side of the road the chicken was on, but it was moving very fast.

DAVID HUME: Out of custom and habit.

SADDAM HUSSEIN: This was an unprovoked act of rebellation and we were quite justified in dropping 50 tons of nerve gas on it.

JACK NICHOLSON: 'Cause it (censored) wanted to. That's the (censored) reason.

RONALD REAGAN: I forget.

JOHN SUNUNU: The air force was only too happy to provide the transportation, so quite understandably the chicken availed himself of the opportunity.

THE SPHINX: You tell me.

MR T: If you saw me coming you'd cross the road too!

HENRY DAVID THOREAU: To live delibeately . . . and suck all the marrow out of life.

MARK TWAIN: The news of its crossing has been greatly exaggerated.

MOLLY YARD: It was a hen!

ZENO OF ELEA: To prove it could never reach the other side.

Index

THE PENGUIN BOOK OF SCHOOLYARD JOKES

collected by Phillip Adams
and Patrice Newell

Penguin Books

ACKNOWLEDGEMENTS

Hundreds of children across Australia contributed to this collection. Special thanks go to our technical advisers, Vidas Kubilius, Vavia Kubilius and Rory Adams.

And a huge thank you to all the teachers and school kids who sent us jokes and gave us lots of laughs, especially Scone Public School; St Mary's, Scone; St James, Muswellbrook; Mullumbimby Adventist Primary School and Colonel Light Gardens Primary School.

Contents

A FEW WORDS TO THE GROWN-UPS

When introducing our first collection of jokes for Penguin we speculated on the origins and evolutionary purpose of humour. While the experts passionately disagreed, as experts tend to do, there seemed to be a scholarly consensus on how kids learned to smile and laugh.

'Both have their origins as expressions of fear or fright. Thus laughter begins when a baby is shocked by something – such as being lifted aloft by a playful parent. Within a nanosecond it discovers that it is not, after all, being threatened, that all is well, that it's going to survive. The lung full of air that was to provide a drawn out scream is, instead, employed in an explosive release of tension. The scream becomes a laugh, just as the gasp becomes a chuckle. And the smile, which began as a grimace of terror, softens as panic passes.'

In the adult, jokes are frequently little acts of exorcism – attempts to deal with fears and anxieties. We laugh about what we dislike, about what frightens us. Hence the abundance of jokes on sex, illness, politicians, foreigners, lawyers and old age. Adult jokes abound in bigotry and cynicism.

But what amuses kids? Having been shocked into smiling and laughing, is their humour as concerned with the human condition? Or does it reflect a more innocent experience of life? And if so, will that innocence long survive in a world of mass media – in which there are no secrets? It's becoming impossible to protect children from images of natural and man-made disasters, from images of war, accidental death and murder. Even if they can be deflected from watching or reading the news, their mass entertainment is increasingly violent.

It is our pleasant duty to report that, thus far, kids' humour remains childish, in both senses of the term. There is little evidence that it has become polluted or corrupted by the terrors of television or the horrors of Hollywood. Whilst emphatically earthy, involving a fascination with poo-poos and wee-wees (or whatever the approved term is in your family), the jokes are, by and large, amiable and nonsensical, sharing none of the nasties that amuse anxious adults. In fact, the words that children use to entertain themselves are, first and foremost, about words themselves. Children's jokes are expressions of delight in the very idea of language. Children like to play with words in the same way that they play with

Playdough or plasticine. The big, dark issues are put aside, awaiting the onset of puberty and, beyond that, maturity.

In the early teens, hormones begin the process of sexual blossoming. At more or less the right time the body will manufacture some powerful chemicals that will hit the appropriate receptors that will, in turn, produce a rising sap in the young of both sexes. With a delighted sense of gender, of sexuality, the pubescent child will start to suffer all the well advertised pangs, whilst at the same time, enjoying some unprecedented pleasures.

Something very similar happens with language.

If Noam Chomsky and his followers are right, language – the unique human ability to communicate an infinite variety of information and ideas through noises invented in the mouth – also begins with a specific hormone. At just the right time, a young human being begins to manufacture a chemical that, impacting on the brain, triggers the learning of any language to which the child is habitually exposed. No hormone – no language. Indeed, if the child hasn't learnt language between birth and puberty it will never learn to speak.

Chomsky's theories have been given substance by studies of feral children. Over the past few hundred years a number of children have turned up in human society who have apparently been raised by animals, or in inhuman conditions. Never having been exposed to language they tried to communicate by grunts and other simple noises. Whilst they can be taught a limited vocabulary of isolated words – so as to ask for food and drink – if they've passed the age of puberty they will never develop comprehensive language skills. The evidence suggests that they cannot, for the life of them, learn to grasp grammar or syntax. They will be unable to form even simple sentences. (About twenty years ago a feral child was discovered living in the suburbs of Los Angeles. She'd been locked in a room for most of her life, kept apart from other human beings and had no experience of speech. Once rescued it was possible to teach her a wide variety of human behaviour but language defeated her.)

What is impossible after puberty is a breeze for the very young. Once the hormone hits, words fill the mind and tumble from the mouth. The synapses crackle and the neurones oblige by storing a growing amount of information on both vocabulary and the structure of sentences. In fact, the human infant is primed to learn any language on earth. Chomsky demonstrates that all languages have an underlying structure, a similar mathematics to them, so that the baby will quickly become competent in Italian or Greek or Russian or Tagalog or Mandarin. And if it's living in a bilingual household it will learn both languages, at the same time, without the slightest effort. All in response to the detonation of a hormone.

Clearly children love language. The child is thrilled by its growing ability to use words. So he or she begins to play with them. To laugh with them. To laugh at them. Whatever else a child may play with – from blocks to dolls – words are the first play thing and remain the most popular.

As they thrill to their new skills in using words, they find them full of surprises and paradox. The same word can mean entirely different things – and there are jokes for that. Every child is an incipient Spike Milligan who likes to make puns and create surreal images. Indeed, the popularity of the *Goon Show* in the fifties is a testament to a child's tenacity. Milligan, like Edward Lear and Lewis Carroll before him, plays with words in a way that is at once innocent and sophisticated. He belongs to a great tradition of humourists who simply refuse to grow up.

What do cats read in the morning?
Mewspapers.

What do you call a duck with fangs?
Count Quackula.

How do you take a sick pig to hospital?
In a ham-bulance.

What goes zzub zzub zzub?
A bee flying backwards.

There are thousands of jokes like this – jokes in the ancient tradition of the riddle. Kids delight in such silliness. And they also enjoy repetition – hence the infinite numbers of knock knock jokes, where the words are given a uniformity of structure.

They delight in hearing old stories retold too – look at the durability of Cinderella against some pretty stiff competition from new technologies. And because kids are reassured by repetition they'll happily watch the same *Wallace and Gromit* video a hundred times. For all their delight and fascination with the new, they're also immensely comforted by the familiar.

When collecting adult jokes we discovered that overwhelmingly, jokes have ancient lineages. Old jokes are endlessly recycled, updated in setting and language. Thus a variety of jokes about Paul Keating turned out to have originated in Munich in the 1930s when the original target was Hitler. As well, adult jokes come rushing into the culture from films, novels and the Internet.

With kids, jokes are overwhelmingly traditional. Many, if not most of the jokes in this book will be painfully familiar to adults because they laughed at exactly the same jokes in kindergarten or primary school. Jokes are handed down from generation to generation like fairy stories and, yes, like nursery rhymes. An idiom will disappear for a time and then suddenly reappear in the playground – a bit like the game of marbles. It's as if children belong to a secret society full of rituals that must be protected and passed on. This is not to say that this secret society doesn't admit to new possibilities, to new traditions. You see that in the way a recent invention like the yo-yo can be added to the repertoire of marbles and hopscotch. And the same thing happens with humour.

Visiting schools – both State and multi-denominational – to gather this collection, we were astonished by the enthusiasm of the response. It wasn't necessary to beg kids or bribe them for contributions. Every hand in a class went up as kids competed for the opportunity to tell their favourites. And we could detect no significant difference between the sexes or various demographics. Kids all over Australia seem to be telling the same jokes at more or less the same time. If they weren't Irish jokes they were fatty and skinny jokes or elephant jokes.

Children live in a world where animals freely interact with human beings. A world of blind mice and eggs toppling off walls. Consequently, an overwhelming majority of jokes concern animals that talk or have traumatic experiences. Human beings play second fiddle to the menagerie – even parents, whom you'd expect to be dominant figures in kids' jokes, are few and far between. Perhaps that's why there was one particular joke that proved to be a marvellous ice-breaker. Trial and error showed that this was the one joke that all kids enjoyed. And perhaps it's an intimation of where jokes will, later, take them.

Why did the koala fall out of the tree?
Because it was dead.

Simple, emphatic, no nonsense. The dead koala invariably provoked hilarity in the classroom. And the matter-of-factness of the joke defines another characteristic. 'Ask a silly question, get a simple answer.'

In that joke about the little furry creature subject to the dictates of gravity, we see perhaps the beginning of an ironic response to a world of growing dangers and difficulties. For finally that's what humour exists to do. To help you deal with life, in all its delights and difficulties.

The editors

Animal Antics

‘Who’s the king of the jungle?’ cried the lion to the zebra.

‘You are, of course,’ said the zebra shyly.

‘Who’s the king of the jungle?’ asked the lion to the giraffe.

‘Why you are dear lion,’ said the giraffe.

‘So who’s the king of the jungle?’ asked the lion to the elephant.

In an instant the elephant picked up the lion in its trunk and hurled him into the air.

‘Now, now,’ said the lion, ‘no need to get nasty just because you don’t know the answer!’

The Mummy and the baby camel were having a cuddle one day when the baby camel asked: ‘Why do I have such long eyelashes?’

‘Because they protect your eyes in a dust storm.’

‘Why do I have such big feet?’

‘So you won’t sink in the sand my dear.’

'Why have I got such a big hump on my back?'

'So you can carry a large quantity of water when you're in the desert.'

'Well Mum, what am I doing in a zoo then?'

'I just ran into a great big bear!'
'Did you let him have both barrels?'
'Heavens no, I let him have the whole gun.'

What do you get if you cross a cocker spaniel, a poodle and a rooster?
Cockapoodledoo.

How did the skunk phone her mother?
On her smellular phone.

Where do steers party?
At the meat ball.

'If you see a leopard, shoot him on the spot!'
'OK, there's a leopard, now quick, which spot?'

What's the difference between a fish and a piano?
You can't tuna fish.

What do you call a bull that's sleeping?
A bull dozer.

What do you call a cow that doesn't give milk?
A milk dud.

What did the snake give his girlfriend on their first date?
A goodnight hiss.

What do cats put in their soft drink?
Mice cubes.

What goes wow wob?
A dog walking backwards.

What TV show is about investigating mysterious cattle?
'The Ox-Files.'

What do worms do in a cornfield?
They go in one ear and out the other.

What do you get when you cross a cow with a duck?
Milk and quackers.

The Queen has corgies, but what sort of cats does she have?
Aristocats.

Why did the farmer buy a brown cow?
Because he wanted chocolate milk.

If a snake and an undertaker were married, what would they inscribe on their towels?
Hiss and Hearse.

If you crossed a dog with a fax machine, what would you get?
A fax terrier.

What do they make at Telecow?
Moobile phones.

What do you call a cow with no legs?
Ground Beef.

What do you need to do if your chooks aren't laying?
Give them an eggs-ray.

Why do cats put mice in the freezer?
To make micey poles.

How does a dog stop a VCR?
He presses the paws button.

What's a cow's favourite TV show?
'Steer Trek.'

Where can you find the most cows?
Moo York.

What do you get from a nervous cow?
A milk shake.

What do you call a cold puppy sitting on a rabbit?
A chilli dog on a bun.

What's more fantastic than a talking dog?
A spelling bee.

What do you get if you cross a skunk with a bear?
Winnie the Pooh.

Where do jellyfish get their jelly from?
From ocean currants.

What do you get when you cross a dog with a hen?
Pooched eggs.

Why aren't turkeys ever invited to dinner parties?
Because they always use fowl language.

What do bees do with their honey?
They cell it.

What do you call a duck with fangs?
Count Quackula.

Where should you never go with a dog?
To the Flea Market.

What is a slug?
A snail with a housing problem.

What's black, white, smelly and noisy?
A skunk with a drum kit.

What did the dog say when he sat on sandpaper?
'Rough! Rough!'

Why did the girl keep tripping over lobsters?
Because she was accident prawn.

What goes zzub zzub zzub?
A bee flying backwards.

What do cats read in the morning?
Mewspapers.

'Has your cat ever had fleas?'
'No, but it's had kittens.'

What do you call a three-legged dog?
Skippy.

What animal always goes to bed with its shoes on?
A horse.

Why did the Dalmatian go to the cleaners?
His coat had spots all over it.

Why do dogs wag their tails?
Because no one will wag them for them.

What did Mr and Mrs Chicken call their baby?
Egg.

What's a dog's favourite fruit?
Paw paw.

Where do sheep do their shopping?
At Woolies.

Why did the dog tick?
Because it was a watchdog.

What has a coat all winter and pants in summer?
A dog.

'My father went hunting, and he shot three ducks.'
'Were they wild?'
'No, but the farmer who owned them was.'

What petrol do snails use?
Shell.

What do cows drink?
Cowpuccino.

Where do foxes go if they lose their tails?
To the retail shop.

What do you call a camel with three humps?
Humphrey.

What happens when a frog's car breaks down?
It gets toad away.

'My dog has no nose.'
'How does it smell?'
'Terrible.'

What do you call high-rise flats for pigs?
Sty scrapers.

Why did the man bring his dog to the railway station?
To train him.

How can you stop your dog barking in the hall?
Put him in the backyard.

Why did the two boaconstrictors get married?
Because they had a crush on each other.

Why did the lion spit out the clown?
Because he tasted funny.

What kind of tie does a pig wear?
A pigsty.

How do you spell 'mouse trap' using three letters?
C A T.

What sort of work do mice do?
Mousework.

What's a bear's favourite drink?
Ginger bear.

If a cat fell into a rubbish bin what would you call it?
Kitty litter.

What does an invisible cat drink?
Evaporated milk.

'Did you know it takes three sheep to make a jumper?'
'I didn't even know they could knit.'

Why do cats change their size?
Because they are let out at night and taken in in the morning.

What do pigs do after school?
Their hamwork.

What is long and slippery and goes 'hith'?
A snake with a lisp.

What do polar bears have for lunch?
Ice burgers.

What do you get when you cross a karate expert with a pig?
A pork chop.

'It's raining cats and dogs.'
'I know, I just stepped in a poodle.'

What do you call a travelling flea?
An itch hiker.

What do frozen cows do?
They give ice-cream.

What do you call a penguin in the desert?
Lost.

A very expensive dog is drowning in the river when a man jumps into the freezing water, swims over to the dog, brings it back to the shore, gives it mouth to mouth resuscitation and revives it. Meanwhile the dog's owner is running towards them having seen the whole episode.

'That was amazing, thank you so much. Are you a vet?'

'Of course I'm a vet, I'm absolutely soaking!'

'Ouch, I thought you said your dog didn't bite?'
'That's not my dog.'

What do you call a monkey with a banana in each ear?
Anything, because it can't hear you.

What did the echidna say to the cactus?
'Mummy!'

'My horse is a blacksmith.'
'What do you mean?'
'Well, if I shout at him, he makes a bolt for the door.'

What do you call a cow that eats your grass?
A lawn mooer.

What's worse than a giraffe with a sore throat?
A centipede with blisters.

What do you get when you stack toads together?
A toadempole.

Why do tigers eat raw meat?
Because they can't cook.

Why did the farmer name his pig 'ink'?
Because it kept running out of the pen.

What do you call a donkey with three legs?
A wonkey.

Why don't snakes have a sense of humour?
Because you can't pull their legs.

What goes oom oom oom?
A cow walking backwards.

Where do rabbits go after they get married?
On a bunny moon.

'Are you aware your dog barked all night?'
'Yes, but don't worry, he got plenty of sleep during the day.'

What does the buffalo say when he sends his son off to school each morning?
'Bison.'

What do you call one hundred rabbits jumping backwards?
A receding hare line.

What did the doctor prescribe for the bald rabbit?
Hare tonic.

What do you get when you pour hot water down a rabbit hole?
Hot cross bunnies.

Where do baby apes sleep?
In apricots.

What do cats eat at parties?
Mice cream.

What is a small turkey called?
A goblet.

Why do fish have such huge phone bills?
Because when they get on the line, they can't get off.

What is a squirrel's favourite ballet?
'The Nut Cracker Suite.'

What are the knees of baby goats called?
Kidneys.

What works in a circus and meows when it swings?
An acrocat.

What kind of key doesn't unlock any door?
A monkey.

What do you get when you cross a rabbit with a spider?
A hare net.

What's grey with a blue face?
A mouse holding its breath.

Why do cows wear bells?
Because their horns don't work.

How did the rodeo horse get so rich?
It had a lot of bucks.

Why don't fish go near computers?
They're afraid of getting caught in the Internet.

What did the rabbit give his girlfriend?
A five carrot ring.

How do you catch a squirrel?
Climb up a tree and act like a nut.

Which side of a chicken has the most feathers?
The outside.

Why is it easy to weigh fish?
Because they come with scales.

Why did the fox bang his head on the piano?
He was playing by ear.

Why did the kitten join the Red Cross?
Because it wanted to be a first aid kit.

What's a fish's favourite game show?
'Name that Tuna.'

Why do mother kangaroos hate rainy days?
Because their kids have to play inside.

What do you call a skunk in court?
Odour in the court.

Why did the crab go to jail?
Because it was always pinching things.

Why do bees buzz?
Because they can't whistle.

What are the most commonly used letters in the skunk alphabet?
'P' and 'U'.

What did the boy octopus say to the girl octopus?
'I want to hold your hand, hand, hand, hand, hand, hand, hand, hand.'

What mouse won't eat cheese?
A computer mouse.

Why couldn't the pony talk?
He was a little horse.

Where does a whale sleep?
On the sea bed.

What do you call a shy lamb?
Baaaashful.

Why do giraffes have such long necks?
Because their feet stink.

What do you get when you cross a snowball with a shark?
Frostbite.

How can you stop a rhinoceros from charging?
Take away its credit cards.

What should you do if you find a gorilla in your bed?
Find somewhere else to sleep.

What do you call an owl with a sore throat?
A bird that doesn't give a hoot.

When does a mouse need an umbrella?
When it's raining cats and dogs.

Why did the turtle cross the road?
To get to the shell station.

If chickens get up when the rooster crows, when do ducks get up?
At the quack of dawn.

What does a polar bear telephone operator say?
'Thank you, and have an ice day.'

What happened to the snake when it had a cold?
She adder viper nose.

Why shouldn't you play cards in the jungle?
Because there are too many cheetahs.

What did the little bird say when it found an orange in its nest?
'Look at the orange mama-laid!'

One cow said to the other: 'Are you worried about this mad cow disease?'
'No, why should I be? I'm a possum.'

What has six legs, bites, is noisy at night and talks in code?
A morse-quito.

What is the opposite of a cool cat?
A hot dog.

What does a snake learn when it goes to school?
Hiss-tory.

'Two of our chooks have stopped laying eggs.'
'How do you know?'
'Because I just ran over them with the tractor.'

How can you talk to a fish?
Drop it a line.

What animal can pray?
A praying mantis.

Why shouldn't you cry if a cow slips on the ice?
Because it's no use crying over spilt milk.

What's green and slimy and lives in my hanky?
My pet frog.

What's the difference between a buffalo and a bison?
You can't wash your hands in a buffalo.

What happened to the cat who ate a ball of wool?
She had mittens.

What animals on Noah's ark didn't come in pairs?
Worms. They came in apples.

Where do tadpoles change into frogs?
In the croakroom.

When is the best time to buy a budgie?
When they're going cheap.

What's a dog's favourite food?
Anything that's on your plate.

What do you get if you cross a rabbit and a sheep?
A Jumper.

What's a frog's favourite drink?
Croaka cola.

How do sheep keep warm in winter?
They turn on the central bleating.

Why did the chicken cross the road?
He saw a man laying bricks.

What do you call a duck that can't read?
A blind duck.

What is the sharpest pine?
A porcupine.

Why does the kookaburra laugh?
Because there's nothing to cry about.

Why did the chicken cross the football field?
Because the umpire cried foul.

What did the lion say when he saw two rabbits on a skateboard?
'Meals on wheels.'

Now you see it, now you don't, now you see it, now you don't. What is it?
A black cat on a zebra crossing.

What makes a dog meow?
A chainsaw. Meeeeeooooow!

Why do snakes have forked tongues?
Because they can't use chop sticks.

Why do gorillas live in the jungle?
Because they can't afford to live in the city.

How come koalas carry their babies on their backs?
They can't push a pram up a tree.

Two bats were out one night looking for blood, but after a few hours of unsuccessful hunting decided to go home. In the wee hours of the morning one of the bats was so hungry he said he had to go out hunting again. An hour later he came back all covered in blood.

'Where did you get that blood?' said the other bat full of envy.

'Come with me and I'll show you.' So out they went into the night.

'See that tree over there?' said the bat covered in blood.

'Yeah.'

'Well, I didn't!'

What's green and smells of eucalyptus?
Koala vomit.

Cow one: Moo.
Cow two: Baa Baa.
Cow one: What do you mean Baa Baa?
Cow two: I'm learning a second language.

What do you get if you sit under a cow?
A pat on the head.

How do goldfish go into business?
They start on a small scale.

'Hey! Your dog has just eaten my hat.'
'He'll be OK, he likes hats.'

What's a bear's second favourite drink?
Coca koala.

Two very big turtles and a very little turtle were sitting in a cafe drinking apple juice when it began to pour with rain. Since the little turtle was the quickest they decided that he should go back home and get their raincoats. But the little one objected. He was worried that when he left, the others would drink his apple juice. It took a lot of convincing, but finally, he was persuaded to head off for the raincoats. Three weeks later one of the big turtles said: 'Let's drink his juice.'

'I'd been thinking exactly the same thing,' said the other.

And from just a few yards away, on the footpath, a little voice said: 'Oh no you don't. If you do, I won't go home and get the raincoats.'

Where do you find the biggest spider?
In the World Wide Web.

Why did the chicken cross the playground?
To get to the other slide.

What happened to the two bedbugs who fell in love?
They got married in the spring.

What does a toad say when it sees something wonderful?
'Toad-ally awesome.'

What kind of shoes does a toad wear?
Open toad sandals.

What are spider webs good for?
Spiders.

Why does a polar bear have fur?
Because it would look silly in leather.

Two men were walking along Bondi early one morning with a shaggy dog. The dog's owner threw the stick into the ocean and the dog ran across the top of the water, collected the stick and bought it back. The other man couldn't believe his eyes.

'That is one amazing dog you have there,' said the man.

'Amazing my foot,' said the dog's owner. 'After all the lessons he's had he still can't swim.'

Who went into the lion's den and came out alive?
The lion.

What do ants take when they are sick?
Antibiotics.

What game do hogs play?
Pig pong.

Where do you find rabbits in Paris?
They're in the hutch, at the back of Notre Dame.

Baby snake: My head hurts.
Mummy snake: Come here and let me hiss it.

'My dog's head is always hanging down so I'm taking him to the vet's.'
'Neck's weak?'
'No, tomorrow.'

'I knew someone who thought he was an owl.'
'Who?'
'Make that two people.'

Why was Mummy centipede so upset?
All the kids needed new shoes.

What did the mother bee say to the naughty baby bee?
'Beehive yourself.'

Why do bees itch?
Because they have hives.

What did the mother glow worm say to the father glow worm?
'Wow, our baby sure is bright.'

Where do you take sick kangaroos?
To the hop-ital.

Where do you take sick dogs?
To the dog-tor.

How do you take sick pigs to the hospital?
In a ham-bulance.

How many toes does a monkey have?
Take off your shoes and count them.

Why don't monkeys live on the moon?
Because there aren't any bananas there.

What is every cat's favourite nursery rhyme?
'Three Blind Mice.'

Why does a dog sit on its hind legs?
If it didn't it would be standing up.

How do baby hens dance?
Chick to chick.

Why did the ibis cross the road?
To prove it wasn't chicken.

'Have you got any dogs going cheap?'
'No, all my dogs go "woof".'

What do you call a good looking emu?
Rare.

Where do you find a tortoise with no legs?
Where you left it.

What does a frog drink when he's on a diet?
Diet croak.

How many monkeys does it take to change a light globe?
Two. One to do it, and one to scratch his bottom.

A man goes into a shop with a pig under his arm. The manager spots him and says: 'That's the ugliest looking animal you've got there. Where on earth did you get it?'

And the pig says, 'I won it in a raffle.'

What year do frogs like the best?
Leap year.

One morning Daddy Bear came down to breakfast to find his porridge bowl empty.

'Somebody's been eating my porridge,' said Daddy Bear.

'And somebody's been eating my porridge,' said Baby Bear.

At that moment Mummy Bear came out of the kitchen and said: 'You silly bears. I haven't made it yet!'

Which birds are religious?
Birds of prey.

Why did the farmer light a fire next to his goat?
Because he wanted to boil his billy.

What bird is a good cook?
A kookaburra.

What kind of cat is found in a library?
A catalogue.

What do you call a bird with a cold?
A cocka choo.

What's the hardest part about milking a mouse?
Getting a bucket under it.

What bird can't you trust?
A lyrebird.

What's a cat's favourite holiday destination?
The Canary Islands.

'I don't like these flies buzzing around me!'
'Well, pick out the ones you like and I'll try to get rid of the rest.'

One flea says to the other as he walks down the road: 'Shall we keep on walking or catch a dog?'

'I want that bird!'
'It's all yours Madam, but it costs twenty dollars.'
'Will you send me the bill?'
'No, you have to take the whole bird.'

I saw a bird up in the sky,
Who dropped a message from up high,
As I wiped it from my eye,
I thanked the Lord that cows don't fly.

Why do bees have sticky hair?
Because they use honey combs.

What did the mosquito say the first time it saw the camel's hump?
'Did I do that?'

Why didn't the butterfly go to the dance?
Because it was a mothball.

What do frogs sit on?
Toadstools.

Where do wasps go when they're sick?
To waspital.

What do you call a mosquito that likes cheese?
A mozzie-rella.

Why were two flies playing football on a saucer?
Because they were practising for the cup.

What lays around 100 feet up?
A dead centipede.

Why does a dog turn around twice before sitting down?
Because one good turn deserves another.

Where do frogs keep their money?
In the riverbank.

'Does your dog have a licence?'
'No, he isn't old enough to drive.'

What did the spaniel say to the bird?
'I'm a cocker too.'

Why do birds fly north?
Because it's too far to walk.

Do cows give milk?
No, you have to take it from them.

Three bees decided to build a car. One worked on the motor, the second on the body and the third on the upholstery. Finally they completed the task and were very proud of themselves. All they needed was some petrol and they could have their first drive.

Whereupon a grasshopper arrived and asked: 'Can I help?'

'Sorry,' chorused the bees. 'This car only takes BP.'

What kind of horses go out at night?
Night mares.

What goes through a grasshopper's mind when it hits the windscreen of a car going at 100 kilometres per hour?
Its legs.

Why do bees hum?
Because they don't know the words.

What do you get when you cross a black sheep with a bra?
'Bra Bra Black Sheep.'

What's the best way to keep a dog off the street?
Keep it in a barking lot.

What did the rat do when his girlfriend fell into the dam?
He gave her mouse to mouse resuscitation.

Why are fish poor tennis players?
Because they don't like to get close to the net.

Why are fish smart?
Because they always go to school.

What did the duck say when she finished shopping?
'Just put it on my bill.'

What kind of shoes are made of banana skins?
Slippers.

How do you catch a runaway dog?
Make a noise like a bone.

What did the pig say when the farmer got hold of his tail?
'That's the end of me!'

What did Mrs Spider say to Mr Spider when he broke her new web?
'Darn it!'

Why is it hard to have a conversation with a goat around?
Because it always butts in.

Why couldn't the leopard escape from the zoo?
Because he was always spotted.

If ten cats were on a boat and one jumped out, how many would be left?
None, they were all copycats.

Why did the three little pigs leave home?
Because their father was a crashing boar.

Why does a monkey scratch itself?
Nobody else knows where it itches.

What horse never wears a saddle?
A seahorse.

Where do you find dinosaurs?
It depends where you leave them.

If horses wear horse shoes, what do camels wear?
Desert boots.

What kind of horse can become a head of a council?
A mare.

What horse can give you a cold?
A draught horse.

'My dog's missing.'
'Put an ad in the paper.'
'But dogs can't read!'

If a man has a dog with no legs what can he do?
Take him for a drag!

How do you find your lost dog in the Botanical Gardens?
Put your ear to a tree and listen to the bark.

What dog never barks?
A hot dog.

What do you get when you cross a bear and a kangaroo?
A fur coat with big pockets.

What did the farmer put on the pig's sore nose?
Oinkment.

What type of shoes do koalas wear?
Gum boots.

What do you get when you cross a pig with a car?
Another kind of crashing boar.

Where do you find wombats?
It depends where they are lost.

Why is a bilby like a one cent piece?
Because it has a head one end and a tail on the other.

What can you do with a short-sighted kangaroo?
Get it to a hop-tician.

A young woman was out bush walking when she came across a friendly wombat on the side of the road. She picked it up and took it to a police station.

'What should I do with this?' she asked the policeman.

'Take him to the zoo,' he replied.

The next morning the policeman saw the woman with the wombat again.

'I thought I told you to take it to the zoo?'

'I did, and this afternoon we're going to the movies.'

How many animals can you put in an empty cage?
One. After that it is not empty.

What do cows eat for breakfast?
Mooslie.

What did the shopkeeper say to the cow?
'Do you want this one or the udder?'

Why did the koala fall out of the tree?
Because it was dead.

What sort of lollies do koalas eat?
Chewing gum.

What's a horse after it's six months old?
Seven months old.

What do you get if a sheep studies karate?
Lamb chops.

What did the rabbit say to the carrot?
'It's been nice gnawing you.'

What's green, red, disgusting and makes a gluggy noise?
A frog in the blender.

What does a giraffe have that no other animals have?
Baby giraffes.

When is it OK to drink rhinoceros milk?
When you're a baby rhinoceros.

Where was the donkey when the light went out?
In the dark.

What's a horse's favourite TV show?
'Neighbours.'

What do you get when you cross a sheep and a kangaroo?
A woolly jumper.

What can you do when a tiger eats your dictionary?
Take the words out of its mouth.

How do you know when you have a hundred wombats trying to get into your fridge?
You can't shut the door.

Why don't kangaroos ride bikes?
Because they don't have a thumb to ring the bell.

Why did the cow jump over the moon?
Because the farmer had cold hands.

Why did the dinosaur cross the road?
Because the chicken hadn't been invented yet.

Why did the bee cross his legs?
Because he couldn't find the BP Station.

What kind of animal can jump higher than a house?
All kinds because houses can't jump.

What do you get if you cross a rabbit with a bumble bee?
A honey bunny.

Dingdong bell,
Pussy's in the well.
If you don't believe me,
Go and have a smell.

What do you call a mouse if you put it in the freezer?
Mice.

Why do wombats dig with their claws?
Because they can't use bulldozers.

How can you tell if a bee is on the phone?
You get a busy signal.

'Sally, have you given the goldfish fresh water today?'
'No, they haven't finished the water they had yesterday.'

Johnny went into the cafe to order a milkshake for himself and a diet soda for his pet giraffe. Soon after they finished their drinks, the giraffe fell off its chair and dropped dead. A man walked in and stared at the dead animal and said: 'What's that lying on the floor?'

'Don't be stupid, that's not a lion. It's a giraffe,' said Johnny.

There are three dogs and three men, and they have to get across the desert without the dogs making a mess. The first man gets a quarter of the way across when, unfortunately, his dog does a poo. The second man gets halfway when his dog also does a poo. But the last man gets all the way. How did he do it?

'Me not silly, me not dumb, me shove cork up doggy's bum.'

An old man is walking along the street when he sees a frog. The frog says: 'Hey, mate, come over here.' The old man walks over and the frog says: 'Pick me up.' So the old man picks up the frog. The frog says: 'If you rub me, I'll turn into a genie and give you lots of money.' The old man puts the frog in his pocket and starts to walk on. The frog squirms and wiggles and yells: 'Hey, take me out of your pocket!' So the old man takes him out of his pocket. The frog stares at the man and shouts: 'I said, I'd turn into a genie and give you whatever you wanted!'

To this the old man replied: 'Look, at my age, I'd rather have a talking frog!'

Which animal is best at cricket?
A bat.

What did the cat have for breakfast?
Mice crispies.

What sort of fish go meow?
Catfish.

What should you do if you find a snake in your bed?
Sleep somewhere else.

How does an octopus go to war?
Well armed.

What do you get when you put a Tasmanian devil into a chicken coop?
Devilled eggs.

Where are you most likely to see a man-eating fish?
In a seafood restaurant.

What did the fish say to the seaweed?
'Kelp, Kelp!'

'Have you ever hunted bear?'
'No, but I've been fishing in my shorts.'

Why did Little Bo-Peep lose her sheep?
Because she had a crook with her.

What kind of cat helps you fix things?
A tool kit.

In what book do ducks look up words?
A duck-tionary.

What gives milk, goes moo and makes all your wishes come true?
Your dairy godmother.

How do you move cows?
In a moo-ving van.

What kind of cow can you sit on?
A cow-ch.

Why was the sheep arrested on the dual carriageway?
Because he did a ewe turn.

What dance do you get if you cross a fox and a horse?
The fox trot.

What's the easiest way to count cows?
On a cow-culator.

Where do sheep go for their holidays.
To the Baa Haa Maa's.

Which singer do cows prefer?
Moodonna.

What type of underwear do zebras wear?
Z-bra.

What do pigs wear to bed?
Pig-jamas.

What's a lion's favourite dance?
Lion-dancing.

What's a monkey's favourite dance?
The orang-a-tango.

How do rabbits travel?
By hare-plane.

What's an octopus's favourite lolly?
A jelly bean.

Why did the dog have to go to court?
Because he got a barking ticket.

'Did you ever see a catfish?'
'Don't be mad. Cats don't fish.'

What do you get when you cross a rooster with a steer?
A cock and bull story.

What do you get if you cross a giraffe with a hedgehog?
A ten metre toothbrush.

How many skunks does it take to stink out a room?
A phew.

What kind of fish do they serve on airplanes?
Flying fish.

Family Life

'Darling,' said the pregnant woman, 'I know how excited you are about becoming a father, but I have to tell you something. In my family we have a tradition that the wife's brother always gets to name the children. I was too nervous to tell you before, but it just has to be that way.'

'But your brother is a complete idiot,' said the husband, 'he'll make a mess of it.'

A little later, beautiful, healthy twins were born. A boy and a girl. So the father asked his wife what names her brother had chosen for his children.

'Well, the girl is Denise,' the mother said quietly.

'That's a pretty name. Perhaps this won't be so bad after all. And what's our son's name?'

'Denephew.'

'Mum, I'm tired of looking like everyone else, could you part my hair from ear to ear please?'

'Are you sure?'

'Yeah.'

That day Johnny came home from school really depressed.

'Can you do my hair back the other way again Mum?'

'What's the matter Johnny, are you sick of being different already?'

'It's not that, I can't stand people whispering in my nose.'

'Now little Mary eat your greens up, or you won't grow up to be beautiful!'
'Nanna, didn't you eat your greens?'

'Mum, can I have a dollar for the man who's crying in the park?'
'What's he crying about?'
He's crying, "Hot dogs, one dollar!"'

How did the farmer mend his pants?
With cabbage patches.

'What are you doing there Johnny, digging that hole?'
'I'm burying my radio. The batteries are dead.'

'Johnny, why have you put sugar in your pillow?'
'So I'll have sweet dreams, Mum.'

'Johnny, why aren't you playing tennis with Simon any more?'
'Mum, would you play with someone who always lies about the score?'
'Absolutely not.'
'Well, neither would Simon!'

'Polly, take that hose out of Johnny's ear!'
'But I'm trying to brainwash him.'

'Daddy, Daddy, can I have another glass of water please?'
'You've already had eight.'
'Yes, but my bedroom's on fire!'

'Johnny, you can't take that sweet to the dentist's appointment!'
'Why not, I want a chocolate filling.'

What do fairy children do when they get home from school?
Their gnome work.

'Johnny, it's time to get up. It's five to eight.'
'Who's winning?'

'Get your father out of that fridge!'
'But I want a cool pop, Mum.'

'Johnny, I think your dog really likes me, he hasn't taken his eyes off me all night.'
'That's because you're eating off his plate.'

Why did Nanna have roller blades fitted to her wheelchair?
So she could rock and roll.

'Johnny, I've told you not to let Rover into the house. It's full of fleas.'
'Rover, you keep out of the house, it's full of fleas.'

'Why is your baby so full of joy?'
'Because she's full of nappiness.'

'Dad, why have you painted rabbits on your head?'
'Can you tell? I thought from a distance they'd look like hares.'

'Dad, I'm really homesick.'
'But this is your home.'
'I know, I'm sick of it.'

'Dad, what did the X-ray of your brain show?'

'Uh, nothing much, son.'

Mum and Dad decided to take all their relatives out to dinner.

Both Mum and Dad ordered a mixed grill. 'And what about your vegetables?' asked the waiter.

'Oh, they can order what they like!' said Dad.

'Johnny, why did you sleep last night with a ruler?'

'Because I wanted to see how long I slept, Mum!'

'Johnny, you are disgusting, why do you pick your nose?'

'Because I can Mum.'

'You're an actor right?'
'Yeah.'
'Well how much will you charge to dress up as a ghost and scare my brother?'
'For $100, I'll scare him out of his wits.'
'Here's $50, he's only a half wit.'

'Mum, I have to write an essay on the High Court.'
'Well that's going to be difficult, paper would be much easier.'

'Johnny, you've got your shoes on the wrong feet again.'
'But they're the only feet I've got!'

'Daddy, can you see any change in me?'
'No, why son?'
'Because I just swallowed twenty cents.'

'Mum, I want to learn to play the piano by ear.'
'Well it's much easier if you use your hands.'

'Johnny, that essay you wrote about your dog is exactly the same as your sister's.'
'Of course teacher, it's the same dog.'

'Teacher, my Dad said there were three kinds of people in the world, those who can count and those who can't.'

'Johnny, did you put the cat out?'
'Why? Was it on fire?'

'Mum, can I swim on a full stomach?'
'No Johnny, it's better to swim on water.'

'Mum, why isn't my nose twelve inches long?'
'Because then it would be a foot.'

'Dad, a man came to see you this afternoon.'
'Did he have a bill?'
'No. He had a nose like yours.'

'Johnny, how are you enjoying your new guitar?'
'I threw it away Dad. It had a hole in the middle.'

Why did Johnny wear wet trousers?
Because the label said wash and wear.

'Why are you jumping up and down Johnny?'
'I took my medicine, but I forgot to shake the bottle.'

'Dad, have your socks got holes in them?'
'Certainly not, Johnny.'
'Well, how do you get your feet in them?'

'Johnny, which month has twenty-eight days?'
'They all have, Miss.'

'Dad, there's a man at the door collecting for a new swimming pool.'
'Give him a glass of water son.'

'My Dad owns a newspaper.'
'Yeah? He must be rich.'
'Not really. He bought it at the newsagent this morning.'

'My Dad can hold up a car with one hand.'
'Yeah? He must be really strong.'
'No. He's a policeman.'

'Mum, are we poisonous snakes?'
'No, of course not.'
'Just as well, because I just bit my lip.'

'Dad, are you still growing?'
'No, why do you ask?'
'Because your head is growing through your hair.'

'Mum, how can I get rid of my BO?'
'Hold your nose.'

'Mum, what has a purple spotted body, ten hairy legs, and big eyes on stalks?'
'I don't know.'
'Well, one just crawled up your dress.'

What's brown, hairy and has no legs but walks?
Dad's socks.

Little Belinda is playing with her mother's purse, pulls out all the coins and swallows one. Mum and Dad rush her to hospital.

'How is our precious little daughter?'

'Not much change yet,' says the nurse.

Mum and Dad go to dinner at the local

restaurant. Dad's halfway through his meal when he has a long, hard look at the potato. He calls the waitress over and says: 'This potato is bad.'

The waitress picks it up, smacks it, and puts it back on the plate.

'Now, if that potato gives you any more trouble, just let me know.'

When is a mummy not a mummy?
When it's a daddy.

'Dad, have you ever seen an oil well?'
'Why, no son I haven't. But I haven't seen one sick either.'

'Look out son! There's a ten foot snake behind you!'
'You can't fool me Dad. Snakes don't have feet.'

'Wow, your microscope magnifies three times.'
'Oh no! I've already used it twice.'

'Could I get a puppy for my son?'
'No Madam, we don't swap.'

Mum and Dad were driving in the country when they realised they were desperate for a cup of tea. Finally they arrived at a small town with a cafe. They pulled up, went inside and were just about to order when a horse walked in and sat at the table next to them. To their astonishment the horse ordered a coffee. Dad was so surprised that he asked the waitress if it was normal.

'No, he usually orders a lemonade!' she said.

Why do little brothers chew with their mouths open?
Flies have got to live somewhere.

'Hey Sis, what's that brain sucker doing on your head wasting its time?'

'Where does your sister live?'
'Alaska.'
'Don't worry, I'll ask her myself.'

'What's small, annoying and really ugly?'
'I'm not sure, but it comes when I call out my little sister's name.'

'Darling, what do you think? I just got back from the beauty parlour.'
'Too bad it was closed.'

Why did the parents call both their sons Jonathan?
Because two Jonathans are better than one.

When do you put a frog in your sister's bed?
When you can't catch a mouse.

What's grey, wrinkled and hangs out your underwear?
Your Grandma.

'Mum, can I have a parrot for Christmas?'
'No, you'll have turkey like the rest of us.'

Johnny came home with one thong.
'Did you lose a thong again?'
'No, I found one.'

Johnny and Mary are sitting on the beach playing with their navels.

'What are these?'

'Well, when you're born there's a piece of rope hanging out of there. They cut it off and twist the end around and tape it inside.'

'What for?'

'So you won't go pssssshhhhh and go down.'

Little Johnny was six and still hadn't spoken a word. Finally, one morning at breakfast he cried out, 'Mum, the toast's burnt!' His amazed mother gave him a big kiss and hug and asked: 'Johnny, why haven't you ever spoken before?'

'Well, up until now everything was fine.'

I've got five noses, seven mouths and six ears, so what am I?
Really ugly.

What goes up on your birthday but never comes down?
Your age.

Husband: Darling, there's a fat hairy ugly thing on your neck!
Wife: Where?
Husband: Oh don't worry, it's just your head.

'Mummy, Mummy, the kids at school say I look like a werewolf.'
'Shut up son and comb your face.'

What did the girl say to her Grandfather when he was drowning?
'Paddle Pop!'

'My nose keeps growing.'
'Stop telling so many lies then.'
'I never tell lies.'
'There it goes again.'

'Johnny, what time is it please, it must be after midnight?'
'I don't know Mum, my watch only goes to twelve.'

'Johnny, I'm sorry to have to tell you this, but we had to shoot Rover today.'
'Was he mad?'
'Well he wasn't too happy about it.'

A little boy kept wiping his nose on his sleeve, when another boy came up and asked: 'Haven't you got a hankie?'

'Yeah, but I don't think my Mum would like me to lend it to anyone.'

Fatty & Skinny

Fatty and Skinny climbed a tree,
Fatty fell down the lavatory.
Skinny went down to pull the chain,
And Fatty was never seen again.

Fatty was on the dunny.
Skinny was in the bath,
Fatty let off a fart,
and made poor Skinny laugh.

Fatty and Skinny went to bed,
Fatty rolled over and Skinny was dead.

Fatty and Skinny had a car.
Fatty had the crash. And Skinny had the scar.

Fatty and Skinny went to Mars,
Fatty came back with lots of bras.

Fatty and Skinny climbed up a tree,
Fatty got sick and did a big pee.

Fatty and Skinny went to the zoo,
Fatty stepped in elephant's poo.
Skinny went home to tell his Mum,
And all he got was a kick up the bum.

Fatty and Skinny went to the movies,
Skinny got excited when he saw some
boobies.

Food Glorious Food

The gourmet food contest was underway and each chef was explaining their recipes.

'I use exactly 239 beans in my taco mix, one more and it would be too farty,' said the Mexican cook.

What's worse than finding a worm in your apple?
Half a worm.

What's the difference between a soft drink and a glass of water?
About a dollar twenty.

What kind of bean will never grow in a vegetable garden?
A jelly bean.

Why won't you ever be hungry at the beach?
Because of all the sand-which-is there.

Where do vegetables take their rusty cars for a service?
To the car-rot station.

Ummm, I like kids, but I don't think I could eat a whole one.

What is a potato's favourite TV show?
'MASH.'

A sandwich walks into a cafe and says: 'Hey, can I have a milkshake?'

The waitress says: 'Sorry mate, we don't serve food here.'

How do you mend a broken pizza?
With tomato paste.

Baby corn: Where did I come from, Mum?
Mummy corn: The stalk brought you.

What's yellow, brown and hairy?
Cheese on toast, dropped on the carpet.

Why should potatoes grow better than any other vegetable?
Because they have eyes and can see what they're doing.

What day do chickens hate the most?
Fry days.

Why were the baby apricots crying?
Because their mummy was in the jam.

What kind of vegetable do they make Lassie's dog biscuits with?
Collie-flour.

Why did the apple turn over?
Because it saw the swiss roll.

What kind of food do scarecrows like?
Strawberries.

Why did the biscuit go to the hospital?
Because he was feeling crummy.

Where were potatoes first fried?
In Greece.

What's in Paris, and is really high and wobbly?
The trifle tower.

Which vegetable is good at snooker?
A cue-cumber.

What do you get when you cross a potato with an onion?
A potato with watery eyes.

What kind of apple isn't an apple?
A pineapple.

Why didn't the duck eat his soup?
He couldn't find his quackers.

If I had six grapefruit in one hand and seven in the other, what would I have?
Very big hands.

What's red and green?
A tomato working part-time as a cucumber.

Why do skeletons drink milk?
Because it's good for their bones.

What do hungry stars do?
Chew on the Milky Way.

What kind of cheese comes with a house?
Cottage cheese.

Where does Superman buy his groceries?
At the supermarket of course.

Why did the chicken lay the egg?
Because if she dropped it it would break.

'Have you seen the salad bowl?'
'No, but I've seen the lunch box.'

What did the mayonnaise say to the refrigerator door?
'Shut the door, I'm dressing.'

How do you help deaf oranges?
Give them a lemon aid.

Should you eat your soup with your right or left hand?
Neither, you should use a spoon.

Why should you never tell secrets in a greengrocers?
Because potatoes have eyes and beans talk.

Why did the egg go to the jungle?
Because it was an eggs-plorer.

A peanut sat on the railway track,
His heart was all a flutter.
The five fifteen came rushing by,
'toot! toot!'
Peanut butter!

How do you make an artichoke?
Strangle it.

What vegetable has a heart in its head?
A lettuce.

What do traffic wardens have in their sandwiches?
Traffic jam.

If you were locked in a room with only a calendar and a bed, how could you survive?
You could eat the dates from the calendar and drink from the springs in the bed.

'Dad, I just can't work on an empty stomach!'
'Well, try the table then!'

'Why are you dancing with that jar of honey?'
'It says "Twist to open".'

What did the tomato say to his friend who was running behind him?
'Ketch-up!'

Why did the peanut go to the police?
Because it had been assalted.

What do you call a train full of toffee?
A chew chew train.

What stays hot in the refrigerator?
Mustard.

There was a young lady from Surrey,
Who cooked up a large pot of curry.
She ate the whole lot,
Straight from the pot,
And ran to the tap in a hurry.

What did the mother cabbage say to her son when he told a lie?
'You better turn over a new leaf.'

What do you call two rows of vegetables?
A dual cabbageway.

Why did twelve people walk out of the cafe at the same time?
Because they had all finished eating.

What do eskimos eat for breakfast?
Ice Krispies.

What has bread on both sides and is scared of everything?
A chicken sandwich.

What nuts can be found in space?
Astronuts.

How do you make a sausage roll?
Push it down the hill.

How do you make an apple puff?
Chase it around the garden.

Why did the steak feel suffocated?
Because it was smothered in onions.

Why did the biscuit cry?
Because his mother had been a wafer so long.

Why did the banana go to the doctor?
Because it wasn't peeling very well.

What should a prize fighter drink?
Punch.

What do you get when you cross a hairy monster and a dozen eggs?
A very hairy omelette.

What's white, fluffy and lives in the jungle?
A meringue-utan.

What do you get if you feed a chicken whisky?
Scotch eggs.

What is small, round and giggles a lot?
A tickled onion.

What's the hardest thing in the world to do?
Milk arrowroot biscuits.

What is wrapped in gladwrap and lives in a bell tower?
The lunch pack of Notre Dame.

What looks like half a loaf of bread?
The other half.

What type of bread is the best for an actor?
A large roll.

What do you call a mushroom who makes you laugh all day?
A fun-gi to be with.

Why is watermelon filled with water?
Because it's planted in the spring.

Why did the banana go out with the prune?
Because it couldn't find a date.

What's a monster's favourite soup?
Scream of tomato.

What's the best time to eat lunch?
After breakfast and before tea.

What kind of flower can you eat?
Forget-me-nuts.

What's the difference between a soldier and a fireman?
You can't dip a fireman in your boiled egg.

What's the difference between a banana and a tiger?
It takes ages to peel a tiger.

What do you call a thief who only steals meat?
A hamburglar.

What did one melon say to the other melon on St Valentine's day?
'Honeydew, I do love you!'

What do cavemen eat for lunch?
Club sandwiches.

What nut is like a sneeze?
A cashew.

What is the strongest vegetable?
A muscle sprout.

What do space aliens eat for breakfast?
Flying sausages.

What do astronauts put in their sandwiches?
Launch meat.

What did one kitchen knife say to the other kitchen knife?
'You're looking sharp today.'

What vegetable can draw water from a well?
A pump-kin.

What tastes hot but always has ice in it?
Spice.

What is bad tempered and goes with custard?
Apple grumble.

What makes the Tower of Pisa lean?
It doesn't eat.

What do you call a robbery in Beijing?
A Chinese takeaway.

Why don't bananas use sunscreen?
So they can peel more easily.

What do ghosts eat with meat?
Grave-y.

What makes suits and eats spinach?
Popeye the Tailorman.

What did the astronaut see in his frying pan?
An unidentified frying object.

What do you get when a monster steps on a house?
Mushed rooms.

What do you get from an educated oyster?
Pearls of wisdom.

Why did the lettuce close its eyes?
Because it didn't want to see the salad dressing.

What letter of the alphabet makes pies sneaky?
'S'. Because it turns pies into spies.

What would you get if you crossed a book of nursery rhymes with an orange?
Tales of Mother Juice.

What do you call a carrot who talked back to the farmer?
A fresh vegetable.

'There is no chicken in this chicken pie.'
'Well do you expect to find dogs in dog biscuits?'

'And how did you find your steak?'
'It wasn't hard, it was just between the potato and the peas.'

'Waiter, waiter, I'm in a hurry, will my pizza be long?'
'No, it will be round.'

'Waiter, waiter, there's a spider in my soup, get me the manager!'
'He won't come, he's scared of them too.'

'Waiter, waiter, this soup tastes funny!'
'Then why aren't you laughing?'

'Waiter, waiter, do you serve crabs in this restaurant?'
'We serve anyone, please take a seat.'

'Waiter, waiter, this apple pie is squashed!'
'You told me to step on it sir because you were in a hurry.'

'Waiter, waiter, how long will my sausages be?'
'Oh, about four inches sir.'

'Waiter, waiter, do you have frog's legs?'
'No, sir, I've always walked like this.'

'Waiter, waiter, there's a button on my plate!'
'I'm sorry sir, it must have fallen off the jacket potato.'

'Waiter, waiter, there's a button in my soup!'
'It must have come off while the salad was dressing.'

'Waiter, waiter, there's a dead fly in my soup!'
'Yes sir, the hot water killed it.'

'Waiter, waiter, what's this?'
'It's called a tomato surprise.'
'I can't see any tomatoes.'
'Yes, that's the surprise.'

'Waiter, waiter, this coffee tastes of mud!'
'That's right, it was only ground this morning.'

'Waiter, waiter, this soup is full of toadstools!'
'I know sir, there wasn't mushroom for anything else.'

'Waiter, waiter, I need something to eat and make it snappy!'
'How about a crocodile sandwich?'

'Waiter, waiter, what is wrong with this fish?'
'Long time, no sea, sir.'

'Waiter, waiter, there are holes in my cheese!'
'Just eat the cheese and leave the holes.'

'Waiter, waiter, there's a small slug on my plate!'
'Wait a minute, I'll try and get you a bigger one.'

'Waiter, waiter, you've got your finger on my steak.'
'Well, I didn't want it to drop on the floor again.'

'Waiter, waiter, there's a twig in my soup.'
'Yes, we have branches everywhere.'

'Waiter, waiter, this egg is bad.'
'Don't blame me, I only laid the table.'

What is the hottest letter in the alphabet?
'B'. Because it makes oil, boil.

What did the egg say to the dinosaur?
'You're egg-stinct.'

'Go over and trip that waiter, and we'll see some flying saucers.'

What turns without moving?
Milk, it can turn sour.

What goes up in the air white and comes down yellow and white?
An egg.

What animal hides in a grape?
An ape.

What's a hedgehog's favourite food?
Prickled onions.

Why did the orange stop rolling down a hill?
Because it ran out of juice.

What letter of the alphabet can make a plum fatter?
'P'. Because it makes plum, plump.

'Eat your cabbage up Johnny, it will put colour in your cheeks!'
'But I don't want green cheeks Mum.'

What do you call a biscuit that's good at school?
A smart cookie.

How do oceans cook?
In micro waves.

What do you call a rich fish?
A goldfish.

Why is this bread full of holes?
Because it's wholemeal bread.

Why did the potato cry?
Because the chips were down.

What is bright orange and sounds like a parrot?
A carrot.

What vegetable is like a chicken farm?
An egg-plant.

Why did the baker stop making doughnuts?
Because he got tired of the hole business.

What did Mary have when she went out to dinner?
Every one knows Mary had a little lamb.

What do thieves eat?
Takeaway.

What is golden brown, flat, has maple syrup on it, and doesn't want to grow up.
Peter Pancake.

What do you call an angry chocolate bar?
A violent crumble.

What do you call a chocolate easter bunny that has stayed in the sun too long?
A runny bunny.

What pies can fly?
Magpies.

What's the best thing to put into a pie?
Your teeth.

What did the older egg say to the younger egg?
'Life is a great egg-sperience.'

What's an egg that does gymnastics?
An egg flip.

What do you call a silly egg?
An egg-nog.

What do you call an egg that knows everything?
An eggs-pert.

What made the biscuit box?
It saw the fruit punch.

What starts out as batter and ends up flattened?
A pancake.

What did one egg say to another?
'You're cracked.'

What did the horse say when he had nothing else left to eat in the paddock but thistle?
'Thistle have to do!'

Why did the cucumber need a lawyer?
Because it was in a pickle.

Why did the strawberry need a lawyer?
Because it was in a jam.

What sweet does Jaws like best?
Shark-o-late.

What happened to the very bad egg?
It was egg-secuted.

What did the egg say to the blender?
'I know when I'm beaten.'

Which birds are on every person's meal?
Swallows.

What do you get if you cross a cat with a lemon?
A sour puss.

What do you call a pig in a restaurant?
A pig out.

What do you call a Grandma banana?
Nana.

A piece of bacon and a sausage are in the frying pan being cooked. The sausage says: 'It's hot in here isn't it?'

And the bacon replied: 'Wow! A talking sausage.'

Why can any hamburger run a mile under four minutes?
Because it is fast food.

Why did the orange cross the road?
Because he wanted to show his girlfriend how to play squash.

How do you make Holy water?
You burn the Hell out of it.

What did the apple tree say to the farmer?
Stop picking on me.

What's the most dangerous vegetable on a ship?
A leek.

What tables are cooked and eaten?
Vegetables.

What can you serve but not eat?
A tennis ball.

Why did the banana stop in the middle of the road?
Because he wanted to be a banana split.

What did the cannibal have for breakfast?
Baked Beings.

What's a cannibal's favourite game?
Swallow the leader.

Did you hear about the restaurant on the moon?
Great food but no atmosphere.

What did the cannibal say when he found the hunter asleep?
'Ah, breakfast in bed.'

Why are cooks so mean?
Because they beat the eggs and whip the cream.

What did one plate say to the other plate?
'Lunch is on me.'

Have you heard the joke about the butter?
No, better not tell you, you might spread it.

'Johnny, this salad tastes awful, did you wash the lettuce like I asked you?'
'Yes Mum, and I used soap too.'

What cup can't you drink from?
A hiccup.

If a radish and a cabbage ran a race who would win?
The cabbage because it's a-head.

Why do bakers bake for a living?
Because they need the dough.

Why didn't the hot dog star in the movies?
Because the rolls weren't good enough.

How do monkeys cook their toast?
Under a gorilla.

What do you do if you find yourself stuck in a lolly shop with a bomb?
Grab a Life Saver.

Why is a cookbook exciting?
It has many stirring events.

Why did the girl throw the butter out the window?
Because she wanted to see the butterfly.

How do you make gold soup?
Add fourteen karats.

Have you heard the joke about the biscuit?
Better not tell you, it's too crumby.

What can a cook make with the letter 'Y'?
A cooky.

Did you hear about the big fight at the lolly shop last night?
Two suckers got licked.

What did Johnny's mother say when she saw him eat twenty pancakes for breakfast?
'Oh, how waffle!'

What do you get if you feed a baby too much cantaloupe?
A melon-colic baby.

Where do lollies come from?
Sweetzerland.

What is the egg capital of the world?
New Yolk City.

Why did the watermelon have a formal wedding?
Cant-elope.

Why is milk the fastest thing on earth?
Because it's pasteurised before you know it.

Heffalumps

‘What do you call a group of elephants?’
‘A herd of elephants.’
‘Of course I’ve heard of elephants!’

What do you do if an elephant sits in front of you at the movies?
Miss most of the movie.

How do you make an elephant fly?
Push him off the top of a highrise building.

Where can you buy elephants?
At Jumbo sales.

What do you call an elephant that never washes?
A smellyphant.

What did the grape say when the elephant trod on it?
Nothing, it just let out a little wine.

What do you get if you cross an elephant with a biscuit?
Crumbs.

What do you give a sick elephant?
A very big paper bag.

Why aren't there many elephants at university?
Because so few finish high school.

What's the difference between an Indian and an African elephant?
Six thousand kilometres.

Why do elephants live in the jungle?
Because they don't fit in houses.

What do elephants play in the car?
Squash.

What do you get if an elephant sits on your best friend?
A flat mate.

What do you call an elephant in a telephone booth?
Stuck.

What happened to the elephant who drank too much beer?
He got trunk.

Why did the elephant go backwards into the telephone box?
He wanted to reverse the charges.

Why did the elephant tie a knot in his trunk?
So he wouldn't forget his hankie.

What is big, red and has a trunk?
A sunburnt elephant.

What do you get if you cross an elephant with a loaf of bread?
A sandwich you'll never forget.

What's the same size and shape as an elephant but weighs nothing?
An elephant's shadow.

What's the difference between an elephant and a grape?
A grape is purple.

When do elephants have sixteen feet?
When there are four of them.

Why did the runaway elephant wear green striped pyjamas?
So he wouldn't be spotted.

What do you call a hitchhiking elephant?
A two-tonne pick up truck.

Why are elephant rides cheaper than pony rides?
Because elephants work for peanuts.

How do you get elephants upstairs?
In an ele-vator.

What has four legs, eight feet and three tails?
An elephant with spare parts.

Why are elephants wrinkled all over?
Because they're too big to put on the ironing board.

How do you get an elephant out of a small car?
The same way you got it in.

How do you get five elephants into a small car?
Two in the front, one in the back and one in the glove compartment.

How do you fit five rhinoceroses in a car?
Chuck the elephants out.

What is grey, has large wings, a long nose and gives money to elephants?
The Tusk Fairy.

What is beautiful, grey and wears glass slippers?
A Cinderelephant.

Why didn't the elephant cross the road?
Because he saw the zebra crossing.

How do elephants talk to one another?
On the elephone.

What kind of elephant flies a jet?
A jumbo.

What do you get when you cross an elephant with a kangaroo?
Great big holes all over Australia.

How do you know if there is an elephant under the bed?
Your nose is touching the ceiling.

Why do elephants paint the soles of their feet yellow?
So they can hide upside down in bowls of custard.

'Do you ever find elephants in your custard?'
'No.'
'So it must work.'

Why weren't the elephants allowed on the beach?
Because they couldn't keep their trunks up.

What time is it when an elephant sits on your fence?
Time to get a new fence.

Why have elephants got trunks?
Because they can't afford suitcases.

How can you find an elephant in your bed?
Because it'll have a big 'E' on it's pyjamas.

Why did the elephant paint her nails red?
So she could hide in the strawberry patch.

What's the difference between an elephant and a flea?
An elephant can have fleas, but a flea can't have elephants.

Why did the elephant wear blue pyjamas to bed?
Because the yellow ones were dirty.

Knock

Knock

Knock knock.
Who's there?
Who.
Who, who?
What are you an owl?

Knock knock.
Who's there?
Cows go.
Cows go who?
Cows don't go who, they go moo.

Knock knock.
Who's there?
Far out.
Far out who?
Far out man.

Knock knock.
Who's there?
Sawyer.
Sawyer who?
Sawyer lights on, so I thought I'd drop by.

Knock knock.
Who's there?
Freeze.
Freeze who?
Freeze a jolly good fellow.

Knock knock.
Who's there?
The Sultan.
The Sultan who?
The sultan pepper.

Knock knock.
Who's there?
Gotta.
Gotta who?
Gotta go to the toilet.

Knock knock.
Who's there?
Robin.
Robin who?
Robin you, so hand over your money.

Knock knock.
Who's there?
Roach.
Roach who?
Roach you a letter, did you get it?

Knock knock.
Who's there?
Olive.
Olive who?
Olive here. Who are you?

Knock knock.
Who's there?
Snow.
Snow who?
Snow good asking me.

Knock knock.
Who's there?
Major.
Major who?
Major answer a knock knock joke.

Knock knock.
Who's there?
Dwayne.
Dwayne who?
Dwayne the bathtub, I'm drowning!

Knock knock.
Who's there?
Isabel.
Isabel who?
Isabel necessary on a bicycle?

Knock knock.
Whose there?
Yah.
Yah who?
Ride on cowboy!

Knock knock.
Who's there?
Tank.
Tank who?
My pleasure.

Knock knock.
Who's there?
Turnip.
Turnip who?
Turnip for school tomorrow or you're expelled.

Knock knock.
Who's there?
Oscar.
Oscar who?
Oscar a silly question, get a silly answer.

Knock knock.
Who's there?
Ivor.
Ivor who?
Ivor you let me in or I'll climb through the window.

Knock knock.
Who's there?
Mandy.
Mandy who?
Mandy boats are sinking.

Knock knock.
Who's there?
Scott.
Scott who?
Scott nothing to do with you.

Knock knock.
Who's there?
Wood.
Wood who?
Wood you believe I've forgotten.

Knock knock.
Who's there?
Upton.
Upton who?
Upton no good, as usual.

Knock knock.
Who's there?
Granny.
Granny who?
Knock knock.
Who's there?
Granny.
Granny who?
Knock knock.
Who's there?
Granny.
Granny who?
Knock knock.
Who's there?
Aunt.
Aunt who?
Aunt you glad Granny's gone!

Knock knock.
Who's there?
Nanna.
Nanna who?
Nanna your business.

Knock knock.
Who's there?
Lion.
Lion who?
Lying won't get you anywhere.

Knock knock.
Who's there?
Las.
Las who?
That's what a cowboy uses.

Knock knock.
Who's there?
Bear.
Bear who?
Bear bum.

Knock knock.
Who's there?
Herman.
Herman who?
Herman eggs.

Knock knock.
Who's there?
Let her in.
Let her in who?
Better let her in or she'll knock your house down.

Knock knock.
Who's there,
Woo.
Woo who?
Woo do you think?

Knock knock.
Who's there?
Fang.
Fang who?
Fang you very much.

Knock knock.
Who's there?
Lettuce.
Lettuce who?
Lettuce in. It's cold out here.

Knock knock.
Who's there?
The boy who can't reach the door bell.

Knock knock.
Who's there?
Betty.
Betty who?
Betty late than never.

Knock knock.
Who's there?
Egg.
Egg who?
Eggslent.

Knock knock.
Who's there?
Nick.
Nick who?
Nick off.

Knock knock.
Who's there?
Luke?
Luke who?
Luke through the keyhole and you'll see.

Knock knock.
Who's there?
Will.
Will who?
Will you sit down and keep quiet please.

Knock knock.
Who's there,
Funny.
Funny who?
Funny the way you keep saying, 'Who's there?' every time I knock.

Knock knock.
Who's there?
Boo.
Boo who?
What are you crying for?

Knock knock.
Who's there?
Amos.
Amos who?
A-mos-quito.

Knock knock.
Who's there?
Mary.
Mary who?
Mary Christmas.

Knock knock.
Who's there?
Evan.
Evan who?
Evan's above.

Knock knock,
Who's there?
Adelaide.
Adelaide who?
Adelaide an egg.

Knock knock.
Who's there?
Canoe.
Canoe who?
Canoe please get off my foot.

Knock knock.
Who's there?
Barbie.
Barbie who?
Barbie Q.

Knock knock.
Who's there?
Caribbean.
Caribbean who?
You don't Caribbean that I'm standing out here in a storm.

Knock knock.
Who's there?
Carrie.
Carrie who?
Carrie me inside, I'm exhausted.

Knock knock.
Who's there?
Celia.
Celia who?
Celia later alligator.

Knock knock.
Who's there?
Dutch.
Dutch who?
Dutch me and I'll scream.

Knock knock.
Who's there?
Eiffel.
Eiffel who?
Eiffel down and hurt my foot.

Knock knock.
Who's there?
Harley.
Harley who?
Harley ever see you anymore.

Knock knock.
Who's there?
Hertz.
Hertz who?
Hertz me more than it hurts you.

Knock knock.
Who's there?
Justin.
Justin who?
Justin time for dinner.

Knock knock.
Who's there?
Kenya.
Kenya who?
Kenya keep it quiet down there?

Knock knock.
Who's there?
Nobel.
Nobel who?
Nobel, so I knocked.

Knock knock.
Who's there?
Rover.
Rover who?
It's all rover for you.

Knock knock.
Who's there?
Liz.
Liz who?
Lizen only once because I'm not going to repeat myself.

Knock knock.
Who's there?
Sancho.
Sancho who?
Sancho a letter, but you never answered.

Knock knock,
Who's there?
Satin.
Satin who?
Who satin my chair?

Knock knock.
Who's there?
Minnie.
Minnie who?
Minnie people want to know.

Knock knock.
Who's there?
Sue.
Sue who?
Sue-prise, it's me.

Knock knock.
Who's there?
Troy.
Troy who?
Troy if I may, I can't reach the bell.

Knock knock.
Who's there?
Dismay.
Dismay who?
Dismay be the last knock knock joke you ever hear!

Medical Matters

'The doctor told me to take these pills for the rest of my life.'
'So what's the problem?'
'He only gave me eight pills.'

What happened when the plastic surgeon sat too close to the fire?
He melted.

'The doctor has given me two weeks to live.'
'What did you say?'
'I said I'd take the first two weeks in January.'

'Doctor, doctor, I'm having trouble breathing.'
'Don't worry, I'll put a stop to that.'

'Doctor, doctor, my son swallowed a bullet.'
'Don't point him at anyone.'

'Doctor, doctor, my husband thinks he's a clock.'
'Are you sure you haven't been winding him up?'

'Doctor, doctor, my hair keeps falling out, can you give me something to keep it in?'
'Sure, what about this clean jar?'

'Doctor, doctor, come quickly! My boy has just swallowed a pen!'
'How are you managing?'
'I'm using a pencil.'

'Doctor, doctor, I've got beans growing out of my ears.'
'How did that happen?'
'I have no idea, I planted leeks.'

'Doctor, doctor, everyone hates me.'
'Don't be stupid, everyone hasn't met you yet.'

'Doctor, doctor, I've got jelly in one ear and custard in the other.'
'Don't worry, you're just a trifle deaf.'

'Doctor, doctor, Johnny's become a kleptomaniac!'
'Has he taken anything for it?'

'Doctor, doctor, I think I'm a billiard ball!'
'Go to the back of the queue.'

'Doctor, doctor, I'm suffering from hallucinations.'
'I'm sure you're only imagining it!'

'Doctor, doctor, can you give me anything for wind?'
'Sure, here's a kite.'

'Doctor, doctor, how can I stop smoking?'
'Stop setting fire to yourself.'

'Doctor, doctor, I keep thinking I'm a fruitcake!'
'What's got into you?'
'Flour, raisins, sultanas and cherries!'

'Doctor, doctor, I think I'm a goat!'
'How long have you thought this?'
'Since I was a kid.'

'Doctor, doctor, I feel like a bell.'
'Well take these, and if they don't work give me a ring.'

'Doctor, doctor, I can't sleep at night.'
'Well lie on the edge of the bed and you'll soon drop off.'

'Doctor, doctor, I've swallowed my camera!'
'Lets hope nothing develops.'

'Doctor, doctor, everyone keeps ignoring me!'
'Next please.'

'Doctor, doctor, I keep seeing green monsters with orange spots.'
'Have you seen a psychiatrist?'
'No, just green monsters with orange spots.'

'Doctor, doctor, I think I'm turning into a dustbin!'
'Don't talk such rubbish.'

'Doctor, doctor, I feel like an apple.'
'Don't worry, I don't bite.'

'Doctor, doctor, I feel like a pack of cards.'
'Wait here, I'll deal with you in a minute.'

'Doctor, doctor, I feel like a curtain.'
'For heaven's sake pull yourself together.'

'Doctor, doctor, I feel like a dog!'
'Sit!'

'Doctor, doctor, I keep hearing ringing in my ears.'
'Well, where did you expect to hear it?'

'Doctor, doctor, there's an invisible man in the waiting room!'
'Well tell him I can't see him!'

'Doctor, doctor, you've got to help me, I think I'm a bridge!'
'What's come over you?'
'So far two cars, a truck and a motorbike.'

'Doctor, doctor, I keep thinking no one can hear me.'
'What seems to be the trouble?'

'Doctor, doctor, my hands won't stop shaking.'
'Do you drink a lot?'
'No. I spill most of it.'

'Doctor, doctor, I get this really bad stabbing pain in the eye whenever I drink a cup of coffee.'
'Try taking the spoon out.'

'Doctor, doctor, I think I'm getting smaller!'
'You'll just have to be a little patient.'

'Doctor, doctor, you've got to help me. I just swallowed my harmonica!'
'Lucky you weren't playing the piano.'

What did the first tonsil say to the second tonsil?
'Better get dressed up tonight, we're going out.'

Did you hear the one about the boy who loved his operation?
The doctor had him in stitches.

I wanted to be a doctor but I didn't have the patients.

'Doctor, tell me, can a child of twelve take out his appendix?'
'Certainly not Madam.'
'Did you hear that Johnny? Now put them back!'

'I think you need glasses.'
'But I already wear glasses.'
'In that case I need some too.'

'You need glasses Miss.'
'How can you tell? You haven't examined me yet.'
'Well, I knew as soon as you walked through that window.'

A doctor had to inform a patient he had only a few minutes to live.
'Doctor, can't you do something?'
'Well, I could boil you an egg.'

A young boy arrives at the doctor's crying his heart out.

'Doctor, doctor, no matter where I touch myself it hurts.'

'Show me where you mean,' said the doctor.

So the boy touched himself on the nose and cried because it hurt. He touched himself on his chest and cried because it hurt. He touched himself on his tummy and cried because it hurt. And then he touched himself in another twelve places and every time it really, really hurt.

'What's wrong with me doctor?' he asked. 'How come I hurt all over?'

'Because,' said the doctor, 'you've got a broken finger.'

'Are you hurt?'

'Yeah, better call me a doctor.'

'OK, you're a doctor.'

Multiculturalism

Why did the Irishman drown?
Because he was practising his river dance.

What do you need to blind an Asian?
A flash.

'What have you got in your pocket?' one Irishman asks another.

'I'll give you a clue. It begins with 'N'.'

'A napple,' said the first Irishman.

'No, I told you it begins with 'N'.'

'A norange!'

'No, I'm telling you for the last time, it begins with 'N'.'

'Would it be a nonion?'

'You got it at last.'

'What's that on your shoulder, Paddy?'
'A birthmark.'
'How long have you had it?'

What do you call an aborigine in a Ferrari?
A jaffa.

What do you get if you cross a Japanese girl with a fish?
Sushi.

What has two legs, two arms and looks just like an Indian?
A photo of an Indian.

An American, a New Zealander and an Australian are sentenced to death. The American is bought out first. The firing squad takes aim. Suddenly the American yells: 'Avalanche!' In the confusion he escapes.

The New Zealander is impressed and decides to try something similar. As the squad takes aim he yells: 'Flood!' And in the confusion, he too makes his escape.

The Australian has observed this closely. He decides to follow their example. So just as the firing squad takes aim, he yells: 'Fire!'

A Chinaman, an Englishman, an American and an Australian are boasting about which country is the best. The Chinaman says: 'We've got the best country because we've got the great wall of China.'

The others say: 'What's so great about that?'

The Englishman says: 'We've got the best country because we've got the Botanical Gardens.'

The others say: 'What's so great about that?'

The American says: 'We've got the best country because we've got the stars and stripes.'

The others say: 'What's so great about that?'

Finally the Australian speaks: ‘Look we’ve got the best country because we’ve got the kangaroo.’

‘What’s so great about that?’ the others cry.

‘Well, it can jump over the Great Wall of China, skip through the Botanical Gardens, and go to sleep on the flag.’

Why did the Irishman wear pearls around his neck?
So he’d know where to stop shaving.

Why was the Egyptian boy confused?
Because his Daddy was a Mummy.

How do you confuse an Irishman?
Give him a jaffa and tell him to eat the chocolate first.

A man walked up to a sheep farmer and said: 'If I can tell you exactly how many sheep you have down there, can I keep one?'

The farmer glanced at the vast array of sheep, and sniggered: 'Yep.'

The man looked over the sheep carefully and said: 'You have 2,471 sheep.'

The farmer was amazed: 'How did you do that?'

'I'd rather not say, can I have my sheep now?'

'Of course.'

The man picked up an animal and walked away.

'Wait!' called the farmer. 'If I can guess where you come from, will you give me back my animal?'

'Sure.'

The farmer waited a minute and then said: 'You're from New Zealand.'

'You're right, how'd you guess that?'

'Well, I'd rather not say, but can I have my dog back now?'

Why do Irish dogs have flat faces?
Because they chase parked cars.

How do you confuse a Pole?
Put him in a room and tell him to go to his room.

How do you confuse an Australian?
Put him in a round room and tell him to go to the corner.

What is a shark afraid of?
A Japanese tourist.

What took over Japan?
Cameras.

Why do Irish men wear two pairs of underpants?
To be sure, to be sure.

I'm an Australian born and bred,
Long in the leg and short in the head.

Naughtiness

The Queen was showing the Archbishop around her stables, when one of her prize thoroughbreds let off a huge, loud fart.

'Oh I am sorry,' said the Queen. 'How embarrassing.'

'It's perfectly all right Your Majesty, as a matter of fact, I thought it was the horse.'

Humpty Dumpty sat on the loo,
Humpty Dumpty did a big poo.

Mrs Jones took her poodle, Tits Wobble, for a walk and lost him. Finally she reported her dog missing to the police.

'Have you seen my Tits Wobble?' she asked the sergeant.

'No,' he said. 'But I'd like to.'

A man steps into an elevator, where a very dignified woman is standing in front of the buttons. He soon realises there's a bad smell in the lift so he turns to the woman and asks: 'Excuse me, but did you fart?'

'Of course I did, you don't think I smell like this all the time?'

A bear and a rabbit are doing a poo in the forest, when the bear turns to the rabbit and enquires: 'Does your poo ever stick to your fur?'

'No.'

So the bear wiped his bum with the rabbit.

'Doctor, I have a terrible problem breaking wind all the time. But fortunately they're not noisy, nor do they smell.'

The doctor made notes in his patient book,

wrote out a prescription, and handed it to the lady.

'What's this doctor, nasal drops?'

'Yes, we'll fix your nose up first and then we'll try and do something about your hearing.'

An American tourist was driving across the Nullarbor Plain, when he saw a man sitting on the side of the road. He pulled up, opened his car door and offered the man a lift. The man declined, so the tourist shut the door and kept driving. For the next 500 kilometres he noticed that the man who said no to the lift was running beside the car. Finally he stopped again. 'Hey, are you sure you don't want a lift?' he asked.

'No.'

'How come you can run so fast?'

'You would too if you had your dick stuck in the door.'

What did Beethoven get when he ate baked beans?
Classical gas.

Why do farts smell?
For the benefit of the deaf.

'What do mothballs smell like?'
'How do I know? I can't find their bottom.'

Quickly, quickly, I feel sickly.
Hasten, hasten, get the basin.
Kerplop, get the mop.

What are hundreds and thousands?
Smarties' poo.

What do you call a smelly Father Christmas?
Farter Claus.

Why did the lobster blush?
Because the sea weed.

'Hold my hand. Now, how old are you?'
'I'm ten.'
'Where do you go to the toilet?'
'I use the public toilets.'
'How do you wipe your bottom?'
'I use my hand.'

Three children are smoking behind the toilet block.

'My dad can blow smoke through his nose,' says one boy.

'That's nothing,' says another boy. 'My dad can smoke through his ears!'

'So what,' says the third boy. 'My dad can smoke through his bum. I've even seen the nicotine stains on his undies.'

Oddities & Insults

A man was driving along a country road when he saw a sign up ahead saying DIP. 'Oh no,' the driver said, 'I forgot the chips.'

People like you don't grow on trees, they swing from them.

Three friends went skydiving, landed in the ocean and were eaten by a shark. Three hours later they all arrived in heaven. There they met an angel who said they could each make a wish. All they had to do was go down a slide and say what they wanted and it would come true. The first bloke went down and said 'gold' and that's what he got, the second said 'chocolate' and that's what he landed in, the third said 'weeee . . .' and that's what he landed in.

I could say nice things about you, but I'd rather tell the truth.

If you ever need a friend, buy a dog.

There's a house with no doors, no windows, no chimney and there's a table in the room, how do you get out?

Bang your arm against the wall until it gets sore. Saw the table in half – two halves make a whole. Climb out of the hole, scream until your voice gets hoarse, then hop on the horse and ride away.

Mary had a little lamb and all the doctors fainted.

What did one elevator say to the other elevator?
'I think I'm coming down with something.'

I never forget a face but in your case I'll make an exception.

I hear you're not allowed to visit the zoo because your face scares all the animals!

What did the hat say to the necktie?
'I'll go ahead, and you hang around.'

Went to pub
feeling nifty,
hit a pole
doing fifty,
poor old soul,
Doctor's fee,
cemetery.

I'd like to hear your opinion, but isn't there enough ignorance in the world already?

I'd like to make a formal complaint about you, but I hate standing in a queue.

'Here's a thousand dollars.'
'What's this for?'
'I steal from the rich and give to the poor.'
'Wow! I'm rich.'
'All right then, stick 'em up.'

'My watch needs a new band.'
'I didn't even know it could sing.'

Escaped prisoner: I'm free, I'm free!
Little girl: So what, I'm four.

You remind me of a goat that's always butting in.

I know I'm talking like an idiot. I have to otherwise you wouldn't understand me.

Have you heard the joke about the garbage truck?
Better not tell you. It's a load of rubbish.

Today all the toilets were stolen and so far the police have nothing to go on.

Most of us live and learn, you just live.

'You've burnt both your ears, how did that happen?'

'Well, I was ironing when the phone rang.'

'But how did you burn both of them?'

'Well, as soon as I put the phone down it rang again.'

You're not really such a bad person, until people get to know you.

The next time you wash your neck, wring it.

There were three boys, Pig, Shut-up, and Manners. One day the three of them were digging for treasure when Pig and Shut-up found gold. Pig and Shut-up went to the Police Station. 'What are your names?' said the sergeant.

'Pig,' said Pig.

'I beg your pardon,' said the sergeant. 'Well, what's your friend's name?'

'Shut-up,' said Shut-up.

'Now listen you two, where are your manners?' said the policeman.

'He's running down the road with our gold!'

Beauty isn't everything, in your case it's nothing.

Your ideas are just like diamonds, very rare.

A full jumbo jet was flying over the Pacific ocean, when the pilot said: 'Ladies and Gentlemen, don't be alarmed, but our number one engine has just failed, we'll be all right but we'll be an hour late.'

A few minutes later: 'Ladies and Gentlemen our number two engine has just crashed, we'll be two hours late now.'

Five minutes later: 'I'm sorry to announce this, but engine number three has just failed, we'll still arrive, except it will be three hours late now.'

Two minutes later: 'Ladies and gentlemen, I'm sorry to announce this latest news, but engine number four has just collapsed.'

'Oh, no,' said the Irish passenger. 'I'm already late, now we're going to be up here all day!'

Look, you made a big mistake today, you got out of bed.

Watch how you sit down, you could give your brain concussion.

Your singing voice is OK if you don't like music.

You remind me of a one storey building. There's nothing upstairs.

If ignorance is bliss, you must be the happiest person alive.

I could break you in half, but who would want two of you?

It's not the ups and downs of life that bother me, it's the jerks like you.

What a shame you can't get anyone to love you the way you love yourself.

Don't complain about the tea, you'll be old and weak one day yourself.

You'd make a great football player, even your breath is offensive.

I hear your friends threw you a big dinner, what a pity they missed.

I can't believe your age, you must be older because no one gets so dumb so fast.

I've got a spare minute so tell me everything you know.

There was an old woman from Leeds,
Who swallowed a packet of seeds.
In less than an hour,
Her nose grew a flower,
And her hair was all covered in weeds.

You could improve this conversation by keeping your mouth shut.

I enjoy talking to you when my mind needs a rest.

There was a young man from Dungall,
Who went to a fancy dress ball.
He thought he would risk it,
And go as a biscuit,
But a dog ate him up in the hall.

You remind me of a jigsaw puzzle, so many of the pieces are missing.

You're obnoxious, mean, rude and ugly and they're your good points.

Little Miss Muffet,
Sat on her tuffet,
Eating her chicken and chips.
Her sister who's hateful,
Nicked half a plateful,
And strolled away licking her lips!

Got a match?
If I had a match for you I'd start a circus.

One more wrinkle and you could pass for a prune.

Your tongue is so long, when it hangs out people think it's your tie.

The only thing you ever give away is secrets.

Don't lose your head,
To gain a minute.
You need your head,
Your brains are in it.

No diet works for a fat head.

Better hide, here comes the garbage collector.

'Did you hear about the wooden car?'
'No.'
'It wooden go.'

I wish you were on TV so I could turn you off.

Wipe your nose, your brain is leaking.

'My cabin on the ship was OK, but that washing machine on the wall was hopeless.'
'That wasn't a washing machine it was a porthole.'
'No wonder I never got my clothes back.'

The only exercise you get is stretching the truth.

The more I think of you the less I think of you.

There were three tall men standing under the umbrella and none of them got wet. How could that be?
It wasn't raining.

You couldn't tell which way the lift was going even if you had two choices.

Look, where have you been all my life, and furthermore, when are you going back there?

‘Dinosaur?’
‘No.’
‘Do you think he saurus?’

Every time I pass a garbage truck I think of you.

You must have been a surprise to your parents. Were they expecting a boy or a girl?

Why did the light turn red?
Wouldn’t you turn red if you were caught changing in the middle of the street?

How many country and western singers does it take to change a light globe?
Three. One to change the globe and two to sing about the old one.

When I watch you eat, I know where they got the idea for *Jaws*.

The nearest you'll ever get to a brainstorm is a light drizzle.

People

Who made the first plane that couldn't fly?
The Wrong Brothers.

Why did Santa Claus grow a vegetable garden?
So he could go hoe, hoe, hoe.

'Hey farmer, what do you do with all the fruit around here?'
'Well, we eat what we can, and what we can't we can.'

If a steamroller ran over Batman and Robin, what would you have?
Flatman and Ribbon.

How do you confuse a gardener?
Take him to a room full of shovels and tell him to take his pick.

What do you call a flying policeman?
A heli-copper.

What does a farmer give his wife on St Valentine's day?
Hogs and kisses.

What is Beethoven doing in his grave?
Decomposing.

What game do spacemen play?
Astronauts and crosses.

Why does a cowboy ride a horse?
Because they're too heavy to carry.

Where did Captain Cook stand when he first landed in Australia?
On his feet.

What is Tarzan's favourite Christmas song?
'Jungle Bells'.

What would you call Superman if he lost all his powers?
Man.

What did the cowboy say to the pencil?
'Draw partner.'

Where do astronauts go for fun?
Lunar park.

What do astronauts make their pyjamas out of?
Saturn.

What's an astronaut's favourite food?
A Mars Bar.

What walks through the forest with sixteen legs?
Snow White and the Seven Dwarves.

Why are hairdressers never late for work?
Because they take short cuts.

What did Tarzan say when he saw elephants coming over the hill with sunglasses on?
Nothing, he didn't recognise them.

Where does Tarzan get his clothes from?
The jungle sale.

Tarzan flying through the air,
Tarzan lost his underwear,
Tarzan said, 'me no care,
Jane make me another pair.'

Boy flying through the air,
Boy lost his underwear,
Boy said, 'me no care,
Jane make me another pair.'

Jane flying though the air,
Jane lost her underwear,
Jane said, 'me no care,
Tarzan like me better bare.'

When is a farmer like a mystery writer?
When he's digging up a plot.

'Johnny,' said the dentist, 'you've got the biggest cavity I've ever seen. The biggest cavity I've ever seen.'

'Well, you don't have to repeat it.'

'I didn't Johnny, that was an echo.'

What's the difference between a well-dressed man and a dog?
The man wears a suit and the dog just pants.

What was Batman doing up tree?
Looking for Robin's nest.

How does Sherlock Holmes sneeze?
A-clue, a-clue.

What is green and plays the guitar?
Elvis Parsley.

What goes black, white, black, white
THUMP!
A nun rolling down the stairs.

What goes black, white, black, white,
ha ha ha.
The nun that pushed her.

What did the blonde call her pet zebra?
Spot.

How many jugglers does it take to change a light globe?
One, but it takes at least three light globes.

How many magicians does it take to change a light globe?
It depends on what you want to change it into.

What did Adam say on the day before Christmas?
'It's Christmas, Eve.'

What do you get if you cross Santa with a tiger?
Santa Claws.

Riddles

Why did the dog keep chewing the furniture?
Because it has a suite tooth.

What causes the death of a lot of people?
Coffin.

What word is always spelt incorrectly?
Incorrectly.

What do you call small rivers that flow into the Nile?
Juveniles.

What do you call a boomerang that won't come back?
A stick.

Where did they sign the Constitution?
At the bottom.

Can a shoe box?
No, but a tin can.

What's big, hairy and flies to New York faster than the speed of sound?
King Kongcorde.

Why does a steak taste better in space?
Because it's meteor.

What's black and white and red all over?
A newspaper.

Can February March?
No, but April can.

What is a specimen?
An Italian astronaut.

What are pilots' favourite biscuits?
Plain biscuits.

What is red and white?
Pink.

What colour is a shout?
Yell-Oh.

Why does a cat purr?
For a purr-pose.

Where do fleas go in winter?
Search me!

How do you make seven an even number?
Take the 'S' off.

What do you always see running along the streets in town?
Pavements.

What's an astronaut's favourite game?
Moonopoly.

What did one computer say to the programmer at lunchtime?
'Can I have a byte?'

What musical instrument is found in the bathroom?
A tuba toothpaste.

What's long, skinny and beats a drum?
Yankee Noodle.

What pop group gets your clothes cleaner?
The Bleach Boys.

What elf was a famous rock star?
Elf S. Presley.

What kind of music do you get when you drop a rock into a puddle?
Plunk rock.

What do you give a sick car?
A fuel injection.

What would happen if everyone had a pink car?
We'd have a pink car-nation.

What type of pants do scientists wear?
Genes.

What kind of phones do musicians use?
Saxophones.

What did the boulder wear to the party?
A F-rock.

What does your Nanna play records on?
The gran-ma phone.

What's the best way to cross a moat?
In a moater boat.

What happens when you kiss a clock?
Your lips tick.

What planet has the biggest bottom?
Sat on.

What did one petrol tanker say to the other petrol tanker?
'What do you take me for, a fuel?'

What lolly is always late?
Choc-o-late.

What do you get when you throw a piano down a mine shaft?
A flat miner.

How do angels answer the phone?
'Halo.'

Where do you study dancing?
At the disco-tech.

What sort of jockey do you see at the disco?
A disc jockey.

What is rude and only comes at Christmas?
Rude-off.

When do people with the flu get exercise?
When their noses run.

What do you get when you cross a computer programmer with an athlete?
A floppy diskus thrower.

What starts with 'P' ends in 'E' and has lots of letters in between?
A Post Office.

What do you call a fairy who never takes a bath?
Stinkerbell.

Which clown has the biggest shoes?
The one with the biggest shoes.

What kind of dress do you have that you never wear?
Your address.

What's faster, heat or cold?
Heat, you can catch a cold.

Why does the ocean roar?
You would too if you had crabs in your head.

What did the teddy bear say when he was offered dessert?
'No thank you I'm stuffed.'

What did the dirt say when it began to rain?
'If this keeps up, my name will be mud.'

How did the piano get out of jail?
With its keys.

What goes over and through eyes?
Your shoe laces.

What falls in the winter and never gets hurt?
Snow.

What did the paper clip say to the magnet?
'I find you attractive.'

What do you call a scared tyrannosaurus?
A nervous rex.

Why are flowers so lazy?
Because they always stay in bed.

Why do bagpipe players walk while they play?
To get away from the noise.

Why couldn't the bicycle stand up?
Because it was tyred.

Why did the bankrobber have a bath?
So he could make a clean getaway.

What kind of people live at the sea?
Buoys and gulls.

How do you get a baby astronaut to sleep?
You rock-et.

How do you start a teddy bear race?
Ready, teddy, go.

What has a bottom at the top?
A leg.

What kind of bow is impossible to tie?
A rainbow.

How do mountains hear?
With their mountain-ears.

What gets wetter as it dries?
A towel.

What's an Ig?
An eskimo's house without a toilet.

Why did the cleaning lady stop work?
Because she worked out that grime doesn't pay.

Why did the hand cross the road?
Because it wanted to go to the second hand shop.

What is always coming, but never arrives?
Tomorrow.

Why is playschool dangerous?
Because there's a bear in there.

What did the bell say when it fell into the water?
'I'm wringing wet.'

What are bugs on the moon called?
Luna-tics.

Why did the chewing gum cross the road?
Because it was stuck to the chicken's foot.

What sport do judges play?
Tennis, because it's played in court.

Who gets the sack every time he goes to work?
The postman.

Why do people laugh up their sleeves?
Because there are funny bones there.

What do fairys use to clean their teeth?
Fairy floss.

What do you put in a box to make it lighter?
A hole.

Why are tall people cleaner than short people?
Because they're in the shower longer.

What trees do hands grow on?
Palm trees.

What star can't shine at night?
The sun.

How do you get rid of unwanted varnish?
Take away the 'R' and it will vanish.

What sort of nails do you find in shoes?
Toenails.

Why did the sailor grab a bar of soap when his ship was sinking?
He was hoping he'd be washed ashore.

Where do astronauts leave their spaceships?
At parking meteors.

What kind of clothes did people wear during the Great Fire of London?
Blazers.

How do you make a bandstand?
Hide all the chairs.

What kind of ears does an engine have?
Engin-ears.

What did the piece of wood say to the electric drill?
You bore me.

Why is the sky so high?
So birds won't bump their heads.

What would you never find in a nudist camp?
A pickpocket.

What happened to the criminal contortionist?
He turned himself in.

Why did the pilot crash into the house?
Because the landing light was on.

What does the sea say to the sand?
Not much, it mostly waves.

Why did the man jump from the Empire State Building?
Because he wanted to make a hit on Broadway.

Why couldn't the sailors play cards?
Because the captain was standing on the deck.

What did the traffic light say to the car?
'Don't look now I'm changing.'

Why did the lady put a sock on her head?
Because she grew a foot.

What goes around the corner and stays in the corner?
A postage stamp.

What room can't you ever enter?
A mushroom.

Did you hear about the man who stayed up all night trying to find out where the sun went?
It finally dawned on him.

'I'd like a return ticket to the moon please.'
'Sorry, the moon's full tonight.'

What do you do when your smoke alarm goes off?
Run after it.

Why should you never marry a tennis player?
Because love means nothing to them.

What did the policeman say to his stomach?
'You're under my vest.'

Where did the inventor of the toupee get his idea from?
Off the top of his head.

Did you hear the story about the hospital?
No.
It's sick.

What letters in the alphabet are the best looking?
'U' and 'I'.

What can you hold without touching?
Your breath.

What has wheels and flies?
A garbage truck.

Why did the baby pen cry?
Because its mother was doing a long sentence.

Where does a general keep his armies?
Up his sleevies.

What sort of lights did Noah's Ark have?
Flood lights.

What did the cloud say to the sun?
'Don't move, I've got you covered.'

The more you take away the bigger it gets. What am I?
A hole.

Why is it hard to keep a secret on a cold day?
Because you can't stop your teeth chattering.

When is water like fat?
When it's dripping.

Have you heard the joke about the three wells?
Well, well, well.

Why did the milking stool only have three legs?
Because the cow had the udder.

What do you call two robbers?
A pair of nickers.

What do you do if your toe drops off in the middle of the road?
Call a toe truck.

When you lose something, why do you always find it in the last place you look?
Because you always stop looking when you find it.

Did you hear about the boy who ran away with the circus?
The policeman made him bring it back.

What do composers write in the bath?
Soap operas.

What burns longer, candles on a boy's birthday cake, or candles on a girl's?
Neither, they both burn shorter.

Did you hear about the man who didn't clean his glasses?
He gave people dirty looks.

What cars do hot dogs like driving?
Rolls.

What goes into the water pink and comes out blue?
A swimmer on a cold day.

What did one eye say to the other?
'Something's come between us that smells.'

What do you find up a clean nose?
Fingerprints.

Why is an old car like a baby?
It never goes anywhere without a rattle.

Why was Cinderella bad at football?
Because she had a pumpkin for a coach.

What did one ear say to the other?
'Between you and me we have brains.'

What goes up and wobbles?
A jelly-copter.

What is clear, but is seen by the naked eye and can be put in a barrel?
A hole.

What kind of music do mummies like?
Rap.

What goes ha ha ha ha THUMP!
A person laughing their head off.

What lies in a pram and wobbles?
A jelly baby.

Have you heard the joke about the bed?
It hasn't been made yet.

How do you make a hankie dance?
Put a little boogie in it.

What did Mrs Cook say when Captain Cook died?
'That's the way the cookie crumbled.'

What has a hole in the middle and no beginning or end?
A doughnut.

Do you need a hammer in maths?
No, you need multi-pliers.

What is the tallest building in any city?
The library because it has the most storeys.

What did one candle say to another?
'Are you going out tonight?'

What starts with an 'E' and ends with an 'E' but only has one letter in it?
An envelope.

What's the easiest way to get on TV?
Sit on it.

Why did the candle fall in love?
It met the perfect match.

How is a song like a locked door?
You need the right key for both.

What goes up when you count down?
A rocket.

If you invited all the alphabet to tea who would be late?
The letters 'UVWXYZ' because they all come after 'T'.

What do misers do when it's cold?
They sit around a candle.

What do misers do when it's really, really cold?
They light it.

What did the baby computer say when it got hurt.
I want my da-ta.

What is a computer's first sign of old age?
Loss of memory.

Did you hear the joke about the airplane?
Never mind, it just took off.

Did you hear the one about the express train?
Never mind, you just missed it.

Did you hear the one about the water bucket that had holes in it?
Never mind, I don't want it to leak out.

Did you hear the joke about the ocean?
Never mind, it's too deep for you.

What do you give someone who has everything?
A burglar alarm.

How do you keep from getting wet in the shower?
Don't turn the water on.

What lies at the bottom of the sea and whimpers?
A nervous wreck.

What has four legs and doesn't walk?
A table.

What did the shoes say to the socks?
'You're putting me on.'

Why did Cinderella get kicked out of the football team?
Because she ran away from the ball.

Why was number six sad?
Because seven eight nine.

What starts with 'T' ends with 'T' and is full of 'T'?
A teapot.

When is a car not a car?
When it's in a driveway.

If two is company, and three a crowd, what are four and five?
Nine.

What does the sun drink out of?
Sunglasses.

Where does Thursday come before Wednesday?
In the dictionary.

Why did the car stop in the middle of the road?
Because it was wheely, wheely tired.

What has many rings but no fingers?
A telephone.

What do you do when you wear your shoes out?
You wear them home again.

What did one hair say to the other?
'It takes two to tangle.'

How much does it cost a pirate to get his ears pierced?
A buck an ear.

Why did the heart get kicked out of the band?
It skipped a beat.

What has a hundred pairs of legs but can't walk?
Fifty pairs of pants.

Why are Saturday and Sunday so strong?
Because the rest are week days.

What did one phone say to the other?
'You're too young to be engaged.'

What did the jeans say to the bra?
'I'll meet you at the clothesline, because that's where I hang out.'

What loses its head every morning but gets it back at night?
A pillow.

Who do mermaids date?
They go out with the tides.

What is a ten letter word that starts with gas?
Automobile.

What is a waste of energy?
Telling hair raising stories to a bald man.

What is the best thing to take into the desert?
A thirst aid kit.

What did the apple say to the pear?
'Why don't you act like a banana and split.'

Why didn't the skeletons go to the movies?
Because they had no guts.

What is black and white and red all over?
A nun on fire.

What did the big chimney say to the small chimney?
'You're too young to smoke.'

Why do clocks seem so shy?
Because they always have their hands in front of their faces.

What did Cinderella say when her photos didn't come back?
'One day my prints will come.'

What's the difference between Cinderella and Tony Modra?
Cinderella gets to the ball first.

What can you serve but not eat?
A tennis ball.

What did one library book say to the other?
'Can I take you out?'

What did the cuffs say to the collar?
'Sleeve us alone.'

How do you make a fisherman's net?
Just sew a lot of holes together.

How do you say I love you in Italian?
'I love you in Italian.'

Why did the man pour veggies all over the world?
He wanted peas on earth.

What goes up when the rain comes down?
An umbrella.

When is a green book not a green book?
When it's read.

Which dinosaur knows the most words?
A thesaurus.

Do babies go on safari?
Not safari as I know.

When is a door not a door?
When it's ajar.

What do you call a dinosaur in high heels?
Myfeetaresaurus.

Scary Stories

Why did the sea monster eat five ships that were carrying potatoes?
No one can eat just one potato ship.

What do you say when you cross a two-headed monster?
'Hello, hello, goodbye, goodbye.'

What kind of lolly do ghosts like the best?
Booble gum.

What do ghosts wear when it snows?
Boooooots.

What happened when the monster ate the electricity company?
He was in shock for a week.

Where do ghosts put their mail?
In the ghost office.

What happens when a banana sees a ghost?
The banana splits.

What do you call two witches who live together?
Broom mates.

Why is the Jolly Green Giant a good gardener?
Because he had two green thumbs.

What's a skeleton afraid of?
A dog. Because it likes bones.

Why doesn't anyone kiss a vampire?
Because they have bat breath.

So, what is a skeleton?
Bones with the person scraped off.

What is Dracula's motto?
The morgue the merrier.

What do sea monsters eat for tea?
Fish and ships.

What do you call a skeleton who tells jokes?
Funny bones.

What's a skeleton's favourite instrument?
A saxa-bone.

What is a devil's picket line called?
A demon-stration.

What did Johnny ghost call his Mum and Dad?
His transparents.

Why do ghosts go to parties?
To have a wail of a time.

What do ghosts do every night at one a.m.?
Take a coffin break.

What's a vampire's favourite drink?
A Bloody Mary.

What is a ghost's favourite dessert?
Boo-berry pie with I-scream.

What did the ghost buy his wife for her birthday?
A see-through nightie.

What do you think the tiniest vampire in the world gets up to at night?
Your ankles.

Who is the most important member of the ghosts' football team?
The ghoulie.

How does a vampire clean his house?
With a victim cleaner.

What do you call a swarm of ghost bees?
Zombees.

What can a vegetarian cannibal eat?
Swedes.

If you want to hunt ghosts, what is the best way to keep fit?
Exorcise yourself.

Where do vampires keep their savings?
In a blood bank.

What job did the lady ghost have on the jumbo jet?
Lady ghostess.

Why did the ghost look in the mirror?
To make sure it really wasn't there.

What do ghosts eat for lunch?
Goulash.

When does a ghost become two ghosts?
When it's beside itself.

What do you call a play that's acted by ghosts?
A phantomine.

How do you make a witch itch?
Take away the 'W'.

What do cannibals eat at parties?
Buttered host.

What do you call a friendly, good looking wizard?
A failure.

Why do witches get plenty of bargains?
Because they love to haggle.

Why do ghosts hate rain?
It dampens their spirits.

Why did the skeleton run up the tree?
Because a dog was after his bones.

What's the first thing a ghost does when it gets into a car?
It fastens the sheet belt.

What do you call a skeleton that doesn't do any work?
Lazy Bones.

How long did the ghost plan to stay in Sydney?
Not long. He was just passing through.

Why are vampires stupid?
Because they're suckers.

How do ghosts like their eggs?
Terror-fried.

What do ghosts eat?
Dread and butter pudding.

How do ghosts learn songs?
With sheet music.

Which musical instrument does a skeleton play?
A trom-bone.

Why didn't the vampire want to play cricket?
Because he didn't want to damage his bats.

Why did the little girl eat a box of bullets?
She wanted to grow bangs.

What does a monster call his parents?
Deady and Mummy.

How does a vampire cross the ocean?
In a blood vessel.

A giant green monster from Blister,
Decided to eat up his sister.
And when he was through,
He cried: 'What did I do?'
Now he's sorry he did, 'cause he missed her.

Why do wizards drink tea?
Because sorcerers need cuppas.

What do you call a wizard from outer space?
A flying sorcerer.

What kind of jewels do monsters wear?
Tombstones.

'How many times Little Johnny monster must I tell you to play with your food before you eat it?'

What's a monster's favourite sport?
Squash.

What's a monster's favourite game at night?
Swallow my leader.

Why did Frankenstein have indigestion?
He bolted his food.

What do you call a city full of monsters?
A monstro-sity.

What medicine do ghosts take when they get the flu?
Coffin drops.

Why aren't vampires welcome in blood banks?
Because they only make withdrawals.

'Johnny Monster, I told you not to speak when you've got someone in your mouth.'

What do good monsters try to remember to say?
Fangs very much.

Did you hear about the bald-headed man who met a man-eating monster?
He had a hair raising experience.

Why did the vampire ask the ghost to join their hockey team?
Because they needed some team spirit.

What do you call ghost children?
Boys and ghouls.

What did the monster say when introduced?
'Pleased to eat you.'

Why did the monster fall in love with a piano?
Because it had such beautiful straight teeth.

A monster adrift on a raft,
Had never been on such a craft.
He fashioned a sail,
With his body and tail,
While the fishes around him just laughed.

What do you call a dumb skeleton?
A numbskull.

What do you call a skeleton who always tells lies?
A boney phoney.

Why did the two ghosts go to the scary movie?
Because they both loved each shudder.

What kind of dog does a ghost have?
A boo-dle.

What happened to the author who died?
He became a ghost writer.

What do ghosts eat for breakfast?
Shrouded wheat.

How does a ghost count?
One, *boo*, three, four, five, six, seven, *hate*, nine, *frighten*.

Why did the girl marry the ghost?
She didn't know what possessed her.

'I called the Vampire gang and told them the card game is on tonight at eight at the cemetery.'
'Why there?'
'Well, if someone doesn't turn up we'll be able to dig up another player.'

What weighs a thousand kilograms but is all bone?
A skele-tonne.

How do you make a skeleton laugh?
Tickle its funny bone.

What do you call a wicked old woman who lives on the beach?
A sandwich.

Why are skeletons usually so calm?
Because nothing gets under their bones.

What did the baby witch want for her birthday?
A haunted doll's house.

What did the ghost teacher say to the ghost student?
'You've lost your spirit.'

What motto do ghosts hate?
'Never say die.'

How many hamburgers do you give to a huge, mean monster?
As many as it wants.

What do women ghosts who have been in hospital love to do?
Talk about their apparitions.

Why are ghosts always drunk?
Because they're too fond of spirits.

What do you call a sorceress without a broomstick?
A witch hiker.

What did the ghost say to the other ghost?
'Do you believe in people?'

What's big and ugly with red spots all over it?
A monster with measles.

How do you tell a good monster from a bad one?
If you meet a good monster, you'll be able to talk about it later.

Where would you find a one-handed monster?
In a second hand store.

What do you do with a green monster?
Put it in the sun until it ripens.

Why are vampires like stars?
Because they only come out at night.

How do you greet a three-legged monster?
'Hello, hello, hello.'

What did the vampire catch after staying up all night?
A bat cold.

What do witches have for dinner?
Spooketti.

What do ghosts call their navy?
The ghost guard.

Why was the ghost arrested?
Because he was haunting without a licence.

How do you know when a skeleton is upset?
He gets rattled.

Why did the mother ghost take her child to the doctor?
Because it had booping cough.

Why did the ghost want to go to Africa?
Because he wanted to be a big game haunter.

What do you flatten a ghost with?
A spirit level.

What do you get if you cross a ghost with a boy scout?
A boy that scares old ladies across the street.

Why don't monsters cross the road?
Because they don't want to be mistaken for a chicken.

What does a witch ask for when she books into a hotel?
'I want a room with broom service.'

Why does a witch ride a broom?
Because vacuum cleaners are too heavy.

'Mummy, I've got a stomach ache.'
'Must have been someone you ate.'

Did you hear about the stupid ghost?
He climbed over walls.

Where do ghosts go swimming?
In the Dead Sea.

What song do ghosts hate the most?
'Staying alive, staying alive, ha ha ha ha staying alive.'

How many vampires does it take to change a light globe?
None, they prefer the dark.

What's every monsters' favourite part of the newspaper?
The horror-scope.

How does a monster count to 13?
With one hand.

What happened when Frankenstein met a girl monster?
They fell in love at first fright.

What do you call a monster who eats his father's sister?
An aunt-eater.

Which street does a ghost live in?
A dead end street.

Who do vampires invite to parties?
Blood relations.

What do you call the winner of a monster beauty contest?
Ugly.

What's a ghost's favourite bird?
A scarecrow.

Why did Dracula go to the dentist?
To improve his bite.

What did the mother ghost say to the baby ghost?
'Don't spook until your spoken to.'

What games do you play at a ghost party?
Haunt and seek.

Why did they put a fence around the graveyard?
Because everyone was dying to get in.

'Who's that at the door darling?'
'It's a ghost!'
'Tell him I can't see him.'

What do you call the spot in the middle of a cemetery?
The dead centre.

What did the skeleton say to its friend?
'I've got a bone to pick with you.'

How do ghosts travel?
On fright trains.

There was once a ghost from Darjeeling,
Who got on the train bound for Ealing.
It said at the door,
'Please don't sit on the floor,'
So he floated up and sat on the ceiling.

What kind of spook can you hold on the end of your finger?
A bogey.

Why was Dracula lost on the freeway?
Because he was looking for the main artery.

What do ghosts put in their coffee?
Evaporated milk.

Did you hear about the ghost that ate all the Christmas decorations?
He got tinsellitis.

What is a ghost's favourite Christmas song?
'I'm dreaming of a fright Christmas.'

What happened to the wolf that fell into the washing machine?
It became a wash and werewolf.

'Hey brother ghost, how did you get that terrible bump on your head?'
'I was floating through the key hole when some moron put the key back in the lock.'

Why was the headless ghost sent to hospital?
Because he wasn't all there.

'Mummy, Mummy, tell me another story about the haunted house.'
'I can't little one, it was a one story building.'

What sort of society do vampires join?
A blood group.

There was once a young ghost from Gloucester,
Whose parents imagined they'd lost her.
From the fridge came a sound,
And at last she was found,
But the problem was how to defrost her.

Why don't ghosts make good magicians?
You can see right through their tricks.

When do ghosts haunt skyscrapers?
When they are in high spirits.

'Mummy, Mummy, am I a real ghost?'
'Of course you are, why do you ask?'
'Are you absolutely sure?'
'Of course! Why?'
'Because, I really hate the dark!'

Did you hear about the skeleton that was attacked by a dog?
It ran off with some bones and left him without a leg to stand on.

How do we know the letter 'S' is scary?
Because it makes cream, scream.

Why didn't the skeleton go to the dance?
He had no body to go with.

What does a ghost look like?
Like nothing you've ever seen before.

Why do demons and ghouls get on so well?
Because demons are a ghoul's best friend.

Why is Dracula a cheap person to take to dinner?
Because he eats necks to nothing.

Lady Jane Grey
Had nothing to say,
What could she have said
After losing her head?

What do witches put on their hair?
Scare spray.

How do vampires fall in love?
Love at first bite.

Where do ghosts go to church?
Westmonster Abbey.

What does a postman deliver to ghosts?
Fang mail.

Who is a vampire likely to fall in love with?
The girl necks door.

'I want a ghoul friend!'
'All right, all right, I'll see what I can dig up.'

'Do ghosts like the dead?'
'Of corpse they do!'

What is Dracula's favourite breed of dog?
Bloodhound.

Why do ghosts love living in high-rise buildings?
Because they have lots of scarecases.

What's the difference between a vampire with toothache and a rainstorm?
One roars with pain and the other pours with rain.

'I've just bought a haunted bike.'
'How do you know it's haunted?'
'Because it's got spooks on the wheels.'

What does a monster eat after he's been to the dentist?
The dentist.

How do ghosts begin a letter?
'Tomb it may concern.'

What do you find in a haunted cellar?
Whines and spirits.

What do vampires put in their fruit salad?
Neck-tarines and blood oranges.

What do little ghosts play with?
Deady bears.

How do skeletons communicate?
They use the telebones.

Where do cowgirl ghosts live?
In ghost towns.

Why wasn't the ghost very popular with the girls at parties?
He wasn't much to look at.

The ghoul stood on the bridge one night,
Its lips were all a quiver.
It gave a cough,
Its leg fell off,
And floated down the river.

What happened when the ghost went to the theatre?
All the actors got stage fright.

Five ghosts were sitting in the barn playing cards one windy night, when another ghost opened the door to come in and blew all the cards off the table.

'For heaven's sake, why didn't you come through the keyhole like everyone else?'

What do you call twin ghosts who keep ringing doorbells?
Dead ringers.

What sort of eyes do ghosts have?
Terror-ize.

What trees do ghosts like?
Ceme-trees.

Who is Dracula's favourite composer?
Bat-hoven.

School Days

'Miss, can I go to the toilet please?'

'Yes Johnny, but I want you to say the alphabet first.'

'OK . . . ABCDEFGHIJKLMNO QRSTUVWXYZ.'

'But where's the 'P'?'

'Running down my legs, Miss.'

'Welcome boys and girls to the start of a new year, now I want to ask you all some questions so I can get to know you better. Peter, what does your father do?'

'He's a fireman, Miss.'

'Paul, what does your father do?'

'He's a train driver, Miss.'

'And what does your father do, Johnny?'

'He's dead Miss.'

'Well, what did he do before he died?'

'He let out a groan, grabbed his chest and fell on the bathroom floor.'

What did one maths book say to another maths book?
'I've got more problems than you.'

Why did the teacher put her hands in the alphabet soup?
Because she was groping for words.

'OK class, who knows who defeated the Philistines?'
'The Swans?'

'Johnny, I hope I didn't see you looking at Mary's work then.'
'I hope you didn't too, Miss.'

'Johnny, put "gruesome" in a sentence.'
'I was short once then I gruesome.'

'Now Johnny, what's a comet?'
'A star with a tail Miss.'
'Name one then.'
'Mickey Mouse.'

What do you call a boy with a dictionary in his pocket?
Smarty pants.

'OK Johnny, give me a sentence with the word "indisposition" in it.'
'I always like playing centre forward because I like playing indisposition.'

What happened to the pot plant on the window-sill in the maths class?
It grew square roots.

Why did the science teacher put a knocker on her door?
She wanted to win the NoBell prize.

'Now that you've sat for your exams Johnny, how did you find the questions?'
'The questions were easy, but I found the answers hard.'

How do you know if your teacher loves you?
She puts kisses by your sums.

'Oh teacher, I would do anything to pass my exams.'
'Anything?'
'Yes, anything.'
'Well try studying.'

What's a good way of stopping pollution in schools?
Use unleaded pencils.

Why was the science teacher's head wet?
Because she had a brainstorm.

'Johnny, I told you to be at school by 9.15 a.m.!'
'Why, what happened?'

What's the difference between a teacher and a train?
A teacher says, 'Spit out that chewing gum!'
And a train says, 'Chew chew.'

‘Johnny, who was the first woman on earth?’
‘Give me a clue Miss, please?’
‘Well, think of an apple.’
‘Granny Smith, Miss.’

Why didn’t the astronaut go to space school classes?
Because it was launch time.

‘Johnny, your homework is in your father’s writing.’
‘I know Miss, I borrowed his pen.’

‘Now class, what is the difference between a stormy sea and this class?’
‘We don’t know, Miss.’
‘A stormy sea only makes me sick sometimes!’

'Now class, who can tell me where you find elephants?'
'How can you lose an elephant?'

Why didn't anyone take the bus to school?
Because it wouldn't fit through the door.

'Now Katherine, can you spell kangaroo?'
'Cangaroo.'
'That's not the way the dictionary spells it.'
'You didn't ask me how the dictionary spells it.'

'Now, who can name five animals that live in the jungle?'
'One lion and . . . um, um . . . four elephants.'

'Now class, if I had fifteen chips in one hand and seventeen chips in the other, what do I have?'
'Greasy hands, Miss.'

Why did the boy take a car to school?
Because he wanted to drive his teacher up the wall.

Why was the teacher cross-eyed?
Because she couldn't control her pupils.

Why did the thermometer go to college?
Because it wanted to get a degree.

What do you call a teacher and twenty children?
A bolt and twenty nuts.

'Johnny, you missed school yesterday didn't you?'
'No teacher, I didn't miss it at all!'

'Now what's the letter after "O" in the alphabet?'
' "K"?'

'Class, class! I wish you'd pay a little attention!'
'Well we are,' said Johnny, 'as little as possible.'

Why did the boy bring a ladder to school?
Because he wanted to go to high school.

What do music teachers give you?
Sound advice.

'Now Johnny, what can you tell me about the Boston Tea Party?'
'Nothing, I don't think I was invited.'

'We're going to study the English Kings and Queens today. Now, who can tell me who came after Mary?'
'One of her little lambs?'

'Dad, there's going to be a small P&T meeting at the school tomorrow.'
'How small, Johnny?'
'Just you, me, and the headmaster.'

'Now, if you asked your mother for a dollar and then you asked your father for a dollar, how much would you have?'
'One dollar.'
'Can't you add up?'
'Well, Miss, you don't know my Dad.'

'Now class, there will only be half a day of school this morning.'
'Hooray!'
'The other half will be this afternoon.'

'Polly, did your mother help you with your homework last night?'
'No. She did it for me.'

What's the maths teacher's favourite instrument?
A triangle.

Why is a car like a classroom?
Because there's a crank in the front and nuts at the back.

'Daniel, if you had five dollars in one pocket and twenty dollars in the other, what would you have?'
'Somebody else's pants.'

'Teacher, can I get into trouble for something I didn't do?'
'No.'
'Good, because I didn't do my homework.'

'Why are you writing so slowly, Johnny?'
'Because it's a letter to my friend who can't read fast.'

'Johnny, it gives me great pleasure to give you 89 out of 100 for your science project.'

'Why not give me 100 out of 100 and really enjoy yourself?'

Sporting Events

Why do you need to take a cricket player with you when you go camping?
To help pitch the tent.

Why did the basketball player throw the ball in the water?
Because his coach told him to sink it.

Why shouldn't you tell jokes when you ice skate?
Because the ice might crack up.

What did one football player say to the other football player?
'I get a kick out of you.'

Why do soccer players have so much trouble eating?
They think they can't use their hands.

When is the best time to long jump?
In a leap year.

'Mum look, I've just found a lost football.'
'How do you know it's lost?'
'Well, the kids down the road are still looking for it.'

When is a baby like a basketball player?
When it dribbles.

What race is never run?
A swimming race.

'Hey Johnny, how come you don't have your football uniform on?'
'My doctor said I can't play football.'
'I could have told you that ages ago.'

Why did the policeman run across the baseball field?
Someone stole second base.

Why was Melbourne cricket ground so hot after the match?
Because all the fans had left.

'Why didn't you stop that ball, goalkeeper?'
'Well, I thought that's what the nets were for.'

Why were all the cricketers given cigarette lighters?
Because they lost all their matches.

Why are snooker players patient?
Because they don't mind standing at the end of a cue.

'Johnny, what are you doing home so early, I thought you had baseball practice?'
'I did, but I hit the ball over the fence and the coach told me to run home.'

What did the bowling ball say to the bowling pins?
'Don't stop me, I'm on a roll.'

Why is bowling called a quiet sport?
Because you can always hear a pin drop.

Why does a golfer always wear two pairs of trousers?
In case he gets a hole in one.

What is the ski instructor's favourite song?
'There's no business like snow business.'

Who can go as fast as a race horse?
The jockey.

Why does a football player always carry a spare pen?
In case he needs an extra point.

How does a hockey player kiss?
He puckers up.

What kind of dog is a fighter?
A boxer.

Why can't a car play football?
Because it's only got one boot.

'According to my watch, I can run 100 metres in ten seconds.'
'Yeah, my watch runs slow too.'

'How's the fishing around here?'
'It's OK.'
'Then how come you haven't caught any fish?'
'You asked me about fishing not catching.'

'I won't play tennis, it's just too noisy!'
'Noisy?'
'Yeah, everyone raises a racket.'

Why did all the bowling pins go down?
Because they were on strike.

Why did the jogger go to the vet's?
Because his calves hurt.

What Do You Call...?

What do you call a woman with one leg shorter than the other?
Eileen.

What do you call a girl with one foot on either side of the river?
Bridget.

What do you call a man with no arms and no legs floating out at sea?
Bob.

What do you call a person who's a talented painter?
Art.

What do you call a man with a spade on his head?
Doug.

What do you call a girl who gambles?
Betty.

What do you call a camel with no humps?
A horse.

What do you call a girl with a frog on her head?
Lily.

What do you call a person who's always around when you need them?
Andy.

Who was Russia's favourite gardener?
Ivan Hoe.

What do you call a man in a pile of leaves?
Russell.

Which rock singer has a vegie garden on her head?
Tina Turnip.

What do you call a woman in the distance?
Dot.

What do you call a lawyer?
Sue.

What do you call a man with a number plate on his head?
Reg.

What do you call a boy with a rabbit cage on his head?
Warren.

What do you call a man with a car on his head?
Jack.

What do you call a person who can sing and drink lemonade at the same time?
A pop singer.

Word Play

The Hungry Dog by Norah Bone

Cliff Tragedy by Eileen Dover

The Man Vanishes by Peter Out

The Ghost in the Attic by Howey Wailes

Walking to School by Mr Bus

Broken Window by Eva Brick

Ghosts by Sue Pernatural

The Omen by B. Warned

Poltergeists by Eve L. Spirit

Camel Rides by Mr Bumsore

A Hole in the Bucket by Lee King

Holidays in Britain by A. Pauline Weather

Infectious Diseases by Willie Catchit

Ghosts by I. C. Spooks

How to Grow Taller by Stan Up

How to Grow Shorter by Neil Down

Bell Ringing by Paula Rope

Tea for Two by Roland Butta

Driving through Germany by Otto Mobile

All About Explosives by Dinah Mite

Help for a Jail Breaker by Freida Prisner

Sahara Journey by I. Rhoda Camel

Rocket to the Sun by R. U. Nuts

Gone Chopin, Bach in a moment.
Out to Lunch, Offenbach sooner.

One One was a racehorse
Two Two was one too
One One won one race
Two Two won one too.

Four still standers
Four dilly danders
Two cookers
Two lookers
And one swish
That's a cow.

Good King Wenceslas looked out
From his kitchen winder
Something hit him on the snout
'Twas a red hot cinder.
Bright shone his nose that night
Though the pain was cru-el
When a poor man came in sight
Riding on a mu-el.

There are four people named Everybody, Somebody, Anybody and Nobody.

There was an important job to be done and Everybody was asked to do it.

Everybody was sure Somebody would do it.

Anybody could have done it, but Nobody did it.

Somebody got angry about that, because it was Everybody's job.

Everybody thought Anybody could do it but Nobody realised that Everybody wouldn't do it.

It ended up that Everybody blamed Somebody for what Anybody could have done.

I'd like to have your picture
It would look very nice.
I'd put it in the cellar
And frighten all the mice.

Little Miss Muffet
Sat on her tuffet
Eating her Irish stew.
Along came a spider
And sat down beside her
So she ate him up too.

If a blue house is made out of blue bricks, and a yellow house made out of yellow bricks, and a red house made out of red bricks, what is a green house made out of?
Glass.

Mary had a little lamb
Her father shot it dead.
Now it goes to school with her
Between two chunks of bread.

Poor old Nelly's dead
She died last night in bed.
They put her in a coffin
And she fell right out the bottom.

Dr Bell fell down the well
And broke his collar bone.
Doctors should attend the sick
And leave the well alone.

Unfortunately one day a man fell out of a plane.
Fortunately there was a haystack under him.
Unfortunately there was a pitch fork in the haystack.
Fortunately he missed the pitchfork.
Unfortunately he missed the haystack.

The Thunder God went for a ride
Upon his favourite filly.
'I'm Thor,' he cried.
The horse replied,
'You forgot your thaddle, thilly.'

ndex